Public Speaking

The Evolving Art

Public Speaking
The Evolving Art

FOURTH EDITION

Stephanie J. Coopman
San José State University

James Lull
San José State University

CENGAGE Learning

Australia • Brazil • Mexico • Singapore • United Kingdom • United States

CENGAGE
Learning

Public Speaking: The Evolving Art, Fourth Edition
Stephanie J. Coopman, James Lull

Product Director: Monica Eckman

Product Manager: Kelli Strieby

Content Developers: Jessica Badiner, Kassi Radomski

Marketing Manager: Sarah Seymour

Content Project Manager: Dan Saabye

Art Director: Marissa Falco

Manufacturing Planner: Doug Bertke

IP Analyst: Ann Hoffman

IP Project Manager: Kathryn Kucharek

Production Service: MPS Limited

Compositor: MPS Limited

Text Designer: Diane Beasley

Cover Designer: Niloufer Moochhala, NYMDesign

Cover Image: rawpixelimages/Dreamstime.com

Library of Congress Control Number: 2016944754

Student Edition:
ISBN: 978-1-337-09056-8

Book-only:
ISBN: 978-1-337-10756-3

Loose-leaf Edition:
ISBN: 978-1-337-10984-0

Cengage Learning
20 Channel Center Street
Boston, MA 02210
USA

Cengage Learning is a leading provider of customized learning solutions with employees residing in nearly 40 different countries and sales in more than 125 countries around the world. Find your local representative at **www.cengage.com**

Cengage Learning products are represented in Canada by Nelson Education, Ltd.

To learn more about Cengage Learning Solutions, visit **www.cengage.com**

Purchase any of our products at your local college store or at our preferred online store **www.cengagebrain.com**

Printed in the United States of America
Print Number: 02 Print Year: 2017

Brief Contents

Contents

PART III Presenting Yourself and Your Ideas

Bonus Chapter

This bonus chapter can be accessed through MindTap Communication. For more information about MIndTap go to page xiv.

Preface

Public Speaking: The Evolving Art deftly links time-honored, classic public speaking instruction with today's emerging technologies. Students develop the confidence and skills essential for effective public speaking across a range of contexts in our fast-changing, digitally oriented world. Taking a practical, audience-centered, culturally up-to-date approach, *Public Speaking: The Evolving Art* and MindTap for *Public Speaking: The Evolving Art* address the ways in which the latest technologies, social transitions, and cultural shifts have affected students and the communication discipline.

Public Speaking Is an Evolving Art

Although the foundations of effective public speaking have endured since classical times, the Internet and other new media have influenced every aspect of public speaking—from the initial stages of topic selection and research to the final stages of practicing and delivering a speech. Consider these current trends:

- Unprecedented access to digitized content is exceptionally easy to appropriate, making the ethics of public speaking increasingly complex.
- Communication technologies—including smartphones, Internet telephony (such as Skype), social media (such as YouTube and Snapchat)—make connecting with others, both locally and globally, faster and easier than ever, and give speakers numerous speech-delivery options, such as podcasting, webcasting, and presentation software.
- Globalization and increased cultural awareness require that communicators consistently demonstrate a high degree of multicultural and intercultural knowledge and sensitivity.
- Audiences often expect a friendly, conversational delivery style, the correct use of presentation media, and messages targeted to their interests.

Embracing the multiplatform realities of today's textbooks, *Public Speaking: The Evolving Art* meets the needs of in-person, hybrid (or blended), and online classes. The book includes a wealth of resources in MindTap Communication—an online, highly personalized learning experience integrated with *Public Speaking: The Evolving Art*. MindTap combines student learning tools—readings, multimedia, and assessments—into a Learning Path for each chapter that guides students through course material. Instructors customize the learning experience with their own and Cengage Learning content and tools that integrate into the MindTap framework. MindTap public speaking apps include the following:

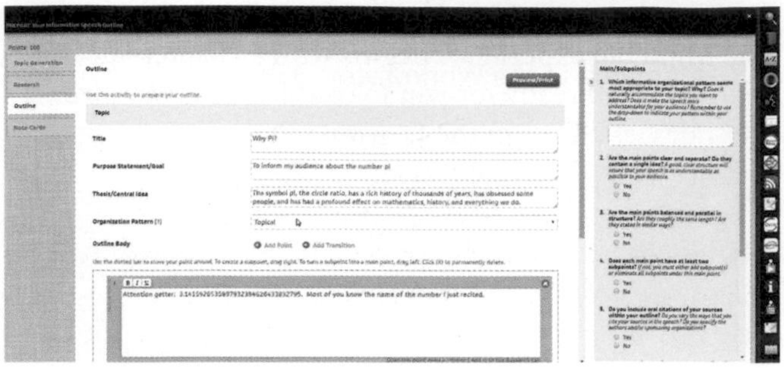

- Outline Builder guides students step by step through the speech preparation process—from topic generation, to research aggregation and source citation, to outline and note card preparation.

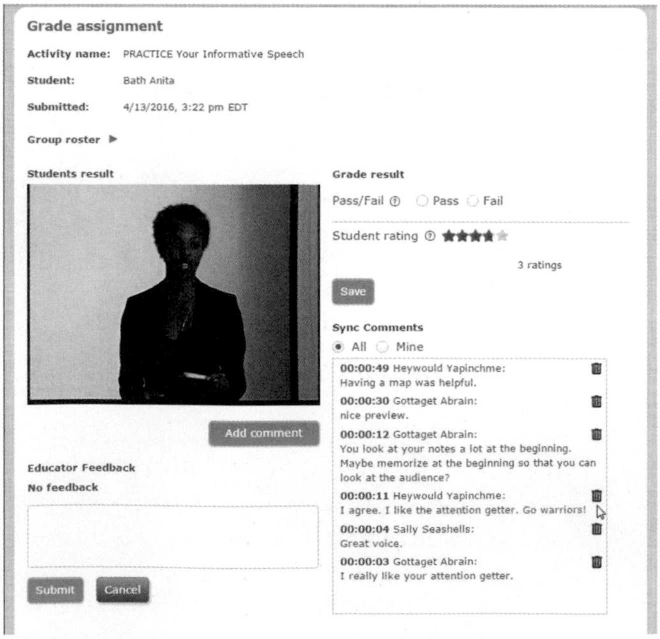

- Practice and Present with YouSeeU is a synchronous and asynchronous speech video delivery, recording, and grading system with robust tools, including rubrics, to facilitate comprehensive instructor and peer evaluation.

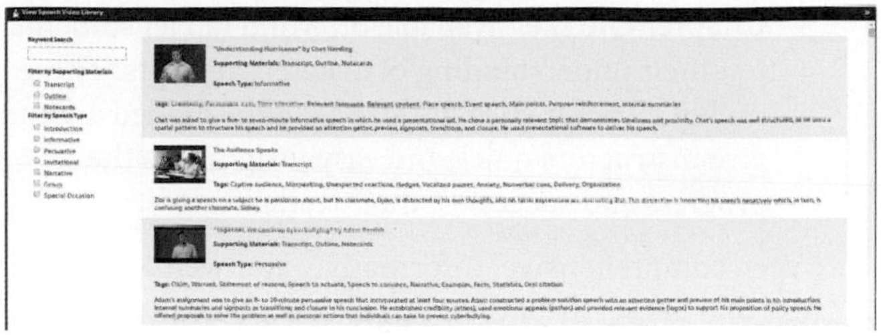

- Available to instructors to add to the Learning Path, the Speech Video Library provides current, realistic examples students can model to improve their speaking skills and gain confidence. Critical thinking questions, a transcript, an outline, and note cards accompany each speech video.

The MindTap experience begins with a chapter-specific Learning Path ready for you to use as is or customize for your class. Design the Learning Path to match your syllabus exactly—hide, rearrange, change, add, and insert campus- or course-specific resources, such as handbooks, school catalogs, web links, your favorite videos, activities, current events materials, or any resource you can upload to the Internet. Some specific resources *Public Speaking: The Evolving Art*'s Learning Path include:

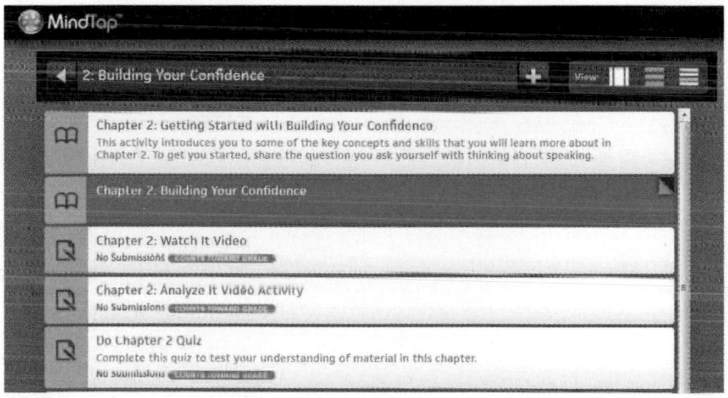

- **Getting Started.** A polling activity where students can view how their responses to chapter-related topics compare with their peers' responses.
- **Read It in the MindTap Reader.** The MindTap Reader is more than a digital version of a textbook. Videos bring the book concepts to life. The robust functionality of the MindTap Reader allows learners to make notes, highlight text, and even find a definition right from the page. After completing the reading, students can review vocabulary with the flashcards and check their comprehension with assignable chapter quizzes.
- **Watch It.** Addressing topics like building confidence, avoiding plagiarism, selecting the best supporting materials, and managing physical delivery, videos and animations of peer mentors offer first-hand strategies and tips for student success in the public speaking course.

MindTap can be bundled with every new copy of the text or ordered separately. Students whose instructors do not order these resources as a package with the text may purchase access to them at **cengagebrain.com.** *Contact your local Cengage Learning sales representative for more details.*

Look for the MindTap icon in the pages of *Public Speaking: The Evolving Art* to find MindTap resources related to the text.

> "*Public Speaking: The Evolving Art* is an excellent Public Speaking text! The information in it is current, relevant, and extremely accessible for the average college student. The Mindtap program associated with it makes it even better. There are a wealth of resources available to students, including an Outline builder to make constructing outlines effortless!"
>
> —Christopher Wood, University of Idaho

Clear and Thorough Examination of the Speech Development Process

Regardless of where on the digital-immersion spectrum your students fall, *Public Speaking: The Evolving Art* is committed to enriching their learning experience, helping them maximize their effectiveness, and greatly enhancing the quality and impact of their public communication.

Public Speaking: The Evolving Art also provides a sound pedagogical approach in sync with how today's students learn: **Read It, Watch It, Analyze It, Apply It, Review It.** Each chapter's material, both in the book and via MindTap, engages students with a user-friendly text, content-rich videos, opportunities to analyze student and professional speeches, and an unparalleled array of study and self-assessment resources.

Touted by instructors for its accessible, conversational writing style, *Public Speaking: The Evolving Art* offers cutting-edge content and coverage of all the essential topics instructors and students need to succeed in an introductory public speaking course. Some unique highlights instructors praise include:

- **Chapter 1, The Evolving Art of Public Speaking,** offers **strong grounding in the classical history** of public speaking that **traces the historical evolution of public speaking** so that students see its place in human development.

- **Chapter 5, Adapting to Your Audience,** provides comprehensive coverage of audience analysis and **using audience research questionnaires**, defines **psychographics** and introduces **speaker credibility**.
- **Chapter 6, Researching Your Topic,** delivers a thorough overview of **research databases** and **current research options**.
- **Chapter 7, Supporting Your Ideas,** includes **five types of supporting material** and differentiates between **types of stories and testimony**.
- **Chapter 12, Delivering Your Speech,** includes specific information for **speakers with dis/abilities** and reinforces an **audience-centered approach**.
- **Chapter 14, Persuasive Speaking,** offers coverage on **persuading different types of audience**—hostile, sympathetic, apathetic, uninformed, divided—to help students design persuasive strategies in order to reach these audiences. New to this edition, this chapter also differentiates between **practical persuasive speaking** (e.g., give blood, register to vote) and **issue-based persuasive speaking** (e.g., death penalty, withdraw from the Middle East).

To help students retain chapter concepts, Review It features the following:

- **Reflecting On questions** encourage students to review key chapter topics on their own or discuss them in groups.

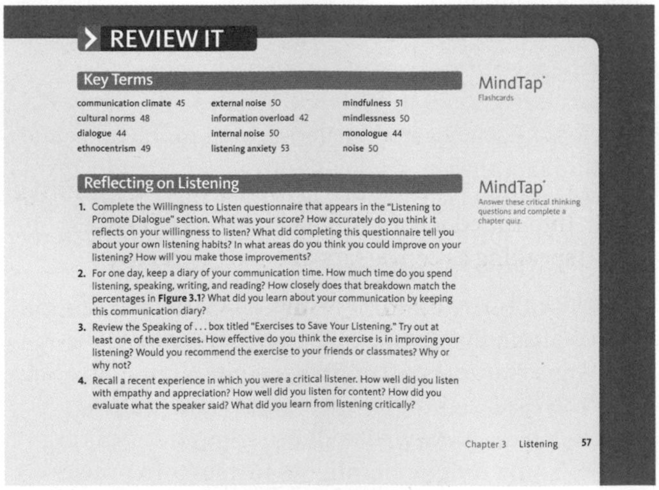
> REVIEW IT

Key Terms

communication climate 45	external noise 50	mindfulness 51
cultural norms 48	information overload 42	mindlessness 50
dialogue 44	internal noise 50	monologue 44
ethnocentrism 49	listening anxiety 53	noise 50

MindTap®
Flashcards

Reflecting on Listening

1. Complete the Willingness to Listen questionnaire that appears in the "Listening to Promote Dialogue" section. What was your score? How accurately do you think it reflects on your willingness to listen? What did completing this questionnaire tell you about your own listening habits? In what areas do you think you could improve on your listening? How will you make those improvements?
2. For one day, keep a diary of your communication time. How much time do you spend listening, speaking, writing, and reading? How closely does that breakdown match the percentages in **Figure 3.1**? What did you learn about your communication by keeping this communication diary?
3. Review the Speaking of . . . box titled "Exercises to Save Your Listening." Try out at least one of the exercises. How effective do you think the exercise is in improving your listening? Would you recommend the exercise to your friends or classmates? Why or why not?
4. Recall a recent experience in which you were a critical listener. How well did you listen with empathy and appreciation? How well did you listen for content? How did you evaluate what the speaker said? What did you learn from listening critically?

MindTap®
Answer these critical thinking questions and complete a chapter quiz.

Chapter 3 Listening 57

- **Key Terms** coupled with marginal definitions throughout the chapter assist students with learning public speaking vocabulary. Flashcards available on MindTap help students study basic concepts and terminology.
- **Chapter Quizzes** available on MindTap let students test their understanding of chapter concepts. These multiple choice style quizzes are auto-graded and give instructors quick and easy insight into the progress and success of their students.

"Very comprehensive, informative, and well written text that is user-friendly, with excellent online supplements."

—Diane DeRosier, Eastern University

Contemporary and Relatable Examples Appeal to Today's Diverse Students

With a distinct 21st-century, student-centered approach, *Public Speaking: The Evolving Art* and its companion resources were developed with an abundance of culturally relevant examples, models, figures, and tables to help students gain the practical public speaking skills they need to reach their full potential as public speakers and to contribute positively to society as confident, accomplished communicators.

> ANALYZE IT

Katherine Heigl, Tribute to Shirley MacLaine

Actor Katherine Heigl spoke at the American Film Institute's tribute to Shirley MacLaine.[50] In this short speech, Heigl honors MacLaine's work and notes how she has served as a role model for other female actors. At the start of the speech, Heigl tells her audience about her fear of public speaking. Read the transcript here to find out how Heigl managed her speech anxiety.

It's such an honor for me to be here tonight to celebrate the wonderfully talented exceptional Shirley MacLaine. I'm kind of petrified of speaking in public. I know it seems ridiculous. But when they first asked me my first thought was fear and my second thought was, but it's Shirley MacLaine. And as I've been sitting here and getting more and more nervous I've also been getting really excited to tell you how significant and important and inspirational you have been to me for a very long time.

I was 12 when I first fell in love with you. It was when I first saw "Steel Magnolias," and "Terms of Endearment," and "Postcards from the Edge," for the first of many, many, many times. I was too young to understand what made you so special and unique. I just knew that you were my 12-year-old heart's favorite actress and I have spent the last 21 years trying to perfect your zingers from "Steel Magnolias." Like, "I'm not crazy M'Lynn, I'm just been in a very bad mood for 40 years." Which is really fun to say to people for no reason.

Shirley you taught me how important, how significant a movie could be in a person's life to help them not feel so alone and isolated in their grief and their loss. And that laughter and tears could be delivered in the same breath. And that strong take-no-prisoners women could be vulnerable and fragile, too. My love for you has grown with each of these astounding performances and my respect for you has deepened when I realized you're more than just an actor. You're a woman who isn't afraid to speak your truth and to laugh at yourself and take a stand. You gave me a woman in Hollywood to look up to. And you've taught me this exceptional lesson to hold my freakin' own and to honor the 12 year old that's still in me.

Can I get your autograph?

Getty Images Entertainment/Getty Images

Chapter 2 Building Your Confidence 37

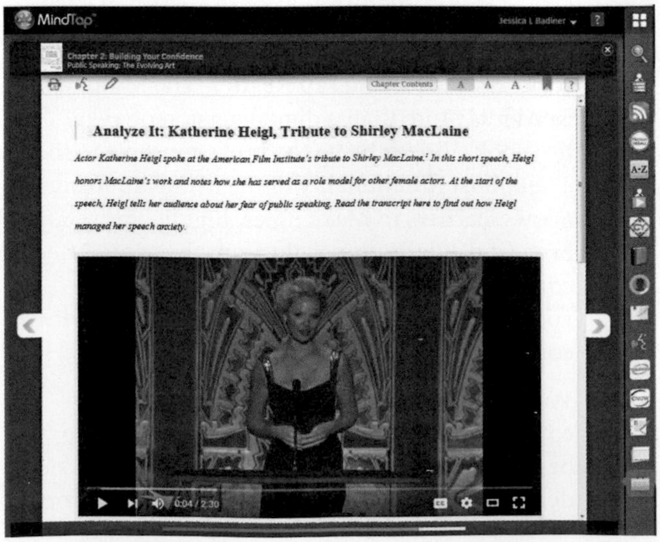

- **Analyze It.** A diverse collection of sample student and professional speeches at the end of Chapters 2 to 16 coupled with video of live delivery of the speech on MindTap allow students to consider chapter concepts in the context of real speeches. Each speech is accompanied by a brief overview of the speech's context and questions for discussion. Read and watch Katherine Heigl's Tribute to Shirley MacLaine (Chapter 2) or a student's persuasive speech on cyberbullying (Chapter 15).

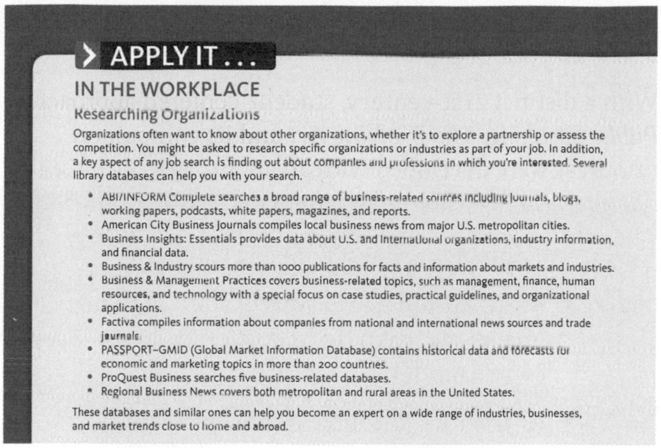

> APPLY IT . . .

IN THE WORKPLACE

Researching Organizations

Organizations often want to know about other organizations, whether it's to explore a partnership or assess the competition. You might be asked to research specific organizations or industries as part of your job. In addition, a key aspect of any job search is finding out about companies and professions in which you're interested. Several library databases can help you with your search.

- ABI/INFORM Complete searches a broad range of business-related sources including journals, blogs, working papers, podcasts, white papers, magazines, and reports.
- American City Business Journals compiles local business news from major U.S. metropolitan cities.
- Business Insights: Essentials provides data about U.S. and International organizations, industry information, and financial data.
- Business & Industry scours more than 1000 publications for facts and information about markets and industries.
- Business & Management Practices covers business-related topics, such as management, finance, human resources, and technology with a special focus on case studies, practical guidelines, and organizational applications.
- Factiva compiles information about companies from national and international news sources and trade journals.
- PASSPORT–GMID (Global Market Information Database) contains historical data and forecasts for economic and marketing topics in more than 200 countries.
- ProQuest Business searches five business-related databases.
- Regional Business News covers both metropolitan and rural areas in the United States.

These databases and similar ones can help you become an expert on a wide range of industries, businesses, and market trends close to home and abroad.

- **Apply It in the Workplace and in Your Community.** These features encourage students to apply their public speaking skills in professional and local organizational settings. The activities demonstrate the ways in which public speaking skills can foster greater social awareness, civility, personal responsibility, service learning, and active learning.

Katherine Heigl, Tribute to Shirley MacLaine

Amanda Wagemann, Winning Speech for the South Dakota Department of Agriculture, 2012 Resource Conservation Speech Contest

Chris, Impressionistic Painting

Katie, Why Pi?

Emily, About ALS

Malkia Cyril, Keynote at the Computers, Freedom and Privacy Conference, October 13, 2015

Alicia, How Guinea Pigs Help Autistic Children

Nathaneal, The 54th Massachusetts

Sierra, The Role of Spots in Society

Dr. Michael Marx, Getting Off Oil

Chase Roberts, First Place Speech at the 2015 Houston 19th Annual Gardere Martin Luther King, Jr., Oratory Competition

Lishan, Chinese Valentine's Day

Carly, Eat Healthier in College

Alicia, Sexual Assault on University Campuses

Adam, Together, We Can Stop Cyberbullying

Tara, My Grandfather, John Flanagan Sr.

"I continue to be impressed with how the authors are using a more modern, student centered set of references and examples."

—John Reffue, Hillsborough Community College

"A visually engaging, comprehensive look at public communication with an abundance of helpful examples and models for students."

—Brian Zager, Merrimack College

New to This Edition

Global revisions to the include:

- Chapter openings that emphasize the continuity and change over time in public speaking styles, approaches, and perspectives.
- Updated and expanded research to provide students with the most relevant and current information related to public speaking.
- Updated photographs, examples, charts, and tables that reflect the evolving art of public speaking.
- Learning outcomes added at the beginning of every chapter and reflection questions that match those learning outcomes.

Chapter revisions to the text include:

- **Chapter 1, The Evolving Art of Public Speaking**: Intensified focus on audience-centered public speaking as conversational and interactive.
- **Chapter 2, Building Your Confidence**: In-depth discussion of relaxation techniques for managing anxiety, inclusion of the Communication Anxiety Regulation Scale, added attention to building confidence for giving online speeches.
- **Chapter 3, Listening**: Completely redesigned with a single focus on listening, the chapter provides a feedback form for classroom speeches, detailed discussion of barriers to effective listening, specific exercises to improve listening. Discussions of ethics and public speaking now are distributed throughout the text.

- **Chapter 4, Developing Your Purpose and Topic:** Highlights the presence of Malala Yousafzi, Neil deGrasse Tyson, Mark Zuckerberg, and Ayaan Hirsi Ali as global public speakers with a well-defined purpose.
- **Chapter 5, Adapting to Your Audience:** Links fundamental principle of evolutionary adaptation to public speaking; integrates current research on audience diversity.
- **Chapter 6, Researching Your Topic**: Updated online resources for searches, such as DuckDuckGo, Google Scholar, Artcyclopedia, and FindSounds; streamlined discussion of information interviews; expanded discussion of evaluating research materials; detailed coverage of plagiarism and strategies for avoiding itthat demonstrates integrating research in to a speech.
- **Chapter 7, Supporting Your Ideas**: Facts and statistics discussed as two separate types of supporting materials; clear distinctions drawn among facts, inferences, and opinions.
- **Chapter 8, Organizing and Outlining Your Speech**: Integrated description and comparison of working, complete-sentence, and speaking outlines.
- **Chapter 9, Beginning and Ending Your Speech**: Clearer discussion of primacy and recency effects student speech for analysis.
- **Chapter 10, Using Language Effectively**: Comprehensive discussions of gender-fair and inclusive language.
- **Chapter 11, Integrating Presentation Media:** Up-to-date discussion of latest presentation media; improved examples of digital slides; new section on citing digital slides in speeches; transcript and new video example that demonstrate how to use digital slides in a speech.
- **Chapter 12, Delivering Your Speech**: Expanded discussion of gender and delivery; added section on effective breathing techniques for reducing anxiety.
- **Chapter 13, Informative Speaking:** New culturally relevant informative speech topic examples that spark student interest; new material to help students differentiate between informative and persuasive speech topics.
- **Chapter 14, Persuasive Speaking:** Practical and issue-based topics treated separately; innovative new section on practical persuasion speech topics and patterns of organization.
- **Chapter 15, Understanding Argument:** New approach to argumentation linked to development of personal leadership skills.
- **Chapter 16, Special Occasion, Distance, and Group Speaking:** Major new section with guidelines on videoconferences, online graphical presentations, and telephone meetings as distance speaking events.

Instructor Resources

Instructors who adopt this book may request the following resources to support their teaching.

- **Instructor Companion Website.** The password-protected Instructor Companion Website includes:
  - Computerized test bank via Cognero®
  - Ready-to-use PowerPoint® slides (with text and images that can also be customized to suit your course needs)
  - Instructor's Resource Manual presents its own Prepare It, Teach It, Assess It, Adapt It framework to parallel the student text's Read It, Watch It, Analyze It, Apply It, Review It pedagogy. This manual offers guidelines for setting up your course, sample syllabi, chapter outlines, suggested topics for lectures and discussion, and activities and assignments for individuals and groups. It also includes a test bank with diverse types of questions and varying levels of difficulty.

  Visit the Instructor Companion Website by accessing **http://login.cengage.com** or by contacting your local sales representative.
- **Digital Course Support.** Get trained, get connected, and get the support you need for the seamless integration of digital resources into your course. This unparalleled technology service and training program provides robust online resources, peer-to-peer instruction, personalized training, and a customizable program you can count on. Visit **cengage.com/dcs** to sign up for online seminars, first days of class services, technical support, or personalized, face-to-face training. Our online and onsite training sessions frequently are led by our Lead Teachers, faculty members who are experts in using Cengage Learning technology and can provide best practices and teaching tips.

Acknowledgments

This project was a team effort, and we appreciate all the work others have contributed to *Public Speaking: The Evolving Art.* Our Cengage Learning team included Monica Eckman, Product Director; Kelli Strieby, Product Manager; Marita Sermolins, Senior Content Developer; Jessica Badiner, Senior Content Developer; Karolina Kiwak, Associate Content Developer; Dan Saabye, Content Project Manager; Marissa Falco, Art Director; and Edward Dionne, Project Manager at MPS Limited.

Many thanks to those who helped with the development of the ancillary materials that accompany the text, including Sheryll Reichwein, who assisted with the MindTap assets.

Many thanks to the reviewers for this edition: Julie Allee, Ivy Tech Community College; Suzanne J. Atkin, Portland State University; Lisa Bamber, Otero Junior College; Cameron Basquiat, College of Southern Nevada; Chantele Carr, Estrella Mountain Community College; John Chamberlain, Santa Fe College; Ronald E. Compton, McHenry County College; Amber Davies-Sloan, Yavapai College; Aaron S. Deason, Ivy Tech; Diane DeRosier, Eastern University; Vance Elderkin, Alamance Community College; Sharon Ewing, University of North Carolina, Charlotte; Lucy Ferguson, Meridian Community College; Kristina Galyen, University of Cincinnati; Kathleen M. Golden, Edinboro University of Pennsylvania; Erin Hammond, Faulkner State Community College; April Hebert, College of Southern Nevada; Ronald Hochstatter, McLennan Community College; Teresa Horton, Baker College; LaToya Jackson, Yuba College; Jody Jones, Alabama A & M University; Sandy King, Anne Arundel Community College; David Kosloski, Clark College; Marilyn Kritzman, Western Michigan University; David Moss, Mt. Saint Jacinto College; Steven Netti, Vincennes University; Kekeli Nuviadenu, Bethune-Cookman University; Amy Powell, Central Michigan University; Narissra Punyanunt-Carter, Texas Tech University; Brandi Quesenberry, Virginia Tech; John Reffue, Hillsborough Community College; Elizabeth Rogers, Huntingdon College; Lynn Rogoff, New York Institute of Technology; David Schreindl, Dickinson State University; Holly Shiveley, Cleveland State Community College; Christy Takamure, Leeward Community College; Sarah Vaughn, Elizabethtown Community & Technical College; Sherri L. Wallace, University of Louisville; Janice Watson, Oakwood University; Arthur Williams, Olivet College; Caitlin Wills-Toler, University of North Georgia; Christopher Wood, University of Idaho; Donata Worrell, Rockingham Community College; and Brian Zager, Merrimack College.

Special thanks to our Student Advisory Board: Montell Boone, Franklin University; Danny Bugingo, University of Idaho; Taylor Caldwell, University of Idaho; Melanie Harvey, Stonehill College; Lindsey Heflin, University of Idaho; Monica Rommens, University of Idaho; and Robert Seger, Ivy Tech, Bloomington.

Special thanks to our Faculty Advisory Board for their constructive criticism and continued support of *Public Speaking: The Evolving Art:* Diane Carter, University of Idaho; Diane DeRosier, Eastern University; Kathleen M. Golden, Edinboro University of Pennsylvania; Erin Hammond, Faulkner State Community College; Sherri L. Wallace, University of Louisville; Carrie West, Schreiner University; and Brian Zager, Merrimack College.

About the Authors

Ted M. Coopman

Stephanie J. Coopman (Ph.D., University of Kentucky) is Professor of Communication Studies at San José State University. She served as department chair for five years and chair of the SJSU University Council of Chairs and Directors for three years. In addition to teaching public speaking since the start of her career, she has conducted numerous training sessions on public speaking and communication pedagogy. Professor Coopman has published her research in a variety of scholarly outlets, including *First Monday, Communication Education, Western Journal of Communication, Communication Yearbook, American Communication Journal, Journal of Business Communication,* and *Management Communication Quarterly.* She contributes 20 percent of her royalties from the sale of *Public Speaking: The Evolving Art* to the Robert R. Zimmermann "Dr. Bob" Scholarship fund for students and the Dr. Robert R. "Dr. Bob" Zimmermann Endowed Teaching Chair Award for faculty at Delta College in University Center, Michigan.

East Side Books

James Lull (Ph.D., University of Wisconsin–Madison) is Professor Emeritus of Communication Studies at San José State University. Winner of the National Communication Association's Golden Anniversary Monograph Award, he has taught public speaking for more than twenty-five years. An internationally recognized leader in media studies, cultural analysis, and evolutionary communication, Professor Lull is author or editor of twelve books with translations into many languages as well as articles published in the top journals in the field. Dr. Lull holds honorary doctorates and professorships from several universities in Europe and Latin America where he regularly gives plenary addresses and seminars.

A Brief Guide to Successful Public Speaking

Use this guide as you prepare for your first speech and as a checklist for all the speeches you give in your public speaking class. The guide also serves as a handy reference for speeches you give after college.

Presenting a speech involves six basic stages:

1. Determining your purpose and topic (Chapter 4)
2. Adapting to your audience (Chapter 5)
3. Researching your topic (Chapter 6)
4. Organizing your ideas and outlining your speech (Chapter 8)
5. Practicing your speech (Chapter 12)
6. Delivering your speech (Chapter 12)

These stages blend together—they're integrated parts of a whole, not discrete units. For example,

- As you're analyzing your audience (stage 2), you revise your topic focus (stage 1).
- What you find out about your audience (stage 2) will influence how you research your topic (stage 3).
- When practicing your speech (stage 5), you may decide that the flow of your ideas won't work for your audience (stage 2), so you go back and modify the organization of your ideas (stage 4).

Although public speaking may seem to be all about presenting, most of a successful speaker's work takes place behind the scenes, well before the speaking event. Let's go through each activity in the speechmaking process.

1. Determine Your Purpose and Topic

a. **Decide on your overall goal,** or the general purpose of your speech.
  - First speeches in a public speaking class usually aim to inform or enhance listeners' knowledge of a topic. *Example:* In introducing a classmate, you'd want your audience to learn a few key bits of information about the person.
  - Some first speeches seek to entertain listeners by sharing anecdotes and using humor. *Example:* In introducing yourself, you might tell your audience a funny story about your summer vacation.
  - Speeches to persuade focus on influencing people's behaviors, values, or attitudes. ***Example:*** Trying to convince audience members to exercise regularly involves persuasion.

b. After you've identified the speech's general purpose, **choose your topic.**
  - Sometimes your instructor will assign a topic for your first speech, such as introducing yourself to the class.
  - In other cases, your assignment may be more broad, like informing the audience about an important campus issue.
  - Pick something of interest to you that you think will appeal to your audience too.

2. Adapt to Your Audience

a. In choosing a topic, **keep your audience in mind** so your speech will interest them.
  - In-depth research allows you to design a speech tailored to your audience.
  - You probably won't be able to do in-depth research for your first speech, but just looking around the classroom gives you some clues about your audience. Demographic characteristics such as ethnic background, age, sex, and educational level tell you a lot. *Example:* If you wanted to give a speech about affordable housing in your community, you'd probably want to approach the issue from the point of view of renters, not landlords, because your student audience is far more likely to rent than to own their own home.

b. Adapting your speech to your audience means that you **apply the information you've gathered about them** when designing your speech.
  - Target your message to *this* particular audience at *this* particular time and place.
  - Use audience-centered communication that engages your listeners and helps you achieve your goal for the speech.
  - You want your audience to feel as if you're speaking directly to them.

3. Research Your Topic

a. **You have many sources of information** for your speech topics.
  - Common sources are websites, books, magazines, newspapers, government publications, and interviews with individuals.
  - But begin with yourself and what you already know about the topic.

b. Once you've identified your knowledge base, **seek out additional sources of information.**
   - You've probably already searched the Internet for information about a wide range of topics. However, finding what you need for a speech is another matter. Locating relevant information online requires determining the right key terms associated with your topic. *Example:* If you're introducing a classmate who enjoys surfing, you may want to find out more about this activity. Typing in "surfing" on Google produces about 33 million webpages, ranging from Internet surfing, to the surfing lawyer, to mind surfing—not exactly relevant to your speech. However, adding key terms to "surfing," such as "sport," "ocean," and "surfboard," refines your search.
   - All campus libraries include extensive electronic databases that serve as gateways to academic journals, newspapers, legal opinions, trade publications, and numerous other sources.
   - A trip to the library and a brief conference with the reference librarian help locate any additional information on paper that you might need.

4. Organize Your Ideas

a. Organizing your ideas involves identifying the main points you want to cover in your speech and putting them in a logical order: introduction, body, and conclusion.

b. With your introduction, you **gain your audience's attention and preview your main points.**
   - Encourage listeners to focus on your ideas by gaining their attention with startling statistics, engaging quotes, rhetorical questions, brief anecdotes, or vivid visual materials that are relevant to your topic.
   - Preview your main points in your thesis statement or in a separate preview statement. *Example:* "The two campus services I'll cover today are the university credit union and the computer recycling program."

c. Once you've introduced your speech, you've **set the stage for the body of your speech.**
   - The body of your speech includes all your main points organized in some logical way. *Example:* If you were describing a stadium, you might begin with the outside, then take the audience through the gates, then into the first level, and on through the arena using a spatial organizational pattern.
   - However you organize your ideas, the pattern must be clear to your audience.

d. In your conclusion, you'll summarize the main points and let your audience know you're finished.
   - *Example:* Signal that you're finishing your speech by saying something like, "Let's review what I've covered today …" or "To summarize, the most important aspects of …."
   - End with a memorable statement. *Example:* "Now you've met Bailey—political science major, entrepreneur, and future mayor of this city."

e. With an outline, you develop a numbered list of your main points and all the points supporting them.
   - Outlining your speech shows how you've arranged your ideas.
   - Successful public speaking requires creating and using three different kinds of outlines for different stages in the development of your speech: working, complete-sentence, and presentation.
   - The following table "Types of Outlines" provides an overview of each type of outline, including what it's used for (function), what it includes (key features), and in which chapter of this text you'll find it covered.

5. Practice Your Speech via Practice and Present in MindTap

a. **Begin rehearsing your speech** by running through your outline and editing it as needed.
   - Go through your complete-sentence outline, talking out loud, listening for how your ideas flow and fit together.
   - Then give your speech aloud again, checking that you're within the time limit.
   - Based on how well you meet the time limit and how your ideas work together, edit and revise for clarity and ease of understanding.

b. Create your presentation outline via Speech Builder Express in MindTap
   - Transfer keywords from your complete-sentence outline to note cards, including only those words that trigger your memory. What you write on your note cards will become your presentation outline—the outline you'll use when you give your speech to the audience.
   - Holding your note cards in one hand, stand up and say your speech, just as you would if your audience were there.

- If you plan to use presentation media like digital slides or posters in your speech, practice incorporating them into your presentation at this point too.
- Because you're using your notes only as a reminder, you'll need to glance at them only briefly and infrequently.

c. Strive to give an excellent version of your speech rather than a perfect speech.
- As you're practicing, your speech will sound a little different each time.
- Aim for a conversational presentation that you adapt to your audience as you're speaking.

6. Present Your Speech via Practice and Present in MindTap

a. When you present your speech, **manage your voice and your body.**
Dress for the setting, audience, and topic.
- It's perfectly normal to feel a little nervous before and during your presentation. Think of any anxiety you feel as energy, then rechannel that energy into enthusiasm for your topic and audience.
- Maintain good eye contact with your audience, glancing at your note cards only to remind you of what you plan to say.
- Speak loudly so your audience can easily hear you.
- Move with purpose and spontaneity, using gestures that appear natural and comfortable.

b. For your first speech, you probably won't have slides, videos, or other presentation media. For longer speeches, **manage your presentation media,** arriving early on the day of your speech and checking the equipment you're going to use.

c. It will help you **manage your audience** as you present your speech if you analyze audience members beforehand.
- What you know about your listeners gives you clues about their possible reactions to your speech.
- Maintaining good eye contact gives you a sense of how they're responding to what you say.

d. **Monitor your time and adjust your speech as needed** if you find you're going to go on too long or fall short of the time limit.
- Effective public speaking means having the flexibility to adjust your presentation as you go along.
- Having a good grasp of the content of your speech will give you the confidence to make whatever adjustments you deem necessary during your presentation.

Types of Outlines

Type of Outline	Functions	Key features	Chapter
Working	Assists in initial topic development; guides research	Includes main points and possible subpoints; revised during research process	4: Developing Your Purpose and Topic
Complete-sentence	Clearly identifies all the pieces of information for the speech; puts ideas in order; forms the basis for developing the presentation outline	Uses complete sentences; lists all sections of speech and all references; revised during preparation process	8: Organizing and Outlining Your Speech
Presentation	Assists you in practicing and giving your speech	Uses keywords; revised as you practice your speech; often transferred to note cards for use during practice and the final presentation	12: Delivering Your Speech

1 The Evolving Art of Public Speaking

READ IT

After successfully completing this chapter, you will be able to:

- Explain why public speaking is considered to be an audience-centered "evolving" art.
- Describe how the foundations of public speaking were formed.
- Discuss specific ways public speaking helps you develop life skills.
- Summarize how public speaking ability can be used outside the classroom.
- Describe the elements of the public speaking model.

MindTap®

Start with a quick warm-up activity and review the chapter's learning outcomes.

As societies evolve and new technologies are introduced, the roles of public speakers and audience members also change.

EyeEm/Getty Images

The essential skills of face-to-face public speaking were established centuries ago and have an impressive track record. You'll learn how to develop and use those time-tested skills in this course. But as societies evolve and new technologies are introduced, the roles of public speakers and audience members also change. The skills you'll learn in this class will prepare you to adapt successfully to whatever traditional and nontraditional speaking opportunities you may have in the future.

Communications technology has evolved rapidly in recent years and provides you with tremendous resources to help you prepare and deliver your speeches. For instance, you can search the Internet and online databases when researching and organizing a speech topic. You can administer an audience survey online. When you deliver your speech, you have the option of using presentation software such as PowerPoint or Keynote to enhance your message. You may even have future opportunities to give presentations by means of a video conference or webcast.

You'll learn how to be an effective public speaker during the weeks ahead, but you already have a head start. You use basic public speaking skills every day, although not in the way most people associate with speaking in public. You answer questions in class, talk with colleagues at work, tell classmates about a concert you attended, and persuade friends to go to a restaurant you like. What you'll learn in your public speaking course builds on face-to-face experiences like these and helps you improve the communication skills you already have.

Maskot/Getty Images

The Craft of Public Speaking

MindTap®

Read, highlight, and take notes online.

public speaking
When an individual speaks to a group of people, assuming responsibility for speaking for a defined length of time.

optimized speaker
A public speaker who consciously selects relevant topics, adapts to the audience, speaks personally and conversationally, and uses technology when appropriate.

It's no wonder that so many college graduates say **public speaking** was one of the most beneficial classes they took in school. Here's what Naomi, a blogger, posted on an educational review blog: "Everyone's scared of public speaking, and they still wind up finding out that this is one of the most valuable classes you can take in college. No matter what you do with your life, you're going to need to communicate with others verbally, and this class is one of the best ways to help you get over your fears and learn."[1]

Your goal for the public speaking class is not just to "get by" or "pass the course." You have an opportunity to become an excellent speaker, so why not take advantage? You do that by becoming an **optimized speaker**. This means you consciously pay full attention to all the factors that contribute to effective public speaking. You engage your audience by selecting topics that are relevant to them, connecting with them personally during your speech, establishing a conversational mood, adapting your message and delivery to fit the audience and situation, and using technology to enhance and extend your message when appropriate.

The basic foundations of effective public speaking don't change over time. You'll learn how to develop and use those time-tested skills in this course. But successful public speakers today also take advantage of the great opportunities that modern communications technology provides. That's why this book refers to public speaking as "the evolving art."

It's All About the Audience

audience centered
Acknowledging an audience's expectations and situations before, during, and after a speech.

Public speaking is **audience centered**, which means speakers have to understand their audience's expectations and situations before they speak in order to connect with them during the presentation. Audiences demand that what they hear is relevant to them or they will tune the speaker out. With good information about *who* the speaker will be addressing, audience-centered speechmaking strategies can be applied to capture and keep the audience's attention.

Make a Personal Connection

Despite all the benefits provided by modern technologies, face-to-face communication will always remain an essential and necessary form of human interaction. Even though it's often less convenient, young people prefer communicating face-to-face with their friends more than texting, tweeting, or interacting with them on social media. They say they enjoy face-to-face interaction more and can better understand what people mean when they express themselves.[2] Meaningful and direct human communication even improves people's overall sense of personal well-being.[3] So how can you make that personal connection with your audience?

Don't Just Speak, Converse!

Audiences respond favorably to speakers who take a conversational approach in their presentations.[4] Think of public speaking as "entering into a conversation with friends." Conversations are relaxed, familiar, and enjoyable. Most important, conversations are not just one-way. When you converse with friends you really try to help them understand what you are trying to explain. You respect the fact they may not agree with you on a controversial topic. You set a friendly and respectful tone that encourages your audience to respond to you as if they were participating with you in a conversation.

Why is a personal, face-to-face connection so powerful? Because unmediated communication helps fulfill basic human needs at the biological, psychological, social, and cultural levels, regardless of the technological resources available.[5] Conversing with friends is good for your health! That's the feeling you'll want to create when you speak this term. You want to become a good public speaker by being a good conversationalist—a speaker that openly invites the audience to listen and respond by welcoming them into the experience.

Earliest Origins of Human Communication

Because speech leaves no fossil trace, it is impossible to know precisely when humans first began to talk. However, some of the conditions that led to the development of modern communication *have* been discovered. For instance, it is certain that our hominid ancestors were physically able to utter sounds more than 3 million years ago.[6] To coordinate hunting, care for offspring, and create communities, the original human populations that began to migrate out of Africa more than 50,000 years ago must have already developed a prototype of language.[7] Since then, the ability to use complex language has developed over thousands of years.

Early humans used rudimentary speech to convey their thoughts, experiences, and instructions to others. This instinctive cooperative behavior forms the foundation of public communication.[8] Gradually, the ability to speak well became a valuable social skill that formed the basis for the various languages and cultures we see around the world today. The entire history of Western civilization is rooted in the ability to communicate in public effectively. Starting with the Classical Era, the developing forms of human communication began to evolve more rapidly and become increasingly complex, as **Figure 1.1** shows.

Influences on Public Speaking Today

Successful speakers today understand that communications technology impacts all of public life. For example, they know that our political, cultural, and social worlds have become profoundly interactive, blurring traditional distinctions between the senders and receivers of messages—in our case, between the public speaker and audience. Overall, most Americans benefit tremendously from the dynamic changes brought by today's communications technology. But that is *not* the case for everyone, especially at the global level. Even with the exciting advantages that technology provides people here in the United States, today's communications technology also creates new challenges for public speakers.

Interactivity The way we get information, participate in politics, converse with each other, and experience culture is shaped by our interactive involvement with mass media, the culture industries, and the Internet. For example, when the president addresses Congress in the annual State of the Union speech, millions of people can watch the speech on national and international television or view it online. People everywhere can also watch the presidential debates every four years, even on mobile devices. Viewers can react by commenting on social media.

At the same time, popular culture collides with communications technology to form a big part of everyday life. For instance, an appearance on *The Late Show with Stephen Colbert* or *Saturday Night Live* can stoke interest in a new indie band or singer. Then consumers can download the artist's songs onto their MP3 players or smartphones. Twitter feeds from celebrities influence their followers' opinions on every imaginable issue.

John Lund/Sam Diephuis/Blend Images/Jupiter Images

Public speaking has global reach. Today, many speeches are uploaded to the Internet for anyone in the world to read or watch at any time. Or speakers can talk in real time to audiences that are thousands of miles away.

**Classical Era (500–100 BCE)
through
Middle Ages (1000–1500 CE)**

- Earliest democratic societies emerge
- Speeches delivered by well-educated men only
- Oral address to live audiences only
- Principles of rhetoric established
- First print media technologies appear

**Information Age
(1960–Present)**

- Greater diversity in public discourse develops
- Birth of new media and advanced personal communications technology
 - Cable/Satellite TV • FM/Satellite Radio
 - Personal computer • Cell phone • MP3 players
 - Smart devices
- Personalization of cultural experience
- Media/cultural globalization

**Industrial Age
(Mid-1700s to Early 1900s)**

- Birth and expansion of mass media
 - Flyers • Books • Newspapers • Magazines
 - AM Radio • Film • Black-and-white TV
- Literacy rate increases greatly
- Mass audiences form
- Marketing and advertising develop
- Birth of precursors of today's personal communication devices
 - Home telephone • Instant camera • Phonograph
- Audio recorders

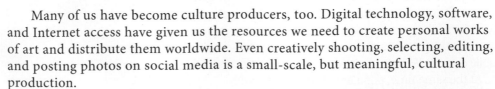

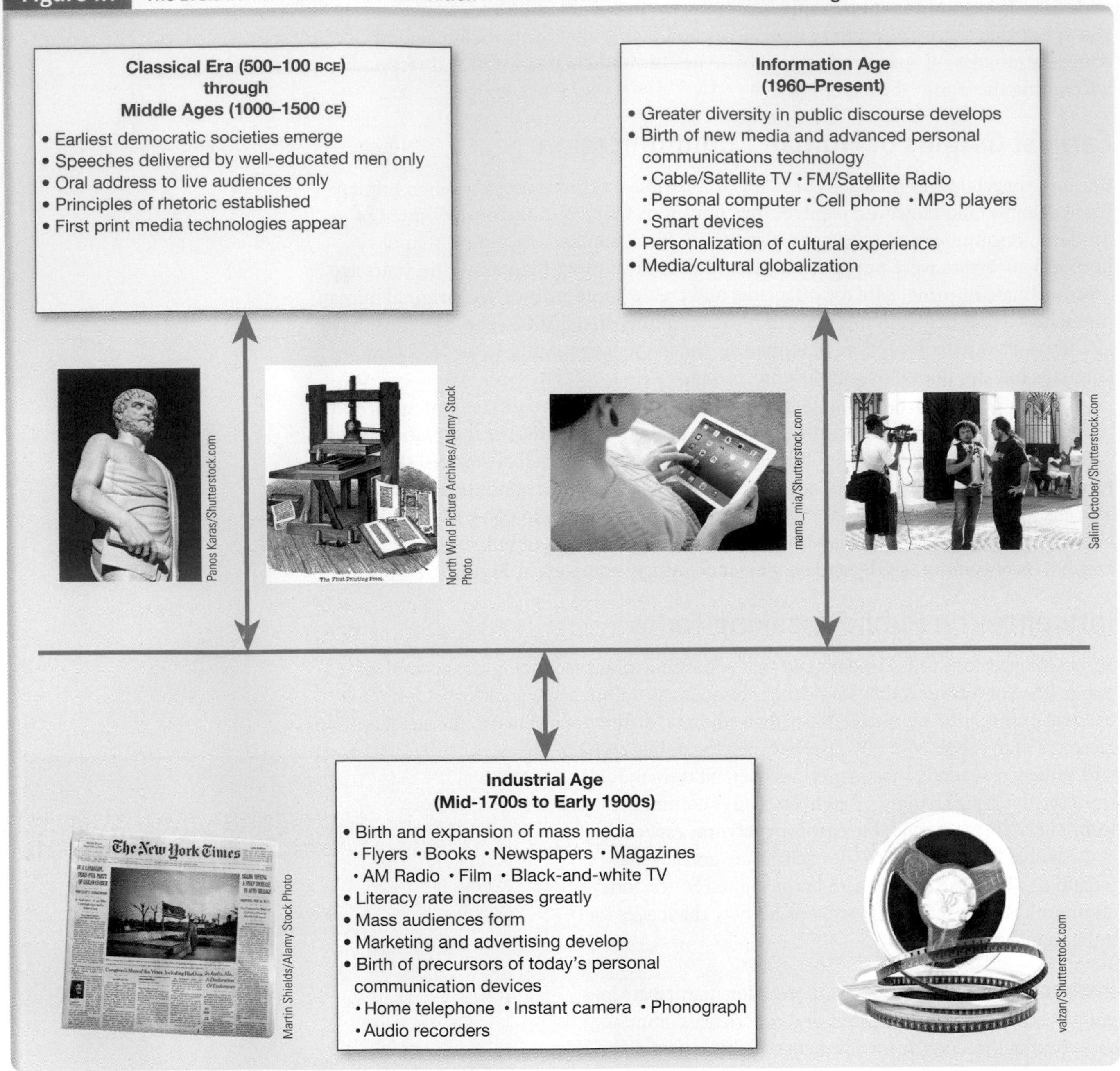

Many of us have become culture producers, too. Digital technology, software, and Internet access have given us the resources we need to create personal works of art and distribute them worldwide. Even creatively shooting, selecting, editing, and posting photos on social media is a small-scale, but meaningful, cultural production.

Speakers today in America and other developed countries know that most people in their audiences are skilled users of media and communications technology. People born in the 1990s and 2000s—the Millennials and Generation Y—are especially technologically literate. They use smartphones, cell phones, all kinds of computers, e-book readers, television, MP3 players, digital cameras, and other electronic devices in combination more than 11 hours a day.[9] More than 87 percent of all Americans and more than 97 percent of American young adults are online.[10] Communications technology has become so ubiquitous that it defines cultural identity and experience—we expect instant access to information and other people.

The Digital Divide On the other hand, today's speakers must realize that the technological and social advantages most of us take for granted in modern Western societies aren't distributed evenly to everyone around the world.

Right here in our own country a **digital divide** reveals differences among the 13 percent of Americans who don't use the Internet. Elderly, poor, less educated, and rural people are less likely than the rest of American society to be online.[11] Therefore, even today, speakers can't assume that everyone in their audience is fully up to speed in online technology and culture. Knowing to what extent your listeners are immersed in technology is part of being audience centered.

digital divide
The gap between groups that have a high level of access to and use of digital communications technology and groups that have a low level of access and use.

Technology: Use with Caution As our communication landscape continues to evolve, speakers and audiences will face new challenges. For example, independent blogs and social media like Facebook, Twitter, Instagram, Snapchat, Pinterest, Vine, and LinkedIn have become major parts of everyday life, but how do they fit into speechmaking? Can you trust the authenticity of the digital images you grab off the Internet? Can you use a clip from YouTube, Netflix, Vimeo, Metacafe, or Yahoo! Screen without permission? Is Wikipedia a reliable source of information? These are among the many important questions today's public speakers must consider.

Information literacy involves not only the ability to access, select, evaluate, and use information effectively, but to do so responsibly.[12] Knowing how to sort through less useful or questionable information is a fundamental public speaking skill. Personal responsibility is key. Speakers must ask themselves tough questions when evaluating sources such as "Where did this information come from?" and "Is the source credible?"

information literacy
The ability to access, select, evaluate, and use information effectively and responsibly.

This text and its accompanying electronic materials have been designed to provide an up-to-date guide for navigating both the foundations of public speaking and what we need to know to be successful *and* responsible public speakers.

MindTap®
Watch It: View a video on the craft of public speaking.

Foundations of Public Speaking

Public speaking in the Western tradition begins with the Sophists (500–300 BCE)—teachers in ancient Greece. As they traveled from place to place, the Sophists lectured students on how to communicate well in a young democratic society. They considered the manner of presenting ideas—delivery—to be the hallmark of an eloquent speaker.

But effective public speaking is by no means limited to delivery techniques. The Greek philosopher Socrates (c. 470–399 BCE) and his student Plato (428–348 BCE) identified logic, evidence, and reasoning as the foundation of true knowledge and the basis for effective public speaking.[13] Aristotle (384–322 BCE), a student of Plato, focused on argument and audiences. Aristotle's ideas about oratory were so influential that he became a key figure in the development of communication as an academic discipline many centuries later. Roman philosophers built upon the established Greek tradition by identifying the "five arts of public speaking."

Aristotle's *Rhetoric*

Aristotle developed a systemic approach to studying **rhetoric**, as public speaking was then called.[14] In Aristotle's major work, *Rhetoric,* he emphasized the importance of adapting speeches to specific audiences and situations. Today we call this approach *audience-centered communication.* Adapting to audiences and building your credibility as a speaker with the specific groups you are addressing form major parts of the audience-centered approach. If, for example, you're attempting to convince your fellow

rhetoric
Aristotle's term for public speaking.

students to get more involved in the local community, you might stress the benefits of listing volunteer work on a résumé. In discussing the same topic with parents of young children, you could focus instead on how volunteer activities help make the community a place where their kids can be safe and thrive.

Aristotle also described various approaches—or *proofs*—a speaker can use to appeal to a specific audience on a particular occasion. He identified three types of proofs: logos, pathos, and ethos. A fourth proof not identified by Aristotle, mythos, was added later.

Logos The term *logos* refers to rational appeals based on logic, verifiable facts, and objective analysis. Traditional examples of logos include the deployment of scientific evidence and the kinds of arguments prosecutors and defense attorneys use in courts of law when they attempt to establish the true facts of a case. But presenting a detailed set of recommendations at a committee meeting or praising a friend's accomplishments when you nominate him or her for a leadership position is also an appeal based on logos.

Pathos Successful speaking usually requires more than logic. Aristotle's second proof, *pathos,* refers to a speaker's appeals to our emotions. Speakers might use pathos to arouse the audience's feelings, such as when they display poignant photos to convince us to contribute to charitable organizations. Public speakers who endeavor to persuade their audiences about sensitive topics often use the power of emotion to support their argument.

Ethos Appeals based on *ethos,* the third proof, rest on the speaker's personal character and credibility. When you speak at a campus meeting or offer comments in class, the listeners, even subconsciously, evaluate your trustworthiness and believability—key components of good character and credibility.

Mythos A fourth type of appeal to the audience, *mythos,* focuses on values and beliefs embedded in cultural narratives or stories.[15] Contemporary communication scholars added this concept to Aristotle's original proofs because stories represent important cultural values that can also appeal to an audience. For instance, American audiences are likely to respond positively to appeals concerning individual freedom, equality of opportunity, or the right to privacy. Chapter 15 further explains all four types of appeals—logos, pathos, ethos, and mythos—and provides detailed guidance about how to use them to support your message.

The Five Arts of Public Speaking

Roman philosophers and scholars later categorized the elements of public communication into five "arts of public speaking" that still apply today.[16] They argued that these five arts—invention, arrangement, style, memory, and delivery—form the broad foundation of public speaking.

invention
Discovering what you want to say in a speech, such as by choosing a topic and developing good arguments.

arrangement
The way ideas presented in a speech are organized.

style
The language or words used in a speech.

1. **Invention** focuses on what you want to say. As the first art, invention refers to the moment when you find an idea, line of thought, or argument you might use in a speech. Choosing a topic (Chapter 4) and developing good arguments (Chapter 15) are both part of invention.
2. **Arrangement**, the second art, refers to how you organize your ideas. This art accounts for the basic parts of a speech (introduction, body, and conclusion) as well as the order in which points are presented (Chapter 8). Good organization helps maintain the audience's attention and keeps them focused on the ideas the speaker presents.[17] For example, sometimes a speaker tells the end of a story first because the audience will then be curious about how the ending came about. At other times, the speaker tells a story in the order in which events happened, leading to a surprise ending.
3. The third art, **style**, involves the imagery you use to bring a speech's content to life (Chapter 10). Consider the differences between saying, "My trip last summer was fun"

and "My adventures last summer included a strenuous but thrilling trek through the Rocky Mountains." Both statements reflect the same idea, but the second one grabs the audience's attention so they want to know what made the trek so thrilling.

4. **Memory**, the fourth art, refers to using your knowledge and abilities as a communicator to give an effective speech. Memory goes beyond simple memorization, referring instead to the importance of using the totality of your public speaking skills comprehensively (Chapter 12).[18] In other words, when you present a speech, you rely on everything you've learned about public speaking, your topic, the audience, and the occasion.
5. As the fifth art, **delivery** reflects the moment when a speech goes public—when it is presented to an audience. Delivery involves how you use your voice, gestures, and body movement when giving a speech. Chapter 12 covers how to achieve the natural, conversational delivery style today's audiences expect and prefer. Today's speakers often incorporate presentation media like PowerPoint seamlessly into their speeches, and there is an art to doing that, too (see Chapter 11).

SPEAKING OF ...

Buddhist Preaching and the Five Arts

The five arts of public speaking come from the Western cultural tradition, but other cultures also emphasize these core ideas. For example, Buddhist preaching in Japan follows similar principles. Established guidelines specify what topics preachers can discuss (invention), the way ideas are organized (arrangement), the type of language used (style), what information requires memorization (memory), and how the voice and body should be used when preaching (delivery). Many of these guidelines are highly detailed, such as those for using a specific organizational pattern for a sermon: recite a verse from a written text, explain the verse's central theme, tell a relevant fictional story, tell a true story, and make concluding comments. Although not all Buddhist preachers rely on this way of organizing their sermons, many still use this traditional organizational pattern.[19]

Storytelling

Most people love to hear stories. Stories not only entertain but also help people understand their worlds. Beyond just making your words clear to your audience, as a speaker you want to achieve understanding. It makes good sense to take advantage of the natural attraction humans have to stories to accomplish this goal. In this key regard, stories form an essential part of the foundation of public speaking.

memory
Using the ability to recall information about all aspects of public speaking to give an effective speech.

delivery
The presentation of a speech to an audience.

Storytelling's appeal is embedded deep in our DNA.[20] Long before our forebears had media to inform them of the news, people told stories to warn each other about threatening things that were happening around them. Listeners depended on the information they got from stories so they could respond in ways that assured their survival.

Consequently, we've been conditioned since childhood to use our instinct for narrative thinking and develop it as a social skill. **Narrative** thinking relies on the power of stories to connect our sense of self with the world, envision what could be, apply logic to identify patterns and causal connections, and structure events in a logical order.[21] Stories stimulate the imagination in ways that bridge cultural differences between people.[22] They often touch our emotions, helping to bind the storyteller to the audience. Because storytelling is so basic to human nature, today's audiences welcome narratives in speeches like their ancestors did long ago.

narrative
A story used in a speech or other form of communication.

Telling a story will probably amuse your audience, but the story itself does not make for a great or even good speech. To influence audiences most effectively, stories must be used in conjunction with other aspects of good speechmaking. Being able to combine the magnetism of storytelling with well-supported arguments and inclusive language is a communication skill that can benefit you in countless academic, professional, and social situations.

Public Speaking Is a Life Skill

When you think about public speaking, you probably conjure up an image of yourself or someone else in the act of delivering a speech. But that's only the final step in the speechmaking process. No doubt your public speaking course will help prepare you to deliver excellent speeches when the time comes, but there's more to this course than that. A public speaking course gives you a chance to develop transferable skills that you can use inside and outside the classroom. For instance, you'll learn how to critically analyze almost any subject, manage nervousness in any situation, listen effectively, adapt what you have to say to the people who are listening to you, build credibility for yourself, find and use many different types of information, organize ideas, and present those ideas and information clearly and persuasively for any purpose. Skills like these naturally carry over from one social context or occasion to another. So, for example, when you learn to manage anxiety in your public speaking class, you'll be able to apply that skill in other settings such as giving presentations in other courses or answering questions in job interviews. **Table 1.1** summarizes the transferable skills learned in a public speaking course, how they're developed, and how they benefit you in everyday life.

Critically Analyzing a Topic or Idea

With easy access to so much information from so many sources, public speakers and their audiences must be especially vigilant and put their critical thinking skills to good use. From the start, it's important to realize that the term *critical* in this context does not mean judgmental. A critical analysis aims at examining the component parts of a topic or idea for clarity, factual integrity, and the logic of the relationships that can be drawn to connect elements of the topic or idea. These critical factors are fundamental to good thinking and good communication generally.

Table 1.1 Transferable Life Skills Gained in a Public Speaking Course

Transferable Skill	How Public Speaking Helps You Develop the Skill	Examples of How the Skill Might Benefit You in Everyday Life
Being more confident and managing communication anxiety	• Habituation • Using proven strategies	Feeling more comfortable talking with people in unfamiliar social situations
Being a good listener	• Understanding listening • Listening reciprocally	Understanding better what a friend has to say, and the friend understanding you better
Adapting to different audiences and building your credibility	• Knowing how to research and analyze audiences • Increasing competence and dynamism	Being able to confront a friend or coworker about a difficult issue without damaging the relationship
Finding and evaluating information	• Recognizing appropriate and reliable sources • Assessing the accuracy and validity of information	Researching a company you think you would like to work for
Critically analyzing ideas for speech topics	• Examining the logical, emotional, and ethical value of idea • Determining fit of idea with intended audience	Evaluating the merit of a proposed project at work
Organizing ideas	• Understanding patterns of organization • Understanding how people process information	Explaining to a classmate the advantages and disadvantages of joining a fraternity or sorority
Presenting ideas effectively	• Communicating mindfully • Knowing how to plan and prepare effective presentation materials	Using presentation software in a speech about college life that you give at your former high school

Whenever we express our thoughts, we want to avoid being vague: Critical analysis helps us clarify what we say or hear. We certainly want to prevent misrepresenting the truth: Critical analysis demands we support our ideas with valid evidence. And we don't want to be sloppy or illogical in what we argue: Critical analysis requires us to carefully examine how sensibly our ideas relate to each other.

You and your ideas will win the attention and respect of others only when you hold what you have to say up to honest self-examination. Public speaking success relies largely on your ability to do that, but success in life generally comes to those who apply a high standard of analysis to everything they say and hear. Your public speaking class will sharpen your ability to recognize the strengths and weaknesses of your ideas and those of others in ways that will help you make critical analysis a transferable and enjoyable life skill.

Becoming More Confident

Nearly everyone gets nervous when speaking in public. Good speakers learn to cope with that feeling. Successfully completing a public speaking course helps to build your confidence, which helps you manage whatever nervousness you may experience in the future.[23]

The process of *habituation*—fearing a situation less as it becomes more familiar, or *habit-like*—helps you manage nervousness over time, just as doing almost anything repeatedly makes you more comfortable doing it. For example, you probably experienced some nervousness the first time you attended a college class. After a few class meetings, though, you likely became more comfortable because you had a better idea of what to expect.

Repetition alone isn't enough, however; you also need positive experiences. You didn't become comfortable taking college courses simply because you attended several class sessions. Your comfort level increased because you got to know your classmates, you made a comment that your instructor praised, or you successfully completed the first assignment. In other words, you were encouraged by the positive weight of your prior experiences to come back and feel more confident.

In the same way, affirming experiences in a public speaking course can help you get used to speaking outside the classroom. You'll get positive feedback about your speeches, and you'll get constructive suggestions about what you might change so that you give a more effective speech next time. Both kinds of feedback give you direction and remind you that you have the support of your instructor and classmates.

The increased confidence and decreased nervousness you experience as your public speaking class progresses will transfer to speaking situations outside of class. When speaking opportunities arise, such as stating your opinion about a controversial issue at a meeting, asking a question in a lecture hall, giving a toast at a friend's party, or explaining an idea to colleagues at work, you'll feel more enthusiastic about doing so. Chapter 2 covers specific strategies for increasing your confidence and managing the common psychological and physiological effects of speaking publicly.

Becoming a Better Listener

Poor listening skills cause all sorts of problems—like missing a key point during a staff meeting at work, misunderstanding a doctor's advice, or giving an inappropriate response to a client or customer's question. A public speaking course sharpens your listening skills.[24]

As you build your various communication skills, one goal you should set is learning how to listen reciprocally. This means that all participants in any social interaction listen to one another with open minds and full attention. Responsible communicators listen openly even when they disagree with someone. Chapter 3 presents specific strategies that help you become a more effective listener and able to compensate for the listening skills some participants might lack.

Adapting to Different Audiences

Gathering and analyzing information about an audience helps you identify audience members' interests and concerns, what they know about your topic, and how they might respond to what you say. Whether you're telling coworkers about a new smartphone app, running for election to student government, or just entertaining people with stories from your travels, knowing your audience is essential to getting your message across well. Chapter 5 explains the best methods for analyzing and adapting to audiences.

Building Your Credibility

Another related skill is building your credibility as a communicator. *Speaker credibility* refers to how much an audience views the speaker as competent, friendly, trustworthy, and dynamic. How you establish and maintain your credibility as a speaker varies from audience to audience and topic to topic. As a result, knowing how to demonstrate your credibility helps you get your ideas across to others no matter what the context. Suppose, for instance, that you'd like to get your college to provide more funding for student organizations on campus. Your message will be much more persuasive if the school's administrators view you as a credible spokesperson. Chapter 5 describes the four components of credibility and explains how you can become a more believable and respected speaker.

Finding and Using Reliable Information

Knowing how to locate information, evaluate its reliability and usefulness for your purpose, and apply it responsibly and effectively can serve you well in all aspects of your personal and professional life. Finding and assessing information for school or work is an obvious example. But research skills are essential for your home life as well. One study found that 80 percent of Internet users in the United States search for health information online, yet very few check the sources of that information.[25] As a result, millions of Americans rely on health information that may or may not be accurate or reliable. Learning how to systematically find, analyze, and evaluate information in your public speaking class will help you avoid poor and discredited information. Chapter 6 covers the research process in depth.

Organizing Ideas and Information Effectively

Listeners in any situation expect and need to hear information that is clearly organized or they lose interest. One of the best ways for you to provide this clarity is to use standard patterns of organization such as *chronological* (how something develops over time), *spatial* (what physical relationships exist between things), *cause and effect* (how one thing results in another), and *problem–solution* (which identifies a problem and discusses how to solve it). Public speaking students develop ways to organize their ideas effectively outside the classroom, too.[26] Whether you're planning a party with others or explaining how to use a new piece of equipment, organizing what you want to say makes it easier for other people to understand you. In the same way, organizing the points of your speech beforehand will give your ideas greater impact. Chapter 8 covers how to organize and outline your ideas. An outline keeps you on track and gives you a basic plan for researching, constructing, and delivering what you want to say about your topic.

Presenting Ideas and Information Effectively

Effective communication requires *mindfulness:* consciously focusing on the situation you're in and maintaining awareness of what you say and how others respond.[27] A mindful public speaker is an audience-centered speaker. Being mindful in your public speaking course also helps you be more mindful as you present ideas and information in your other social interactions.

Mindfulness also applies to planning, preparing, and using presentation media effectively. Integrating PowerPoint, Keynote, or other digital slide software into speeches has become nearly a requirement for many business presentations, but it's not appropriate for every speaking situation. For instance, when you get together with friends you wouldn't use digital slides to tell them about your whitewater kayaking trip in Colorado—they probably already saw your photos on social media anyway. However, you might put together a digital slide show to share your adventure at a meeting where you try to recruit new members to your kayaking club. The audience and context determine your use of presentation media—you must be mindful of that too. Chapter 11 gives you strategies for using all presentation media.

Speaking Effectively in "Public"

In many ways, the term *public speaking* doesn't accurately describe most situations in which we try to inform or persuade other people. Giving a speech in a classroom or making a presentation at work, for example, isn't "public" in the same way that addressing an open forum on campus or a hearing at city hall is. Many of the opportunities you have for using your public speaking skills are more semiprivate or private than public. The following are some of the common contexts where your public speaking skills can be applied: the college classroom, the workplace, your community, social events, and online.

In Classes

You've probably already answered instructors' questions, asked questions yourself, given reports, or explained ideas in class. You've certainly told a few stories to other students in and out of class, had many spontaneous conversations, expressed your views in discussion groups, and collaborated on assignments. These are all informal speaking opportunities. Clearly, your public speaking course is not the only place on campus where you can apply the communication skills you are learning.

Instructors in departments all across college campuses increasingly expect students to make classroom presentations.[28] For instance, students majoring in science, technology, engineering, or mathematics (the STEM disciplines) are asked to explain concepts or describe projects in class. Psychology, sociology, and other social science majors are called on to report the findings of research undertaken during the term. Public performance often makes up an important part of the requirements for a degree in the humanities and arts. Degrees in education naturally involve speaking before classroom audiences.

In the Workplace

As the base of our economy continues to shift from manufacturing to information, the ability to communicate well becomes increasingly essential to professional success.[29] Being able to think creatively and innovate is extremely important in today's economy.[30] But that's not enough. You've got to be able to describe your creative, innovative ideas to others effectively. That's one reason why employers in all types of organizations and industries rank oral and written communication ability as the most important professional skill set for college graduates to have when they enter the workforce (**Figure 1.2**).

Communication skills provide the foundation for the development of other important abilities too, like working well with others and solving problems. The good news is that the ability to communicate well in professional settings can be learned. Students who successfully complete a class in public speaking bring better communication skills to the workplace than those who don't take the class.[31]

You may think, "I'll never do any public speaking in my job." At first, you might even try to avoid situations at work where you have to express your thoughts to others

Figure 1.2 Communication-Related Skills Employers Rated Most Important

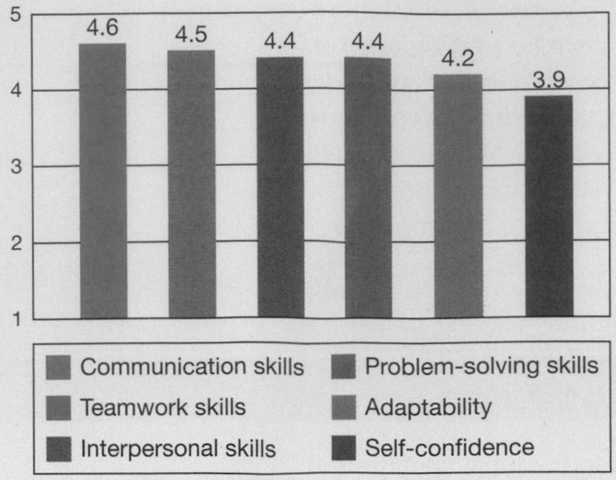

in groups. However, you'll need excellent communication skills to advance your career no matter where you work. Employees in any field must attend meetings frequently where they are expected to contribute to the discussions. Even in professions such as accounting—usually not associated with public speaking—very good oral communication skills are essential for developing business contacts and getting promoted.[32] Some companies even hire speech coaches to help employees improve their speaking abilities before considering them for promotion.[33] Clearly, it's far better to arrive at hiring or promotion interviews with those personal presentational skills already developed.

In Communities

Citizens who are willing to speak in their communities make up the very foundation of a vibrant democracy.[34] When you use your public speaking skills to discuss issues with others in your community, you contribute to a more informed society and feel a greater sense of belonging. By communicating publicly, you participate in democracy at its most basic level.[35] The skills you develop in your public speaking class can help you play an active part in the various communities to which you belong.

The demographic face of our communities is changing. As Latino and Asian populations across the country grow, so too does the public participation and impact of these traditionally underrepresented groups. Consider the effect young Latino leaders Julián Castro and Marco Rubio are having on American politics. Castro, of Mexican descent, was born in San Antonio, Texas, and graduated from Stanford University with a double major: political science and communication. Rubio, whose parents emigrated from Cuba, was born in Miami and graduated from the University of Florida in political science. Castro became Democratic mayor of San Antonio and the U.S. Secretary of Housing and Urban Development. Rubio became a Republican U.S. senator from Florida and presidential candidate. Both are political figures from diverse communities who became superb public speakers in their second language.

Robin Jerstad/ZUMA Press, Inc./Alamy Stock Photo

Julián Castro

Christopher Halloran/Shutterstock.com

Marco Rubio

At Social Events

Many social events, such as graduations, bachelor and bachelorette parties, wedding receptions, *quinceañeras*, charity events, and family reunions call for public speaking. Casual get-togethers like birthday celebrations, holiday gatherings, going-away parties, neighborhood barbeques, and dinners with friends often become more meaningful when attendees mark the moment with a few brief comments to the group. Such rituals endure in our societies because they strengthen ties between people and help transmit cultural values.

When you celebrate graduating from your college or university, for example, you may be called on to say a few words, even if the event is an informal gathering. Successfully completing a class in public speaking will help you prepare a short speech your audience will remember and that truly expresses the meaning of the occasion for you. It will probably be captured on video as well, so why not make it memorable in a positive way? Social events offer fairly regular opportunities to demonstrate and further develop your public speaking skills throughout your life.

Online

As communications technology has evolved, so too have the opportunities for public speaking. If you're like most people, you spend a considerable part of your life online. You go online for school and work; to get caught up on news, entertainment, and sports; and to connect with friends. But you probably aren't just a consumer of online media—you likely create content, too. For example, you may post photos on Instagram or Snapchat, updates on Facebook, or commentaries on HuffPost, upload a resume or video biography to job websites, make and post videos on YouTube, start up a blog, or provide status updates to your colleagues in online business meetings. Being able to present yourself well online is key to success in all these endeavors.

Distance speaking is fast becoming part of the public speaking landscape. **Distance speaking** is the planned and structured presentation of ideas transmitted from one physical location to other locations by means of information and communications technology. You can adapt the skills you learn in your public speaking class to all kinds of online communication. Although the technologies used for distance speaking create their own advantages and challenges, the skills you need for effective public speaking don't change. Distance speaking still involves a human source sending a message to a human audience, just as face-to-face speaking in a classroom does. Knowing how to come up with good ideas, research a topic, organize the content, and deliver a message effectively all transfer smoothly from face-to-face speaking in a single location to distance speaking received in various locations online.

distance speaking
The planned and structured presentation of ideas transmitted from one physical location to other locations by means of information and communications technology.

Public Speaking and Human Communication Today

Public speaking shares some characteristics with other types of communication, but it also differs in several important ways. Knowing the similarities and differences will help you understand the place of public speaking within the spectrum of human communication and help you see how your speaking skills apply in other contexts.

Traditional Categories of Human Communication

Communication scholars traditionally use the following categories to identify contexts for human communication:

- *Interpersonal communication* occurs when two or more people interact with each other as unique individuals. You develop personal relationships with friends, family, and coworkers through interpersonal communication.
- In *small-group communication,* three or more people interact to accomplish a task or reach a shared objective. Local theater groups, committees, and collaborative work groups are examples of small groups.
- *Organizational communication* refers to the flow of information that takes place within and among organizations for the purpose of accomplishing common goals, such as creating products and offering services. Organizations often provide the setting for speeches, as when a department manager gives a presentation to senior executives.

- *Mass communication* originates with a media organization such as NBC, *People* magazine, XM Satellite Radio, or *The New York Times* and is transmitted to large, fairly anonymous, and often diverse audiences.
- *Public communication* occurs when, for a limited amount of time, an individual speaks or otherwise sends a message to people outside that individual's known social group—a political speech or a post on a message board, for example.

But personal communications technology has changed the nature of all traditional forms of human communication. We connect interpersonally offline and online. Small groups and organizations use the Internet to meet and plan their activities. The mass media industries rely on social media for sources of news and entertainment. Public communication, including public speaking, is often mediated by communications technology.

Evolution of Communication Models

Scholars create graphical models to help us understand the dynamics of human behavior. In the field of communication, the models reflect the complicated nature of social interaction and how technology influences the ways we connect.

Models visually represent the nature of human communication by describing the elements involved. The very first models portrayed human communication simply as information that moves in one direction, from a *sender* to a *receiver*. These models became known as the *transmission* or *linear* models of communication.[36]

But communication is not strictly a one-way affair. Over the years, scholars developed increasingly complex models of communication to account for the *feedback* that goes back and forth between individuals as they interact and to describe more fully the *channels* through which people exchange *messages*.[37] These more complex models, which described communication as an interaction or a transaction, emphasize the active role of listening and responding as well as speaking.

The later, more sophisticated communication models added three more elements: noise, context, and environment. *Noise* refers to any interference that prevents messages from being understood. The *context* is the setting for any social interaction, such as a conference room or grocery checkout line. The *environment* includes all the outside forces that might affect communication, such as current events or the weather.

Any contemporary general model of human communication must start by considering the individual communicator—you. You are right in the middle of everything that's going on in the Information Age. Individualized lifestyles and the personalization of experience have become dominant cultural trends.[38] And because today's information and communications technologies give you tremendous individual freedom and flexibility, the most recent models of human communication also describe a **pervasive communication environment**. In this environment, information can be accessed and shared in multiple forms from multiple locations in ways that transcend conventional ways of thinking about time and space.[39]

pervasive communication environment
The ability to access and share information in multiple forms from multiple locations in ways that transcend conventional ways of thinking about time and space.

Spheres of Communication We express ourselves and engage other people within four principal spheres of communications activity (see **Figure 1.3**):

- *Mass media.* This is the least interactive sphere of communication. Nonetheless, mainstream media still occupy an enormous amount of our time as we search for information and entertainment.
- *Mediated personal communication.* Mobile technologies and the Internet have become dominant forms of social interaction, giving us the ability to connect instantly with others by voice, text, and image.

Figure 1.3 The Spheres of Communication

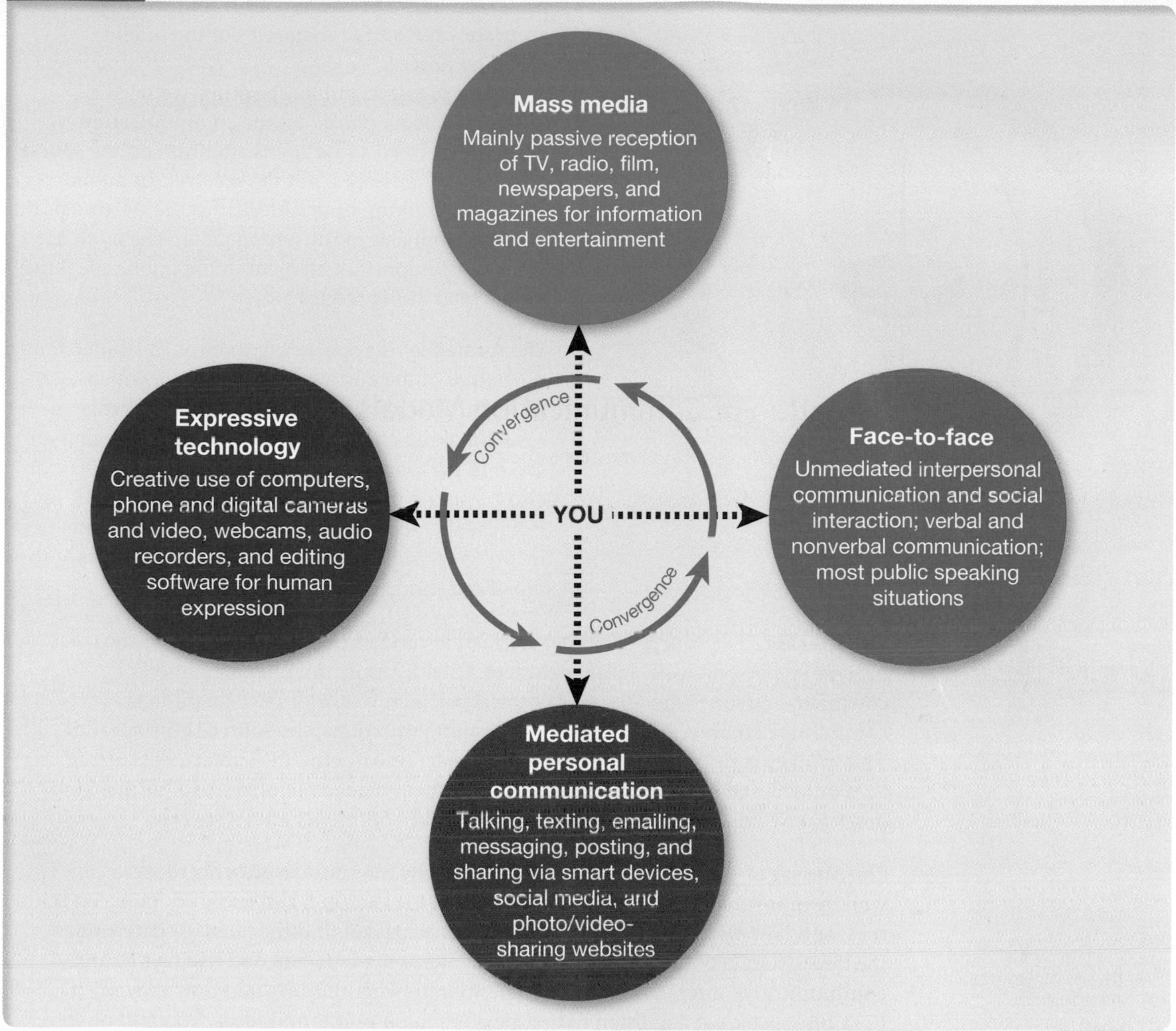

- *Expressive technology.* Digital technology has opened up endless ways for people to gather information and creatively express themselves, fulfilling a basic human need.
- *Face-to-face.* This type of communication encompasses unmediated contact with other people, including most public speaking situations.

Although each sphere has its own form and function, people often interact in multiple spheres simultaneously. This process is known as **convergence**. For example, expressive technology converges with mediated personal communication when a creative idea is passed from one person to another. Or, in another example, public speakers use a form of expressive technology—presentation media software—to inform, persuade, or entertain their live audience.

convergence
When people interact in multiple communications spheres simultaneously.

The Elements of Audience-Centered Public Speaking Every one of us is constantly immersed in the four spheres of communication where technologies converge in a pervasive communication environment. We have a stunning richness of resources and options that enable us to communicate with almost anyone, anywhere,

Figure 1.4 A Model of Public Speaking

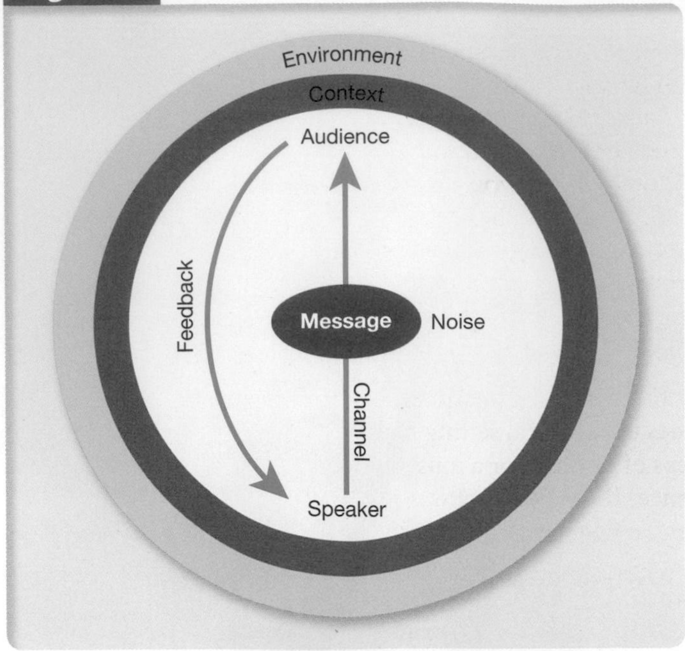

at any time. But do the communication models presented in the previous section of this chapter accurately reflect the dynamics of the public speaking process?

Not exactly. In public speaking, we need a different starting point. All the communication models described so far focus attention on the source or sender of messages, not the receiver. In public speaking, thinking of the speaker as the starting point puts the emphasis in the wrong place. The audience is the most important element in the public speaking model seen in **Figure 1.4**.

The Audience If a speaker ignores or misunderstands the nature of the **audience**, the message will not get through. This principle applies across the range of speechmaking contexts. Although most speeches are given in person to a live audience, presentations can also be linked up via webcam for distance speaking. Because the needs and interests of listeners come first in any speaking situation, the audience appears at the top of our model of public speaking.

audience
The intended recipients of a speaker's message.

speaker
The person who assumes the primary responsibility for conveying a message in a public communication context.

The Speaker The source or sender element in models of communication is the individual person—you, another student, friend, family member, neighbor, or coworker—anyone who assumes a central role as initiator or participant in a communicative interaction. In public speaking situations, the source is the **speaker**. The speaker is responsible for choosing a topic, researching the subject, organizing the content, and presenting the speech. In turn, audience members also fulfill a kind of speaker role when they ask questions or make comments after a speech.

message
The words and nonverbal cues a speaker uses to convey ideas, feelings, and thoughts.

The Message The words a speaker uses and how the speaker presents those words—nonverbal communication—to get an idea across to an audience make up the **message**. The way an audience responds to the speaker and the message determines the effectiveness of the speech. When you interpret what someone else says in any communicative interaction, you pay attention to what they say and how they say it. In public speaking, you listen to the speaker's main points and ideas. You also observe how the speaker moves, incorporates gestures, makes eye contact, and uses his or her voice. All these factors interact to influence how the message is received.

channel
A mode or medium of communication.

The Channel The **channel** is the mode or medium that is used to communicate—in person, in print, or by electronic media. Public speaking often involves multiple channels. For instance, in addition to vocal delivery, a speaker may display a graph, play a relevant musical clip, or make available a paper handout with additional information. Communications technology also allows speakers to give speeches via webcam or videoconference and make their digital slides available to an audience anywhere in the world. Especially in business, digital slides make up a key component of many speeches. Audience members may respond through multiple channels as well, such as texting or emailing a question to the presenter after the speech.

noise
Anything that interferes with the understanding of a message.

Noise Any distraction that interferes with the audience's ability to hear and understand a message represents **noise**. In public speaking, noise may be internal to the listener, as with daydreaming, being hungry, or feeling tired. External noise includes sounds or actions that prevent listeners from easily hearing what the speaker has to say, such as other people talking or moving around, traffic noise, or a cell phone going off. Poor lighting, difficulty seeing the speaker, and cluttered digital slides are other sources of unwanted external noise.

Feedback Gaining and keeping the audience's attention is most important, so speakers feel encouraged when the audience appears to be listening with interest. Nods and smiles indicate that listeners understand and perhaps agree. Shaking heads, frowns, and quizzical looks suggest that audience members may disagree, feel confused, or not understand the speaker's point. Getting **feedback** from listeners lets you know how well you are coming across as a speaker and indicates areas in which you might improve. In your public speaking class, you gather feedback informally by observing your audience as you speak, listening to their questions, and asking them after class what they thought of your presentation. Your instructor provides you with comments that are more formal and may even collect feedback from your audience, such as written or oral peer evaluations.

feedback
Audience members' responses to a speech.

The Context The **context** refers to the circumstances or situation in which a particular interaction takes place. In public speaking, the context includes the physical setting for a speech—an auditorium, classroom, conference room, the steps of city hall, or a museum gallery, for instance. The place where a speech is given influences the way the message is delivered and how the audience responds. A classroom or conference room is generally less formal than a large auditorium filled with hundreds of people. Trying to keep listeners' attention poses different challenges on the steps outside city hall than inside a quiet museum gallery. The occasion for the speech also shapes the context. For instance, audience members have different expectations for a speech commemorating an historic event than for a speech supporting a candidate for political office.

context
The situation within which a speech is given.

The Environment The **environment** consists of the surroundings that extend beyond the immediate context that influence any communicative interaction. In public speaking, audience members can't help but respond to the speaker's message even subconsciously in terms of what's happening in their world. The effect can be negative or positive. For example, a speech to a student audience on why your university should build a fancy new swimming pool probably would not be well received at a time when tuition costs are skyrocketing. But the same audience might respond positively to a speech advocating the installation of economical solar energy technology on campus.

environment
The external surroundings that influence a public speaking event.

Summary

As a constantly evolving art, public speaking has changed in ways that benefit you tremendously. You can easily use communications technology to help you research, organize, and present your speeches. But the core of effective public speaking depends on basic communication ability, and you have that already. What you'll learn in this course builds on your innate communication abilities to develop something truly valuable—the ability to speak confidently in front of a group.

Public speaking is a craft that is centered on connecting with the audience effectively. You achieve that goal by keeping the audience first and foremost in your mind throughout the speechmaking process and entering into a conversation with them when you speak. From the dawn of human evolution, our ancestors have had to convey their ideas and instructions accurately and convincingly to others in order to survive and thrive. From the Classical Age through the Industrial Age to the Information Age we live in today, the rise of democratic societies and creation of new technology have broadened the stage so that many more people now have opportunities to speak publicly. Yet, a digital divide still exists, so speakers who are fortunate enough to have access to today's technological resources must be sure to use them responsibly.

The foundations of public speaking were established in Greek and Roman societies during the Classical Era in the history of Western civilization more than two thousand years ago. Many of the great teachers and philosophers of the time—the Sophists, Socrates, Plato, Aristotle, and the Romans—created the evolving art of rhetoric, as public speaking was then known. Aristotle's proofs—logos, pathos, and ethos—form the theoretical basis of public speaking that has endured through time. Later, the five arts—invention, arrangement, style, memory, and delivery—became the core components of public speaking, then and now. Public speaking's foundation is also built upon the power of the narrative—storytelling. Long before the media arrived, our ancestors told stories to each other to warn of danger and form primitive cultures. Consequently, narrative thinking is embedded deep in our DNA and serves us well as a public speaking technique.

Your public speaking course will help you develop valuable life skills by sharpening your analytical ability. By preparing your own speeches and listening to others speak, you'll learn how to critically analyze a wide range of subjects. You'll develop confidence as a speaker and learn how to listen closely and smartly when others present. You'll discover how to adapt the content of your speeches to your audience and build your speaker credibility. You'll learn how to systematically find, organize, and present information in ways that engage and influence people.

The public speaking class you're taking will benefit you in practical ways. In the classroom, many instructors across a wide variety of fields of study require students to participate in discussions, debates, and presentations. Communication ability is ranked at the top of the list of desirable workplace skills by employers and managers. Our diverse communities today offer great opportunities for individuals to make presentations that can influence plans and policies. Good presentational skills will give you confidence to speak up at graduations, receptions, parties, and other social gatherings. And what you'll learn in the public speaking class can also be applied to online meetings and distance speaking.

Our motivations for communicating have remained the same over the millennia, but the nature of how we communicate constantly evolves. Four spheres of communication have emerged in the modern era—the mass media, expressive technology, mediated interpersonal communication, and face-to-face interaction. General models of human communication attempt to account for the elements involved. The models have evolved from the limited one-way transmission approach to more sophisticated models that reflect today's complex communication environment, with you at the center of the action. But in public speaking the focus is always on the audience. The public speaking model comprises eight elements: audience, speaker, message, channel, noise, feedback, context, and environment.

> REVIEW IT

MindTap®
Use flashcards to learn key terms and take a quiz to test your knowledge.

Key Terms

- **arrangement** 8
- **audience** 18
- **audience centered** 4
- **channel** 18
- **context** 19
- **convergence** 17
- **delivery** 9
- **digital divide** 7
- **distance speaking** 15
- **environment** 19
- **feedback** 19
- **information literacy** 7
- **invention** 8
- **memory** 9
- **message** 18
- **narrative** 9
- **noise** 18
- **optimized speaker** 4
- **pervasive communication environment** 16
- **public speaking** 4
- **rhetoric** 7
- **speaker** 18
- **style** 8

Reflecting on the Evolving Art of Public Speaking

1. How has the art of public speaking evolved from the Classical Era to the Information Age?
2. Why should you consider the "audience" to be so important when you prepare and deliver your speeches?
3. How do Aristotle's five "proofs" work as ways to appeal to audiences?
4. Specifically, in what ways can learning to become an excellent public speaker help you develop other valuable life skills?
5. Why do employers rank communication skills first among abilities they want college graduates to have when hiring? Why do you think leaders in business especially need to communicate well? How will the communication skills you are learning in this course transfer to settings outside the classroom in your life?
6. "You" exist right in the middle of the spheres of communications activity in which you are involved. So why does the public speaking model presented at the end of this chapter consider the audience, not you, to be more important? Can you begin to analyze the people who will hear your speeches this term just by looking around the room? How would you describe your audience?

2 Building Your Confidence

READ IT

After successfully completing this chapter, you will be able to:

- Identify and discuss the causes of speech anxiety.
- Describe the uncertainties associated with public speaking.
- Explain and apply general strategies for building your public speaking confidence.
- Describe and apply the strategies you can use to build your confidence as you prepare your speech.
- Discuss and apply techniques for building your confidence during a speech.

MindTap®

Start with a quick warm-up activity and review the chapter's learning outcomes.

Successfully completing a public speaking class will raise your confidence, lower your speech anxiety, and improve your public speaking skills across a variety of speech contexts.

JT Vintage/Glasshouse Images/Alamy Stock Photo

Type "public speaking" into any online search engine and you'll find "fear of public speaking" and "conquer your speech anxiety" on the first page of results. If you get anxious just thinking about getting in front of an audience and giving a speech, you are not alone. Throughout history, many famous people who were well known for their public speaking skills also experienced speech anxiety. Aristotle, who as you learned in Chapter 1 developed many public speaking theories and practices still used today, wrote about his fear of speaking in public. Other famous people with speech anxiety include American Red Cross founder Clara Barton, former British Prime Minister Winston Churchill, actor Samuel L. Jackson, singer Carly Simon, actress Emily Blunt, musician Chris Trapper, and boxing champion Jermain Taylor.

Like the vast majority of people, college students rank public speaking as more frightening than loneliness, insects and bugs, financial problems, flying—even death. Fear of public speaking cuts across gender, ethnic background, and age—and for students, even grade point average.[1] But you've already taken the first step in conquering your fear of public speaking—multiple studies have demonstrated that successfully completing a public speaking class will raise your confidence, lower your speech anxiety, and improve your public speaking skills across a variety of speech contexts.[2]

Decades of research studies have shown you can mitigate many of the causes of speech anxiety, reduce its symptoms, and use your nervous energy in productive ways.[3] You may always feel somewhat nervous when speaking in public. That's natural, normal, and even beneficial. In this chapter, you'll learn about why you get nervous in public speaking situations, how you can manage that anxiety, and ways to build your confidence.

Getty Images Entertainment/Getty Images

What Causes Speech Anxiety?

MindTap®

Read, highlight, and take notes online.

speech anxiety
Fear of speaking in front of an audience.

Speech anxiety refers to fear of speaking in front of an audience. Before, during, and after giving a speech, speakers experience a wide range of sensations, thoughts, and behaviors that spring from the internal causes of nervousness. These may include quavering voice, shaky hands, changes in body temperature, itchy skin, dry mouth, the mind going blank, increased heart rate, shortness of breath, increased rate of speech, trembling legs, sweaty palms, or cold hands and feet.[4]

Fear of public speaking stems from two sources: your temperament and how you've learned to respond to uncertainty.[5]

Temperament

The communibiology perspective addresses how speech anxiety is related to temperament. This approach suggests that a fear response to public speaking is rooted in the basic biological brain activity underlying your personality. In other words, your temperament or personality directly influences your level of speech anxiety.[6]

According to this perspective, people who are more genetically prone to speech anxiety tend to have personalities that cause them to feel uncomfortable in many social situations. For example, they tend to be preoccupied with themselves and their own thoughts, often having a rich imagination and enjoying activities on their own. They also tend to exhibit anxiety, low self-esteem, shyness, guilt, and similar traits. In contrast, people who are less genetically prone to speech anxiety tend to display personality traits that cause them to enjoy social situations more. Such people focus on their surroundings and the people in them, so they're outgoing and assertive. In addition, they are more calm, self-assured, and easygoing.[7] Few individuals are *always* shy and anxious or *always* outgoing and calm. But the more you exhibit personality traits that cause you to feel socially uncomfortable, the higher level of speech anxiety you'll experience.

A useful tool that can help you get an idea of your speech anxiety level is the Personal Report of Public Speaking Anxiety (PRPSA).[8]

MindTap®

Access and complete the Personal Report of Public Speaking Anxiety (PRPSA) online.

uncertainty reduction theory
A theory that posits when individuals face an uncertain or unfamiliar situation, their level of anxiety increases.

Response to Uncertainty

Uncertainty reduction theory addresses the other source of speech anxiety. When individuals face an uncertain or unfamiliar situation, their level of anxiety increases. For most people, speaking in public is not an everyday activity. The change in context from your regular, everyday interactions with others to an unfamiliar, public interaction naturally makes you nervous.[9] The next section identifies the areas of uncertainty associated with public speaking.

The Uncertainties of Public Speaking

The public speaking context produces seven different areas of uncertainty, presented below and summarized in **Table 2.1.**

Uncertainty about Your Role as a Speaker

If you're like most people, you're probably much more familiar with listening to a speech than giving one. In the speaker role, you may ask yourself, What should I do when I give a speech? Uncertainty about your role as a speaker can begin long before you present a speech—even in the early stages of preparation you might feel your heart rate go up as you think about your speech.[10] The less certain you are about your role as speaker, the more nervous you will feel about presenting a speech.

Table 2.1 Uncertainties and Questions about Public Speaking

Uncertainty about . . .	Question Speakers Ask Themselves
the speaker's role	What should I do?
my speaking abilities	What am I able to do?
my ideas	How well do I know my topic?
the audience's response	How will others react?
how others will evaluate me	What impression will I make?
the setting	How familiar/unfamiliar is the space?
the technology	Will the technology work?

Uncertainty about Your Speaking Abilities

A second uncertainty associated with public speaking concerns your speaking abilities. You may wonder, What am I able to do as a speaker? You likely haven't had many opportunities to test your skills as a communicator in formal, structured situations. You may lack confidence in your public speaking proficiency—you may not be sure you have the skills you need to speak effectively. If English is not your first language, you also may feel uncertain about any accent you may have or of your ability to pronounce words correctly.[11] The less confidence you have in your speaking skills, the more apprehension you will feel about public speaking.[12]

Uncertainty about Your Ideas

In everyday conversations, you don't expect people to research thoroughly every topic they talk about. In contrast, your public speaking audience expects you to demonstrate expertise about your subject. As a public speaker, you want to appear knowledgeable in front your audience, especially your peers. You may ask yourself, "How well do I know my topic?" The less sure you are about your knowledge of your topic, the more nervous you will feel about giving the speech.

Uncertainty about the Audience's Response

When you have a pretty good idea about what will happen in a given situation, you feel fairly comfortable. In public speaking, you don't know exactly how audience members will respond to your message. There's no doubt the audience's response influences the speaker's confidence. If audience members smile and nod their heads, you're more likely to feel confident about your speech and ideas. If audience members avoid eye contact or frown, you're more likely to feel anxious about your speech.[13] So you might ask yourself, How will listeners react to my speech? When you present a speech, you risk having your ideas rejected. The less you believe you can predict a positive response from your audience, the more anxious you will feel.[14]

photo by Neal Waters, 07 Geography, 15 MS Mass Communications

You can't predict your audience's response with exact certainty, which results in some nervousness. However, observing your listeners smiling and nodding will increase your confidence.

SPEAKING OF ...

Information that Increases Anxiety

A study of middle school children found that when a peer related a negative public speaking experience, the children's anxiety decreased. The reverse was true as well—a peer's positive story about public speaking increased the children's speech anxiety. Why? The researchers believe that the negative information led the children to think public speaking was something they could do: They could certainly do a better job than the peer who told the dismal story. On the other hand, the positive story made effective public speaking seem unattainable because the peer seemed so extraordinarily skilled at it.[15]

Uncertainty about Evaluation

Fear of negative evaluation plays a major role in students' anxiety about public speaking and contributes to physical symptoms such as elevated heart rate and queasiness.[16] Even after you learn how your instructor grades speeches, you may feel nervous about how your classmates will respond. In other public speaking situations, such as giving an oral report at work or nominating someone at a meeting, speakers also are concerned about how the audience will view them.[17] Research shows, however, that the **spotlight effect** leads a speaker to *think* people observe her or him much more carefully than they actually do.[18] Many minor speaking errors, such as stumbling over a word, briefly losing your place, or skipping to the wrong digital slide, are far more noticeable to you than to the audience. Of course, listeners will evaluate your presentation, but the spotlight probably isn't nearly as bright as you might think.

spotlight effect
An overestimation of how much others are paying attention to you, your appearance, your actions, and what you say.

Uncertainty about the Setting

As a student, you're used to the instructor standing in the front of the room. As a speaker, you're the one up there in front. The room seems very different—and often more intimidating—from this vantage point. Although you may be accustomed to public settings as an audience member, you're probably less used to such settings as a speaker.[19] When considering where you'll give your speech, you might ask, How familiar is the speaking space? The more unfamiliar the setting, the more nervous you may feel about your speech.

Uncertainty about Technology

You connect to your social world with your smartphone. If the phone's battery goes dead, you may be annoyed and frustrated, but you're not embarrassed. In contrast, when you can't access the online video clip you'd planned to show, you panic and your anxiety level soars. When thinking about giving a speech, you'll probably ask, Will the technology work? Lack of familiarity with technical equipment and concerns about it working increase a speaker's nervousness.

Strategies for Building Your Confidence

MindTap®
Watch It: View a video on how to build your confidence.

The remainder of this chapter takes you through the complete public speaking experience, from the weeks before the speech to the hours afterward, to identify what you can do at each stage to effectively manage speech anxiety and build your confidence. These strategies focus on the two root causes of speech anxiety: your temperament and your uncertainties about public speaking. So whether your speech anxiety comes primarily from your personality or uncertainties—or both—these approaches to addressing anxiety can help.

Relaxation Techniques

Relaxation techniques help reduce the physical symptoms of stress, such as increased heart rate and tense muscles. When you practice relaxation techniques, you feel calmer and have a sense of well-being.[20] Two relaxation techniques are especially helpful for managing the physical stress associated with public speaking: deep breathing and progressive relaxation.

Deep Breathing Exercises Developing good breathing habits provides the foundation for reducing stress and relaxing.[21] Three different types of exercise can help you increase breathing efficiency, reduce nervousness, and help you relax when you're feeling anxious about giving a speech.

- The first exercise, *diaphragmatic breathing,* relies on smooth, even breathing using your diaphragm. Sit or stand with your feet flat on the floor, shoulder-width apart. With your hands just below your rib cage, breathe in with an exaggerated yawn while pushing your abdomen out. Exhale slowly and gently, letting your abdomen relax inward.
- The second exercise, *meditation breathing,* helps your body relax. Begin by breathing with your diaphragm, but this time focus on every aspect of the breathing process and how it feels. Clear your mind of all thoughts and concentrate on the rhythm of your breathing: in breath, out breath, in breath, out breath.
- The last exercise, *tension-release breathing,* combines diaphragmatic breathing with relaxing specific parts of your body. Begin by finding a comfortable position and breathing naturally. While you're breathing, identify tense muscle areas. Then inhale fully through your nose, using your diaphragm. As you slowly exhale through your mouth, relax one tense muscle area. Continue this process until you feel completely relaxed. This exercise can be done systematically by starting at your head and progressing to your toes or vice versa.[22]

Progressive Relaxation Also called progressive muscle relaxation or progressive muscle relaxation meditation, this method facilitates the release of tension you've built up in your muscles due to stress. Progressive relaxation also helps you identify how differently your muscles feel when they are relaxed and when they are tense. Practicing progressive relaxation makes you feel calmer, reduces your anxiety, and improves your brain's ability to learn and retain information.[23] These exercises can help you reduce your anxiety in the weeks before you give your speech and even the day of your speech.

With progressive relaxation, you focus on relaxing the muscles in three main areas of your body, starting with your feet.[24]

Feet and Legs. Lie down on your back on a carpeted floor or mat and follow the steps below. Start with your toes pointed toward the ceiling. Now point your feet down and gently curl your toes. Keep your toe muscles tightened for a few moments, then release them. Repeat this several times. Notice how your leg and foot muscles feel when they're tightened and when they're relaxed.

Abdomen. For this part of the exercise, either remain lying down or stand up, whichever is most comfortable for you. Tighten your abdomen muscles, but avoid straining yourself. Pay attention to how you feel with those muscled tightened. Release your muscles, letting your belly pouf out a bit. Reflect on how you feel with your muscles relaxed. Repeat this several times.

Shoulders and Neck. Stand or sit for this exercise, making sure your arms are unrestricted and can drop down to your sides. Start by shrugging your shoulders up to your ears and keeping them there for a moment. Note how your muscles feel when they are tense. Now drop your shoulders so they are relaxed. Your neck should feel relaxed as well. Think about the difference in how you feel when your shoulders are tense and then they're relaxed. Repeat this exercise several times.

These relaxation exercises for your feet, abdomen, shoulders, and neck help with overall tenseness in your body. Other exercises focus specifically on relaxing your body in preparation for a speech. Try these additional progressive relaxation techniques before you practice your speech or the day of your presentation.[25]

Hands. With your arms and hands relaxed at your side, close your hands tightly to form a fist. Hold for a few seconds, then release. Focus on how your muscles feel when your hand is closed and when it's open. Repeat several times.

Mouth. You might not realize it, but your mouth muscles can tense up. Get into a comfortable position—lying down, sitting, or standing. Inhale and close your mouth tightly, pressing your lips together, for several seconds. Note how your mouth, face, and jaw muscles feel when they're tense. Now gently exhale, slightly opening your mouth and releasing your mouth muscles. Consider how you feel with your mouth and jaw relaxed. Repeat several times.

Tongue. Your tongue is the strongest and most flexible muscle in your body, and like all your other muscles, it can get tense, too.[26] Because your tongue is essential for speaking, you want your tongue to feel relaxed when you give your speech. For this activity, you want to be comfortably sitting or standing. With your mouth slightly open, press your tongue to the roof of your mouth with the tip of your tongue right behind your top front teeth and hold it there for a few seconds. Concentrate on how it feels to have your tongue tensed up. Then gradually relax your tongue so it's flat in your mouth. Notice how your mouth and jaw now also are relaxed. Repeat several times.

When you relax the various muscles in your body, you reduce the tension you're experiencing. Combining deep breathing and progressive relaxation techniques can help increase your positive emotions, such as happiness, optimism, and assurance, and lessen your anxiety about public speaking.[27]

Relabeling

What is your first response when you find out you need to give a speech? Do you avoid thinking about it, work to suppress any anxious feelings, tell others about how nervous you feel, or view it as an opportunity to develop your skills? Before reading more about relabeling, complete the Communication Anxiety Regulation Scale here to find out how you typically respond to public speaking situations.[28]

In this public speaking class, you'll learn to manage your speech anxiety productively, such as reappraising or relabeling that nervous energy.

relabeling
Assigning more positive words or phrases to the physical reactions and feelings associated with speech anxiety.

visualization
Imagining a successful communication event by thinking through a sequence of actions in a positive, concrete, step-by-step way.

Relabeling involves assigning positive words or phrases to the physical reactions and feelings associated with speech anxiety. You stop using negative words and phrases like *fearful* and *apprehensive* and instead use positive words like *thrilled* and *delighted.* When your voice quavers a bit and your hands shake, attribute those sensations to your body and mind gathering the energy they need to prepare for and present the speech. Say to yourself, "I'm really excited about giving this speech!" rather than, "I'm so nervous about this speech." Your anxiety won't magically disappear, but relabeling puts your response to public speaking in a positive light and increases your ability to manage your anxiety.[29]

Visualization

Research demonstrates the effectiveness of visualization across a wide variety of contexts, such as quitting smoking, solving math problems, completing complex tasks in a team, and managing interpersonal conflict.[30] For example, student groups working on a complicated economics case performed better both individually and as a group when they used visualization to consider the problem and possible solutions.

When you apply **visualization** to public speaking, you think through the sequence of actions that will make up the speech with a positive, detailed, concrete, step-by-step approach. As you practice your speech, imagine the place, the audience, and yourself successfully presenting your speech. Focus on what will go right, not what will go wrong. But also imagine how the event will unfold in a realistic way, including what you will say and how your audience will respond.[31] Use all your senses to *feel* what will

SPEAKING OF ...

Can-Do Language

How you label things shapes your experiences with them. Do you view difficult times as challenges or as problems? Do you focus on opportunities or on barriers? When you think of public speaking as a chore, you're probably not going to get very excited about your next speech. In contrast, if you think of public speaking as talking about your ideas and getting feedback from an audience, then you're more likely to anticipate your next speech with enthusiasm. That enthusiasm can motivate you to thoroughly plan and prepare your presentation.

COMMUNICATION ANXIETY REGULATION SCALE

Imagine that you have to give an unprepared speech in front of an audience. In the two minutes before you are to give your speech, you may do any of the activities listed. Rate how likely you would be to choose each of the following in order to deal with your anxiety. Use this scale for your ratings:

1 = Definitely would not	4 = Maybe would
2 = Probably would not	5 = Probably would
3 = Maybe would not	6 = Definitely would

_____ **1.** I would think about how this could be a good opportunity to practice my public speaking skills.

_____ **2.** I would watch a brief video clip from a TV show I enjoy.

_____ **3.** I would bury my face in a pillow and scream.

_____ **4.** I would think about how giving the speech will make me a more competent individual and help me learn how to think fast on my feet for the future.

_____ **5.** I would think about all of the other things I need to do this week and try not to think about the speech I will be giving.

_____ **6.** I would show my anxiety so that everyone would know how I am feeling.

_____ **7.** I would try to control my anxiety by not expressing it.

_____ **8.** I would make a conscious effort to keep my face and body language from appearing anxious.

_____ **9.** I would play a video game on a computer or handheld device.

_____ **10.** I would brainstorm all of the positive things that could come about from giving this speech.

_____ **11.** I would mask any anxiety that I am feeling.

_____ **12.** I would show my anxiety in order to get people to comfort and help me.

SCORING:

Now add up your ratings in this way:

Add your ratings from Questions 1, 4, 10 _____

Add your ratings from Questions 2, 5, 9 _____

Add your ratings from Questions 3, 6, 12 _____

Add your ratings from Questions 7, 8, 11 _____

If your scores were highest for Questions 1, 4, and 10, you manage your public speaking anxiety by reappraising or relabeling it. If your scores were highest for Questions 2, 5, and 9, you manage your public speaking anxiety by avoiding it. If your scores were highest for Questions 3, 6, and 12, you manage your public speaking anxiety by venting to others about it. If your scores were highest for Questions 7, 8, and 11, you manage your public speaking anxiety by suppressing your feelings.

happen. Move through the visualization process in stages, so you give your full attention to all aspects of the speaking event. Start at the point right before your turn to speak and visualize yourself:

- Feeling some nervousness but relabeling that feeling *positive energy.*
- Breathing in through your nose and out through your mouth in a calm and relaxed way.
- Listening attentively to the speakers who are presenting before you.

Now it's your opportunity to speak. Focus on the moments before you start speaking and on your introduction, imagining yourself:

- Gathering your notes and any other materials and going to the front of the room.
- Checking any technology you're using, such as digital slides.
- Facing the audience.
- Making eye contact and smiling.
- Remaining still until the audience has settled.
- Beginning the speech.

For the next step, concentrate on the main part of the speech, visualizing yourself:

- Transitioning from your speech introduction to the first main point.
- Incorporating effective presentation media.
- Observing audience members nodding, jotting down a few notes, and listening intently.
- Continuing your speech, presenting each main point.
- Giving the conclusion.
- Listening to audience members clapping.

Your speech is over, but you're not quite done. Visualize yourself:

- Breathing normally and easily.
- Answering questions readily.
- Thanking the audience.
- Going back to your seat and sitting down.
- Congratulating yourself on giving an effective speech.

As you visualize your presentation, consider your abilities and preparation for the speech. Your goal is to create a close match between what likely will happen and the actual event. If your imagined performance far exceeds your skills, then as you give your speech your anxiety level will soar.[32] Keep your visualization positive yet plausible.

Psychologists, teachers, athletes, actors, and many others emphasize the importance of controlling your feelings when facing the challenge of a public presentation. You may already have visualized success in challenging situations. When you visualize your speech going well, you will reduce your anxiety, build your confidence, and give a more dynamic presentation.[33]

Universal Press Syndicate

Table 2.2 Relaxation, Relabeling, and Visualization

Strategy	Brief Definition	Example
Relaxation techniques	Reducing physical symptoms of stress	Engage in meditation breathing by focusing on how it feels to breathe.
Relabeling	Assigning positive words to anxious feelings	Use "lively" or "energetic" instead of "nervous."
Visualization	Imagining successful presentation	Envision audience's positive response to speech introduction.

Using relaxation techniques, relabeling anxious feelings, and visualizing a successful presentation are three proven ways to reduce anxiety. If you anticipate the benefits of implementing these methods for decreasing your anxiety, research shows you'll enjoy an even better outcome.[34] **Table 2.2** summarizes these strategies.

Building Your Confidence before the Day of Your Speech

In addition to using visualization, relabeling, and relaxation techniques to build confidence and manage nervousness, effectively completing all the planning and preparation steps in the speechmaking process reduces many of the uncertainties associated with public speaking. Use the following strategies to manage anxiety as you develop your speeches

Start Planning and Preparing Your Speech Early

Getting an early start on speech preparation reduces speech anxiety. Schedule plenty of time to work on your speech— and stick with that schedule. Students who procrastinate invariably experience higher levels of speech anxiety than those who get an early start.[35]

Universal UClick

Choose a Topic You Care About

If you're highly interested in your topic, you'll focus more on it and less on yourself.[36] Chapter 4 goes into greater detail about how to choose a topic. For now, consider some topics you might want to discuss with an audience. Are you willing to speak out about them, even with people you may not know very well? How nervous will you feel talking about those topics in front of your audience? Some nervousness is okay, but if you think

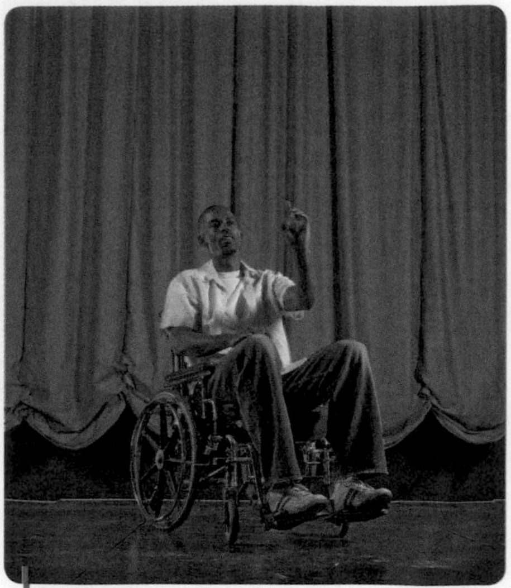

iStockphoto.com/MotoEd

Choosing a topic you care about motivates you to talk with your audience about it and reduces your anxiety about giving a speech.

speaking on a particular topic will make your anxiety unmanageable, avoid that topic. Choose topics you feel confident talking about, find compelling, and believe will interest your audience.

Become an Expert on Your Topic

Thoroughly researching your topic, discussed in depth in Chapter 6, will greatly increase your confidence and success as a public speaker.[37] What you present in your speech comprises only a small portion of what you know about the topic. If you *don't* do your research, you *will* be nervous about your speech.

Research Your Audience

Learn all you can about your listeners to reduce your uncertainty about who they are, what they know about your topic, how they feel about it, and how they are likely to respond (Chapter 5). Becoming familiar with the people in your audience makes it easier to design your speech for them and increases the likelihood they will respond positively to it.[38]

Practice Your Speech

When you practice your speech, you discover what body movements are appropriate for you and your speech. You also identify effective ways to use your notes and integrate presentation media. Best of all, your confidence increases.

Before presentation day, rehearse your speech in stages until you feel comfortable talking about your topic.

Stage 1. Read through your outline a few times in a conversational tone, as if you're talking with a friend about your topic.

Stage 2. After you've developed your notes based on your outline, stand up and go through your speech by yourself, listening carefully to what you're saying.

Stage 3. Record yourself giving your speech, using all the presentation media, such as digital slides, you plan to use the day you present. If possible, practice in a location similar to the one where you'll give your speech—classroom, conference room, auditorium—to reduce your uncertainty about the setting. Review the recording, noting both your strengths and areas for improvement. Although you may think watching your speech might increase your anxiety, research with college students who were especially anxious about public speaking found that this step greatly reduced their anxiety.[39]

Stage 4. This stage is the most important for boosting your confidence. Practice in front of an audience, recording your speech *and* the audience's reactions during the speech. Ask your audience for constructive feedback. Research shows that practicing your speech before an audience—especially an audience of four or more people—not only reduces your anxiety but also results in a higher evaluation of your presentation.[40] Review the recording, observing what you said and did and how your audience reacted.

More outgoing and assertive people may not experience much anxiety when anticipating a public speaking situation. Although low anxiety may seem like an advantage, it can result in little motivation to plan and practice a speech. Failing to rehearse a speech increases your speech anxiety and negatively affects your presentation.[41] Even the best speakers practice.

In any public speaking situation, rehearsing beforehand can help you develop a polished presentation and increase your confidence that you'll do well.

Know Your Introduction and Conclusion Well

Successfully presenting the introduction of your speech will boost your confidence, help calm your nerves, and reduce worrisome thoughts that increase anxiety.[12] Knowing that you'll finish with a coherent, smooth, and memorable conclusion will increase your confidence and lessen your nervousness throughout your speech. Write out your introduction and conclusion word for word. Then read them aloud a few times, listening to how they sound and making any necessary changes. Once you're satisfied with your introduction and conclusion, commit them to memory as best you can. Although generally you don't want to memorize your entire speech, memorizing your introduction and conclusion will help you present them more fluently and lessen your anxiety.

Careful planning and preparation reduce some of the uncertainties public speakers face. Implementing these long-term strategies won't change your personality, but they will increase your confidence. The next section explains additional short-term strategies for managing speech anxiety.

Building Your Confidence on the Day of Your Speech

If you have planned, prepared, and practiced your speech, you should feel more confident about your presentation. But still—your hands are shaking, your stomach is queasy, and your mouth is dry. How can you calm these last-minute jitters? The following strategies will help you manage your anxiety on the day of your speech.

Before Presenting Your Speech

The following techniques provide ways to boost your confidence the day you give your speech:

- *Dress for the occasion.* Great clothes can't make up for a poorly prepared speech. However, dressing appropriately for the setting will increase your comfort level and decrease your nervousness. If you're not sure what to wear, consider how a speaker would dress to gain your respect. Choose clothes that convey a professional appearance and fit the occasion.
- *Keep all your notes and materials organized.* Put all the materials for your speech in a single location where you'll remember to bring them with you. When you

arrive, arrange them so you can calmly and confidently go to the front of the room when it's your turn to speak. If you're giving your speech online, set up all your materials so they're easily accessible when you start your presentation.

- *Arrive early.* Give yourself plenty of time to get to your speaking location. Rushing in at the last minute or arriving late will increase your stress level. For an online speech, log into the speech presentation site early and run a quick microphone and video check. Making sure there are no technical issues will reduce your anxiety. And if you do encounter problems, you'll have plenty of time to address them.
- *Talk with others at the event.* Engage in informal conversation with audience members and other speakers at the event. These brief, casual interactions will warm up your voice, reduce your nervousness, and help you feel more comfortable in the situation.[43] If you're giving your speech online, you'll likely have the opportunity for a brief greeting with your classmates. Then you'll need to mute your microphone. But you still can warm up your voice before the presentations start.
- *Use positive self-talk.* Pump yourself up with supportive thoughts about yourself and your speaking abilities. Either to yourself or aloud say, "I'm excited to be here!" It may sound silly, but research on public speaking has found that relabeling your nervousness as enthusiasm and excitement reduces your anxiety and builds your confidence far better than trying to suppress your emotions. In addition, negative self-talk, in which you evaluate yourself poorly, only increases your anxiety and lowers your confidence.[44]
- *Make sure all technical aspects of your speech are ready to go.* This is especially important for online speeches as you're depending on technology to connect you with your instructor and classmates. If possible, try out the speaking software your class is using in advance so you can troubleshoot any problems. For in-person presentations, check that any equipment you are using, such as a laptop computer and LCD projector, are working properly. By taking care of these details, you will reduce technological uncertainty (Chapter 11).
- *Concentrate on the other speakers.* Focusing on yourself only increases your anxiety.[45] Instead, actively listening to others can help calm your nerves. You might even gather some information you can weave into your speech so that you'll better adapt your message to your audience (Chapter 5). Writing down speakers' main points and participating in the question-and-answer sessions after their speeches will keep your attention on what others have to say.

Building your confidence and reducing your anxiety before you give your speech will help prepare you to manage the nervousness you'll likely feel during your presentation.

During Your Speech

Even with the most thorough preparation, you'll probably experience some anxiety as you give your speech. You can use the following strategies to manage anxiety during your presentation:

- *Display a confident attitude.* You've chosen a topic you find interesting, done your research, analyzed your audience, organized your ideas, and practiced your speech. You're dressed for the occasion and you arrived early. You're an expert on your topic and look forward to talking with your audience about it. So when it's your turn to speak, put into motion the positive scenario you previously visualized:
    - Calmly go up to the front of the room.
    - Face your audience and look at all your listeners. Or, if you are giving your speech online, look directly into the camera.
    - Wait a moment to give the audience time to get ready to listen.

- Breathe naturally.
- Briefly smile.
- Clearly, confidently, and enthusiastically begin your speech.

- *Expect to experience some speech anxiety.* Speakers naturally become nervous before they give a speech, with anxiety generally decreasing after they present the introduction, although your anxiety may fluctuate throughout your speech.[46] With more experience, you'll have a better idea of when you'll feel anxious and you can plan how to manage it.
- *Turn your anxiety into productive energy.* Relabel speech anxiety as a positive source of body energy. Put that nervousness to work in appropriate gestures, body movement, facial expressions, and tone of voice. For example, use the little energy jolt you feel when facing an audience to increase your voice volume and gesture expressively to highlight key points in your speech.
- *Avoid overanalyzing your anxiety.* Concentrating on your speech anxiety distracts you from what you want to say and makes you more nervous. Acknowledge your anxiety, but don't dwell on it. Later you can reflect on your presentation and how you felt.
- *Never comment on your speech anxiety.* Most people experience the **illusion of transparency**, believing their internal states, such as speech anxiety, are easily observable by others. Studies show that speakers consistently rate themselves as more nervous than audience members do.[47] However, if you point out your nervousness, listeners will search for signs of anxiety, distracting them from what you're saying. Also, you'll sense their scrutiny and feel even more anxious.

illusion of transparency
The tendency of individuals to believe that how they feel is much more apparent to others than is really the case.

- *Focus on your audience, not on yourself.* Analyzing your audience (Chapter 5) helps you concentrate on their needs and interests rather than on yourself. Putting your efforts toward effectively presenting your message reduces your self-consciousness and nervousness. Viewing audience members as friends rather than opponents also diminishes anxiety.[48]
- *Pay attention to audience feedback.* When you appear confident, your audience will return that energy with nods, smiles, and eye contact. All audience members may not agree with your message, but most will find your confidence agreeable. As you present your ideas, seek out the friendly faces among your listeners and make eye contact with them. Positive audience feedback reduces uncertainty about your role as a public speaker and lessens your anxiety.[49]
- *Make no apologies or excuses.* If you misstate a point, get your ideas out of order, or mispronounce a word, simply make the correction and go on. For example, if you realize you've missed a major point, finish the point you're discussing, then say something like, "To put this in context . . ." and go back to the point you accidentally skipped. Avoid excuses that hurt your credibility such as, "My computer crashed last night, so I don't have my digital slides." Your audience may respond negatively, heightening your own nervousness.

Nearly all speakers experience some speech anxiety during their presentations. Use that anxiety or energy to your advantage for a more focused and dynamic speech.

Craig F. Walker/The Denver Post/Getty Images

Appearing confident, as U.S. Supreme Court Justice Sonia Sotomayor does as she speaks, helps you manage your speech anxiety.

After You've Presented Your Speech

Like many speakers, you might still feel some anxiety after you've finished your speech. Here are some ways to manage that anxiety.

- *Listen carefully to audience members' questions.* Give yourself time to formulate your responses. Ask for clarification if you're not sure you understand a question. For example, you might say, "I'm not exactly sure what you mean by that. Would you elaborate on your question?" Attending to audience members' questions with full concentration will keep the focus on your audience and help you manage anxiety. Many speakers find that their feelings of nervousness decrease considerably during the question-and-answer period after the formal speech.
- *Recognize that speech anxiety can occur even after you finish your speech.* Some speakers say that reflecting back on their speeches makes them more nervous than actually giving their speeches. When this happens, think about your overall presentation. Review what you did well and what you could improve next time, but don't blame yourself for any feelings of nervousness that you experience after your speech.
- *Reinforce your confidence.* Congratulate yourself on completing your speech. Reflect on all the work you put into your presentation.
- *Identify useful strategies for managing speech anxiety.* Recall the times during your speech when you felt most comfortable. What strategies worked well in managing your nervousness?
- *Develop a plan for managing anxiety to use in future public speaking situations.* You've learned about ways to manage speech anxiety, but you need to adjust those strategies to fit your personality and speaking style. List ways to manage anxiety that you'll apply in future speeches. Then consider additional strategies that will increase your confidence and decrease your nervousness.

For most speakers, speech anxiety tapers off at the end of the speech. But some speakers still experience anxiety after the formal speech is completed.

Nearly everyone experiences speech anxiety, and you probably will, too. Speech anxiety won't go away, but you've learned about many ways to manage it. **Table 2.3** summarizes strategies for increasing confidence before, during, and after your speech.

Table 2.3 Strategies for Building Your Confidence

Time Leading Up to Your Speech	Before You Speak	While You're Speaking	After You Speak
• Start speech preparation early. • Choose a topic you care about. • Become an expert on your topic. • Research your audience. • Practice your speech. • Know your introduction and conclusion. • Use relaxation techniques. • Use relabeling. • Use visualization.	• Dress appropriately. • Keep all speech materials organized. • Arrive early. • Talk with others. • Use positive self-talk. • Check on technical equipment. • Listen to other speakers. • Use relaxation techniques. • Use relabeling. • Use visualization.	• Display a confident attitude. • Expect to feel some anxiety. • Turn anxiety into productive energy. • Avoid overanalyzing your anxiety. • Do not comment on your anxiety to your audience. • Focus on the audience, not yourself. • Attend to audience feedback. • Make no apologies and give no excuses.	• Listen to audience members' questions. • Know that anxiety may occur. • Reinforce your confident attitude. • Identify effective anxiety management strategies. • Develop plans for managing future speech anxiety.

Summary

You'll never be completely free of your fear of public speaking, but you can use that to your advantage. That stress you feel motivates you to prepare for your speech. When you think about the day you're scheduled to speak, you should feel a little jolt and think, "I need to finish my research," "I need to learn more about my audience," or "I need to practice my speech again." Without nervousness to motivate you, you might not prepare thoroughly for your speech and likely will do poorly as a result.

Relaxation, relabeling, and visualization techniques help you increase your confidence as a speaker and decrease your nervousness. Still, you need more than the right mental framework to manage your fear of public speaking. Thorough planning, preparation, and practice give you the confidence that you truly are ready for your presentation. All speakers must learn to live with feelings of nervousness. In this chapter, you learned about many concrete strategies to cope with these feelings. As you develop ways to manage your speech anxiety, you'll become more confident as a speaker. Rather than overwhelming you, the nervousness you feel can help you present a dynamic, engaging, and audience-centered speech.

ANALYZE IT

Katherine Heigl, Tribute to Shirley MacLaine

Actor Katherine Heigl spoke at the American Film Institute's tribute to Shirley MacLaine.[50] *In this short speech, Heigl honors MacLaine's work and notes how she has served as a role model for other female actors. At the start of the speech, Heigl tells her audience about her fear of public speaking. Read the transcript here to find out how Heigl managed her speech anxiety.*

It's such an honor for me to be here tonight to celebrate the wonderfully talented exceptional Shirley MacLaine. I'm kind of petrified of speaking in public. I know it seems ridiculous. But when they first asked me my first thought was fear and my second thought was, but it's Shirley MacLaine. And as I've been sitting here and getting more and more nervous I've also been getting really excited to tell you how significant and important and inspirational you have been to me for a very long time.

I was 12 when I first fell in love with you. It was when I first saw "Steel Magnolias," and "Terms of Endearment," and "Postcards from the Edge," for the first of many, many, many times. I was too young to understand what made you so special and unique. I just knew that you were my 12-year-old heart's favorite actress and I have spent the last 21 years trying to perfect your zingers from "Steel Magnolias." Like, "I'm not crazy M'Lynn, I'm just been in a very bad mood for 40 years." Which is really fun to say to people for no reason.

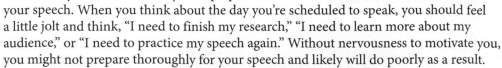

Getty Images Entertainment/Getty Images

MindTap®
Watch and analyze this speech on MindTap.

Shirley you taught me how important, how significant a movie could be in a person's life to help them not feel so alone and isolated in their grief and their loss. And that laughter and tears could be delivered in the same breath. And that strong take-no-prisoners women could be vulnerable and fragile, too. My love for you has grown with each of these astounding performances and my respect for you has deepened when I realized you're more than just an actor. You're a woman who isn't afraid to speak your truth and to laugh at yourself and take a stand. You gave me a woman in Hollywood to look up to. And you've taught me this exceptional lesson to hold my freakin' own and to honor the 12 year old that's still in me.

Can I get your autograph?

Questions for Discussion

1. Katherine Heigl says at the start of her speech, "I'm kind of petrified of speaking in public." Based on what you've read in this chapter, how might she have conveyed her feelings about the occasion in a more positive way?
2. When Heigl says, "But when they first asked me my first thought was fear and my second thought was, but it's Shirley MacLaine," how would you respond as an audience member? Heigl is admitting her fear of public speaking again, yet then says, "but it's Shirley MacLaine." What do you think Heigl means by that?
3. Heigl goes on to say, "And as I've been sitting here and getting more and more nervous, I've also been getting really excited to tell you how significant and important and inspirational you have been to me for a very long time." How would you describe what's she's doing with her nervous energy here?
4. When you watch Heigl's speech, how can you sense that she's nervous? How does she handle her nervousness? Observe her anxiety for the entire speech. When does she appear the most nervous? The least nervous?
5. As you watch the speech, identify the ways Heigl makes her speech interesting for her audience. How does the audience respond? How does that seem to affect her nervousness?
6. If you were giving Katherine Heigl suggestions for improving her public speaking skills, what would you say?

> APPLY IT . . .

IN THE WORKPLACE

Facing Your Public Speaking Fears at Work

Presentations at work often involve some aspects that are more predictable than others. For example, if you're presenting a report to your coworkers, you usually know quite a bit about your topic and your audience. However, you may be less comfortable with your role as speaker and more concerned about how your coworkers will evaluate you. Reflect on the following seven questions about speech anxiety sources (**Table 2.1**) in relationship to your workplace or other organizational context:

- What should I do? (your role)
- What am I able to do? (your abilities)
- How well do I know my topic? (your ideas)
- How will others react? (your audience's likely response)
- How familiar or unfamiliar is the space? (the setting)
- Will the technology work? (technology you plan to use)
- What impression will I make? (others' evaluations)

Which questions were more difficult for you to answer? Which questions were you able to answer more easily? Identifying the key sources of your anxiety in advance can help you prepare for your workplace presentation and reduce your anxiety.

IN YOUR COMMUNITY

Practicing with Audiences in Your Community

Giving the same or similar speech for multiple audiences is one of the best ways to build your confidence and reduce your speech anxiety.[51] Consider other groups that might benefit from your ideas, such as middle school students or a local nonprofit organization. Contact a few of those groups and arrange to give your speech. After your presentation, reflect on your performance, your degree of nervousness, and the audience's response. Compare your community experience with your classroom speech.

> REVIEW IT

Key Terms

illusion of transparency 35
relabeling 28
speech anxiety 24
spotlight effect 26
uncertainty reduction theory 24
visualization 28

MindTap®
Use flashcards to learn key terms and take a quiz to test your knowledge.

Reflecting on Building Your Confidence

1. Review the section on the communibiological perspective and speech anxiety. Would you describe yourself as generally uncomfortable in social situations, or do you tend to enjoy them? Considering your personality, which strategies for managing speech anxiety work best for you?
2. Speakers who are generally uncomfortable in social situations tend to experience greater levels of speech anxiety. How might that be a positive response to giving a speech? In contrast, speakers who generally enjoy social situations tend to have lower levels of speech anxiety. How might that cause problems for those speakers?
3. One uncertainty speakers face in public speaking is how the audience will respond to their ideas. Reflect on situations in which you think an audience might reject your ideas. How might fear of rejection lead you to avoid possible speech topics? What might be some positive aspects of such avoidance? What might be the drawbacks of avoiding possible speech topics?
4. The spotlight effect suggests that speakers overestimate how much others notice their actions. Consider recent public speaking situations, such as a classroom lecture or a presentation at work, in which you've been an audience member. Describe the speaker's attire and mannerisms, gestures, voice, main ideas, and other speech content. How observant were you? What are the implications of the spotlight effect? Are audience members not observant enough? Or are speakers too worried about themselves and how they appear to others?
5. What do you think of relabeling as a technique for managing speech anxiety? Have you tried it? What positive words can you come up with to describe the anxiousness you feel about giving a speech? How might you try using those positive words to build your confidence?
6. Knowing your audience goes a long way toward reducing speech anxiety and building confidence. How well do you know the other students in the class? What are some strategies you can use to get to know your classmates better?
7. Review the ways you can build your confidence as you're giving your speech. Which are the top three that you think will help you the most to reduce any anxiety you might have? Why do you think those strategies will work well?

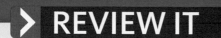

3 Listening

READ IT

After successfully completing this chapter, you will be able to:

- Discuss the role of listening in public speaking, including the components of listening and the types of listening.
- Employ the guidelines for listening to promote dialogue.
- Identify and discuss barriers to effective listening.
- Identify techniques for improving your listening effectiveness.

MindTap®

Start with a quick warm-up activity and review the chapter's learning outcomes.

Effective listening requires a commitment to giving speakers your full attention and responding appropriately to their ideas and perspectives.

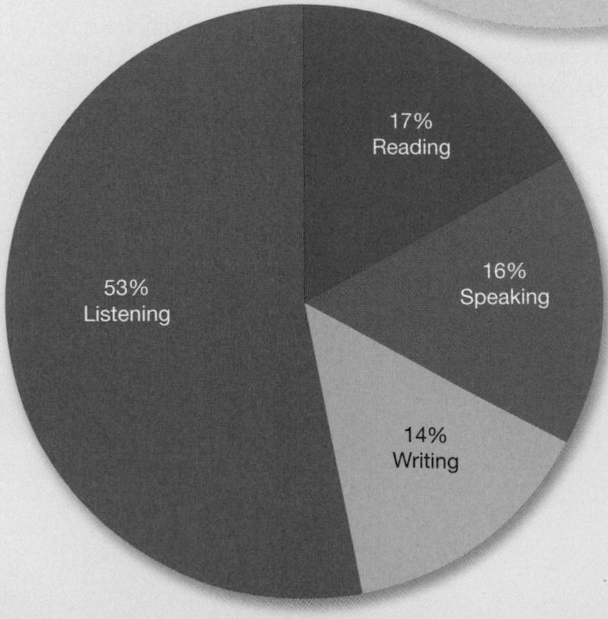

Figure 3.1 Average Daily Communication Time Today

Philanthropic organizations interested in funding projects in Colorado's San Luis Valley had a problem—getting money to areas and people who needed it the most. Located high in the Rocky Mountains of Southern Colorado, the region includes six rural counties of small towns and farms. Community residents and leaders could offer the most relevant information. But how best to get their input? The answer: a listening tour in which organizational leaders would listen and community members would speak. Along with the state's Commission on Community Service, the organizations launched the San Luis Valley Rural Philanthropy Days Listening Tour. Representatives from philanthropic foundations and government officials traveled to six towns, convening public forums at each location, to ask three questions:

1. How would you describe the personality and character of your community?
2. What are the challenges facing your community?
3. What are the successes facing your community?

In listening to local residents speak publicly about their communities and the issues they faced, the philanthropic organizations were able to pinpoint the region's needs more precisely and develop effective strategies for distributing funding.[1] This provides just one example of the role of listening in public speaking.

Even though you may equate *communication* with speaking, research shows that listening dominates communication activities in your everyday life. On average, 53 percent of your communication time each day is spent listening, 17 percent reading, 16 percent speaking, and 14 percent writing (**Figure 3.1**).[2] Compare that with 60 years ago, when people spent *less* of their communication time listening (45 percent) and writing (9 percent) and *more* time speaking (30 percent) (**Figure 3.2**).[3] But whatever the era, people engage in listening more than any other communication activity.

Like speaking, you *perform* listening as you engage with the speaker's message, the time and place of the speech, and the other audience members.[4] Effective listening requires a commitment to giving speakers your full attention and responding appropriately to their ideas and perspectives. In this chapter, you'll learn about the basics of listening, the benefits of engaging in dialogic listening, barriers to effective listening, and how to improve your listening skills.

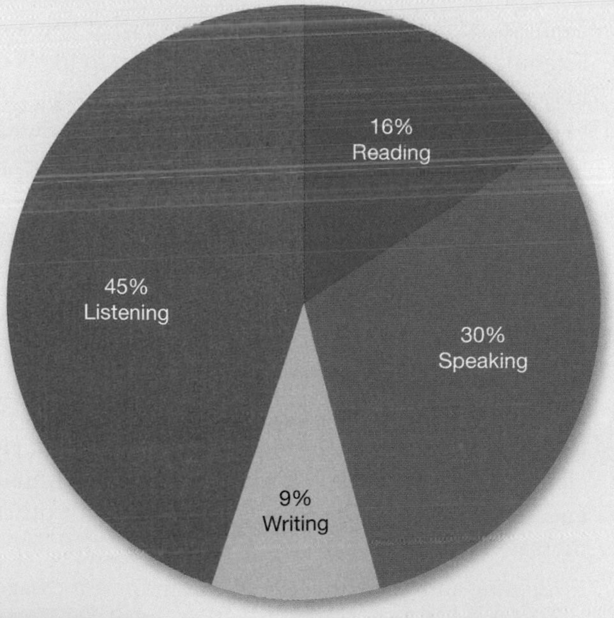

Figure 3.2 Average Daily Communication Time, 1950s

Listening and Public Speaking

MindTap®

Read, highlight, and take notes online.

When you think of a public speaking class, you probably focus on the speaking part. Yet public speaking is as much about listening as speaking because speeches are incomplete without listeners. In fact, for most of the class, you'll be listening. Let's do the math. Suppose your class meets in person for 150 minutes each week for 16 weeks, or 2400 minutes. Also suppose that you present four speeches that average 7 minutes each, and five speaking activities (very short mini-speeches) that average about 2 minutes each, for a total of 38 minutes. You'll likely have other opportunities to talk, such as participating in class discussions, asking speakers questions, and answering questions your instructor poses. So, you might have another 300 speaking minutes—or 338 minutes total. That means there's 2062 minutes—about 85 percent of class time—when you're *not* talking! And if you're taking the class online or mixed-mode (part in person, part online), you'll likely have even less speaking time and more listening (and reading) time.

Listening to your classmates helps you better analyze your audience, provides ideas for presenting your own speeches, and builds your confidence. Understanding the components and types of listening will help you improve your listening skills.

Components of Listening

The HURIER model identifies six components that combine to form the listening process in any context: hearing, understanding, remembering, interpreting, evaluating, and responding. The model depicts listening as a dynamic process—an ongoing, ever-changing collaboration between the speaker and the listener.[5]

information overload
Occurs when individuals receive too much information and are unable to interpret it in a meaningful way.

- *Hearing* is the physical reception of sounds. When you listen, you selectively receive and attend to sounds and other sensory stimuli. At times, you make a conscious decision to listen (or not listen) to what others are saying. At other times, you are not aware of the choices you make. You experience **information overload** when you receive too much information and are unable to interpret it in a meaningful way.[6] Selective listening helps you identify what is important and what is not from all the information you receive every day.
- *Understanding* involves comprehending what you have heard. Effective listening requires your conscious intention to focus on the speaker and strive to understand the meaning of the speaker's message. As a listener, dedicate yourself to listening carefully to each speaker. As a speaker, listen to your audience's responses and questions.
- *Remembering* allows you to think about and recall auditory information. To recall what you've heard and understood, your brain must first commit the information to the immediate memory or what is happening in the moment. Then the information is passed to the short-term, or working, memory. At this stage of remembering, you need to actively engage with and think about the information so that it is retained in the long-term memory.
- When you *interpret,* you assign meaning to the sounds you've received based on your own experiences and knowledge. However, the interpretive element of listening is not a completely individualistic process—your culture and society provide meanings you share with others that help you interpret messages.[7]
- *Evaluating* allows you to critically examine a message, such as when you test a speaker's logic. To effectively evaluate a speech, listeners attend to *all* aspects of a speaker's message, including gestures, movements, vocal qualities, eye contact,

and facial expressions.[8] In addition, listeners take into account the setting for the speech and the presentation materials the speaker uses, such as video and digital slides.

- Finally, listening requires *responding* to what the speaker has said. Appropriate verbal and nonverbal responses demonstrate your involvement in the speech and reflect your effectiveness as a listener. Smiling, making eye contact, nodding in agreement, and other nonverbal cues show that you're listening.[9] You might also ask questions at the end of a speech.

Your individual listening filters, such as your culture and values, influence each component. You routinely apply your imagination, past experiences, and knowledge to what others say. A speaker's words, tone of voice, and body movements also play a role in how you create the meaning of a message. For example, when others talk about their childhood adventures, you might associate what they say with your own experiences while growing up.

Figure 3.3 demonstrates how those components work together in the listening process.

Types of Listening

There are different reasons for listening and different ways of listening. In *empathic* listening, you want to know the feelings and emotions the speaker is conveying. When a speaker is giving a eulogy, for instance, you listen with compassion and understanding to the emotional components of the message. In *appreciative* listening, you listen for enjoyment, as when listening to a stand-up comedy routine or an after-dinner speech. When you listen for *content,* you gather information, focusing on the speaker's main ideas, as when an instructor lectures. Finally, *critical* listening requires that you evaluate the speaker's credibility, ideas, and supporting evidence.

Most public speaking situations call for critical listening. For example, when listening to a persuasive speech, you might try to identify the feelings that motivated the speaker to choose her or his topic. You might also laugh at a humorous story and smile as you recall a similar situation. You might want to take a few notes on the main ideas presented. Once you've listened with empathy, with appreciation, and for content, you're ready to evaluate the speech.

Figure 3.3 HURIER Listening Model

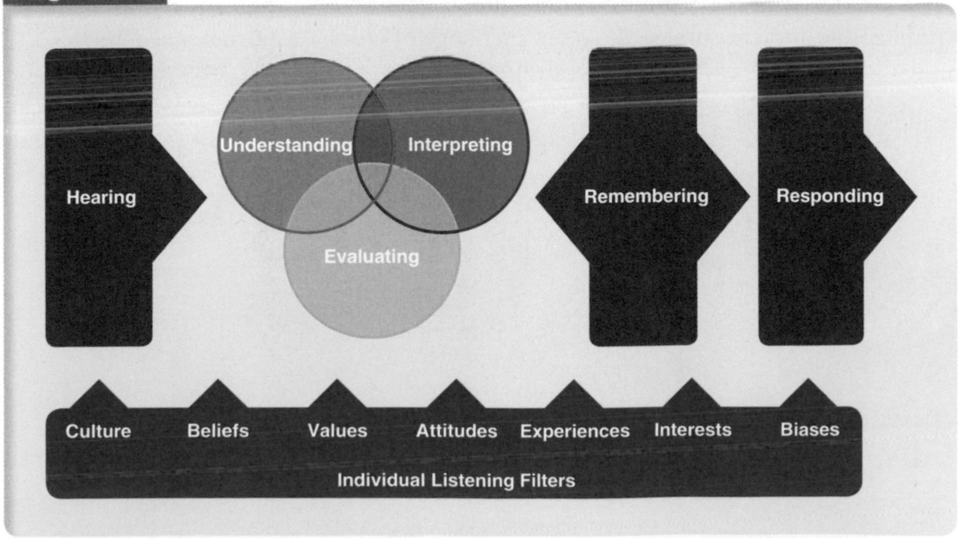

Source: Brownell, J. (2012). *Listening: Attitudes, principles, and skills* (5th ed.). New York: Pearson.

Listening to Promote Dialogue

dialogue
Occurs when communicators are sensitive to each other's needs and communicative goals, actively listen, and respond appropriately and effectively.

monologue
Occurs when communicators are concerned only with expressing their own ideas and their own individual goals.

As a listener in your public speaking class, you can help create a dialogue between speakers and listeners that promotes the free and open exchange of ideas. With **dialogue** communicators are invited to express their ideas with the goal of listening to and understanding each other.[10] The question-and-answer session after a speech provides an opportunity for such dialogue. As a listener, you want to ask fair and thoughtful questions that encourage the speaker to elaborate on an idea. The speaker, in turn, carefully listens to each question and answers as completely and honestly as possible. In contrast, **monologue** occurs when communicators are only concerned with voicing their own ideas and achieving their own individual goals. For instance, when listeners make confrontational statements rather than ask genuine questions, they're promoting their own goals. Similarly, if speakers aren't willing to give others a fair hearing, then they're engaging in monologue. Creating true dialogue requires a passion for comprehending the speaker and performing well as a listener.[11] How willing are you to listen to others and promote dialogue? Examine your orientation to listening by completing the Willingness to Listen Questionnaire here.

Respect, open-mindedness, and active listening form the basis of dialogue. The principles associated with this approach to listening are discussed in the next section. You can use them as guidelines for facilitating a productive communication climate in public speaking contexts.

Facilitate a Supportive Communication Climate

communication climate
The psychological and emotional tone that develops as communicators interact with one another.

Effective listening skills form an important basis for a productive **communication climate**—the psychological and emotional tone that develops as people interact with others.[12] Effective listeners come to a speaking event prepared to use active listening skills and provide meaningful feedback. Working together, listeners and speakers promote a supportive communication climate in which everyone feels free to express ideas in a respectful manner. Listeners' responses are descriptive, problem-oriented, spontaneous, empathic, provisional, and promote equality. In contrast, a defensive communication climate develops when listeners and speakers behave disrespectfully and inhibit the free expression of ideas. Listeners' defensive responses are judgmental, controlling, strategizing, indifferent, certain, and superior.[13]

Creating a supportive communication climate gives everyone an equal opportunity to communicate and encourages the open exchange of ideas. As a listener seeking to promote dialogue, give each speaker your undivided attention—turn off your phone,

Universal UClick

WILLINGNESS TO LISTEN QUESTIONNAIRE

Directions: The following 24 statements refer to listening. Please indicate the degree to which each statement applies to you by marking whether you:

1 = Strongly disagree, 2 = Disagree, 3 = Are neutral, 4 = Agree, 5 = Strongly agree

_____ **1.** I dislike listening to boring speakers.
_____ **2.** Generally, I can listen to a boring speaker.
_____ **3.** I am bored and tired while listening to a boring speaker.
_____ **4.** I will listen when the content of a speech is boring.
_____ **5.** Listening to boring speakers about boring content makes me tired, sleepy, and bored.
_____ **6.** I am willing to listen to boring speakers about boring content.
_____ **7.** Generally, I am unwilling to listen when there is noise during a speaker's presentation.
_____ **8.** Usually, I am willing to listen when there is noise during a speaker's presentation.
_____ **9.** I am accepting and willing to listen to speakers who do not adapt to me.
_____ **10.** I am unwilling to listen to speakers who do not do some adaptation to me.
_____ **11.** Being preoccupied with other things makes me less willing to listen to a speaker.
_____ **12.** I am willing to listen to a speaker even if I have other things on my mind.
_____ **13.** While being occupied with other things on my mind, I am unwilling to listen to a speaker.
_____ **14.** I have a willingness to listen to a speaker, even if other important things are on my mind.
_____ **15.** Generally, I will not listen to a speaker who is disorganized.
_____ **16.** Generally, I will try to listen to a speaker who is disorganized.
_____ **17.** While listening to a nonimmediate, nonresponsive speaker, I feel relaxed with the speaker.
_____ **18.** While listening to a nonimmediate, nonresponsive speaker, I feel distant and cold toward that speaker.
_____ **19.** I can listen to a nonimmediate, nonresponsive speaker.
_____ **20.** I am unwilling to listen to a nonimmediate, nonresponsive speaker.
_____ **21.** I am willing to listen to a speaker with views different from mine.
_____ **22.** I am unwilling to listen to a speaker with views different from mine.
_____ **23.** I am willing to listen to a speaker who is not clear about what he or she wants to say.
_____ **24.** I am unwilling to listen to a speaker who is not clear, not credible, and abstract.

SCORING:

Scores can range from 24 to 120. To compute the score on this instrument complete the following steps:

Step 1: Add scores for items 2, 4, 6, 8, 9, 12, 14, 16, 17, 19, 21, and 23.

Step 2: Add scores for items 1, 3, 5, 7, 10, 11, 13, 15, 18, 20, 22, and 24.

Step 3: Total score = 72 − Total from Step 1 + Total from Step 2.

Scores above 89 indicate a high willingness to listen. Scores below 59 indicate a low willingness to listen. Scores between 59 and 89 indicate a moderate willingness to listen.

Source: From Richmond, V. P., & Hickson, M. III. (2002). *Going public: A practical guide to public talk*. New York: Pearson.

Kayte Deioma/PhotoEdit

Giving the speaker your undivided attention and actively listening help create a supportive communication climate.

avoid irrelevant comments and distracting movements, and focus on the speaker's message. **Table 3.1** provides examples of supportive and defensive listener responses. In most public speaking situations, you'll respond verbally during the question-and-answer session after the speech.

Demonstrate Mutual Respect as an Audience Member

Dialogic listening involves respecting commonalities as well as differences between yourself and others.[14] You show respect for a speaker's ideas by demonstrating your interest—maintaining eye contact, taking notes, and giving relevant feedback. As the speaker is talking, consider the main points presented in light of what you already know about the topic. Also, fully understand the speaker's message before responding. For example, if you disagree with a speaker's position on gun control, you might want to first check for clarification, saying something like, "If I understand you correctly, you support our current laws on gun ownership and want no changes in those laws. Is that a fair interpretation?" Dialogic listeners accept differing viewpoints on a topic as inevitable. They recognize that working through disagreements can produce positive change.

Demonstrate Mutual Respect as a Speaker

When you give a speech, listen carefully and respectfully to questions. Try to gather more information from listeners if they object to your ideas. You might say, "In my research, I found strong support for changing our current gun laws. But I know not everyone agrees with that position, including some experts. So I'd like to hear more about your thinking on the issue." In addition, listen to questions without interruption before responding.

Convey a Positive Attitude for Learning

When listeners possess a positive attitude for learning, they want to learn all they can about a topic. This may mean, for example, listening to speakers whose views

Table 3.1 Supportive and Defensive Listener Responses

Supportive Messages	Listener Orientation	Example	Defensive Messages	Listener Orientation	Example
Description	Makes "I" statements	"I don't fully understand your point."	*Judgment*	Makes "you" statements	"You did a poor job explaining your point."
Problem orientation	Takes a collaborative approach to interaction	"Let's try to figure this out together."	*Control*	Attempts to dominate the interaction	"Let's get back to my idea."
Spontaneity	Free of hidden motives	"How do you think your plan would work?" while thinking, "That plan seems quite interesting."	*Strategizing*	Uses deception to achieve own goals	"How can you plan work?" while thinking, "Now you owe me a favor."
Empathy	Recognizes others' emotions	"You seem really excited about your research."	*Indifference*	Shows lack of enthusiasm	"I guess what you found out is okay."
Provisionalism	Considers new information	"I hadn't thought about the alternatives you're suggesting."	*Certainty*	Unwilling to consider alternatives	"There's no way your ideas will work."
Equality	Fosters respect and trust	"Although I disagree with you, I respect the careful consideration you've given the topic."	*Superiority*	Presents self as being better than others	"Your position on the topic clearly is wrong."

you may not agree with so you have a better understanding of perspectives different from your own. You might also develop your own knowledge base on a topic a speaker will be discussing so you can engage in a productive discussion. The dialogic listener thoughtfully considers and responds to what others say, thereby increasing all participants' access to information.

Provide Effective Feedback

Respectful audience members listen completely to a speaker's message and provide constructive feedback. For instance, during the question-and-answer session that often follows a speech, make relevant comments that demonstrate you are listening carefully to the speaker's ideas.

In your public speaking class, your instructor may ask you to evaluate classmates' speeches. When you give this kind of feedback, identify both what the speaker did well and areas for the speaker to work on. Offer specific examples, such as a particularly good transition, and concrete suggestions for improvement, such as more clearly previewing main points. When you provide evaluation, your goal is to engage the speaker in a conversation about the speech content and delivery, rather than point out every flaw you observed. The evaluation form in **Table 3.2** offers one way to structure your feedback on your classmates' speeches.

MindTap®

Watch It: View a video on how you can promote dialogue.

Table 3.2 Feedback Form for Classroom Speeches

	Excellent	Good	Fair	Missing	Comments
Introduction					
Thesis and Preview					
Research					
Organization					
Conclusion					
Delivery					
Presentation Media					
Audience Impact					

Barriers to Effective Listening

Much as good listening skills are essential in public speaking, there are many barriers to effective listening; a few of the most common ones are discussed here. As you review this section of the chapter, consider the degree to which these barriers apply to you, especially in public speaking situations.

Flaws in Individual Listening Filters

cultural norms
Prescriptions for how people should interact and what messages should mean in a particular setting.

Recall from the HURIER model of listening that individual listening filters influence every aspect of the listening process. As shown in **Figure 3.4**, those filters include culture, values, attitudes, experiences, beliefs, interests, and biases. For example, your cultural background plays a role in how you listen to others, especially the cultural norms you've internalized.[15] **Cultural norms**, or rules for how members of a culture should behave, can be explicit or stated, as with military codes of conduct. Most norms, however, are implicit or unstated, such as how to act when attending a guest lecture on campus. No one tells you how to behave or how to listen at a lecture. Some cultural norms support good listening habits, such as not interrupting a speaker. But other cultural norms may present barriers to effective listening, such as encouraging individuals to express their ideas. For instance, research on listening among legal professionals found that those in the United States focused more on evaluating the person speaking and those in Finland were more concerned with evaluating the facts.[16] Your orientation toward listening—based in cultural norms—influences what you hear

Figure 3.4 Individual Listening Filters

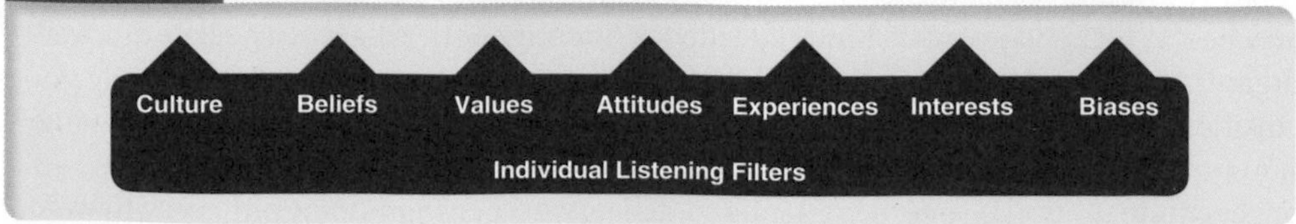

and how you interpret it. In addition, what is appropriate in one culture may not be appropriate in another.

Beliefs are assumptions that you think are true. You might believe that hard work is essential for success and that people should be rewarded based on their efforts. Some beliefs, such as ethnocentric ones, can interfere with effective listening because they prevent you from truly attending to the speaker. **Ethnocentrism** occurs when individuals think their view of the world is better than anyone else's. Often, rather than explicitly stating, "My perspective is the best," communicators might think, "How can *those people* believe in *that*?" or "People over 40 just don't know what's really going on in the world." When you start thinking that anything different from your point of view is inherently wrong, strange, or bad, you're experiencing ethnocentrism.

ethnocentrism
The belief that your worldview, based on your cultural background, is superior to others' worldviews.

Ethnocentrism influences how listeners evaluate a speaker's competence and credibility.[17] That is, the more ethnocentric listeners are, the more likely they are to think speakers who appear different from them are less trustworthy and capable. Ethnocentric listeners, for instance, may respond negatively to a speaker simply because they don't share a similar cultural background.[18]

Ethnocentrism also can prevent people from speaking out about and listening to difficult issues, especially those associated with race, class, and gender.[19] When listeners think ethnocentrically, they avoid questioning societal and cultural practices that promote discrimination against people based on their ethnic background, religious beliefs, socioeconomic status, sexual orientation, disability, sex, and other demographic categories. Stepping out of your own cultural beliefs can prove challenging because your cultural worldview is so much a part of your sense of self. But when people believe their way of thinking is superior to other ways, they're practicing ethnocentrism and creating a barrier to effective listening.

Values refer to your standards and principles in life. For instance, you may consider a college education especially important and completing your degree something that guides what you do in life. You might consider respect, integrity, and loyalty the most important values in a friendship. Values can enhance your listening skills when they encourage you to listen to something, such as a guest lecture on a topic related to your college major. Values also can serve as a listening barrier when they keep you from fully attending to a speaker, as when a speaker supports values different from your own.

An *attitude* refers to how much you like or dislike something. Whereas values are strongly held because they provide an orientation to behaving in the world, attitudes are more open to change and often change over time. Something you liked when you were younger, for instance, may evolve into something you dislike now. Attitudes can influence your willingness to listen. If you dislike someone, you may find yourself less motivated to listen to that person. Conversely, if you like the person, you might listen more attentively.

Your *experiences* influence how you listen and what you listen to. You can't control the experiences you've had—they're a part of you. But you can reflect on how they might interfere with your listening. If you've had favorable experiences with a speaker or topic, you're more likely to listen. Unfavorable experiences can have the opposite effect. Say you had a disagreement with a coworker, who now is presenting a report to your work group. Your negative experience may lead you to dismiss what the speaker has to say.

Your personal *interests* influence what you listen to and what you ignore. The more you're interested in speakers and their topics, the more likely you'll focus your attention on them. Conversely, if you find speakers and topics uninteresting, you'll put less effort into listening. A recruiter providing tips on how to prepare for a job interview might get your attention as you near graduation and start the job search. A first-year college student may find the talk less relevant and not listen as closely.

Everyone has *biases*, or preconceived notions about people, objects, places, and topics. Your biases can lead you to avoid listening to something altogether, as with not attending a guest lecture on campus because you think the person's position on the topic is wrong.

Flaws in individual listening filters can negatively impact your ability to listen effectively. Recognizing those flaws is the first step to reducing these listening barriers.

Mindlessness

mindlessness
Occurs when individuals view something as unimportant, trivial, routine, or habitual and fail to focus their attention on it.

When you view something as unimportant, trivial, routine, or habitual, you experience **mindlessness**. As a barrier to effective listening, mindlessness prevents you from fully attending to what the speaker is saying. You miss important parts of the message and fail to truly comprehend the ideas the speaker is presenting. For instance, mindlessness can result in more compliant listeners because they're not completely processing and evaluating the speaker's message.[20] Most people experience mindlessness throughout the day as they engage in routine interactions with others. You walk by a friend on campus, you both wave and say hi, and you keep going to class. Your communication was automatic—you didn't really think about it. But if your friend had stopped and said, "I've been sick all week and missed our public speaking class. Do you have some time later to go over with me what was covered?" you would have to think about your response. If you continued to listen mindlessly, you might respond inappropriately or not at all.

Noise

noise
Distractions that interfere with an individual's ability to listen.

external noise
Conditions in the environment that interfere with listening.

Noise refers to distractions that interfere with the listening process. These distractions shift your attention away from the speaker to something else. **External noise** occurs in the environment. These distractions may be sounds, such as other audience members talking, or other environmental factors, such as glaring lights or a stuffy room. External noise can serve as a physical barrier preventing you from hearing a speaker or a mental barrier that keeps you from concentrating on the speaker's message. Even if you hear what the speaker is saying, these distractions shift your attention and your cognitive processing to them and away from the presentation.[21]

internal noise
Thoughts, emotions, and physical sensations that interfere with listening.

Internal noise refers to distractions within the individual, such as emotional responses, thoughts, and physical sensations.[22] You might have an upcoming midterm exam, so you think about that rather than your classmate's speech. Or you may have skipped breakfast and now that lunchtime is approaching your stomach is growling and thoughts turn to a trip to the campus food court.

Defensiveness

As an effective listener, you want to promote a supportive communication that encourages the open exchange of ideas. In contrast, defensive responses hinder open communication and present a barrier to effective listening. When you listen defensively, you focus on yourself, your ideas, and your thoughts, without giving the speaker a fair hearing. You might jump to conclusions, display indifference, demonstrate an unwillingness to even consider the speaker's points, or think to yourself that your viewpoint simply is better than the speaker's. Sometimes a defensive orientation is

Some external noise is unavoidable, as with poor acoustics or outside noises. Effective listeners work to block out those distractions and concentrate on the speaker's message.

understandable if you feel the speaker is attacking you and your ideas. Nonetheless, defensiveness prevents you from fully attending to the speaker's message and applying your active listening skills.

Faking Attention

Faking attention, or pseudolistening, occurs when you appear to be listening to the speaker but you're actually thinking about or doing something else. You might be in class sending a text instead of listening to your instructor or checking email during a conference call at work. You could even look at the speaker directly and still fake attention if you're daydreaming about something else. You may be giving all the appropriate head nods, occasionally saying "uh huh," and making eye contact with the speaker, but you're not really attending to the person's message. Faking attention can be especially problematic because the speaker thinks you're getting all the information when in fact you're completely missing it. Pseudolisteners are ineffective listeners.

Listening Effectively to Speeches

Research shows that immediately after a lecture, listeners recall only about 50 percent of what the speaker said.[23] Follow the strategies presented here to help you improve your listening skills and better evaluate the speaker's message.

Listen Mindfully

mindfulness
Occurs when individuals actively focus their attention on themselves and others in the present moment.

In contrast to mindlessness, **mindfulness** involves your active, focused attention on yourself and others at the present moment. When you listen mindfully, you set aside

SPEAKING OF ...

The Mindfulness App

A phone app for mindfulness may seem counterintuitive—don't smartphones, tablets, and laptops keep you from a mindful state? But apps such as Headspace, developed by meditation and mindfulness expert Andy Puddicombe, provide exercises for you to train your brain to be more mindful and present. Download a free app or a free trial. Try out the activities. Did they help you become a more mindful listener?

your plans for the day, thoughts about work or school, ideas you have for a project, and all the other internal distractions you may encounter. Instead, you give the speaker your undivided attention and concentrate on understanding what the person has to say. When you listen more mindfully, you reduce barriers to effective listening and improve your own listening habits.[25]

Set Goals

Different public speaking situations call for different types of listening. Setting goals that correspond with a specific situation improves your listening skills. For example, after-dinner speeches are generally meant to entertain, so the listener's goal might be to simply enjoy the presentation. When a speaker toasts a newly married couple at a wedding reception, listeners would likely focus on the feelings associated with the occasion. However, in most classroom speaking situations, the listener's ultimate goal is to critique speeches. As an audience member in your public speaking class:

- Listen for the speaker's emotions (empathic listening).
- Enjoy the speaker's sense of humor (appreciative listening).
- Identify the speaker's main ideas (content listening).
- Evaluate the speaker's overall message (critical listening).

Block Distractions

The human brain processes information about three times faster than speakers can talk.[26] That leaves listeners time to get distracted by internal and external noise. Arriving at a speaking event prepared to listen can help prevent internal distractions. For instance, if your public speaking class is early in the morning, be sure you go to bed early the night before and get plenty of sleep so you're not tired. If you have a particularly busy day, write out your schedule ahead of time rather than think about it while speakers are talking. If you find yourself daydreaming, focus your attention on the speaker, take notes, consider how the topic applies to you, and develop a few questions to ask after the speaker has finished.

Some external distractions are unavoidable, as with audience members coughing or a noisy plane flying overhead during a crucial point in the speaker's presentation. But you can prepare for possible distractions and thus avoid them. If you know the room will be warm, for example, wear loose-fitting and comfortable clothes. If you're listening to your classmates' speeches online, use ear buds or headphones so outside sounds won't bother you. Avoid texting, checking email, and similar activities. External distractions can challenge your active listening skills. By blocking these distractions, however, you can concentrate on what speakers are saying.

listening anxiety
Anxiety produced by the fear of misunderstanding, not fully comprehending, or not being mentally prepared for information you may hear.

Manage Listening Anxiety

Just as speakers experience anxiety when giving a speech, listeners sometimes become anxious. **Listening anxiety** stems from the fear of misunderstanding, not fully comprehending, incorrectly recalling, or being unprepared mentally for information you may hear. Students often experience anxiety when listening to a lengthy lecture they know they'll be tested on.[27] The physical symptoms are similar to those of speech anxiety. Manage listening anxiety by focusing on the speaker, clearing your mind of extraneous thoughts, and maintaining a positive attitude.

Suspend Judgment

Effective listeners first listen for content and empathy and then evaluate the speaker's message. Controversial topics such as sex education in public schools, capital punishment, welfare policies, and nuclear power can trigger immediate emotional responses. Recognize your emotional responses and then listen carefully to the speaker's ideas, even if they don't correspond with your own. In addition, avoid judging the speaker based on gender, ethnic background, dis/ability, or other demographic attributes. Instead, concentrate on the information the speaker presents.

Focus on the Speaker's Main Points

Focusing on the speaker's main points is particularly important in content listening and critical listening. To evaluate what the speaker has said, you first need to understand the main ideas being presented. Speakers often call attention to their main points by stating them in the introduction and reviewing them in the conclusion.

Take Effective Notes

Taking effective notes when listening to a speech helps you recall what the speaker said and prepare good questions.[28] Your notes need not be extensive—a few keywords will do. Here's a system that promotes effective listening: Divide a piece of paper into three columns. Label the first column "Important Points," the second column "My Response," and the third column "My Questions." As you listen to the speaker, write down your notes in the appropriate column.

SPEAKING OF ...

Exercises to Save Your Listening

Sound consultant Julian Treasure argues that people are losing their listening due to a whole host of factors, including a noisy environment, fast-paced society, and an increasingly video and audio recorded culture.[24] Not only can individuals not hear each other, they don't have the time for listening and don't recognize its importance. Treasure suggests five exercises that will help you save your listening.

1. *Silence.* Experience three minutes of silence or quiet every day.
2. *In the mix.* Stop for a moment and identify the mix of sounds you hear. Can you pick out different voices in your classroom? Can you hear footsteps in the hallway? Is there a humming noise from the heater or air conditioner? What sounds can you hear from outside the building? Try this in a range of locations—at home, while commuting, outdoors, at a party.
3. *Savoring.* Listen to everyday sounds that you usually ignore, such as water running from a faucet, a bus as it whooshes by you, a purring cat, an elevator as it descends. Enjoy these sounds that Treasure calls a "hidden choir."
4. *Positioning your listening.* Consider the individual filters that you bring to any public speaking event. How can you position those filters to get the most out of your listening experience? For example, how can you relate your interests to those of the speaker?
5. *Receive-appreciate-summarize-ask.* This exercise is especially useful in your public speaking class. Receive or pay attention to the speaker. Appreciate what the speaker has to say by nonverbally signaling your attention. Summarize the speaker's main points as you listen to the presentation. Ask questions that demonstrate your interest in the speaker's topic.

Effective and ethical listeners ask good questions—ones that are open-ended, direct, on topic, and genuine requests for information.

Use All Your Senses

To improve your listening, use all your senses, paying attention to how speakers talk as well as what they are saying. While you listen to the speaker's main points, observe nonverbal cues such as gestures and tone of voice. Your senses will give you clues to the speaker's feelings about the topic.

Ask Good Questions

Ethical listeners ask questions that help the speaker clarify or elaborate on the main ideas presented. Even when you disagree with a speaker, focus your questions on gaining more information, not on presenting your point of view. Each question should take just a few seconds to ask. Good questions are:

- *Open-ended.* Begin questions with *how, why, what,* or *where.* For example, ask, "How do you think your proposal will affect local residents?" rather than, "Will your proposal affect local residents?"
- *Direct.* Just ask the question, avoiding a long, drawn-out preface. For example, ask, "What do you think will be the impact of these changes over the next 10 years?"
- *On topic.* Stick with the topic. If you think there's a weakness in the speaker's argument, ask about it, but be sure it relates to the speaker's message. For example, ask, "You discussed a few drawbacks associated with this new assessment program in K–12 schools. What have teachers and administrators

done to address these issues?" Compare this with, "I know this isn't really related to what you talked about, but I was wondering what you think about the amount of homework teachers assign in their classes."

- *Genuine requests for information.* Ethical listening fosters a supportive communication climate. Conversely, using derogatory language and intentionally distorting the speaker's message produce a defensive communication climate.

As an active listener, ask questions that encourage speakers to provide more information. Compare these questions:

1. "You mentioned some statistics on college students' use of file sharing. What are the sources of those statistics?"
2. "I'm sure you're wrong about those statistics you mentioned on college students and file sharing. What sources are you using? I want to look them up."

In the first question, the listener respectfully asks for the information, giving the speaker a chance to state the sources more precisely. In the second question, the listener attacks the speaker, who will in turn feel compelled to respond defensively. Dialogue evaporates, and a battle ensues over who is "right" and who is "wrong."

With good questions, listeners continue the conversation the speaker began. Listening attentively during speeches and asking good questions that promote the free exchange of ideas are the hallmarks of an ethical listener.

Summary

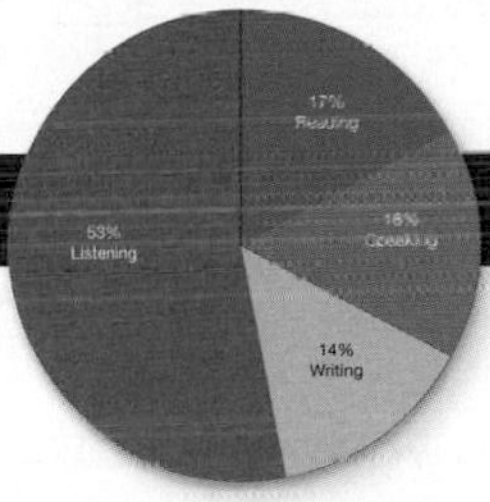

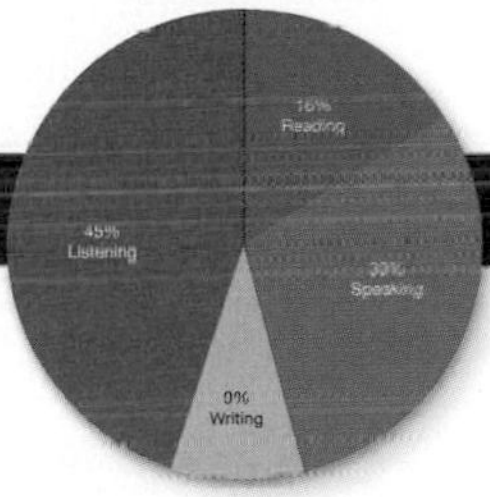

Listening involves hearing, understanding, interpreting, evaluating, remembering, and responding to speakers' messages. Individual listening filters, including culture, values, attitudes, experiences, beliefs, interests, and biases influence the listening process. Although you may experience all the types of listening in public speaking situations, critical listening is the most common as you often must evaluate the speaker's message.

Listening to promote dialogue facilitates a conversation between listeners and speakers. Developing a supportive communication climate, demonstrating mutual respect, conveying a positive attitude for learning, and providing constructive feedback all contribute to listener–speaker dialogue.

Some of the more prominent barriers to effective listening are flaws in individual listening filters, mindlessness, noise, defensive listening, and faking attention. Effective listening practices, including mindful listening, setting goals, blocking distractions, managing listening anxiety, suspending judgment, focusing on the speaker's main points, taking effective notes, using all your senses, and asking good questions, can counteract listening barriers. When listeners become fully engaged, they create a meaningful conversation between speaker and audience.

ANALYZE IT

Amanda Wagemann, Winning Speech for the South Dakota Department of Agriculture, 2012 Resource Conservation Speech Contest

Source: South Dakota Department of Agriculture

MindTap®

Watch and analyze this speech on MindTap.

At the 51st annual South Dakota State Finals of the Resource Conservation Speech Contest, first-place winner Amanda Wagemann, a junior at Central High School in Aberdeen, South Dakota, gave this speech in response to the competitions topic, "75 Years of Conservation: What's Next?" As you read and view the speech, note the ways in which she invites her audience to listen.

My grandparents live on a farm. And consequently you could say that I've grown up there quite a bit too. Now while I may not appreciate driving the baler back and forth in the field on hot summer days or tagging calves while their angry mothers snort behind us, I do enjoy being out there. Running through the pasture and down washed-out gravel roads or playing hide and seek through rows of trees with my brother are all memories I hold close to my heart.

However, I have begun to worry that there will come a time when children of South Dakota will no longer be able to enjoy these simple pleasures. I worry that the next generation won't know the difference between cropland and concrete or what conservation really means. So, 75 years of conversation, what's next? Some suggest this may be where the road ends. Where we can drop our hard hats and freely plow up and cut down once more. This, however, is not so. We've gotten this far and now we must push further. So how do we continue to improve?

First, we'll observe our surroundings and see how we got to where we are today in terms of conservation. Then we'll dig up some dirt and examine the negative effects that will occur if we once again lack in our conservation efforts. And finally, we'll plant some solutions that can benefit us all.

Thanks to the hard work and determination of the South Dakota Association of Conservation Districts our state is growing and developing in agriculture and our environment. For example, the Rifled Lake Wildlife Tree Planting Project was completed in the spring of 1994. Now it thrives as it provides excellent coverage and food for deer, pheasants, rabbits, and birds. The recognition for such projects often falls on our adult generation today. But oddly enough, this isn't who we should actually be thanking. Instead, we owe our debt to those who started this conservation revolution. Yes, we're proud for having 45 foot tall trees lining your roads and fields now, but what about the individuals who invested time and money into planting and caring for them so many years ago? The Rifled Lake Project wouldn't have stood a chance without the efforts of Game, Fish and Parks officials who protected and replaced trees, and cultivated the land for three years. We need to appreciate those who saw the opportunity for repairing our broken and destroyed agricultural system of the 1930's, and made a difference.

Now before we let our egos get the better of us, it's time to take a glance at reality. Although we are still seeing much progress, our arrogance is steering us straight back to where we came from. For example, people are continuing to bring in their own firewood, while we fight the Emerald Ash Bore, and while South Dakota's Forestry Department declares a full scale war against mountain pine beetles, which have infested ponderosa pine trees on over 400,000 acres of Black Hills National Forest. Farmers are also choosing to put down record amounts of fertilizer in order to produce bin busting crops and

CRP [Conservation Reserve Program] acres are dropping 11 percent every other year. This problem is manifesting itself right before our eyes once again. Conservation can't just be tossed behind us in hopes that the increases now will continue, because they won't. In Dr. Seuss' book, *The Lorax,* the Onceler becomes so preoccupied with how well his Truffula Trees are selling that he ignores the side effects that are impacting the environment and animals living among him. Soon, all of the Truffula Trees have been destroyed and the land becomes uninhabitable. We don't need a rhyme to see that we are heading towards the same fate. Whether it be by planting as much as possible without taking the time to care for the land through something as simple as crop rotation, or by building further and further into wildlife habitats because the housing settlement just can't be without a golf course, we have become a society that is fixated on nothing but materialism now. However, if we pursue this by destroying the lives of animals and depleting the land for generations to come, are we really winning?

So, let's raise the disc, tum around, and reverse our already growing issue. As funding decreases significantly, the conservation districts must work to do more with less. Therefore, give the officials your gratitude, and then get to work and help them out! We can help with funding by contacting our legislature and advocating a penny tax on rural water systems. These districts do so much, from planting shelter belts, to providing weed control. We owe them our assistance. You don't need to be a farmer in order to guard this precious land. Saving water by taking shorter showers, using safe, chemical-free pesticides, and keeping fertilizers away from any creeks or ponds are all changes that will have huge impacts. We can't just rely on what has happened already, but how we can make this progress stronger. By continuing to monitor what we do, we will maintain our uphill climb towards more effective conservation and protection.

When I was young, I didn't really know why we had miles of trees to run through or why my dad alternated between corn, wheat, and beans every year. As I've grown up, though, I've learned to understand and really appreciate how we do the things we do, because you never know when it could be gone. Now that we've seen how important conservation is and what we must do to preserve it, let's throw out the excuses and start anew. After 75 years of conservation: What's next? Well, these acres of rolling plains could quickly tum into a country club, complete with a swimming pool and waterslide, but, as long as I'm around, South Dakota's agriculture and conservation are going to go nowhere but up.

Questions for Discussion

1. What did Amanda say at the start of her speech to help build a supportive communication climate? How did her narrative encourage her audience to listen?
2. How did Amanda encourage her audience to engage in a dialogue? Give an example.
3. In what ways did Amanda help her listeners pay attention to her speech? How did she relate her topic to the audience?
4. If you had been in the audience, what questions would you have asked Amanda after her speech?
5. If you were giving Amanda suggestions for improvement, what would you say?

APPLY IT . . .

IN THE WORKPLACE

Polishing Your Listening Skills at Work

Especially in today's multicultural workplace, effective listening is essential to accomplishing tasks and achieving goals.[29] Develop a plan for yourself to promote dialogue with your coworkers. Identify concrete ways you can:

- Facilitate a supportive communication climate, as with taking a problem orientation during a meeting.
- Demonstrate respect for your coworkers, as with not interrupting others.
- Convey a positive attitude for learning about them and their ideas, as with encouraging a coworker whose point of view differs from yours to offer her or his opinion.
- Provide effective feedback, as with noting things your coworker did well.

Now try out your plan in a one-on-one conversation, with a group, or in a public speaking setting. How well did your plan work? How did others respond to your attempts to promote dialogue? Reflect on what you learned as a dialogic listener at work.

IN YOUR COMMUNITY

A Listening Tour of Your Community

How much do you know about your neighborhood and your community? Whether you live on campus, commute, or go to school online, you may not have an in-depth understanding of the varying viewpoints your neighbors and community members hold. A listening tour is an excellent way to find out. You can do this on your own or with some of your classmates. Recall the three basic questions asked in the San Luis Valley Rural Philanthropy Days Listening Tour:

1. How would you describe the personality and character of your community?
2. What are the challenges facing your community?
3. What are the successes facing your community?

Develop three simple questions of your own, such as:

1. How would you describe your community to others?
2. What do you like most about your community?
3. What makes your community unique?

Arrange to meet with a few neighborhood groups. Using your skills as an effective listener, learn everything you can about the community. How did community members respond to your listening tour? How did you feel serving in the listener role rather than the speaker role? After you've gathered the information, arrange to give brief presentations to the groups that summarize your results.

REVIEW IT

Key Terms

communication climate 44
cultural norms 48
dialogue 44
ethnocentrism 49
external noise 50
information overload 42
internal noise 50
listening anxiety 53
mindfulness 51
mindlessness 50
monologue 44
noise 50

MindTap®
Use flashcards to learn key terms and take a quiz to test your knowledge.

Reflecting on Listening

1. Complete the Willingness to Listen questionnaire that appears in the "Listening to Promote Dialogue" section. What was your score? How accurately do you think it reflects on your willingness to listen? What did completing this questionnaire tell you about your own listening habits? In what areas do you think you could improve on your listening? How will you make those improvements?
2. For one day, keep a diary of your communication time. How much time do you spend listening, speaking, writing, and reading? How closely does that breakdown match the percentages in **Figure 3.1**? What did you learn about your communication by keeping this communication diary?
3. Review the Speaking of . . . box titled "Exercises to Save Your Listening." Try out at least one of the exercises. How effective do you think the exercise is in improving your listening? Would you recommend the exercise to your friends or classmates? Why or why not?
4. Recall a recent experience in which you were a critical listener. How well did you listen with empathy and appreciation? How well did you listen for content? How did you evaluate what the speaker said? What did you learn from listening critically?

4 Developing Your Purpose and Topic

READ IT

After successfully completing this chapter, you will be able to:

- Understand clearly the general purpose of your speeches.
- Use brainstorming techniques to generate speech topics.
- Employ criteria to evaluate and select topic ideas.
- Write a specific purpose statement tailored to a speech topic.
- Write a clear thesis statement.
- Develop a working outline.

MindTap®

Start with a quick warm-up activity and review the chapter's learning outcomes.

You have to know what is expected of you, what you plan to do in response, and what you can expect to accomplish as a result.

Getty Images Entertainment/Getty Images

When Pakistani teenager Malala Yousafzi—shot in the face by religious extremists for encouraging girls to attend school—spoke at the United Nations, she called on the leaders of all nations to ensure free compulsory education for every child. Her purpose for speaking was to persuade, and thanks to the Internet her vital message has been heard around the world. In a speech to the general public in Mountain View, California, astrobiologist John Baross described how extreme environments on Earth, like the bottom of the ocean, give clues about possible life elsewhere in the universe. His purpose was to inform, and the crowd who heard him shared Baross's insights with friends and colleagues through social media. And when Sydney Seau, the daughter of famous professional football player Junior Seau, spoke at her deceased father's induction into the Pro Football Hall of Fame, she talked about the Polynesian American's relentless passion for the game. Sydney Seau's purpose was to honor her father and help family and friends deal with the absence of their loved one at that special moment. Her emotional speech can still be viewed or read on lots of news and sports websites.

Malala, John, and Sydney were passionate about the topic of their speeches and clear about their purposes. That's why their messages were successful. You should strive for the same result in your public speaking class—and you've got lots of help. Today's information technology gives you extraordinary access to online resources that can help you choose and conduct research on a topic you really care about.

Whenever you talk with other people in everyday life, you usually have a goal, or purpose, in mind.[1] You may be trying to make them understand an idea you came up with or appreciate an experience you've had. Perhaps you're trying to influence their opinion about an issue or motivate them to do something. Maybe you're just trying to create the right mood for a special situation. Having a well-defined purpose is especially important in public speaking and starts at the beginning of your speech preparation. You have to know what is expected of you, what you plan to do in response, and what you can expect to accomplish as a result. Four key steps make up the early part of speech preparation. You:

1. Determine your general purpose.
2. Evaluate and select your speech topic.
3. Combine your general purpose and topic to identify your specific purpose.
4. Phrase the thesis of your speech as you develop your topic.

New York Times Syndicate

Determining Your General Purpose

MindTap®

Read, highlight, and take notes online.

general purpose
The speaker's overall objective: to inform, to persuade, or to entertain.

topic
The main subject, idea, or theme of a speech.

The **general purpose** of your speech refers to your overall goal, and answers the question, "What do I want my speech to do?" The general purpose of your speech typically corresponds to one of the most common types of speeches: informative, persuasive, or entertaining.

Speaking to Inform

When you give a speech to inform, your goal is to describe, explain, or demonstrate something. Informative speeches serve to increase listeners' knowledge about a **topic**, or the main subject, idea, or theme of your speech. When the general purpose is to inform, your objective is to help the audience understand and recall information about a topic. In the professional world, informative presentations include employee orientations, training sessions, product demonstrations, and project reports. Within communities, they include project proposals, status reports, art and cultural lectures, and policy updates.

Speaking to Persuade

When you speak to persuade, you attempt to reinforce, modify, or change audience members' beliefs, attitudes, opinions, values, and behaviors. Your objective is to prompt the audience to alter their thinking and possibly take action. Attempts at persuasion dominate the world of advertising and politics. Yet when a student nominates a friend for president of a fraternity, a football coach gives a half-time pep talk, a community member advocates disaster preparedness, or a university president presents a five-year vision to the faculty, these are persuasive speeches, too.

Speaking to Entertain

In a speech to entertain, the speaker seeks to captivate audience members and have them enjoy the speech. Special occasions like awards ceremonies, company parties, roasts, and toasts often provide the context for such speeches. After-dinner speakers, for instance, typically try to charm and humor the audience. Entertaining speeches often feature jokes and stories.

Keeping Your General Purpose in Mind

For any particular speech, you'll concentrate on a single general purpose: to inform, to persuade, or to entertain. As you develop your speech, always keep your general purpose in mind. Although you might include humor in an informative speech, your ultimate goal is to inform, not to entertain. Similarly, you might offer explanations in a persuasive speech, but your primary objective is to persuade, not to inform. Moreover, you might give your opinions in an entertaining speech, yet in the end you want to entertain, not to persuade, your audience. If you try to entertain *and* persuade, for example, you won't do either one very well.[2] Think about humorous television commercials in which you can recall the joke but not the product advertised. Focusing on one general purpose helps you achieve your overall goal for the speech.

Giving speeches of these types and for these purposes extends and refines the communication skills you already have, because you inform, persuade, and entertain people all the time. In turn, they inform, persuade, and entertain you. In your public speaking class, your instructor usually assigns speeches to inform, persuade, or entertain—so you may not have to figure out your general purpose. Once you know your speech's general purpose, your next step involves coming up with possible speech topics. You'll have great creative freedom to do this; however, your instructor may want to approve acceptable topics.

Brainstorming for Possible Topics

A public speaking event gives you an opportunity to speak to an audience, but what will you inform them about, persuade them to do, or entertain them with? Carefully selecting a topic that fits your general purpose will set you on the road to delivering an effective speech. So where do you begin? You begin by **brainstorming**—a free-form way of generating ideas without immediately evaluating them.

MindTap®

Use MindTap to help you generate topic ideas.

brainstorming
The free-form generation of ideas for speech topics and content in which individuals think of and record ideas without immediately evaluating them.

Brainstorming Techniques

Brainstorming happens in many ways. As you go about your daily routines, topic ideas may pop into your head, so be ready to record them. An online news article, webpage image, radio talk show, television program, or conversation with an interesting person may trigger ideas for your speech. Trying out something new may also help you think of appealing topics.[3] Take an alternative route to a friend's apartment, listen to some new music, or spend some time in a coffeehouse outside your usual stomping grounds, for example.

At some point, you'll want to set aside a specific time to generate ideas or add to the ones you developed previously. Choose a place where you feel relaxed, yet still alert and attentive. The main point of brainstorming is to make a list of topics you might want to talk about. Don't evaluate the topics at this point. Simply record whatever comes to mind. Be creative. When brainstorming, you don't want to censor yourself.[4] The rules for productive brainstorming are few but important (**Figure 4.1**).

Asking yourself key questions can help you jump-start and focus the brainstorming process. The questions should be broad enough to encourage creativity, but not so broad that you stray far from your original goal. Here are some examples:[5]

- What do I talk or text about with my friends?
- What are my interests and hobbies?
- What unique experiences have I had?
- What am I passionate about?
- What would I like to learn about?

Brainstorming Sources

If this kind of self-inventory doesn't get ideas flowing, you have other sources for possible speech topics. Check the headlines from a major news source or web portal, or use search engine pages that list issues, such as globalissues.org, procon.org, or dmoz.org. Current events often appeal to audiences. Subjects discussed in blogs, message boards, and podcasts can also provide topics to consider. When you find an article or post that interests you, write down the topic, as well as any others you associate with it.

When brainstorming for topics, think not only in terms of ideas or words that come to mind but also of images that have impressed you. A news photo or video may give you an idea for a speech topic. For example, people worldwide see images from uprisings and terrorist attacks shortly after they become available. These images could prompt you to speak about the history of the regions involved, the reasons for terrorism, or the wisdom of American foreign policy. Images of natural disasters suggest a range of topics, such as volunteer relief efforts, disparities between rich and poor people in affected areas, and the use

Figure 4.1 Rules for Brainstorming

- Generate as many ideas as possible
- Write down every idea—whatever comes to mind
- Avoid evaluating your ideas
- Be as creative and imaginative as possible

John Marshall Mantel/ZUMA Press, Inc./Alamy Stock Photo

High-impact images of significant events can help you brainstorm a range of possible speech topics.

of technology to prepare and issue warnings. A disturbing image of a child being bullied at school could prompt you to research and speak on what qualifies as bullying, the causes of bullying, school policies, or campaigns like National Bullying Prevention Month. YouTube videos and personal postings on social networking sites can also spark topic ideas.

Start brainstorming for topic ideas well before you're scheduled to present your speech. Research shows that brainstorming works best when done over several sessions.[6] The most useful ideas usually emerge from brainstorming on your own, but asking another knowledgeable person to brainstorm with you can work well, too.[7] Trying to brainstorm under the pressure of having to give your speech in a few days will not help you come up with your best ideas, make the best choice, or do justice to the topic you choose.

Evaluating and Selecting Topic Ideas

MindTap®

Watch It: View a video on brainstorming and evaluating topics.

Good public speakers always carefully consider the needs and interests of their audiences. However, as you begin to select a topic, you also must think about your own interests and knowledge, the availability of resources, and the time and setting for your speech. Evaluating possible topics based on the following considerations can speed up your topic selection process:

- Your own interests
- The audience
- Available resources
- The time limit
- The setting and occasion

Consider Your Own Interests

In evaluating possible topics, first consider your own interests and what you already know. Ask yourself these questions:

- How interested am I in this topic?
- What do I know about this topic?
- How comfortable will I be talking about this topic?

If your answer to the first question is, "not very interested," cross that topic off your list. Your audience will immediately know if you're not enthusiastic about it. A topic you feel passionate about will energize you and produce a more dynamic and interesting speech. Knowing a lot about a topic provides much of the background information needed to create a well-researched, dynamic, and inspiring speech. But having little knowledge of a topic may also motivate you or give you a chance to learn more about it. Just be sure you have enough time and resources to research the topic fully. Finally, consider how comfortable you are talking about a topic. Be willing to explore new ground. But if it's something you don't like discussing with your friends and family, you probably won't want to give a speech about it.[8]

Consider Your Audience

Although you'll do more research on your audience after you've chosen your topic, at this early stage in the process you need to do some basic screening to give yourself a general idea of audience members' knowledge and interests. Ask yourself these four questions about your audience when evaluating the topics on your list:

- How relevant is this topic to my audience?
- Why do audience members need to know about this topic?
- Will I be able to interest my audience in this topic?
- How much does my audience already know about the topic?

As you evaluate topics, always put yourself in the audience's place. Choose speech topics that are likely to interest and engage your listeners. Some topics may not seem directly relevant to audience members; you may need to create that link. For instance, a persuasive speech advocating a new privacy law might seem too abstract until you reveal how it affects audience members' personal password protection on social media sites. An informative speech about DNA may not resonate with listeners until you connect it to the ability to predict an individual person's future illnesses and diseases. However, if you believe the topic probably won't pique listeners' interest and you can't think of any reasons why they should know about the topic, cross it off your list. In addition, balance relevance and interest with knowledge level. If a topic is relevant and of interest to audience members but they already know quite a bit about it, you need to take a fresh approach to the topic or remove it from your list.

Consider Available Resources

As you narrow your list of possible topics, think about what resources you can use to develop the content of your speech. Audience members want to know if you have sufficient supportive information from credible sources. They quickly discern if the base of your speech is too thin. So, when choosing a topic, be sure you can locate and access relevant and valid resources—books, online articles, news reports, interviews with experts, and the like.

Consider Time

Successful public speakers stay within their time limits. Examine your list of topics. Would you be able to cover each of the topics you're considering within the allotted time? Beginning speakers often think they won't have enough to say unless they choose a big, comprehensive topic. Then, when they give the speech, they run out of time before covering all the main points. Depending on the time frame, you may need to either narrow or broaden particular speech topics.

Consider the Setting and the Occasion

The place where you'll present your speech influences the selection and treatment of possible topics. A typical college classroom works well for most speech topics. But for speeches given outside the classroom, the physical setting must be considered. Will you be speaking in a large auditorium, a conference room, or online? Are you speaking to 1000, 100, or 10 people? The way you present a topic in a small meeting room may not prove effective in a large auditorium. In the meeting room, the setting is more personal; in an auditorium, there's greater distance between the speaker and the audience. In the less spacious setting, your close physical presence adds to the power of your words, in particular when you use facial expressions and body language to reinforce certain points or arguments. In the more spacious setting, you

> **SPEAKING OF ...**
>
> **Know Your Audience**
>
> Choosing a topic that's irrelevant or antithetical to your audience can lead to unfavorable responses. Audience members may become bored and distracted. For instance, a speech about how to restore antique furniture would not interest most members of a college audience. Some topics can even make the audience feel insulted or angry. Speeches that advocate particular religious philosophies always risk aggravating general audiences. Knowing your audience—its members' interests, needs, knowledge level, values, attitudes, and beliefs—greatly increases the likelihood that the topic you select will interest your audience.

NG Images/Alamy Stock Photo

Getty Images News/Getty Images

Neil deGrasse Tyson is not only the director of the Hayden Planetarium at the Museum of Natural History in New York and host of *Star Talk* on the National Geographic Channel, he is a masterful public speaker who adapts very well to big and small venues and audiences.

are physically less prominent and must ensure that this does not translate into a loss of attention. And online, you want to balance the great physical distance between speaker and audience with the interpersonal intimacy that web-based communication can create.

For most speeches given outside the public speaking classroom, the topic, setting, and occasion are already known. In these cases, you've probably been invited to speak on a particular subject. But when you have a choice, the content and presentational style of the speech must match the event and size of the venue. For example, if you're presenting an after-dinner speech, you don't want to talk about a serious topic like skin cancer. For any topic, large audiences in big rooms generally expect a more forceful, passionate style of delivery than they would get in a small meeting room. Online audiences usually expect a more informal, conversational presentation.

Identifying Your Specific Purpose

specific purpose
A concise statement articulating what the speaker will achieve in giving a speech.

After settling on a topic, you next want to identify your **specific purpose**—that is, what you expect to achieve with your speech. To craft your specific purpose, you merge your general purpose (to inform, persuade, or entertain) with your particular topic and what you believe would interest or inspire your audience to act. For example, if the general purpose is to inform and your topic is your campus's student government, your specific purpose might be, "To inform my audience about the two branches of our campus's student government, executive and legislative." This statement integrates your general purpose (to inform) with your topic (student government) and what you want your audience to know about (the two branches of student government).

Specific Purpose to Inform

The specific purpose is a clear, concise statement about your topic that focuses on a single goal and incorporates the response you want from the audience. For a speech to inform, your specific purpose will begin with something like this:

- to inform my audience about . . .
- to explain to my audience why . . .
- to make my audience aware of . . .
- to demonstrate to my audience how to . . .

Each statement begins by placing the audience at the center of attention and refers, directly or indirectly, to the general purpose—in this case, to inform. Then you add in the topic:

- to inform my audience about how face recognition systems work
- to explain to my audience why strategies for time management are useful
- to make my audience aware of the services offered at the campus career center
- to demonstrate to my audience how to take a dramatic photograph

Corbis

Facebook CEO Mark Zuckerberg explains his company's mission in Mandarin to an appreciative student audience in China, where Facebook is usually blocked.

Identifying a specific purpose helps you conceptualize your speech from the audience's point of view. It centers your attention on what you want your audience members to know and why they should listen to you. Thinking this way keeps you clearly focused on the reason you're speaking in the first place—to inform the audience.

Specific Purpose to Persuade

Speeches to persuade often aim to produce a rational or emotional response or prompt audience members to take a specific action, such as "exercise daily," "donate blood," "demand an increase in veterans' benefits," or "sign a petition guaranteeing free speech on campus." A statement of specific purpose for a persuasive speech might begin with

- to persuade my audience to . . .
- to convince my audience that . . .
- to deepen the empathy my audience feels for . . .
- to motivate my audience to . . .

When merged with a topic, these examples become

- to persuade my audience to support a campus-wide smoking ban
- to convince my audience that genetically modified dairy products are safe
- to deepen my audience's empathy for people living in poverty
- to motivate my audience to vote in the upcoming election

Specific Purpose to Entertain

In speeches to entertain, the specific purpose is to engage and amuse the audience. Your statement of specific purpose would begin like this:

- to entertain my audience with . . .
- to amuse my audience with . . .
- to delight my audience with . . .
- to inspire my audience with . . .

AP Images/Bas Czerwinski

Somalian refugee and author Ayaan Hirsi Ali calls for reform in mainstream Islam in speeches she gives throughout the United States and the Western world.

We are used to seeing former President Barack Obama give serious speeches about policy, but he has also been asked to give entertaining speeches, such as this moment before the national press corps in Washington, D.C.

When merged with a topic, these examples become

- to entertain my audience with an inside story of working at a fast-food restaurant
- to amuse my audience with the zaniness of family summer vacations
- to delight my audience with unusual inventions of the past
- to inspire my audience with offbeat ways to simplify their lives

Putting It All Together

Writing down your specific purpose brings together the general purpose, topic, and the response you want from your audience, providing a reference point that will keep you on track throughout the speechmaking process (see **Figure 4.2**).[9] **Table 4.1** provides additional examples of how the general purpose, topic, specific purpose, and audience link up in coherent ways.

The specific purpose of your speech determines important decisions in later stages of the speech process, such as researching your topic, deciding on supporting materials,

Figure 4.2 Developing Your Specific Purpose

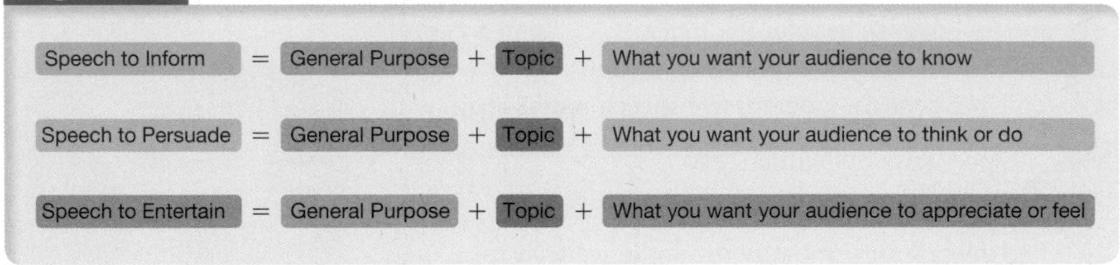

Speech to Inform = General Purpose + Topic + What you want your audience to know
Speech to Persuade = General Purpose + Topic + What you want your audience to think or do
Speech to Entertain = General Purpose + Topic + What you want your audience to appreciate or feel

Table 4.1 Examples of General Purpose, Topic, and Specific Purpose

General Purpose	Topic	Specific Purpose
To inform	Latinos in films	To inform my audience about the history of Latinos in U.S. films
To inform	Memes	To teach my audience how memes create and spread cultural themes
To inform	Online pinboards	To demonstrate to my audience how to use the latest online pinboards
To persuade	Zoos	To persuade my audience that zoos help many animal species survive
To persuade	Skateboarding	To convince my audience that campus rules prohibiting skateboarding should be eliminated
To persuade	Video games	To help my audience appreciate the positive effects of video games
To entertain	Funny tweets	To entertain my audience with fictional tweets they can send in sticky social situations
To entertain	Nutrition	To amuse my audience with the college student's version of the food pyramid
To entertain	Sports	To inspire my audience with true stories of accomplished athletes in little-known sports

organizing your ideas, making language choices, and integrating presentation resources. As you work on your speech, ask yourself, "Will this quote, statistic, video clip, or other material help me achieve my specific purpose?"

The vast majority of the work you'll do preparing your speeches takes place long before you stand in front of your audience. The considerable amount of time you'll spend thinking about and researching your speeches is another good reason to choose topics you truly care about.

Phrasing Your Thesis

Your general purpose points you in the direction your speech must take—to inform, persuade, or entertain. Your specific purpose addresses how you want your speech to affect your audience about the topic you selected. Your **thesis** describes how you intend to achieve the specific purpose. A thesis is presented in a single sentence that captures the central idea of your speech. In that sentence, you crystallize your speech in a way that embodies your topic and the main ideas you'll address. Ask yourself, "What is the central idea I want my audience to get from my speech?" How you answer that question is your thesis.[10]

thesis
A single declarative sentence that captures the central idea of a speech.

A well-phrased thesis statement briefly summarizes your main points. The thesis statement helps make your audience aware of what's coming in your speech and keeps them on track and involved throughout your presentation. Why is this important? Consider that by the time you give your speech, you will have become very familiar with the subject matter you plan to present. However, the members of your audience have little or no clue about what you're going to say. *The more you help them organize the structure of your presentation in their minds, the better your chances for successfully informing, persuading, or entertaining them.*

The thesis plays a key role in your speech, so you must put it together very carefully. Think of the thesis statement as a little work of art. Make sure the language is clear and concise, not vague or wordy. Say it out loud—how does it sound? If it sounds clunky or doesn't give your audience the information it needs to understand your speech, rework it until it sounds right. For instance, compare these two theses by saying each out loud.

> Creativity is a good thing everybody has potential for and can be improved through interactions with other people, always staying open, trying to connect with yourself, and going out into nature.
>
> Creativity can be developed by surrounding yourself with creative people, being open-minded, spending time alone, and appreciating nature.

Your thesis incorporates the topic, flows from the specific purpose, and directly addresses how you will elicit the response you want from your audience. It summarizes the main points of your speech, helping you clarify your approach and giving your audience a sense of what to expect during the Introduction (see Chapter 9). Formulating a thesis statement well is one of the most important skills an effective public speaker masters.[11]

Here are some more examples of thesis statements:

TOPIC:	Telemedicine
GENERAL PURPOSE:	To inform
SPECIFIC PURPOSE:	To educate my audience about the role of telemedicine in health care
THESIS:	Telemedicine uses new communication technologies for consultations between doctors, interactions between patients and doctors, and monitoring patients at remote locations.

TOPIC:	Mobile payment apps
GENERAL PURPOSE:	To persuade
SPECIFIC PURPOSE:	To convince my audience to use mobile payment apps
THESIS:	Mobile payment apps are safe, convenient, and inexpensive ways to pay for almost anything.

TOPIC:	Online dating services
GENERAL PURPOSE:	To entertain
SPECIFIC PURPOSE:	To amuse my audience with stories about my experience using an online dating service
THESIS:	From setting up my profile to searching through the online personals and finally going on a date, my first experience with an online dating service is one I'll never forget.

Each of these thesis statements plainly states the topic and frames the main points for the speech. Composing a clear thesis at an early stage of speech preparation provides excellent guidance for researching your topic.

Sometimes you'll determine the thesis as soon as you've written the specific purpose—you have a clear idea of your topic, what you want to accomplish, and how you'll get there. More commonly, the thesis emerges as you begin developing your topic.[12] As you start thinking about your topic and conducting preliminary research, you'll identify specific points or ideas that will help you achieve your specific purpose. Composing a good thesis statement forces you to clarify exactly what you want to say, which makes developing the rest of your speech much easier.

Building Your Working Outline

working outline
An outline that guides you during the initial stages of topic development, helping to keep you focused on your general purpose and clarify your specific purpose.

Once you know your general purpose, select a topic, and determine the specific purpose of your speech, you're ready to begin putting together your working outline. The **working outline** guides you during the initial stages of topic development, helping to keep you focused on your general purpose and to clarify your specific purpose. As your working outline evolves, you'll include the speech topic, general purpose, specific purpose, thesis, and keywords for the main ideas and subpoints you want to address. Later, you'll construct a complete-sentence outline. Then, in the final stages of preparing your speech, you'll create a presentation outline. **Table 4.2** shows where you are in the process of giving a speech based on the type of outline you're creating or using.

MindTap®
Use MindTap to help you begin building your outline.

Imagine that for an informative speech, you decide to tell your classmates about the most important factors students should consider when choosing a major. Every college student has dealt with this problem, so this subject will be familiar to your audience. Your topic is "Choosing a Major," and your specific purpose is "To make my audience understand how to choose a college major." Let's take a look at how

Table 4.2 Types of Outlines

Type of Outline	Functions	Key Features	Chapter
Working	Assists in initial topic development; guides research	Includes main points and possible subpoints; revised during research process	Chapter 4: Developing Your Purpose and Topic
Complete-sentence	Clearly identifies all the pieces of information for the speech; puts ideas in order; forms the basis for developing the presentation outline	Uses complete sentences; lists all sections of speech and all references; revised during preparation process	Chapter 8: Organizing and Outlining Your Speech
Presentation	Assists you in practicing and giving your speech	Uses keywords; revised as you practice your speech; often transferred to note cards for use during practice and the final presentation	Chapter 12: Delivering Your Speech

◀ **You are here**

you can apply what you've learned in this chapter to building a working outline for this topic.

Brainstorming for Topic Development

You've already learned how to brainstorm for speech topics. Now you'll brainstorm for ideas you may want to include in your speech.[13] The two processes are similar. Without trying to separate major points from minor points, just write down whatever you think could be said about your topic. Imagine, for example, that the general purpose of your speech is to inform and the topic you settled on is "How to choose a college major." Brainstorming for ideas to include in a speech for college students about choosing a major might produce the following list:

- career goals after college
- the university's reputation in the chosen field
- how long it will take to graduate
- the student's life goals
- majors the student really would not like
- areas of strongest skills
- whether the department is admitting new majors
- potential earnings in jobs related to the major
- quality of instructors
- things the student really likes to do
- job market for students graduating in the major
- requirements for the major
- whether the university offers the major
- department resources to help students

SPEAKING OF ...

Limit Your Working Outline

Including too many points is one of the biggest problems students encounter when learning how to develop a topic. You'll have to make some tough decisions to avoid cluttering your speech with points that may be interesting to you, but don't advance your specific purpose. For each idea you want to include, ask yourself, "Does the audience *really* need or want to know this? "Do I have to mention this point to get the outcome I want"? Learning how to edit your ideas effectively at this stage will save you time and effort as you progress through the speechmaking process, and it will greatly improve the flow and impact of your speech.

Grouping Ideas to Select Main Points

Research on innovation and developing good ideas shows that building connections between concepts is the main key to success.[14] Same for your speeches. Once you have a list of ideas for your topic, distill each one down to a single key word or short phrase. This will make it easier to identify links among them. Choose accurate and clear terms that capture your ideas, like these:

- career goals after college (career goals)
- the university's reputation in the chosen field (reputation)
- how long it will take to graduate (time needed)
- the student's life goals (personal goals)
- majors the student really would not like (dislikes)
- areas of strongest skills (strengths)
- whether the department is admitting new majors (openings)
- potential earnings in jobs related to the major (money)
- quality of instructors (instructors)
- things the student really likes to do (likes)
- job market for students graduating in the major (job market)
- requirements in the major (requirements)
- whether the university offers the major (curriculum)
- department resources to help students (student support)

internal consistency
A logical relationship among the ideas that make up any main heading or subheading in a speech.

Next, group the key words or phrases into categories that represent main themes. You're striving for **internal consistency** in each group of keywords. Internal consistency means that the ideas that make up any main heading or subheading have a logical relationship to one another. What you name the category should describe the elements contained within it. For the speech on choosing a major, the ideas fall into three major categories (**Table 4.3**): (1) practical considerations (reputation, time needed, job market, money, and requirements), (2) academic resources (openings, instructors, curriculum, and student support), and (3) personal considerations (career goals, personal goals, likes, dislikes, and strengths).

By grouping ideas into main themes, you reduce a topic to logical categories. This helps you visualize what the skeleton, or main points, of the speech might look like. The thematically arranged categories provide an initial structure for your main ideas and what you might talk about for each one. For example, in the speech on choosing a major, the "practical considerations" category includes reputation, time needed, job market, money, and requirements. The categories provide the basis for

Table 4.3 **Idea Groupings for "Choosing a Major"**

Practical Considerations	Academic Resources	Personal Considerations
Reputation	Openings	Career goals
Time needed	Instructors	Personal goals
Job market	Curriculum	Likes
Money	Student support	Dislikes
Requirements		Strengths

your initial working outline (see **Figure 4.3**), which helps you accomplish the following tasks:

- Design your speech so that it connects well with your audience.
- Research your main themes using keyword searches.
- Create the complete-sentence outline you will use as you organize the information you've gathered.

Figure 4.3 Initial Working Outline for "Choosing a Major"

Topic: Choosing a major

General purpose: To inform

Specific purpose: To inform my audience about how to choose a college major

I. Practical considerations
  A. Reputation
  B. Time to graduation
  C. Job market
  D. Money
  E. Requirements
II. Academic resources
  A. Openings
  B. Instructors
  C. Curriculum
  D. Student support
III. Personal orientations
  A. Career goals
  B. Personal goals
  C. What you enjoy
  D. What you don't like
  E. What you're good at

Writing the Thesis

The initial grouping of ideas for the topic of choosing a major suggests the following thesis: "Three factors influence how to choose a major: practical considerations, academic resources, and personal considerations." This sentence sums up the core of the speech, indicates how you intend to fulfill your specific purpose, and can serve as your preliminary thesis statement. Add it to the information at the beginning of your working outline (**Figure 4.4**). This preliminary thesis may change as you analyze your audience and research your speech, but it's a good place to start.

As you analyze your audience and research your topic, refer back to your working outline to keep yourself on track. Although you may make important changes in your outline as you develop your speech, you want to stay focused on your main points. A working outline is a reliable tool that helps you do that.

Figure 4.4 Adding the Thesis to the Working Outline for "Choosing a Major"

Topic: Choosing a major

General purpose: To inform

Specific purpose: To inform my audience about how to choose a college major

Thesis: Three factors influence how to choose a major: practical considerations, academic resources, and personal considerations.

Summary

Every speech you present has one overall goal or general purpose: to inform, to persuade, or to entertain. The general purpose determines the nature of your speech.

In brainstorming for topics, list all the topic ideas you can think of without evaluating them. Often brainstorming begins long before you finally write down your topic ideas. Nevertheless, setting aside some time to identify and consider all your ideas will help you choose a topic that suits your speaking purpose.

Evaluate possible topics in terms of five basic considerations: yourself, your audience, available resources, time limit, and setting/occasion. Choose a topic that is appropriate for you, the audience, and the situation. Also, make sure you can find enough information to present a well-researched speech.

Your specific purpose—what you want to achieve—brings together your general purpose and topic with the response you seek from your audience. As you work on choosing a topic, you'll determine and frame the specific purpose.

Phrasing the thesis is a crucial step in topic development. Your thesis flows from your specific purpose and indicates how you will achieve the objective of your speech. Written as a single declarative sentence, the thesis captures the essence of your speech by incorporating the main points you plan to address.

Developing the content of your speech starts with brainstorming for ideas associated with your topic. The next step is to identify themes that arise from your brainstorming and group them into categories. These categories become the main points of your speech and suggest the thesis—the essence of what you'll cover.

Your topic, general purpose, specific purpose, thesis, and main points form the basis of your working outline. The working outline provides a tentative plan for your speech that may change as you learn more about your topic and audience. This early work gives you a solid foundation for analyzing your audience, researching your topic, identifying appropriate supporting materials, and determining the best way to organize and present your ideas.

> ANALYZE IT

Chris, Impressionistic Painting

Often the first major graded speech in a public speaking course is the speech to inform. In the following speech, Chris tells his student audience about a true love of his—impressionistic painting. For this first major speech, Chris's instructor required students to use the topical pattern of speech organization—where main points are of about equal importance. When reading the transcript or watching the speech on video, see how Chris identifies, organizes, and delivers his main points for an informative speech.

Good afternoon. My name is Chris Lucke, and today I'm going to give an informative speech about Impressionistic painting.

The French artist Claude Monet once said, "I paint as the bird sings." Well, this quote describes the lights and vibrant nature of Impressionistic painting. Impressionism is defined as a practice in painting among French painters of the late 1800s, depicting subject matter in its natural setting. The way people view Impressionistic painting has changed remarkably since its creation over a century ago. Today this form of artwork is viewed with great admiration. However, in the eighteenth century, well, critics looked at it in a very negative light.

As an admirer and former student of arts, I've had several opportunities to view these paintings in person as well as to learn a little bit about each one that I've seen. Today I'd like to talk to you a little bit about the three defining aspects of Impressionistic paintings. These aspects are the subject matter is all from nature, the scenes and subjects are painted in vibrant hues and unmixed color, and each painting is done with broad, fragmented brushstrokes.

MindTap®

Watch and analyze this speech on MindTap.

Let's start with the subjects painted. Unlike the typical artwork of the eighteenth century, which included paintings of fruit baskets and bouquets of flowers, Impressionistic paintings focused purely on things from nature. Examples include landscapes, as well as water scenes like this one done by Claude Monet, which shows a bunch of sailboats drifting on a calm pond.

Now that you're a little more aware of the subject matter that is used in these types of paintings, let's take a look at the hues and the unmixed color that make them so attractive. When some of you have gone to a museum, I'm sure you've all seen portraits of war scenes and presidents, and when you've looked at these paintings, the colors may look solid and mixed and very rich in texture. Well, with Impressionistic paintings, it's really the opposite: the colors are unmixed and the hues are vibrant, meaning they're energetic, they're scattered, they're all over the place.

Natural subject matter, as well as vibrant hues and unmixed color, are two important aspects of this type of painting. Now I'd like to give you some insight and a little bit of information about the third aspect of Impressionistic painting. This aspect is that these pieces of artwork are painted with broad, fragmented brushstrokes. The effect that Impressionistic paintings usually have on people is similar to the effect that a TV screen has on us. That is, if you go up close to a TV and look at it right in the screen, you see just a lot of tiny colored dots. Well, the same is with Impressionistic paintings, and when you step back from the painting, you see a solid colored picture.

So now that I've told you a little bit about the three defining aspects of Impressionism and the paintings, which, again, are natural subject matter, the scenes and subjects are all created from vibrant hues and unmixed color, and each painting is done with broad and fragmented brushstrokes. I hope that the next time you go to an art museum, you take some time to look at at least one Impressionistic painting, if they're around, of course, and hopefully appreciate the beauty that you see in it with these three aspects in mind.

Questions for Discussion

1. What was the specific purpose of Chris' speech to inform?
2. How did Chris attempt to establish his credibility as a speaker on this topic? Could he have enhanced his credibility even more? How so?
3. What were the main points of Chris' speech?
4. Did Chris support his main points well? What did you like or not like about the way he developed the flow of ideas in his speech? What more could he have done to support his ideas?
5. Did Chris keep you on track with the flow of main points in his speech? How did he try to do this?
6. How could Chris have improved his speech in terms of delivery?
7. Do you believe Chris achieved his specific purpose with this speech?

› APPLY IT . . .

IN THE WORKPLACE

Brainstorming

You use brainstorming techniques twice as you develop your speeches—first for identifying possible speech topics and later for coming up with material to use in your presentation. Brainstorming is a skill you can use in work settings, too. For instance, managers sometimes ask work groups to brainstorm together to come up with ways to solve problems or generate new ideas. However, research shows that the best results usually emerge when each person brainstorms independently and then brings the ideas that emerge to the manager or group in person or online.[15] Of course, you can and should ask other people for their input about your ideas in any situation. But the individual brainstorming skills you're developing for public speaking will serve you well in work settings too.

IN YOUR COMMUNITY

Coordinating with Speakers

Consider the settings and occasions for the speaking opportunities you'll have after you leave college. Professional employees routinely make presentations in meetings, panels, training sessions, or seminars. In these situations, you often present in a format where other speakers make presentations too. This means you have to coordinate well with the other speakers beforehand to insure that your presentations complement each other well. As always, you and your copresenters must first understand who the audience is (supervisors, other colleagues, clients, trainees?) and what they need to hear from each of you. As a group, you want to cover all the necessary information but not overlap. You also must coordinate your presentation to fit in the time frame, the size of the room where you'll speak, the possible use of presentation media, and whether your presentation will be delivered face-to-face or online. Learning how to blend your talents into an organizational structure is a valuable professional skill, and the way you communicate in those settings will be closely observed and appreciated by your supervisors.

REVIEW IT

MindTap®
Use flashcards to learn key terms and take a quiz to test your knowledge.

Key Terms

brainstorming 63
general purpose 62
internal consistency 72
specific purpose 66
thesis 69
topic 62
working outline 70

Reflecting on Developing Your Purpose and Topic

1. Why is it so important to keep the general purpose in mind as you develop your speeches?
2. Being open to new ideas and perspectives helps you exercise your critical thinking skills. How can you brainstorm for topic ideas with an open mind? Can you apply the strategy of trying out something new to come up with creative topic ideas?
3. When evaluating possible speech topics, how do you balance your own interests against what you believe to be the interests of the audience? Do you have to find common ground?
4. What role does the audience play in your thinking when you form the specific purpose of your speech? Can you come up with a good specific purpose for a speech without including the audience? Why or why not?
5. Using the topic "superstitions," can you create a separate specific purpose for an informative, persuasive, and entertaining speech on the topic of "superstitions"?
6. Developing a speech well is a fluid process. Getting feedback from your student community or the place where you live can help you narrow down your topic and make it relevant to your audience. How might community feedback help you find the best way to choose a tropic, decide on your specific purpose, and phrase your thesis? What kinds of questions would you ask members of your community on a topic like gun control?
7. In what ways do a clear specific purpose and thesis help you research your speech topic?

8. What do you achieve by brainstorming in order to develop the organization of your speech? Can you think of other ways to organize the main points for the extended example of "Choosing a Major" given toward the end of this chapter?
9. As you develop your topic—generating ideas and grouping them together—consider the assumptions you are making about the subject matter and the audience. What would you change if you were speaking to a group in your community rather than a student audience? How would you develop your topic to make it truly engaging for a club or organization you belong to or would like to address? Would the general purpose, specific purpose, and thesis remain the same? How might they differ?

5 Adapting to Your Audience

READ IT

After successfully completing this chapter, you will be able to:

- Explain what good speakers do to connect with their audiences.
- Adapt your speeches to reach diverse target audiences.
- Gather and use demographic information about your audience.
- Discern among audience standpoints, values, attitudes, and beliefs.
- Develop an audience questionnaire.
- Use audience research data in your speeches.
- Prepare a speech considering the physical location, occasion, and time of the presentation.
- Discuss the four dimensions of speaker credibility.

MindTap®

Start with a quick warm-up activity and review the chapter's learning outcomes.

While animals like the arctic fox can adapt through genetic change over many generations, we humans can consciously adjust our behavior right away to meet the challenges we face, like tailoring a speech to fit your audience.

outdoorsman/Shutterstock.com

Throughout the animal kingdom, the individuals and species that survive and thrive are the ones that adapt best to their changing environments. Human beings are no different. But while animals, like the arctic fox whose coloring adapted to the snow through genetic change over many generations, we humans can consciously adjust our behavior right away to meet the challenges we face. Our brains are wired to adapt.[1] Although your long-term survival might not hang in the balance from your performance as a public speaker, the evolutionary principle still applies. You greatly increase your effectiveness as a speaker when you adapt to the particular needs and interests of your audience.

Fortunately, you can take practical steps that will make your speech relevant and interesting to any audience. For instance, when Microsoft founder Bill Gates speaks at colleges and universities, he talks about the empowering role of computers at all the schools he visits, but he adjusts his speech for each audience. At the University of Michigan he said, "Microsoft hires about 30 people from the University of Michigan a year, including a lot of our top people. So, let me thank you for that, and hope we can keep up that incredibly strong relationship." When Gates spoke to graduating seniors at Stanford University, he praised the students for their "flexibility of mind" and "openness to change." He told them, "This is where people come to discover the future and have fun doing it." He began his speech at Canada's University of Waterloo with, "Well, it's great to be here. As you heard from some of your alums, Waterloo has contributed an amazing amount to Microsoft."[2] Those brief acknowledgments let audience members know that Gates had prepared his speech with them in mind. Audience analysis and adaptation begins with the first stages of speech preparation and continues through the presentation of the speech and beyond.[3]

Jamie McCarthy/WireImage/Getty Images

What Is an Audience?

MindTap®

Read, highlight, and take notes online.

The term *audience* originally referred to a group of people who share a common interest and physically gather together, usually in a public or semipublic setting such as a plaza, theater, or stadium. With the arrival of film, movie theaters became another common gathering place for audiences. Radio, television, and the Internet also have audiences, of course. History shows that as new communications technologies arrive, audiences also evolve.[4] For example, when radio and television were new, it was common for family and friends to listen or watch in real time as a communal audience. Now these and other media can be experienced on demand by individual people anytime and anywhere.

Today's communications technology allows us to be in the audience for many types of media simultaneously and often quite anonymously. Consequently, we often don't know who our fellow audience members are. Yet the essential idea of audience remains much the same as it was in the public forums of ancient Greece—speakers send messages to human receivers. With or without technology, **audience** refers to the intended recipients of a speaker's message.

audience
The intended recipients of a speaker's message.

The Speaker–Audience Connection

audience analysis
Obtaining and evaluating information about your audience in order to anticipate its members' needs and interests and designing a strategy to respond to them.

Tailoring a speech to fit your audience begins with **audience analysis**—getting to know the people you'll be addressing—their interests, views, and familiarity with your topic. That knowledge allows you to anticipate your listeners' needs and interests and design your speech in a way that responds to them. Even as you deliver your speech, audience feedback becomes a key source of information.[5] Are audience members smiling, frowning, making eye contact with you, or looking out the window? You'll react appropriately to listeners' nonverbal cues, adapting your speech based on that feedback. If there is a question-and-answer exchange following the presentation of your speech, listen carefully to what the audience has to say and respond thoughtfully and non-defensively.

Speakers succeed to the degree they connect with their audience. To make that vital connection happen, it helps to think of your audience members as partners who want to work with you to create a good experience.[6] Most audiences are extremely supportive. They want you to succeed. But the audience will cooperate fully only if it believes what you are saying truly applies to them and fits reasonably well with their viewpoints and experiences. To get audience members to listen attentively and consider your ideas, you must be able to interest them, intrigue them, or otherwise respond to their needs or advance their interests.[7]

Former Los Angeles mayor and California gubernatorial candidate Antonio Villaraigosa knows how to connect well with his audiences. Villaraigosa grew up in East Los Angeles, a poor Latino part of the city. Before he turned 17, Villaraigosa had dropped out of high school—twice. But soon he straightened himself out, started working hard, learned to appreciate education—and developed outstanding speaking skills. Through many inspirational public speeches, Los Angeles's first elected Latino mayor in modern history convinced many of the city's residents to envision a brighter future, even in times of declining budgets and economic instability. In his first state of the city address, Villaraigosa said:

David Hume Kennerly/Getty Images

Antonio Villaraigosa became a successful politician by inspiring diverse audiences to pursue a common dream.

> This day isn't about addressing the state of things as they are. It's about the state of our city as it should be. Over nine months ago, I stood before you on the south steps of City Hall, and I asked you to dream with me about a different kind of future for Los Angeles. A future where LA is taking

> the lead as the great global city of the twenty-first century. . . .I asked you to imagine a future where it doesn't matter who you are or where you come from. . . .Whether you're African American, Latino, Caucasian, or Asian. . . .Whether you're gay or straight, rich or poor. . . .Where every Angelino has a chance to show their talent.[8]

By speaking to the audience in ways they can identify with, Antonio Villaraigosa connects with people, stirs their hopes and dreams, and moves them to act.

Understanding how to prepare a speech with the audience firmly in mind applies to every aspect of **audience-centered** speechmaking. Some speakers make the mistake of focusing too much on preparing the content of their speeches, without sufficiently taking into consideration *who* they're talking to. This principle applies to every kind of public communication. Analyzing and adapting to specific audiences is crucial to the success of media producers, writers, theater producers, politicians,[9] and every professional and amateur public speaker, including you.

audience-centered
Describes a speaker who acknowledges the audience by considering and listening to the diverse and common perspectives of its members before, during, and after the speech.

Classroom Audiences

A college speech class differs from most public speaking situations. As a college student, you have some built-in advantages when you prepare your speeches. You and your classmates can't avoid getting to know one another. You'll share more about yourself than you do in almost any other class. For most students, that's an enjoyable part of the experience. And even though any audience can be challenging to win over, the students you speak to this term want you to do well.[10]

This unusual access to your audience means you'll have a basic impression of who they are even before you give your first graded speech. By applying good listening skills, you'll learn even more about your audience as the term progresses. However, becoming familiar with your audience involves more than gaining basic impressions. Even in the classroom environment, adapting your speech to your audience requires determining in advance, as precisely as possible, who will be listening to you and what they know and think about your speech topic.

Reaching Your Target Audience

Only if you understand the basic characteristics of your audience members and have some idea of their knowledge and feelings about your topic can you tailor your speech to reach them effectively. Politicians and advertisers convince people to vote for them or buy their products by shaping their messages to appeal to their **target audience**—the particular group or subgroup they are trying to reach. Marketing to target audiences has accelerated in the Information Age. For instance, by analyzing your personal data, the websites you visit, and the purchases you make, online marketers like Amazon.com and social media like Facebook identify target audiences for particular products and send them personalized sales messages.

target audience
The particular group or subgroup a speaker most wants to inform, persuade, or entertain.

For public speakers, the target audience comprises the people the speaker most wants to inform, persuade, or entertain. You might, for instance, give a speech at a community center on the need for installing a traffic light at a dangerous intersection. Although your audience may be mostly neighborhood residents who agree with your position, your target audience is the city council members in attendance who can actually do something about the problem. Similarly, if you wanted to advocate curriculum changes at your college, you'd target faculty and administrators—the people with the power to make the changes you seek. The field of marketing is based on two key objectives: (1) sellers of goods and services must know who their target audiences are, and (2) they must know how to connect with them. Just like marketers, public speakers must analyze their target audience in order to determine the best way to present their ideas.

That's not always an easy task. There is never just one audience in a room, even a public speaking classroom.[11] Particularly in today's media-driven world, students—like all audiences—have a range of personal experiences and easy access to lots of information about a variety of topics. Thus, although the students in your public speaking class will have some history in common, they'll also differ in many ways. Part of your responsibility as a speaker is to recognize the diversity of backgrounds, knowledge, interests, and opinions that exist among the members of your audience and plan your presentations accordingly.

Meeting the Challenges of Audience Diversity

The United States ranks as one of the most diverse countries in the world, with people from a wide variety of cultural, religious, educational, and economic backgrounds. In U.S. colleges, the number of African American, Latino, Native American, and Asian American students has increased steadily since the 1970s to about 40 percent of the overall student population today.[12] This trend will only increase in the future.[13]

Diversity is a dynamic phenomenon. Women—who used to be underrepresented on college campuses—account for much of the increase in minority enrollment, especially among black and Hispanic populations.[14] Overall, women now outnumber men among students of all ethnic groups.[15] The presence of openly lesbian, gay, bisexual, and transgender students has increased on campus.[16] Diversity of religious affiliation, including a soaring number of nonaffiliated and atheist students, has proliferated in recent years.[17] Disabled students, including wounded military veterans, make up about 11 percent of the college population.[18] More than one million international students have enrolled in colleges and universities in the United States, more than a 50 percent increase since 2010.[19]

These trends make clear that when you present a speech to a student audience, more than likely you'll face a very diverse group. You may not even be able to recognize the full measure of diversity that is present just by looking at the people who make up your audience. Adapting your speech to individuals with a range of backgrounds, experiences, and interests may seem difficult, but that diversity can work to your advantage and result in a successful experience for you and your audience.[20]

When you interact with people whose backgrounds differ from your own, you learn how to:

- Promote a supportive communication climate that welcomes differing perspectives on topics and issues.
- Draw from a wide pool of knowledge and information that contributes to a better learning experience for all participants.
- Foster positive intergroup relationships in a cooperative fashion.
- Better articulate your own cultural identity and understand that of others.
- Acknowledge and respect differences while avoiding ethnocentrism.
- Advocate constructive dialogue about contentious topics.

At the same time, diverse audiences pose challenges. For example, most humor relies on cultural context: If members of your audience don't share that context, they likely won't find your attempts at humor very funny. Worse, they may feel uncomfortable and become distracted. Excluding some members of your audience with the language you use, the information you present, or the images you show hinders your ability to achieve the goal of your speech—to affect everyone positively with your ideas.

Techniques for Speaking to Diverse Audiences

Five particularly effective techniques can help you adapt your speeches to diverse audiences. Successfully applying the techniques described here depends on a careful and thorough analysis of your audience.[21] Taken together, the techniques allow you to respond to the challenges of audience diversity and promote an inclusive communication climate.

Identify Commonalities Search for commonalities related to your topic among audience members. For instance, if you're giving an informative speech on home schooling to a group with mixed opinions and knowledge of the topic, you might begin by establishing the importance of a good education in general—something all audience members can agree on.

Establish Specific Credibility Demonstrating expertise on the speech topic and sincere concern for the particular interests of your listeners in a friendly and approachable manner will help you win your audience's favor. Regardless of their beliefs and attitudes about your topic, audience members are more likely to listen carefully when you exhibit true knowledge of the subject, seem honest and committed to the topic and to them, and demonstrate interest and enthusiasm by giving an engaging presentation. For example, for a persuasive speech on lowering the blood-alcohol level for a DUI arrest from .08 to .05, you'd have to have credible data that clearly shows the change would save lives. An emotionally touching example of a family member or friend who was victimized by a drunk driving incident would add another strong dimension to your personal credibility.

Include Supporting Materials Relevant to Specific Audience Groups Use supporting materials that will likely resonate strongly with one segment of your audience and leave everyone else with positive or at least neutral feelings. For example, in an informative speech about women's college basketball, you might mention that women started playing basketball at Smith College in 1892—just one year after the game was invented. Audience members who follow women's basketball will likely find this fact particularly important, while others may at least view it as interesting.

Use Appropriate Language Choose language that can be understood by all members of the audience. Select words audience members find clear and meaningful by taking into account what you think the words mean to *them,* not you. This may require defining unfamiliar ideas or concepts and avoiding jargon (like "pushing the envelope" or "burn rate"), acronyms or initialisms (such as "WASP" or "DIY"), and colloquialisms (like "He didn't have a leg to stand on" or "The crowd was totally dead") that not all audience members, especially in a diverse group, will understand.

Continuously Attend to All Segments of Your Audience Acknowledge the variety of your audience's feelings about your topic throughout your presentation rather than addressing each subgroup in separate sections of your speech. For example, in a persuasive speech encouraging listeners to vote for climate change legislation, you should integrate appeals to the full range of audience members, from completely uninformed to highly informed, in all parts of the speech rather than dedicating a specific section to each group. Showing how the legislation you support responds to the particular threats posed by climate change would allow you to quickly mention the basic facts of climate science throughout the speech while at the same time keeping the focus on what must be done.

Monkey Business/Fotolia LLC

No matter who you are talking to or where, you connect with your audience by identifying commonalities, establishing credibility, providing supporting materials when needed, using appropriate language, and continuously attending to the group.

Using Demographic Information

Implementing the techniques of speaking to diverse audiences requires knowing your audience as thoroughly as possible. You'll now learn how you can begin to analyze your audience by examining its basic demographic characteristics.

Understanding the Value of Demographics

demographics
The ways in which populations can be divided into smaller groups according to key characteristics such as, gender, ethnicity, age, and social class.

In any situation, successful speakers initially assess the size of the audience and who its members are—their demographics. **Demographics** are the primary characteristics that describe an individual or group of people. Important demographic categories include age, gender, race and ethnicity, educational level, income level or social class, urban or rural residence, dis/ability, religious affiliation (if any), political affiliation (if any), and relationship status.

Effective communicators use demographics to begin to identify their target audiences. Demographics do not paint a complete picture of any individual or group, but knowing the demographics of your audience gives you a good place to start understanding their possible needs and interests. They help keep your audience foremost in your mind when deciding how to approach your topic.

Gathering Demographic Data

Demographic information about an audience can be obtained through personal observation, consulting with people who are familiar with the group, relying on public resources, or using a questionnaire (discussed later in this chapter).

Personal Observation Student speakers have an advantage over speakers in other settings. For speeches you give in class, some demographic categories—educational level, for instance—will be obvious. You can also note the ratio of women to men and get a good sense of audience members' age range. In addition, you may have some idea of their ethnic backgrounds. Some demographic information is less observable, however. For example, you may not know the income level or socioeconomic class of audience members, although you can sometimes make reasonable assumptions by considering the type of school you attend and noting how your classmates dress and talk.

People who give presentations in their place of employment or other familiar settings also often know a lot about their audience beforehand. For instance, you would probably have a good sense of the demographic composition of the audience for a report given to colleagues at work or in a speech to members of a club to which you belong.

Consulting People Familiar with the Audience In many other settings you don't have personal access to the audience before the event. In such situations, the best source of information is the person or organization that invited you to speak. Ask for information about the audience—the size and purpose of the group, members' demographic characteristics, what they know about the topic, how they feel about it, what they might expect from the speaker, and even how best to reach them with your message. Gathering this information helps you prepare and present your message effectively to that group. Because you will have a better idea of what to expect, it also helps reduce your nervousness.

Public Resources When the options just described aren't available, you might find general demographic information about the American public to be useful. For example, current political affiliations of men and women, number of people of different ethnicities living in various states, or employment statistics among various age groups can be found on the websites of national opinion polling organizations like the Pew Research Center, the Gallup Poll, the Zogby Poll, and the National Opinion Research Center at the University of Chicago. You also may be able to find online resources that reveal useful information about more specific populations, like the demographic composition of a particular college campus, business organization, governmental agency, state, city, or town.

No Demographic Stereotyping

Although demographics can provide valuable insights into attitudes that tend to differ according to people's ethnicity, age, gender, social class, and so on, each person in a community must be treated as an individual who may have different views from others in the same demographic group. When you have an opportunity to speak in your community, avoid stereotyping your audience. You do that by being sensitive to real differences among audience subgroups without making assumptions about any particular audience member. Men don't all think alike because they're men. Not all teenagers are rebels. Every Asian is not a good student. This careful treatment of the audience can be a challenge because the demographic composition of our communities is becoming more and more complex today.

Using Psychographic Information

Demographics give you basic information about who the members of your audience are. **Psychographics** tell you something about how they think. In many ways, that's more important. Many people in the business world certainly think so. Marketers and advertisers rely on psychographic data to develop strategies that might motivate consumers to buy a company's products or services. For example, healthy and unhealthy eaters differ not only in their eating behaviors but also in the values they associate with overall health, exercise, and other lifestyle issues. Marketing a product to healthy and unhealthy eaters thus requires different strategies that address each group's psychological orientations. Likewise, understanding the psychographics of your audience will help you develop your speech effectively for that particular group. The following four concepts explain how psychographics can help you adapt your speech to your audience and show how they can shape a person's thinking (**Figure 5.1**).

psychographics
Psychological data about an audience, such as standpoints that draw from a person's values, attitudes, and beliefs.

Audience Standpoints

Standpoint refers to the mental place from which an individual views, interprets, and evaluates the world. An individual takes a "stand" about her or his "point" of view. Having a standpoint signals independence of mind, personal commitment, and a willingness to act on one's convictions.[22] A person's standpoint stems to a significant degree from the individual's objective position in society, based on demographic categories such as socioeconomic status, gender, and age. The demographic groups to which an individual belongs—for example, a Catholic Latina college student with a learning disability who comes from a working-class family or a 40-year-old African American gay man from an upper-middle-class family—influence the person's view of society.[23] But

standpoint
The psychological location or place from which an individual views, interprets, and evaluates the world.

Figure 5.1 Levels of Psychographic Data

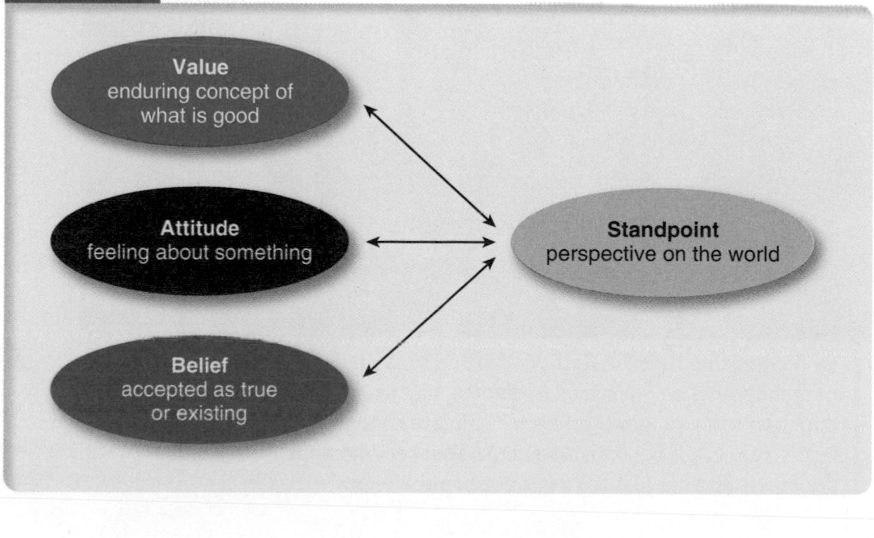

personal standpoints also evolve according to each individual audience member's values, attitudes, and beliefs.

Considering standpoints moves audience analysis beyond categorizing individuals solely on the basis of demographics. Standpoints reflect how audience members differ in ways that are more subjective—how they feel about a topic and their willingness to act in ways that reflect their feelings. In the case of a classroom audience, for instance, everyone shares the experience of being a college student. However, individuals in the group always have different standpoints arising from their personal experiences in life. For example, first-generation college students likely view the value of higher education differently than do second-, third-, and fourth-generation college students. That life experience will affect their evaluation of a speech about policies concerning educational opportunity. Non–native-English-speaking students see the world in ways that differ from those who are native born. They will likely hold strong views about immigration issues. Suburban rockers and hip-hop fans may share demographic similarities but often manifest very different lifestyles. Individuals from those groups often see cultural trends quite differently. In all these cases, diverse standpoints influence how audience members will respond to a speech topic, especially one that hits close to home.

As a speaker, you want to recognize the differences among your audience members and give everyone something they can relate to in your presentation. Acknowledging their diversity is one way to inspire all the audience members to pursue a common goal.[24]

Audience Values

values
Enduring concepts of what is good, right, worthy, and important.

Values reflect what a person thinks is good, right, worthy, and important. You learned your own values from the people you interact with, especially your family, and from the mass media, your society, and culture. You express your values when you judge something to be good or bad, desirable or undesirable, right or wrong, worthy or unworthy. Your values influence your standpoint and behavior. For instance, if you value social justice deeply, you will likely take a strong stand against racist language when you hear it.

Conversely, sometimes your standpoint influences your values. For example, research on environmentalism found that women view altruism as a more important value than men do, which in turn leads women to be more concerned about the environment.[25] If you were giving a speech on an environmental issue, knowing that the women and men in your audience likely have differing value priorities would help you adapt your speech to both groups.

attitude
How an individual feels about something.

But a word of caution: Values are broad concepts that can be misleading. Some values—like respect for life—can manifest very different applied meanings and consequences. For example, someone who is "pro-life" (or "antiabortion") could still support a deadly war. Honesty is a universal value, but most people find ways to justify dishonest behavior in certain situations. Even widely shared values—such as respect for others—are influenced by culture. Giving someone constructive but direct criticism is a positive value in many Western cultures, for instance, but it is often considered unseemly and obnoxious commentary elsewhere.[26]

CLAUDIO PERI/EPA/Corbis

By recognizing that the Catholic faithful today represent a diversity of standpoints on questions of divorce, gay marriage, women's rights, contraception, religious tolerance, climate change, and many other issues, Pope Francis has become a powerful speaker who appeals to a global audience, and not just to religious people.

Audience Attitudes

An **attitude** reflects how a person feels about something in particular. Attitudes indicate approval or disapproval and liking or disliking of a person, place, object, event, or idea. You might like your biology instructor, approve of the new student union building, dislike a music video you just watched, and disapprove of your city's plan for redeveloping the downtown area. Your attitudes are related to your standpoint, values, and beliefs, but these psychographic concepts are not always consistent. For example, from the standpoint of a person with a disability, you might value universal access to public transit and believe that public transit is essential to your community and yet dislike your local public transit system. These conflicting psychological factors may stem from a negative experience or from a conflict between two competing beliefs.

Audience Beliefs

A **belief** is something a person accepts as true or existing. Beliefs can be changed by exposure to new evidence or a good argument. For instance, you may have believed that hypnosis is some kind of gimmick with no value until you learned from a trusted source that it can help treat eating and sleep disorders, compulsive gambling, and depression. Still, some people seldom question their beliefs, even when new information seems to contradict them. For example, research indicates that consuming large quantities of antioxidants can have negative health consequences. Yet if you believe that antioxidants can improve your health, you might interpret the research with skepticism, thereby keeping your belief intact.

belief
Something an individual accepts as true or existing.

Gathering Psychographic Data

In your public speaking class, careful observation will help you gather psychographic data about your audience. It pays to be a good listener. What do your classmates talk about outside class? What topics do they choose for their speeches? How do they respond to other students' speeches? The more you interact with and observe the other students in your class, the more familiar you'll become with who they are and how they think.

In many other instances you'll be familiar with your audience through routine work or social interactions. In those cases, reflecting on what you know about your audience will give you important insights into their standpoints, values, attitudes, and beliefs. For example, you would consider their demographic characteristics but also the topics they talk about, the ideas they argue about, the emotions they express, and what you know about their lifestyles generally. Observing audience members carefully before you present your speech helps you adapt to their particular characteristics.

In some situations, you may have little or no access to your audience beforehand. In those circumstances you'll need to make educated guesses about the audience based on general knowledge about the setting and the situation where you'll make your presentation (such as students at an urban high school or members of a community theater group at their playhouse).

Developing an Audience-Research Questionnaire

Speakers can use **audience-research questionnaires** to gather useful information about audience demographics and psychographics. Getting a better sense of your audience's demographics but also their values, attitudes, and beliefs—especially those related to your topic—will greatly influence the way you research, organize, and present your speech. Developing and distributing your questionnaire well in advance of speech day will help keep your audience at the forefront throughout the speechmaking process.[27]

audience-research questionnaire
A questionnaire used by speakers to assess the knowledge and opinions of audience members; can take the form of email, web-based, or in-class surveys.

An effective audience-research questionnaire features two basic types of questions: closed-ended and open-ended.

Asking Closed-Ended Questions

closed-ended question
A question that limits the possible responses, asking for very specific information.

Closed-ended questions give the respondent a set of possible answers from which to choose. For instance, to gather demographic information, you might ask questions such as

- What is your gender?
  ___ Female ___ Male
- To which ethnic group do you belong?
  ___ African American ___ Asian American ___ European American
  ___ Latin/Hispanic American ___ Native American ___ Other

Similarly, you may want to learn basic facts about the audience that helps you develop an effective approach to your speech topic. If you want to persuade your audience to stop watching television, for instance, or to watch it more selectively, you would first want to have accurate information about members' viewing habits. This information would give you an idea of how to craft your argument for your particular audience. You might include closed-ended questions like these:

- On average, how many hours do you watch TV each week?
  ___ 0–9 ___ 10–19 ___ 20–39 ___ 40 or more
- Do you have a television in your bedroom?
  ___ Yes ___ No
- Why do you usually watch TV?
  ___ Because I'm bored ___ To socialize with family or friends ___ To escape
  ___ As a reward ___ To learn things ___ For entertainment ___ Other

You can also use the questionnaire to gather psychographic data related to your topic. If you are developing an informative speech about your school's 150th anniversary, for example, you might ask these questions in order to get an idea of audience members' opinion of the school and their interest in promoting it:

- Our school has a long history of excellent education.
  ___ True ___ False
- It's important to me that people in the community have a positive view of our school.
  ___ Agree ___ Disagree
- I would enjoy participating in events to celebrate our school's 150th anniversary.
  ___ Yes ___ No ___ Maybe

You can find out about audience members' beliefs by using a sliding scale closed-ended format that ascertains the strength of respondents' views. For example:

- Women make excellent bosses.
  ___ Strongly agree ___ Agree ___ Neither agree nor disagree
  ___ Disagree ___ Strongly disagree
- Marijuana should be made legal for recreational purposes.
  ___ Strongly agree ___ Agree ___ Neither agree nor disagree
  ___ Disagree ___ Strongly disagree

Responses to these questions give you an idea of what respondents believe as well as how strongly they believe it. Your classmates probably already have experience with these kinds of questionnaires, so they should be able to give you informed responses. When analyzing data from sliding scale questions, you'll get a good idea of how strongly your audience agrees or disagrees with the statement.

Asking Open-Ended Questions

Open-ended questions are designed to elicit more in-depth information about an audience by asking respondents to answer in their own words. You want clear, succinct responses. Insights can be gained by asking questions such as

open-ended question
A broad, general question, often specifying only the topic.

- Briefly, what do you know about identity theft?
- In a few words, why do you think some people don't think climate change is real?
- What basic changes, if any, would you make to our school's basic course requirements?
- In a nutshell, what does the word *freedom* mean to you?

Combining Question Types

Combining closed-ended and open-ended questions can clarify audience positions and elicit additional useful information. Here are some examples:

- Should the academic year for high school be extended to 12 months?

  ___ Yes ___ No

  Why did you answer that way? ______________________________
- Have you ever thought about joining a fraternity or sorority?

  ___ Yes ___ No

  Why or why not? ______________________________
- Do you think it's a good idea to keep a handgun at home?

  ___ Yes ___ No

  Why do you think this? ______________________________

Leave enough room after each open-ended item for respondents to give useful answers, but keep your questionnaire short overall.

Distributing Your Questionnaire

If your instructor provides class time, you may be able to distribute questionnaires to your audience in paper form. However, the easiest way to administer an audience-research questionnaire is online through a free survey-building website like SurveyMonkey, KwikSurveys, or Zoomerang. These websites offer much more than ease of use and anonymous responses; often they provide tools for organizing and tabulating survey data. Once you've developed your survey, you'll have to contact your audience, provide the link, and set a deadline for completion.

Keep the length of your questionnaire manageable. Five to ten questions usually will give you plenty of data and avoid burdening your audience. If your questionnaire is too long, respondents will tire of answering questions and may not respond as fully as you'd like (or at all). In addition, you'll end up with far more data than you need, causing you to waste time sifting through irrelevant information.

Questionnaires for Nonclassroom Audiences

Putting your audience-research questionnaire on a survey-building website works well for audiences outside the classroom as well. But surveying an entire audience outside class in any systematic way often isn't possible. Sometimes you'll have to make do with asking key people a few questions, doing an Internet search, or both. For instance, for a speech you've been invited to give to a local community group, you might ask the person who organized the event to tell you how many people will probably attend and what

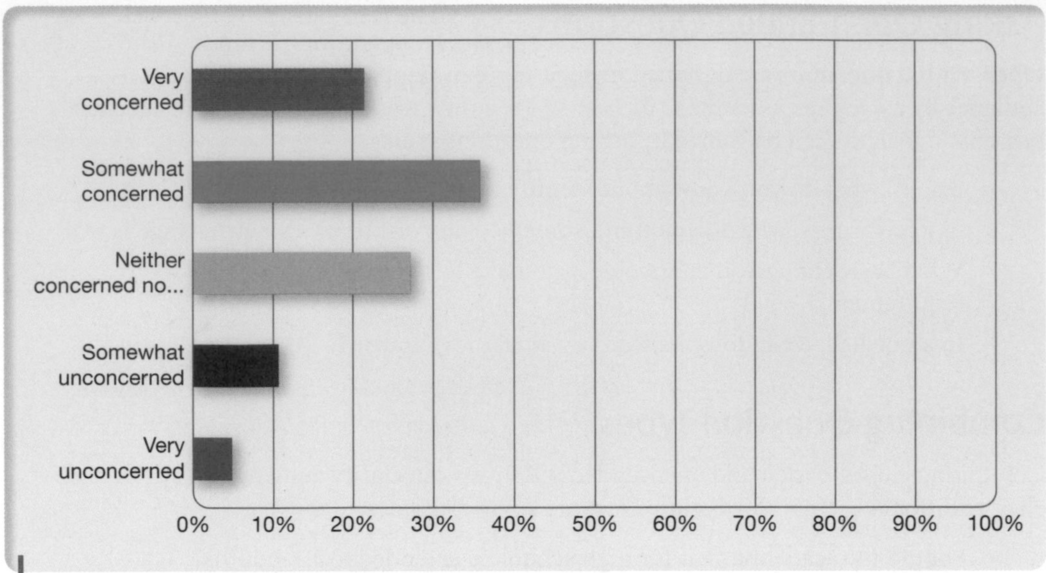

Results from an online survey website can help you analyze your audience's position on any speech topic.

they know or how they feel about the topic. You can often research the group online, too. What you never want to do is walk into a speaking situation completely cold. The more information you have about the audience—even if it's just a rough idea—the better you can prepare a speech that will be appropriate for the group and thus more effective.

Using Audience-Research Data in Your Speech

MindTap®

Watch It: View a video on analyzing and using audience-research data.

Information gathered from a well-constructed audience-research questionnaire can help you prepare and deliver your speech in two ways. First, you will learn more about who your audience members are, what they know about your topic, and how they feel about it. Second, the questionnaire gives you data and comments you can refer to in the speech itself.

Types of Audience Data

Just mentioning questionnaire data in your speech will catch your audience's attention: They know their personal opinions form part of the data set and that fact alone intrigues them. But you can also use specific questionnaire data to achieve the best possible effect by mentioning two types of information in your speech.

summary statistics
Information in the responses to an audience-research questionnaire that reflects trends and comparisons.

Summary Statistics **Summary statistics** reflect trends and comparisons. For instance, you may find that 75 percent of an audience of adult women you plan to speak to believe that annual screening for breast cancer is necessary despite research to the contrary. That is a statistic you obtained by asking the question, "Do you believe women over 40 should be screened every year for breast cancer?" Because you also asked respondents to state their age, you can make some useful comparisons. For instance, you may have found that older women in your audience are much more likely than younger women to support the idea of annual screenings. Comparisons like this allow you to break down summary statistics into useful subcategories that help you identify individual audience members' standpoints.

direct quote
Comments written in response to open-ended questions in an audience-research questionnaire.

Direct Quotes **Direct quotes** are provided by your questionnaire respondents as answers to open-ended questions. For example, after asking college students the closed-ended question "Should the U.S. military draft be reinstated?" you probably will get some heartfelt responses to the following open-ended question: "Why do you think that way?" In selecting quotes, choose short, well expressed statements that are clearly linked to the point you want to make, such as

> The draft should not be reinstated because a voluntary military is more motivated, professional, and dedicated.
>
> I don't want to die in a war I don't believe in!

Select comments that serve your speech purpose well and that will make sense to the audience. Be sure that the quotes you use accurately reflect the respondents' overall sentiments. As a responsible speaker, avoid quotes that would obviously identify the person who made the comment or embarrass audience members or portray them in a negative way. Even if such quotes support your point, using them violates the ethical principles of public speaking, hurts your credibility, and makes the audience less inclined to listen.

Referring to Audience Data in Your Speeches

Summary statistics and direct quotes are valuable material you can use to get the audience's attention, support your main points, make transitions from one point to another, and conclude your speech. For example, you could begin a speech promoting public transportation this way:

> More than 90 percent of the people sitting in this room say they support toughening environmental standards against air pollution, yet very few of you say you carpool or use public transportation. Today I'm going to show you how you can personally follow through on your interest in protecting the environment by making informed and responsible decisions about the forms of transportation you use every day.

Or you could use a quote as your attention getter:

> "It's the biggest scam out there!" That's what one of you said about all the weight-loss programs we see advertised on TV. Let's take a closer look at just what those magical weight loss programs are really all about.

Data from your audience-research questionnaire can also be used to support your main points. For instance, you might integrate summary statistics into your speech in this way:

> According to the questionnaire you filled out last week, more than three-fourths of you say you expect to take at least five years to finish your college degree—exactly the national average. For most students in the United States, the four-year college degree is a thing of the past.

In addition, summary statistics and direct quotes can provide effective transitions from one point to the next. For example:

> Cutting worker benefits might reduce costs, but does it accomplish what someone in the audience calls "the single most important thing we have to do in America today—stop exporting good jobs to foreign countries"? Let's talk about how that might be done.

Statistics and quotes gleaned from the audience-research questionnaire can prove effective in speech conclusions as well, because a key statistic or compelling quote will stay with the audience long after the speech is over. You can leave the source of your data implicit and try something like this:

> Finally, I encourage each of you to do the right thing and what the vast majority of you say must be done. Demand that the university adopt a strong hate speech policy and implement it now!

When using a quote in a conclusion, you might say something like this:

> You've heard my appeal for reforming the way presidential debates are conducted in this country. As one of your classmates asked, "How can the most democratic country in the world fail to represent the full range of diverse voices in this vital exercise of democracy—the presidential debates?" Think about it. Thank you.

Adapting to the Setting

The setting for your speech plays an important role in audience-centered public speaking. During speech preparation and delivery, consider the following factors.

The Physical Location

Where you give your speech—a small conference room, large auditorium, outside on the steps of your school's student union, or online—influences what you say and how you say it. Identify in advance the advantages and disadvantages of the location where you'll be speaking.

Indoors For example, a small conference room allows for a more informal presentation in which you can personalize your speech and easily make eye contact with each audience member. However, that informality may also lead listeners to whisper comments to each other or check their phones. Even in a casual setting, you'll want to maintain a degree of formality so that audience members will focus on you.

Large auditoriums likewise come with both positive and negative features. These settings usually have built-in systems for displaying digital slides, video, and audio. Using presentation media can prove crucial in maintaining the attention of a large audience. However, in this setting listeners become more anonymous—especially if the room is dark and the spotlight is on you—and may be tempted to talk, arrive late, or leave early. You should expect these types of distractions and stay focused.

Outdoors An outdoor setting can be very fitting for certain topics or occasions, but speaking outdoors also brings special challenges—especially noise. The speaker has less control over the situation in general, so the rule of thumb for outdoor speaking is "be flexible." Outdoors, speakers have to adapt minute-by-minute not only to the audience but also to the conditions. When speaking to more than a few people, you'll have to increase your vocal volume and make a concentrated effort to maintain eye contact with audience members because they will have a tendency to look around and not listen to the speech. For many outdoor events, speakers amplify their voices with a sound system. Physical demonstrations in a speech can often be done successfully outdoors, but visual presentation media like digital slides usually can't be used because ambient light makes it impossible for audience members to see images on screen.

Online If you make a presentation on a webcast or in a videoconference—which has become common in professional settings—your audience may be located in several physical places, even in other states or countries. Distance speaking like this brings unique challenges because technological interventions between speaker and audience allow listeners to become distracted easily. Gathering and using information about the places where your audience members are located can help you personalize your presentation and keep your listeners engaged. Chapter 16 provides useful strategies for effective public speaking in the online environment.

Evaluate the Setting Always analyze the room or outdoor space where you will be speaking before the day of your presentation. You may be accustomed to the setting, but probably from the vantage point of the audience, not the speaker.

If indoors, note the room's configuration and the availability of technical equipment. Identify possible sources of noise, such as open windows or doors. If you plan to use visual presentation media, be sure you can darken the room sufficiently so your images will show up clearly. If necessary, arrange ahead of time to have a screen put in place. Determine whether you'll use a podium, a desk, or nothing at all.

If outdoors, imagine where the audience will sit or stand and determine if you'll have to use a sound system. Identify possible sources of noise. Plan on not having a podium available. Figure out how you'll incorporate any physical items or other people into your talk, and where you'll position them before you begin. Knowing the possibilities and constraints of the location in advance helps you adapt to the setting.

Use the Setting Sometimes it pays to refer to the location where you speak during the speech itself. Doing so lets the audience know you're not coming in cold and unaware. You've thought about the place or space in advance, showing a kind of respect that people like. That's why rock bands shout out "Hello, Minneapolis!" when they play a concert there. We saw at the beginning of this chapter how Bill Gates localizes his comments to connect with audiences on the campuses he visits. Non-Hispanic politicians earn some measure of respect from Latino audiences by speaking a bit of passable Spanish. Showing awareness of local values also makes the audience more receptive to the speaker's message. For instance, when real estate developer Joe Verbalis—a communication arts and sciences graduate from Pennsylvania State University—addressed the city council in Revelstoke, British Columbia, about a new housing project, the first thing he stressed was the importance of protecting Canada's pristine wilderness where Revelstoke is located.

The Occasion

Why have people gathered for the speech? Is the audience voluntary or captive? **Voluntary audiences** choose to attend (or not attend) a speaking event, as when you attend a guest lecture on campus because you find the topic interesting or listen to a political candidate's campaign speech in a public venue. **Captive audiences**, in contrast, feel they *must* attend. Mandatory staff meetings at work and required college orientations are examples of occasions when audience attendance is involuntary. The audience for your public speaking class may be captive if the course is required. Generally, voluntary audiences are motivated to listen. They've made an effort to attend. Speakers may have to work harder to engage captive audiences.

voluntary audience
Individuals who can choose to attend or not attend a speaking event.

captive audience
Individuals who feel they must attend an event.

Knowing what an audience expects or hopes for can help a speaker adapt nicely to the occasion. After thanking the school president for inviting him to speak at Lafayette College's graduation ceremony, historian Michael Beschloss[28] dispelled a common fear in this setting:

> Have no fear. I know the lesson that commencement speeches should not be too long. I learned it at Williams College, where I graduated exactly 30 years ago this month. It was about 98 degrees, and we had a commencement speaker who droned on for at least 45 or 50 minutes. People were getting very hot; some people were about to faint; people were in danger of losing their airplane reservations because they were about to fly out that afternoon. Finally, he seemed to be coming to the end, and there was a collective sigh of relief, at which point the speaker said, "Now for the second half of my talk." There was a groan from the audience, and I guess if I learned nothing else from Williams, I learned one thing: Keep it brief if you ever speak at a commencement.

Michael Beschloss showed his audience respect. He demonstrated sensitivity toward them by considering the occasion from the audience's perspective, not his own.

Mark Ralston/AFP/Getty Images

Many occasions for speaking arise from events that affect the speaker directly, like a college or university fee increase. How might you adapt your speech to your audience on the occasion depicted here, a protest outside a university board meeting?

SPEAKING OF ...

Adapt, Don't Mislead

Public speakers, especially politicians, used to be able to say or promise one thing to an audience in one location and something quite different to another audience in another place. Too often the speakers were "adapting" to the audience by misleading them. Such behavior was unethical but often went unnoticed. Not today. Digital communications technology allows anyone to record and later examine what a speaker says. As you develop your life skills as a public speaker, keep in mind that a change of location or audiences does not give you license to alter your message in ways that are misleading. Keep the core of your speeches true to the facts no matter where you speak.

The Time

Adapting to time means taking into account the time of day you'll give your speech, thoughtfully considering when you'll speak during an event (for example, your position in the order of speakers on the day you speak in class) and relating your topic to current events that could make your speech more relevant to your audience.

Time of day influences your audience's alertness and interests. Clearly, listeners are likely to be more alert at 8:30 in the morning than at 8:30 in the evening. Speaking close to a mealtime can prove challenging because audience members can be distracted by hunger before eating and feel drowsy afterward. Late afternoons can also be difficult for keeping an audience engaged. Given these potential drawbacks, mentioning the time of day can actually help you connect personally with the audience: "Well, good morning everyone. Thanks for taking time out of your busy morning schedule to attend my talk. . . ." or, "It's getting late and I don't want to keep you too long, but there is one more point I would like to cover briefly before we go. . . ."

As you prepare your speech, consider at what point you'll be called on during the occasion for your talk. Even if you're the only speaker, your speech will take place within a larger context—the flow of presentations that make up meetings, workshops, seminars, and conferences. Be fully aware of the circumstances that surround your speech and do your best to fit in. In your public speaking class, being alert to what other speakers have talked about earlier that day or previously in the term will help you integrate your topic into the occasion. It's often a good idea to even refer briefly to other speakers in your speech. Doing so demonstrates spontaneity and sensitivity to the audience, which helps gain their attention and respect.

Finally, showing how current events relate to your topic can help make your speech come off as fresh and credible. Placing your topic within the larger framework of happenings at the local, regional, national, or global level makes your presentation seem particularly timely and relevant, especially if the news applies to the audience. For example, referring to recent hiring trends in a vocational field might encourage audience members to pay close attention to what you have to say about that field.

Developing Credibility with Your Audience

credibility
An audience's perception of a speaker's competence, trustworthiness, dynamism, and sociability.

Regardless of who makes up your audience, appearing credible to them is critical to your success. Speaker **credibility**, or what the Greek philosopher Aristotle called *ethos,* arises from audience perceptions of a speaker's competence, trustworthiness, dynamism, and sociability. The four dimensions of credibility work together to give the audience an overall impression of the speaker, as shown in **Figure 5.2**. That impression greatly influences whether or not the audience will listen to and believe the speaker, so it makes good sense to learn how to maximize your credibility.

Competence

competence
The qualifications a speaker has to talk about a particular topic.

Competence refers to the qualifications a speaker has to talk about a particular topic. Naturally, listeners view speakers as more credible when they appear well informed about their topic.[29] This expertise may stem from a speaker's overall training and experience related to the topic or from careful research carried out specifically for the speech. Speakers can demonstrate competence by explicitly establishing their prior credentials on the topic. For example, if you were to give a speech on swimming or lifesaving skills, you would want to let your audience know if you are a certified lifeguard. All good speakers show competence by presenting sufficient relevant and up-to-date information that supports their thesis.

Nothing undermines a speaker's credibility more than the perception that he or she is not well prepared. But keep in mind that different audiences will have varying expectations about what constitutes effective and appropriate supporting materials.[30] For instance, an audience of specialists on the topic will hold the speaker to an especially high standard of credibility. Carefully analyzing your audience will give you insights into what they'll find interesting and convincing.

Figure 5.2 The Dimensions of Speaker Credibility

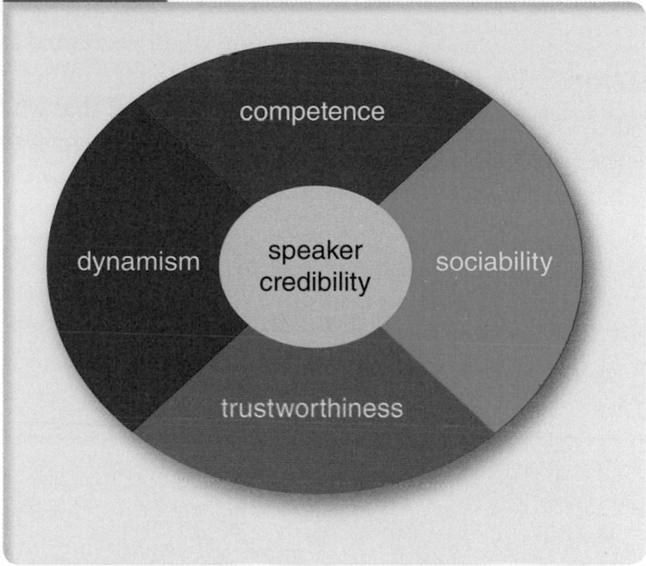

Trustworthiness

The second dimension of speaker credibility is **trustworthiness**. Unlike competence, which relates to specific qualifications, information, and authority, trustworthiness is a much more general idea. In some ways, it's more difficult for speakers to appear trustworthy than competent because trustworthiness stems from overall perceptions of the speaker as a person. Nonetheless, you can develop strategies for generating the trust of your audience. Audiences regard you as trustworthy when they consider you to be honest, ethical, sincere, reliable, sensitive, and empathic.

trustworthiness
An audience's perception of a speaker as honest, ethical, sincere, reliable, sensitive, and empathic.

Audiences want to know, "Who benefits from what the speaker is advocating? What's in this for me?" Aristotle argued that a trustworthy public speaker demonstrates **goodwill** by showing he or she has the audience's true needs, wants, and interests at heart.[31] So if you employ language in your speech that makes clear what you are saying can benefit members of the audience, and speak to the group sensitively, your listeners will be more inclined to find you worthy of their trust.

goodwill
An audience's perception that a speaker shows he or she has the audience's true needs, wants, and interests at heart.

Dynamism

The third dimension of credibility, **dynamism**, refers to how the audience regards your activity level during your presentation.[32] Activity level doesn't mean just moving around a lot, although body language does play a role. Dynamism has more to do with the overall level of enthusiasm you display. Dynamic speakers appear lively, strong, confident, and fluent in what they say and how they present their ideas. Being dynamic makes a speaker more charismatic.[33] Audience members listen to, remember, enjoy, and are convinced by speakers who are dynamic.

dynamism
An audience's perception of a speaker's activity level during a presentation.

Sociability

Sociability reflects the degree to which an audience connects with a speaker. Sociable speakers are those the audience considers to be friendly, accessible, and responsive.[34] Appearing sociable requires establishing rapport with the audience. An effective way to achieve rapport is to show how you share some common ground or similarities with the audience. In her spirited graduation speech from the University of Chicago, Sophie Nunberg used the idea of "emerging" together as a way to connect with her fellow students:

sociability
The degree to which an audience feels a connection to a speaker.

> . . . Here, together, we endured. We wallowed. We reveled. And now we've emerged. We've emerged better read, more passionate than when we had begun.

> . . . We've emerged as the selves we were meant to be. Whole and complete. No postscripts, asterisks, or footnotes. I can't predict the future; what the world will be when we return for our 25th reunion in 2037. Will we have sustainable energy? Will global conflict cease to exist? Will Pierce Hall's plumbing finally be working? I only know that whatever paths we take, they won't be the easy ones. And we know we will emerge, again. And however we emerge, each and every time, we will be marked as University of Chicago alumni, as people who know that what's too easy is apt to be boring. And let me tell you, Class of 2012, boring is the one thing we definitely are not.[35]

With clear and direct language, the speaker used sentimentality, humor, and pride to establish common ground and create a strong emotional bond with her audience.

Summary

Adapting to your audience requires thorough analysis, which will help you design a speech that is likely to accomplish your objective. Especially today, audience members represent many different backgrounds, knowledge levels, and interests. Appealing to everyone in the audience is a key quality of a successful public speaker. Speaking to diverse audiences entails techniques such as finding commonalities, establishing credibility, incorporating relevant supporting materials, using language that all audience members understand, and being sensitive to all audience members throughout the speech.

When analyzing your audience, you gather two types of information: demographic and psychographic. Demographic information includes categories such as age, gender, educational level, socioeconomic status, religious affiliation (if any), and ethnic background. Psychographic information refers to psychological data about audience members, including their standpoints, values, attitudes, and beliefs. This information adds important insights to demographic data about what might motivate your audience.

One method for gathering demographic and psychographic data is the audience-research questionnaire. Carefully designed closed- and open-ended questions can elicit valuable information about your audience's interests and needs as well as those of subgroups within the larger audience.

You can integrate information from the audience-research questionnaire into your speech. Closed-ended questions provide trends and averages you can cite. Open-ended questions elicit audience members' feelings expressed in their own words. Quoting clever or insightful remarks by audience members is a great way to capture their attention, support your main points, make transitions from one point to the next, or create an effective conclusion.

Adapting to your audience also means adapting to the physical location, occasion, and time of your speech. The physical location is the place where you give your speech, such as an auditorium, a classroom, or the steps of the county courthouse. The occasion is the purpose of the event. The time of the speech includes time of day, speaking order, and current events.

Whatever your audience and setting, developing your credibility is crucial to your success as a speaker. Competence, trustworthiness, dynamism, and sociability work together to form a speaker's credibility.

> ANALYZE IT

Katie, Why Pi?

Katie's main objective for the informative speech she gave was to get her audience interested in a subject they don't know or care much about. To accomplish this, she had to adapt her approach to fit the knowledge and interest level of her listeners. Notice how she attempts to appeal to her uninformed audience by establishing credibility on the topic and using an upbeat, personable style of delivery. By adapting smartly to her audience and humanizing the topic, Katie was able to attract and hold the audience's attention in her successful speech to inform.

3. 1415926535897932384626433832795 …. Most of you know the name of the number that I just recited. It is a number found in rainbows, pupils of eyes, ripples in the water, sound waves, and even DNA. It is a number that both nature and music understand, but the human mind cannot quite comprehend. This number has sparked curiosity in many minds over the past 4,000 years. I am talking about pi—not the dessert, but the circle ratio.

Now, a class of speech majors is probably wondering if they can survive a five-minute speech on math, but I will try my hardest to present pi as a fascinating topic, for that's what I believe it to be.

I have researched this topic, finding information both technical and historical, and also fanatical. My own interest came about when I was challenged to memorize more digits than a friend of mine. I plan to inform you on what pi is, the history of pi, and why pi has caused obsessions in people's lives.

Pi is a symbol that most everyone is familiar with, even if they don't know what it represents. When you take the circumference of a circle, and divide it by the diameter, which is the line that goes through it, your result will always be pi. It doesn't matter how large or how small the circle; whenever you divide a circumference by the diameter, the answer will always be the constant pi. This is called the "circle ratio."

Now, most of you know pi to be 3.14, or 22 over 7. But the truth is that pi is an irrational number, which means it can't be represented as a fraction. Much of pi's mysticism is due to the fact that it's never-ending. Or is it? This has boggled mathematicians for ages. They're puzzled and almost ashamed that it's so difficult to find a number as simple as the ratio of a circle.

But pi goes beyond the circle ratio. According to David Blatner, who wrote *The Joy of Pi*, this value can be found in all fields of math, science, architecture, the arts, and even the Bible. The world record to this date, of the most digits calculated, is 206 billion decimal places. This was calculated by Dr. Kanada at the University of Tokyo.

MindTap®

Watch and analyze this speech on MindTap.

Although 206 billion digits have been calculated thus far, there was a time when there was uncertainty of even the second decimal place, back in the days of antiquity. Woven between pi's infinite digits is a rich history, ranging from the great thinkers of the ancient cultures to the supercomputers of the twentieth century.

Imagine 4,000 years ago. There's no decimal system, no compass, no paper, no pencil, but people still found ways to do math. All the Egyptians needed was a stick, a piece of rope, and the sand, and they were able to approximate pi as "a little over three." Also, the Greeks, Babylonians, Israelites, Chinese, and Mesopotamians studied the circle ratio, but all of them uncertain of even the third decimal place.

Pi's finality remained a mystery until the sixteenth century. Peter Beckmann, a former professor of engineering at CU, likes to call this period "the age of the digit hunters," with each generation popping on more digits than the one before it. I will spare you the technical details of the methods they used, but keep in mind, there was still no calculator. Great thinkers like Archimedes, Richter, Shanks, and several other mathematicians that you've never heard of continued to break records. But in the mid-1900s, along with the invention of the computer, came the breakthrough in the hunt for pi. After IBM printed out 16,000 digits, it was confirmed that pi was totally random, and that no pattern was to be found in its strand.

Well, the question still remains. Why do people devote their lives for searching pi when the number's completely useless after 20 digits? Why not the square root of 2? Or the sine of 1 degree? Or any other number with an infinite strand of digits? What's the fascination with pi?

Well, the mysticism and mystery behind this unknown value has caused people to become both fascinated and obsessed. Blatner also states that more people have memorized, philosophized, calculated, and expounded upon this value more than any number in history.

I want to share with you a few stories on how pi has impacted certain individual lives. I'll start with the Chudnovsky brothers. David and Gregory were two brothers who were mathematicians and moved here from Russia so they could freely entertain their obsession with pi. From their own apartment in Manhattan, they built a supercomputer from scratch, just so they could calculate more digits and study its use in various formulas.

Have you ever known anyone who has tried to memorize pi? Maybe a few weirdos or math nerds here and there. Some do it for sport, others to be silly; but some people are much more serious about memorizing pi. Blatner states that five years ago, the record was blown out of the water when Hiroyuki Goto spent over nine hours reciting 42,000 digits of pi, from memory. Now this was a rare case, but there are methods in memorization for the average memory—some people have translated the digits into poems, clever mnemonics, and songs; or you can just memorize them in groups of four, which is the method that I have found the easiest.

And lastly, the celebration of Pi Day on March 14th—3/14. It is suggested on the Ridiculously Enhanced Pi Page on the web that you gather with your friends at 1:59 p.m. to eat pie and to share personal stories about pi.

So ends my analysis on people's obsessions. The question was never answered though. No one knows why pi has caused such a craze, or why several books, movies, and fanatical web pages have been produced on the subject. What inspired the Chudnovsky brothers to devote their whole lives in search for pi? What inspired me to write a speech on a silly number? I think the answer lies in the mystery. Exploring pi is an adventure! That's why people do it.

I want you to remember pi. But not just as the circle ratio, and not just as the biggest influence on math over history, but as a number that has greatly impacted people, and has had an influence on everything we do.

In William Schaaf's book, *The Nature and History of Pi*, he concludes that no other symbol in mathematics has ever evoked as much mystery, romanticism, misconception, and human interest, as the number pi.

Questions for Discussion

1. What did Katie do to adapt her topic to a general college student audience? Do you think she was successful at doing this? What more could she have done?
2. Reflecting on each of the four main factors of credibility—competence, trustworthiness, dynamism, and sociability—did Katie come across as a credible speaker on this topic?
3. Specifically, what did the speaker do to connect with her audience?
4. If you were to develop an audience research questionnaire on this topic, what questions would you include?
5. Were you able to detect the main points of Katie's speech? What were they? Did she use transitions effectively?
6. Evaluate the effectiveness of her introduction and conclusion to the speech.

APPLY IT . . .

IN THE WORKPLACE

Meeting Colleagues' Expectations

Audiences don't exist only in classrooms or meeting rooms. We are audience members of one kind or another every waking minute of our everyday lives. We routinely consume communications media in bite-sized chunks, skipping from one medium to the next or paying attention to several media simultaneously.[36] In a world of 140-character tweets, 30-second video games, 2-minute versions of rock music classics, and 11-minute online TV episodes, we all expect rapid information delivery. This expectation prevails in the workplace as well, where wasted time is not well tolerated. But, while your coworkers expect efficiency when listening to professional presentations, they also need substance.[37] You should respect their desire to get the information they need quickly, but don't compromise on quality. Keep your presentations on track, concise, and informative. Provide necessary detail, support your ideas with up-to-date information, and make sure your presentation media are always clean, clear, and truly useful to your fellow employees. Can you list areas in a potential presentation in a work environment where you would be able to keep your presentation brief and others where precision might require more expansive explanations?

IN YOUR COMMUNITY

Audience Follow-up

Audience analysis involves gathering and interpreting information about people who will hear a speaker's message. That helps speakers adapt their remarks to their audiences. But the process of knowing the audience does not have to stop when the speech is finished. When possible, it can also be very beneficial to measure the effect of a speech—especially for speeches about issues that are important to a particular group. To accomplish this, leaders of businesses, government agencies, and community organizations can gather contact information from individuals who attend presentations made to their employees or members. The leaders can then conduct a follow-up survey to determine the effectiveness of a speaker and message. For example, analyzing how hospital employees respond to an administrator's presentation of new hygiene rules in the facility would help the staff understand if the rules were well understood and what adjustments might have to be made. Follow-up audience analysis can be crucial for making a speech truly impactful in the community.

> REVIEW IT

Key Terms

attitude 86
audience-centered 81
audience-research questionnaire 87
audience 80
audience analysis 80
belief 87
captive audience 93
closed-ended question 88
competence 94
credibility 94
demographics 84
direct quote 90
dynamism 95
goodwill 95
open-ended question 89
psychographics 85
sociability 95
standpoint 85
summary statistics 90
target audience 81
trustworthiness 95
values 86
voluntary audiences 93

MindTap®
Use flashcards to learn key terms and take a quiz to test your knowledge.

Reflecting on Adapting to Your Audience

1. How do audience analysis, adaptation, and connecting with your audience work together for public speakers? In what ways might you adapt your speeches to appeal to your audience this term?
2. Can you assume that men and women differ on sensitive issues like accepting new immigrants to the United States? On what information or impressions do you base your assumptions? How might age and ethnicity influence what women and men think about this issue?
3. You've been asked by another student to explain the difference between "demographic" and "psychographic" information. What would you tell them? Can you give them a good example of how demographics and psychographics can be used in audience analysis and speech preparation on the topic of raising the minimum wage to $15 per hour?
4. Audience-research questionnaires can provide speakers with summary statistics and direct quotes to be used in their presentations. Of what real use is this data? In what ways are statistics and quotes best used by speakers?
5. You hear your boss at work say, "It doesn't matter where or when I speak. My message is so strong it comes through anywhere, for any group, at any time!" What friendly advice would you give her about the location, occasion, and time of her presentations?
6. Competence and trustworthiness are key dimensions of a speaker's credibility. A speaker can demonstrate competence by being qualified and informed on a topic. But how does a speaker inspire trust? What public figures do you trust? Why?

6 Researching Your Topic

READ IT

After successfully completing this chapter, you will be able to:

- Prepare to research your topic by examining your own experience and multiple perspectives and sources.
- List and describe the various online resources for researching your speech topic.
- List and describe the various library resources for researching your speech topic.
- Identify and discuss strategies for maximizing the effectiveness of your information searches.
- Effectively plan and conduct a research interview.
- Evaluate information sources about your topic for relevance, purpose, and validity.
- Recognize plagiarism and identify strategies to avoid it.

MindTap®

Start with a quick warm-up activity and review the chapter's learning outcomes.

Students view online information with a healthy skepticism and report a desire to better identify reliable and valid sources.

Library of Congress Prints and Photographs Division [LC-USW3-000386-C]

You and your friends can't decide where to go for spring break. How do you research your options? You find you're not getting enough exercise. Where is the first place you check for ideas on fitness programs? The deadline to give your speech in this class is fast approaching. Where do you go to learn more about your topic? Whereas in the past you would have made a trip to your public or campus library and hunted through paper card catalogs, today you'll go online using your smartphone, tablet, or computer to track down the information you need. Surveys of college students in the United States have found that 95 percent use an online search engine when seeking information about a topic. Most rely on Google and Wikipedia for their searches because students view the search engine and online encyclopedia as efficient time-savers.[1] However, students view online information with a healthy skepticism and report a desire to better identify reliable and valid sources.[2] Not surprising, many students find locating the information they need an overwhelming and anxiety-producing experience.[3]

This chapter provides you with the skills and strategies you need to effectively research your speech topics. You will learn how to use the right navigation tools to search out information from the Internet, the library, and interview sources. Thoroughly researching your speech topic builds your confidence, enhances your credibility and contributes to a polished and engaging presentation.

© David Schmitz Photography

Preparing to Research Your Topic

MindTap®

Read, highlight, and take notes online.

Researching your speech topic consists of three phases: (1) preparing for the search, (2) gathering the information, and (3) evaluating the information found. **Table 6.1** summarizes these phases.

The first step on your path to a well-researched speech that you can present with confidence is developing a clear research plan, which involves determining: (1) what you already know about the topic, (2) how you found out about it, and (3) possible sources of information about your topic. This section suggests strategies you can use in formulating your research plan.

Examining Your Own Experience

MindTap®

Watch It: View a video on researching speech topics.

To begin, create a list of words you associate with your topic. Then write out a few sentences for each phrase, explaining what you know about the topic.

Second, identify how you learned about the topic. Did you read about it online? Discuss it in a class? Hear a story about it on a radio or TV program? View an image on Instagram or Pinterest? You may have acquired information about your topic from multiple sources.

In exploring how you learned about a topic, what you already know is important, but serves only as a starting point. You must become an expert on your topic and draw information from many diverse sources. In addition to reducing speech anxiety and building your confidence as a speaker, becoming an expert on your topic allows you to determine the reliability of what you know and the credibility of your original sources.

Table 6.1 Phases in Researching Your Speech Topic

Prepare	Identify • What you know • How you learned it • Multiple perspectives and sources
Gather → Internet	• Websites • Social media • Documents • Images • Video/audio files
Gather → Library	• Books • Academic journals, magazines, newspapers • Government publications • Reference materials • Nonprint resources
Gather → Interviews	• Research interviews with experts
Evaluate	Assess information's • Reliability • Validity • Currency

Universal Press Syndicate

Identifying Multiple Perspectives and Sources

As you conduct your research, seek multiple perspectives, regardless of your topic. Identifying a full range of perspectives challenges your assumptions, gives you an idea of what kind of resistance from your audience you might face when you speak, and makes you a more credible speaker.

Considering multiple perspectives on your topic also encourages you to explore multiple sources of information. People often develop habitual ways of accessing information that greatly narrow the possibilities for a search, such as relying exclusively on one search engine.[4] To find multiple points of view on your topic, ask the following questions to guide your search for information.

Who Might Be Knowledgeable about This Topic? Identify people who are experts on your topic. If you're giving a speech on campus safety, for instance, then a member of your school's police department would be a good source of information. Alternately, for a speech on tourism in your state, you might want to talk with a local tourism official. For a speech on the latest job search strategies, a career counselor on your campus or a recruiter for a large company likely can give you insight into the topic. Also consider people you know who may have expertise on your topic, such as instructors, coworkers, family members, and friends.

What Organizations Address the Topic You Are Researching? Particularly if your topic touches on a community issue, local organizations often can provide information not available from any other source. For example, suppose you're conducting research for a speech on hospice, which provides spiritual, emotional, and medical care to terminally ill people and their families. Although you can get general information from the National Hospice and Palliative Care Organization's website, your audience will appreciate information about hospice care in their community.

Not every organization has a website, but basic contact information likely is available on websites such as Yellow Pages (yellowpages.com) or Superpages (superpages.com). In the case of hospice, once you find a local one, you can contact its staff, request pamphlets or other information, and possibly schedule an interview with the director.

What Events Are Happening Related to Your Topic? The answer to this question may lead you to information posted in your social media network, such as Twitter or Facebook, or to an event such as a book reading or a public lecture. Campus

© David Schmitz Photography

Many public and campus libraries have special collections with materials on particular topics that you can access only in the library's building.

SPEAKING OF ...

Primary versus Secondary Sources

Primary sources express the authors' original ideas or findings from original research. For example, research reports produced by the Pew Research Center (pewinternet.org) present data that the project's researchers collect.

Secondary sources are others' interpretations or adaptations of primary sources. For example, a secondary source would consist of a newspaper article that incorporates findings from a particular Pew Research Center report. In this case, the journalist is interpreting and reusing that report's primary information. In researching your speeches, generally it's best to use primary sources so you're not depending on someone else's interpretations, which may not be accurate or complete.

websites often list diverse and interesting weekly events. Yahoo! Local (local.yahoo.com) allows you to identify traditional as well as online events for most cities in the United States. Check your local newspaper—online or print version—as well.

How Can I Find the Information I Need? For nearly all topics, there are many sources of information and many ways to get to those sources. Although you probably first think of a search engine, such as Google, as the starting place for your research, you have many other options to find the information you need. Online databases available through your library, for instance, will produce an array of articles and stories about the same topic.

Keywords, terms associated with a topic that are used to search for information related to it, influence the direction your research will take. In addition to determining the best keywords to use in searching online for information about your topic, identify the best physical places to search. Libraries often have special collections dealing with local topics. For example, the San José State University Library features the Steinbeck Center, the Beethoven Center, and the California Room, with resources pertaining to their particular topic. Public libraries typically have extensive reference sections that include specialized dictionaries, topical encyclopedias, and historical documents.

Finding Research Materials

keyword
A term associated with a topic and used to search for information related to that topic.

primary source
Information that expresses an author's original ideas or findings from original research.

secondary source
Others' interpretations or adaptations of a primary source.

In the past when college students needed to find information for class assignments, they often started with their favorite search engine.[5] But more recent research has found that college students use a variety of search strategies for their school work, including library databases, the library catalog, Wikipedia, and Google Scholar.[6] In this section you'll learn the best strategies for using Internet and library information search tools.

Accessing Internet Resources

relevance
How closely a webpage's content is related to the keywords used in an Internet search.

To develop a well-researched speech you'll need to effectively use metasearch engines, search engines, specialized search engines, and web directories that help you locate relevant information on your topic. **Relevance** refers to how closely a webpage's content is related to the keywords used in a search. The better your keywords represent the topic you're researching, the greater the likelihood you'll find relevant information.

metasearch engine
A search tool that compiles the results from other search engines.

Metasearch Engines These tools rely on other search engines to find information on the web. Several **metasearch engines** are listed in **Table 6.2**. Metasearch engines provide information breadth rather than depth. For example, if you were giving an informative speech on the history of TV, you'd want more general information about the topic. In contrast, a speech focusing on a specific TV genre, such as reality shows, would require more in-depth information. In combining the results of several search engines, metasearch engines reveal the websites and webpages most frequently listed by the different search engines. The results from metasearch engines represent only a small portion of the websites you'd find if you used each search engine individually. The results listed may be the most popular websites each search engine has identified,

Table 6.2 Metasearch Engines

	Web Address	Features
Dogpile	dogpile.com	Favorite Fetches lists most popular searches.
Info.com	info.com	Focus searches by type, such as research, jobs, health, and classifieds.
Ixquick	ixquick.com	Rates each result by how many search engines choose it.
Mamma	mamma.com	Targets searches by categories, including jobs, videos, and travel.
Symbaloo	symbaloo.com	Customize webmixes to search specific sites and categories.
Yippy	yippy.com	Sorts similar results into clouds.
ZapMeta	zapmeta.com	Fine-tune your search with clusters and keyword highlighting.

but they may not be the best or most relevant sources of information. Metasearch engines can be useful as a starting point in your research: They give you a sampling of websites associated with your topic.

Search Engines Using sophisticated software programs, **search engines** hunt through computer documents to locate those associated with particular keywords. Search engines like those listed in **Table 6.3** search only files that they've indexed—and no search engine has indexed the entire web. Each search engine applies its own methods to scour the web. Thus, different search engines will produce different results, and the same search engine will produce different results on different days. In addition, research shows that search engine users rarely go past the first page of results and will click on only a few links before giving up.[9] But if you keep digging, use multiple search engines, and search with a variety of keywords, you're more likely to locate information relevant to your topic.

search engine
A sophisticated software program that hunts through documents to find those associated with particular keywords.

As an example, let's explore the topic *urban agriculture,* also called *urban* or *community farming,* which involves growing and distributing food within a city or town, and compare how the results vary between search engines.

- *Google.* The keywords *urban agriculture* produce more than 26 million results in Google, with the first page including:
  - an entry in Wikipedia,
  - a link to the U.S. Department of Agriculture's Alternative Farming Systems Information Center, and
  - an article in *The Detroit News* on the topic.

  Google also suggests additional keyword phrases, such as *urban farming, benefits of urban agriculture,* and *urban agriculture sustainable cities.*
- *DuckDuckGo.* A search on DuckDuckGo overlaps somewhat with Google but also includes links to:
  - an article on rooftop gardens in *National Geographic,*

SPEAKING OF ...

Weighing in on Wikipedia

Should you use Wikipedia when researching your speech topics? A survey of college students in the United States found that three-quarters of respondents used Wikipedia at least some of the time for their classes.[7] However, many instructors do not allow the use of Wikipedia as a source for college-level research papers and oral presentations. But as first-year college students reported in a recent survey, Wikipedia provides general background information on a topic and can offer a useful first step for Internet searches.[8] For example, you might use Wikipedia to help you identify keywords for Internet and library database searches. In addition, the Talk tab at the top of entry allows you to view conversations about the entry's content, tone, and style. These conversations can provide useful insight into varying perspectives on the topic.

- the Food and Agriculture Organization of the United Nations, and
    - a research article on urban farming in Japan.
- *Qwant.* Finally, searching Qwant provides links to:
    - a nonprofit organization that promotes urban farming,
    - a news article on edible landscaping, and
    - a tweet about an urban agriculture symposium.

This simple example gives you an idea of the benefits of using multiple search engines when gathering information online.

Table 6.3 **Search Engines**

	Web Address	Features
Ask	ask.com	Offers question-based searching and ideas for related topics.
Bing	bing.com	Keeps a list of your search history for easy backtracking.
DuckDuckGo	duckduckgo.com	Gives instant answers and suggests related topics.
Exalead	exalead.com/search	Presents page thumbnails and charts of results by country and language.
Gigablast	gigablast.com	Includes Giga Bits that offer suggestions for refining your search.
Google	google.com	Offers specialized search engines, such as Finance, Patents, Blogs, Google Scholar, and Trends.
Qwant	qwant.com	Sorts results by web, news, and social media.
Yahoo!	yahoo.com	Allows you to use tabs to search images, news, local, video, and other specialized content.

Specialized Metasearch and Search Engines Traditional metasearch engines and search engines index only a fraction of the web's content. For example, medical research, financial information, and legal cases often are available only through direct queries to specialized databases.[10] Google Scholar, for instance, is a specialized search engine that searches about 165 million documents in U.S. and European scholarly books and journals as well as conference papers, theses, dissertations, and technical reports. In addition, journals indexed in the library database ProQuest are now searchable with Google Scholar.[11] **Table 6.4** lists several specialized metasearch and search engines that access specific topic areas, such as science, education, government, and businesses; social media and blogs; and documents, images, and audio files.

Web Directories With the number of indexed webpages approaching five billion and the number of active websites nearly one billion, quickly finding useful information requires precise searching.[12] Metasearch engines, search engines, and specialized search engines provide useful tools for sifting through all that information. In addition, web directories like those listed in **Table 6.5** can help you refine your search strategies, especially if you're not exactly sure which keywords best fit your speech topic. **Web directories**, also called *search indexes,* organize webpages hierarchically by categories. For example, Best of the Web includes subject areas such as arts, finance, health, games, science, and sports, which in turn are broken down into subcategories. You can browse directories by category or search using keywords.

web directory
An online list that organizes webpages and websites hierarchically by category; also called a search index.

Table 6.4 **Specialized Search Engines**

	Web Address	Features
Topical		
Artcyclopedia	artcyclopedia.com	Search by artist's name, title of artwork, or museum name or location.
Google Scholar	scholar.google.com	Suggests related articles; save your searches to your library folder.
healthfinder.gov	healthfinder.gov	Sponsored by U.S. Department of Health and Human Services, searches health news and information from more than 1500 health organizations.
History Engine	historyengine.richmond.edu	Includes thousands of summaries or "episodes" of a wide range of U.S. history topics.
iSEEK-Education	education.iseek.com	Searches resources from universities, government, and established noncommercial providers.
INFOMIME	infomime.ucr.edu	Built by librarians, searches scholarly online resources, such as book, journals, and articles.
pipl	pipl.com	Search for people by name, email address, or phone number.
USA.gov	usa.gov	Centralizes browsing and searching for all U.S. government websites.
Social Media and Blogs		
Addict-o-matic	addictomatic.com	Customize your search of social media with the results dashboard.
IceRocket	icerocket.com	Offers specialized real-time searches of blogs, Twitter, Facebook, images, and Big Buzz.
Regator	regator.com	Searches selected blogs; use the setup wizard to get started.
Social Mention	socialmention.com	Searches all social media or select specific sources; sign up for social media alerts.
Technorati	technorati.com	Monitors blogs in real time; lists top blogs and tags.
Topsy	topsy.com	Searches real-time tweets, links, photos, and videos; follow what's trending.
Whos Talkin	whostalkin.com	Search more than 60 of the most popular social media sites.
Documents and Media		
blinkx	blinkx.com	Searches for video on hundreds of media sites.
Clipblast	clipblast.com	Finds videos from sites such as Disney, ESPN, CBS, the Discovery Channel, the Sundance Channel, and Showtime.
DocJax	docjax.com	Search e-books, documents, spreadsheets, digital slides, PDFs, and text documents.
FindSounds	findsounds.com	Search for sound effects in multiple formats; mobile app available.

Table 6.5 **Web Directories**

	Web Address	Features
Best of the Web	botw.org	Includes local and blog directories.
Galaxy.com	galaxy.com	Highlights new listings as well as recent headlines in the news.
JoeAnt.com	joeant.com	Organizes information by subject, blog type, and region of the world.
Open Directory Project	dmoz.org	An international network of volunteers gives this directory a global scope.
SoMuch.com	somuch.com	Links updated daily; features today's historical events.
The WWW Virtual Library	vlib.org	The oldest web directory; experts review each site listed in the library.

Courtesy of SJSU.edu

The reference desk at your campus library is a key resource in your search for information: trained librarians can provide valuable leads and sources.

Exploring Library Resources

Although Internet search engines can provide you with many sources related to your speech topic, a recent study of college students' search strategies found that the databases available from the campus library produce higher quality sources, especially current publications, such as newspapers and journal articles.[13] Your campus library's website provides access to books, academic journals, magazines, newspapers, government publications, reference materials, and nonprint resources.

You may not be familiar with all the services that your library offers.[14] A trip to the library to discuss your topic with a librarian may quickly and efficiently narrow your search for relevant information. A visit to your library also allows you to examine various resources available only at the library, including many books, complete periodicals such as journals, magazines and newspapers, government publications, reference works, and nonprint resources such as films and material on microform. In addition to in-person assistance, many college libraries offer online-guided tours that explain the library's resources and how to access them. Most libraries have email and real-time chat reference services.

Books Books remain a key source of information, even in today's online environment. Typically, they are credible information sources because they have gone through an intense editorial process, often including peer review. However, because of the time it takes to write and publish a book, the information may be somewhat dated. Books, therefore, are most useful for historical information or topics that are not especially time sensitive. For example, if you were developing a speech on trends in surfing culture, you might find valuable information and photographs in a book about the early days of surfing. But if you need information about the latest developments in surfing equipment and styles, you would be better off searching for information in periodicals such as magazines and trade journals.

For extremely current information, such as the most recent unemployment figures or college graduation rates, books are not the right choice. If you find a book that appears promising, however, always check its copyright page (usually following the page displaying its author, title, and publisher) to determine when it was published. Library catalog entries also note a book's year of publication if it's known, as do online booksellers.

Begin your search for books related to your topic by checking your campus library's online catalog. Unless you know the title of a book or author, use the keyword function to search for relevant books. When you identify a book you think will be useful, write down its **call number** so you can check it out from the library the next time you're on campus. Or, if it's an e-book, you can review it on screen.

A library's online catalog entry for a book often includes links to related topics. For example, a search for books about immigration in the United States produced nearly more than 5700 titles, including *Dreams and Nightmares: Immigration Policy, Youth, and Families* by Marjorie Sue Zatz and Nancy Rodriguez, published by the University of California Press in 2015. The subject list included links to related resources in four areas:

© David Schmitz Photography

Your campus library has many resources not available online.

- Immigrant youth United States Social conditions
- Unaccompanied immigrant children United States Social conditions
- Emigration and immigration law United States
- Immigrant families Law and legislation United States

call number
The number assigned to each book or bound publication in a library to identify that book in the library's classification system.

By clicking on the links to these areas, you could browse other library materials that might be useful for a speech on U.S. immigration.

Journals, Magazines, and Newspapers Published at regular intervals, or periods, periodicals include journals, magazines, and newspapers. Your library provides access to full-text databases of articles from periodicals. Follow the library's instructions for accessing those databases, such as:

- Academic Search Complete (scholarly journals across a range of disciplines in the humanities and arts, social sciences, sciences, engineering, business, and more),
- LexisNexis Academic (newspapers, magazines, trade publications, and company information),
- Newspaper Source (extensive collection of U.S. and international newspapers, including more than 300 regional U.S. newspapers), and
- ProQuest Newsstand (full text articles from worldwide news sources and news wires).

Newspapers often have the most current information about your topic. Although you could search the websites of individual newspapers, using a database such as ProQuest Newsstand allows you to search multiple news sources simultaneously. ProQuest Newsstand gives you many options for searching, such as selecting specific databases and limiting the date range. Another news database, Alt-PressWatch, allows you to search independent and alternative newspapers, magazines, and journals.

Government Publications Cybercrime, endangered species, housing, nursing, solar power, water—these are just a few of the topics addressed in U.S. government publications. The Catalog of United States Government Publications, available free online (catalog.gpo.gov), indexes documents from the three branches of the U.S. government dating back to July 1976. New publications are added every day. Reports, monographs, handbooks, pamphlets, and audio files are among the types of resources you'll find in government publications. If you were conducting research for a speech on solar power, for instance, a keyword search would yield NASA documents,

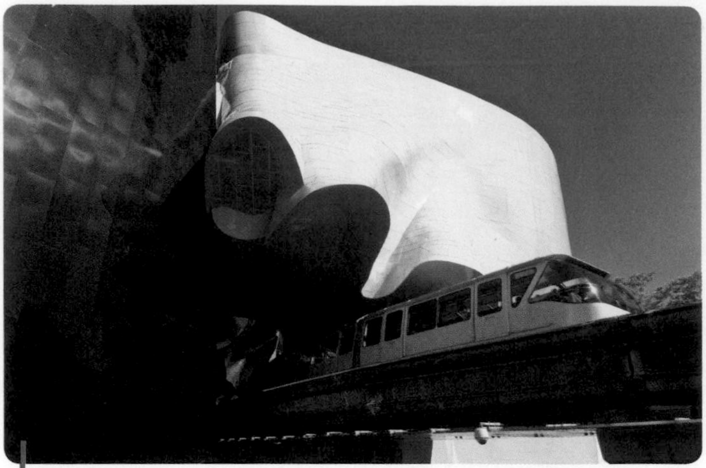

The Experience Music Project Museum in Seattle has sources such as audio files not available online.

consumer guides, Senate testimony, and reports from the National Renewable Energy Laboratory related to solar power and other forms of alternative energy.

Reference Works Use your library's online catalog to locate reference materials such as paper versions of maps, atlases, encyclopedias, dictionaries, and various print indexes. Although traditionally you had to go to the library to access reference materials, increasingly they are available online. For example, *The African-American Almanac* must be used in the library, but the African American Experience database includes similar full-text online articles about African American history and culture. The United States Geography database includes online maps and images that in the past only were available in paper at the library.

When it's helpful to define precisely the terms you use in your speeches, you can find dictionaries online, but some specialized dictionaries are found only in print or as e-books. The *Morris Dictionary of Word and Phrase Origins* traces the etymology of words as well as how their use developed over time. Such dictionaries not only provide definitions but also cover a wide range of topics from dance to women artists. *Dow's Dictionary of Railway Quotations*, for instance, includes excerpts from songs, films, novels, TV broadcasts, and other sources. Visual dictionaries can prove particularly helpful for informative speeches. They include photographs, drawings, diagrams, and illustrations that help readers understand the meanings of words. For example, the *Firefly Visual Dictionary with Definitions* contains more than 35,000 terms with detailed illustrations, many in color. *A Visual Dictionary of Chinese Architecture* includes detailed descriptions and line drawings.

Nonprint Resources If you've seen Martin Luther King, Jr.'s "I Have a Dream" speech on film, you understand the potential impact of visual or multimedia resources. Although the words alone move people, seeing and hearing Dr. King deliver this landmark speech influences the audience much more profoundly. His image—gesturing, nodding, scanning the crowd, the deep voice compelling listeners to fight for freedom—stays with you even if you forget his exact words.

Audio sources may also convey an image or set a tone that a simple verbal description cannot accomplish. For example, an exhibit at the Experience Music Project Museum in Seattle includes interviews with local hip-hop artists. Hearing their stories in their own voices generates an emotional force that visitors can't experience just by reading printed statements.

Your campus library includes many nonprint resources you can explore via electronic databases. *Oxford Art Online* includes more than 6000 searchable images ranging from a chart of the Arabic alphabet to a photograph of the Zigzag Bridge in the Jiangsu Province of China. *ARTstor* boasts more than a half million images associated with the arts, humanities, and social sciences that you can browse by topic, collection, geography, or classification. With *Naxos Music Library,* you can listen to streaming audio of classical, jazz, world, and other music genres and read artist biographies and opera synopses.

Table 6.6 summarizes examples of general and specialized library databases you'll find useful as you research topics for your speeches. Not all libraries will have all the databases listed. Your librarian will help you find the databases most relevant to your speech topics.

Table 6.6 Examples of General and Specialized Library Databases

Database	Description	Useful for Searching . . .	Search Hint
General			
Academic Search Complete	Full-text articles from more than 9000 publications in multiple disciplines dating back to 1887.	A wide variety of sources, including academic journals, newspapers, and magazines.	Search by document type, such as speech, short story, poem, book review, and case study.
Ingenta	Full-text of nearly 6 million articles in more than 13,000 publications.	Scholarly and academic journals in the humanities, sciences and social sciences, including chemistry, engineering, nursing, psychology, and philosophy.	Sign up for a free account to save searches and receive alerts when new material becomes available related to your searches.
JSTOR	Full-text archive of more than 1400 older issues of scholarly journals in the arts, sciences, humanities, and social sciences.	Historically important research and scholarly work.	Explore collections such as African Cultural Heritage Sites and Landscapes, and 19th-Century British Pamphlets.
LexisNexis Academic	Full-text articles and reviews as well as radio and TV transcripts from news, industry, medical, legal, and governmental sources.	Specific publication types, such as public records, reference materials, law directories, and government reports.	Conduct specialized searches for news, legal cases, company information, and people.
Oxford Reference	More than 2 million entries from the Oxford Quick Reference and Oxford Reference Library.	Multiple dictionary and reference publications simultaneously.	Search more than 250 historical timelines and more than 15,000 quotations.
Opposing Viewpoints in Context	Opinion pieces, pro–con essays, newspaper stories, and scholarly articles on current social issues.	A wide range of viewpoints on contested topics such as offshore drilling and online gambling.	Browse by general topic area, such as society and culture, energy and environmentalism, and business and economics.
Project MUSE	More than 700,000 full-text scholarly journal articles and chapters in many academic disciplines.	Peer-reviewed journal articles on the latest topics of interest in the arts, humanities, sciences, and social sciences.	Browse journals by disciplines, such as music, philosophy, and women's studies.
ProQuest Direct	Includes 32 databases on a wide range of topics.	Across multiple subject areas and multiple media in a single search.	Use the search forms in specific areas, such as the arts, business, history, and social sciences to customize your search.
Web of Knowledge	A compilation of databases such as Web of Science, Global Health, Biological Abstracts, and Index Chemicus.	Multiple databases simultaneously, with a special focus on the sciences.	Get citation alerts, save searches, and create a list of frequently read journals when you set up a free account.
WorldCat	A network of thousands of libraries that allows you to search for library content and services from around the world.	Research articles and digital content such as audiobooks and e-books.	Click on "Ask a Librarian" for help with your search.

(*Continued*)

Table 6.6 Continued

Database	Description	Useful for Searching . . .	Search Hint
Specialized			
Alt-Press Watch	More than 670,000 full-text articles from more than 260 independent and alternative presses.	Sources and perspectives not found in mainstream media outlets.	Locate biographical profiles of individuals active in social justice and free-press issues.
Black Thought and Culture	Essays, letters, song lyrics, interviews, and speeches by African Americans from the 17th century to the present.	Historical and current information on the African American experience in the United States.	Browse by authors, interview questions, sources, historical events, and personal events.
Communication & Mass Media Complete	Full-text articles from more than 650 scholarly journals in communication and media studies as well as more than 5500 author profiles.	Research related to all aspects of communication, including public speaking.	Choose visual search to map results by relevance, date, and category.
Gilded Age	Full-text documents, photos, songs, letters, cartoons, interviews about and from the Gilded Age in the United States (1865–1900).	Primary sources related to key topics of this era, such as race, woman suffrage, and immigration.	Review the critical documentary essays that focus on central issues of the time.
GreenFILE	Indexing, abstracts, and full-text articles for scholarly and general-interest publications related to the environment.	Topics associated with the environment, including global climate change, recycling, sustainable agriculture, and renewable energy.	Limit your search by document type, including bibliography, case study, or science experiment.
Latino American Experience	Full-text database that includes primary sources, images, and vetted websites.	Resources on the history and culture of Latinos and Latinas living in the United States.	Go The Idea Exchange for the advisory board's discussion of key Latino and Latina issues.
Music Online	Cross-searches all of your library's Alexander Street Press music databases.	All types of music in your library.	Categories such as Historical Events, Places, and Cultural Groups allow you to browse for music in novel ways.
North American Indian Thought and Culture	A collection of autobiographies, biographies, oral histories, photographs, audio files, and similar primary sources on North American indigenous people.	First-person accounts of life for Native Americans, Alaska Natives, and Canadian First Peoples.	Browse by topic areas such as individuals, peoples, places, and historical events.
Women and Social Movements in the United States (1600–2000)	Nearly 5000 documents, 1000 images, and 900 links to related websites.	Primary documents related to the U.S. women's movement, as well as newspaper articles, pamphlets, books, and images.	Search or browse document projects that group together documents related to a specific question, such as "How did women participate in the Underground Railroad?"

Maximizing Your Searches

In addition to using a variety of sources and search tools, the following search strategies will maximize your ability to get the most out of the wide array of sources found on the Internet and in your campus library in an efficient manner.

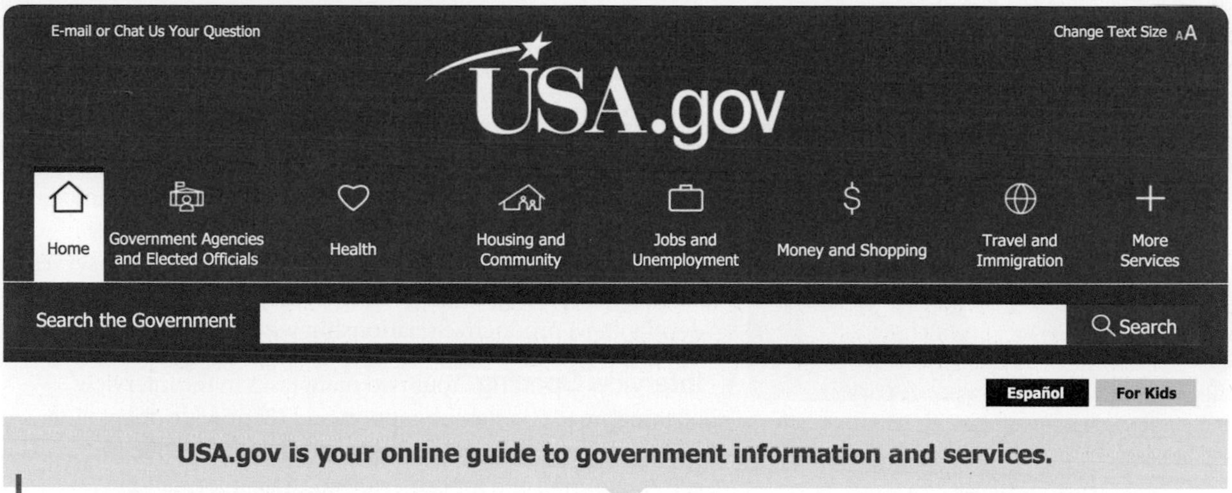

USA.gov

U.S. government sites offer many reliable sources you can access on the Internet. Browse and search these sites from USA.gov, the web portal for all U.S. government offices and departments.

Use a Variety of Keywords

Search tools produce results based on the keywords you enter. Different libraries, databases, search engines, and web directories use different indexing and keyword systems. Choose your keywords carefully and consider alternatives to your original choice. For example, for *free speech* also try *freedom of speech, first amendment, first amendment rights,* and *bill of rights.* Each set of keywords produces different results. Most search engines and databases will give you suggestions for additional search terms.

Use the Advanced Search Option

Many search tools offer an advanced or guided search option that allows you to refine your search by keyword, date, type of media, and other specific parameters. In addition, nearly all search tools include a section on "tips for searching" that explains the best strategies for using that particular search tool.

Search for More than Text

As you're searching for information, consider more than text. Nearly all metasearch engines and search engines allow you to search for image, video, and audio files. Read the **copyright information** carefully before using any files you download. Copyright information is a statement about the legal rights of others to use an original work. Use of website images and similar files in classroom speeches generally is allowed under fair use laws if you properly credit the author.

copyright information
A statement about the legal rights of others to use an original work, such as a song (lyrics and melody), story, poem, photograph, or image.

Conducting Research Interviews

Research interviews with experts on your topic can help you obtain valuable information. Particularly in classroom speeches—where much of your credibility derives from accurate information—interviews must be carefully planned and implemented. The research interview process consists of the steps described here.

Select Interviewee(s)

Select interviewees based on their expertise, availability, and willingness to answer your questions. If an interviewee views you as credible, you'll have a better chance of getting the information you want. To enhance your credibility, research the topic and the interviewee,

Jupiterimages/Comstock/Getty Images/Thinkstock

A warm and personable opening can put your interviewee at ease.

carefully prepare for the interview, use active listening skills, and demonstrate sensitivity to the interviewee's cultural background.

Develop Your Interview Guide

The questions you plan to ask form the basis of your **interview guide**, the list of all the main questions and possible follow-up questions you will ask in the interview, as well as how you'll begin and end the interview. The interview guide serves as a road map for gathering the information you seek and developing a productive relationship with your interviewee.

interview guide
A list of all the questions and possible probes an interviewer asks in an interview, as well as notes about how the interviewer will begin and end the interview.

Interview Opening Your two main tasks in the interview opening are to (1) establish rapport and (2) provide orientation. Accomplishing these early on provides a basis for effective communication and for gathering accurate information throughout the interview.[15] For instance, personable and friendly communication at the start will help you establish rapport with your interviewee. A clear orientation lets your interviewee know how you're going to proceed, such as stating the purpose of the interview, the topics you'll cover, the expected length of the interview, and how the information will be used.

Interview Body Your interview questions make up the body, or main portion, of the interview and should follow a logical sequence. Begin with general questions so you get a sense of the interviewee's breadth of knowledge; then ask more specific questions. Group questions by subtopic. Within each subtopic, ask general questions and then move to more specific ones.

A student who conducted an interview on public transportation organized questions into four groups:

1. How the interviewee got started working in public transportation
2. Promoting public transportation
3. Responding to critics of public transportation
4. The interviewee's predictions regarding future innovations in public transportation

This grouping follows a logical order: asking fairly easy questions about how the interviewee got involved in public transportation, then asking how the interviewee promotes public transportation and responds to critics, and finally inviting the interviewee to speculate about possible innovations in public transportation.

Interview Closing The closing of an interview should leave the interviewee feeling positive and satisfied with the exchange. Generally, the closing progresses through three stages:

1. The *conclusion preview* signals that the interview is drawing to a close, as with saying, "My final question is . . . " or "We have just a few minutes left. . . ."
2. In the *closure statement,* summarize the main points you gleaned from the interview and thank the interviewee for participating. Ask if you may contact the interviewee should you have any questions while preparing your speech.
3. Finally, *post-interview conversation* occurs after the formal interview and may include small talk or general discussion of the topic. The interviewee may relax and reveal important information related to your topic. During the post-interview discussion, you'll say your final goodbyes and once again express appreciation for the interviewee's cooperation.

In structuring your questions and determining the opening and closing, you'll complete your interview guide. Effective interviewers remain flexible, diverging from the interview guide if the interviewee provides useful, but unexpected, information. **Figure 6.1** presents a sample interview guide.

Figure 6.1 Sample Interview Guide

Interviewee: Lauria Quijas, founder and CEO

Organization: Internet Ideas

Purpose: To gain a better understanding of what is involved in founding a company

Opening: My name is Barrett Yip, and I am a student at City College taking a class in public speaking. Thank you for taking the time to meet with me. I've browsed through your company's website, and I'm so interested to learn more about it. As I mentioned in my email when we scheduled this interview, I'm researching a speech on the steps involved in starting your own company. This interview should take about 45 minutes. The questions I have cover four main topics: your motivations for starting Internet Ideas, its current status, your view of the company's future, and your advice for anyone wanting to start their own business. As we discussed previously, I will record the interview so I have an accurate record of what you said. What questions do you have before we get started?

1. First, I'd like to ask you about the origins of Internet Ideas. What motivated you to start this company?
- 1.1. Tell me more about your initial motivation.
- 1.2. What else prompted your decision?

2. How did others influence your decision to form Internet Ideas?
- 2.1. Please give me an example of what people said.
- 2.2. How did you respond?

3. How did you choose the name *Internet Ideas?*
- 3.1. What other names did you consider?
- 3.2. How difficult was it to make the final choice?

4. Let's talk about Internet Ideas as it is today. How do you describe your organization to someone who is entirely unfamiliar with it?
- 4.1. Why do you say that?
- 4.2. I understand.

5. On the Internet Ideas website, the mission statement emphasizes the "open exchange of ideas to revolutionize the internet." How do you go about achieving that mission?
- 5.1. How do you encourage employees to exchange ideas openly?
- 5.2. Is there anything that's kept you from achieving that goal?

6. A recent article in the local newspaper about Internet Ideas both praised and criticized you and the company. What was your response to the article?
- 6.1. How did employees respond?
- 6.2. What effect overall did the article have on the company?

7. Now, thinking about the future: In what ways do you think Internet Ideas will be different in five years?
- 7.1. What about in ten years?
- 7.2. What other changes do you foresee?

8. As you know, I'd like to start my own company someday. What are the positive aspects of starting your own company?
- 8.1. What other pluses have you experienced?
- 8.2. Does that apply to any new company?

9. What are the pitfalls in starting your own company?
- 9.1. Please give me an example.
- 9.2. How can founders avoid that pitfall?

10. What advice do you have for entrepreneurs interested in starting their own company?
- 10.1. What other suggestions do you have?
- 10.2. Any other bits of wisdom?

11. Is there additional information related to the topic I should be sure to include in my speech?
- 11.1. What else should I know that I haven't covered?

Closing:

Those are all the questions I have for you. Let me briefly summarize the main points you covered in your responses [*quickly review interviewee's responses here*]. If I need clarification on something we covered, may I email or phone you? You've given me a lot of firsthand information on starting a company that I'm sure my listeners will be eager to learn about. I know how busy you are, so I really appreciate your answering all my questions. Thank you again for your time.

Conduct the Interview

Following these strategies will help ensure a more productive interview.

- *Review your interview guide.* Being familiar with your interview guide allows you to use it the way you use note cards in your speeches—to trigger your memory.
- *Choose an appropriate setting.* Ideally, conduct the interview in a quiet, private place free from interruptions, for in-person interviews. For other real-time interviews, such as online or telephone interviews, minimize distractions at your location and ask the interviewee to do the same.
- *Record the interview.* With the interviewee's permission, record the interview electronically for later review. Also take notes, writing down main points and key ideas that will help you recall what the person said. In addition, record important nonverbal cues, your general impressions, and ideas that occur to you during the interview.
- *Ask one question at a time.* If you ask multiple questions, the interviewee will become confused and likely only answer one part of the question asked.[16] For example, instead of asking, "How and why did you begin your own business?" phrase the question as two separate ones. First ask, "What led you to start your own business?" and then, after the interviewee has responded, ask, "How did you go about opening your business?"
- *Monitor your verbal and nonverbal cues.* This strategy helps avoid unintentionally biasing the interviewee's responses. To indicate that you're listening, say "I understand" or "I see." The interviewee should be doing most of the talking, not you. Put all your active listening skills to work. Use eye contact and other nonverbal cues to let the interviewee know you are paying attention.[17]

Integrate the Information

Information from experts on your topic can personalize, enliven, and add credibility to each section of your speech.

In the Introduction A catchy quote in the introduction can grab your audience's attention, as well as establish your credibility. Here's an example:

> Ever think about the information websites gather when you're online? Jamie Anderson, professor of information science here at Southern University for 10 years, has. Dr. Anderson told me in a recent interview, "If people knew how much information corporations gathered on each visitor to their websites, they would be shocked—even embarrassed—and much more careful about their Internet use."

The speaker underscores the importance of the topic, making it relevant to her audience by identifying the interviewee as a "professor of information science here at Southern University." To enhance her credibility she points out the interviewee's own credibility when she mentions "for 10 years."

In the Body Information from an interview can also be a source of personal, recent evidence in the body of your speech. When including quotes or summarized information from research interviews, clearly state your interviewee's full name and title and explain what makes that person an expert on the topic, as the speaker does in the following example:

> Mae Hawthorne, a local organic farmer for more than 15 years, predicts three trends in organic farming innovations: incorporating effective farming methods from

thousands of years ago, using social media to link together farmers from around the world, and community-supported agriculture. Recent research suggests similar trends. For example . . .

Here, the speaker first presented a summary of the interviewee's predictions and then included supporting information from other sources.

In the Conclusion Speakers use interview information in the conclusion of a speech in two ways: (1) to provide a sense of closure and (2) to leave listeners in an appropriate state of mind. For example, if you quote an interviewee in your introduction, you could quote the same person in your conclusion, as in the following example:

> When you go online, you focus on the information you *get*. But information scientists recognize the dangers in the information you *give* others in your Internet travels. Professor Jamie Anderson believes, "The hallmark of the Internet is the free exchange of information. However, individuals must know what information they're revealing when they visit websites, and corporations must restrict and safeguard the personal information they gather."

This quote ties in neatly with the one the speaker used in the introduction, reminding the audience of information presented early in the speech. In addition, a good quote in the conclusion can leave audience members with a lasting, personalized impression of the topic.

Evaluating Your Research Materials

As you locate information for your speech, apply three primary evaluation criteria: relevance, purpose, and validity.[18]

MindTap®

Learn more about evaluating your research materials.

Relevance

Relevance is the least complicated of the evaluation criteria to apply. You examine the source to determine how closely it matches the topic you are researching. For instance, if you're researching a speech on blood diamonds, which are mined to finance an insurgency or war, you could search the library database Academic Search Complete using the keywords *blood diamonds*. A recent search produced these sources:

- Baker, A., Kabanda, C., & Kalombo, F. (2015). Dirty diamonds. *Time, 186*(9/10), 62–69.
- Patrick, R., @PatRyanWrites, & USA, T. (n.d.). Surprise! Madonna releases six songs. *USA Today*.
- Penn, A. (2014). Eclectic youth. *Artforum International, 53*(3), 175.
- Saunders, R. (2014). Geologies of power: Blood diamonds, security politics and Zimbabwe's troubled transition. *Journal of Contemporary African Studies, 32*(3), 378–394.

Which of those sources seem the most relevant to you? "Surprise! Madonna Releases Six Songs" and "Eclectic Youth" likely aren't relevant—when you review the article summaries you know they're about a band, Blood Diamonds. The other two seem promising and when you check the full text, you note that they're directly concerned with your topic.

Purpose

In examining the purpose of the information, you want to identify why it was created. Just like the purpose of speech, determine if the source's purpose is to inform, persuade, or entertain. Editorials and opinion pieces, for instance, are designed to persuade audiences. Scholarly research articles are written to inform others about important research findings. Satires and comedy skits are meant to entertain.

Determining a source's purpose also involves identifying its scope and depth. *Scope* refers to what information is included and what is left out. In a report on climate change, for instance, is the focus on a specific geographic area or on worldwide conditions? *Depth* involves the extent to which the topic is covered. Does the author provide detailed and expansive coverage of the topic? Or is the coverage fairly general?

The usefulness of a source's scope and depth depends on your research needs. If you want a basic overview of a topic, then a broad scope with little depth is sufficient. If you're interested in how a topic affects a specific population, group, or locale, then you'll want information that's narrow in scope and provides much depth. In all cases, use what you already know about the topic to consider what information might be left out.

The language or *style* an author uses provides additional insight into the purpose. Review the words the author chooses to discuss the topic. For example, in discussing voting laws, does the author use *voter fraud, voting rights, voter ID laws, voting restrictions,* or *voter suppression*? Authors' specific language choices can reveal the response they seek from the audience.

Validity

The soundness of the logic underlying the information is called *validity.* Validity has three components: currency, accuracy, and authority. The recency of the information is its *currency*. You want information that is as up to date as possible. Even when researching a topic considered ancient history, such as dinosaurs, what is known about the topic changes over time. For example, although the most popular explanation for why dinosaurs became extinct centers on the theory that an asteroid hit Earth at about that time, more recent explanations posit an exploding star or volcanic eruptions as the cause. Checking the date when printed material was published, a television or radio show was broadcast, or a webpage was revised reveals the currency of your information.

Accuracy refers to the consistency and reliability of the information. Information is accurate when it fits with what other experts have concluded. An article in *Science* on how carbon monoxide contributes to global climate change, for instance, would be reliable because the findings are consistent with those of other researchers and the magazine is well respected in the scientific community.

To test the accuracy of your information, examine the author's logic, evidence, and conclusions. For example, when researching a speech about people's shopping preferences, suppose you interview the president of the local chamber of commerce. Your interviewee claims that all downtown parking should be free because having to pay for parking drives away shoppers. However, the only evidence provided to support this assertion is the interviewee's own experience that parking downtown can be expensive, whereas parking at a suburban mall is free. There are at least two reasons not to trust this evidence. First, you don't know that people are avoiding downtown shopping. Second, even if they are, they could be doing so for other reasons, such as the types of stores available and the distance from their homes. In this case, the interviewee's conclusion *might* make sense, but there's no evidence to back it up.

Authority refers to who produced the information—both the person who created it and the platform for presenting it. Review the author's credentials to determine if she or he is an expert on the topic. If the author's credentials aren't readily apparent, a quick

Universal UClick

Internet search with the person's name likely will reveal her or his level of expertise. Any source the author cites also provides insight into expertise. Just as you research your speech topics to become an expert on them, you want to be sure your information sources have done the same.

Where the information is published or presented also contributes to a source's validity. A peer-reviewed scholarly journal is considered a highly respected information source because articles have undergone a rigorous review process before publication. In contrast, a weekly community newspaper has less credibility because the review process is less rigorous. As another example, a research university's YouTube channel, such as Arizona State University's compilation of speeches, lectures, and tutorials, is considered a credible source due to its reputation as a world-class university. At the other end of the spectrum, a company's marketing videos posted on YouTube are less credible because the organization is naturally biased in favor of its products or services.

Regardless of its source, critically examine the information you gather. Asking the questions summarized in **Table 6.7** will help you determine the relevance, purpose, and validity of information.

Table 6.7 **Critical Questions for Evaluating Information**

Critical Question	Goal
How relevant is the source?	Determine if the information fits with your topic and purpose.
What are the author's purposes?	Determine the author's reasons for presenting the information, revealed in scope, depth, and style.
How current is the information?	Determine if the author's information is as up to date as possible.
Who is the author?	Determine who produced the information and if the author is an expert on the topic.
Who is the publisher?	Determine the organization that published the information and if the source is unbiased.
What evidence has the author provided?	Determine if the author has used a variety of types of information from knowledgeable sources.
Has any information been omitted?	Determine if the author has left out any information that might lead to alternate conclusions.
What are the author's underlying assumptions?	Determine the assumptions the author is making and if different assumptions might produce different conclusions.
What inferences or conclusions has the author drawn?	Determine if the author's conclusions are valid and if other conclusions could be drawn from the same information.

Recognizing and Avoiding Plagiarism

MindTap®

Watch It: View a video on how to avoid plagiarism.

plagiarism
Presenting someone else's ideas and work, such as speeches, papers, and images, as your own.

copyright
A type of intellectual property law that protects an author's original work (such as a play, book, song, or movie) from being used by others.

fair use
Using someone else's original work in a way that does not infringe on the owner's rights, generally for educational purposes, literary criticism, and news reporting.

Plagiarism refers to taking someone else's ideas and work, including speeches, papers, and images, and presenting them as your own, whether intentionally or unintentionally. However, plagiarism is not a universal concept. In Aristotle's time, because ideas were considered public property, speakers freely quoted others' work without attribution. The same is true for many cultures today, especially those with a strong oral tradition. Cultures with a print tradition, such as the United States and most of Europe, view ideas and words as commodities owned by individuals or organizations.[19] Therefore, you must credit the authors of materials you use in your speeches.

In the United States and many other countries, presenting others' work as your own not only violates basic ethical principles but also is illegal. Article I, Section 8, of the U.S. Constitution provides the basis for **copyright** or intellectual property laws:

> The Congress shall have power . . . to promote the progress of science and useful arts, by securing for limited times to authors and inventors the exclusive right to their respective writings and discoveries.

Copyright laws, including the Digital Millennium Copyright Act of 1998, require you to get permission from authors if you want to use their original published and unpublished works. **Fair use**, however, allows you to use *limited* portions of an author's work *if* you credit the source of the information.

Universal Press Syndicate

Research shows that about 50 percent of U.S. college students admit they've plagiarized, and more than a third report copying information directly from an Internet source without providing a reference. Colleges and universities are well aware of plagiarism on their campuses, with 55 percent of college presidents reporting that the problem has increased over the past 10 years.[20] Learning about plagiarism will help you understand and avoid it. Also, research shows that students who participate in training on academic integrity are much less likely to plagiarize than those who do not.[21]

In a survey of nearly 900 college and high school instructors, antiplagiarism software company Turnitin found that student plagiarism falls into 10 general categories, ranging from completely copying someone else's work to poor paraphrasing.[22] **Figure 6.2** lists and defines these common types of plagiarism.

In his book *Doing Honest Work in College: How to Prepare Citations, Avoid Plagiarism, and Achieve Real Academic Success,* University of Chicago professor Charles Lipson identifies three essential principles for academic integrity:

1. When you say you did the work yourself, you actually did it.
2. When you rely on someone else's work, you cite it. When you use their words, you quote them openly and accurately, and you cite them, too.

3. When you present research materials, you present them fairly and truthfully. That's true whether the research involves data, documents, or the writings of other scholars.[23]

Accurate note-taking, paraphrasing, and orally citing sources will help you achieve academic integrity in your speeches.

Figure 6.2 Common Forms of Plagiarism from Most to Least Severe

1. CLONE:
An act of submitting another's work, word-for-word, as one's own.

2. CTRL-C:
A written piece that contains significant portions of text from a single source without alterations.

3. FIND–REPLACE:
The act of changing key words and phrases but retaining the essential content of the source in a paper.

4. REMIX:
An act of paraphrasing from other sources and making the content fit together seamlessly.

5. RECYCLE:
The act of borrowing generously from one's own previous work without citation; To self plagiarize.

6. HYBRID:
The act of combining perfectly cited sources with copied passages–without citation–in one paper.

7. MASHUP:
A paper that represents a mix of copied material from several different sources without proper citation.

8. 404 ERROR:
A written piece that includes citations to non-existent or inaccurate information about sources.

9. AGGREGATOR:
The "Aggregator" includes proper citation, but the paper contains almost no original work.

10. RE-TWEET:
This paper includes proper citation, but relies too closely on the text's original wording and/or structure.

Source: From Turnitin. (2015). *White paper: The plagiarism spectrum: Instructor insights into the 10 types of plagiarism*. Retrieved from turnitin.com

Taking Accurate Notes

Sometimes plagiarism results from poor note-taking. For example, an early version of the honor code at the University of Texas at San Antonio contained sections identical to the honor code at Brigham Young University. The plagiarized passages were traced to materials from a conference on academic integrity. As it turned out, the students who attended the conference failed to take accurate notes on the sources for sample honor codes.[24]

As you research your speech, you may jot down notes from various sources without fully recording quotes and citations. But clearly identifying quoted passages and writing out the complete citation will help you give credit where it's due, as shown in the following examples.[25]

- *Use **boldface** to mark quotations.*

  Article on international students' views of plagiarism: **Generally, our group of international students has a point of view on intellectual property and copyright that is similar to the Western definitions.** (p. 826) *Source:* Datig, I., & Russell, B. (2015). "The fruits of intellectual labor": International student views of intellectual property. *College & Research Libraries, 76*(6), 811–830.

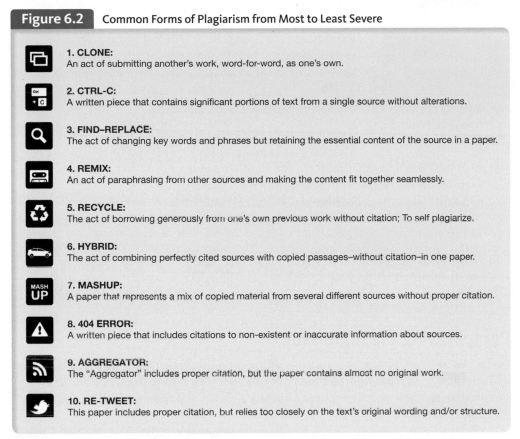

Hero Images/Getty Images

You can avoid plagiarism by taking careful notes that clearly identify quotes and their sources as you research your topic.

- *Use a different font color to mark quotations.*

Article on digital plagiarism and achievement goals: Rather than simply being driven by a fundamental drive to cheat, the results of this study suggest that individuals perceive and act on the affordances made available by the online learning environment in context and not solely based on their pre-existing goal structures or personal beliefs. (p. 54). *Source:* Kauffman, Y., & Young, M. F. (2015). Digital plagiarism: An experimental study of the effect of instructional goals and copy-and-paste affordance. *Computers & Education, 83,* 44–56.

- *Use highlighting to mark quotations.*

Article on how students perceive self-plagiarism: Many students perceive they own their own previously unpublished works, and feel they should be able to use their previous thoughts and ideas in new assignments. (p. 102)
Source: Halupa, C., & Bolliger, D. (2015). Student perceptions of self-plagiarism: A multi-university exploratory study. *Journal of Academic Ethics, 13*(1), 91–105.

Following a clear and consistent system to identify quotes and their sources as you gather information on your speech topics will help you avoid unintentional plagiarism.

Paraphrasing the Right Way

Paraphrasing involves putting a source's information into your own words. You consider what the author said or wrote and then provide your own interpretation rather than simply altering a few words or phrases. **Table 6.8** shows you right and wrong ways to paraphrase.

Your goal when paraphrasing is to capture the essence of what the author said, using language that fits with your way of speaking.[26] If that doesn't work and you find yourself relying on the original quotation too much, then consider using the quote in your speech. Whether paraphrasing or quoting from a source, provide an oral citation in your speech to avoid plagiarism.

Acknowledging Your Sources

Public speakers acknowledge their sources in two ways: orally in the speech and in written form in the bibliography.

oral citation
A source of information that a speaker mentions, or cites, during a speech.

With **oral citations**, speakers mention, or *cite,* the sources of their information during the speech. Here are some examples that demonstrate both how to set up an oral citation and how to punctuate it:

- In an August 2015 TED Fellow Retreat talk, artist Christine Sun Kim, who born deaf, said this about American Sign Language (ASL): "We live in a very audio-centric world. And just because ASL has no sound to it, it automatically holds no social currency. We need to start thinking harder about what defines social currency and allow ASL to develop its own form of currency—without sound. And this could possibly be a step to lead to a more inclusive society."
- Life on Mars is no longer just for science fiction. NASA scientists announced in a September 2015 press release on the agency's website that evidence of hydrated salts indicates there is water on Mars—and where there's water there's life.

Table 6.8 Right and Wrong Ways to Paraphrase

Source	Quote	Wrong Paraphrase	Right Paraphrase
Jacobs, S. P. (2015, November 5). Slacking off. *TIME, 186*(19), 44–47. *(quote on p. 44)*	If you've used Facebook or Twitter, you'll understand why Slack is hot. The program—it's not that different from the instant messengers that were popular on the early Internet—helps different parts of a company communicate in real time. Slack preserves every comment in one easily searchable archive, and all those messages now skip your dreaded inbox.	Facebook or Twitter users will understand why Slack is popular. It's like instant messaging that was used in the early days of the Internet. Slack helps the various units in a company communicate in real time. The program keeps every message in an archive you can search, and the messages don't go to your inbox.	Slack is like social media for the workplace in that you don't have to worry about messages piling up in your inbox. Instead, the program lets you communicate with coworkers in real time and saves the messages so you can search them later.
Sandberg, S. (2013). *Lean in: Women, work, and the will to lead.* New York: Alfred A. Knopf. *(quote on p. 78)*	Communication works best when we combine appropriateness with authenticity, finding that sweet spot where opinions are not brutally honest but delicately honest. Speaking truthfully without hurting feelings come naturally to some and is an acquired skill for others.	If you combine appropriateness with authenticity, that's when there's the best communication. You find the optimal spot between callous honesty and thoughtful honesty. Some people naturally are good at speaking the truth without hurting others, but other people have to develop that skill.	Communicating truthfully means that you are honest while still taking into account the other person's feelings. It's a skill that you may already have or one that you need to learn.
Zhang, S. (2015, Nov 2). Helping refugees isn't just about designing better shelters. *Wired.* Retrieved from http://www.wired.com/2015/11/helping-refugees-is-not-about-designing-better-shelters /*(quote from paragraph 8)*	For new tech to help, it has to help bridge the transition from temporary to permanent shelter. And nothing has done that better than plastic tarpaulin. Yes: basically the stuff that blue IKEA bags are made of. The tarp can become roofing or walls. But it can also be incorporated as a waterproofing layer in more permanent mud huts. And more—much more.	New technology must bridge the transition from temporary to permanent shelter to be helpful. The plastic tarpaulin, like what blue IKEA bags are made of, can be used for a roof or walls. Tarps also can be used for waterproofing mud huts, which are more permanent, and much, much more.	The basic plastic tarp is the versatile new technology that can help refugees build permanent shelters. For instance, tarps can make a mud hut waterproof.

The scientists say the water is actually liquid brine that flows when the weather is warm and freezes during colder times on the planet. So there may not be little green people on Mars, but there may be little organisms living in the liquid brine.

- University of Kentucky communication professor Jessalyn Vallade and her colleagues found in their research that instructor misbehaviors, such as verbal abuse and apathy toward students, negatively affected student learning. However, student forgiveness of instructor behavior lessened the impact. The authors conclude in their 2015 *Western Journal of Communication* article that instructors must be more aware of misbehaviors and develop strategies to repair their relationships with students when misbehaviors occur.

In these examples, the speaker tells the audience who authored or published a particular piece of information.

If a speaker must also provide a written reference list, these sources would be cited like this:

Kim, C. S. (2015, August). The enchanting music of sign language. Presented at TED Fellow Retreat. Retrieved from http://www.ted.com/talks/christine_sun_kim_the_enchanting_music_of_sign_language

National Aeronautics and Space Agency. (2015, September 28). NASA confirms evidence that liquid water flows on today's Mars. Retrieved from https://www.nasa.gov/press-release/nasa-confirms-evidence-that-liquid-water-flows-on-today-s-mars

Vallade, J. I., Martin, M. M., & Vela, L. E. (2015). An investigation of students' forgiveness, instructional dissent, and learning in the college classroom. *Western Journal of Communication*, *79*(4), 389–412.

bibliographic information A source's complete citation, including author, date of publication, title, place of publication, and publisher.

Table 6.9 shows how to format written citations, or **bibliographic information**, for a variety of types of information sources. The bibliographic information is a source's complete citation, including author, date of publication, title, place of publication, and publisher. You'll need this information to attribute your sources correctly in your speech and reference list. Most communication researchers use either Modern Language Association (MLA) or American Psychological Association (APA) style to record citations.[27] Ask your instructor which style you should use.

Table 6.9 Documenting Source Information

APA Style	
Book	Dickerman, L., & Smithgall, E. (2015). *Jacob Lawrence: The migration series.* Boston: The Museum of Modern Art and the Phillips Collection.
Essay in book	Kühne, O., & Antrop, M. (2015). Concepts of landscape. In D. Bruns, O. Kühne, A. Schönwald, & S. Theile (Eds.), *Landscape culture—culturing landscapes: The differentiated construction of landscapes* (pp. 41–66). Berlin: Springer VS.
Journal article	Maurantonio, N. (2015). Material rhetoric, public memory, and the post-it note. *Southern Communication Journal, 80,* 83–101.
Newspaper article	Arum, M. (2015, November 2). Driverless cars' fatal flaw may result in an ethical dilemma. *The Atlanta Journal - Constitution,* p. B3.
Blog	Hinduja, S. (2015, October 9). How empathy, kindness and compassion can build belongingness and reduce bullying [Web log comment]. Retrieved from http://cyberbullying.org/blog
Webpage	National Centers for Environmental Information: National Oceanic and Atmospheric Administration. (2015). *State of the climate: Global analysis September 2015.* Retrieved from http://www.ncdc.noaa.gov/sotc/global/201509
MLA Style	
Book	McGonigal, Jane. *SuperBetter: A Revolutionary Approach to Getting Stronger, Happier, Braver and More Resilient—Powered by the Science of Games.* New York: Penguin, 2015. Print.
Essay in book	Dunwoody, Sharon. "Environment Scientists and Public Communication." *The Routledge Handbook of Environment and Communication.* Eds. Anders Hansen and Robert Cox. New York: Routledge, 2015, 63–72. Print.
Journal article	Buckner, Marjorie M., and Brandi N. Frisby. "Feeling Valued Matters: An Examination of Instructor Confirmation and Instructional Dissent." *Communication Studies* 66.3 (2015): 398–413. Print.
Newspaper article	Moore, Daniel. "Duty Calls: Mobile Work Policies Left Up in the Air for Employees." *San Jose Mercury News* 01 November 2015: E1, E5. Print.
Blog	Nakhimovsky, Sharon. "Taxing Unhealthy Foods and Beverages: A Burden or Blessing for the Poor?" *The Collective Voice.* Global Health Council. 02 Nov. 2015. Web. 04 Nov. 2015.
Webpage	"What's in your Job Search Toolkit?" *Career Center.* San José State University, 13 July 2015. Web. 04 Nov. 2015.

Research Guidelines

The guidelines summarized here will make researching your topic a more positive and productive experience.

- *Start early.* How early to start developing your speech depends on the length of your class (semester, quarter, or condensed session), access to the resources you need, and your own approach to research. So get out the calendar, note when your speaking materials and speech are due, and work backward from there. Build in enough time to identify your supporting materials (Chapter 7), organize and outline your ideas (Chapter 8), integrate effective language (Chapter 10), develop relevant presentation materials (Chapter 11), and practice (Chapter 12).
- *Schedule research time.* Block out research time in your daily planner. Think of that time as an appointment and make a commitment to keep to it.
- *Ask questions.* Campus librarians and your instructor are key resources in your search for information that meets the criteria for reliability, purpose, currency, accuracy, and authority. When you encounter a sticking point in researching your topic, ask for help. If you wait until speech day, it will be too late.
- *Keep accurate records.* Carefully record the publication information for each source you find.
- *Take notes on each source.* When you record a source's bibliographic information, also write down the ideas that seem most relevant to your topic.
- *Revise as needed.* As you do your research, you may find yourself going off in a direction you hadn't planned on. Review your specific purpose and thesis. Decide whether you need to revise them or refocus your research.
- *Know when to move on.* You have a set amount of time to prepare your speech. If you spend too little time on research, your speech will lack substance; if you spend too much time, you'll neglect the other steps in the speechmaking process. When you feel comfortable talking about your topic with others and think you can answer your audience's questions, it's time to move on.
- *Know when to go back.* Later in the process of developing your speech, you may find gaps in your research or a question you want to answer. Do the additional research necessary to close those gaps and answer that question. Your audience and your confidence depend on your expertise.

MindTap®

Use MindTap to help you collect your research and cite your sources.

Summary

Researching your speech topic requires three activities: preparing to do your research, gathering information, and evaluating what you've found. Preparation begins with determining what you know and don't know about your topic. Use your own experiences as the basis for developing your research strategy. Preparation also requires identifying multiple perspectives and sources, particularly those that challenge your assumptions.

Metasearch engines, search engines, web directories, and specialized search engines assist you in your quest for information available on the Internet. Your campus library is a key information source for your speech topics. Library databases often contain hundreds of full-text articles that you can read online or download.

Interviews with experts can yield personal and current information about your topic. Planning and preparation form the basis of a successful interview. Developing a solid interview guide with thoughtfully phrased questions that are logically organized facilitates productive interaction during the interview. Flexibility and a genuine interest in knowing more about your topic will aid to conduct a successful interview.

As you gather information, evaluate it for relevance, purpose, and validity. In evaluating information, ask critical questions such as "What are the author's assumptions?" and "What evidence is presented to support the conclusions drawn?"

Avoiding plagiarism is an essential part of the research process. Taking accurate notes, effectively paraphrasing source material, and acknowledging your sources will help you avoid plagiarizing others' works and ideas.

Doing sound research means starting early, setting aside specific time to research your topic, asking questions when you run into problems, keeping accurate records, taking accurate notes on each source, revising and refocusing when necessary, knowing when you have enough information, and knowing when to continue your research.

> ANALYZE IT

Emily, About ALS

Emily gave this informative speech on amyotrophic lateral sclerosis (ALS), also known as Lou Gehrig's disease, in her public speaking class. Observe how she integrates the research she did on the topic into her speech.

Whenever I woke up crying in the middle of the night when I was a baby, my mom would always have my dad go and get me out of my crib and bring me back into their room. He would place me on her chest. She couldn't move her arms, but this was the way that she was able to comfort me. My mom had ALS. She died when I was three years old.

Most people that I talk to have no idea what ALS is. They've never heard of it before. ALS is a horrible disease that can affect anyone. People need to understand what it is, how it's diagnosed, what treatments are available, and what research is being done to try and find a cure.

MindTap®
Watch and analyze this speech on MindTap.

ALS stands for amyotrophic lateral sclerosis. And according to ALSA.org, it is a progressive neurodegenerative disease that affects nerve cells in the brain and in the spinal cord. In a way it's similar to Parkinson's or multiple sclerosis in the fact that it affects a patient's motor functions in their body. Writer Dudley Clendinon, who was diagnosed with ALS, described the disease in an article he did for the *New York Times*. He said, "The nerves and muscles pulse and twitch, and progressively they die. From the outside it looks like a ripple of piano keys in the muscles under my skin. From the inside it feels like anxious butterflies."

The disease affects each patient differently, but in a typical case of ALS the disease starts in a patient's hands and in their feet. Every day activities like walking, like holding a pen, those things will be difficult for people with ALS. As the disease progresses, it moves up a patient's arms and legs, and it causes them to become paralyzed. Then, once the disease is in the final stages, it moves into a patient's torso, and that's when it affects their ability to eat, to speak, and to breathe on their own. Throughout all of this, the disease does not affect a patient's mind, so they have a complete understanding of what is happening to them. Arleen M. Kaptur said in *Today's Caregiver* that 50 percent of patients die within 18 months of being diagnosed.

There is no cure for ALS. The symptoms of ALS will become obvious over time, but it's a difficult disease to diagnose. There's no test for ALS, and it shows up differently in each patient. So, doctors essentially have to work backwards. They have to rule out everything else before they can make that eventual diagnosis of ALS. Arleen M. Kaptur said in her article that there are certain tests that can be done, blood tests, biopsies, MRIs—those are the type of tests that are done to rule out everything else before they make that final diagnosis.

Once the disease is diagnosed, there are certain treatments that patients can use. In her article, Arleen M. Kaptur said that there is one drug that is available, which is called Rilutek. And what Rilutek does is it slows down the symptoms of the disease. So, patients are, they can live a little bit longer, but it is not a cure for the disease. Patients can treat specific symptoms. So, they can work with a physical therapist to help them with their movements, and they can also work with a nutritionist because patients will typically lose a lot of weight when they have the disease. And then at the very end they can use a feeding tube or ventilation when they can no longer eat and breathe on their own.

There are only a few treatments available for ALS, but research is being done to try and find a cure. Research has to be done in a lot of different areas because so little is still known about the disease. ALSA.org says that research is being done into the causes of the disease, so they're looking at different environmental factors that may cause it. They are also looking at different gene mutations that may cause the disease. They also have to research how the disease progresses because it does show up differently in each patient. And then, of course, they're looking at different treatments for the disease. So, they are experimenting with clinical trials and different drugs. And they're also looking into stem cell research.

But there is no cure yet for the disease. ALS is a disease with no cure, and people need to understand what it is, how it's diagnosed, what treatments are available, and what research is being done to try and find a cure. People diagnosed with ALS face death in their near future, but scientists are researching the disease and every day we get closer to finding a cure.

Questions for Discussion

1. How does Emily's speech reflect multiple perspectives and sources?
2. What experts does Emily rely on in her speech? How effective are her choices?
3. What sources does she use to support her ideas? How appropriate are these sources for the topic of her speech?
4. How does Emily orally cite her sources?
5. How would you evaluate her research materials? Are they relevant, purposeful, and valid?
6. What have you learned from analyzing this speech about researching a speech topic?
7. If you were a speech consultant for Emily, what advice would you give her about researching a speech topic based on your analysis of her speech?

APPLY IT . . .

IN THE WORKPLACE

Researching Organizations

Organizations often want to know about other organizations, whether it's to explore a partnership or assess the competition. You might be asked to research specific organizations or industries as part of your job. In addition, a key aspect of any job search is finding out about companies and professions in which you're interested. Several library databases can help you with your search.

- ABI/INFORM Complete searches a broad range of business-related sources including journals, blogs, working papers, podcasts, white papers, magazines, and reports.
- American City Business Journals compiles local business news from major U.S. metropolitan cities.
- Business Insights: Essentials provides data about U.S. and international organizations, industry information, and financial data.
- Business & Industry scours more than 1000 publications for facts and information about markets and industries.
- Business & Management Practices covers business-related topics, such as management, finance, human resources, and technology with a special focus on case studies, practical guidelines, and organizational applications.
- Factiva compiles information about companies from national and international news sources and trade journals.
- PASSPORT–GMID (Global Market Information Database) contains historical data and forecasts for economic and marketing topics in more than 200 countries.
- ProQuest Business searches five business-related databases.
- Regional Business News covers both metropolitan and rural areas in the United States.

These databases and similar ones can help you become an expert on a wide range of industries, businesses, and market trends close to home and abroad.

IN YOUR COMMUNITY

Interviewing in Your Community

For thousands of years, humans relied on the spoken word to pass along stories, values, and beliefs from one generation to the next. Although most cultures now rely primarily on the written word for such information exchange, the oral tradition retains a key place in transmitting community knowledge. Practice your interviewing skills by identifying a member of your community—at school, at work, or at home—who can provide insight into the community's history. Arrange the interview, develop your interview guide, and conduct the interview. Reflect on what you learned about your community, your role in that community, and the interview process. How might you use the information you gathered in the interview to promote positive change in your community? How might you share the information with others?

REVIEW IT

MindTap®

Use flashcards to learn key terms and take a quiz to test your knowledge.

Key Terms

bibliographic information 124
call number 109
copyright 120
copyright information 113
fair use 120
interview guide 114
keywords 104
metasearch engine 104
oral citation 122
plagiarism 120
primary source 104
relevance 104
search engine 105
secondary source 104
web directory 106

Reflecting on Researching Your Topic

1. The first step in researching your topic is to determine what you already know. How might what you know get in the way of doing good research? How might you check the reliability, currency, and validity of what you already know about a topic? Blogs are criticized for their lack of gatekeepers such as editors and publishers. But *who* is blogging may be just as important. When searching blogs for information about your topic, consider the authors. Are you finding a diversity of perspectives? How might you find a variety of blogs that represent multiple points of view?
2. In using information gathered from interviews, you need to consider what information to include in your speech and what to leave out. For example, how you frame an interviewee's remarks or how you place a quote in your speech can greatly influence how others interpret that information and how they perceive the interviewee. As an ethical speaker, what steps should you take to ensure that you accurately represent what the interviewee said?
3. If something is in a book, journal article, magazine, newspaper, or other printed source, is it necessarily accurate? Gatekeepers such as editors can miss both intentional and unintentional errors, as *The New York Times* did in the case of journalist Jayson Blair, who fabricated or plagiarized hundreds of stories. Moreover, desktop publishing allows authors to bypass traditional gatekeepers. How can you apply your critical thinking skills to evaluate the accuracy of printed materials?
4. One way to avoid plagiarism is to take accurate notes. If you already have a note-taking system, describe what you do and how it helps you avoid plagiarism. If you don't have one, identify a system that will work for you. How will your new note-taking system help you avoid plagiarism?
5. Review the research guidelines section. Which one is the most helpful to you? How do you think it will improve your research skills?

7 Supporting Your Ideas

READ IT

After successfully completing this chapter, you will be able to:

- Identify the various types of supporting material used in a speech.
- Critique narratives for how they maintain structure, engage the audience, and create a sense of drama.
- Evaluate speakers' examples for concreteness and generalizability.
- Evaluate definitions used in a speech for how well they clarify the topic and the speaker's position on the topic.
- Evaluate testimony for bias, credibility, and expertise.
- Evaluate facts for bias and recency.
- Evaluate statistics for comprehension currency.

MindTap®

Start with a quick warm-up activity and review the chapter's learning outcomes.

Although Aristotle's work has stood the test of time, more recent scholars observe that in addition to ethos, pathos, and logos, speakers rely on mythos, or appeals to cultural values and beliefs.

Pictorial Press Ltd/Alamy Stock Photo

The Greek philosopher Aristotle argued that when speakers present their ideas, they rely on three types of appeals: ethos, or appeals to the speaker's credibility, logos, or logical appeals, and pathos, or emotional appeals.[1] In 1872, Susan B. Anthony, a leader of the women's suffrage movement in the United States, voted in the U.S. presidential election, knowing that her action was illegal, and was arrested. In a speech explaining her decision to vote, she began by quoting the U.S. Constitution to establish her credibility on the topic:[2]

> "We, the people of the United States, in order to form a more perfect union, establish justice, insure domestic tranquility, provide for the common defense, promote the general welfare, and secure the blessings of liberty to ourselves and our posterity, do ordain and establish this Constitution for the United States of America."

Then she went on to present her logic for why women should have the right to vote, arguing that "We, the people" referred to all persons, including women:

> It was we, the people; not we, the white male citizens; nor yet we, the male citizens; but we, the whole people, who formed the Union. And we formed it, not to give the blessings of liberty, but to secure them; not to the half of ourselves and the half of our posterity, but to the whole people—women as well as men.

Finally, she used strong language in appealing to her audience's emotions:

> To them [women] this government is not a democracy. It is not a republic. It is an odious aristocracy; a hateful oligarchy of sex; the most hateful aristocracy ever established on the face of the globe . . . .

Incorporating all three appeals into her speech made Anthony's position more persuasive than if she had relied on only one or two types of appeals. Still, she was fined $100 for casting her vote and nearly 50 years passed before women were allowed to vote in the United States.

Although Aristotle's work has stood the test of time, more recent scholars observe that in addition to ethos, pathos, and logos, speakers rely on mythos, or appeals to cultural values and beliefs.[3] In her commencement speech to the 2015 graduates of Carthage College, journalist Laura Ling stressed the value of diversity.[4] She reflected on her frightening capture and 140 days of imprisonment in North Korea for documenting the plight of women in that country. During her captivity,

Ling explains that she did what she could to take charge of her life, such as exercising and meditating. In addition, she decided to try to learn about her captors:

> I knew I couldn't just sit around and wait for somebody else to decide my fate. I tried to engage my captors every chance I could to try to find out what was necessary to get us home. . . . One day one of my guards had gone home to visit with her family. And when she returned I asked if she had a nice time seeing them. And she looked down a bit, forlorn, and she said, "I did. But I felt badly that I could see my family when you've been separated from yours for so long."

Summarizing what she learned from these and similar encounters while she was in the North Korean prison, Ling told her audience:

> I mention these moments because I do think that they're a testament to what can happen when people from enemy nations or opposite ends of a spectrum get a chance to interact and communicate. Our perceptions of one another can grow and widen if we only take that chance to engage with those we consider different, we might find out how much we actually have in common.

Ling's speech demonstrates the power of appealing to cultural values and beliefs in presenting your ideas. She applied the simple act of communicating one-on-one with someone to show her audience the importance of reaching out to others they may think of as different.

supporting material
Evidence used to demonstrate the worth of an idea.

ethos
Appeals to the speaker's credibility.

pathos
Appeals to emotion.

logos
Appeals to logic.

mythos
Appeals to cultural beliefs and values.

Supporting materials—narratives, examples, definitions, testimony, facts, and statistics—illustrate, clarify, and provide evidence for ideas. For instance, Susan B. Anthony defined "We, the people" as all people, not just white men. Laura Ling recounted a personal story about her imprisonment in North Korea. The different types of supporting materials use **ethos**, **pathos**, **logos**, and **mythos** to appeal to audiences in different ways. When you're researching your topic, you're gathering the supporting materials that you'll use to inform, persuade, and entertain your audience. **Table 7.1** summarizes the types of supporting materials discussed in this chapter.

Table 7.1 **Types of Supporting Materials**

Type	Appeal	Useful for	Strengths	Weaknesses
Narratives	Emotional Cultural	Engaging audience	• Dramatize topic • Encourage audience to identify with topic	• Single view on topic • Distract from speech thesis
Examples	Emotional	Personalizing topic	• Make topic concrete • Simplify complex concepts	• Lacks generalizability • Not representative
Definitions	Emotional Logical	Establishing common meaning	• Clarify concepts • Delineate topic boundaries	• Inaccurate or inappropriate • Ignore connotations associated with terms
Testimony	Emotional Cultural Logical	Enhancing speaker credibility	• Provides specific voices on topic • Demonstrates expertise	• Biased information • Source's hidden agenda
Facts	Logical	Establishing the parameters of a topic	• Promote agreement • Provide foundation for topic's importance	• Subject to multiple interpretations • Confined to the past or present
Statistics	Logical	Demonstrating the scope of a problem	• Allow for comparisons among groups • Offer future predictions based on trends identified	• Overwhelming or difficult to comprehend • Subject to manipulation

Narratives

Sometimes called **anecdotes**, **narratives** describe events in a dramatic way, appealing to audience members' emotions. Well-known cultural, societal, and group narratives appeal to deeply held beliefs and values. Narratives generally include a beginning, middle, and end. Compelling stories seem plausible and dramatize a topic. When effectively told, narratives help the audience identify with the speaker's ideas, making this form of evidence one of the most persuasive.[5] In addition, integrating narratives into your speech increases audience engagement with the topic and builds your confidence.[6]

Effective storytelling involves creating a sense of drama, developing compelling characters, and using evocative language and images to transport audience members' imaginations into the narrative.[7] Also, you must choose what information to include and what to leave out, where to begin the story and where to end it, how much of the story's moral or main point you want listeners to figure out for themselves and how much you want to state outright. Too much rambling in telling your story can distract audience members from the main points of your speech.

Speakers rely on four types of narratives: their own stories, stories about others, institutional stories, and cultural stories.

MindTap®

Read, highlight, and take notes online.

anecdote
A brief narrative.

narrative
A description of events in a dramatic fashion; also called a story.

Your Own Stories

Relating your own narrative personalizes the topic and helps listeners understand why you choose it. In his keynote address at South by Southwest (SXSW), the annual music and film festival in Austin, Texas, Bruce Springsteen[8] explained the role of country music in his own work:

> So now I'm in my late twenties, and I'm concerned, of course—getting older. I want to write music that I can imagine myself singing on stage at the advanced old age, perhaps, of 40? I wanted to grow up. I wanted to twist the form I loved into something that could address my adult concerns. And so I found my way to country music.
>
> I remember sitting in my little apartment, playing "Hank Williams Greatest Hits" over and over. And I was trying to crack its code, because at first it just didn't sound good to me. It just sounded cranky and old-fashioned. But it was that hard country voice and I'm playing it, and it was an austere instrumentation. But slowly, slowly, my ears became accustomed to it, its beautiful simplicity, and its darkness and depth. And Hank Williams went from archival, to alive for me, before my very eyes.

Springsteen's personal account provided audience members with a powerful image of his connection to country music. Visualizing a young Springsteen in his apartment listening to a Hank Williams album gave the audience a deeper understanding of how he evolved as a musician.

Others' Stories

Stories about others relate events that the speaker didn't directly observe or participate in. Artist Candy Chang included this story in her keynote address at the Lead On Silicon Valley Conference for Women:

> This is a true story about a man named Joseph Paxton, who was a gardener in the 1800s and he was the first person in England to grow the giant water lily plant. The giant water lily is the biggest flowering plant in the world. It can grow up to eight feet in diameter. It has this special cross-ribbed structure that gives a lily pad a really rigid form. This made Joseph wonder just how strong it really was. So he put his child on it and it still

© David Schmitz Photography

Telling your own story associated with a topic helps your audience identify with you and your topic.

> floated, but he didn't stop there. He somehow found other people's children and loaded them onto the lily pad, too. He discovered it could support a whopping five kids. When he realized just how strong the lily pad was, he wondered, What if this structure could be applied to other things? So he used the same structure to create experimental greenhouses and then he made this—the Crystal Palace—this gigantic cast iron and glass building in London for the Great Exhibition of 1851. More than 14,000 people came together in this space to celebrate the latest technology during the Industrial Revolution. . . . I aspire to have the openness of mind where the strength of a leaf can lead you to reimagine the way we build our buildings.[9]

In her speech, Chang's story about a man who went from gardening to designing buildings helped her audience visualize in a concrete way how an open mind can lead people to imagine what might appear impossible.

Institutional Stories

Institutional stories center on specific organizations, such as a university, corporation, church, or social club. These stories identify how individuals should act in the organization and the values it emphasizes. The president of a student organization might explain to new members the story of how the group got started to give listeners a sense of what they're expected to do. For example, if students founded the organization to provide outreach to neighborhood elementary schools, then the story of the group's origins would highlight the emphasis on community involvement. Similarly, a project leader might describe how a product was developed to demonstrate how team members should approach their own work on a current product.

Cultural Stories

You hear and read cultural stories from the time you're very young. Cultural stories best represent mythos in the way they transmit basic values and accepted behaviors, often told in the form of a fable or myth. In a recent speech, filmmaker Ken Burns recounted a pivotal moment in the classic American Mark Twain novel, *The Adventures of Huckleberry Finn*. Burns used this iconic cultural story to examine equality and racism in the United States.[10] He began by reminding this audience of the book's premise:

> Set near here, before the Civil War and emancipation, *The Adventures of Huckleberry Finn* is the story of two runaways—a white boy, Tom Sawyer's old friend Huck, fleeing civilization, and a black man, Jim, who is running away from slavery. They escape together on a raft going down the Mississippi River.

Burns then identified the key moment in the book:

> The novel reaches its moral climax when Huck is faced with a terrible choice. He believes he has committed a grievous sin in helping Jim escape, and he finally writes out a letter, telling Jim's owner where her runaway property can be found. Huck feels good about doing this at first, he says, and marvels at "how close I came to being lost and going to hell."
>
> But then he hesitates, thinking about how kind Jim has been to him during their adventure. . . . Huck remembers the letter he has written. "I took it up, and held it in my hand," he says. "I was a-trembling because I'd got to decide, forever, betwixt two things, and I knowed it. I studied a minute, sort of holding my breath, and then says to myself: 'All right then, I'll go to hell'—and tore it up."

Minneapolis Star Tribune/ZJMAPRESS.com/Alamy Stock Photo

The classic American story, *The Adventures of Huckleberry Finn*, provides a cultural narrative on race and equality in the United States.

Arguing that racism still exists and the United States has yet to achieve complete equality for all its people, Burns offered this advice to his audience:

> And if you ever find yourself in Huck's spot, if you've "got to decide betwixt two things," do the right thing. Don't forget to tear up the letter. He didn't go to hell—and you won't either.

Using the example of Huckleberry Finn, Burns presented the moral of the story in a way that would resonate with his audience.

Examples

Examples are illustrations or cases that represent a larger group or class of things. Examples make ideas more concrete and personalize the topic, appealing to audience emotions.

example
An illustration or case that represents a larger group or class of things.

Especially for complex ideas, an example can help audience members get a better grasp of key points and concepts related to the topic. Listening to a speech on the importance of community service, audience members might have a vague notion of what that entails. A few examples, such as volunteering at the local public library and tutoring elementary school students in math, provide the audience with a clear picture of what community service involves.

Yet examples may give misleading information if they fail to represent accurately the group to which they belong.[11] For instance, Microsoft chairman and cofounder Bill Gates never completed his college degree at Harvard, yet he has become one of the wealthiest people in the world. However, using Gates as an example of the earning power of college dropouts would be misleading because few people have Gates's computer programming abilities. In addition, while audiences tend to find examples persuasive used in conjunction with other forms of supporting materials—especially statistics and facts—examples alone usually are not convincing.[12]

In your speech, you might use three types of examples: general examples, specific examples, and hypothetical examples.

General Examples

General examples provide little detail; the speaker expects audience members to be familiar with the situation, person, object, or event cited. For instance, if you refer to the Everglades or the Grand Canyon, most people in your audience probably will know about these places—you don't need to explain where they're located or that they're part of the U.S. national park system. Similarly, if you mention common U.S. holidays such as Memorial Day and the Fourth of July, your audience likely knows about them. However, both these examples assume that you're speaking with people who live in the United States or are familiar with the country and its culture. If you were speaking with a group of visitors to the United States, for instance, you would use general examples related to their experiences.

Specific Examples

Specific examples give listeners much more detail. One of our public speaking students presented specific examples that demonstrated the impact of the Ford Motor Company on U.S. culture:

> Although the Ford Motor Company has influenced American culture in many ways, four events stand out. First, Ford's production of the first Model T in 1908 paved the way for an automobile-centered society. Assembly line technology dramatically lowered production costs and greatly increased the affordability of a car for the general public.
>
> Second, in 1914 Ford offered wages of five dollars per day, over twice the previous pay rate. Paying workers more encouraged them to spend more, launching what has become known as a consumer culture.
>
> Third, and much more recently, the first Ford Explorer SUV rolled off the assembly line in 1990. The Explorer came to represent what Americans love—and hate—about suburban life.
>
> Fourth, the latest addition to the Ford Motor Company line up, the Fusion, demonstrates an America of the future—practical and environment-friendly.

With each specific example, the student linked a company event with a trend in U.S. lifestyles. Providing concrete examples that are familiar to the audience clearly demonstrated to listeners the connection between each event and the long-term impact on American culture.

Anadolu Agency/Getty Images

The Ford Fusion hybrid provided a specific example in a student speech on the Ford Motor Company's influence on American culture.

Hypothetical Examples

In contrast to general and specific examples, which are based on actual events, hypothetical examples stem from conjecture or supposition. In other words, with hypothetical examples, speakers ask the audience to imagine something. In a speech on exercise, the speaker might use a hypothetical example such as "Let's go through a typical day for the average person. Rather than getting out of bed and going immediately to the kitchen, our average person stretches and then warms up by jogging in place for a few minutes. Next, our average person . . . ."

Effective hypothetical examples contain a high degree of plausibility—audience members must believe the situation could actually occur. During his presidency, Franklin Delano Roosevelt became well known for his radio-broadcasted fireside chats that resonated with listeners in part due to his effective use of examples.[13] In his September 6, 1936, radio speech, Roosevelt compared two hypothetical examples to explain the federal government's decision to fund a comprehensive water-conservation effort in response to extreme drought in the Great Plains states:

Underwood Archives/Archive Photos/Getty Images

President Franklin Delano Roosevelt during one of his "fireside chats" on AM radio.

> If, for example, in some local area the water table continues to drop and the topsoil to blow away, the land values will disappear with the water and the soil. People on the farms will drift into the nearby cities; the cities will have no farm trade and the workers in the city factories and stores will have no jobs. Property values in the cities will decline. If, on the other hand, the farms within that area remain as farms with better water supply and no erosion, the farm population will stay on the land and prosper and the nearby cities will prosper too. Property values will increase instead of disappearing. That is why it is worth our while as a nation to spend money in order to save money.[14]

Using hypothetical examples of what the future might hold, Roosevelt encouraged his audience to imagine not only what might happen if the federal water-conservation program were *not* implemented but also what might happen if it were. Listeners could relate to the examples because they appealed to those living in city and rural areas. In using hypothetical examples, you're asking your listeners to imagine something, so what you suggest can't be too far-fetched. During this time of extreme drought conditions, listeners did not find Roosevelt's examples difficult to imagine.

Definitions

definition
A statement that describes the essence, precise meaning, or scope of a word or a phrase.

denotative meaning
An agreed-upon definition of a word found in a dictionary.

connotative meaning
A unique meaning associated with a word based on a person's own experiences.

Definitions explain or describe what something is. Words have both denotative and connotative meanings. **Denotative meanings** appeal to logic and are the definitions you find in dictionaries—what speakers and writers of a language generally agree a specific word represents. **Connotative meanings** appeal to emotion and are the personal associations individuals have with a particular word. Even a simple word like *chair* has multiple denotative meanings—the *Compact Oxford English Dictionary* lists six—and infinite connotative meanings. Speakers use definitions to clarify for audience members how they should interpret a term. At the 10th Nelson Mandela Annual Lecture, Mary Robinson, former U.N. High Commissioner for Human Rights, relied on denotative and connotative meanings to connect with her audience:

> *Meitheal* is an Irish word that describes a traditional, rural practice of people coming together to work, farmers lending support to their neighbors as the need arises. It expresses the idea of community spirit and self-reliance. I can remember as a child going out with my father, a doctor, on his calls to rural areas at harvest time: practically everyone would be working in a particular field to save the hay, the women bringing sweet tea and bread and jam. If a farmer was sick, his field would be done willingly by neighbors. I find *meitheal* similar to the African ethic of *Ubuntu*, that idea of human interconnectedness and solidarity, described in the phrase which Archbishop Tutu often uses with us, the phrase "I am because you are."[15]

First, Robinson defined the word Irish word *meitheal* for the audience to establish a common meaning for the word. Second, she explained what the word meant to her and the memories she associated with meitheal. Third, she tied the Irish term *meitheal* to the African term *Ubuntu* to show similarities in cultural experiences.

Speakers commonly use two types of definitions: definitions by function and definitions by analogy.

Definition by Function

When speakers define something by its function, they explain what it does or how it works. At the Romance Writers of America National Conference, Stephanie Laurens said early in her speech:

> What is the definition of success in our business? Recently I've heard some contend that success for an author is getting published. Really? Getting published is you handing your manuscript over for transmittal—how can that be success? No—we're entertainers, and as an entertainer's success is measured by their box office draw, our success is measured by the number of readers lining up to buy our next book. Not the book that just went out, but our next book. Our success is measured by the size of our already captured audience.[16]

Laurens took an abstract concept *success* and explained how it works—achieving success means having an audience waiting for the next book, rather than simply getting a book published. Dictionary and functional definitions appeal to audience members' logic by defining words in concrete, agreed-upon ways.

Definition by Analogy

analogy
A type of comparison that describes something by comparing it to something else that it resembles.

metaphor
A figure of speech that makes an implicit comparison between two things.

simile
A figure of speech that makes an explicit comparison between two things, using the words *like* or *as*.

An **analogy** describes something by comparing it to something else it resembles. Speakers often use analogies to help listeners understand something new to them—that is, they use an analogy referring to something familiar to define something unfamiliar. For example, in emphasizing the importance of learning first-aid techniques, a speaker might say, "It's like studying for an exam—you want to be prepared for any situation that might arise." In explaining the analogy, speakers typically identify how the two things are both similar and dissimilar. So the speaker might go on to say, "But, unlike in the case of an exam, if you're not prepared for a first-aid situation, someone could needlessly suffer—or even die."

Metaphors and **similes** are sometimes grouped with analogies. A metaphor relies on an implicit comparison—something *is* something else, while a simile makes an explicit comparison—something *is like* something else. Sheryl Sandberg, Facebook COO, argued at the 2012 Harvard Business School commencement that *jungle gym* has replaced *ladder* as a career metaphor. She explained that in a career you "move sideways, move down, move on, move off."[17] Comparing the two metaphors—ladder and jungle gym—visualized for the audience that the traditional idea of a career as an upward trajectory no longer applies.

Similes often juxtapose objects, processes, or ideas in unique and novel ways, heightening the audience's interest. In a recent interview, Culinary Institute of America chef Jonathan Zearfoss described the school's integration of science and cooking this way: "A traditional kitchen is like a pirate ship. We like our flames, we like our noise, we have our scars. We'd like to create a kitchen that's more like a yacht."[18] This comparison offers a rich visualization of cooking that conveys this new scientific approach to food preparation.

Definitions of all types help audience members understand a topic's scope and increase the likelihood that the speaker and the audience think about the topic in similar ways. Definitions also tell your audience what you *won't* be talking about or how you *won't* use a word. In a speech on stress, for instance, the speaker might talk about the differences between situational stress, which arises in specific contexts, and chronic stress, which never goes away, and then say, "Today I'm going to focus on situational stress."

Although definitions may clarify your topic, they can also cause problems. No matter how clearly you define your terms,

SPEAKING OF ...

Making Your Topic Shine with Similes and Metaphors

Audiences find similes and metaphors engaging because these forms of analogies provide mental links between two things they might not ordinarily think go together. You probably wouldn't think of pirate ships and kitchens in the same sentence, yet comparing old ways of cooking to pirate ships and cooking based in science to yachts sparks your imagination, providing intrigue to a topic that on the surface may seem dull. Consider the topic for the speech you're currently working on or plan to give soon. What terms associated with your topic require clear definitions? What comes to your mind when you think of those terms? How are those terms like something with which your audience may be familiar? How might a simile or metaphor help visualize the terms for your audience?

Bettmann/CORBIS

Dalibor Brlek/Alamy Stock Photo

How effective is Chef Zearfoss's simile comparing kitchens to a pirate ship and a yacht?

audience members always will have connotations associated with those words. For example, Chapter 1 defines the term *style* as the language used in a speech, but you might associate style with fashion or having a flair for doing something. Definitions may be inappropriate. This often happens when speakers use a standard dictionary definition for a technical term. Chapter 1 also defines the term *invention* as Cicero did, to refer to discovering what a speaker wants to say in a speech. However, using a dictionary definition of *invention*—creating something new—to describe Cicero's approach would be inadequate because it wouldn't offer the precision needed to apply the term to public speaking.

Testimony

When speakers use **testimony**, they rely on an individual's or group's opinions related to a particular topic. Using testimony to support your points works only if listeners believe in the source's credibility and feel a personal connection to the source or topic.[19] Speakers use three different types of sources: testimony from experts, celebrities, and laypeople.

testimony
An individual's opinions or experiences about a particular topic.

Expert Testimony

In identifying expert testimony for your speeches, choose sources the audience will perceive as highly qualified on your topic. One of our students recently presented a speech on invasive plants in California. He incorporated quotes from his interview with a campus biology professor who had conducted extensive research on invasive plants. Although the student was a biology major, the professor was a stronger authority on invasive plants, so her testimony was more convincing. The effectiveness of expert testimony rests on the audience's belief that the source truly is an expert on the topic.[20]

Celebrity Testimony

Audiences find celebrity testimony compelling because of the person's fame or star power, not necessarily the person's knowledge about the topic. For example, actor William Macy played a person with cerebral palsy in *Door to Door*, a film based on a true story. Macy later joined United Cerebral Palsy's (UCP's) board of trustees. Listeners consider what he has to say about this disability credible because of his celebrity status, role in the film, and participation in UCP. Actor and *Superman* star Christopher Reeve became a strong advocate for stem cell research after an accident in which he broke two vertebrae in his neck. Both his reputation as an actor and his experience as a person with a disability gave credibility to his views, although he had no scientific knowledge related to stem cell research.

Lay Testimony

Lay testimony involves individuals who have experience with a topic but aren't experts or well known. Journalists often use lay testimony when reporting on human-interest stories. For example, in a speech on keeping costs low for college students, the speaker might interview a few students to find out their strategies for saving money.

Facts

fact
An observation based on actual experience.

inference
An interpretation of facts.

opinion
A way of thinking or judgment about something.

Facts provide support for speakers' logical appeals. Your senses serve as the basis for **facts**, observations you make based on your experiences. In contrast, statements of **inference** are conclusions or interpretations you draw based on facts. For instance, you can observe how many students are in your class right now and how many are absent. Let's say 21 students are in attendance and 4 are not—that's a statement of fact. You can draw an infinite number of inferences about that fact. For instance, you might conclude the four students are ill, had to work, are attending an event on campus, or just decided to skip class. **Table 7.2** outlines the differences between facts and inferences.

Inferences are not the same as opinions. An **opinion** is a way of thinking or judgment about something that may have nothing to do with observations or facts. For example, you may have an opinion about a course, such as organic chemistry, without knowing anything about it. Your opinion may be that it's a difficult course. To draw an *inference* about the course, you'd need to know something about it, such as how many students pass the course each semester or statements from students who have completed it. You might base an opinion on facts, but facts aren't necessary to form an opinion about something.

For the most part, speakers rely on others when gathering facts. An author's credibility, or ethos, influences the degree to which audience members think information is accurate. Source credibility is especially important when presenting facts. As explained in Chapter 6, you want to carefully evaluate the sources for your information.

When you include facts in a speech, you accept others' observations as well as your own. For example, you weren't alive when George Washington became president, but you accept his presidency as a fact based on what others have reported. To support this, you can examine historical documents located in the Library of Congress collections (loc.gov), and read accounts of Washington's inauguration.

Facts generally foster agreement because they often can be verified as true or false. However, audiences do not always interpret facts the same way speakers do.

Table 7.2 Facts vs. Inferences

Statement of Fact	Statement of Inference
Made after observation	Made during or after observation
Confined to observations—cannot be made about the future	Goes beyond observations—may involve the past, present, or future
Limited number possible	Unlimited number possible
High probability	Some degree of probability
Tends to further agreement	More likely to lead to disagreement

© David Schmitz Photography

One interpretation of the fact that Apple hires San José State University graduates is that the company wants a diverse workforce. A different interpretation is that Apple hires those students for relatively low-paying retail positions.

For example, in a speech on diversifying the workplace, a student cited a Business Insider report[21] comparing the college backgrounds of Apple and Google employees. To no one's surprise, the top five universities Google employees graduated from are Stanford University; the University of California, Berkeley; the Massachusetts Institute of Technology; Carnegie Mellon University; and the University of California, Los Angeles. However, the top five universities for Apple employees did surprise listeners: San José State University; Stanford University; the University of California, Berkeley; the University of Texas at Austin; and Santa Clara University. The speaker argued that Apple's ability to succeed and dominate the technology industry, especially in smartphones, tablets, and music players, stemmed in part from the company's broad-based strategy of hiring employees from a diverse range of schools—not all of them known for their engineering programs. However, listeners might have interpreted the same facts as simply reflecting Apple's greater retail presence and the need for more employees in that sector. To counterbalance this interpretation, the speaker underscored the elite nature of the Google list and the more middle-class roots of the Apple list, particularly San José State.

As a speaker, recognizing that your audience may not infer what you do about the facts you present will help you use facts that truly support your ideas.

Statistics

Statistics are numerical data or information, such as the average price of a home or how many students are enrolled at your university this year. Like facts, speakers rely on statistics for logical appeals.

statistics Numerical data or information.

Statistics allow speakers to quantify the magnitude of a problem and make comparisons across groups and time periods. For example, a speaker might claim that the Internet provides an easy avenue for consumer fraud. How could you find out if this claim is true? By going to the Federal Trade Commission (FTC) website (ftc.gov), you can view the latest statistics on consumer complaints: The FTC reported that it received more than 1.5 million fraud-related complaints in 2014, costing consumers more than $1.7 billion. Telephone (54 percent) was the top source of initial contact, followed by email (23 percent), websites (11 percent), and traditional mail (4 percent). These statistics have changed over time, with fewer initial contacts via email and websites today than in 2012.[22] If you were preparing for a speech on the Internet and fraud, these statistics would suggest that online fraud is increasing while telephone fraud is on the rise.

In her keynote address at the NETmundial, Nnenna Nwakanma, Africa Regional Coordinator for the World Wide Web Foundation, used statistics to argue that Internet access remains a critical issue worldwide:

> As much as two-thirds of the world's population is not connected to the Internet. The penetration rates in less-developed countries average around 31 percent. In the African continent, this figure drops to 16 percent. In the world's 49 least-developed countries, over 90 percent of people are not online. We have one billion people living with disability. Eighty percent live in developing countries. Each one deserves access: to information, to libraries, to knowledge, to affordable Internet.[23]

In this case, statistics offered a platform for demonstrating the extent to which so many people do not have Internet access. Nwakanma used statistics to underscore the magnitude of the problem.

You may think of statistics as objective, yet these supporting materials are still subject to interpretation—and manipulation. For example, if a speaker said, "The number of bicycles stolen on this campus has quadrupled in the past year," listeners would reasonably conclude that bicycle theft was a major problem. However, if only two bicycles had been stolen in the previous year, "quadrupled" would mean eight had been stolen in the current year. In contrast, if 50 bikes were stolen the previous year and 200 in the current year, the speaker would have a stronger case for identifying bicycle theft as a serious problem.

Because they appeal to logic, audience members generally find statistics convincing in persuasive situations.[24] But if you overwhelm audience members with statistics, they will tune out. As you select statistics for your speeches, consider how your audience will interpret the data and respond.

AFP/Getty Images

Statistics can show the extent of a problem as Nnenna Nwakanma, Africa Regional Coordinator for the World Wide Web Foundation, demonstrated in arguing that many people worldwide do not have reliable Internet access.

SPEAKING OF ...

Finding Credible Statistics

As you know, not all Internet sources are created equal: Some are more credible than others.

1. For domestic data, USA.gov (usa.gov), the portal for the U.S. government's websites, provides a reliable place to start in your search for statistics about the United States. To find statistics on national health issues, for instance, visit the National Center for Health Statistics site (cdc.gov/nchs), part of the Centers for Disease Control and Prevention.
2. For international statistics, visit the United Nations website (un.org). This site hosts a vast array of databases, including:
   - FAOSTAT (faostat.fao.org), which covers topics associated with food and agriculture;
   - the International Labor Organization (ilo.org), which focuses especially on child labor issues; and
   - the UNESCO Institute for Statistics (uis.unesco.org), which compares statistics across countries in education, technology, literature, science, and culture.
3. Specific countries and groups of countries also sponsor their own statistics websites, such as:
   - EUROSTAT (ec.europa.eu/eurostat), part of the European Union's website;
   - the National Bureau of Statistics of China (stats.gov.cn/english); and
   - Statistics South Africa (statssa.gov.za).

Summary

As you research your topic, you'll find information related to your points and ideas. These supporting materials form the substance of your speech. They bring your ideas to life, demonstrate the weight and seriousness of your topic, and help you build credibility. Supporting materials may appeal to your audience's emotions, logic, and cultural beliefs.

There are six basic types of supporting materials. Narratives dramatize a topic and help your audience identify with it. Examples make ideas less abstract and personalize a topic. Definitions establish a common meaning between the speaker and the audience. Experts, celebrities, and laypeople may provide testimony or their experiences about a topic. Facts are based on observations and appeal to an audience's logical thinking processes. Statistics provide numerical representations of information, and like facts, are used in logical appeals.

MindTap®

Watch It: View a video on selecting the best supporting materials.

ANALYZE IT

Malkia Cyril, Keynote at the Computers, Freedom and Privacy Conference, October 13, 2015

Malkia Cyril/Center for Media Justice
Malkia Cyril

MindTap®

Watch and analyze this speech on MindTap.

Malkia Cyril, cofounder and Executive Director of the Center for Media Justice (CMJ), presented the keynote address at the 2015 Computers, Freedom and Privacy Conference. As you read this excerpt from the speech (or view the complete speech online), note the different types of supporting materials she used in her speech.

Thank you. I am honored to be here. I am honored to represent those who, too often, aren't called to this table, aren't heard in these halls.

I'm talking about the 450,000 migrants in U.S. detention centers. The 2 million people incarcerated in the U.S. The 9 million under the control of the justice system. I am talking about the 883 people killed by police this year. I am here for people like my Uncle Kamou Sadiki, a former Black Panther who will spend the rest of his life in prison for a crime he did not commit. People like my mom, Janet Cyril, also a Black Panther, who faced the FBI head on when they burst into our house and demanded she testify against the San Francisco 8 in a secret court proceeding. She said no, and died two weeks later from sickle cell anemia. I'm here for Walter Scott, Eric Garner, and 12-year-old Tamir Rice, whose Black bodies were murdered on video, and still incited zero police accountability.

I am here for the thousands who have taken to the streets in the name of Black Lives Matter. I'm here for the 200 organizations of the Media Action Grassroots Network. I am honored to speak for them. Martin Luther King said in 1958, everything we see is a shadow cast by that which we do not see. I hope I am a long shadow.

I'm especially grateful to speak with you today, because we are on the precipice of an outstanding political moment. A moment when migrant activists have put their bodies on the line to block deportation buses; when a movement for Black Lives has taken to the streets led in large measure by women, queer people, the disabled, and those whose voices are usually ousted from the collective practice of democracy. A moment like 1963, when in all parts of this country, attacks on Black bodies by white police officers and vigilantes went unaccounted for, despite being in full view of a historically divided public.

It sounds familiar, doesn't it?

1963, when the U.S waged a seemingly never-ending war halfway across the world for a democracy we could not taste, touch or see right here at home.

1963, when widespread outrage over these epic inconsistencies between the story of America and her truth transformed into a civil rights movement. We are living in that kind of moment today. We know what this moment looks like, because we've lived through it before as a nation. We know that moments like these don't come often, and while it's hot right now, they don't stay.

So, we have some tough decisions to make. The decentralized power of the Internet has made much of this moment possible. But I ask myself, will the technology serve a future of equity and democracy? Will it fuel a new era of civil action, a renaissance of human rights? Or will it drive a widening wealth gap, a more militarized state, a political economy characterized by structural inequality and persistent discrimination?

I submit that the answer to that question is up to you. Look around, see who is and who is not in this room.

On the one hand, this digital age and era of big data holds extraordinary promise for all of us. It allows us to reach into parts of the world we never could before, learn in seconds what might have taken months or years. But, while these technological advances may speed and ease what this nation and economy *can* do, the issue at hand is what we *will* do.

For Black people to move about the streets safely in 1700's America, we needed a pass. That was the surveillance technology of that time. A white person had to vouch for you, and every white person was deputized to enforce that system. I do not want you to vouch for me today, I vouch for myself. In the 21st century, almost two thirds of incarcerated people and those under the control of the justice system are racial and ethnic minorities. Over 40% of us are Black. We live on databases, in ankle bracelets, between checkpoints. This did not start with the NSA revelations and it will not end with policies that limit the NSA, this is embedded into the structure of this nation—we need more. Today, we have some new technology doing some very old work.

Here's the thing. Technology can only serve democracy to the degree that it is democratized. People like me have always been watched. The only difference is the tool, and the time.

It was August, 2013. A man, Jimmy Barraza, a migrant worker in New Orleans, was unloading a carful of groceries when agents pulled up with pistols drawn, handcuffing him as well as his teenage son, a United States citizen. It was a typical random raid. The probable cause? He was Latino. A mobile fingerprint check of Mr. Barraza, who is also Honduran, revealed an old court order for his deportation. A judge said the ends justified the means. I disagree. I say, not in my name. We have some tough choices to make.

Will we be a nation that uses the Internet to bypass existing legal protections and facilitate mass deportation? That uses sound technology to clear protestors from the streets? Uses federally funded drones to spy on Muslim American communities with neither their consent nor probable cause? Will our right to record police officers in the commission of their duties be consistently violated with threats, arrests, and illegal searches, and by the law itself in places like Texas? How much longer will the communities I speak for here today live scanned, tracked, and traced?

Cause that's how we live today. . . .

Last year, New York City Police Commissioner Bill Bratton said 2015 would be the year of technology for law enforcement. And indeed, it has been. Predictive policing has taken hold as the big brother of broken windows policing. Total information awareness has become the goal. Across the country, local police departments are working with federal law enforcement agencies to use advanced technological tools and data analysis to "pre-empt crime." I have never seen anyone able to pre-empt crime, but I appreciate the arrogance that suggests you can tell the future in that way. I wish, instead, technologists would attempt to pre-empt poverty. Instead, algorithms. Instead, automation. In the name of community safety and national security we are now relying on algorithms to mete out sentences, determine city budgets, and automate public decision-making without any public input. That sounds familiar too. It sounds like Black codes. Like Jim Crow. Like 1963. . . .

We need a new civil rights act for the era of big data, and we need it now. No more piecemeal approaches. No more federal bills that leave people like me out. Without this level of rigorous constitutional protection, it means the 21st century will supplement 1963's informants with 2016's facial recognition software. . . .

At my mother's funeral in 2005, my uncle Jamal Joseph, one of the Panther Party's youngest members talked about J. Edgar Hoover's targeted attack against Black communities. He reminded us that files obtained during a break in at an FBI office in 1971 revealed that African Americans, Hoover's largest targeted group, didn't have to be perceived as dissident to warrant surveillance. They just had to be Black. Not much has changed, today.

Speaking of surveillance, my niece sent me a quote on Facebook that said, "War is when the government tells you who your enemy is. Revolution is when you decide for yourself." Surveillance has always been used to define our enemy for us, both foreign and domestic. To create racialized profiles that would determine who has access to the state, to its resources and its protection, based on "empirical observation." The point of surveillance at this level is not simply to invade our privacy, but to carry out the primary economic and social objectives of both state and economy, which too often are at odds with our own, at odds with human rights and the course of humanity. It's time to revolt and reject the use of technology to uphold the caste system in this country.

MLK said, "Everything we see is a shadow cast by that which we do not see." I've always wondered what he meant by that. Though the iconic civil rights leader spoke those words in 1958, almost 60 years ago, they are no less true in today's digital age, when inequality is driven by an information economy whose Black codes and Jim Crow laws are coded in 1's and 0's; automated and hidden from view, but no less of a yoke around the neck, no less a warrantless search of the selves I carry in my cell phone, my computer; no less discriminatory and dangerous today.

But thank goodness there are victories. In L.A. my colleagues at the Stop LAPD Spying Coalition are fighting against the use of suspicious activities reports and drones. The ACLU and others just won the passage of an unprecedented Electronic Privacy Act by California's Governor Brown. The national online civil rights group ColorOfChange.org is making FOIA requests right now to shed light on the secret surveillance of Black Lives Matter by law enforcement agencies.

We are fighting back; because we are 1963, we are 2016. We are the culture jedi of the 21st century, armed with our bits and our bytes and our love and our humanity. We are a rising tide, and we will rise again and again and again until we win. Thank you.

Questions for Discussion

1. How did Malkia Cyril use narratives in her speech? Identify the type(s) of narratives she included.
2. How did she use examples in her speech? Identify the type(s) of examples she included.
3. Malkia Cyril draws analogies between 1963 and today. How effective are those analogies?
4. How does Cyril use testimony in her speech?
5. What facts did she state in her speech?
6. What statistics did she include in her speech?
7. Overall, how effective was Malkia Cyril in providing supporting materials for her main points?
8. If you were advising Malkia Cyril on how to improve her use of supporting materials, what would you say?
9. What have you learned about supporting materials that you'll apply in your own speeches?

APPLY IT . . .

IN THE WORKPLACE

Framing the Facts

Gathering data and presenting facts clearly and concisely are essential skills in the workplace. Yet, as you know, facts may be interpreted in different ways. When you give a presentation to your coworkers, supervisors, clients, or customers, you can't guarantee they'll view your facts in the way you intended, but you can anticipate your audience's various perspectives. Here are some ways you can prepare yourself for presenting facts in the workplace:

- List the facts you plan to include in your presentation. Identify at least two different interpretations for those facts.
- Meet with several coworkers to discuss their perspectives on the facts you plan to present.
- Contact clients or customers and ask them for their thoughts on a few of the facts you've gathered.
- Choose the most persuasive or important facts from your presentation and ask for your supervisor's interpretation.

Even informal conversations can help you gain multiple perspectives on the facts you've gathered for a workplace presentation As you interact with coworkers, supervisors, clients, and customers, pay special attention to their views on various topics so you can make informed guesses about how they'll respond to facts you'll include in future presentations.

IN YOUR COMMUNITY

Gathering Community Stories

Humans are storytellers and story listeners. Much of what you've learned about yourself, your family, your neighborhood, your society, and your culture comes from stories you've heard and stories you've told. Because they're such a natural part of human interaction, you may not have examined the important role stories play in the life of your community. Begin by identifying a few key people and organizations in your community. Develop a list of questions you plan to ask, following the interview guidelines described in Chapter 6. Consider what you want to know about your community. For example, you might ask about memorable events or people. After you've conducted the interviews, determine which stories are the most compelling or provide the greatest insight into your community. Arrange to share the stories with the people and organizations where you collected them. You might give a brief talk about the stories, providing your audience with examples. How do these stories help those both in and outside of your community better understand it? In gathering and speaking on community stories, what have you learned about narratives and public speaking?

REVIEW IT

Key Terms

analogy 138
anecdote 133
connotative meaning 137
definition 137
denotative meaning 137
ethos 132
example 135
fact 140
inference 140
logos 132
metaphors 138
mythos 132
narratives 133
opinion 140
pathos 132
simile 138
statistics 141
supporting material 132
testimony 139

MindTap®
Use flashcards to learn key terms and take a quiz to test your knowledge.

Reflecting on Supporting Your Ideas

1. Humans love to tell and listen to stories, so listeners find stories in speeches especially engaging. What are the negative aspects of using narratives in speeches? How can audience members enjoy a story yet listen critically at the same time?
2. Critical listeners closely examine how speakers define words. Definitions can be very powerful in a speech if audience members simply accept the definitions the speaker offers. Reflect on a recent public speaking situation in which you were in the audience. Did you question the speaker's definitions? In what other ways might the terms have been defined? How would those definitions change the nature of the speech and the speaker's conclusions?
3. Examples can help audience members identify with a topic if the examples are familiar to the audience. How have you used general examples in your speeches in the past? How well did they work? How have you used specific examples? How did the audience respond?
4. When you're listening to a speaker, how convincing do you find expert, celebrity, and lay testimony? What makes you skeptical of testimony?
5. Suppose you enter a classroom and observe that 20 out of 25 students have umbrellas. Based on this fact, what inferences can you draw? Consider all possible inferences, no matter how fanciful. What insight does this brief activity give you into using facts in your speeches?
6. You've probably heard the saying, "There are three kinds of lies: lies, damned lies, and statistics." The source of the quote is unclear, but the meaning is not: Statistics can be used to support a weak or even false claim. What can you do to make sure the statistics you use in your speech are correct and support a valid claim?

8 Organizing and Outlining Your Speech

MindTap

Start with a quick warm-up activity and review the chapter's learning outcomes.

> READ IT

After successfully completing this chapter, you will be able to:

> Identify the main parts of a speech.

> Describe and give examples of the organizational patterns for arranging the body of your speech.

> Use transition words, phrases, or sentences to connect the ideas and main points in your speech and identify where to place them in your speech.

> Describe how to put together a working outline, complete-sentence outline, and speaking outline.

When you organize a speech well, audience members follow your ideas more easily and better understand what you have to say.

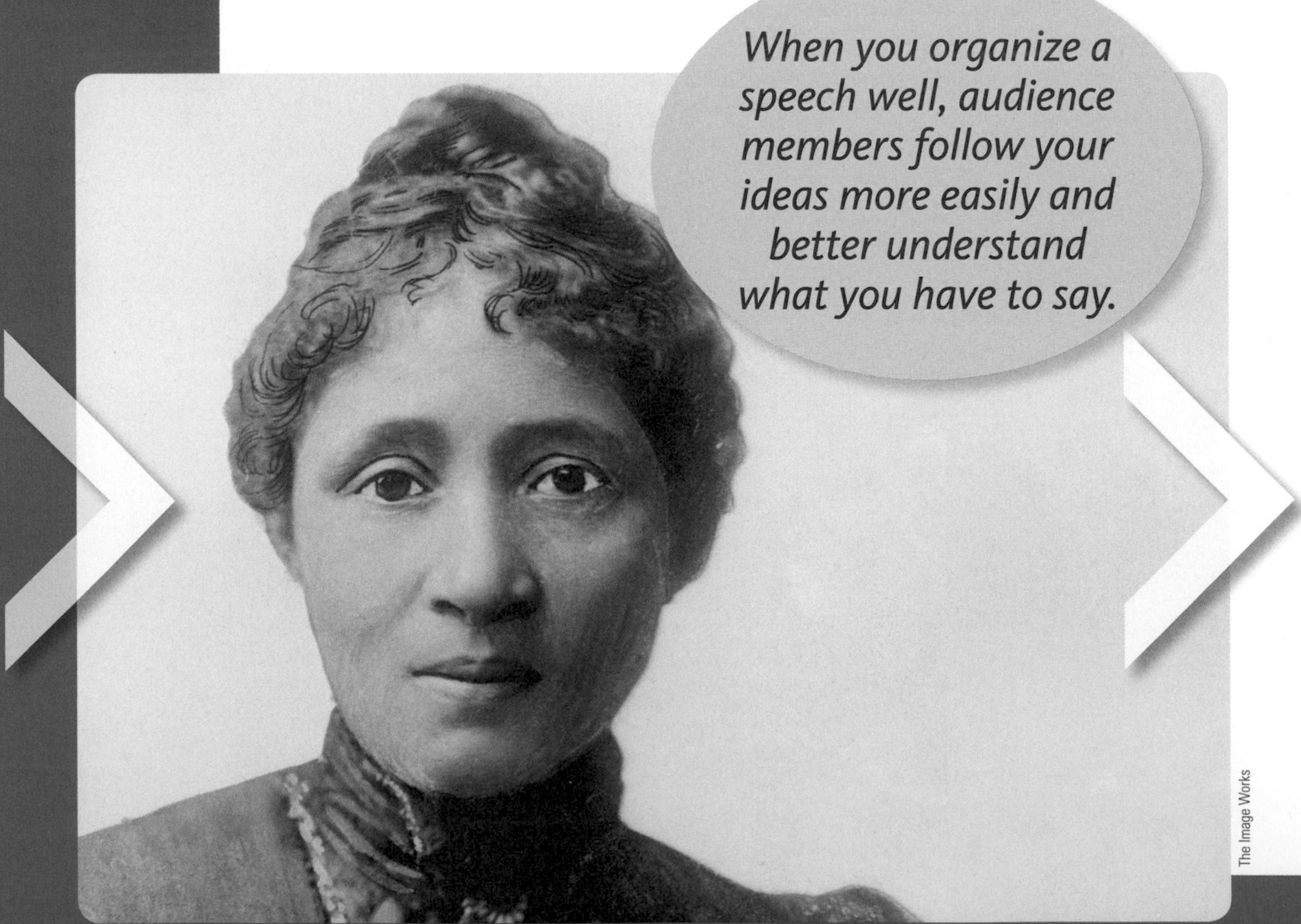

The Image Works

Speakers and listeners long have recognized the importance of effective organization in public speaking. In *Rhetorica ad Herennium*, likely written about 80 BCE and the first known textbook on public speaking, the author identified the five canons of rhetoric—invention, arrangement, style, memory, and delivery.[1] As you learned in Chapter 1, *arrangement* refers to the ways in which speakers organize their ideas to best reach their goals. Just as effective organization was essential to public speakers in ancient Rome, having sound organization provides a necessary foundation for public speaking today.

When you organize a speech well, audience members follow your ideas more easily and better understand what you have to say. In addition, good organization helps you stay on track, keeping your purpose and thesis in mind. With a thoughtful plan for the order in which you want to present your points, you'll feel more confident. In addition, carefully organizing your speech increases the chances you'll achieve your specific purpose and your audience will respond as you'd planned. For example, Lucy Gonzalez Parsons, activist and cofounder of the Industrial Workers of the World labor organization in 1905, organized her points in impassioned speeches to motivate her audience to take action. Activists today, such as actor America Ferrera, who works with Voto Latino to promote Latina/o empowerment and leadership, know that effective idea organization is key to winning over their audiences.

Getty Images Entertainment/Getty Images

The Parts of a Speech

MindTap®

Read, highlight, and take notes online.

Every speech has four main parts as shown in **Figure 8.1**.

- *The introduction:* In this first part of the speech, the speaker must get the audience's attention, indicate the purpose and thesis, establish credibility, and preview the speech's main points.
- *The body:* It includes all the speaker's main points and subordinate points.
- *Transitions:* These words, phrases, sentences, or paragraphs help the speaker move from the introduction to the body, from one point to the next, and from the body to the conclusion.
- *The conclusion:* It ends the speech, with the speaker reviewing the main points, restating the thesis, and providing closure.

When you present a speech, you proceed from the introduction through the body to the conclusion. But when you put together a speech, you typically develop the body and transitions first, the introduction second, and the conclusion last. **Figure 8.1** shows the logic underlying this seemingly illogical order. You need to know what you're going to say in the body before you develop the introduction and the conclusion. You may find, however, that as you work on the body of your speech you'll think of something you want to say in the introduction or get an idea for a great way to end your speech. Organizing your speech, like speechmaking in general, doesn't always follow a linear path.

This chapter focuses on developing the body of your speech and connecting your points together, as those are the starting points for most speakers. Chapter 9 discusses how to begin and end your speech.

Organizing the Body of Your Speech

MindTap®

Watch It: View a video on organizing your main points.

body
The middle and main part of a speech; includes main and subordinate points.

The **body** is where the action of your speech takes place—where you inform, persuade, or entertain your audience. This section identifies and describes the main elements of this part of your speech (**Figure 8.2**).

Developing Your Main Points

Your working outline, introduced in Chapter 4, provides a useful guide for developing your main points. The working outline includes your topic, general purpose, specific

Figure 8.1 The Parts of a Speech

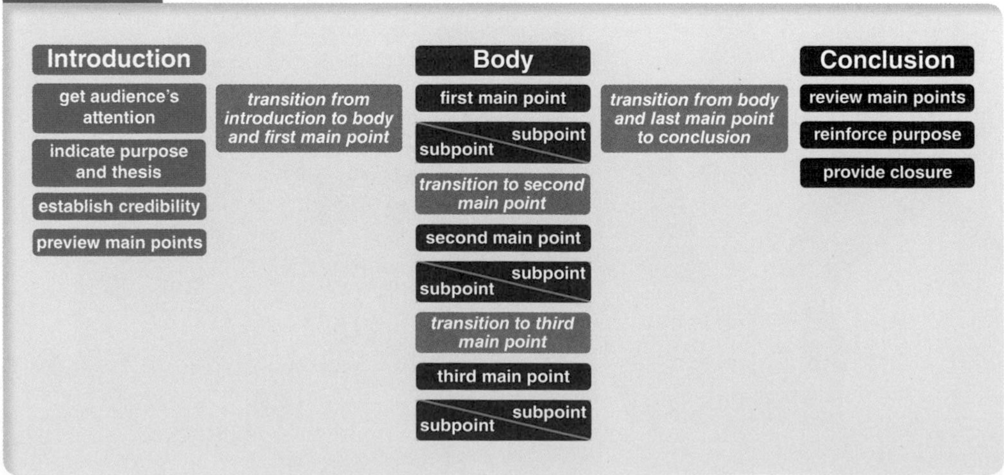

purpose, thesis, and keywords for the main ideas and subpoints. In addition, you'll start your list of references on your working outline. As you review your working outline, applying the principles of clarity, relevance, and balance will help you identify what points to include and what points to leave out of your speech.

Clarity Your main points should identify for your audience what your speech is about and the response you seek. They must also clearly support your specific purpose and be consistent with your thesis. In the following example, notice how the main points elaborate the ideas expressed in the thesis, providing clarity on the topic of happiness. They also support the specific purpose, allowing the speaker to reach the goal of informing the audience.

TOPIC:	A Scientific Approach to Happiness
GENERAL PURPOSE:	To inform
SPECIFIC PURPOSE:	To inform my audience about the science of happiness
THESIS:	According to scientists, people achieve happiness through involvement with daily activities and other people, contributing in meaningful ways to larger goals, and finding pleasure in everyday life.

MAIN POINTS:

I. The first component of happiness is being engaged in activities and interacting with others.

II. The second component of happiness is feeling like what you do contributes in meaningful ways to some larger goal or objective.

III. The third component of happiness is simply finding pleasure in the everyday things you do.

Figure 8.2 Elements of the Body

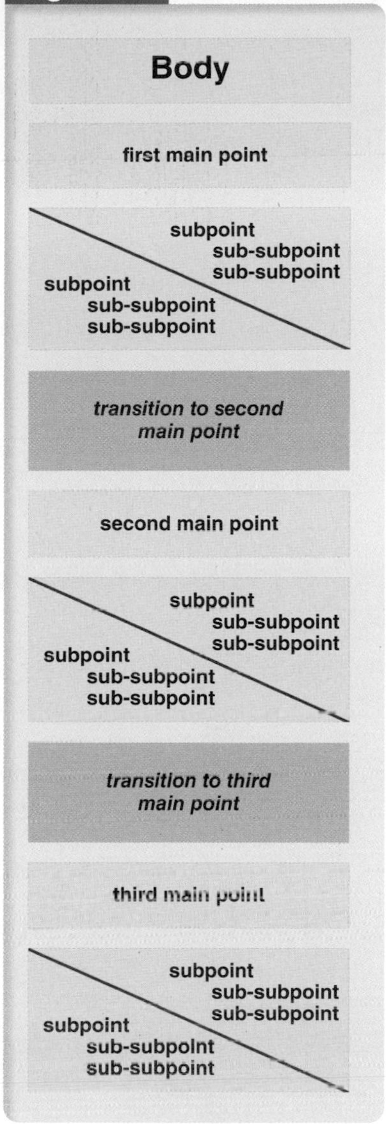

Even slightly altering what you want to say about a topic changes the specific purpose and thesis. In turn, the main points must also change to clearly reflect different focus. For example:

TOPIC:	The Myths of Happiness
GENERAL PURPOSE:	To inform
SPECIFIC PURPOSE:	To make my audience aware of myths about happiness
THESIS:	Scientists have dispelled three common myths about happiness: Money makes you happy, intelligence makes you happy, and being young makes you happy.

MAIN POINTS:

I. "Wealth makes you happy" is one myth scientists have proven false.

II. "Greater intelligence makes you happier" is a second myth scientists have proven false.

III. "Youth as the key to happiness" is a third myth scientists have dispelled.

oneinchpunch/Shutterstock.com

You can take many approaches to the same topic, such as happiness. Each approach will change the specific purpose, thesis, and main points you cover in your speech.

These examples of two approaches to the same topic, happiness, demonstrate the importance of the early steps you take in topic development: clearly refining your topic, phrasing your specific purpose, and writing your thesis statement (Chapter 4).

Relevance The main points of your speech must pertain directly to your topic. As you research your topic, you'll gather more information than you'll use in your speech. Continually review your specific purpose and thesis to identify the points that are truly relevant to your specific purpose. You'll always know more about your topic than what you include in your speech—you're the expert—but avoid including information that would detract from your specific purpose.

Main points must be relevant to one another as well as to the topic. Consider the main points for this informative speech about U.S. science fiction writer Octavia E. Butler:

Matthew Jordan Smith/Corbis

An informative speech about Octavia E. Butler might focus on the major writing awards she won rather than everything she accomplished in her entire career.

TOPIC:	The Achievements of Octavia E. Butler
GENERAL PURPOSE:	To inform
SPECIFIC PURPOSE:	To increase my audience's awareness of some of Octavia E. Butler's important achievements
THESIS:	Octavia E. Butler's many achievements include winning two Hugo and two Nebula awards, a MacArthur genius grant, and a lifetime achievement award from the PEN American Center.

MAIN POINTS:

I. Butler won two Hugo and two Nebula awards for her science fiction stories.

II. In 1995, Butler became the first, and so far only, science fiction writer to win a "genius grant" from the MacArthur Foundation.

III. In 1999, Butler won the PEN American Center Lifetime Achievement Award in writing.

Each main point focuses on an important award that brought Butler recognition. She also achieved success in other ways, such as writing a science fiction movie at age 12 and selling 250,000 copies of her novel *Kindred.* Although these are important accomplishments, they're not directly relevant to a discussion of the awards she won.

Balance Also consider how balanced your main points are. Each point should be about equal in importance relative to both your topic and the other points. All your points may not be *completely* equal in importance, but one point shouldn't be much more or much less important than the others. Let's consider an example for an informative speech about an event.

TOPIC:	The Ann Arbor Street Art Fair
GENERAL PURPOSE:	To inform
SPECIFIC PURPOSE:	To teach my audience about the many interesting facets of Ann Arbor's annual Street Art Fair
THESIS:	The people, the place, and the art make the annual Ann Arbor Street Art Fair an exciting event to attend.

MAIN POINTS:

I. Performers, artists, volunteers, and fairgoers make the Ann Arbor Street Art Fair lively.

II. Home to the University of Michigan, Ann Arbor is no stranger to making people feel welcome.

III. The nearly 20 different types of art—from pottery to fine jewelry—provide a feast for the senses.

In this example, the three aspects of the Ann Arbor Street Art Fair contribute about equally to the event. You'd likely plan to talk about each of them for about the same amount of time.

If the main points you want to discuss are of unequal importance, you can still achieve a rough balance by spending less time on less important points. Consider a speech about the people who come together for the Ann Arbor Street Art Fair:

TOPIC:	The People of the Ann Arbor Street Art Fair
GENERAL PURPOSE:	To inform
SPECIFIC PURPOSE:	To inform my audience about the people of Ann Arbor's annual Street Art Fair
THESIS:	The people of the Ann Arbor Street Art Fair include the organizers, volunteers, artists, performers, and fairgoers.

MAIN POINTS:

I. The organizers work all year planning the event.
II. Volunteers do everything from giving tours of the fair to reuniting lost parents and children.
III. The nearly 200 artists display their creative work.
IV. Performers keep everyone in good cheer.
V. Thousands of fairgoers from around the world attend the event every year.

Joseph Sibilsky/Alamy Stock Photo

The Ann Arbor Street Art Fair

You'd probably spend more time talking about the artists and performers because they're the reason people attend the fair. Or you could emphasize the behind-the-scenes work of the organizers and volunteers. Whatever your emphasis, maintain balance by spending a similar amount of time on each point. For example, you could spend two minutes each on the artists and performers, and one minute each on the organizers, volunteers, and fairgoers.

Evaluating the balance of your main points also requires that you identify the appropriate number of points to include in your speech. To help you determine the right number of main points, consider:

1. what information you must cover to achieve your specific purpose and
2. how much time you have to present your speech.

Say you have five minutes to present the informative speech about the people of the Ann Arbor Street Art Fair. Can you adequately talk about each main point and give sufficient attention to the introduction and conclusion in that amount of time? No. You'd have less than one minute for each main point, giving you little time to provide the audience with any in-depth information. You need either more time or fewer points. If you can't change the amount of time allotted, you must reduce the number of main points. You could, for instance, focus just on the creative people associated with the fair—the artists and the performers. Or you could talk about the behind-the-scenes people—the organizers and the volunteers. Or you could concentrate on the two groups that interact with each other—the artists and the fairgoers.

Patterns for Organizing Your Main Points

Once you've selected the main points for your speech, organize them in a clear and logical pattern. **Patterns of organization** are structures for ordering the main points of your speech that help audience members understand the relationships among your ideas. A clear pattern of organization increases the likelihood that you'll give a successful speech and achieve your specific purpose.[2] Choosing an effective pattern of organization requires careful consideration of your speech topic, general purpose, specific purpose, and thesis.

pattern of organization
A structure for ordering the main points of a speech.

SPEAKING OF ...

A Time Machine

A chronological pattern of organization allows you to move backward as well as forward through time. Filmmakers sometimes use this strategy, essentially revealing the movie's end and then going back to the beginning, as with Steven Spielberg's film *Munich*, about the terrorist attacks on the Israeli Olympic team at the 1972 Games. Presenting events out of chronological sequence works only if your audience members don't know the first step, stage, or event. You need an element of suspense to hold your audience's attention so they'll listen with anticipation to find out what led up to the end—an ending they already know. For example, most people are familiar with today's Internet, but few know about yesterday's (or yesteryear's) Internet, so it's one topic that could fit this pattern.

Table 8.1 Patterns of Organization	Brief Definition	Useful for . . .	Provides Your Audience with . . .	Examples from Student Speeches
Chronological	The way in which something develops or occurs in a time sequence	Recounting the history of a subject, a sequence of events, or a step-by-step procedure	A sense of how a topic unfolds over time	*Topic:* The Job Search *Thesis:* Finding a job requires four steps: self-analysis, résumé development, application, and follow-up.
Spatial	The physical or geographical relationship between objects or places	Describing an object, a place, or how something is designed	A visual understanding of the relationship between the parts of the topic	*Topic:* Badlands National Park *Thesis:* The terrain in the Badlands National Park ranges from soaring pinnacles and spires to flatland prairies.
Topical	Arranged by subtopics of equal importance	Explaining the elements that make up a topic	An image of the subpoints within the topic	*Topic:* Local Public Transportation Can Work for You *Thesis:* The primary modes of public transit in our area are light rail, trolley, and bus.
Narrative	Dramatic retelling of events as a story or a series of short stories	Encouraging audience involvement and participation	A basis for sharing the speaker's point of view	*Topic:* Kayaking Adventure *Thesis:* Kayaking the Menominee River on the Wisconsin–Michigan border was filled with whitewater, white knuckles, and fun.
Cause and Effect	Shows how an action produces a particular outcome	Demonstrating a causal link between two or more events	A view of the relationships between conditions or events	*Topic:* Diabetes and Dieting *Thesis:* Eating too much sugar has caused the recent increase in the number of people with diabetes in the United States.
Problem–Solution	Describes a problem and provides possible solutions	Convincing audience members to agree with a course of action	A rationale for considering a particular solution to a problem	*Topic:* Telecommuting *Thesis:* Because too many people commute long distances to work, more companies should promote telecommuting.
Monroe's Motivated Sequence	Each step designed to facilitate audience involvement and interest	Gaining audience interest or agreement	Reasons to listen and take action	*Topic:* Recycling Old Computers *Thesis:* Recycling old computers protects landfills and groundwater from contamination caused by chemical toxins in computer components.

Speakers commonly rely on seven patterns of organization. **Table 8.1** provides an overview of the organizational patterns discussed in this chapter.

Chronological When you use a **chronological pattern** of organization, you arrange your ideas in a time sequence. For example, in a speech on how to build a birdhouse, you'd start with what listeners need to do first, then explain what they need to do second, and so on, covering each step in order of completion.

chronological pattern
A pattern that organizes a speech by how something develops or occurs in a time sequence.

You can also use the chronological pattern to trace the history of a topic. For example, a speech on the history of the Internet might focus on major events such as the development of ARPANET—the precursor to the Internet—in 1969 and

Tim Berners-Lee's idea for the web 20 years later.[3] These events or turning points would provide main points for the speech:

TOPIC:	History of the Internet
GENERAL PURPOSE:	To inform
SPECIFIC PURPOSE:	To teach my audience about important events in the history of the Internet
THESIS:	There are five key turning points in the history of the Internet: the Advanced Research Projects Agency Network (ARPANET) connects four major U.S. universities, emoticons are first used, Tim Berners-Lee develops the idea for hypertext, Napster is launched, and the Internet of Things outpaces the Internet of people.

MAIN POINTS:

I. In 1969, the ARPANET connects four major U.S. universities.

II. In 1979, members of a science fiction email list use the first emoticons as a way to express emotions online.

III. In 1989, Tim Berners-Lee develops the idea for hypertext, which becomes the basis for the World Wide Web.

IV. In 1999, Shawn Fanning invents Napster, the peer-to-peer file-sharing program.

V. In 2009, the Internet of Things becomes official as more objects than people are connected to the Internet.

spatial pattern
A pattern that organizes a speech by the physical or directional relationship between objects or places.

Spatial Speeches that rely on a **spatial pattern** of organization link points together based on their physical or geographical relationships, such as their locations. This pattern works particularly well for informative and entertaining speeches about places and objects. For example, when you describe a room you identify the objects in it and

A spatial pattern of organization would work well for an informative speech on the solar system.

their place in terms of each other: "As you walk in the room, the bright orange couch is on the far wall, facing the television and the aquarium." An informative speech on the solar system might discuss each planet in order of increasing distance from the sun: Mercury, Venus, Earth, Mars, Jupiter, Saturn, Uranus, and Neptune. Similarly, a speech to entertain about intriguing places you've visited could start with the location farthest from where you're speaking and progress to the closest one.

TOPIC:	Intriguing Places I've Visited
GENERAL PURPOSE:	To entertain
SPECIFIC PURPOSE:	To amuse my audience with the features of some intriguing places I've visited
THESIS:	Maine's haunted Hitchborn Inn, Tennessee's Salt and Pepper Shaker Museum, the Mice Graves of Montana's Boot Hill Cemetery, and Seattle's Underground City are four intriguing places I've visited.

MAIN POINTS:

I. Maine's haunted Hitchborn Inn, near Penobscot Bay, may be the greatest distance from us, but sometimes I still feel the ghosts are right here.

II. As we travel west and south, we come to the Salt and Pepper Shaker Museum in Gatlinburg, Tennessee.

III. Heading west and north, we reach Virginia City, Montana, and the graves of three rogue mice buried in Boot Hill Cemetery.

IV. Finally, as we continue west, we reach the intriguing place closest to us, the Underground City of Seattle.

Topical A **topical pattern** of organization divides a topic into subtopics that address its components, elements, or aspects. For example, in a speech on what you learn about people when they play golf, one of our students discussed the following three points.

topical pattern
A pattern that organizes a speech by arranging subtopics of equal importance.

TOPIC:	Learning about People on the Golf Course
GENERAL PURPOSE:	To inform
SPECIFIC PURPOSE:	To inform my audience about what it can learn about people when they're playing golf
THESIS:	When people play golf, they reveal how they handle the unexpected, their level of patience, and their concern for others.

MAIN POINTS:

I. Observing people as they play golf gives you insight into how they handle unexpected events.

II. Observing people as they play golf gives you a good indication of how patient they are.

III. Observing people as they play golf lets you know how—or if—they show concern for other people.

Patrick Tuohy/Shutterstock.com

A topical pattern of organization works well for a speech on what you can learn about people when they play golf.

These points are clearly relevant to the main topic, what you learn about people by observing them playing golf. However, points also related to golf, such as "Golf is a great game to play" or "You can play golf at any age," would not be appropriate for this speech because they are not subtopics of the topic the speaker is focusing on.

Narrative With a **narrative pattern** of organization, you structure your main points in story form. Speeches of tribute and introduction often follow a narrative format. Listeners find stories compelling and memorable, which makes the narrative pattern an engaging organizational option.[4]

Many stories follow this sequence: setting the scene, describing an initial conflict, increasing action, escalating conflict, taking conflict to its peak, and arriving at the final outcome.[5]

Consider an informative speech on the Atlantic City Boardwalk.[6]

narrative pattern
A pattern that organizes a speech by a dramatic retelling of events as a story or a series of short stories.

TOPIC:	The History of Atlantic City's Boardwalk
GENERAL PURPOSE:	To inform
SPECIFIC PURPOSE:	To inform my audience about the history of Atlantic City's Boardwalk
THESIS:	The history of Atlantic City's Boardwalk involves sand, bootleggers, soldiers, casinos, resorts, and hurricanes.

MAIN POINTS:

I. The Boardwalk in Atlantic City was first built in 1870 to keep sand out of buildings and public transportation near the beach. (*setting the scene*)

II. In the 1920s—during Prohibition—lax enforcement of liquor laws in Atlantic City made the Boardwalk a popular spot for tourists and bootleggers. (*initial conflict*)

III. World War II brought soldiers to the Boardwalk for training and beachfront exercises. (*increasing action*)

IV. Legalized gambling in 1976 brought new attention—both good and bad—to the Boardwalk. (*escalating conflict*)

V. Controversy erupted over tax breaks for resorts near the Boardwalk in the early 2000s (*peak conflict*)

VI. Finally, Hurricane Sandy demolished part of the Boardwalk in 2012. (*final outcome*)

cause-and-effect pattern
A pattern that organizes a speech by showing how an action produces a particular outcome.

Cause and Effect The **cause-and-effect pattern** of organization relies on the idea of one action leading to or bringing about another. When using this pattern, clearly and carefully link the cause with the effect, providing appropriate and effective supporting materials. Although most often used for persuasive speeches, the cause-and-effect pattern also can be applied to informative speeches. For example, an informative speech on the positive effects of meditation works well with a cause-and-effect pattern of organization.

TOPIC:	Positive Effects of Meditation
GENERAL PURPOSE:	To inform
SPECIFIC PURPOSE:	To inform my audience about the positive effects of meditation
THESIS:	By using less oxygen, lowering your heart rate, and altering your brain waves, meditation helps you relax, feel more content, and think more creatively.

MAIN POINTS:

I. Meditation causes three changes in your body.
  - **A.** When you meditate, you use less oxygen.
  - **B.** When you meditate, you lower your heart rate.
  - **C.** When you meditate, your theta brain waves—those associated with daydreaming—increase in frequency.

II. These three changes in your body as you meditate have three main effects.
  - **A.** You feel more relaxed.
  - **B.** You feel more content.
  - **C.** You think more creatively.

When you use the cause-and-effect pattern for a persuasive speech, your audience must come to agree with you about what causes a particular circumstance or event. Consider the topic of homelessness in the United States.

TOPIC:	Homelessness in the United States
GENERAL PURPOSE:	To persuade
SPECIFIC PURPOSE:	To convince my audience that lack of education is one cause of homelessness
THESIS:	Many people in the United States become homeless because they lack educational opportunities.

MAIN POINTS:

I. Serious inequities in the American educational system mean some people have limited educational opportunities.
  - **A.** These inequities start in elementary schools, with unequal funding even within the same city.
  - **B.** These inequities continue in higher education, with students from poorer neighborhoods less likely to attend the top schools.

II. Inequities in the American education system result in two effects that contribute to homelessness in the United States.
  - **A.** Without a good education, individuals can't get the jobs they need to pay for a place to live.
  - **B.** Without a good education, individuals don't have the resources to adapt to economic downturns.

If your listeners agree with the initial cause—inequities in the U.S. educational system—they will be more inclined to agree that the effects contribute to homelessness. In contrast, if listeners disagree with the cause you cite, or identify different causes, your speech will be less persuasive.

problem–solution pattern
A pattern that organizes a speech by describing a problem and providing possible solutions.

Problem–Solution When speakers use a **problem–solution pattern** of organization, they're attempting to convince audience members that a specific dilemma or problem requires a particular course of action or solution. Clearly establishing that a problem exists provides the foundation for persuading the audience that the solution should be implemented. Imagine that the football team at your school perpetually loses money, using more funds than it produces. A persuasive speech that proposes to terminate the football program would be appropriate. If listeners don't think there's a problem, however, they're unlikely to support your solution.

TOPIC:	Ending the Football Program on Our Campus
GENERAL PURPOSE:	To persuade
SPECIFIC PURPOSE:	To convince my audience that we should no longer have a football program at our school
THESIS:	The football program at our school drains resources from our campus, so it should be eliminated.

MAIN POINTS:

I. The football program at our school loses money each year.
II. The football program drains money from the school's budget that could be used for other programs.
III. Our school's football program should be eliminated.

In addition, speakers must demonstrate that the proposed solution will adequately address the issue described and can be reasonably implemented. For example, let's say you identify air pollution as a problem and suggest limiting every household in the United States to one vehicle as a remedy. Audience members, especially in the United States, likely would view your solution as too extreme and difficult to implement. So rather than ask audience members to give up their cars, you could suggest a smaller step and ask them to give up driving one day each week. This solution provides a balanced response to the problem and also presents a behavioral change that listeners might consider reasonable.

Monroe's motivated sequence
A five-step pattern of organization that requires speakers to identify and respond to what will motivate an audience to pay attention.

Monroe's Motivated Sequence This pattern encourages speakers to focus on audience outcomes when organizing ideas. Composed of five steps, **Monroe's motivated sequence** requires that speakers identify and respond to what will motivate the audience to pay attention.[7]

Step 1. Gaining the audience's attention: The speaker relates the topic to listeners, linking it to their lives and providing them with a reason to listen.

Step 2. Establishing the need for something or the existence of a problem: The speaker shows listeners that they lack important information or that there's an issue requiring their attention.

Step 3. Satisfying the problem: The speaker provides audience members with the information they lack or the solution to the problem.

Step 4. Helping audience members visualize an outcome: The speaker describes for them what will happen if they apply or don't apply the solution.

Step 5. Moving an audience to action: The speaker details how audience members can implement the solution.

For the motivated sequence to work, each step must build on the previous one. If earlier steps don't elicit the desired audience response, then the later steps will fall short as well. The motivated sequence can be used for both informative and persuasive speeches (**Table 8.2**).

The first three steps—attention, need, and satisfaction—give you the basic structure for an informative speech (Chapter 13). The motivated sequence can prove especially effective with an informative speech topic that may not instantly resonate with your audience. By focusing on gaining the audience's attention at the start, the motivated sequence helps you encourage your audience to listen. Giving a speech on opera to an audience unfamiliar with it provides a good example. First, get your audience's attention by playing a very short audio clip from a contemporary opera. In the next step, show the audience why they need to know more about opera by highlighting its popularity around the world, the drama and mystery of each opera's story line, and the timeless topics of courage, love, betrayal, and deceit. Finally, in the satisfaction step, explain one of the more popular operas, such as *The Pirates of Penzance,* and demonstrate how its themes resonate with people today, giving your audience the information they need to appreciate opera.

Adding the visualization step to a speech represents a key move from an informative to a persuasive speech—a speech that focuses on changing listeners' beliefs, attitudes, or

Table 8.2 **Monroe's Motivated Sequence for Informative and Persuasive Speeches**

Step	Speaker's Action	Audience's Response	Speech Purpose
Attention	Relate topic to audience to gain attention.	I will listen because this is relevant to me.	
Need	Show that there's information the audience needs to know. (*informative speech*) *or* Establish the problem or current harm. (*persuasive speech*)	There is important information I'm lacking. (*informative speech*) *or* There's a problem that needs my attention. (*persuasive speech*)	Informative
Satisfaction	Present information that audience members lack. (*informative speech*) *or* Describe the solution to the problem. (*persuasive speech*)	Here is the information I need to know. (*informative speech*) *or* Here's the solution to the problem. (*persuasive speech*)	
Visualization	Show audience the benefits of the proposed solution or the costs of not implementing the solution or both.	I can visualize the benefits of this solution or the costs of not implementing this solution or both.	Persuasive (influence attitudes, beliefs, and values)
Action	Explain how the audience can implement the proposed solution.	I will do this.	Persuasive (influence actions)

© David Schmitz Photography

Monroe's motivated sequence works well when you want to convince your audience to take some kind of action.

opinions. In asking listeners to visualize the benefits or costs associated with a particular solution, the speaker seeks to modify how the audience thinks about something. Say you wanted to persuade your audience that video games should promote more cooperation and less competition. In the attention step, you might pique your audience's interest by countering video game stereotypes, providing information such as "Did you know that women account for nearly 45 percent of video game players and that the average age of a player is 35?" You could also provide a new view on the problem by telling your audience about the importance of learning to work with others and about the lack of games that foster cooperation rather than violent competition. The satisfaction step then becomes obvious: Create and promote video games based on cooperation rather than competition. For the visualization step, you could suggest that facilitating the ability to cooperate with others contributes more to society. In this step, you could imagine for your audience situations in which individuals cooperate more to accomplish tasks, rather than competing in unproductive ways.

For a speech in which you want to influence the audience's action, you add the action step (Chapter 14). This step may seem similar to the satisfaction step, but the action step includes much greater detail—you want your audience to implement your suggestions. Consider a speech about simplifying your life. You'd begin your speech with the attention step, possibly presenting statistics on how much Americans work and consume in relation to the rest of the world. In the need step, you might draw attention to the ways in which audience members needlessly complicate their lives and the resulting harms. This leads to the satisfaction step, where you'd discuss in general the idea of simplifying our lives. The topic lends itself to visualizing both the benefits of simplification and the costs of a life grounded in consumerism. The action step then details exactly how audience members might simplify their lives, such as gardening, changing spending habits, reducing clutter, and consuming responsibly.

You've learned about seven patterns for organizing your speech: chronological, spatial, topical, narrative, cause and effect, problem–solution, and Monroe's motivated sequence. **Table 8.3** demonstrates how the discussion of one topic, voting, changes based on which organizational pattern you apply.

Table 8.3 Applying Patterns of Organization to a Single Topic: Voting

Pattern	General Purpose	Specific Purpose	Thesis	Main Points
Chronological	To inform	To teach my audience about key amendments to the U.S. Constitution in the history of voting in the United States.	Three amendments to the Constitution changed voting in the United States: the 15th, 19th, and 24th Amendments.	I. The 15th Amendment to the U.S. Constitution granted all U.S. citizens the right to vote regardless of race, color, or previous condition of servitude. II. The 19th Amendment gave women the right to vote. III. The 24th Amendment ended the practice of poll taxing, or forcing people to pay a tax to vote.
Spatial	To inform	To help my audience understand the layout of a typical ballot.	The layout of a ballot includes four main sections: the election's title and description, the instructions, a list of individuals and items to vote on, and the space to record the vote.	I. The election's title and description are at the top of the ballot. II. How to complete the ballot is explained next. III. Candidates, proposals, propositions, and initiatives are listed in a specified order. IV. Space to record your vote is usually to the right of each item.
Topical	To inform	To make my audience aware of how voting occurs in other democratic countries.	The Philippines, South Africa, and Australia provide examples of democratic countries whose voting systems differ from ours.	I. The Philippines' voting system II. South Africa's voting system III. Australia's voting system
Narrative	To entertain	To share with my audience the lighter side of getting out the vote for student elections on a college campus.	My adventures in getting out the vote for student government elections on my campus nearly ended my college career but finished on an unexpected note.	I. My campus's student election day was more like doomsday for me. II. Getting out the vote almost got me expelled from school. III. My political science advisor suggested I change my major. IV. The ending of this story surprised even me.
Cause and effect	To persuade	To persuade my audience that the United States needs standardized federal voting regulations.	The lack of consistency in voting rules and procedures across states in our country has led to voting problems on election day.	I. Local and state governments are in charge of voting procedures. II. Variation in voting standards has led to ballot counting problems at the national, state, and local levels.
Problem–solution	To persuade	To encourage my audience to consider alternative voting procedures in the United States.	Giving people greater flexibility in how they vote will solve the problem of not being able to reach a polling place on election day.	I. Many people don't vote because they have difficulty getting to their polling places on election day. II. Alternative voting methods, such as mailed ballots, will solve the problem of not being able to get to the polls.
Monroe's motivated sequence	To persuade	To persuade my audience to vote.	One important part of exercising your voice in a democratic society is voting in every election.	I. Although voter participation in the last election was up, only about 50% of eligible voters cast a vote. (*attention*) II. A healthy democracy requires voter participation. (*need*) III. You must vote. (*satisfaction*) IV. There are benefits to voting and costs to not voting. (*visualization*) V. These are the steps you need to take to vote. (*action*)

Connecting Your Ideas with Transitions

coherence
An obvious and plausible connection among ideas.

transition
A word, phrase, sentence, or paragraph used throughout a speech to mark locations in the organization and clearly link the parts of a speech together.

Effective speaking demands more than researching your topic well and developing a logical way to organize your material. Your speech must also have **coherence**, an obvious and plausible connection among your ideas. **Transitions** play an important role in creating coherence: They help direct your audience from one idea or part of your speech to the next.[8] Effective transitions allow you to:

- Move smoothly and clearly from the introduction to the body of the speech.
- Move from one main point to the next main point within the body of the speech.
- Exit from the body of the speech to the conclusion.

Table 8.4 provides examples of transition words and phrases.

Use brief, clear transitions to make it as effortless as possible for listeners to navigate through the content of your speech. This section more closely examines how you can use transitions in three key places identified below.

Introducing the First Main Point

signpost
A transition that indicates a key move in the speech, making its organization clear to the audience.

After you've given your speech introduction, you're ready to move on to the first main point in the body of your speech. To accomplish this task smoothly, include a brief transition to **signpost** the direction of your speech. Signposts, which include ordering transitions such as *first, next,* and *finally,* let audience members know where you are in a speech, where you're going, and how your points relate to one another. You might say,

- "Now, let me elaborate on that first point I referred to in the introduction (*then refer to the first point*) .... "
- "As I mentioned, we'll first consider (*first point*) ...."
- "To begin, I'll describe (*first point*) ...."

After voicing the transition, begin discussing your first main point.

Transitions between Main Points

When you shift from one main point to the next within the body of the speech, use internal transitions that clearly signpost the direction in which you're going. Here are

Table 8.4 Types of Transitions

Type of Transition	Word or Phrase	Example
Ordering	*first, second, third; next, then, finally*	First, I'll review the history of the missions in California.
Reinforcing	*similarly, also, likewise, in addition, moreover, further*	Also, you could volunteer as a tutor in a local elementary school.
Contrasting	*however, yet, in contrast, whereas, unless, although, even though, instead*	However, your best strategy is to prepare well in advance.
Chronology or time	*when, while, now, before, after, currently, recently then, during, later, meanwhile*	During this process you must keep a close watch on your time.
Causality	*therefore, so, consequently, since, because, for this reason, with this in mind*	Therefore, learning to manage your money now will help you avoid problems in the future.
Summarizing or concluding	*in summary, let me summarize, finally, let's review, as I've discussed*	Finally, good study habits require evaluating what works and what doesn't.

some examples of what you might say as you move through the body of a speech on human biological cell cloning:

- "Now that I've described what human biological cell cloning is, let's turn to my second main point, the advantages human cloning offers to medical research...."
- "We've learned the basics of human biological cell cloning. Now let's consider what it offers to medical research...."
- "As you can tell, human biological cell cloning is a complex and intriguing subject. Equally intriguing is the potential for medical research, which I want to elaborate on...."

Internal summaries are longer transitions that also help listeners move from one main point to the next. These transitions remind listeners of previously presented information so that they have a solid grasp of those ideas before you move on to the next point. The following example, from an informative speech on the International Spy Museum in Washington, D.C., uses chronological transitions.

internal summary
A review of main points or subpoints given before going on to the next point in a speech.

> So you'll start your tour of the museum by learning about the basics of espionage and choosing your own cover identity. Fully engaging in this first part of the museum provides the essential framework for enjoying the remainder of your tour. The spy gadgets, weapons, and bugs you'll find in the next exhibit are all the more fascinating when you think about them in terms of your spy identity. Then you'll view those tricks of the trade in action in the third part of the museum, which focuses on the history of spying. Some of the secret spies will surprise you. Now let's turn to more recent history presented in the International Spy Museum.

With eight main exhibits, as well as special exhibits, listeners may well lose track of the information presented earlier. Refreshing their memories about the first three exhibits discussed allows the speaker to move with confidence to the next main point, the fourth exhibit.

In the next example, the speaker uses reinforcing and contrasting transitions in an internal summary during a persuasive speech on the need for greater security in radio frequency identification tags.

> Before I move on, let's briefly review the basics of radio frequency identification tags, or RFIDs. These ID tags are becoming commonplace. We use them for our pets—the computer chips we implant that contain information in case our pets get lost. RFIDs are used in the new electronic passports issued by the U.S. government. These tiny chips contain personal information such as your name, birthplace, and date of birth. Additionally, the electronic passports include a digital photograph designed for use with face-recognition software. RFIDs can hold a great deal of information—your medical records, financial history, and other personal data. They're cheap to produce and easy to manufacture. However, as we'll see next, they're also easy to infect with computer viruses.

This internal summary provides an essential link between the explanation of what RFIDs are used for and the potential problems computer viruses could cause.

Internal summaries perform two functions for the speaker:

1. They remind the audience of the key points the speaker has talked about, and
2. they link previous points with the upcoming one.

The more you reinforce your ideas by reminding audience members of what you said—without becoming repetitious and long winded—the greater the likelihood they'll remember your points.

Transitions to the Conclusion

Letting your audience know you're moving from the final main point to the end of your speech prepares them for the conclusion. The transition to the conclusion requires little more than a few words or a phrase. Link the transition from your last main point to the actual content of the conclusion as seamlessly as possible. Consider these examples that use summarizing, or concluding, phrases:

- "In summary, I've covered key points about (*transition and review main points*)...."
- "Let's review the main issues to keep in mind (*transition and review main points*)...."

When you use a transition to signal your audience that the end of your speech is near, they will expect you to finish shortly. For speeches of 10 minutes or less, that generally means no more than a minute for the conclusion.

Outlining Your Speech: The Working, Complete-Sentence, and Speaking Outlines

MindTap®

Go to your MindTap for help with developing your outlines.

Outlining your speech helps you identify the order for your ideas and develop a map or plan for how those ideas fit together.[9] Recall that as you're developing your speeches you'll create three different outlines:

1. the working outline for initially identifying the main ideas you want to address (Chapter 4),
2. the complete-sentence outline for elaborating on your points (covered in this chapter), and
3. the speaking outline for giving your speech (Chapter 12).

Table 8.5 reviews these outlines.

The Purpose and Format of the Working Outline

working outline
An outline that guides you during the initial stages of topic development, helping to keep you focused on your general purpose and clarify your specific purpose.

The **working outline** helps you through the initial phases of developing your speech, especially researching your topic. You start the working outline when you first decide on your topic. Begin your working outline by identifying the topic, general purpose, specific purpose, thesis statement, and possible main points. You may revise your specific purpose and thesis as you research your speech topic, but having an idea at the start of

Table 8.5 Types of Outlines

Type of Outline	Functions	Key Features	Use When . . .
Working	Assists in initial topic development; guides research.	Includes main points and possible subpoints; revised during research process.	developing your speech topic and conducting your research.
Complete-sentence	Clearly identifies all the pieces of information for the speech; puts ideas in order; forms the basis for developing the speaking outline.	Uses complete sentences; lists all sections of speech and all references; revised during preparation process.	you've completed your research and you're ready to put together your ideas and construct your entire speech.
Speaking	Assists you in practicing and giving your speech.	Uses keywords; revised as you practice your speech; often transferred to note cards for use during practice and the final presentation.	you practice and present your speech.

what you plan to do will help keep you on track. For example, if you're giving a speech on the World's Fair, your working outline based just on what you know about the topic might look like this:

TOPIC:	World's Fair
GENERAL PURPOSE:	To inform
SPECIFIC PURPOSE:	To educate my audience about the history of the World's Fair
THESIS:	The World's Fair has a nearly 200-year-old history that reflects major cultural changes around the globe.

MAIN POINTS:

I. Origins in France.
II. 16 in the U.S.
III. Focus has changed over time
IV. World's Fair today.

As you research the World's Fair, you find that you need to update your working outline; your revisions are something along these lines:

TOPIC:	Historical Themes of the World's Fair
GENERAL PURPOSE:	To inform
SPECIFIC PURPOSE:	To educate my audience about the major themes in the history of the World's Fair
THESIS:	In the course of its more than 150-year history, the World's Fair has centered on these three themes: technological innovations, intercultural communication, and national image.

MAIN POINTS:

I. Mid-1800s–early 1900s—focus on latest advances in technology
II. Mid-1900s—focus on improving intercultural understandings
III. Late 1900s—focus on promoting national image
IV. Today—combination of all three

REFERENCES:

Greenhalgh, P. (2011). *Fair world: A history of World's Fairs and Expositions from London to Shanghai 1851–2010*. Winterbourne, Berkshire, UK: Papadakis.
Harvey, B. (2014). *World's Fair in a southern accent: Atlanta, Nashville, and Charleston, 1895–1902*. Knoxville, TN: University of Tennessee.
Kunitake, K., & Sheinberg, H. (2015). It happened at the World's Fair. *National Geographic Traveler*, *32*(3), 49–54.

As you can observe, the main points are quite basic—just keywords. However, you've found several useful sources that you can mine for more information and ideas. As you learn more about your topic, you'll add subpoints to your main points and develop a more complete list of references.

Figure 8.3 Basic Outline Format

I. First main point
    A. First subpoint
        1. First sub-subpoint
        2. Second sub-subpoint
            a. First sub-sub-subpoint
            b. Second sub-sub-subpoint
                i. First sub-sub-sub-subpoint
                ii. Second sub-sub-sub-subpoint

The Purpose and Format of the Complete-Sentence Outline

While the working outline gives you general directions for researching and organizing your speeches and the speaking outline helps you practice and present your speech, the **complete-sentence outline** offers a highly detailed description of your ideas and how they're related to one another. The complete-sentence outline provides much greater depth than the other two types of outlines. In the complete- or full-sentence outline, you'll use complete sentences that clearly reflect your thinking and research on your topic.[10]

complete-sentence outline A formal outline using full sentences for all points developed after researching the speech and identifying supporting materials; includes a speech's topic, general purpose, specific purpose, thesis, introduction, main points, subpoints, conclusion, transitions, and references.

All outlines use symbols and indentation to provide a visual representation of how a speech is organized. Outlines show the priority of your ideas, from first to last, and how they're related. Typically, uppercase roman numerals (I, II, III) indicate the main points of the speech, and these points sit at the left margin of the page. For the first subpoints under a main point, indent one level and use a capital letter (A, B, C). For sub-subpoints, use arabic numbers (1, 2, 3) and indent another level. For lengthy speeches, you might need to add sub-sub-subpoints, using lowercase letters (a, b, c) and indenting another level, and sub-sub-sub-subpoints, using lowercase roman numerals (i, ii, iii,) and indenting once again. A period follows each number or letter, as shown in **Figure 8.3**.

Some basic rules provide the guidance you need for formatting your complete-sentence outline.

Preface the Outline with Identifying Information Just like with the working outline, listing your topic, general purpose, specific purpose, and thesis at the top of your complete-sentence outline keeps you on track as you develop your speech. Clearly label each item, as in this example:

TOPIC:	Taking Good Photographs
GENERAL PURPOSE:	To inform
SPECIFIC PURPOSE:	To demonstrate to my audience how to take good photographs
THESIS:	Key guidelines for taking good photographs are to get close, avoid background clutter, go for the action, and check your light source.

List Your Main Points in Order List main points in the order you'll present them. You'll identify the main points of your speech like this:

I. First main point
II. Second main point
III. Third main point

State Points and Subpoints in Complete Sentences Writing out your points and subpoints as complete sentences helps you elaborate on your thoughts. Your working outline, which includes just keywords or phrases, represents the rudiments of your speech—your ideas before you fully developed them. In the complete-sentence outline, you articulate your thoughts more clearly by writing out your points and subpoints in

Table 8.6 Main Points for the Working and Complete-Sentence Outlines

Main Points in the Working Outline	Main Points in the Complete-Sentence Outline
I. Mid-1800s–early 1900s—focus on latest advances in technology	I. From their start in 1851 to the early 1930s, World's Fairs or Expos featured the latest advances in science and technology, displaying recent inventions and innovations.
II. Mid-1900s—focus on improving intercultural understandings	II. In the mid-1900s, the World's Fairs promoted culture exchange and intercultural understanding, encouraging attendees to learn more about world cultures.
III. Late 1900s—focus on promoting host country	III. In the late 1900s the World's Fairs became a platform for nations to present a positive image to the world, with countries building elaborate structures to showcase their successes.
IV. Today—combination of all three	IV. Today, the World's Fairs integrate all three themes, highlighting technological innovations, facilitating intercultural communication, and offering a venue for countries to polish their images.

complete sentences. In addition, each main point or subpoint expresses only one idea, so use just one sentence for each point.

Comparing the main points of the working and complete-sentence outlines for the speech on the World's Fair, demonstrates key differences between the two types of outlines (**Table 8.6**). The complete-sentence outline shows how each point is developed. For example, the sentence "Practical considerations in choosing a major include the department's reputation, the time it will take to graduate, the job market, possible salary, and requirements for the major" suggests five subpoints within that main point. In the working outline, the phrase "practical considerations" doesn't give enough information about how the speaker might elaborate on that point.

Maintain Levels of Importance All items at the same level on the outline should have the same level of importance—that is, all main points must be equally important in relation to your topic, all subpoints must be equally important in relation to a main point, and so on. For example, in a speech on business etiquette, the main points might be:

I. Telephone etiquette is necessary for the four parts of a phone conversation.
II. Face-to-face etiquette is necessary for the three parts of an in-person conversation.
III. Online etiquette is necessary for the three parts of a message exchange.

All three items are of equal importance because they discuss ways to communicate. A fourth main point about "etiquette with the boss" wouldn't fit because it refers to a specific person you might communicate with at work, an idea that is subordinate to the main points about ways in which people communicate.

Subordinate Ideas That Support Your Main Points Subordinate points are those that fall under your main points, providing evidence and information that support your main ideas. In the speech on business etiquette, the first main point and subpoints might look something like this:

I. Telephone etiquette is necessary for the four parts of a phone conversation.
 A. There are etiquette rules for answering the telephone.
 B. There are etiquette rules for placing a call.
 C. There are etiquette rules for fulfilling your obligations during the phone conversation.
 D. There are etiquette rules for ending a call.

In this example, each subpoint provides a piece of information that supports the main idea that etiquette rules apply to different parts of a telephone conversation.

Check the Number of Subpoints If you can't identify at least two pieces of information to support a point or subpoint, then reexamine how you're organizing your ideas, consider conducting additional research, or determine whether the point really requires additional explanation. An informative speech on media literacy might include the following main points and subpoints:

I. Media literacy requires that an individual be an effective consumer and producer of mediated communication.
    A. Media literacy differs from information literacy.
    B. Media literacy differs from digital literacy.
II. Media literacy has three components.
    A. The first component is analyzing mediated communication.
    B. The second component is evaluating mediated communication.
    C. The third component is creating mediated communication.
III. There are three ways to determine whether you're media literate.
    A. Analyze media messages such as television news.
    B. Evaluate media messages such as magazine advertisements.
    C. Create media messages such as webpages.

Notice that each main point has at least two subpoints. For example, if the third main point had been as follows, you'd have to question the strength of the main idea:

I. There's a test for media literacy.
    A. Take the test for media literacy.

Should you just drop it from the speech? Search for more information? Audience members probably would be curious about their media literacy, so stating the main point more clearly and then elaborating on it would be the best choice.

Include and Label Your Introduction, Conclusion, and Transitions Because the preparation outline includes every detail of your speech, incorporate your introduction, conclusion, and transitions into your outline. Some instructors may ask you to write out your introduction and conclusion word for word in paragraph form. Others may ask you to outline those parts of your speech, as shown in the sample complete-sentence outline at the end of this chapter. In addition, label your transitions as shown in the sample outline. This will help you remember to use them when you give your speech.

Use a Consistent System of Symbols and Indentation Generally, speakers use the following system of symbols and indentation:

I. First main point
    A. First subpoint
        1. First sub-subpoint
            a. First sub-sub-subpoint
            b. Second sub-sub-subpoint
        2. Second sub-subpoint
    B. Second subpoint

List References for Your Speech At the end of your outline, list the references for your speech—the sources of all the supporting material you included. In the sample complete-sentence outline in the next section of this chapter, the references are listed using the formatting rules of the American Psychological Association. Some instructors require students to use the Modern Language Association reference formatting rules.[11] Check with your instructor to find out how you should format your references. **Figure 8.4** provides an example of a complete-sentence outline.

Figure 8.4 Sample Complete-Sentence Outline

Tyler Schmidt, San José State University

Courtesy of Tyler Schmidt

Tyler Schmidt

TOPIC: California State Parks

GENERAL PURPOSE: To persuade

SPECIFIC PURPOSE: To convince my audience to take steps to save California's state parks

THESIS: California parks face many problems, but working together, we can implement solutions to save them.

INTRODUCTION: Finals week is just a few weeks away here at San José State University and, like many of the students here, the next few weeks will be very stressful to me. The best way I have found to relieve this stress is to get outside, get some much-needed fresh air, and enjoy some beautiful scenery. All the amazing parks that we explored during my speech on public land given in this classroom on November 7th offer these sources of stress relief, but if we are not careful these parks will start disappearing. Today I am going to discuss the problems these great parks face, solutions to the park's problems, what will happen if we do not implement the solutions, and what we can all do to implement these solutions.

I. California state parks have been put in danger due to the economic status of our state.

- **A.** Due to state budget cuts m any California state parks, including some of the parks I showed you right here near SJSU, have faced the possibility of closure in the past year.
  - **1.** The *Huffington Post* stated on November 17th that 70 California state parks were slated to close as of July of this year, but 65 were able to remain open due to nonprofits, local governments, and other sources.
  - **2.** Save Our State Parks, a campaign to save California's state parks, states that even with all of the help that saved 65 out of the 70 parks, "We are not out of the woods yet, not even close. California's entire state park system remains threatened."
- **B.** "In the more than 40-year history of CSPF, we've never seen our state parks system at as much risk as it is today," said Elizabeth Goldstein, president of California State Parks Foundation.

II. Solutions to saving the state parks that surround us come in many different forms of support.

- **A.** When somebody asks me to support something, the first thing that comes to mind is a donation of time or money.

(Continued)

Figure 8.4 Continued

1. Seventy percent of us in this class stated that they would donate money or time on the survey that was taken on October 17th, 2012.
2. It is stated that California state parks rely heavily on volunteers for survival on the Save Our State Parks website.

B. In addition to volunteering, we can all support and enact legislation that keeps state parks open and protected.

C. Considering that only 61 percent of us in this class know about the endangerment of many California state parks, the parks could be supported simply by spreading the word about California state parks.

D. Also, many people may not realize it but we can support the parks just by going and enjoying them without any inconvenience to ourselves.

III. Supporting the parks provides several benefits, while not supporting the parks will have negative consequences.

A. If we support the parks and enjoy what they have to offer we will receive physical health, mental health, and social health benefits.
1. If we make a habit of going to any of these parks and being active it is going to increase our fitness level.
2. In addition, the beautiful scenery of these parks can take our mind off of other stresses in our lives.
3. Also, these parks provide activities to do with family and friends and open up opportunities to meet new people.

B. If we do not support these parks, we are only going to hurt ourselves and the community surrounding the parks.
1. We will lose the benefits and resources that these parks have to offer if they start closing down.
2. In addition, there are many businesses that rely on these parks to stay afloat.
   a. "With over 70 million visits annually, California's state parks are an important economic engine to the local communities in which they are located, generating over $6 billion in overall economic activity across the state" states Save State Parks.
   b. Also, Save State Parks states, "California's travel and tourism industry including hotels, locally-owned bed and breakfast establishments, restaurants, retail shops, tour operations and many more businesses that rely on parks for visitation and economic activity will be negatively impacted."

IV. Many of us may be wondering how we are supposed to go about supporting all of these parks.

A. For those of us willing to donate time and/or money, every little bit helps.
1. There are a number of organizations that support local parks that are endangered of closing.
   a. The Pine Ridge Association supports Henry Coe State Park in Morgan Hill.
   b. Castle Rock State Park in Los Gatos, another park I talked about in a previous speech, would have been shut down if it were not for the support of organizations like the Portola and Castle Rock Foundation.
2. If you research these organizations, they will provide information on how you can help.

B. In order to spread the word about state parks, I would like us all to take a challenge.
1. I want everybody in here to tell five friends about what our local state parks have to offer and how we can all easily support them.
2. Then we all need to challenge our friends and family to do the same.

Figure 8.4 **Continued**

C. You may be wondering how just going to these parks will benefit you personally.
   1. These parks offer hiking trails and areas for picnicking that could make for an adventurous and romantic date with a loved one.
   2. In addition, you could get a group of friends together and turn visiting these parks into a fun social experience.
   3. Moreover, anyone of us could make visiting these parks a new family tradition.
      a. We could make plans to go on an annual holiday hike with our families.
      b. Also, we could show our families these parks when they come to visit.
      c. I know from personal experience visiting these parks offer excellent bonding experiences; I often visit parks with my father, and it opens up opportunities to spend time and socialize with him.

CONCLUSION: Beautiful parks all over the state are endangered because our state government is cutting the parks budget in order to make up a huge deficit, but we can all help through many forms of support. Supporting these parks benefits us all personally as well as the parks, and we can all do our part without creating much of a burden for ourselves. By supporting our local parks we can preserve areas that enable us to experience a natural environment.

WORKS CITED:

Dearen, J. (2012, June 28). California state parks closure: 65 of 70 slated to close will stay open. *The Huffington Post*. Retrieved from huffingtonpost.com/2012/06/28/california-state-parks-closure_n_1635713.html

Save Our State Parks. (2011). Closing parks is bad for business. Retrieved from savestateparks.org/badforbusiness.html

Save Our State Parks. (2011). Parks in crisis. Retrieved from savestateparks.org/parksincrisis.html

Save Our State Parks. (2011). Support legislation. Retrieved from savestateparks.org/supportlegislation.html

State of California Resources Agency. (2005). The health and social benefits of recreation. Retrieved from parks.ca.gov/pages/795/files/benefits%20final%20online%20v6-1-05.pdf

The Pine Ridge Association at Henry W. Coe State Park. (2013). Uniformed volunteer program. Retrieved from http://coepark.net/pineridgeassociation/support-coe/ununifomed-volunteer-program

The Portola and Castle Rock Foundation. (n.d.). Retrieved from http://www.portolaandcastlerockfound.org/

The Purpose and Format of the Speaking Outline

speaking outline
An outline that distills a complete-sentence outline, listing only the words and phrases that will guide the speaker through the main parts of the speech and the transitions between them.

The **speaking outline** for a speech distills your complete-sentence outline into key words and phrases that capture the essence of your speech. When you give your speech, the speaking outline allows you to:

- Refer comfortably and precisely to the information you have gathered.
- Present that information in a clear and organized way.
- Engage your audience personally and professionally during the speech.

As you practice your speech, you'll revise your speaking outline so that it serves as a reliable resource for presenting your speech. A speaking outline makes it possible for a well-prepared speaker to deliver an abundance of ideas effectively.

keywords
Words that identify a subject or a point of primary interest or concern.

The **keywords** in a speaking outline are very similar to the keywords or search terms you use online: They identify subjects or points of primary interest or concern. Keywords represent the most important points you want to talk about in your speech and serve as reminders for the ideas you want to cover. Because they're listed in the same order as the sentences in your complete-sentence outline, they indicate the order in which you want to present those points.

Although speaking outlines are usually quite short, they can be created only after you've fully researched and developed your speech. As you use your speaking outline or note cards to practice your speech, you'll find that you need to move back and forth between your complete-sentence outline and your speaking outline, revising the former and then the latter several times. Each time, you'll be challenged to condense your ideas and information into keywords for your speaking outline that will trigger your memory as you present your speech. **Figure 8.5** shows an example of a speaking outline.

Summary

Organizing your speech effectively helps you provide a clear message for your audience. Every speech includes four key parts: introduction, body, transitions, and conclusion.

The body of the speech comprises most of what you'll present: your main points and supporting materials. As you select and then develop your main points, apply the principles of clarity, relevance, and balance. Your main points must support your specific purpose and clearly indicate the response you want from your audience. In addition, main points must be relevant both to your topic and to one another, and they must be balanced in terms of their relative importance.

Seven patterns of organization are commonly used to organize a speech: chronological, spatial, topical, narrative, cause and effect, problem–solution, and Monroe's motivated sequence. An effective pattern of organization complements your topic, specific purpose, and audience.

Transitions link together the elements of your speech. Types of transitions include ordering, reinforcing, contrasting, chronology, causality, and summarizing or concluding. Key places to use transitions are between the introduction and the first main point, between main points, and between the last main point and the conclusion.

Figure 8.5 Sample Speaking Outline

TITLE: The History and Etiquette of Chopsticks

ATTENTION GETTER: [hold chopsticks and click together twice] Why are these called chopsticks?

Because [click, click] they help you eat fast!

THESIS: Chopsticks have a central place in the eating etiquette of several Asian cultures.

PREVIEW: First, I'll tell you about the history of chopsticks in the four "chopstick" countries: China, Vietnam, Japan, and Korea. Then I'll talk about how each culture has developed its own chopsticks etiquette.

I. History
- **A.** China: origin—5000 years ago
  - **1.** Confucius influence
  - **2.** Cook over fire
  - **3.** 12 inches
  - **4.** Bamboo/wood
- **B.** Vietnam: 2000 years ago
  - **1.** Like China
  - **2.** Old: wood; now: plastic
- **C.** Korea: 2000 years ago
  - **1.** 8–9 inches
  - **2.** Old: silver; now: wood/ stainless
- **D.** Japan: 1500 years ago
  - **1.** Shorter and sharper
  - **2.** 10 inches
  - **3.** Lacquered wood

II. Etiquette
- **A.** China
  - **1.** Hold up bowl
  - **2.** Don 't tap
  - **3.** Don' t spear
- **B.** Vietnam
  - **1.** Eat from own bowl
  - **2.** Don't hold in mouth
  - **3.** Always use two
- **C.** Korea
  - **1.** Use spoon for rice
  - **2.** Spoon and chopsticks
  - **3.** Dishes on table
- **D.** Japan
  - **1.** Use chopstick rest
  - **2.** Don't cross
  - **3.** Don't rub together

REVIEW: I explained the history of chopsticks in four Asian countries and the differences in chopsticks etiquette in those four cultures.

REINFORCE PURPOSE: Chopsticks have a long history, but what they look like and how they're used varies based on cultural practices.

CLOSURE: Learning about chopsticks history and etiquette gave me an appreciation for something I've used all my life. Now I know why I eat so quickly [click, click]. Thank you.

The complete-sentence outline is where you record all the parts of your speech. The most detailed outline you'll produce for your speech, the complete-sentence outline, includes your topic, general purpose, specific purpose, thesis, introduction, main points, subpoints, conclusion, transitions, and references. You'll revise and rework this outline as you research your speech and identify appropriate supporting materials. Developing this comprehensive outline helps clearly identify each bit of information you want to include in your speech and visualize the order of your ideas.

> ANALYZE IT

Alicia, How Guinea Pigs Help Autistic Children

Alicia's assignment was to give an informative speech to her class in which she was to educate them on an unfamiliar subject. To ensure she was objectively informing the audience, she discussed both the benefits and the limitations of her subject.

At 22 months old, Cooper Mullen was diagnosed with autism. With conditions of sensory processing issues and apraxia, Cooper cannot be touched, held, or hugged without screaming. Late into the night his mother, Elizabeth Mullen, would sneak into his room while he was sleeping. With Cooper's condition, this was the only chance Elizabeth had to hold and cradle her autistic child, according to the Child Mind Institute website on September 11, 2012. After years of believing that one day, Cooper's condition would improve, a guinea pig named Cocoa came into the design. Upon three months of Cocoa's arrival, Cooper's tolerance to different sensations changed. Today, I want to inform you about the potential guinea pigs have in helping autistic children cope with the social and communication difficulties associated with autism.

According to *Medical News Today*, last updated August 1, 2013, autism is known as a complex, developmental disability which affects the development of a person's communication and social interaction skills. A new study in science shows that animals, such as guinea pigs, may significantly increase positive social behaviors in children who have autism. To better understand how a guinea pig like Cocoa can help Cooper's condition, I will first begin by discussing the recent research and theories of Maggie O'Haire, a Doctoral candidate of Psychology at the University of Queensland. Second, I will further examine the beneficial results of O'Haire's research. And finally, I will consider the limitations and future implications of her research.

MindTap®
Watch and analyze this speech on MindTap.

First, it is crucial that we understand the role guinea pigs take on toward helping autistic children by discussing the recent research and theories of Maggie O'Haire. In an interview with ABC News accessed January 12, 2013, Maggie O'Haire explains that by interacting with the guinea pig autistic children learn valuable lessons of empathy, nurturing, and caring. An article published by *Vet Street* on October 22, 2013, explains that some of the reasons guinea pigs were chosen are because they are small, mild-mannered animals who are very social and can be kept in a classroom. One of the major reasons guinea pigs were chosen for this study are because they are low maintenance animals, meaning that guinea pigs are easier to take care of than cats, dogs, or horses.

The U.S. National Library of Medicine on August 2, 2013, describes that Maggie O'Haire's research consisted of a total of 99 children in two schools from ages 5 to 13 years old. This research focuses on the social improvement of children with autism in the classroom. First, O'Haire identifies that engaging with their classmates is often a struggle for autistic children. Social isolation, bullying, and stress are some of the problems this struggle creates. These stressful conditions in the classroom can lead to poor academic performance and problematic behaviors. Second, in O'Haire's study, she encounters problems with teachers who also have difficulties interacting with their autistic students. As a result, there are poor student–teacher relations and more teacher burnouts. According to Maggie O'Haire's study published in the Public Library of Science, also known as PLOS, on February 20, 2013, it examined how the presence of guinea pigs affected the interaction of autistic children with adults and nonautistic kids revealing that the presence of a classroom pet stimulates social interaction among humans.

Furthermore, the National Public Radio on February 27, 2013, explores several theories why an animal might have this impact. The first theory illustrates that animals facilitate social interaction by giving people a common focus of attention, meaning that children are more drawn to the attention of an animal than to no animal at all. The second theory initiates that animals have a calming effect on children. Maggie O'Haire argues that by interacting with a guinea pig, autistic children feel more comfortable with their peers. The final theory is that people with animals are seen as friendly, less threatening, and most importantly, are more approachable.

Now that we have examined Maggie O'Haire's research let us explore the benefits of this new, emerging study. First, an article published by the University of Queensland explains that Maggie O'Haire's research is a low cost program compared to all the other alternative programs that are out there. Dr. Tarbox from the Centers for Autism and Related Disorders, also known as CARD, discloses to KTLN News on February 25, 2013, that a program CARD offers that does not involve an animal can cost anywhere between $50,000 and $100,000 per year for three to four years. Now according to PetSmart.com last accessed 30 minutes ago, the retail price for a guinea pig is $37.99. But they are on sale, so you can buy a guinea pig at Pet Smart for $32.99. Needless to say CARD is one of those alternative programs that are costly. Second, an article published by the *Los Angeles Times* on February 28, 2013, reported that autistic children who played with guinea pigs were more talkative, made more eye contact, and displayed a more positive attitude.

Finally, O'Haire states to the *Huffington Post* on February 28, 2013, that children with autism engaged in 55 percent more social behaviors when they were with the animals compared to toys. With the previously cited ABC interview, they interviewed an 11-year-old boy named Angus, who was part of O'Haire's research. Angus stated that having a guinea pig as a classroom pet channeled all his bad moods away. Angus's teacher reports that he is making more friends than she expected. Many autistic children are unable to verbally convey their feelings. Crying, yelling, and physically harming themselves are some of the ways children with autism are able to relieve their stress. Maggie O'Haire's research shows that the presence of guinea pigs led to more smiling and laughing and less frowning. O'Haire states that the presence of an animal appears to encourage socialization among children with autism and their peers.

Now that we know about the beneficial results of guinea pigs from O'Haire's study, we will examine the limitations of the study and its future implications. According to the previously cited PLOS, further exploration into the animal–human relationship may be useful to better understand the influence of animals on autistic children's social and communication development. In O'Haire's study, children with autism demonstrated warmth and affection to the animals but not humans. The guinea pigs in O'Haire's study were not trained therapy animals; they were chosen because they make good classroom pets. According to the *Times* on August 2, 2012, research suggests that interacting with creatures less complicated than humans could help autistic children understand social and communication skills.

The truth is that getting a child with autism a pet will not magically improve their symptoms. And pets are not for everyone. O'Haire's study only investigated whether interacting with an animal could change a child's behavior. Dr. Melissa Nishawala, an assistant professor with the Child Study Center at the New York University Langone Medical Center stated to the *Huffington Post* on July 25, 2013, that animal-assisted therapy is a young area. It has been around for several decades but the past five years have seen a real uptake in research, looking at the possible health benefits tied to human–animal interaction.

So today, I talked about the potential guinea pigs have in helping autistic children by first discussing the recent research and theories of Maggie O'Haire. I then further examined the beneficial results of O'Haire's research before finally considering the limitations and future implications of this research. For the first time in four years, Elizabeth Mullen was able to gently hug her son without him screaming. A story of hope, Cocoa was able to help Cooper in ways that his mother could not. With continued research on animals and their positive influence on children who have autism we can now see that helping autistic children may only be a guinea pig away.

Questions for Discussion

1. Review Alicia's speech and develop a complete-sentence outline for it.
2. From the complete-sentence outline, create a speaking outline that would work well for presenting the speech.
3. Now review Alicia's complete-sentence and speaking outlines on MindTap. How closely do they match the ones you developed?
4. Review Alicia's complete-sentence outline on MindTap. How relevant is each point to Alicia's general purpose, specific purpose, and thesis? How balanced are the main points?
5. Which pattern of organization did Alicia use? How effective was that pattern in helping her achieve her specific purpose? How might she have applied a different pattern of organization?
6. Give examples of the transition words and phrases the speaker used. How effective were those transitions? Were there places in the speech that were missing transitions?
7. If you were advising Alicia on how to improve the organization of her speech, what would you suggest?
8. What have you learned about organizing your ideas and outlining that you'll apply in your own speeches?

> APPLY IT . . .

IN THE WORKPLACE

Identifying Problems and Offering Solutions

You've probably observed that many conversations in the workplace center on problems—processes that often have glitches and procedures that seem convoluted. These may be small problems, such as a form that customers usually fill out incorrectly, or large problems, such as employees not following safety procedures. Identify one of these problems and how you would solve it. Then put together a brief proposal and short presentation using the problem–solution pattern of organization. Ask to meet with your supervisor and present your idea. How effective was your proposal? How well did the problem–solution pattern of organization work in winning over your boss?

IN YOUR COMMUNITY

Organizing Speeches about Service Learning

One key component of service learning is reflecting on what you've learned from your community experience and telling others about it. Identify one aspect of your service learning work that you'd like to share with others. For example, you may have gained insight into how your city makes policies or into teaching strategies to get third graders interested in environmental issues. How might each pattern of organization discussed in this chapter lead to different ways to talk about your topic? Which pattern best fits with your topic, your specific purpose, and your audience? What have you learned about patterns of organization that will help you with your speeches in the classroom and in other speaking contexts?

REVIEW IT

Key Terms

body 150
cause-and-effect pattern 158
chronological pattern 155
coherence 164
complete-sentence outline 168
internal summary 165
keywords 174
Monroe's motivated sequence 160
narrative pattern 158
pattern of organization 154
problem–solution pattern 160
signpost 164
spatial pattern 156
speaking outline 174
topical pattern 157
transition 164
working outline 166

MindTap®
Use flashcards to learn key terms and take a quiz to test your knowledge.

Reflecting on Organizing and Outlining Your Speech

1. Think back to a speech you listened to recently. How readily could you identify the introduction, body, and conclusion? How did recognizing the parts of the speech influence your evaluation of the speaker and the speaker's message?
2. Although you probably think of narratives as unfolding in a linear fashion—starting with the beginning, then the middle, and finally the end—stories can be told in a variety of ways. Consider a topic you might organize using the narrative pattern of organization. What are the different ways in which you might order the sequence of events? Which order do you think will work best for your audience?
3. The section on organizing the body of your speech includes an example of applying the six different patterns of organization to a single topic. Choose a topic and do the same, identifying the main points you'd cover for each pattern. How does the topic change as you apply each pattern of organization?
4. In everyday conversations, communicators often don't use transitions: They just skip from point to point and topic to topic. But in public speaking, audience members rely on speakers to use transitions to show how the different parts of the speech fit together. Choose a speech to view in person or online. How effective are the speaker's transitions? How does the speaker's use of transitions (or the absence of transitions) influence your evaluation of the speech?
5. Outlining helps you visualize all the elements of your speech and determine whether your ideas are organized in the most effective way. Critically examine one of your own complete-sentence outlines. For each section ask yourself, "Is this the best way to say this or present this idea? What are my alternatives?"

9 Beginning and Ending Your Speech

READ IT

After successfully completing this chapter, you will be able to:

- Discuss the four elements of a speech's introduction: attention getter, purpose and thesis statement, reference to the speaker's credibility, and preview of the speech's main points.
- Employ at least one effective strategy for gaining audience attention in an introduction.
- Discuss the three elements of a speech's conclusion: review of main points, reinforcement of the speech's purpose, and closing statement.
- Employ at least one effective strategy for providing speech closure in a conclusion.
- Differentiate between effective and ineffective speech introductions and conclusions.

MindTap®

Start with a quick warm-up activity and review the chapter's learning outcomes.

You never get a second chance to make a first impression.

Glasshouse Images/Alamy Stock Photo

In 1853 former slave, author, and human rights activist Sojourner Truth began her speech at the Fourth Women's Rights Convention in New York City this way:

> Is it not good for me to come and draw forth a spirit, to see what kind of spirit people are of? I see that some of you have got the spirit of a goose, and some have got the spirit of a snake. . . . I am citizen of the state of New York; I was born in it, and I was a slave in the state of New York; and now I am a good citizen of this State. . . . I've been lookin' round and watchin' things, and I know a little mite'bout Woman's Rights, too. I come forth to speak 'bout Woman's Rights, and want to throw in my little mite, to keep the scales a-movin'. I know that it feels a kind o' hissin' and ticklin' like to see a colored woman get up again; but we have been long enough trodden now; we will come up again, and now I am here.[1]

More than a century later, in 1969, U.S. House Representative from New York Shirley Chisholm addressed her colleagues on the same issue of women's rights:

> Mr. Speaker, when a young woman graduates from college and starts looking for a job, she is likely to have a frustrating and even demeaning experience ahead of her. If she walks into an office for an interview, the first question she will be asked is, "Do you type?" There is a calculated system of prejudice that lies unspoken behind that question. Why is it acceptable for women to be secretaries, librarians, and teachers, but totally unacceptable for them to be managers, administrators, doctors, lawyers, and Members of Congress? The unspoken assumption is that women are different. They do not have executive ability, orderly minds, stability, leadership skills, and they are too emotional.[2]

More recently, while attending a meeting in Tokyo, Japan, First Lady Michelle Obama spoke about access to education for girls worldwide, starting her speech with:

> I am so pleased to be here today as the United States and Japan announce a new partnership to educate girls across the globe. . . . Right now, as you heard, 62 million girls worldwide are not in school. And when we talk about this issue, we often focus on the economic barriers girls face—school fees or uniforms, or how they live miles from the nearest school and have no safe transportation, or how the school in their community doesn't have bathroom facilities for girls so they just can't attend.

AP Images/Richard Drew

But we all know that the problem here isn't just about infrastructure and resources. It's also about attitudes and beliefs. It's about whether fathers—and mothers—think their daughters are as worthy of an education as their sons. It's about whether communities value girls simply for their bodies, for their household labor, their reproductive capacities, or whether they value girls for their minds as well. It's about whether societies cling to laws and traditions that oppress women, or whether they view women as full citizens entitled to the same rights and freedoms as men. And if we're being honest with ourselves, we have to admit that these kinds of challenges aren't just limited to the developing world.[3]

How each of these women got her audience's attention differs, but the importance of intriguing their audiences from the start remains the same: You never get a second chance to make a first impression. Chapter 8 focused on how to develop the central element of your speech—the body—and how to link together the parts of your speech with transitions. This chapter completes the discussion of the four parts of the speech, elaborating on the introduction and conclusion.

Beginning and Ending: The Primacy and Recency Effects

MindTap®

Read, highlight, and take notes online.

primacy effect
An audience is more likely to pay attention to and recall what speakers present at the beginning of a speech than what they present in the speech body.

recency effect
An audience is more likely to remember what speakers present at the end of a speech than what they present in the speech body.

introduction
The beginning of a speech, including an attention getter, a statement of the thesis and purpose, a reference to the speaker's credibility, and a preview of the main points.

Researchers have identified the **primacy effect**, in which you're most likely to remember the beginning of something, such as a speech or list of names.[4] That is, individuals tend to recall best the first comments a speaker makes, the advertisements shown during the first quarter of the Super Bowl, and the first people they're introduced to at a party. In addition, the impressions people get from these "firsts" influence later perceptions—in these examples, of the remainder of the speech, later advertisements, and other partygoers.[5]

In public speaking, audiences tend to recall what the speaker says right at the start of the speech so well because this is when they're most attentive. The digital slides or images a speaker shows in the introduction also influence how audiences interpret the remainder of the speaker's message.[6] In addition, often an audience decides whether or not to pay attention to a speaker within the first moments of a speech.[7]

The flip side of the primacy effect is the **recency effect**, in which audience members recall what the speaker presents last better than the information contained in the body of the speech.[8] Moreover, if the speaker concludes with particularly startling, contradictory, or compelling information, the recency effect will outweigh the primacy effect.[9] Still, research suggests that although the recency effect is important, the primacy effect tends to be stronger, especially if the speaker's opening remarks resonate with the audience.[10]

Of course, listeners will remember more than only the beginning and ending of your presentation. However, the primacy and recency effects underscore the key role the introduction and conclusion play in achieving your purpose. The introduction gets your audience ready to listen to your ideas; the conclusion reinforces what you talked about.

Developing Your Introduction

MindTap®

Watch It: View a video on how to develop effective introductions for your speeches.

attention getter
The first element of an introduction, designed mainly to create interest in a speech.

In the **introduction** to your speech you gain your audience's attention, explain what you want to accomplish in your speech, establish yourself as an expert on the topic, and tell your audience what you're going to talk about **(Figure 9.1)**. The introduction's four elements work together to prepare your audience to listen to the main ideas you'll present in the body of your speech.

Get Your Audience's Attention

The introduction's first element is the **attention getter**, a device used to create interest in your speech. Effective attention getters are relevant to your topic and encourage the audience to listen to you.[11] Popular attention getters include asking a question, vividly describing a compelling image, telling a brief story, or playing a short clip from a song. To create an effective attention getter, consider your speech's purpose, the amount of time you have to present your introduction, creative strategies, common attention getters, and presentation media related to your topic.

Figure 9.1 Elements of the Introduction

Introduction
Get audience attention
Indicate purpose and thesis
Establish credibility
Preview main points

Consider Your Purpose The nature of the attention getter depends on the general purpose of your speech, the topic you choose, and the specific purpose you have in mind. Successful attention getters make clear to listeners that the topic merits their time and energy. But more than that, an effective attention getter:

- relates the topic to the audience,
- piques the audience's interest in the topic,
- connects you and your audience,
- gives you a well-designed start to your speech,
- reduces your nervousness, and
- introduces a theme that joins together the elements of your speech.

In the following example, high school student Cynthia Tientcheu Kamga presented an effective attention getter when she accepted a scholarship from the Cameroon Professional Society:

> Good afternoon ladies and gentlemen. As I was sitting at home, wondering what I would say today, I was overcome with joy at my accomplishment this summer. Earlier this year, I saw a high school in a village in Cameroon on Facebook. Seeing the poor condition of the school, I decided to help since I was scheduled to go to Cameroon to visit my family anyway. Instead of being all talk, I put my words into action.[12]

Kamga's initial opening acknowledged her audience and recognized the formality of the occasion. She piqued the audience's interest when she mentioned her summer accomplishment—listeners wanted to know about it. Then she indicated the theme of her speech: putting words into action. The simple phrase provided a natural transition to the body of her speech.

Creating a theme in the introduction helps join together the parts of your speech. As Kamga continued her acceptance speech, she told the story of collecting funds and supplies for a school in Cameroon and traveling to the country to personally deliver them. You also can use stories to provide a theme for your speech. For example, you might begin your speech with a short human-interest story that you purposefully leave unfinished. Then, as you conclude your speech several minutes later, refer back to the story or characters you introduced in the attention getter. Starting with part of a story and finishing with the rest of it gives your speech coherence. The audience views you more positively because your organizational skills tie together the elements of your speech. In the attention getter for a speech to persuade (Chapter 14), you also want to:

- establish the seriousness of your purpose,
- dramatize the controversial nature of your topic, and
- initiate the process of persuasion by presenting a strong logical, cultural, or emotional appeal.

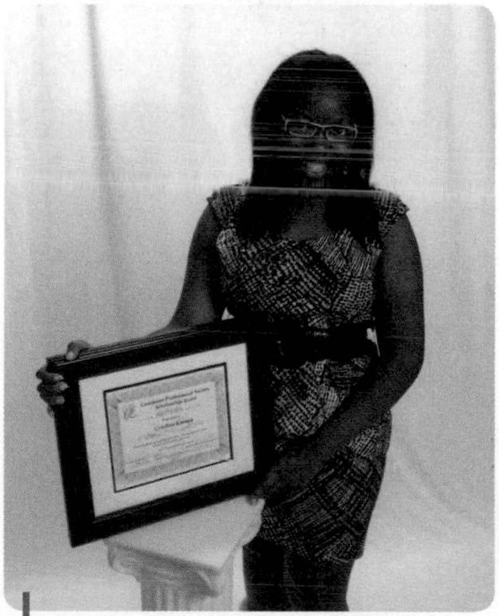

Courtesy of Gertude Kisob

Cameroon Professional Society scholarship winner Cynthia Tientcheu Kamga established a theme in the introduction of her speech.

Jane McGonigal, director of game research and development at the Institute for the Future as well as creator of the online game *Superbetter,* fulfilled these

Game designer, speaker, and author Jane McGonigal dramatized the topic for her audience.

objectives in the introduction to her speech, "Gaming Can Make a Better World," presented at a Technology, Entertainment, Design (TED) conference:

> I'm Jane McGonigal. I'm a game designer. I've been making games online now for 10 years and my goal for the next decade is try to make it as easy to save the world in real life as it is to save the world in online games. Now I have a plan for this and it entails convincing more people, including all of you, to spend more time playing bigger and better games. Right now we spend 3 billion hours a week playing online games. Some of you might be thinking, "That's a lot of time to be spending playing online games—maybe too much time considering how many urgent problems we have to solve in the real world." But actually according to my research at the Institute for the Future, the opposite is true. Three billion hours a week is not nearly enough game play to solve the world's most urgent problems. In fact, I believe if we want to survive the next century on this planet, we need to increase that total dramatically. I've calculated the total we need at 21 billion hours of game play every week.[13]

Referring to the "urgent problems we have to solve in the real world," McGonigal highlighted the seriousness of the topic. Proposing that individuals worldwide spend more time playing games—seven times the current rate—dramatized the topic for the audience by its counterintuitive nature. More than likely, audience members were familiar with arguments *against* online games; here was someone not only promoting online games but also arguing they could save the world. McGonigal appealed to the audience's logic in citing her research and their emotions in referring to human survival on Earth. Her dramatic introduction instantly engaged audience members and made them want to listen to her speech.

Consider Your Time An effective attention getter focuses the audience on your topic but does not cut into the time you need for the body of the speech. Some attention getters last only 15 seconds. Others may take a minute, or even longer in some cases.

Here's how actor Viola Davis began her Emmy Award acceptance speech for Outstanding Actress in a Drama:

Viola Davis quickly got her audience's attention in her acceptance speech for an Emmy Award for Outstanding Actress in a Drama.

> "In my mind, I see a line. And over that line, I see green fields and lovely flowers and beautiful white women with their arms stretched out to me over that line. But I can't seem to get there no how. I can't seem to get over that line." That was Harriet Tubman in the 1800s. And let me tell you something: The only thing that separates women of color from anyone else is opportunity. You cannot win an Emmy for roles that are simply not there.[14]

Davis quickly got her audience's attention with a moving quote from abolitionist and former slave Harriet Tubman. She linked the situation Tubman described to the present-day lack of dramatic roles for African Americans. Within the first few moments of her speech, she made the topic both personal to herself and her listeners.

Use Your Creativity Creating and delivering an effective attention getter presents a special challenge for public speakers. It demands that you use your imagination well. Award-winning author Chimamanda Ngozi Adichie demonstrated her creativity at the start of her Commonwealth lecture given in The Guildhall, London:

> When I was growing up in Nsukka, the university town in southeastern Nigeria, books were the center of my world. I started reading when I was perhaps four years old. I read everything I could find. One day, I read an American novel in which a

character ate something called a bagel for breakfast. I had no idea what a bagel was, but I thought it sounded very elegant, very exotic—I pronounced it "bah-gel." I desperately wanted to have a bah-gel. My family visited the United States for the first time when I was nine. At the airport in New York, I told my mother that, as a matter of the gravest urgency, we had to buy a bah-gel. And she went to a café and bought one. Finally I would have a bah-gel. You can imagine my disappointed surprise when I discovered that this bah-gel, this glorious bah-gel from the novel, was only just a dense doughnut.

Still, even though a bagel ended up not being some sort of exquisite confection, the moments in which I thought it was were well worth it. Because my imagination soared in delight. And there was something comforting and instructive in that discovery of a bagel, in the demystifying ordinariness of a bagel: other people, like me, ate boring food.[15]

Leon Neal/Staff/Getty Images

Chimamanda Ngozi Adichie used her creativity to spark her audience's imagination at the start of her speech.

As a successful author, Adichie's storytelling talents are well known. Here, her story worked well because she first made the ordinary—a bagel—seem extraordinary, and then ordinary again. Taking her audience on this brief adventure provided a connection to listeners on two levels—the everydayness of eating boring food and the imaginative insights books can provoke. Adichie's tactic charmed her listeners and captured their attention.

Try Using Common Attention Getters So far, you've learned about general approaches and ideas for gaining your audience's attention in the speech introduction. You have to decide what you think works best for your audience, your topic, and you. Here are some strategies successful speakers use that you might try.

- *Cite a surprising fact or statistic to call attention to your topic.* Say, for instance, "Did you know that loud noise is more than just an annoyance? It's considered pollution that can increase your stress level, disrupt your sleep, raise your blood pressure, and cause permanent hearing loss." Or, "According to the National Center for Education Statistics, U.S. college library collections contain more than one billion items on site and more than 520 million electronic resources." Although this strategy suffers from overuse, if your fact or statistic really surprises or alarms your audience, you may quickly gain their attention.
- *Tell an emotionally arousing but brief human interest story.* Panashe Chigumadzi began her Ruth First Memorial Lecture at the University of the Witwatersrand, South Africa, with a narrative about her experiences as a child:

  Towards the end of 1997, the year before I was to turn 7 and go to big school, my parents and I began preparations such as interviews, buying the uniform and making sure that I could dress myself. With everything ready, one thing seemed to be missing: "Mama, at big school next year, can they call me Gloria?" (Gloria, by the way is my second name.) My mother looked at me, a little confused and simply said, "No. Your name is Panashe, so they will call you that."

  Without the words to explain why I felt that this new 'calling' name was necessary, I went along with the Shona name that had been so badly mangled in the mouths of my white teachers at my predominantly white pre-school—everything from Pinashe, Panache to Spinasie.

  At the age of six I had already begun the dance that many black people in South Africa know too well. Our names are just one of the many important sites of struggle as we manoeuvre around our blackness in spaces that do not truly accommodate us in our fullness as black people.[16]

By recalling a childhood experience, Chigumadzi appealed to audience members' early recollections of the first day of school. And because your name is an essential part of how you are, listeners could empathize with the young Chigumadzi as she recounted how white teachers had mispronounced her name. Having gained her audience's attention, Chigumadzi presented the thesis of her speech, "Our names are just one of the many important sites of struggle as we manoeuvre around our blackness in spaces that do not truly accommodate us in our fullness as black people."

- *Use humor to introduce the topic and get the audience interested.* Laughing together helps audience members identify with you, one another, and the topic.[17] Humor that audience members perceive as authentic and reflecting your true self puts your audience in a more positive frame of mind about you and your speech.[18] However, offensive or demeaning jokes will alienate your audience, as discussed in this chapter's Speaking of ... box. In addition, joking about serious social issues such as bullying and obesity trivializes the topics and may lead the audience to question your credibility.[19]
- *Use the information you have about your audience.* The audience research you conduct may produce data your listeners will find provocative or interesting. For instance, you could begin an informative speech about managing distractions by saying, "According to the survey you filled out for my speech topic, nearly all of you text during your classes." But getting your listeners' attention in and of itself isn't enough. The data must be sufficiently intriguing to motivate them to continue listening.
- *Ask a question that you want your audience to answer or consider.* To get an idea of how important a topic is for an audience, you might begin with a question such as, "How many of you couldn't find a parking place on campus this morning?" Or, "Have you thought about saving for retirement? If you have, raise your hand." Some speakers ask rhetorical questions—ones listeners aren't expected to answer—to gain attention. Examples of rhetorical questions are "How can we best prepare for the technology of the future?" and "Do we really know what's in our drinking water?" Rhetorical questions encourage listeners to think about the answer to the question, but they expect the speaker to provide that answer.

Integrate Presentation Media Starting your speech with a brief audio or visual clip, a photograph on a digital slide, or other presentation media offers another way to capture the audience's attention and inspire interest. For example, you might display a colorful and richly detailed image of muscle tissue to introduce a speech about magnetic resonance imaging (MRI) technology.

Presentation media can be effective attention getters if they are well designed, well practiced, and clearly relevant to the topic. As with any attention getter, brevity is key. Thirty seconds seems like a brief time, yet in a five-minute speech that's one-tenth of your speaking time. Also consider what you'll be doing as audience members listen to or watch the presentation media you've designed for your attention getter. Especially when you're trying to gain your audience's attention at the beginning of your speech, you don't want to find yourself staring off into space while your listeners watch 30 seconds of a film clip. Chapter 11 discusses designing and using presentation media in detail.

SPEAKING OF ...

Laughing with You, Not at You

Integrating humor into your speeches serves many positive goals, such as gaining attention and helping the audience feel comfortable with you. But some humor can detract from your speech and hurt your credibility. For example, humor that makes you look incompetent or unintelligent will make audience members wonder why they should listen to you. In addition, humor that disparages groups or categories of people, such as jokes based on gender or ethnicity, may offend your audience.[20] And too much humor gets the audience focusing on the jokes rather than on the points you're trying to make—just like television commercials whose comical scenes viewers recall rather than the product advertised.

Indicate Your Purpose and Thesis

Once you have gotten your audience's attention, you want to provide a clear indication of your speech's purpose and thesis. Recall that the specific purpose succinctly expresses the response you want from your audience ("To help my audience learn the basic steps of jazz dance" or "To teach my audience about how arabic numerals replaced roman numerals in mathematics"). When you deliver your speech, you might not state your purpose exactly in those terms. But your audience should know what the purpose of your speech is and what you expect from them. Consider the introduction to a speech by Sam Hodges, a student at Lehigh University double majoring in international relations and history, given at the university's Founder's Day ceremony:

> When Lehigh University was founded by Asa Packer, it was based on a novel, forward-thinking ideal of giving students studying engineering and more technical trades a strong rooting in the liberal arts and sciences. A well-rounded student, Asa Packer thought, would be a leader in their field and in their country.
>
> As time has shown, the approach Asa Packer took to education did produce leaders in their field. A Lehigh alum engineered the escalator; a Lehigh alum revived Chrysler back in the 1980s; and Lehigh alumni built the Golden Gate Bridge.
>
> The approach of producing well-rounded students has stayed at the forefront of Lehigh's mission. While the exact methods and processes used in 1865 are not being used today, the idea of a multifaceted Lehigh graduate still permeates our culture. During my time here, I feel as if this culture has served me well.[21]

How do you know the purpose of the speech? The speaker doesn't declare outright "My purpose is to convince you that all college students should get a liberal arts education." Hodges is more subtle, referring to Asa Packer's reason for founding Lehigh University and highlighting the accomplishments of alumni. So he establishes his purpose—his audience knows why he's there and what he wants them to think. He then states his thesis, "a multifaceted Lehigh graduate still permeates our culture," and underscores his agreement with advantages of a liberal arts education.

Indicating the speech's purpose and thesis typically requires just a few sentences. As with the attention getter, you don't want to go on and on. But you do want your audience members to know the response you expect from them and the basic idea you're conveying.

Establish Your Credibility

Your introduction gives you the first opportunity to show you've thoroughly researched your topic. Presenting yourself as a credible speaker takes only a few moments but plays a key role in getting your audience to listen to you. For example, if your speech topic is how to save people from drowning and you've worked as a lifeguard, you might say, "In my five years as a lifeguard, I've successfully applied three basic techniques to save someone who's drowning." That brief mention of your experience tells the audience you have some expertise on the topic.

You also let your audience know about your credibility when you refer to the research you've done on your topic. For a speech on staying safe and healthy at work, for instance, you might refer to information you've gathered on the topic, as with, "According to the U.S. Department of Labor, more than 3 million people get hurt or become ill at work each year."

Preview Your Main Points

A **preview of main points** concisely tells the audience what the main points of the speech will be, establishing an expectation of what the speech will address. The preview provides the first step in helping the audience follow your main ideas as you move from one main point to the next. Transitions connect the various elements of the

preview of main points The final element of the introduction, in which the main points to be presented in the body of the speech are mentioned.

introduction together. For example, you might start an informative speech about herb gardens in this way:

> Growing a simple indoor herb garden is easy and enjoyable *(indicate thesis).* Today, you'll learn how to set up your own garden *(indicate purpose).* To begin *(transition),* I will explain the basic equipment you'll need that I've found in my many years of herb gardening *(establish credibility).* Next *(transition),* I will show you how to plant your indoor herb garden. Finally *(transition),* I'll give you some tips on keeping your herbs happy and healthy *(preview main points).*

Similarly, a persuasive speech about meditation could begin like this:

> Incorporating meditation into your daily life reduces stress and can even increase your longevity *(indicate thesis).* I meditate regularly—and did so this morning to help manage my speech anxiety *(establish credibility).* As part of a balanced lifestyle, you should take the necessary steps to make meditation part of your daily routine *(indicate purpose).* Different types of meditation will improve the balance in your life and you can incorporate them easily into your day-to-day activities *(reinforce thesis).* To make clear how to start meditating, I will first *(transition)* explain the positive effects meditation can give you. I will then *(transition)* describe several different kinds of meditation. After *(transition)* describing the types, I will explain how you can begin meditating on a daily basis *(preview main points).*

Even entertaining speeches benefit from a clear preview of main points, as in this example:

> Some people claim they learned everything they needed to know in kindergarten, but I learned everything I needed to know in my first year of high school *(indicate thesis).* I think you'll appreciate all the lessons I learned in spite of what my teachers were trying to tell me *(indicate purpose).* I admit this may sound odd, but I was an unusual teenager, recording my first year of high school like I was writing a documentary *(establish credibility).* Before I regale you with my many brilliant insights *(transition),* I will give you some background on my high school. Second *(transition),* I'll explain the three most important lessons I learned. Finally *(transition),* I'll tell you how I've applied those lessons recently, even for this class *(preview main points).*

Developing Your Conclusion

MindTap®

Watch It: View a video on how to develop effective conclusions in your speeches.

conclusion
The end of a speech, in which the speaker reviews the main points, reinforces the purpose, and provides closure.

You've presented your main points, and now you're ready to wrap up your speech. But you're not quite finished. Recall the *recency effect,* in which audience members tend to remember what the speaker presents last better than what the speaker said in the body of the speech.

In the **conclusion** to your speech, you review the main points, reinforce the speech's general and specific purposes, and provide closure so your audience knows your speech is over **(Figure 9.2)**. In addition, integrating visual and auditory imagery in the conclusion can make your topic more memorable and reinforce your purpose.[22] Judicious use of presentation media, such as a few video frames, a particularly poignant photograph, or a very short audio clip, can spark your audience's imagination. Use the conclusion to continue building rapport with your audience and emphasize your points, but do it efficiently. Audiences perk up when they know your speech is coming to an end. They are ready for you to stop talking, but they are also willing to listen closely to your final remarks. Your words, facial expression, and body movement should all indicate that your presentation has purposefully concluded. By preparing, practicing, and presenting an effective conclusion, you will reinforce your key points, strengthen a call to action or a persuasive argument, and give your audience a lasting impression of your message.

Figure 9.2 Elements of the Conclusion

Conclusion
Review main points
Reinforce purpose
Provide closure

Review Your Main Points

Use the conclusion to remind your audience of the main points presented in the body of your speech. The **review of main points** normally follows a transition word or phrase that indicates you're moving from the body to the conclusion. When you review your main points, you remind listeners of the key points you've made, but without the specific details. Here are some examples.

review of main points
The portion of the conclusion of a speech in which the main points presented in the body of the speech are briefly mentioned again.

- *In a speech to inform:* In summary *(transition),* today you've learned how to get started windsurfing. I described the history of windsurfing, the equipment you'll need, and where you can try out this fun sport *(review main points).*
- *In a speech to persuade:* Let's review *(transition)* what I covered in my speech. I told you about how you can improve your study habits and get better grades almost immediately. I've described the most common problems students create for themselves, how those mistakes lead to poor results in the classroom, and what to do about it to improve your grades *(review main points).*
- *In a speech to entertain:* Now *(transition)* you know my secrets of backpacking in style: Treat your backpacking guide very, very well; bring the proper equipment; and make backup reservations at a nearby resort hotel *(review main points).*

Reinforce Your Purpose

The conclusion gives you a final opportunity to reinforce your specific purpose by highlighting the reason your information is important (for a speech to inform), crystallizing your argument and making a final appeal to the audience (for a speech to persuade), or getting that last laugh (for a speech to entertain).

In reinforcing your specific purpose, you provide a **memorable message** to capture the audience's attention in a way that makes the information or persuasive argument you've given impossible to ignore or refute. What you say must be brief, clear, strong, and striking, as in the following examples:

memorable message
A sentence or group of sentences included in the conclusion of a speech, designed to make the speaker's thesis unforgettable.

- "We've finally got the evidence that proves what scientists had long suspected: Humans are evolved apes." *(informative speech reporting new DNA evidence)*
- "Choosing the right profession involves identifying what you ideally want in a job or profession, what you must have, and what you absolutely don't want." *(informative speech on how to choose a job or profession)*
- "It's *your* choice: Are you going to give up or shape up?" *(persuasive speech promoting exercise program for college students)*
- "Every single one of you will have to pay for that new football stadium!" *(persuasive speech against constructing a new stadium)*

Provide Closure

Sometimes speakers find the very end of the speech the most difficult part. You've probably heard speakers say, "That's about it," "Okay, well, that's all I have to say," or "I guess I'm done." Do these endings make the speaker sound convincing, confident, inspiring? Are they likely to impress a listener favorably? The conclusion is the last chance you have to make an impression on your audience, and you want it to be a good one. As with the introduction, the best strategies for providing closure fit you, your audience, and your topic.

Here are some specific techniques you might want to try.

- *End with a quotation.* "As author Rita Mae Brown once said, 'The statistics on sanity are that one out of every four Americans is suffering from some form of mental illness. Think of your three best friends. If they're okay, then it's you.' "[23] *(entertaining speech on staying sane in today's world)*

- *Use presentation media.* In closing her TED Talk on gaming, Jane McGonigal showed her audience a digital slide with just four words: "Let the games begin," and said, "When I look forward to the next decade, I know two things for sure: that we can make any future we can imagine, and we can play any games we want. So, I say: Let the world-changing games begin. Thank you."[24] The stark visual image reinforced her verbal message, making audience members more likely to recall the action she wanted them to take. *(persuasive speech on using online games to solve real-world problems)*
- *Make a dramatic statement.* "And in the 10 minutes I've been talking, 20 people in Africa have died of malaria." *(informative speech on the impact of malaria around the world)*
- *Refer to the introduction.* "Now I'll finish the story I started in my introduction. And this story has a happy ending. I found a great summer job that will pay for my two weeks in Mexico over winter break." *(informative speech on how to find a good summer job)*
- *Refer to subsequent events.* "Later, in coordination with the U.S. Department of Justice, AMBER Alert plans were passed in all 50 states." *(informative speech on Americans Missing: Broadcast Emergency Response program)*
- *Reinforce the speaker–audience connection.* "Like many of you, I thought the idea of freedom was a pretty basic thing. But now that I've learned how people in other cultures view freedom and shared that information with you, we all realize that there are many different ways to think of this common word." *(informative speech on defining freedom)*
- *Thank the audience.* "Thank you for considering my proposal to increase the number of elective courses and reduce the number of required courses for all students attending our school." *(persuasive speech on changing graduation requirements)*

Summary

In the speech introduction, you get the audience's attention, indicate your purpose and thesis, establish your credibility, and preview your speech's main points. In creating the attention getter, consider your specific purpose and how much time you have to give the speech. Also, use your creativity and imagination to find a way to make your audience sit up, take notice, and want to listen to your speech. Present your thesis clearly so the audience understands the response you expect. Let the audience know you're an expert on your topic. Complete the introduction by previewing your main points.

In your conclusion, review your main points, emphasize your general and specific purpose, and provide closure. Strategies for providing closure include ending with a quotation, making a dramatic statement, referring to the introduction, referring to subsequent events, reinforcing the speaker–audience connection, and thanking the audience. Increase the likelihood you'll achieve your specific purpose by leaving your audience with a lasting and positive impression.

MindTap®

Use MindTap to help you develop your introduction and conclusion.

> ANALYZE IT

Nathanael, The 54th Massachusetts

Nathanael's assignment was to give an informative speech on a topic of his choice. Pay special attention to the beginning and end of the speech to assess how effectively you think he introduces and concludes his speech.

MindTap®

Watch and analyze this speech on MindTap.

It was eighth-grade history class, and I hated, absolutely hated, history. But as another boring week began, I heard what was music to my ears: "Class, this week we're going to watch a movie." The movie was called *Glory*. It was about the Civil War and the raising of the first black regiment from the Northeast.

Every year in the month of February, our country celebrates Black History Month. We recognize the efforts of such African Americans as Harriet Tubman, Booker T. Washington, and Martin Luther King, Jr. However, today I will not be speaking on such notable names as these; quite the contrary. I'll be speaking about what review author Jeff Shannon calls a noble yet little-known episode of history: the 54th Massachusetts. After watching *Glory*, I became intrigued with the Civil War and began doing research on it, specifically the events surrounding the 54th Massachusetts. It all began on January 1, 1863, when Abraham Lincoln signed the Emancipation Proclamation, allowing for the first time in this nation's history the opportunity for men of color to sign up and fight for their country. Today, I'll be discussing the formation of the 54th Massachusetts, the racial difficulties they faced, and the Battle of Fort Wagner. Let's begin with the formation of the troops.

In March 1863, the regiment simply known as the 54th was formed in Readville, Massachusetts. The man who would be the colonel in charge of the men was Robert Gould Shaw, the 25-year-old son of a prominent Boston abolitionist family. Although he was young, he was already a veteran of the battlefield. Civil War historian William James notes that from the time Shaw accepted the preferred command, he lived but for one object, and that was to establish the honor of the 54th Massachusetts. On May 28, 1863, a parade honoring the men cheered them on as they left Boston to fight for the Union. With the men trained, suited up, and ready for battle, next I'll be discussing the racial difficulties the men faced.

The 54th was comprised mostly of free men who had never been slaves or had to face the types of racial prejudices that were to come. First, according to Civil War author and lecturer Kathy Dahl of BitsofBlueandGray.com, instead of the promised Army wage of thirteen dollars a month, because they were black troops, they would receive ten dollars a month—minus three dollars for clothing. Then, despite intense training and fighting readiness, the regiment was only ordered to do basic manual labor. Then in June 1863, Shaw was given orders to have his men burn and loot a small town in Georgia. Shaw saw this as a satanic action, and in a letter to his wife he writes, "I fear that such actions will hurt the reputation of black troops and those connected with them." Performing only manual labor with little pay and the possible disgrace brought upon them with the burning of the town, this will take us to the last point: the Battle of Fort Wagner.

On July 16, 1863, the men of the 54th saw action and were successful in their attempts. That night, under the secrecy of darkness and in a torrent of rain, the 54th trudged through mud and hazardous terrain for eight hours, and on the morning of July 18, Colonel Shaw accepted the honor of leading his troops in the assault on Fort Wagner. The fort was to be taken by bayonet in hand-to-hand combat. At dusk, Shaw and his men began their assault. In front of the fort was a moat followed by a 30-foot wall of sand. Confederate fire opened. Nearly blinded by gunsmoke and fire, Shaw led his men up to the top of the hill. With a final charge of "Forward, 54th!" Colonel Shaw was shot through the heart, falling face down into the fort.

William Carney, a member of the regiment, saw that the flag bearer had been shot and lay dead in the moat. Carney climbed down the hill, raced into the moat, grasped the flag, and began his ascent back to the top. In the process, Carney was shot through the leg, the shoulder, the arm, and in the head. With orders to retreat, Carney clutched onto the flag, got on his hands and knees, and crawled back down the hill, which was by then covered with the bodies of fallen comrades, and fled some five hundred yards to safety. Before collapsing, his only words were, "Boys, I only did my duty; the flag never touched the ground." The next day, the body of Colonel Shaw and three hundred of his men were thrown into a sandy ditch and buried. Thirty years later, William Carney would become the first African American in this nation's history to be awarded the Congressional Medal of Honor and become the public symbol of the many unsung heroes of the 54th Massachusetts. Because of the efforts of the 54th, more black troops were enlisted, and President Lincoln credited the raising up of African American troops as helping to secure the final victory.

In conclusion, we have covered the formation of the 54th Massachusetts, the racial difficulties they faced, and the Battle of Fort Wagner. It has been many years since that eighth grade history class, but the images of those brave men serve as constant reminders that although their names may remain unknown, their place in our nation's history will last forever. The courage and legacy of the 54th are encapsulated best in the words of an unknown author: "Glory was not to be found in victory, but in their willingness to keep fighting for what they believed in."

Questions for Discussion

1. What was the purpose of Nathanael's speech? How did he address it in the introduction?
2. How did he get his audience's attention?
3. What did he do to relate his topic to his audience?
4. What did Nathanael say to establish his credibility?
5. What was the thesis of his speech? How did he weave it into the introduction?
6. How did Nathanael summarize his main points?
7. How did he reinforce the purpose of his speech?
8. How did he provide closure?
9. If you were advising Nathanael on how to improve the way he began and ended his speech, what would you suggest?
10. What have you learned about speech introductions and conclusions that you'll apply in your own speeches?

APPLY IT . . .

IN THE WORKPLACE

Connecting with Your Audience

As with the other parts of a speech, a successful introduction relies on how well you connect with your audience. In the workplace, you often know your listeners, which makes appealing to them a little easier. In addition, you and your audience share common experiences either working for the organization (coworkers and supervisors) or working with the organization (clients, customers, vendors, and the like). As you develop the introduction to your workplace presentation, consider the points of commonality between you and your audience, such as organizational goals and values or reaching a specific objective. Here are some questions to ask when developing your introduction:

- What common events have my audience members participated in?
- What common goals do we want to achieve?
- What common values do we share based on our membership in this organization?

Answers to these questions can provide the basis for an introduction that quickly gains audience members' attention and helps them feel connected to each other and to you.

IN YOUR COMMUNITY

Focusing Attention on Service Learning

Telling others about your service-learning experiences promotes this important aspect of your college career and demonstrates how institutions of higher education serve their communities. You might give a formal speech in which you try to persuade classmates to get involved in service learning, or you might talk informally with friends and family members about your experiences. Whatever the context, you must first get your audience's attention. How might you do that? Do you know of some startling fact or statistic about service learning? Do you have a compelling story to tell based on your project? Did something humorous happen related to your service-learning experience? What do you know about your audience in relationship to service learning? Is there a question about service learning you want your audience to consider? Generate a list of attention getters and the audiences they best match.

REVIEW IT

Key Terms

attention getter 182
conclusion 188
introduction 182
memorable message 189
preview of main points 189
primacy effect 182
recency effect 182
review of main points 189

MindTap®
Use flashcards to learn key terms and take a quiz to test your knowledge.

Reflecting on Beginning and Ending Your Speech

1. Getting the audience's attention is a primary function of the introduction to your speech. However, the attention getter must fit with the speech topic, occasion, and audience. How might an attention getter be ineffective and detract from a speech? For example, how might a statistic or fact be too startling? How might a story mislead the audience?
2. Think ahead to the next speech you plan to give in this class. How might you establish your credibility in the introduction?
3. Speakers often neglect the conclusion of a speech and lose the opportunity to take advantage of the recency effect. Think back to a speech you've heard in which the closing was lacking. How did you feel after the speech was over? What do you recall most from the speech? How could the speaker have been more effective in ending the speech?
4. Reflect on the last speech you gave, whether in class or in another situation. How well did you end the speech? What did you say to summarize your main points? How did you reinforce the purpose of your speech? To what extent did you provide closure to your speech? What will you do to make sure you develop effective conclusions for your speeches in the future?

10 Using Language Effectively

READ IT

After successfully completing this chapter, you will be able to:

- Explain how language is arbitrary, ambiguous, abstract, and active.
- Choose words that convey your ideas accurately while avoiding jargon, slang, idioms, euphemisms, clichés, tag questions, and hedges.
- Avoid tag questions and hedges and use gender-fair language.
- Explain how spoken language differs from written language.
- Use appropriate words for the audience and occasion by putting your language in context, personalizing your language, using inclusive language, using visual language, and sparking your audience's imagination with language.
- Apply the guidelines for effectively using language in your speeches.

MindTap®

Start with a quick warm-up activity and review the chapter's learning outcomes.

Effective language in public speaking invites audience members to listen, stirs their emotions, and touches their senses.

Library of Congress Prints and Photographs Division Washington, D.C, LC-DIG-pga-01711

On March 23, 1775, lawyer and planter Patrick Henry gave one of the most famous speeches in the history of the United States at a political meeting in Richmond, Virginia. His speech was remembered both for its passion and its use of language. You're familiar with his final statement, "Give me liberty or give me death!" But you may not know the clever and compelling words he used earlier in his speech to encourage his listeners to fight for independence from the British:

> I have but one lamp by which my feet are guided; and that is the lamp of experience. I know of no way of judging of the future but by the past. And judging by the past, I wish to know what there has been in the conduct of the British ministry for the last ten years to justify those hopes with which gentlemen have been pleased to solace themselves and the house? Is it that insidious smile with which our petition has been lately received? Trust it not, sir; it will prove a snare to your feet. Suffer not yourselves to be betrayed with a kiss. Ask yourselves how this gracious reception of our petition comports with these warlike preparations which cover our waters and darken our land. Are fleets and armies necessary to a work of love and reconciliation? Have we shown ourselves so unwilling to be reconciled that force must be called in to win back our love? Let us not deceive ourselves, sir. These are the implements of war and subjugation—the last arguments to which kings resort.[1]

Today, Henry's language is considered flowery and overwrought. But at the time, his words served to spur the attendees to pass a resolution declaring independence from Great Britain.

More recently, Aung San Suu Kyi, Nobel Prize winner and chairperson of the National League for Democracy in Burma, spoke after accepting the Sakharov Prize for Freedom of Thought. Given the award in 1990, she was under house arrest and unable to travel to Strasbourg, France, to accept it at that time. In her speech nearly 25 years later, like Patrick Henry, she spoke of independence, although she used different words to convey her thoughts:

> When the fathers of the independence movement were working to free our country from colonial rule they said we want the right to shape our own destiny. This is still what we need in Burma, the right of our people to shape our own destiny. We want to be able to decide what we think is best for ourselves. We want to be able to learn to sort out our differences. We want to be able to come to a united position in spite of our differences because Burma is a country of many peoples, of many opinions, of many religions, of many races.[2]

Effective language in public speaking invites audience members to listen, stirs their emotions, and touches their senses. Patrick Henry simply could have said, "We need to fight the British," and Aung San Suu Kyi could have told her audience, "My country hasn't really achieved independence." But in both cases, those words lack the power to evoke the feelings associated with the speakers' experiences. Why not? That's what you'll find out in this chapter.

AFP/Getty Images

Language Fundamentals

MindTap®

Read, highlight, and take notes online.

language
The system of words people use to communicate with others.

symbol
Something, such as a word, that stands for something else, such as a person, place, thing, or idea.

Language refers to the system of words people use when communicating with others. The power of language rests in its ability to create images in the minds of listeners. Those images inform, persuade, and entertain audience members. When you speak in public, your words also encourage your audience to think, reason, contemplate, feel, evaluate, and otherwise respond to what you have to say.

How do words work? Words are **symbols** that stand for something else—material things such as an object, person, place, or event. Symbols may also represent ideas that are more abstract, such as freedom, justice, and happiness. Words don't *transfer* information or ideas from your mind to others' minds. Instead, words *trigger* the meanings and thoughts people have for words in their minds—that's because language is arbitrary, ambiguous, abstract, and active.

Language Is Arbitrary

Researchers have identified about 7000 languages spoken by people around the world.[3] This vast number of languages suggests that the meanings of words are arbitrary. Because there's no direct connection between a word and what it represents, different groups of people have different words that stand for the same things. **Figure 10.1** demonstrates that when you have an idea or thought, there's a clear association between the object that led to your thought and the words you choose to express that thought. But there's no direct link between the object itself and the words you choose.

Consider the word *tree.* In Dutch, the word is *boom.* In Greek, it's *dentro.* In Japanese, *tree* is 木. And in Spanish, you'd say *árbol.* Each language has a different way of representing what is called *tree* in English. That's why language is considered arbitrary.

denotative meaning
An agreed-upon definition of a word found in a dictionary.

connotative meaning
A unique meaning for a word based on an individual's own experiences.

Communicators use words to stand for their thoughts and ideas. The link between a word and what it stands for always goes through your mind.[4] As the example in **Figure 10.2** shows, the person views some palm trees, triggering the memory of a vacation in Florida, and then says, "Palm trees remind me of the Florida Keys."

Figure 10.1 The Arbitrary Relationship among Words, Thoughts, and Objects

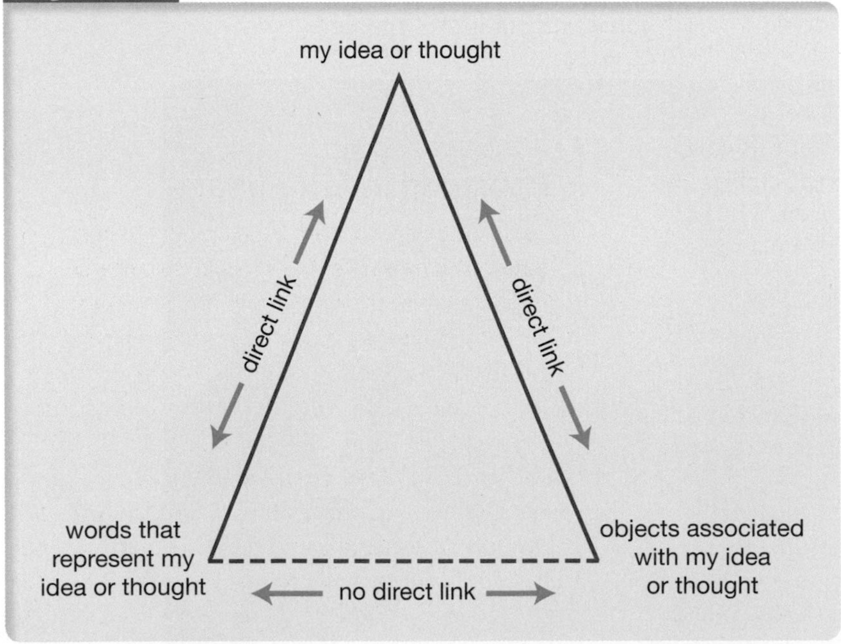

Source: Adapted from Ogden, C. K., & Richards, I. A. (1923). *The meaning of meaning: A study of the influence of language upon thought and of the science of symbolism.* New York: Harcourt, Brace.

Language Is Ambiguous

Speakers usually assume that if they say "X," others will think "X," But that's not necessarily the case. Language is ambiguous—words have multiple meanings and individuals have their own meanings, or associations, for words and the concepts those words stand for. **Denotative meanings** refer to formal, or literal, meanings—the definitions you find in dictionaries. **Connotative meanings** are the unique meanings you have for words based on your own experiences.

Even words you might think of as straightforward, such as *car*, can have multiple meanings. It can refer to a four-wheel road vehicle and also designate the four-wheel vehicles that make up a train. It can describe the part of an elevator or other moving enclosures that hold passengers or freight. The financial world also uses the term in the context of commodity futures contracts. CAR, in capital letters, refers to the Chief of the Army Reserve.[5] These are denotative meanings—you will find different definitions for the word in the *Merriam-Webster Dictionary, The Free Dictionary*, and other online dictionaries. But think about all the connotative meanings you associate with *car*, such as independence, financial burden, and traveling.

The ambiguity of language pervades all aspects of the speechmaking process. When selecting your topic, consider the words you'll choose to identify it. Would you refer to plagiarism as academic *integrity* or academic *dishonesty?* Would a speech on plans to repurpose a local vacant lot refer to *open space* or to *undeveloped land?* In a speech on the effects of our increasingly global society, would you use the term *antiglobalization* or the term *global justice?* To take just one of these examples, consider the differences between academic dishonesty and academic integrity. *Dishonesty* has negative connotations; listeners will likely think of activities such as cheating on a test or plagiarizing a speech outline. *Integrity* brings up positive associations such as studying for a test and carefully documenting sources for a speech. Making the choice between those two words—*dishonesty* and *integrity*—will influence the **tone** or general mood associated with the speech (Chapter 3).

Figure 10.2 Words, Thoughts, and Objects: An Example

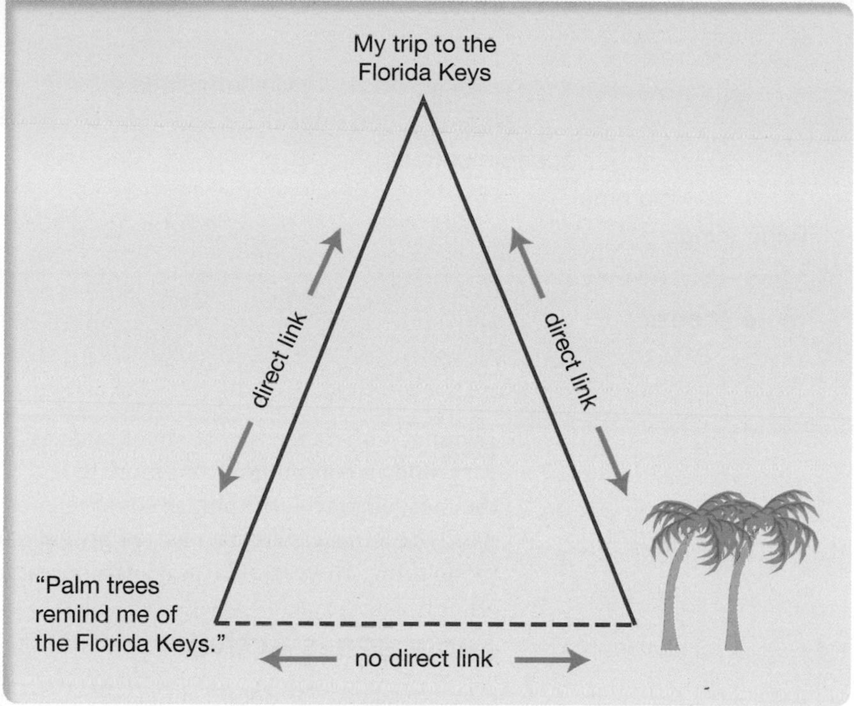

Source: Adapted from Ogden, C. K., & Richards, I. A. (1923). *The meaning of meaning: A study of the influence of language upon thought and of the science of symbolism*. New York: Harcourt, Bace.

tone
Use of language to set the mood or atmosphere associated with a speaking situation.

How you phrase your topic will guide you in the development of the idea, the analysis of your audience, the research you conduct, and the selection of your supporting materials. When you deliver your speech (Chapter 12), the language you use to frame and define your topic will influence how your listeners interpret your message. It's during delivery that the ambiguous nature of language will have its most obvious effects. The way your audience responds to your speech depends in part on the language you choose.

Language Is Abstract

You experience your world with all your senses—you smell bread baking, you see a friend smiling, you taste a square of chocolate, you touch the surface of your smartphone, you hear a coworker laughing. These sensations exist in the physical world. Although communicators say, hear, write, and read words, what those words represent is abstract. You can place your hand on this page or screen and touch the words, but the meanings those words conjure up exist in your mind.

Although all words are abstract, they vary in their level of abstractness. Some words are fairly specific, such as "my friend

SPEAKING OF ...

Engaging in Lexpionage

Global Language Monitor estimates that English gains one new word every 98 minutes or nearly 15 new words each day.[6] Want to find out more about those new words? Websites such as Word Spy (wordspy.com), the *Macmillan English Dictionary* (macmillandictionary.com), and World Wide Words (worldwidewords.org) will clue you in on the latest additions. The American Dialect Society (ADS) identifies the most influential words of the year. For example, ADS members voted the singular use of *they* (rather than using she or he) the Word of the Year for 2015 and *google* the word of the decade. In 1999, *Y2K* was the top choice, *web* was the word of the decade, and *jazz* was the word of the 20th century.[7]

Figure 10.3 Levels of Abstraction in Language

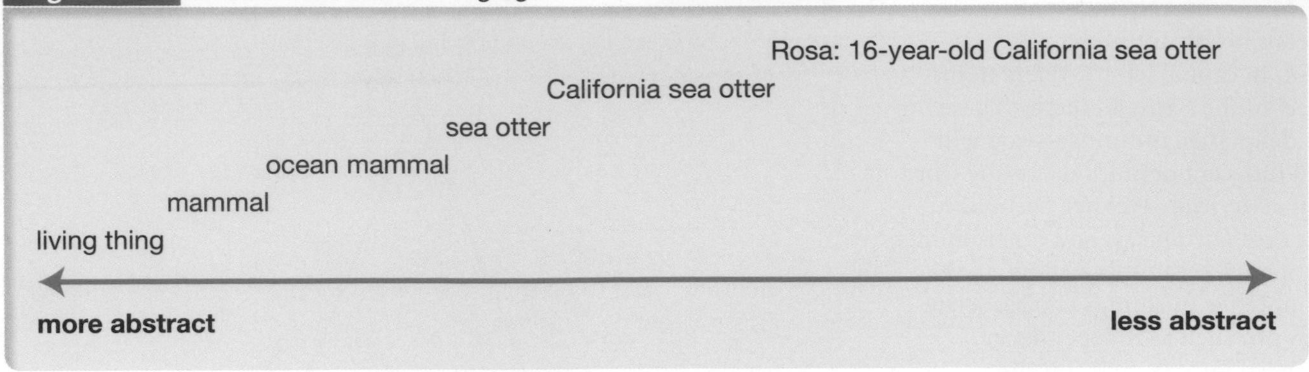

Kyoung." Others are very abstract, such as "human being." **Figure 10.3** shows how words vary along a continuum from more to less abstract. In the example, "living thing" is the most abstract—the phrase could refer to plants or animals, humans or insects. The words become less abstract as you progress up the levels until you reach a particular living thing, 16-year-old Rosa, a famous sea otter living at the Monterey Bay Aquarium.

Language Is Active

Like time, language doesn't stand still. As people learn new things about the world and encounter new experiences, they develop new words. Before the Internet, words such as *cyberbullying, hyperlink,* and *phishing* didn't exist. Each year, *Oxford Dictionaries* adds about 1000 words to its online edition. Recent additions include *awesomesauce, hangry,* and *bruh.*

Communicators continually alter the meanings of words. The advent of the Internet brought with it new meanings for *spam, zombie,* and *cookie.* You might think the term *webpage* traces its origins from the pages of a printed book. Yet scrolling through a page on a website is more like unrolling and reading a papyrus document from ancient Egypt.[8]

Language is dynamic in another way, too. You've probably heard sayings such as "All talk, no action" and "Actions speak louder than words." Yet language *is* action. You accomplish goals when you use words. In public speaking, speakers inform, persuade, and entertain. Speakers get listeners to think more deeply, laugh out loud, learn something new, change their views, and alter their behaviors.

You take similar actions with words in your everyday conversations. You promise, calm down, cheer up, compliment, accuse, blame, support, and criticize—that is, you affect those around you with words.

Language and Culture

Language and culture are inseparable. How you use language reflects your culture, and your culture influences the language you use and how you interpret it. Consider how people in the United States refer to time. You probably say things like, "That's a waste of time," "I like spending time with you," and "Time is money." Most Americans view time as a commodity that can be given ("I can give you a few minutes of my time") and taken away ("I won't take much of your time"). You likely think of time as something you "own," referring to "my" time and "your" time. The words people use give strong clues about what's important in a culture and what's not.

Americans generally consider speech and speaking extremely important, in part because the U.S. Constitution guarantees free speech. FreeThesaurus.net lists almost 300 synonyms for *speak*—words such as *articulate, chatter, gab, muse, take the floor,* and *vocalize.* Yet listening—a central aspect of democracy as well—doesn't get nearly the attention that speaking gets. FreeThesaurus.net includes just 31 synonyms for *listen,* about one-tenth the number for *speak.*[9] Even though communicators listen more than they speak, American culture puts a much greater emphasis on speaking than on listening.

In public speaking contexts, culture becomes especially evident when speakers use slang, jargon, idioms, euphemisms, and clichés.

Slang

Informal language typically used in an interpersonal setting, such as *whatever,* or *nah,* and *fam,* is referred to as **slang**. Because public speaking is more formal than conversations with your friends, you'll want to avoid using slang in speeches. Slang can hurt your credibility, giving your audience the impression that you're not taking the event seriously or are unprepared.

slang
Informal, nonstandard language, often used within a particular group.

Jargon

Technical terms and expressions associated with a specific profession or subject are considered **jargon**. For example, jargon associated with new media frequently finds its way into everyday conversations. People *text, blog,* and *Skype.* Internet users are concerned about *spam, viruses,* and *malware,* and search for free WiFi so they can get *online* at their local coffeehouse.

jargon
Technical language used by members of a profession or associated with a specific topic.

Both slang and jargon require an insider's knowledge to understand what the words mean. If you're part of the military culture, for instance, you've internalized its jargon as part of your own vocabulary.

Idioms

Idioms have practical meanings that differ from their literal meanings. Listeners must have a solid command of the language as people use it in everyday conversation to interpret an idiom correctly. Here are examples of the literal meanings of idioms and their common interpretations:

idiom
An expression that means something other than the literal meaning of the words.

- That test was a piece of cake.

  Literal meaning: That test was a confection made of flour, sugar, and eggs.

  Idiomatic meaning: That test was easy.
- You should take your friend's advice with a grain of salt.

  Literal meaning: When your friend gives you advice, you should eat a grain of salt.

  Idiomatic meaning: Don't take what your friend says too seriously.
- Would you lend me your ear for a few minutes?

  Literal meaning: Would you remove your ear and give it to me for a few minutes?

  Idiomatic meaning: Would you listen to me for a few minutes?

You might laugh at the literal meanings if you've grown up speaking English, because you're so accustomed to hearing and using idioms—you don't even think about how you've learned to interpret them.

Euphemisms

Speakers use **euphemisms** in place of words that are viewed as more disagreeable or offensive. For example, pornographic movies are called "adult films," and those who star in such movies become "adult entertainers." Euphemisms can prove useful if you're concerned you might offend your audience. For the most part, though, euphemistic language simply confuses listeners. For example, organizations typically refer to employee layoffs and firings as *downsizing* and *rightsizing,* which may sound less harsh—but not to the people who have lost their jobs.

euphemism
A word used in place of another word that is viewed as more disagreeable or offensive.

Clichés

cliché
An expression so overused it fails to have any important meaning.

Clichés are trite or obvious phrases used so often that they lack any important meaning. At one point, the remark was original, but overuse has made it dull. Examples of clichés include "the big picture," "think outside the box," and "it is what it is." Clichés cause problems for speakers in two ways. First, as with slang, jargon, idioms, and euphemisms, listeners must possess the cultural knowledge to interpret clichés. Second, because clichés are overused, listeners may think they've heard the speaker's message before and lose interest in the speech.

If you've grown up in the United States and English is your first language, you probably wouldn't be fazed by someone saying, "My bad," "Text me the directions," "We're on the same page," "I fell on my tush ice skating," and "Money doesn't grow on trees." But not all your audience members will have the cultural knowledge necessary to understand slang, jargon, idioms, euphemisms, and clichés. Unless they're an essential part of your speech, minimize your use of these types of language.

Language and Gender

Language and gender intersect with public speaking in two ways: how audiences interpret behavior and the language choices speakers make.

Gender-Based Interpretation

How listeners interpret what speakers say can depend on the listeners' gender.[10] Research on powerful and powerless language provides a useful example. Powerful language conveys the speaker's certainty about the topic. "This proposal will win over our client!" and "Our team effort led to our success" make clear the speaker's confidence. Audience members view speakers who use powerful language as dynamic and competent. Powerless language such as "I guess," "sorta," and "right?" indicates uncertainty and hurts a speaker's credibility.[11] Even in everyday conversations, listeners are less likely to believe someone who sounds uncertain.

tag questions
Questions added onto the ends of declarative statements that lessens the impact of those statements.

hedges
Qualifiers, such as *probably* and *maybe*, that make statements ambiguous.

Researchers usually categorize **tag questions** as powerless language. Speakers tack on tag questions at the end of a sentence, as in "This proposal will win over our client, *don't you think?*" Men usually interpret "don't you think?" as uncertainty. But women generally view "don't you think?" as an invitation for others to state their opinions. Similarly, **hedges**—words that qualify what the speaker is saying—often function differently for men than for women. Women might interpret "Our team effort *likely* led to our success" as acknowledging that other factors may have contributed to the group's accomplishments. For men, "likely" could indicate a speaker's self-doubt. In addition, listeners evaluate a woman as less competent when she uses tag questions and hedges, whereas such language has little impact on how listeners evaluate men.[12]

Powerful language can lead to similar misunderstandings. Statements such as "This research leaves no doubt that the program will fail" and "Employee morale has never been higher" convey certainty and conviction. But for women such language can also convey arrogance and disdain for other perspectives.

Table 10.1 **Replacing Gendered Language with Gender-Fair Language**

Instead of Saying This ...	Say This ...
mankind	humankind, humanity
man-hours	staff hours, hours
the common man	ordinary people, average person
chairman	chair, chairperson
freshman	first-year student
waitress/waiter	server
male nurse	nurse
lady lawyer	lawyer
career woman	professional

Gender-Fair Terminology

Using language that excludes or demeans some audience members will cause many of them to stop listening to you. To be sure that you're addressing all members of your audience equally, use **gender-fair language** words that are not associated with or do not privilege either sex.[13] Consider the difference between *stewardess* and *flight attendant*. The first word suggests a woman; the second could be a woman or a man. **Table 10.1** provides examples of gender-fair alternatives to gendered language. Using gender-fair language also refers to the order in which speakers refer to people. Generally, listeners think of the first item in a list as the most important and the last as the least important. Do you always say "men and women," "boys and girls," "husband and wife"? To avoid privileging one sex over the other, rotate the order of gendered terms.

gender-fair language
Words that are not associated with or do not privilege either sex.

Also, avoid language that demeans either women or men. For example, referring to a "female doctor" suggests that women aren't typically physicians—yet the American Medical Association reports that about 33 percent of all U.S. physicians and nearly half of all students in U.S. medical schools are women.[14] Use inclusive pronouns, as in "A bicyclist should always wear her or his helmet." Better yet, use the plural and avoid gendered language, such as "Bicyclists should always wear their helmets."

Using gender-fair language in your speeches also means using similar language for women and men when describing them and their accomplishments.[15] From sports to political campaigns, women and men are often portrayed in very different ways. For example, sportscasters typically describe male athletes in terms of their physical abilities but describe female athletes in terms of their personalities, looks, appearance, and sexual attractiveness.[16] Consider the differences in these two statements: "His ability to make the key shots is amazing!" and "She looks fabulous in the team's new uniform!" The bias works both ways. When talking about a man in the nursing profession, a speaker might say, "He's so sensitive and caring." Yet those are qualities you'd associate with any nurse.

Aspen Photo/Shutterstock.com

When you use gender-fair language in your speeches, you describe women's and men's activities and accomplishments in the same way. For instance, you might talk about a basketball player's ability to quickly move the ball down the court; you would not comment on her hairstyle.

Spoken versus Written Language

So far, you've learned about the general characteristics and qualities of language. Although written and spoken language share these general traits, they differ in important ways. Since audience members listen to your words rather than reading them, use spoken language in your speeches. Audiences often find speeches read word for word ponderous and difficult to follow. Listeners usually prefer an extemporaneous delivery method (Chapter 12), in which speakers use conversational and engaging language.

Dynamic versus Static

Public speaking occurs *in the moment* as the speaker and the audience come together to create a speaking event. As a result, speaking is dynamic. Unless participants record the event in some way, what they say is fleeting and impermanent. Listeners will recall some of what they hear, but they can't go back and rehear what you've said. Redundancy helps overcome the transient nature of spoken language, and audience members expect some redundancy to help them recall what the speaker said. Speakers therefore preview main points, provide internal summaries, and review key ideas in the conclusion. In contrast, written language is static. Readers can reread a passage of text over and over again, so they don't need the redundancy that listeners need.

Immediate versus Distant

The immediacy of spoken language affects public speaking in several ways. First, listeners receive the message right away, while the speaker is talking, and can provide nearly instantaneous feedback. In contrast, writers receive no immediate feedback from their audiences. Second, public speaking involves all the senses—audience members hear how the words are spoken and see how the speaker uses nonverbal communication. Gestures, movements, and vocal intonations provide a context for the words speakers use. Third, immediacy allows speakers to refer to the situation in which the speech is taking place. So speakers can make comments such as "You've dressed for the warm weather we're supposed to get later today" and "How many of you have studied for your finals next week?" Jose Luis Campo, president of the Americas Paralympic Committee (APC) provides an excellent example of referring to the speech situation. In his opening ceremony speech at the fifth Parapan American Games, he referred to the games' location this way:

> Not only are the athletes the best prepared ever for this event, but so is the spectacular city of Toronto. Never in the history of the Parapan American Games has one city shown such dedication and commitment to this event and the legacies it can leave. . . . These Games have already had a huge impact on this city and its surrounding area. Accessible venues have been built with legacy in mind, and I am sure this impact will only be magnified over the coming days, weeks and years.[17]

He went on to describe the future of both the games and city as "bright," demonstrating how the fortunes of Toronto paralleled that of the Parapan American Games. Linking the event's location with his topic established a common experience for audience members.

Informal versus Formal

When you talk with friends, neighbors, coworkers, and others, your language is rather informal. You might say, "Hey, what's up?" and "How's your day?" You use slang and jargon. Your sentences are short and often incomplete. Ordinarily, in these interpersonal situations you're not concerned with choosing the perfect words to express your ideas. In contrast, the language you use when you give a speech is more formal than your everyday conversations, yet still conversational. However, you don't speak as casually in your speeches as you do with your friends, even if your friends are in the audience.

Irreversible versus Revisable

Getty Images Entertainment/Getty Images

Although you can retract your words when you speak, as Steve Harvey did after he announced the wrong contestant's name for the Miss Universe Pageant, you can't change what you said and what the audience heard.

Once you've said something, it's out there. You can try to take it back, but listeners will still have heard what you said. You can immediately correct what you've said, as with, "Oh, sorry. I meant to say North Dakota, not South Dakota." In addition, you can reframe statements. For example, Steve Harvey, host of the 2015 Miss Universe Pageant, announced Ariadna Gutierrez, the contestant from Columbia, as the winner, only to retract that minutes later and award the crown to Pia Alonzo, the contestant from the Philippines. He later explained he misread the card with the winner's name on it.[18] Still, it proved an embarrassing moment for Harvey and the two contestants.

Question-and-answer sessions also allow you to further clarify and elaborate on what you say in a speech. At a recent Commonwealth Club meeting in San Francisco, Liz Fanning, Founder and Executive Director of CorpsAfrica, talked about the organization, its history, and current projects. Audience questions allowed her to provide additional information and further explain the similarities and differences between the work of U.S. Peace Corps volunteers and that of the young Africans who volunteer with CorpsAfrica.[19]

Unlike spoken language, written language allows for nearly infinite revisions—at least until the deadline for submitting a document. For example, this book underwent many, many revisions and multiple drafts as we worked to make the text right for you, our audience.

Narratives versus Facts

Although you often read stories, storytelling has its roots in oral communication. With its informality and immediacy, spoken language provides an ideal vehicle for telling a dramatic and engaging story. Oral language allows audience participation, sometimes including nonverbal feedback and additional information. The next time you're with friends or family, observe what happens when someone starts telling a story. Others likely will jump in with a bit of dialogue or description. When you're telling a story, it often becomes a group effort.

Written language handles facts, statistics, and other technical information more readily than spoken language because readers have time to review numbers and facts. Listeners don't have that luxury. Citing too many facts and statistics during a speech loses their attention because they can't comprehend all the information in one sitting.

Audience-Centered Language

Keep the differences between spoken and written language in mind as you read this section. Language geared toward your audience helps you get your message across in a way that resonates with them. You vary the words you use based on the intended recipients and the situation. For example, you use different language when welcoming

Table 10.2 Audience-Centered Language

Put your language in context by …	• mentioning the location. • referring to current events. • responding to what happens during the speech.
Personalize your language by …	• integrating audience analysis information. • remarking on what other speakers have said. • using *we, us, you,* and *I.*
Use inclusive language by …	• avoiding language that discriminates and stereotypes.
Use visual language by incorporating …	• similes. • metaphors. • parallelism. • rhyme. • alliteration. • antithesis.
Spark imagination with your language by using …	• imaginative invitation. • humor.

newcomers to a student organization than when welcoming friends to a get-together in your home.

Your success as a speaker depends in part on using words that appeal to your audience.[20] **Table 10.2** summarizes the ways to develop audience-centered language in your speech, described in the next section.

Put Your Language in Context

The in-the-moment qualities of public speaking work to your advantage. Integrating comments about the physical location, current events, and the speech situation brings spontaneity to your speech and keeps your listeners interested. For a report you're presenting at work, for instance, you might begin with, "The original idea for this project began in this very room, with many of you who are here today sitting around this conference table." Or maybe you're giving a welcome speech to new students. You could say, "This campus—the people, buildings, and traditions—may seem strange to you now. But by the end of the semester what you see around you today will be familiar and comforting—almost like home." These direct references to the context in which you're speaking help you gain and maintain your listeners' attention and let them know you've designed the speech for them.

Putting context in your language also means responding to events that happen during your speech. If many people were to applaud during a speech of tribute, for example, you could say, "I can tell you agree with me" or "I share your enthusiasm." In your public speaking class, you might acknowledge audience feedback by saying, "I see a lot of heads nodding" or "Some of you look puzzled."

Personalize Your Language

In most public speaking situations, you and your audience share the same physical space. Even with video conferencing, speakers and listeners hear and see each other. When you are the speaker, this gives you an opportunity to personalize your speech, using language tailored to your audience that promotes a productive communication climate (Chapter 3).

In your public speaking class, you get to know your audience from the speeches your classmates give and from your audience analysis (Chapter 5). Integrating information from audience questionnaires can help maintain your audience's attention. You might say something like "Based on your responses to my questionnaire, about half of you exercise once a week and a quarter of you exercise almost every day," or "Your responses to my questionnaire helped me narrow down my topic."

You can make your speeches even more personal by referring to specific people in the class. You might even mention a speech presented earlier in the term, as with "As Sondra mentioned in her speech last month…," or to one given shortly before yours, as with "In his speech a few minutes ago, Trent said…." During your speech, you also could comment on a specific audience member's nonverbal communication: "Mei, you look skeptical. Let me tell you more about my idea…."

Audiences expect some informality in spoken language, such as using the pronouns *we, us, you,* and *I* in your speeches. Using these pronouns includes the audience in your speech and encourages them to listen. For example, if you're speaking at a student organization meeting, you might say, "We've raised awareness of three important issues on this campus," or "I'm proud of the work you've accomplished in raising awareness on these three important campus issues." Words like *we* and *us* let your audience know you share similar experiences, values, beliefs, and attitudes. When you use the pronoun *I,* you let audience members know you're the one who thinks or believes a certain way. "It's important for all college students to take a public speaking class" doesn't have the same meaning—or the same force—as "I think all college students should take a public speaking class." In the first example, the speaker remains distant from the topic; listeners don't know whether she agrees with the statement or not. In the second example, the speaker takes a stand, letting the audience know her position.

SPEAKING OF ...

Hate Speech versus Free Speech

Professor Gerald Uelmen, dean of Santa Clara University's law school and a fellow of the Markkula Center for Applied Ethics, presents arguments both for and against regulating speech on campus in his essay, "The Price of Free Speech: Campus Hate Speech Codes." In arguing for such codes, he notes the harm done to individual students and the campus climate when colleges and universities allow hate speech. He also notes that restricting hate speech encourages logical debates rather than allowing speakers to rely on denigration and oppression. In arguing against such codes, Professor Uelmen observes that they run counter to the First Amendment's guarantee of free speech. In addition, students may remain silent, fearful of violating the hate speech code. To learn more about this issue, read Professor Uelmen's comments on the Markkula Center for Applied Ethics' website, scu.edu/ethics (search terms: hate speech code).

Use Inclusive Language

When you use **inclusive language** in your speeches, you choose words that don't privilege one group over another. Noninclusive language promotes discrimination and stereotyping, even if the speaker's word choices are unintentional.[21] Language that needlessly emphasizes someone's race, class, gender, age, dis/ability, sexual orientation, and the like is noninclusive.

Derogatory language provides a clear example of noninclusive language.[22] **Hate speech**—words that attack individuals or groups based on their race, gender, ethnic background, religious affiliation, dis/ability, or sexual orientation—is hurtful and degrading. That's why many colleges and universities have adopted policies against hate speech. And research shows that those policies work. Although teens and college students generally report welcoming diverse viewpoints, those same students indicate they have little tolerance for hate speech.[23] Refrain from using hate language in your speeches and challenge others who use it.

inclusive language
Words that don't privilege one group over another.

hate speech
Words that attack individuals or groups based on their race, gender, ethnic background, religious affiliation, dis/ability, or sexual orientation.

Gendered language, discussed earlier in the chapter, provides another clear example of noninclusive language, but speakers may exclude groups in other ways. Here are some examples:

- Jeannette and her *Latina friend* Maria volunteer at a local food bank.

  Problem: Why identify Maria as Latina? Should you assume Jeannette is white?

- The *disabled actor* put on a great performance.

  Problem: If the person did not have a disability, would it be okay to say, "The

Neal Waters

Using inclusive language invites all audience members to listen to your speech.

nondisabled actor put on a great performance"? Of course not. What, then, would be the best way to identify the actor you're discussing? Something like "The actor who played the lead role put on a great performance" works fine.

- She's the *senior citizen* on her crew team.

  Problem: Words such as *aged, elderly,* and *senior citizen* suggest the person is frail or impaired in some way. If the person's age is significant to the accomplishment, include it, as in "At 75, she's the oldest active member of her crew team." If age isn't important, don't mention it, as in "She belongs to a crew team."

- The *primitive people* of Africa relied on oral communication to pass along cultural stories.

  Problem: Primitive implies deficiency or incompetence. Because the reference is to a time period, *early* is a more accurate word.

These may seem like small distinctions, but all instances of noninclusive language affect everyone—the people left out and the people singled out.

Use Visual Language

simile
A language device that compares two things that are generally dissimilar but share some common properties, expressed using *like* or as.

metaphor
A language device that demonstrates the commonalities between two dissimilar things.

parallelism
Using the same phrase, wording, or clause multiple times to add emphasis.

The language devices presented below give your speech force and help your audience visualize your ideas.

Similes and metaphors, as Chapter 7 explains, are *analogies*—a shorthand way of comparing two dissimilar things. **Similes** suggest that two things share some similar qualities. Similes use *like* and *as* to make a comparison, as in "That story is like an old friend" and "The car rode as smoothly as a tin can on plastic wheels." **Metaphors** equate one thing with another. They often compare something more abstract with something more concrete, such as "Life is a rollercoaster" and "Ideas are wildflowers." Similes and metaphors make your speech memorable by comparing things that listeners might not ordinarily think of as going together. Similes and metaphors also help audience members understand something unfamiliar by comparing it with something familiar. When using **parallelism**, speakers use the same phrase, wording, or clause multiple times to add emphasis. At a recent Smith College commencement, Juliet V. Garcia, former president of the University of Texas at Brownsville and the first Latina to lead a U.S. college or university, used parallelism when talking about the strength she developed from challenges in her life:

> My strength comes from those two babies that I had between degrees that are now extraordinary parents themselves.
>
> My strength comes from my four grandchildren, one of whom, Carolina Rico, is here with me today and watching them become better versions of themselves.
>
> My strength comes from the 40,000 men and women that we have graduated from The University of Texas at Brownsville, so that never again will someone who grows up in South Texas fail to fulfill their dream of getting a college education because they could not afford to leave to attend college.
>
> My strength comes from having had the great privilege of doing important work in my community on the southern border of the United States. Not because there weren't opportunities for positions elsewhere, but because I could never find another place that seemed to need us so badly to help it succeed.[24]

AP Images/The Brownsville Herald, Brad Doherty

University of Texas at Brownsville President Juliet V. Garcia used parallelism to emphasize the main theme of her speech.

Garcia's repetitive use of the phrase "My strength comes from" emphasized the multiple challenges she faced and how she became stronger because of them. In addition, the items on her list of strengths moves from the personal to professional, demonstrating the different contexts in which she learned important life lessons. Through her use of parallelism, Garcia prepared the audience for her advice later in the speech, "Today, you must seek that which gives you strength. And having discovered it, you must run toward it."

You've likely heard **rhymes** ever since you were a young child. Rhyming words have similar sounds, usually the last syllable. Public service announcements often use rhymes to embed their message more clearly in our memories. For example, the National Highway Safety Administration uses the slogan "Drive Sober or Get Pulled Over" to encourage drivers not to drink and drive. In a recent contest for slogans that remind people to save water, one fifth grader submitted this catchy rhyme, "Even in the heaviest rains, don't let water go down drains."[25]

rhyme
Using words with similar sounds, usually at the end of the word, to emphasize a point.

In her keynote speech at a Stephens College commencement, Anita Parran, associate state director for public affairs at the AARP Missouri, ended with:

> I wish you well and I close with the words that my first-grade teacher wrote in my memory book:
>
> "Good, better, best, never let it rest, Until your good is better, and your better best."[26]

Parran could have said "Do your best" instead of quoting something from elementary school. But the short rhyme provided a more memorable message for the audience and gave her advice greater impact.

Speakers use **alliteration** when they repeat a sound in a series of words, usually the first consonant. Classic tongue twisters provide examples of alliteration, such as "She sells seashells by the seashore" and "Fat frogs flying past fast." Alliteration can increase audience members' recall, but avoid alliterative phrases or sentences you find difficult to say. In his speech on integrity at Tuskegee University, Samuel P. Jenkins, a vice president of Boeing, described the organization's ethics website in this way: "We established a special portal so *anyone* could reach us *anytime* from *anywhere, anonymously* if necessary."[27]

alliteration
Repetition of a sound in a series of words, usually the first consonant.

Antithesis refers to the juxtaposition of two apparently contradictory phrases that are organized in a parallel structure. With antithesis, the *meanings* of the phrases are in opposition, but the *arrangement* of the words within the phrases is in alignment. Antithesis gets listeners' attention because the speaker brings together words in an unexpected, yet balanced, way. For example, during her Nobel Lecture in Oslo, Malala Yousafzai asked her audience:

antithesis
Juxtaposition of two apparently contradictory phrases that are organized in a parallel structure.

> Why is it that countries which we call strong are so powerful in creating wars but are so weak in bringing peace? Why is it that giving guns is so easy but giving books is so hard? Why is it, why is it that making tanks is so easy, but building schools is so hard?[28]

Yousafzai's use of antithesis underscores the contrasts between activities that lead to war and those that lead to peace.

Spark Imagination with Your Language

Two language techniques can spark your audience's imagination: *invitation to imagine* and *humor.* An **invitation to imagine** asks listeners to create a scene or situation in their minds. Visualizing a place or series of events makes the audience feel more involved in your topic. Use your imagination when developing an invitation to imagine with phrases like these:

invitation to imagine
Asking listeners to create a scene or situation in their minds.

- "The miners were trapped 250 feet below ground and the water was rising. How do you suppose they felt, not knowing if anyone knew they were alive?"
- "Does a weekend of snowboarding at Stowe, Vermont, sound like a good idea to you?"
- "What would you have done under the circumstances?"

Some of the best stories are the ones you refer to but don't tell entirely. By reminding your audience of events, circumstances, narratives, or jokes you are confident they already know you can ignite their imagination without repeating something that is already familiar. University of Chicago professor Martha C. Nussbaum used this strategy in a speech at Georgetown University. She began with "I want to ask you to pause for a minute, and to think of the ending of a tragic drama, Euripides's *The Trojan Women,*" and then told the story in four sentences—just enough to help listeners recall the narrative's key turning points.[29]

Speakers sometimes use jokes to connect with their audiences, especially for particular kinds of public presentations, such as after-dinner speeches. Humorous stories and anecdotes can relax the speaker and create common ground with the audience. Appropriate use of humor can also help the speaker gain the audience's confidence, generate an emotional atmosphere consistent with the purpose of the speech, and provide a pleasant, memorable experience for listeners.[30]

Effectively told humorous stories and asides provoke audiences to imagine and visualize, inviting listeners to actively engage with the speaker's topic. Short humorous stories get the audience's attention at the beginning of the speech or help conclude it in a dynamic, unforgettable way. For example, Wabash College senior Dustin DeNeal began his commencement speech, "Katabasis and Anabasis: A Four-Year Journey," this way:

> I know, I know. You're looking at the title and thinking: "What in the world is this supposed to mean?" Well, to be honest, I'm not completely sure. But out of the countless lessons I'll take away from Wabash, one of the most important is that half the game is looking like you know what you're talking about even if you really don't. Big thanks to campus BS artist Chris Morris for that one. No, seriously.[31]

DeNeal's familiarity with his audience allowed him to gently poke fun at the title of his speech and gain his audience's attention.

Incorporating brief stories, quips, and humorous observations throughout your speech can help illustrate a point in the body of the speech and connect the audience with the topic and speaker. DeNeal included humor at several points in his speech, such as "We took the road less traveled and committed four years to an all-male institution. What were we thinking?"

Incorporating jokes and anecdotes into a speech can produce positive results if they're well planned and practiced. Follow these guidelines for using humor in your speeches:

- Tell only jokes or anecdotes appropriate for you, the topic, the audience, and the situation.
- Use humor strategically to attract attention, make a point, illustrate an idea, or conclude in a witty way.
- Keep jokes and humorous stories brief and to the point.
- Avoid trite and unoriginal jokes.

If you're not comfortable telling jokes or making funny comments, don't include humor in your speech. Self-disparaging humor, in which speakers make jokes about their own shortcomings, negatively affects speaker credibility. Poor use of humor damages the dialogue you strive to establish with your audience.[32]

Guidelines for Using Language in Your Speech

MindTap®

Watch It: View a video on making effective language choices in your speeches.

The words you choose to convey your message to the audience play a key role in developing your credibility and achieving your purpose. Your language should fit the topic, occasion, and audience. Speaking ethically requires that you use language that is respectful of yourself and your audience. This section explores the following specific guidelines for using language in your speeches: Use spoken language, choose meaningful words, balance clarity and ambiguity, be concise, avoid offensive and aggressive language, build in redundancy, and don't get too attached to your words.

Use Spoken Language

Audiences quickly lose interest when speakers read from a manuscript. Choose conversational, engaging, personal, and active language that speaks directly to your audience. Compare "It's important to investigate this topic in depth so students can gain more knowledge of their civil liberties on university campuses" with "I researched this topic so we could learn more about our civil liberties on campus."

Choose Meaningful Words

Avoid jargon, idioms, euphemisms, slang, and clichés that listeners won't understand or will find offensive. If you must use technical terms, define them clearly. Groups with specialized interests often use jargon or technical language that speakers can weave into their speeches. But even experts find listening to a speech filled with technical language difficult and tiresome.[33] Thoroughly analyzing your audience will help you strike a balance between precision and comprehension. Use words that are on your audience's level—not above or below it.

Balance Clarity and Ambiguity

Clear language promotes understanding. Compare "Many people believe in this proposal" with "Three hundred fifty-one individuals signed the proposal." By replacing "many" with an actual number, the speaker provides a concrete indication of the proposal's support. *Many* could mean thousands, tens of thousands, millions, or fewer than 10. At times, however, ambiguous language can bring people together. Nearly everyone would agree with "We need to give children the best education possible." Such statements motivate audience members to tackle tough projects. If you begin with specific ideas that not everyone supports, listeners will focus on areas of disagreement rather than agreement.

Be Concise

Concise language avoids unnecessary words. Compare "We must get the up-to-date version of our computer applications and software packages on a regular basis" (17 words) with "We must regularly update our computer software" (7 words). As you practice your speech, listen to the words you use and try out ways to present your points as concisely as possible.

Avoid Offensive and Aggressive Language

Connotative meanings often stir deep emotions. People link emotions with words and words with experience. As a speaker, you don't want to use language with negative connotations. You certainly would never use words that denigrate any group. Language that audience members consider aggressive—such as demanding that they take action or questioning their intelligence—puts up a barrier to listening and damages your credibility as a speaker.[34]

Build in Redundancy

Recall the fleeting nature of spoken language. Listeners can't stop, go back, and relisten to your speech the way they might reread written material. Build in redundancy through previews, reviews, clear transitions, and internal summaries. A few words, such as "Now let's examine," "As I mentioned earlier," and "Last, I'll talk about," serve to remind your audience of what you've covered and where you're headed.

Don't Get Too Attached to Your Words

Sometimes speakers get caught up in finding the perfect words for their speeches and forget about the purpose—informing, persuading, or entertaining the audience. As you practice your speech, try out different phrasing and listen to how it sounds. If you focus on choosing the "right" words, you'll lose the flexibility you need to adapt to your audience.

Summary

Language enlivens your ideas. The words you choose get audience members' attention, help them visualize your main points, and facilitate their ability to remember what you say. Language refers to the system of words you use to communicate with others. It is arbitrary, ambiguous, abstract, and active, characteristics that present speakers with both opportunities and challenges. Because language is arbitrary, audiences may interpret your words in ways you don't intend. Because language is ambiguous, consider both the connotative and denotative meanings of the words you use. Because language is abstract, consider when to discuss ideas and concepts rather than tangible objects and specific actions. Because language is active, the words you use and how you use them change over time.

Language and culture are interdependent. You learn about the meanings of words from your culture, and words help you interpret culture. Slang, jargon, idioms, euphemisms, and clichés highlight the link between language and culture. Because your audiences may not always share your cultural background, it's best to avoid these types of culture-specific words or phrases unless they're essential to the speech. You must also pay attention to gender and language when you give a speech, considering how the gender of your listeners will affect how they interpret your message. In addition, use gender-fair language to avoid alienating some members of your audience.

Spoken language differs from written language in that it is dynamic, immediate, informal, irreversible, and based in narrative, whereas written language is static, distant, formal, revisable, and able to describe multiple facts. When you give a speech to an audience, use spoken language in an engaging conversational manner and use audience-centered language. When you take an audience-centered approach, you put your language in context, personalize your language, use inclusive language, use visual language, and spark imagination with your language.

To use language successfully to engage your audience, use spoken language, choose meaningful words, balance clarity and ambiguity, strive for conciseness, avoid offensive or aggressive language, build in redundancy, and don't get too attached to your words.

ANALYZE IT

MindTap®

Watch and analyze this speech on MindTap.

Sierra, The Role of Sports in Society

Sierra's assignment was to give a 3-5 minute informative speech to her class. She chose a subject with which she was personally familiar to inform her audience about the role of sports in society. Pay particular attention to the various ways she uses language to captivate her audience.

It's full of adrenaline rushes, blood, sweat, tears, cheers, pain, pleasure, joy, and everything in between. Whether it's the roar of the crowd, the swish of the basket, the crack of the bat, or the sound of the buzzer, it's something that we are all familiar with despite the heartbreaks and gut-wrenching defeats, we can never let go of one of the greatest things in the world: sports. No matter if you're young or old, tall or small; sports have something to offer everyone. Maybe you like guys in tight pants, or girls in short shorts, or maybe you just watch for the love of the game. Sports provide unique opportunities that give children an outlet, teach leadership and responsibility, and invoke a sense of camaraderie among us.

As young children, most of us were signed up for one sport or another. Our parents thought it was a great way to get us out of the house and make new friends. Of course, they were right. For me, T-ball was the first sport that I ever played. Back then, there was more fascination with rolling in the dirt than actually playing the game. But none the less, a love for sports stemmed from the experience. Many children all over the world look to sports as an outlet. Some use sports as a way to escape their impoverished lives while others have the ambition to pursue a collegiate or professional career. These children come from different backgrounds and cultures but share one thing in common: their love for the game. For some, their love for sports is the only opportunity they have to learn leadership and responsibility. Sports provide endless opportunities for responsibility and leadership. A precious example would be, for me, to be a coach and to teach small groups of five year old girls how to shoot a basketball and a goal for the first time. Or maybe you're the leader of a baseball fantasy league and are responsible for making sure things run smoothly. It could be your turn to host and provide snacks for your friends, viewing the weekly football game. Or perhaps there's more at stake. You could be the point guard or quarterback responsible for hitting the winning free throw or throwing the winning touchdown to lead your team to victory. Each example provides an opportunity for leadership and responsibility.

However, there is something else that these instances also provide: camaraderie. Across cities, states, and nations, sports bring millions of people together. In South Carolina, most of us unite to cheer for one of two teams, Clemson or South Carolina. Despite the severity of the rivalry, and it is pretty severe, we are all able to come together and share in the fellowship of the game. Even though at the end of the game, one team is left with the sinking feeling of defeat, most recently Clemson, and the other overflowing with the joys of victory, we can still come together for the love of the game. During the Olympics, nations unite under their flag to cheer for their home country. We anxiously await the medal count at the end of each night and hold our breath to see if Michael Phelps will win yet another Gold Medal for the United States. It is the thread of patriotism that unites us under one nation to cheer for the home team.

Whether we experience victory or defeat, we love the game, our love for the game can never be taken away from us. Sports present us with a means to escape our daily lives and enjoy ourselves. Through them we are given opportunities to lead groups of our peers and teach the next generation. Sports allow us the once in a lifetime opportunity to come together and celebrate as a nation. They can stir up emotions that we wouldn't normally express. When it's all over and the fans and athletes alike, we all hang up our jerseys in our respective locker rooms or closets and anxiously await for the next opportunity to compete.

Questions for Discussion

1. How does Sierra's language reflect the qualities of spoken language? For example, how was her language immediate?

2. How was Sierra's language audience centered? Give an example of how Sierra:
   a. Put her language in context.
   b. Personalized her language.
   c. Used inclusive language.
   d. Used visual language.
   e. Sparked imagination with her language.
3. How well did Sierra follow the guidelines for using language in public speaking? Give examples for each area.
   a. Used spoken language.
   b. Chose meaningful words.
   c. Balanced clarity and ambiguity.
   d. Was concise.
   e. Avoided offensive and aggressive language.
   f. Built in redundancy.
   g. Didn't get too attached to her words
4. What have you learned about language from the content of Sierra's speech?
5. What have you learned about language in public speaking from closely examining Sierra's speech that you can apply in your own public speaking experiences?

> APPLY IT . . .

IN THE WORKPLACE

Uncovering Workplace Vocabulary

Organizations develop cultures with their own norms, practices, and vocabularies. For example, consider the language you need to know to function at your particular college or university. At San José State University, for instance, there's BSAC (Business Student Advisement Center), SpartaJobs (job and internship postings for students), and the WST (Writing Skills Test). Students follow road maps (semester-by-semester course plans for each major) and meet with advisors at AARS (Academic Advising & Retention Services). When you're part of an organization, you use the vocabulary without really thinking about it. When preparing a presentation for your workplace, consider your audience. Will people from outside the organization be there? Will they understand the words you use that are specific to your workplace? Also, even those within an organization may not know all the language that's specific to that company. In your college or university, for example, there's probably language students use that faculty don't and vice versa. Identifying the language used in your workplace will help you become more aware of its culture.

IN YOUR COMMUNITY

Using Audience-Centered Language in Service Learning

Whatever type of service learning or similar community project you're pursuing, finding the right words to talk with your audience provides an essential basis for effective communication. You may not give formal presentations to the people you're helping, but you're probably talking with them regularly. Identify ways you can put your language in context (such as referring to current events), personalize your language (integrating what you know about your audience), use inclusive language (avoiding words that stereotype or discriminate), use visual language (such as metaphors and parallelism), and spark imagination (such as telling a humorous story). Observe how others respond when you use audience-centered language. Which strategies work the best? Why do you think they're effective?

REVIEW IT

Key Terms

MindTap®
Use flashcards to learn key terms and take a quiz to test your knowledge.

alliteration 207
antithesis 207
cliché 200
connotative meaning 196
denotative meaning 196
euphemism 199
gender-fair language 201
hate speech 205
hedge 200
idiom 199
inclusive language 205
invitation to imagine 207
jargon 199
language 196
metaphor 206
parallelism 206
rhyme 207
simile 206
slang 199
symbol 196
tag question 200
tone 197

Reflecting on Using Language Effectively

1. Although ambiguity can produce positive results, it can also obscure the speaker's true intentions. Consider your use of ambiguous language. Have you ever used vague language to mislead or deceive others? Or has someone ever misled or deceived you in this way? What was the outcome? How did you feel about what happened? What did you learn from your experience?
2. Here are some common American idioms:
   a. at the drop of a hat
   b. biting off more than you can chew
   c. from rags to riches
   d. icing on the cake
   e. off the hook

   Explain what each idiom means. How would you replace each one in a speech you were giving? How can you check your speeches for idioms?
3. Gender-fair language recognizes that people are equal regardless of gender. How does gendered language influence your interpretations? For example, what image comes to mind when you read this statement, "He is the teacher," versus "She is the teacher"? The American Dialect Society voted the singular use of "they" the 2015 word of the year. What image comes to mind with this statement, "They is the teacher"? How can you integrate gender-fair language into your speeches?
4. Similes and metaphors help audience members visualize your ideas. Brainstorm for similes and metaphors that describe your college. How do those analogies help you visualize your campus? How do different similes and metaphors reveal or hide different aspects of your college or university? How can speakers make sure they use similes and metaphors that accurately represent the things they're comparing? Spoken language is immediate whereas written language is distant. How have you used the immediacy of spoken language in your speeches? How might you use this feature of spoken language in your next speech?
5. Swear words can get your audience's attention and give added impact to what you say. But is it the impact you want? Should you swear in your speech? Recall an instance in which you heard or read about a speaker cursing during a presentation. How did you react? Do you think that's the reaction the speaker intended? Is using such words ever appropriate in public speaking? Why or why not?

11 Integrating Presentation Media

READ IT

After successfully completing this chapter, you will be able to:

- Explain specifically how presentation media can enhance your speeches.
- Prepare presentational aids that reflect the basic principles of visual design.
- Create digital slides for presentation software that are designed to achieve the maximum effect.
- Discuss the advantages and limitations of various audiovisual presentation media.
- Take the necessary steps to ensure you deliver your presentation media effectively to your audience.

MindTap®

Start with a quick warm-up activity and review the chapter's learning outcomes.

Presentation media can add something special to your speech by giving your audience additional sensory input about your topic or argument.

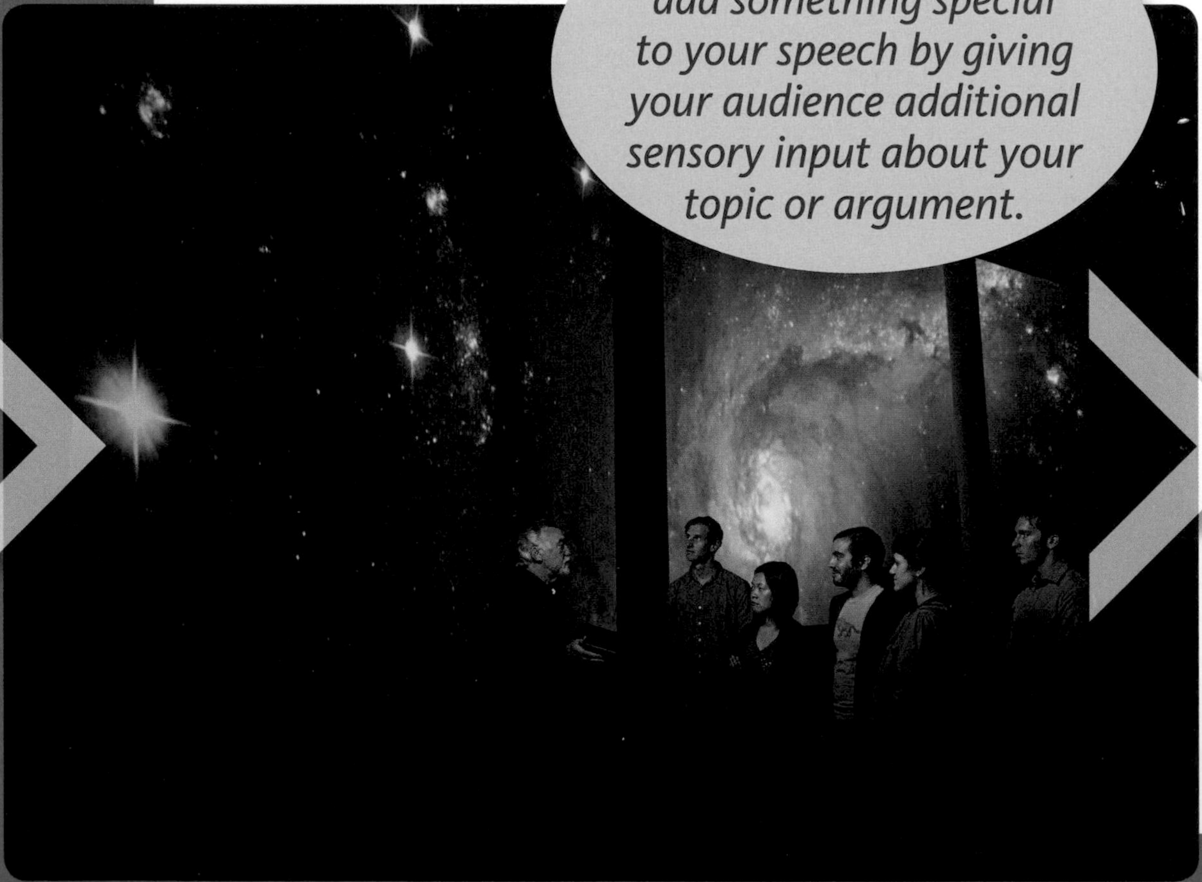

Asteroids, comets, and meteors streak across the night sky as the California Academy of Sciences presenter describes how these planetary bodies travel through our solar system and beyond. The speaker explains how a huge asteroid crashed to Earth more than 65 million years ago, creating a dirt-filled atmosphere that eventually killed off the dinosaurs. He zooms in on a meteor to show detail and then zooms out to show perspective. He warns that a big asteroid could strike Earth again at any time, and then he demonstrates visually how modern technology can redirect the path of incoming threats from space.[1]

Operating a wireless tablet computer from the stage, the planetarium speaker can set extraterrestrial bodies into motion on multiple screens to illustrate the phenomena he is describing. You certainly won't need such sophisticated technology to deliver excellent speeches this term. But you do have a wide array of high-tech and low-tech presentation resources available to you, and you should take advantage of them as much as you can. Even for beginning public speakers, the correct use of presentation media can enhance the quality of your work.

Presentation media have evolved dramatically over time. Communication technology's central place in contemporary public speaking emerged originally in ancient Greece. The philosopher Aristotle spoke of *techne* as the "craft" or "skill" of creating public debate that is based on reason and logic (techno-logy).[2] The rhetorical instrument or "technology" that was used skillfully to shape public address in Aristotle's time was spoken language. The appeal of today's presentation media evolves from and extends the extraordinary power of language.[3]

When integrated effectively into a speech, even low-tech presentation media like paper handouts and flip charts can enhance the look and feel of your speeches, strengthen your message, and help ensure the speech fulfills its purpose. But a warning: Presentation media are often misused. In this chapter, you'll learn about the most popular presentation media used today, the basics of good design, and guidelines for using presentation media effectively.

Jerry Holt/ZUMA Press/Newscom

Why Use Presentation Media?

MindTap®

Read, highlight, and take notes online.

presentation media
Technical and material resources ranging from presentation software and real-time web access (RWA) to flip charts and handouts that speakers use to highlight, clarify, and complement the information they present orally.

Presentation media range from software programs such as PowerPoint and Keynote to flip charts, music, and handouts that speakers use to highlight, clarify, and complement the information they present orally.

When used appropriately, presentation media can become a core feature of your speeches and help make them successful. They can help you attract and connect with audience members, spark their imagination, make sure they get the full meaning and impact of what you have to say, and demonstrate your creativity. Presentation media can add something special to your speech by giving the audience additional sensory input about your topic or your argument.

However, like everything else in your speech, you must have good reasons for incorporating media into your presentation. Learning how to use presentation media well involves much more than mastering a set of technical procedures. Your use of presentation media must be properly motivated and well executed in order to introduce, clarify, support, dramatize, or exemplify the information you present orally.

You can use presentation media to:

- Draw attention to your topic.
- Illustrate an idea that can't be fully described by words alone.
- Stimulate an emotional reaction.
- Emphasize a key point.
- Support your argument with a graphical display of facts and figures.
- Help your audience remember your main ideas.

Each type of presentation media has advantages and limitations, which are summarized in **Table 11.1.** The remainder of this chapter explores the most useful applications of the most popular presentation media and explains how you can best employ them in your speeches.

Table 11.1 **Advantages and Limitations of Presentation Media**

Type	Advantages	Limitations
Presentation software or digital slides	• Blends text, images, video, and/or sound into a speech	• Overused • Boring • Can distract from vocalized speech content • Speaker tends to talk to and read screen
Document camera	• Projects images with great detail • Can zoom in • Captures images • Displays a wide range of items	• Must manage order of items to be projected • Speaker tends to talk to screen
Flip chart	• Records spontaneous thought • Encourages audience participation	• Best for audience-centered brainstorming, not presenting • Difficult for everyone to see
Traditional whiteboard	• Records spontaneous thoughts	• Unprofessional looking • Writing takes away from speaking time • Speaker turns back on audience

(Continued)

Table 11.1 Continued

Type	Advantages	Limitations
Interactive whiteboard	• Encourages audience participation • Is enjoyable to use • Captures and saves boards • Serves as a screen; interfaces with polling technology	• Best used for instructional and professional group activities • Expensive
Video	• Evokes emotions in audience • Portrays impactful examples	• Interferes with speaking pace and audience focus • Often takes up too much time • If video is from web, link reliability and download speed
Handout	• Enhances audience recall after speech by having something to refer to • Reinforces key ideas	• Disrupts continuity of presentation • Is wasteful
Physical model	• Provides specific, memorable references • Helps audiences comprehend abstract materials and concepts	• Can be too small or detailed • Not suitable for large audiences unless projected by document camera
Human assistant	• Helps demonstrate two-person activities • Realistic • Another live body stokes audience interest	• Close coordination with assistant required • Can appear unprofessional • Can encounter human failure
Sound and music	• Sets context or mood • Triggers imagination • Packs entertainment value	• Decreases speaking time • Distracting • Sound quality and volume must be carefully controlled
Real-time web access	• Provides fresh, current information	• Connection and download speed • Absence or change of websites • Institutional access to web can be unreliable
Overhead projector transparency	• Technical simplicity and ease of use • Is portable • Is durable	• Out-of-date technology • Must manage transparency order and placement • Speaker tends to talk to screen

Understanding the Basics of Visual Design

Speakers often choose to enhance their presentations with some form of visual media. The basic principles of good design apply to every visual medium.[4] As always, your main motivation for using visual materials must focus on the needs and interests of the audience. Given this priority, how can you design visual materials to increase the effectiveness of your speech?

Visual materials can be broken into two categories: written information and images. To achieve the maximum impact from any medium that projects visual material, follow these guidelines:

- *Keep it simple.* Avoid including too much information in a graphic. The impact should be immediate and clear. By keeping visual material simple, you maintain maximum personal contact with your audience.

- *Emphasize only key ideas.* When you call attention to ideas with a graphic representation, make sure the graphic clearly illustrates your key points or most important supporting data.
- *Show what you can't say.* The best use of visual media is to reveal material you can't easily describe orally or with plain text. Photographs, drawings, simple charts, and graphs can all accomplish this objective.
- *Use close-up photographs and other images.* Select and present photographs, video, and other images that will create real impact. Close-ups can be very effective, especially to evoke emotional responses from your audience.
- *Keep the number of images you present manageable.* Too many images will tire your audience. Eight or ten relevant images should be the maximum number for most classroom presentations (unless you're giving a speech about a highly visual topic).
- *Combine variety with coherence.* If you use several images, vary the design enough to make them interesting but keep them aesthetically consistent. For instance, use the same colors or type font, but vary the content. Or mix photographs with graphics that maintain the same style throughout.
- *Use large lettering.* Use large lettering so the audience can read the text easily. Avoid presenting lengthy blocks of text.

Using Presentation Software

MindTap®

Watch It: View a video on using digital slides.

presentation software
Computer software that allows users to display information in multimedia slide shows.

The name PowerPoint has become synonymous with presentation software, but other digital slide software is available from Apple (Keynote) and from Prezi, Corel Presentations, Lotus Freelance Graphics, MagicPoint, and others. **Presentation software** allows you to display information as slides, video, and audio on a screen by using a personal computer, laptop, tablet, or smartphone and projector.

Without question, presentation software has become the most versatile and dynamic tool for most public speaking purposes. When presentation software is used effectively, audiences pay increased attention to speakers, understand main ideas better, and retain information well.[5] But not every speech or occasion calls for digital slides.[6] Many people have tired of overblown PowerPoint–driven speeches. Some classrooms and boardrooms have even banned the use of digital slide software.[7]

You may already feel comfortable and confident using PowerPoint, Keynote, or Prezi. But if you're just getting started, consult the online help and documentation that comes with the software. Your school may provide tutorials for learning how to use presentation software. You can find free tutorials online. Friends can help.

When used in moderation, presentation software can help you produce a more conversational and engaging presentation.[8] But remember: *Presentation software will not give your speech for you.* Nor should it be more prominent than you, the speaker.[9] You give a "speech," not a "PowerPoint presentation." You and your message must remain the primary focal points.

Simple slides can be used to emphasize a key point in the body of your speech, increasing the audience's focus and ability to remember your most important ideas (**Figure 11.1**).

Digital slides can present statistical data, helping to support your thesis. A clean, background helps your audience see the data clearly. Keep the statistics simple and readable. Be sure to orally cite the sources of your statistics and graphical material, such as primary uses of the Internet (**Figure 11.2.**).

Keneva Photography/Shutterstock.com

You can use presentation media any time during your speech. For example, you could begin or end your speech with a majestic digital slide of the rock formations at Yosemite National Park for an informative speech about how our national park system was established.

Hardware Setup

The hardware you'll use in class depends mainly on the equipment available at your school and the rules your instructor establishes for using presentation

Figure 11.1 Emphasize Key Ideas

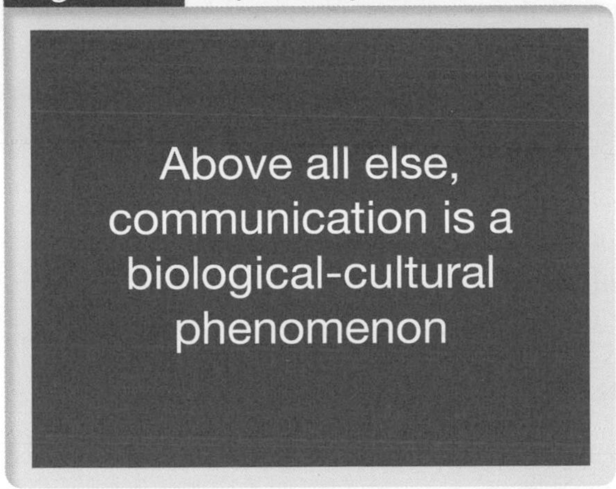

Above all else, communication is a biological-cultural phenomenon

Figure 11.2 Show Simple Data

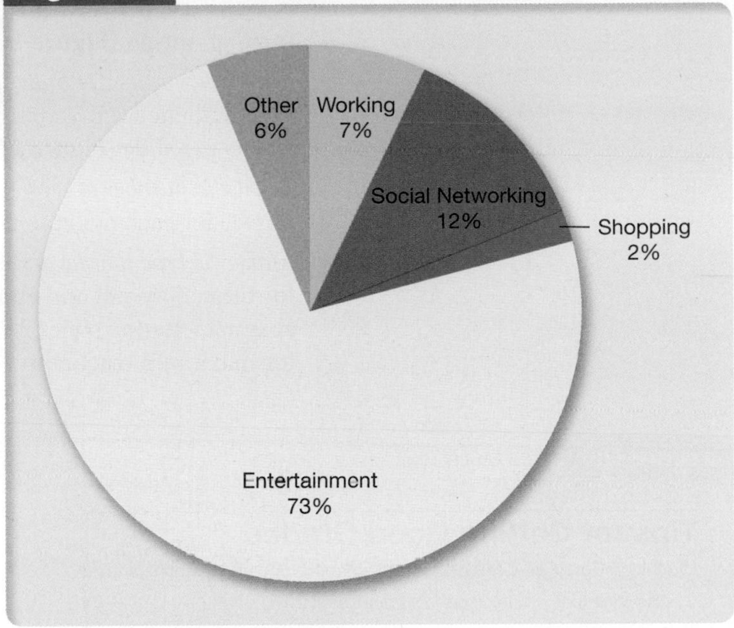

software in speeches. Your institution may provide a computer and projector in the room where you'll speak. In that case, you'll only have to email your slides to your instructor, or whoever is in charge, or save the slides on a flash drive and bring it with you to class. In other cases, you may bring your own laptop, tablet, or smart device to the classroom and connect it to the projector.

You need to know exactly how you're going to project your slides long before the day of your speech. Even if you bring your own equipment, know how to make it function properly in the room where you'll be speaking.

If you want freedom to move around the room during your speech—which is almost always a good idea—use a remote-control device to advance your digital slides.

Designing Digital Slides

The general guidelines for visual design presented earlier in this chapter explain much of what you need to know about designing digital slides. If you use presentation software, keep the following additional guidelines in mind:

- *Carefully develop your speech and then consider how you'll support your oral materials with digital slides.* Avoid taking the reverse approach—overpreparing your digital slides and underpreparing the rest of your presentation. The success of your speech depends primarily on the quality of what you have to say and how you say it.[10]
- *Use digital slides sparingly.* Audiences tire of too much visual information and will tune you out if they feel visually overwhelmed.[11] Digital slides can take the emotion and personality out of a speech and diminish the vital connection between speaker and audience.[12] Use digital slides in a way that keeps your audience connected to you and your topic. Some types of information are better suited to digital slides than others. For example, integrating technical material into a speech can be an effective use of presentation software.[13] But avoid jargon or symbols that your audience is not likely to know.
- *Balance creativity with clarity and predictability with spontaneity.* Avoid depending on the standard templates, clip art, and animation techniques that presentation software programs provide. Because PowerPoint and Keynote are so widely used, everyone immediately recognizes those predictable visual forms. Audiences generally don't like the software's animations and sound effects.[14]

- *Avoid relying on text or numbers.* The most effective use of presentation software is for visual, not textual or numerical, representation. The visuals may be still or moving images (**Figure 11.3**).
- *Limit the number of bullet points for each slide.* If you decide to use text, don't bore your audience with lengthy, wordy slides. Use a maximum of four to six bullet points per slide (**Figure 11.4**).
- *Limit the number of words for each bullet point.* Use just a few words or a brief phrase for each bullet point (**Figure 11.5**).
- *Make the type font large and clean.* Keep the font size large (40-point and above for titles; 20-point and above for text), and stay away from script or overly abstract lettering styles. Use sans-serif fonts, such as Arial, Verdana, and Geneva, for maximum readability (**Figure 11.6**).

Figure 11.3 Too Much Text

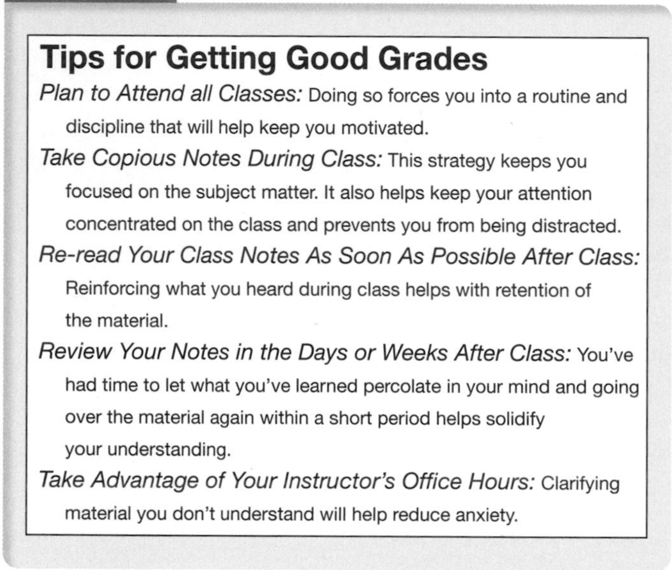

Tips for Getting Good Grades
Plan to Attend all Classes: Doing so forces you into a routine and discipline that will help keep you motivated.
Take Copious Notes During Class: This strategy keeps you focused on the subject matter. It also helps keep your attention concentrated on the class and prevents you from being distracted.
Re-read Your Class Notes As Soon As Possible After Class: Reinforcing what you heard during class helps with retention of the material.
Review Your Notes in the Days or Weeks After Class: You've had time to let what you've learned percolate in your mind and going over the material again within a short period helps solidify your understanding.
Take Advantage of Your Instructor's Office Hours: Clarifying material you don't understand will help reduce anxiety.

Figure 11.4 Too Many Bullet Points

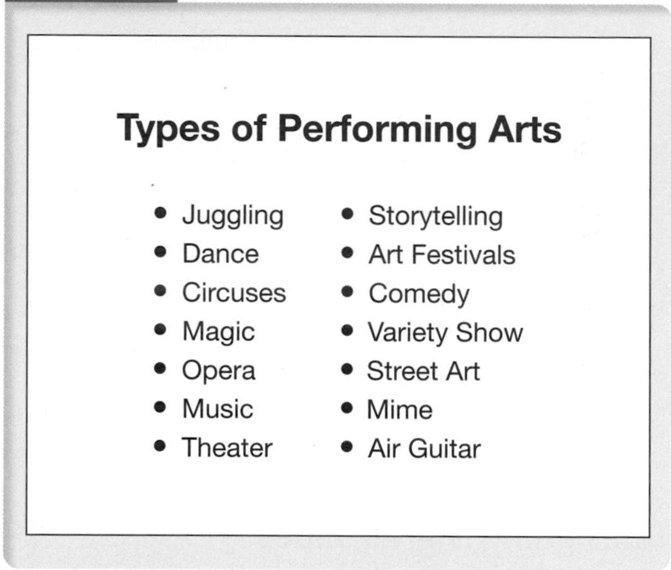

Figure 11.5 Wordy Bullet Points

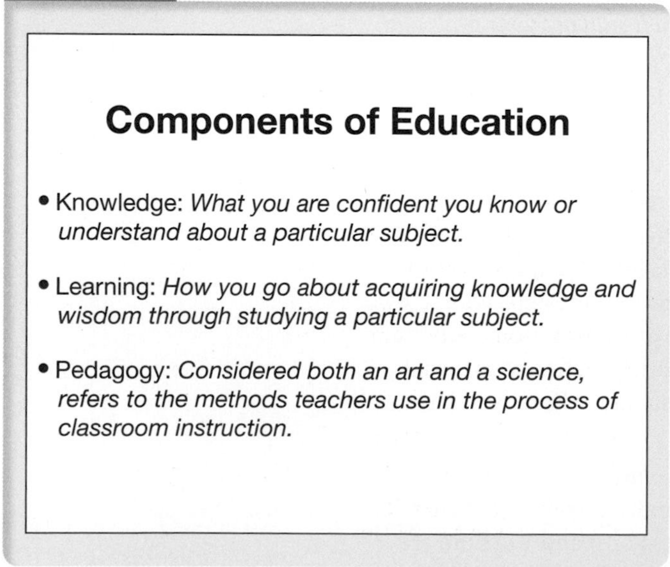

Components of Education
Knowledge: What you are confident you know or understand about a particular subject.
Learning: How you go about acquiring knowledge and wisdom through studying a particular subject.
Pedagogy: Considered both an art and a science, refers to the methods teachers use in the process of classroom instruction.

Figure 11.6 Large, Clean Type Font

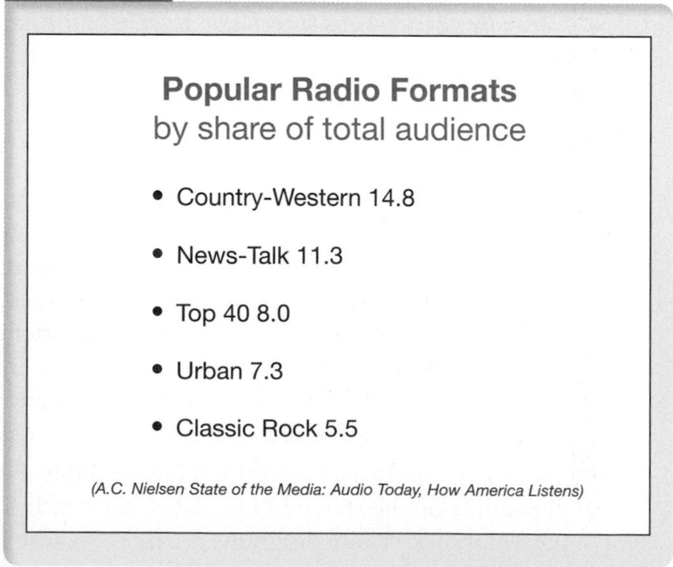

Popular Radio Formats
by share of total audience
Country-Western 14.8
News-Talk 11.3
Top 40 8.0
Urban 7.3
Classic Rock 5.5
(A.C. Nielsen State of the Media: Audio Today, How America Listens)

- *Choose transitions that fit the tone of your topic and visual material.* Presentation software gives you many ways to move from one slide to the next. Keep the transitions simple and don't be cute. Fading or dissolving from slide to slide works well. Within a speech, use the same or similar transitions for all your slides to give the audience a sense of consistency.
- *Use animation effects wisely.* Animation effects allow you to manipulate a digital slide's visual field in order to put portions of the field in motion. For instance, you can have an image "fly" in from top or bottom, left or right. But why? Any special effect you use should function in a way that is directly related to your speech's purpose. You can use the animation feature of your presentation software effectively to reveal bullet points one after the other. For example, you could first discuss the seriousness of sports concussions for high school students overall, then click to speak about the special danger for females, click again to talk about where the injuries usually occur, and so on through the list (**Figure 11.7**).

Figure 11.7 Reveal Bullet Points One by One

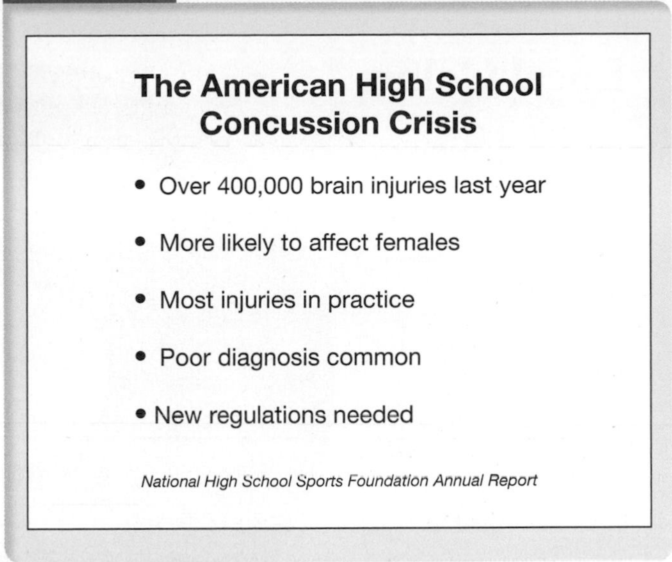

The American High School Concussion Crisis
• Over 400,000 brain injuries last year
• More likely to affect females
• Most injuries in practice
• Poor diagnosis common
• New regulations needed
National High School Sports Foundation Annual Report

- *Use color well.* To make your slides easy to read, choose colors that produce a high contrast between the background and the font. Most speakers prefer a clean white background with dark lettering. Sometimes it makes sense to match the color scheme of the slide set with the speech event or organization, like using your school's colors or logo for a presentation about a campus issue.
- *Don't copy webpages onto slides.* Internet pages can be a great source of information for your speeches (Chapter 6). It's tempting just to cut and paste those pages into your presentation media and use them as a slide during your speech. Doing so is almost never a good idea. Those pages weren't designed to be used in a speech so they don't translate well into a slide format. The pages usually contain way too much information. Cutting and pasting images from the Internet often end up looking like **Figure 11.8.** Your audience will get nothing from a slide like this and will quickly tire of your presentation.

Citing Sources for Digital Slides

Presenting clear and simple statistical data to support your argument can be a very effective use of digital slides. Just as you would do for a term paper in any of your classes, you must acknowledge the sources of information, ideas, or images you use in your speeches (Chapter 3). This includes reference material you present on digital slides. This requirement can be met in various ways. Your instructor may give you specific guidelines about how to cite references for your class.

Your instructor may find it sufficient for you to only cite your sources orally when showing a slide. For example, as you click on a slide that displays basic statistics about a decline in crime committed on your campus **(Figure 11.9)**, you could say, "According to statistics released in their annual report last year, the Valley University police department says that crime on our campus has been steadily decreasing over the past five years…"

Figure 11.8 Copying Internet Pages onto Digital Slides

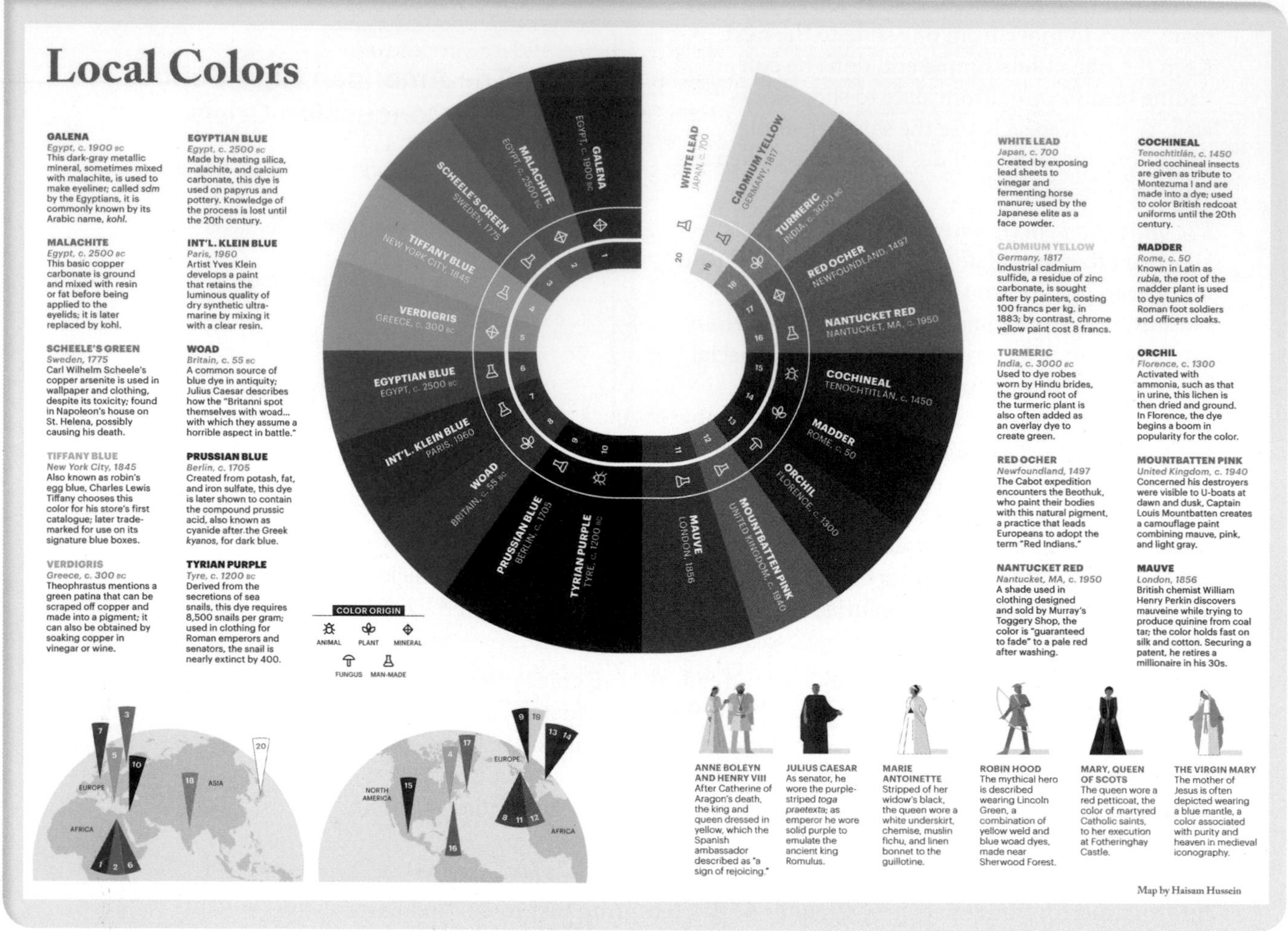

Source: http://www.laphamsquarterly.org/fashion/maps/local-colors

Figure 11.9 Citing Sources on a Digital Slide

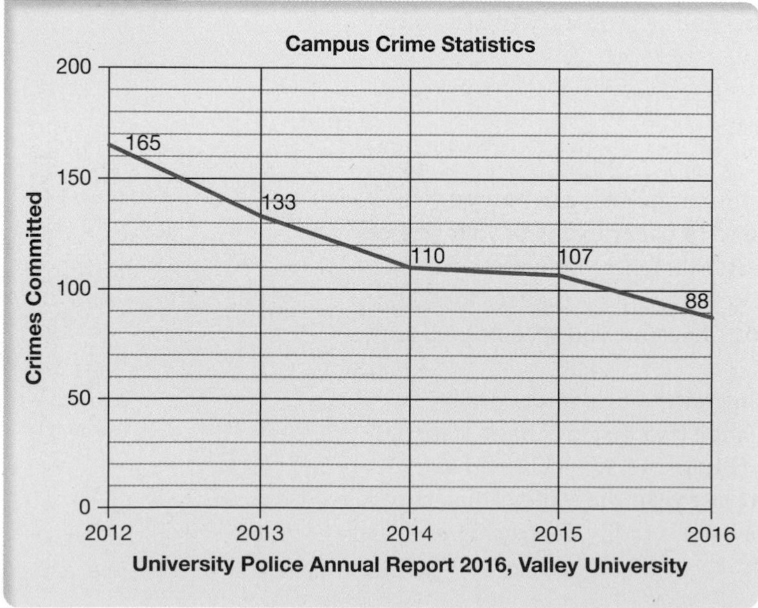

You could present the same slide and cite the campus police department with text at the bottom of the slide (**Figure 11.9**). If you do it that way, you should still acknowledge the source orally when you talk about the statistical trend. You build your speaker credibility, in part, by using respected sources, so make sure your audience plainly hears who or what your sources are. It's usually not enough to simply identify the source on the slide.

If you plan to make your slides available to your instructor or the audience after the speech, then be sure to also include a separate slide that lists your references. Don't show that slide during your presentation, but provide it later so your audience has full access to your sources. Reference page slides for digital slides should look no different than they do for a written essay or report. Your instructor will probably want you to follow one of the major style guides (MLA, APA) for your reference slide.

Using Other Visual and Audio Media

Loading up on presentation media, especially poorly designed digital slides, can destroy your relationship with the audience, get in the way of your purpose for speaking, and diminish the impact of your speech. Very often with presentation media, "less is more." The latest and most complicated technology is not always your best choice. Your topic, the size of the audience and of the room, and the public speaking event should dictate which presentation media you'll want to use, if any.

Each type of presentation media has advantages and limitations; these are summarized in **Table 11.1**. Media other than digital slides you can integrate into your speeches are covered here.

Document Cameras

Common in classrooms and meeting rooms, **document cameras** are used to project high-resolution images of any visual material—printed paper, a photograph, drawing, map, graphic, artwork, or small object. Images captured by the camera are projected onto a screen or blank wall, sent to a television monitor, or integrated into a website or videoconferencing system. Public speakers use document cameras to show something so small, intricate, or complex that the audience would not be able to see it well otherwise.

document cameras
A projection device that uses a video camera to capture and display images.

Document cameras (often referred to by their brand name, like "ELMO" or "Smart Camera") are easy to use. You place what you want to show under the camera. The material is illuminated by the document camera's lighting system, so the entire room does not have to be bright. Mounted on a movable arm, the camera captures an unobstructed view of the object.

Most document cameras focus automatically on the material you want to show, even three-dimensional objects, so you don't have to keep focusing as you move from one item to the next during your presentation.

Document cameras allow you to zoom in on a specific part of an object, show highly detailed images of the object, and capture and store images you create for later use. You can also use document cameras to show something with your hands, like assembling a small handicraft or demonstrating the correct finger positioning for sign language.

Here are some tips for using a document camera to the best advantage:

- *Be well prepared.* As with all presentation media, prepare the visual materials you want to show in advance. Acquaint yourself with the equipment—the camera and the remote control—*before* the day of your speech. Most document cameras are desktop or portable models that rest on a flat surface. The projector should be mounted from the ceiling or placed in such a way that it doesn't obstruct the audience's view or limit your movement.
- *Display your images only when you talk about them.* Just before you begin your speech, place your first item or object under the camera and turn on the camera. When you are sure the equipment is working properly and the image is sharply focused, use the remote control to put the projector in "dim" or "blank" mode so the image disappears from the screen. When you reach the point in your speech where you want to show the image, switch back to camera mode. Keep it there until you plan to talk about material not related to the last image you've shown. Put the projector in the blank or dim mode again. When you finish with your

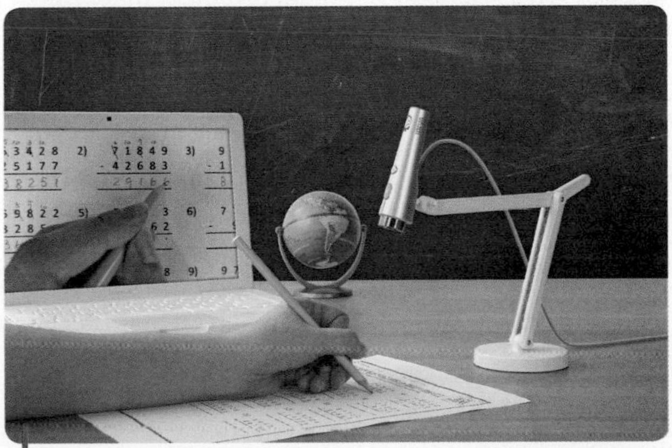

2016 IPEVO Inc

You could use a document camera to illustrate the features of a puzzle, map, or smartphone app.

final image, dim the projector for the rest of your speech. If the document camera is mounted on a mobile stand, you might want to push the stand out of your way to give yourself center stage for the remainder of your speech.

- *Number the materials in the order you'll use them.* If you intend to project several images during your speech, be sure to carefully manage the materials you're going to show. Stack or line up the materials in the order you plan to show them. Place the materials near the camera in such a way that you'll know exactly how to position them to appear properly on the screen. Preparing this way means you won't have to think about shuffling your visual materials while you're giving your speech.

Flip Charts

flip chart
A large pad of paper that rests on an easel, allowing a speaker to record text or drawings with markers during a speech.

Sometimes speakers want to document ideas brought up during an interactive brainstorming session. A **flip chart**, a large pad of paper propped up on an easel placed near the speaker, is an excellent medium for this purpose. Write on the flip chart with a big, bold marker so everyone in the room can see what you've written. Even the biggest high-tech companies routinely use flip charts for their in-person brainstorming sessions. The audience stays engaged during such interactive meetings, especially if the meeting is attended by a relatively small number of people. In large spaces with large audiences—say, more than 50 people—flip charts won't hold the audience's attention very well or serve the purpose of facilitating interaction among audience members.

Traditional Whiteboards

traditional whiteboard
A smooth whiteboard that can be written or drawn on with markers.

Using a **traditional whiteboard** with colored pens (or even a chalkboard with white chalk) can help you achieve the same outcome as a flip chart. The board, however, should be used *only* when brainstorming with the audience about ideas, never for presenting materials. Although it may be tempting, don't use a traditional whiteboard for posting telephone numbers, web addresses, mailing addresses, and the like. Turning your back to the audience while you scribble something on the board can make you look less prepared and professional than you are. You'll be more effective if you include this sort of information on a digital slide that you project during the speech or put in a handout for distribution after you conclude your speech.

Interactive Whiteboards

Interactive whiteboard
Also called *smart board*, a device that can maximize active student involvement in learning; can be very useful in certain situations.

Effective teaching and other forms of instruction promote interactivity between student and instructor, between student and student, and between student and ideas. **Interactive whiteboards** (sometimes called *smart boards)* can help maximize active student involvement in learning. Like traditional whiteboards, interactive whiteboards can be very useful in certain situations. But the use of interactive whiteboards for most public speaking events is limited mainly to group activities.

Interactive whiteboard technology consists of three components: a large touch screen situated in the front of the room, a computer, and a projector. Using electronic pens or just a finger, the user can write directly on the whiteboard or call up a keyboard and toolbar to make commands manually. Graphics can then be created in real time, revised, and moved around by touching the board. Interactive whiteboards come with audio speakers powerful enough for most classroom-sized presentations or activities. Any screen that is created during a presentation can be saved and distributed as an electronic file or as paper copies.

Interactive whiteboards are best used to facilitate activities. They function well in educational settings, often in elementary schools, where instructors ask students to write or manipulate images on the board. Interactive whiteboards can be used to project anything you can prepare on a computer, so they can also function as screens.

The interactive feature of these whiteboards can be taken to another level. Imagine that you want to find out how many people in your audience can correctly answer a question you have in mind. What if you wanted to survey audience members to learn about their opinions on a controversial topic? With polling software and wireless handheld response devices distributed to audience members, presenters can get immediate, confidential data they can display on an interactive whiteboard for viewing and analysis. The raw data—anonymous individual responses from the audience members to questions posed on the board—can be crunched and turned into attractive line graphs, pie charts, and bar graphs. These visual displays can then serve to provoke discussion about the question or topic at hand. Creative instructors and professionals can productively apply polling technology to interactive whiteboards in their classrooms or meeting rooms.

Bob Daemmrich/Alamy Stock Photo

Using an interactive whiteboard

The interactive whiteboard can also be useful in professional settings for activities such as brainstorming by small groups, game-based strategy sessions, participatory training exercises, and polling. But you are better served with presentation software programs like PowerPoint and a screen for almost any public speaking event.

Video

To determine whether you should use a video clip, ask yourself whether it will contribute something truly important to your speech. Showing a video clip can elicit an emotional response from the audience and increase how much listeners remember from your speech.[15] But it also dramatically changes the mood of the speech and may disturb the relationship between speaker and audience.

With the availability of video sites such as YouTube and Hulu, searching for and identifying a relevant video clip have become much easier than before. Audiences seem to appreciate video clips, if used well, as part of a speech. Viewing video clips is part of everyday life. More than 90 percent of Internet users ages 18 to 29 watch content on video-sharing sites, which is more than those who visit social networking sites, download podcasts, or use Twitter.[16] More than half adult Internet users are "online creators"—individuals who also post or share photos or videos online.[17]

Most short speeches are better without video. But if you decide to incorporate a video clip into your speech, consider these guidelines:

- *Keep the clip very short.* With other visual media, speakers continue to talk while showing images or text. Unless you turn off the audio for a video clip, you can't speak while it's playing, so you lose valuable speaking time. In addition, the clip takes the audience's attention away from you. Choose a very short clip for maximum impact and be absolutely sure it adds something to your speech that you cannot otherwise achieve.
- *Treat the video component as an integral part of your speech.* Determine how you will transition into and out of the video to provide a seamless experience for your audience.
- *If possible, embed the video within your digital slides.* Presentation software allows you to insert video into a slide so you can avoid relying on a separate piece of equipment such as a DVD projector.
- *Make sure the video is not offensive.* Video clips can be used to stimulate a strong reaction. Just be sure the content won't offend audience members, which may cause them to stop listening to you or dismiss your message.
- *Cite the source of the video clip.* As you introduce the video segment during your speech, say where it originated, not just where you got it. For example, many videos on YouTube and Hulu come from primary sources such as television networks or movie trailers.

- *Be sure the clip is legitimate.* Just as you have to make sure your written sources of information are credible, be certain your visual sources are too. Anyone can post almost anything on video-sharing sites, including hoaxes. Be sure you know that the clip you're using is authentic and legitimate.

Be wary of incorporating an attention-getting video clip at the risk of neglecting the most important elements of your speech—the content and the delivery. In addition, keep in mind that relating a video clip to your speech in a way that truly advances your purpose can prove challenging. Even if a brief video clip provides an enjoyable experience for an audience, it may not accomplish your goal to inform or persuade.

Handouts

handout
Sheets of paper containing relevant information that are distributed before, during, or after a speech.

A paper **handout** can be effective in some public speaking situations. For example, you might use a handout to provide a list of website addresses where audience members can make donations to a charity you've described in a persuasive speech. You might give your audience a diagram illustrating how to administer emergency cardiopulmonary resuscitation (CPR) treatment. You could hand out copies of a letter you've written to your state senator promoting tougher child pornography laws and encourage your listeners to sign and mail them.

Some speakers use a handout in conjunction with other presentation media. For instance, you might use digital slides to provide photographic detail and graphic summaries of the effectiveness of a new cancer-treating drug, then pass out a handout that provides a list of websites where audience members can find additional information about the new treatment.

If you decide to use a handout, think carefully about when you'll distribute it. You have three options: before you begin the speech, during the speech, or after you conclude. To help you decide which option to use, determine when the audience needs the information. Think about how the physical act of distributing the handout will affect your speech performance. Passing paper around the room is noisy and disrupts your audience's attention and concentration. Worse, the audience will read the handout and not listen to you. All things considered, it's almost always best to distribute handouts after you finish your formal remarks.[18]

Physical Models

physical model
A copy of an object, usually built to scale, that represents the object in detail.

For certain subjects, **physical models** that represent the topic being discussed can add a helpful visual dimension to a speech. Models are especially useful for describing and explaining scientific topics that involve a relatively large or very small physical structure. For instance, a replica of a fossil can help a speaker describe the physical characteristics of an extinct species. A model of a proposed new building in the community or campus helps audience members visualize what the building would look like. The molecular structure of an atom can be demonstrated with a physical model. Speeches about medical and biological topics such as the anatomy of the brain or the physiology of hearing can be difficult to present *without* the appropriate physical model.

You have options for displaying the physical model. Sometimes the best approach is to place the model in view or pick it up at particular times while you talk about it. Audiences usually respond well to this technique by paying close attention to the speaker. Manipulating the model with your hands can also help you show and describe the object well, especially to a small audience. The number of students in a typical public speaking class may be small enough that you can use the model this way.

But even with a small audience, it's often best to display a physical model under the lens of a document camera. By changing the camera angle and direction of the light source, many document cameras allow you to position even fairly large objects in front of the camera.

You might also consider making photographic images of the model and creating one or more digital slides of it using presentation software. You gain convenience by using a digital slide instead of the physical model, but you lose the ability to manipulate the model manually during your presentation. Showing the physical model creates a more realistic and intimate relationship with the audience when compared to digital slides.

Human Assistants

In some cases it can be helpful, even necessary, for the speaker to ask someone to play a supportive part in a speech. Some informative speeches lend themselves nicely to the use of a **human assistant**. For instance, to demonstrate a martial arts maneuver, proper first-aid techniques, the steps of Brazilian samba, or how to play good defense in basketball, a presentation that involves a human assistant can be more effective than digital slide images.

human assistant
A person who plays a supportive part in a speech.

Using another person as an accessory for topics like these can help you gain and maintain the audience's attention. The human dimension shows you have prepared something special—a bit of a show. But you have to control the situation tightly, so strict rules apply:

- Always select your assistant well in advance of your speech. Do *not* try to recruit someone on the spot. You have no idea how that person will react and the audience will be uneasy too. It's often best to ask a trusted individual who is not in your class to be your assistant.
- Give your assistant clear directions about what to do, and then practice the speech with that person until you are both exactly sure of what you will do and when during the presentation.
- Take responsibility yourself for bringing any necessary props or equipment to the place where you will give your speech.
- Make sure your assistant arrives before the scheduled time for the speech.
- Have your assistant remain seated until needed so as not to distract the audience.
- Maintain a professional demeanor with your assistant during the presentation.
- Be prepared to give your speech without your assistant in case of emergency.

Sound and Music

Sound and music, like visual images, can stimulate mental images, triggering the imagination and setting a mood.[19] Sound can provide compelling evidence of something that is difficult to explain with words. How might you convince your audience that a proposal for a new freeway through your city is a bad idea? Play traffic noise—loudly. How might you set the mood for a demonstration of restorative yoga positions? Begin with a few seconds of calming ambient music played softly.

When thinking about possible audio to include, always keep your audience in mind: Avoid sound or music that would offend or alienate audience members, such as songs containing profane or sexually explicit language.

The best way to play sound or music is to embed the audio file in a digital slide so you can transition into and out of your audio clip smoothly. Just be sure that whatever amplifier and speaker system you connect to delivers good sound quality and sufficient volume for the space where you give the speech. Standard tablet or laptop speakers will not be good enough in classroom settings. You'll have to connect to the house system or bring in your own speakers.

Andrey_Popov/Shutterstock.com

There are different kinds of presentation aids. For example, this speaker is using a physical model, the dummy, and a human assistant, the woman in blue, in his CPR presentation.

You can also use audio technology to integrate sound or music into your speech. That can be the best solution if you don't plan to use visuals to accompany the audio. Bring in your own smart device, MP3 player, or portable CD player. But remember, if the room isn't set up with speakers, you'll have to bring them, too. Be sure you've got wireless connectivity or the right connector wires to link your device or player to the house sound system or to your external speakers.

Cue up the audio clip you want to play on your playback device beforehand. Indicate clearly on your presentation outline when you want to play the clip or clips during the speech. Set the volume high enough so everyone can hear the sound clearly, but don't turn it up so loud that it annoys your audience. Be sure that whatever system you use is placed in a convenient location so you can start and stop the audio with minimal disruption.

Live, unrecorded sound or music can also work in a speech. Some public speakers briefly sing or play an acoustic instrument as part of their speeches, for instance. That can be effective; just don't confuse giving a speech with giving a concert.

Real-Time Web Access

real-time web access (RWA)
Employing a live Internet feed as a visual media or information resource during a public speech.

webidence
Web sources displayed as evidence during a speech, found by using real-time web access or webpage capture software.

Many classrooms and meeting rooms provide live Internet access, which gives you the option of displaying websites during your speech. This is a dynamic resource that can be very useful for certain kinds of presentations. When applied to speechmaking, this functionality is termed **real-time web access (RWA).** With RWA, you navigate in real time through webpages associated with your topic. You can use RWA to demonstrate how to do something specific on the web such as checking the current status of any topic or displaying articles found on websites that support your purpose or argument. This web evidence, or **webidence**, gives your presentation an in-the-moment feeling not possible with static digital slides or video.[20] Because the audience understands that you are speaking in real time, you can also encourage the group to participate in your navigations or searches.

The spontaneous nature of RWA and webidence can be used to the speaker's advantage. Still, if you plan to display one or more web pages in real time during your speech, check immediately beforehand to make sure access remains possible and that the site(s) you intend to show are available.

Overhead Projector Transparencies

transparency
An acetate page displayed by means of an overhead projector.

Although most speakers in education and work-related speaking situations use digital slides and document cameras, overhead projector transparencies are still used in some classrooms. The projectors tend to be bulky and noisy, but they are inexpensive, durable, and easy to use.

The basic principles for using an overhead projector are the same as for a document camera. But to use an overhead projector, you must first make transparencies of the material you want to show. **Transparencies** are acetate pages displayed by an overhead projector during a speech. You can create high-quality transparencies in color or black and white by using the presentation, word-processing, or graphics software on your computer. After generating the visual material you want to show, print that material onto sheets of acetate.

Delivering Presentation Media Effectively

Presentation media can not only enhance your effectiveness as a speaker but can also detract from your message if not used correctly. You want to avoid racing quickly through your last slides to get to the end of your speech. You also want to prevent getting stuck in front of your audience fumbling with the technology. Carefully managing your technology greatly reduces these kinds of risks and helps you deliver presentation media effectively. Good planning and practice are required. The following advice will help you integrate presentation media into your speech successfully.

Consider the Room

To get the maximum effect from your presentation media, be sure you become completely familiar with the location where you will speak. You must have unobstructed access to the equipment and to your audience while you speak. *Take charge of the situation. Arrange things the way you want them.* This will boost your confidence and make you appear more comfortable.

Be sure your audience can see any images you display. If you use digital slides or a document camera, project the images at a height and distance that will make them easy for everyone to see. This may require moving a table or a stand to a better position. If you use physical models, be sure they can be seen by everyone. Should you include a human assistant, clear the floor space you'll need *before* you begin your talk.

When using digital slides or other media that require a screen, avoid turning your body toward the screen where the images are projected. Remain facing your audience while they look at the screen. You will always know exactly what's being projected by quickly observing what's on your computer screen. It looks amateurish to glance back at the big screen or monitor.

corbis rf/First Light

There's no need to look at your digital slides while presenting. It's even less effective to read the content of your slides to audience members. Let them view your slides on their own while you engage them directly with your words.

Practice with Your Media

Select, design, and edit the digital slides, video clips, audio clips, or any other technological components of your presentation well before the day of your speech. Then practice using the technology. Discovering the best way to integrate your presentation media into your speech will help you revise and improve the speech during practice sessions. You'll also be much better prepared to give the speech in class.

Sometimes speakers forget about using their media as they give their speeches, so include reminders on your presentation outline or note cards indicating when to use your presentation media. It's a good idea to write these reminders in big letters and in a different color ink from the rest of your cards or outline. Add these reminders before or during the practice stages of your speech preparation. That will help you practice more effectively and ensure that you'll notice the reminders at the right moment when you give your speech in class.

Set Up Early

On the day of your speech, arrive early and verify that the technical equipment you need is working properly. Doing so will help you manage nervousness and avoid most of possible technology mishaps. If you can, check the focal sharpness of projected images before audience members enter the room. When using a document camera, overhead projector transparencies, or physical models, put your visual materials in the order you'll present them. Set the right volume levels if you're using audio.

Although you can take steps to eliminate technical problems, you still must be prepared for presentation media to fail during your speech. Sometimes quick repairs are possible; at other times, you have to continue speaking without the technology you'd planned to use. In these cases, you must improvise. Don't panic. Rely first and foremost on your delivery skills. Always be prepared to give your speech without your presentation media in case something goes wrong.

SPEAKING OF ...

Extend the Speech Whenever Possible

Your speech doesn't have to end when you finish talking. Maintaining contact with your audience, providing them with up-to-date information, and offering opportunities for them to follow through on what you advocate in your speech helps you achieve your purpose for speaking. You can use various techniques to extend and enhance the audience's experience beyond your original presentation. For instance, at the end of a speech, you might distribute a handout that indicates how to contact you or the persons or institutions mentioned in the speech, where to locate relevant web resources, or how to review the digital slides you presented. You could post your slides on a website or collect the email addresses of audience members and send your slides to them after the speech. Some speakers dispense with showing digital slides in their speeches altogether and email the slides to audience members afterward.

Speak to Your Audience, Not Your Media

Whatever presentation media you use, always keep your focus on the audience. You may be tempted to look at the screen when projecting an image. This is a common mistake. When you look at the screen, you turn your back on the audience and become a spectator, not a speaker. Listeners will feel ignored, and their attention will wane. Instead, continue to make eye contact with your audience and glance at the actual image on the media equipment, such as the computer screen, only when you need to. Most important, *never read the content of your presentation media verbatim to your audience.* Keep your slides simple so you won't have to compete with them for the audience's attention. And when you practice with your presentation media, make a conscious effort to face your imaginary audience.

MindTap®

Watch It: View a video on integrating presentation media.

Summary

Speakers use presentation media to draw attention to their topics, illustrate ideas, evoke emotional reactions, clarify points, support arguments, and assist with audience recall. General guidelines for designing effective visual media include keeping them simple, emphasizing only key ideas, showing what you can't say, using close-up photographs and other images, combining variety with coherence, and using large, readable lettering.

Digital slides have become the most popular form of presentation media. But document cameras, traditional and interactive whiteboards, flip charts, video, handouts, physical models, human assistants, sound and music recordings, real-time web access, and overhead projector transparencies can also enrich your speech.

By treating your presentation media as essential components of your speech that require careful preparation and delivery, you can maximize their impact and avoid common problems associated with their use. The key to success in using presentation media is balance: Give media the proper supporting role in your speech. With all the resources available to you, remember that *you,* the living, breathing human being, will always be the best delivery system for communicating ideas to your audience.

› ANALYZE IT

Dr. Michael Marx, Getting Off Oil

Dr. Michael Marx is Executive Director of Corporate Ethics International and the strategic advisor to Climate Works and the Beyond Oil Fund. He regularly speaks to audiences about environmental issues, especially the damaging role of petroleum in the growing global climate crisis. He skillfully uses digital slides in his speeches to demonstrate the severity of climate change, its causes, and the solutions that we can employ to confront the problem.[21]

Every generation faces a challenge that defines its character and sometimes its fate. For my father's generation, that was World War II. For my generation, that was the Vietnam War. And for your generation, that is catastrophic climate change. And the enemy in your war on climate is one of the most powerful industries in the world, big oil. In the next few minutes, I want to convince you of four things. One, that our dependence on oil is harming us. Two, that we need to get off oil as fast as

MindTap®

Watch and analyze this speech on MindTap.

possible. Three, that we have the technical capacity to do this. And four, but it's going to require action on the part of you and me.

My first point, our dependence on oil is harming us. One, it's harming our climate. The Environment Protection Agency has estimated that one-third of all of our fossil fuel emissions in the United States every year are due to burning oil for transportation. The International Panel on Climate Change, which is comprised of the top climate scientists in the world, has concluded that carbon emissions from coal and oil and natural gas are the leading cause of climate change, and they've also concluded that climate change is why we're experiencing record-breaking floods, hurricanes, droughts, and tornadoes.

Two, oil is harming our health. Burning oil produces carbon dioxide, carbon monoxide, nitrogen oxide, and particulate matter. According to the American Lung Association, these pollutants are major causes of bronchitis, asthma, heart disease, and lung cancer. According to the Union of Concerned Scientists, particulate matter alone is responsible for 30,000 premature deaths in the United States every year.

Three, oil is harming our security. The Department of Defense in its 2015 National Security Strategy Report said that climate change is an urgent and growing threat to our national security. It is contributing to increased natural disasters, refugee flows, conflicts over basic resources such as food and water, but they went on to say that these are already occurring, and the scope, the scale, and the intensity of these impacts are going to get worse as climate change accelerates.

Four, oil is harming our democracy. Big oil companies and oil executives are among the largest contributors to political campaigns in the U.S. Charles and David Koch, two of the ten richest people in the world whose wealth is derived from oil, committed to spend $900 million in the 2016 election cycle to influence the outcome of that election. The two major parties, the Democrats and the Republicans, each projected that they would spend about the same amount of money. Now, whether you're a liberal or you're a conservative, a Republican or a Democrat, you should be concerned when a handful of oil executives have the same amount of spending power to influence an election as our two major parties. It is a threat to the health of our democracy. Summary, oil is harming our climate, it's harming our health, it's harming our security, and it's harming our democracy.

My second point is that we need to get off oil as fast as possible. Now, make two points here. One, we have to get off oil as fast as possible to avoid climate catastrophe. The International Energy Agency tells us that we have to use 50% less oil by 2030 and 80% less oil by 2050 in order to avoid going past the tipping point, the point where climate change is out of control and we can no longer stop it. Researchers at the University College of London, after looking at all the data, concluded that we need to leave 80% of all of our current fossil fuel reserves in the ground. We can't burn them. What that means is that we need to stop all new oil exploration and development now. We can't even safely burn the oil that we already have identified in our reserves.

Two, we need to get off oil fast because big oil is ramping up to stop us from being the leaders in the clean energy revolution. Innovation and leadership have been the key to our prosperity for the last hundred years. We invented the radio, the television, the car, the airplane, computers, and they all resulted in economic boom. We are currently the leaders in the development of electric and self-driving cars. But guess what? Charles and David Koch have committed to back a group that will spend $10 million a year to try to block the federal government and state governments from encouraging the adoption of electric vehicles. We're already losing the war to China in terms of solar and wind and being the leaders in that economy. We cannot afford to lose this war where we could be the leaders in electric and self-driving vehicles. We need to get off oil fast.

My third point is that we have the capacity to end our dependence on oil if we do certain things on the oil production side and on the oil consumption side. Let's talk first about the oil production side. Here the theme is we need to stop expanding oil infrastructure. First, we have to convince the President and the Department of Interior to end all oil and gas leases on federal public lands, particularly also in our waters like the Arctic, the Atlantic, and the Gulf. These are some of the last remaining undeveloped oil reserves and we don't need them.

Second, we have to convince the President and a few key governors to stop approving all new oil infrastructure. No new pipelines. No new oil terminals. No expansions of oil refineries. This will scare investors who have clung religiously for several decades to their investments in oil, and when they start to move towards renewable energy, that is a game-changer. On the consumption side, we need to transition our entire transportation system to a grid that is powered by renewable energy. We need to pressure auto companies to meet the 2025 fuel efficiency standards of 54.5 miles per gallon average for their fleet, and then we need to raise it to 75 miles per gallon for 2035. We need to defend and we need to expand driving and purchasing incentives for electric vehicles not only at the federal level but at the state level as well. We need to increase ride and car-sharing so that Uber and Lyft and Zipcar and companies like that become the norm for personal mobility, and we need to stop expanding the urban boundary. We need to build up, not out, and when we build, we need to build close to the transportation corridors so people can very easily reach mass transits. In short, we can end our dependence on oil, but we have to stop expanding oil infrastructure that's going to lock us into that industry for another 30 to 50 years, and we need to transition our transportation system to a clean renewable energy-driven grid.

Which brings me to my fourth point, and that is you have to get involved, and here's what you can do. Number one, don't buy a car unless you absolutely have to, and if you have to buy a car, first buy an electric vehicle, and if you can't afford an electric vehicle, buy a car that gets 50 miles to the gallon. Second, don't vote for any politician that takes oil money and let them know that. Call up their office, send an email, send a letter, get your friends and classmates to do the same. Third, don't be afraid to put your body on the line. Don't be afraid to join demonstrations, and in some instances don't be afraid to get trained and then engage in non-violent civil disobedience. No movement has ever achieved its goals without non-violent civil disobedience, not slavery, not apartheid, not civil rights, not women's rights, not gay rights and marriage equality. And finally, become a digital activist member of the groups that are fighting big oil, groups like 350.org, Sierra Club, Rainforest Action Network, the Natural Resources Defense Council, Energy Action Coalition, and others. Believe me, they want your activism more than they want your money.

So in summary, oil is destroying our climate, our health, our security, and our democracy. We need to get off oil immediately so we can lead the world in the clean energy revolution. We have to stop expanding oil infrastructure and we have to transition our transportation system to a clean energy-driven grid. But we're the key. If we don't act, big oil wins and takes us over the climate change cliff. In conclusion, climate change is the greatest threat to our future. Every generation faces a challenge that defines its character and potentially its fate. If we don't act quickly to marshal our forces to defeat big oil, then our fate is sealed. But if we do, and if we do this together, we get our democracy back, we get better jobs, we get healthier cities, and we get a chance for greater peace in the world. And we can do this. As one of the greatest cultural anthropologists of our time Margaret Mead once said, "Never doubt that a small group of thoughtful, committed citizens can change the world. Indeed, it's the only thing that ever has." I am proud to be one of those committed citizens who doesn't own a car and has put his body on the line in demonstrations and in non-violent civil disobedience to try to end our dependence on oil, and I'm inviting you to join us because your fate may well depend on it. Thank you.

Questions for Discussion

1. How do the slides Dr. Michael Marx used help you understand and appreciate the content of his speech? Would the speech have been just as effective without the slides? Why yes or no?
2. Do the slides appear at the right points in his speech? Did he use too many or too few slides? If any, what changes might you have made to the number or placement of slides?
3. What other images or points he made in the speech could have been illustrated with slides?
4. Were you able to easily grasp the content of each slide? How could Dr. Marx have improved on the way he used presentation media for this speech topic?
5. This was an issue-based persuasive speech. What was the main message of his speech? What action or actions did the speaker ask the audience to take after listening to him?
6. Did the speaker use language about the issue that could be easily understood by a college student audience?

APPLY IT . . .

IN THE WORKPLACE

Digital Literacy and Creativity

Knowing how to use digital slides offers you advantages that extend far beyond the public speaking classroom. You can also incorporate digital slides into presentations for civic organizations, nonprofit groups, public events, clubs, and even family gatherings. But in a competitive job market, being able to use digital slides well gives you a communication skill that is valued, even expected, by professional employers. Don't think of digital literacy strictly as a technical skill. Like all forms of human expression, composing and presenting digital images gives you a great opportunity to exercise your imagination and creativity. Digital media is not just a tool—it's also an art form. As such, it can help create and maintain human connections, which are vital to your professional success and growth. Think of digital slide presentations you have used or seen in your public speaking course: What particular presentation styles, type of content, and organizational structure would likely work best in a workplace and why?

REVIEW IT

Key Terms

document cameras 223
flip chart 224
handout 226
human assistant 227
interactive whiteboard 224
physical model 226
presentation media 216
presentation software 218
real-time web access (RWA) 228
traditional whiteboard 224
transparency 228
webidence 228

MindTap®
Use flashcards to learn key terms and take a quiz to test your knowledge.

Reflecting on Integrating Presentation Media

1. Should you use presentation media for any speech? What are the best reasons for using presentation media?
2. What are the main principles of design that apply to any of the visual presentation media discussed in this chapter?
3. Many public speakers don't know or ignore the most fundamental rules for designing digital slides. What common problems have you noticed when speakers use slides? How can you avoid making those mistakes?
4. Many speakers use digital slides, but other presentation alternatives can be effective too. When might you use a document camera, video, handout, physical model, human assistant, music, or sound in a speech?
5. Why is it important to practice your speech with the presentation media you plan to use? Why do you want to resist the temptation to look at your presentation media while you speak?

12 Delivering Your Speech

READ IT

After successfully completing this chapter, you will be able to:

- Describe the four speech delivery methods.
- Describe how culture, gender, fluency, dialect, and physical impairments may influence how you deliver a speech.
- Explain how to orally cite written and visual sources in your speech.
- Manage your voice effectively through vocal delivery techniques.
- Manage your body effectively through appearance, movement, eye contact, and facial expression.
- Describe strategies for adapting your speech and delivery to different audiences.
- Compose a speaking outline with note cards that aid extemporaneous delivery.
- Demonstrate effective ways for practicing the delivery of your speech.

MindTap®

Start with a quick warm-up activity and review the chapter's learning outcomes.

Audiences today expect a more conversational style of public speaking that is less scripted than speech delivery a century ago.

Popperfoto/Getty Images

If you were taking a public speaking class just over 100 years ago—1916 to be exact—you might have used the textbook, *The Elements of Public Speaking*, by Harry Garfield Houghton, an assistant professor of public speaking at the University of Wisconsin.[1] Eleven of the twelve chapters address the actual presentation of the speech, with titles such as Action, Gesture, The Breath, Enunciation, Pitch, and Force. In the preface, the author explained his reasons for writing the book:

> My observation has been that many people who think very clearly express their thoughts very badly through the voice, and that mere attention to the thought alone is by no means always adequate. This book aims to teach the importance of clear thinking as the foundation of all vocal processes, but no less does it aim to show the necessity for vocal and actional responsiveness as the medium through which thought must find expression.[2]

While Professor Houghton recognized the importance of speech content—what he called clear thinking—he viewed speech delivery as the primary focus for a public speaking course. If you were taking Professor Houghton's class, you would complete practical exercises to improve your breathing, enunciation, physical fitness, sense of rhythm, and vocal flexibility.

There's no doubt presenting your speech remains a critical element in any public speaking course. Giving your speech to an audience is the culmination of all the work you've put into preparing for your presentation. You inform, persuade, or entertain your audience when you actually give your speech. You influence what they think about and how they think about it. In delivering your speech, you even affect the neural responses of their brains.[3] But public speaking courses and textbooks today strike a balance between developing the content of your speech—choosing your topic, finding valid and reliable sources, organizing your ideas—and presenting it. In addition, audiences today expect a more conversational style of public speaking that is less scripted than speech delivery a century ago.

Your audience will not expect perfection from your speech, as there is always room for improvement. However, you want to make the best impression you can and achieve your goals for the speech. This chapter discusses several aspects of effective delivery: selecting an appropriate delivery method; understanding factors that influence a speaker's delivery; managing your voice, body, and audience during your speech; preparing your speaking outline; and practicing your speech.

Getty Images Entertainment/Getty Images

Selecting a Delivery Method

MindTap®

Read, highlight, and take notes online.

delivery
The public presentation of a speech.

Delivery refers to presenting a speech in public. When you deliver a speech, you merge its verbal and visual components into a presentation before an audience. Scholars have long recognized the importance of delivery for the effective public speaker.[4] Effective delivery brings together all the planning, researching, and organizing you've done for your speech. The volume of your voice, your posture, how you manage your time during a speech—all of these and more are aspects of delivery.

Four types of delivery methods are presented here. **Table 12.1** provides an overview of these four methods and the best situations in which to use them. When deciding on a delivery style, choose one that enhances the content of your speech and doesn't distract your audience.

Impromptu Speaking

impromptu speaking
A type of public speaking in which the speaker has little or no time to prepare a speech.

In public speaking, delivery with little or no preparation is called **impromptu speaking**. You engage in impromptu speaking every day as you communicate thoughts and ideas that spring up in the moment with no preparation or practice whatsoever. For example, when you answer a question in class or speak up during a meeting of a campus organization, you're using impromptu speaking. In this respect, impromptu speaking is simply another way to use the basic communication skills you already have and use regularly. Learning how to express yourself on the spot without relying on research, extensive preparation, or notes will help you do well in your public speaking class and in less-structured speaking situations beyond the classroom.[5] In addition, developing your impromptu speaking skills increases your confidence and decreases your speaking anxiety in any presentation context.[6]

Table 12.1 Delivery Methods

Method	Brief Definition	Advantages	Disadvantages	Typical Situations
Impromptu	Speaking without preparation	Flexibility; complete spontaneity	Not researched; can be disorganized; speaker has little, if any, time to practice	Responding to audience questions
Extemporaneous	Giving a speech that has been planned, researched, organized, and practiced	Allows speaker to develop expertise on a topic; allows structured spontaneity; allows speaker to adjust to audience feedback	Researching, organizing, and practicing a speech is time-consuming	Most classroom, professional, and community presentations
Manuscript	Giving a speech that has been written out word for word	Allows speaker to choose each word precisely and time the speech exactly	Speaker uses written rather than spoken language; difficult to modify based on audience feedback	Political speeches
Memorized	Giving a speech that has been committed to memory	Allows speaker to present speech without notes; same speech can be presented many times	Can seem artificial; requires intensive practicing	Short ceremonial speeches

An impromptu speaker is given a topic on the spot and often has a minute or two to think about what to say. **Figure 12.1** provides questions you can ask yourself to quickly develop and organize your thoughts when you're faced with an impromptu speaking situation. As you present your speech, do your best to speak coherently. Keep your general purpose in mind—are you informing, persuading, or entertaining your audience about your topic? Don't worry about making mistakes—no one expects an impromptu speech to be perfect.

David Young-Wolff/PhotoEdit

You engage in impromptu speaking every day—in the classroom, at home, and as you go about your daily life and interact with others.

Extemporaneous Speaking

For **extemporaneous speaking**, you carefully research, organize, and rehearse your speech before you deliver it. This approach to speaking balances adapting to the audience in the moment with thorough planning and practicing. Extemporaneous speaking requires both flexibility and forethought, or structured spontaneity. When you appear spontaneous, your speech comes across as natural and authentic.[7] When you present clear and well-organized ideas, you come across as knowledgeable and confident.[8] Speaking extemporaneously helps you deliver an audience-centered and engaging message, greatly maximizing your chances of connecting with your listeners and having your speech achieve its purpose. For most of the public speaking situations you'll encounter, the extemporaneous method is the most desirable because its structured spontaneity usually makes it the most effective.

extemporaneous speaking
A type of public speaking in which the speaker researches, organizes, rehearses, and delivers a speech in a way that combines structure and spontaneity.

Manuscript Speaking

When politicians and world leaders give speeches, they usually appear to be speaking from just a few notes as they look directly at the audience and the camera. However, they're often reading from a teleprompter that displays a manuscript speech—a speech written out word for word. One advantage of **manuscript speaking** is that you can compose the exact language you want to use for your speech. In situations in which a misspoken word might lead to a tragic misunderstanding—such as when negotiating a peace treaty—manuscript speaking is necessary to maintain absolute precision. However, most public speakers never will have to speak in such sensitive situations.

manuscript speaking
A type of public speaking in which the speaker reads a written script word for word.

Manuscript speaking may seem easy, but reading from a manuscript greatly reduces your ability to make eye contact with your listeners and adapt to their feedback. Audience members may also feel ignored. In addition, when speakers write out their entire speech word for word, they tend to use written rather than spoken language. Because written language is more complex and less personal than spoken language, audience members may struggle to understand a speaker who is using words meant for reading rather than listening. Audiences tend to favor an extemporaneous style, so avoid reading a speech from a manuscript unless the situation calls for it.

memorized speaking
A type of public speaking in which the speaker commits a speech to memory.

Figure 12.1 Developing and Organizing Your Impromptu Speeches

- What is my topic?
- What are my thoughts and feelings about the topic? (Use key words and phrases to capture your ideas.)
- How do I want to organize my ideas on the topic? (Identify an order for your thoughts.)
- What is a good way to begin my speech? (Write down a few sentences or phrases that will help you begin.)
- What is a good way to end my speech? (Write down a few sentences or phrases that will give your speech closure.)

Memorized Speaking

When delivering a memorized speech, the speaker commits the entire speech to memory and then presents it to an audience. **Memorized speaking** can be useful and appropriate in certain situations. For short speeches, such as a wedding toast or acceptance of an award,

Bob Daemmrich/The Image Works

Speakers often use teleprompters when speaking from a manuscript so their delivery appears more conversational.

knowing exactly what you're going to say reduces the chances that you'll sound unprepared or make comments you'll regret later. And memorizing small sections of your speech, such as your introduction, key transitions, and conclusion, helps reduce anxiety and can increase your confidence (Chapter 2). However, memorizing an entire lengthy speech can cause several problems. First, if you forget a line or a word, you may find it difficult to recover and continue your speech. Second, there's little flexibility in a fully memorized speech, so adapting to audience responses is challenging. Third, memorized speeches can seem artificial and lack spontaneity.

Understanding Factors That Influence Delivery

The speaking situation and speech type are external factors that help determine how you will deliver your speech. This section addresses four important factors unique to each speaker that influence delivery.

Culture and Delivery

Cultural factors influence how a speaker behaves in front of an audience and how the audience perceives the speaker. For instance, public speaking forms a central part of Kenyan culture, with people of all ages expected to give speeches at ceremonies and other occasions.[9] In contrast, people from China, Japan, Korea, Vietnam, and other East Asian countries often consider it rude to highlight their own accomplishments. This unwillingness to draw attention to themselves may explain the finding that college students in Thailand perceive themselves as less competent in public speaking than their American counterparts.[10] Similarly, the greater emphasis on public speaking in American and British schools likely contributes to Americans and the British reporting higher levels of communication competence and willingness to communicate than residents of Finland, Germany, and Sweden.[11] Iranian college students as well reported higher levels of comfort interacting in dyads and small groups with friends than in public speaking situations.[12] However, Chinese people living in the United States reported lower levels of communication apprehension and higher levels of communication competence the longer they lived in the United States, suggesting how culture can influence communication behaviors.[13]

Culture also influences how audiences perceive speakers. For example, what American audiences perceive as nervousness in a speaker, Asian audiences may view as modesty or less-direct communication.[14] If based on your cultural, social, or family background, you're used to asserting yourself in more subtle ways, you might have to develop new skills to adapt to the expectations of American audiences.

Gender and Delivery

In the past, audiences evaluated female and male speakers differently. For example, men were granted higher status and greater credibility, while women were typically judged based on their clothing and physical attractiveness.[15] Much has changed over the years, and some of the most powerful and eloquent speakers today, such as Chimamanda Ngozi Adichie, Viola Davis, Gloria Estefan, Michelle Obama, Sheryl Sandberg,

Oprah Winfrey, and Malala Yousafzai are well-respected women. Yet research shows that audiences still tend to evaluate speakers based on their gender.

Even when women and men present the exact same information, they're evaluated differently. In one study, female and male professional newscasters read identical scripts in identical settings with identical camera angles. The female newscaster was rated as less credible—less competent, composed, and extroverted—than the male newscaster.[16] However, research on women's and men's vocal qualities found that listeners viewed a woman's voice as more persuasive than a man's voice in radio advertisements encouraging people to donate blood.[17] These different results could be due to differences in the speakers' purpose—informative in the newscast and persuasive in the advertisement. In addition, the first study involved video and the second only audio. Still, the research is clear that gender plays a role in how audiences evaluate speakers.

Although a study of college student speakers found that peers perceived their classmates as competent regardless of gender, male speakers often were viewed as more influential and persuasive, even when female and male speakers displayed similar behaviors. In addition, student audiences judged men's and women's credibility differently. Female speakers' credibility rested primarily on their use of trustworthy information sources. In contrast, male speakers' credibility enjoyed a broader base, including believable sources, eye contact, organization of ideas, and vocal variety.[18] In another study of classroom speeches, when women looked somewhat more at their notes and somewhat less at the audience, they were viewed as more competent, reliable, and intelligent. For men, the more eye contact they made the higher the audience rated them as speakers.[19]

Of course, many factors contribute to a speaker's perceived credibility and competence, regardless of gender. A woman who avoids making eye contact, speaks in a monotone, and organizes her points poorly risks making a negative impression on the audience. Similarly, a man who relies only on his voice, eye contact, and speech structure to win over listeners likely will earn low marks as a speaker.

Vocal Attributes One challenging delivery issue women face is making themselves heard. Women's voices are generally higher and softer than men's voices, making them more difficult to hear. This difference stems partly from biology—women have shorter vocal cords than men do—and partly from culture—girls are expected to talk more quietly than boys.[20] Whatever the reason, female speakers usually must work harder than male speakers to project their voices. Speaking more loudly and at a slightly lower pitch while delivering a speech may feel odd at first, because you're used to hearing your voice sound a certain way. But good vocal **volume**—the loudness of your voice—is essential to public speaking, because you want your audience to hear your message.

volume
The loudness of a speaker's voice.

pitch
The highness or lowness of a speaker's voice.

The use of vocal **pitch**—the highness or lowness of a speaker's voice—also affects how audiences judge a woman's confidence as a speaker. One way you indicate you're asking a *question* is to raise the pitch of your voice. When a speaker's voice goes up at the end of a *statement,* audience members view the speaker as less confident, more anxious, and less sure of the information presented.[21] Research suggests that women tend to use this practice more than men,[22] so women speakers should watch for this problem and correct it if necessary as they practice their speeches.

© David Schmitz Photography

Because women's voices are often harder to hear than men's voices, women speakers must use strategies to make sure their audiences hear them. Even when women use a microphone, speaking at a higher volume and with a slightly lower pitch will help their audiences understand them.

Fluency and Delivery

Stuttering is one of the more common speech impairments that affect public speakers. Researchers estimate that more than 3 million Americans stutter, although most children stop stuttering as they grow older.[23] People who stutter are often characterized as nervous, shy, quiet, withdrawn, and fearful. Although studies show these characterizations are unfounded, fluent speakers continue to view people who stutter negatively.[24] However, people who stutter can employ four strategies to change those negative perceptions:

- *Anticipation.* When you anticipate ahead of time that you may experience dysfluency, you can identify strategies beforehand that will help you effectively manage your stuttering when it does occur.
- *Acknowledgment.* Research has found that simply acknowledging you stutter reduces the pressure you may feel to speak perfectly, improves your fluency, and causes the audience to view you more favorably.
- *Goal attainment.* Concentrating on the goal for your speech—presenting your ideas to the audience—keeps you focused on your role as a speaker and builds your confidence.
- *Eye contact.* Making eye contact with your audience may not reduce your stuttering, but it will help others view you more positively and react in more supportive ways. When you look at your audience, you're better able to monitor their feedback and respond to it appropriately.[25]

Dialect and Delivery

dialect
The vocabulary, grammar, and pronunciation used by a specific group of people, such as an ethnic or regional group.

Another factor that influences delivery, a **dialect** is the vocabulary, grammar, and pronunciation used by a group of people. Everyone speaks in some dialect, even if they don't recognize it. Although dialects are often associated with specific regions of the United States, such as the South and New England, dialects also can be ethnically based, as with African American English and Cajun or Creole English.[26] Dialects also reflect migration patterns, as in the case of former Alaska governor Sarah Palin. A detailed analysis of her speech found that her dialect—using *goin'* rather than *going* and terms such as *gosh darn* and *you betcha*—reflected features of Upper Midwest speakers, a region of the United States from which many Alaskans can trace their roots.[27]

Dialects can reveal rich cultural traditions and help bind a group together. No dialect is inferior to any other way of speaking. However, an analysis of 20 studies found that audiences gave more negative evaluations in the areas of trustworthiness, intelligence, and dynamism to speakers with dialects or accents different from their own.[28] As a public speaker, your own use of dialect affects how well your audience can understand you. When you're talking with others in your own dialect group, you and your listeners don't notice how you use language. But when you speak in front of an audience, you must be more aware of how you use language so that you can ensure your audience understands your message. If you articulate your words clearly, pronounce them correctly, and define terms that might be unfamiliar to your audience, you will be able to bridge most of the differences between your dialect and your audience's.

Physical Impairments and Delivery

If you are a speaker with a physical impairment, it may affect how you deliver your speech. The following sections offer strategies for speakers using mobility aids and speakers with visual or hearing impairments.

Speakers Using Mobility Aids Speakers who use crutches or a walker must consider several issues before presenting a speech:

1. Identify your plan for approaching and leaving the speaker's area to make the minutes before and after your speech as stress free as possible. Check that your path to and from the area is unobstructed and easy to reach.

2. Decide if standing for your entire presentation will work for you. As you practice your speech, you may find that you become uncomfortable or needlessly tired if you stand up. If that's the case, consider sitting when you give your speech.
3. Find the best way to manage your note cards and presentation media so you easily integrate them into your speech delivery.

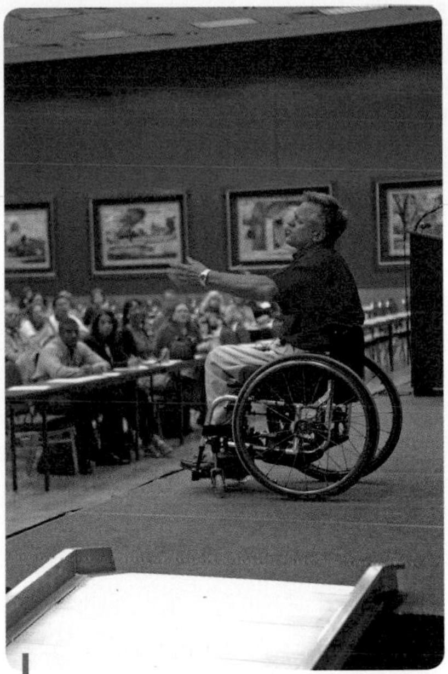
Bob Daemmrich/PhotoEdit

Minimizing the physical distance between the speaker and audience is especially important for speakers who use a wheelchair for mobility.

Speakers who use a wheelchair or need to sit for their presentations must pay special attention to visibility and voice projection. You can increase your visibility by not having a large object, such as a table, between you and your audience. This allows you to get physically closer to your listeners and keeps the focus on you.

Practice speaking aloud to attain the best possible voice projection. Sit up as straight as possible, take a deep breath, and breathe out as you speak. To check your volume, practice with a friend in a room that is similar in size to the one where you'll be speaking. Have your friend sit at the back of the room and tell you when your voice can be heard easily. If voice projection is still a problem, use a microphone.

Speakers with Visual Impairments About 14 million Americans are visually impaired.[29] For public speakers with visual impairments, the key issue is how to recall everything you want to say. Memorization is a safe strategy for short speeches, but committing long speeches to memory is a challenge. Notes in braille are a good solution. If you don't read braille but are able to read large print, try using big note cards with clearly written keywords.

If your visual impairment is such that written notes are not feasible, you might consider three alternatives.

1. Develop your speech by capturing your ideas on a digital audio recording device, such as a smartphone, revising until you are satisfied with the speech. Using an earbud, present the speech as you listen to the recorded version.
2. If you write in braille, write out your speech, have a sighted person record it in a digital format, and use the digital recording as in the first strategy. Keep in mind that listening to and saying your speech at the same time is quite difficult to do and takes considerable practice.
3. Write out your speech and have a sighted person present it for you. You should then be prepared to answer questions after the speech.

Speakers with Hearing Impairments The National Institute on Deafness and Other Communication Disorders (NIDCD) estimates that nearly 38 million people in the United States experience some sort of hearing impairment.[30] As a public speaker with a hearing impairment, consider your ability to hear and your comfort with using your voice. If you usually communicate using American Sign Language (ASL), signing and using a sign-to-voice interpreter is a logical choice. If you're confident about your vocal abilities, present your speech aloud. During the question-and-answer session, ask listeners to state questions loudly and clearly or request a microphone for audience members to use.

People with impairments should adapt the preceding techniques to suit their own physical, cognitive, and sensory requirements. There's no need to tell your audience why you are doing things your way.[31] If you have an impairment that affects your speech delivery, you may want to discuss the matter with your instructor so you'll get the most out of your public speaking class and your audience will get the most out of your speeches.

Hans Gutknecht/ZUMA Wire Service/Alamy Stock Photo

A speaker with a hearing impairment may use an interpreter when giving a speech.

Managing Your Voice During Your Speech

MindTap®

Watch It: View a video on effective vocal delivery.

Your voice is a key tool for getting your audience's attention, emphasizing points, stirring emotions, and conveying the content of your message. Practicing *vocal mindfulness*—attending to your voice and how you use it when you speak—improves your voice as you practice and present your speech.[32] Proper breathing, good voice volume, variations in vocal qualities, minimal pauses, and clear articulation and pronunciation are essential for effective public speaking.

Control Your Breath

In *The Elements of Public Speaking* mentioned earlier in this chapter, Professor Houghton dedicates an entire chapter to correct breathing. He recognized that how you breathe provides a platform for how you use your voice. He used the analogy of a pipe organ to explain how the human vocal mechanism works. The reed, or your vocal chords, vibrates to produce tones. The bellows are your lungs and esophagus, which push air past the reeds. The pipe organ's hollow pipe is your layrnx, mouth, and head, which serve to make the sounds resonate (**Figure 12.2**). Without your breath, you have no voice.

The importance of proper breathing in public speaking hasn't changed since Professor Houghton published his book. The *Harvard Business Review* offers these suggestions for breathing properly while giving a speech.[33]

1. Stand or sit as upright as possible with your shoulders down and back. This posture allows your bellows—your lungs—to fill up as full as possible.
2. Breathe in and out rather than up and down. Breathe with your abdomen rather than your chest. Put your hand on your stomach. If your hand goes in and out, you're breathing properly. If your hand goes up and down, you're breathing high in your chest and not completely filling your lungs. In addition, chest breathing causes vocal problems you want to avoid, such as hoarseness, breathiness, and nasal tone.[34]
3. Speak as you exhale. Inhale completely and quickly; exhale slowly as you talk. This helps you project your voice. Using your breath to carry your words puts less strain on your vocal cords by letting your natural bellows—your lungs—do the work.

Breathing in this way gives your voice a rich and full quality, improves the clarity of your voice, and makes it easier for your audience to hear you.

Figure 12.2 You push air from your diaphragm into your lungs and esophagus (respiration) into your larynx (phonation) and through your vocal cords and mouth (resonance) to produce your voice.

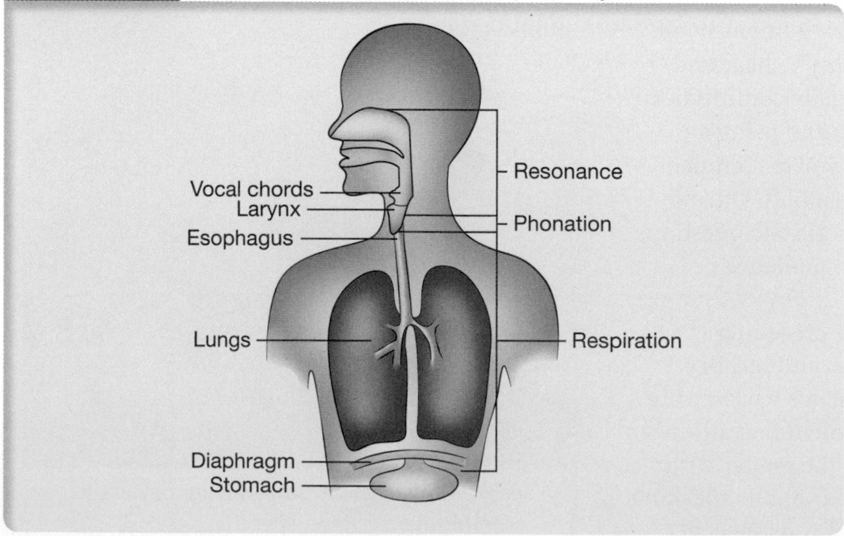

Alila Medical Media/Shutterstock.com

Speak Loudly Enough

Right from the beginning of your speech, speak so that everyone in your audience can hear you. This may take some practice if you feel uncomfortable raising your voice volume above an everyday speaking level. However, sufficient volume is crucial; audience members shouldn't have to strain to hear you. Proper breathing—from your abdomen rather than your chest—provides the foundation for projecting your voice.

You want your audience to hear you easily, but you don't want to be so loud that your vocal volume overwhelms your audience and listeners feel uncomfortable. If you're not sure what "loud enough" sounds like, practice with a friend in the room where you'll present the speech, or in a similar space. Have your friend sit in the farthest corner of the room and raise your voice volume until she or he can easily hear you.

Vary Your Rate, Pitch, and Volume

Differences stand out to listeners; sameness does not. Not every point or statement included in a speech carries the same weight or tone. Some parts of your speech may be on the lighter side; others may be more serious. As you naturally talk in everyday conversation, your **rate** of speaking, or the speed at which you talk, varies over the course of the interaction. Speaking at a faster rate, with a higher pitch, and in a louder volume suggests energy and excitement. A slower rate, lower pitch, and softer volume indicate a more solemn and contemplative tone. Audiences generally find it easier to listen to speech that has a lower pitch, moderate rate, and somewhat loud, although not booming, volume.[35] However, you want to use **vocal variety**—varying the rate, pitch, and volume of your voice—to add interest to your speech. When you alter your voice, even in small subtle ways, your audience notices the differences and pays greater attention to you. Speaking in a **monotone**, or with little alteration in pitch, signals nervousness and boredom to your audience.[36] Use vocal variety to fit your topic and evoke emotion in the audience.

rate
The speed at which a speaker speaks.

vocal variety
Changes in the volume, rate, and pitch of a speaker's voice that affect the meaning of the words delivered.

monotone
A way of speaking in which the speaker does not alter his or her pitch.

Avoid Vocalized Pauses

In everyday conversations, you know it's your turn to speak when the other person pauses. But sometimes you pause even when you're not finished speaking because you're trying to formulate the next point you want to make or you can't quite think of the word you want. You don't want the other person to jump in and start talking, so you say "ah" or "um" to tell the other person, "I'm not done talking yet." This habit carries over to public speaking, even though you know listeners will not start talking if you pause. These **vocalized pauses** or verbal fillers use up time without providing any information, and they hurt your credibility because they make you sound anxious and unsure of yourself.[37] When you hear yourself using a vocalized pause, concentrate on just pausing—your audience will wait for you. Also, as you practice your speech you'll become more certain of what you want to say, reducing those "ahs" and "ums."

vocalized pauses
"Ah," "um," "you know," and other verbal fillers that speakers use when they're trying to think of what they want to say.

Articulate Your Words Clearly and Pronounce Them Correctly

In everyday speech, speakers often articulate poorly, leaving off the endings of words ("I'm leavin' soon"), skipping sounds entirely ("I'm gonna leave in twenny minutes"), and running words together ("Waddaya think?"). Poor **articulation** isn't necessarily a problem in casual conversation, but during a speech it may cause your audience to strain to understand you and may hurt your credibility. Use your lips, tongue, and jaw to fully form each syllable of the words you are saying.

Incorrect **pronunciation** can also damage your credibility. Some common mispronunciations are "git" for *get,* "excape" for *escape,* "pitcher" for *picture,* and "reckanize" for *recognize.* If you're unsure of a word's correct pronunciation, check a dictionary—nearly all online dictionaries include audio files so you can listen to how a word is pronounced. And when you practice your speech in front of a small audience, ask listeners to point out words you pronounce incorrectly, then practice saying the words aloud correctly until you're comfortable saying them.

articulation
The physical process of producing specific speech sounds to make language intelligible.

pronunciation
The act of saying words correctly according to the accepted standards of the speaker's language.

Managing Your Body During Your Speech

Everything about how you present yourself should tell your audience that you're poised, confident, and enthusiastic. In addition, knowing what to do with your body can significantly reduce speech anxiety. This section outlines specific ways to use attire, facial expressions, and body movement effectively when giving your speech. If you live with a dis/ability, you may need to modify some of these guidelines to suit your situation.

MindTap®
Watch It: View a video on effective physical delivery in public speaking.

Tony Freeman/PhotoEdit

When you dress for the occasion, you enhance your credibility, impress your audience, and boost your confidence.

Dress for the Occasion

Appearances count, especially in public speaking. Your clothing should enhance your speech and contribute to listeners' perceptions of your dynamism and overall credibility. Dressing appropriately for your speeches demonstrates respect for your audience: You care enough about your listeners and your speech to look your best. Some instructors require that students dress in corporate business attire for their speeches in order to emphasize the differences between social conversation and public speaking. Your instructor's dress code may not be that formal, but you should dress at least one step up from what you usually wear to class. If you look the part, it will be easier to play the part and manage your nervousness.[38]

Face Your Audience and Make Eye Contact with Them

Your listeners want to know you're talking to them—not the floor, your notes, a tree outside the window, or a spot on the wall at the back of the room. Look at all your listeners, from those in the front row to those in the back corners. Avoid scanning the room from one side to the other, looking only at audience members who happen to be sitting in the middle of the room, or concentrating your attention on the instructor. When you write something on a chalkboard or whiteboard, turn around and speak to your audience after you've finished writing. Talk to your audience—not to the screen—when using digital slides or an overhead projector. Except when presenting an exact quotation, glance quickly and infrequently at your notes, using them to trigger your memory. Good eye contact signals that you are competent, trustworthy, dynamic, and sociable.

Display Appropriate Facial Expressions

posture
The way speakers position and carry their bodies.

You communicate much of how you feel through your face. A smile, frown, or puzzled look can underscore a point. Adjust your facial expression according to the content of your speech and the message you're trying to send. For example, smiling nervously when talking about a serious topic, such as the implications of climate change, sends a mixed message and may cause your audience to misunderstand your intent. However, smiling as you greet audience members before you start your speech lets them know you're pleased to be there.

SPEAKING OF ...

Speaking Around the Podium

Podiums can give a speaking event an air of formality and are essential in some situations, such as a political press conference or a university commencement. And it's useful to know how to use a podium to your advantage when you're speaking at an event that requires one. When you know you'll have to use a podium, practice speaking behind, in front of, and away from it. For example, if you move from the podium and toward the audience, you convey a sense of closeness and informality. When you move behind the podium, you convey a sense of seriousness. Make the podium work for you and the message you want to get across to your audience.

Maintain Good Posture

Your **posture** is the way you position and carry your body. When you have your shoulders back, head up, hands loosely at your sides, knees slightly bent, feet shoulder-width apart and flat on the floor, and weight evenly distributed, you can easily move and gesture. Standing up straight demonstrates your self-assurance; keeping your feet flat on the floor prevents you from shifting your weight from foot to foot or crossing and uncrossing your feet. If you use a wheelchair for mobility or for other reasons need to sit while talking, sit up as straight as possible so you can breathe from your abdomen.

Move with Purpose and Spontaneity

When planning your speech, consider what body movements can help you communicate your message in a dynamic way.

As you practice, experiment with movement that underscores a point, demonstrates your confidence, and captures your audience's attention. For example, you might step closer to your listeners to make them feel included, especially when discussing how a point affects them personally. Or you might take a few steps to the left or right to signal a transition from one main point to the next. Such movement and gestures help your audience get a better idea of what you're saying and can provide a context for your verbal message.[39]

Have a reason or purpose for movements you make while you speak. For instance, you might want to walk toward one side of the room as you begin a narrative and move to the other side for the dramatic ending. However, avoid movements that appear staged or overly dramatic, as with holding up three fingers and saying, "I'll cover three main points in this speech." Your audience will prefer a more conversational style.

a katz/Shutterstock.com

Removing physical barriers between your audience and you allows you to adopt a more conversation style.

Avoid Physical Barriers

Although a few public speaking contexts require using a podium due to convention and formality, in most cases you won't need one. A podium constrains your ability to use your entire body to convey your message and puts a physical barrier between you and your audience. If you need to use a podium or table to support your visual materials, tablet, or laptop, stand to the side, not behind the furniture.

Applying the delivery strategies outlined in these discussions of voice and body will help you give dynamic and engaging extemporaneous presentations. **Figure 12.3** provides a quick summary of these strategies. After awhile, most of this will come naturally. You'll develop your own style as you become more confident about your public speaking abilities.

Figure 12.3 Strategies for Effective Delivery

- Control your breath.
- Speak loudly enough.
- Vary your voice's rate, pitch, and volume.
- Avoid vocalized pauses.
- Articulate your words clearly and pronounce them correctly.
- Dress for the occasion.
- Face your audience and make eye contact with everyone.
- Display appropriate facial expressions.
- Maintain good posture.
- Move with purpose and spontaneity.
- Avoid physical barriers.

Managing Your Audience During Your Speech

Managing your audience begins with researching your listeners and designing your message to achieve their goals as well as your own (Chapter 5). If you have developed a speech that your audience finds useful and interesting, and if you present the speech in an enthusiastic and engaging manner, then listeners more likely will respond the way you expect them to. You can also help influence an audience's response to you by adjusting your speaking space, involving your audience, respecting your audience's time, accommodating audience members with impairments, responding calmly to rude or hostile audiences, and being prepared for question-and-answer sessions.

Adjust Your Speaking Space as Needed

Set up the speaking space in a way that's comfortable for you and your audience. Even small modifications can influence how the audience listens to you. For example, if you're in a small conference room with a large table, suggest that audience members turn their chairs so it's easier for them to see you and your digital slides or other presentation

Neal Waters

In a large auditorium, moving out from behind the podium can help you better connect with your audience.

materials. This also reduces the likelihood that audience members will talk among themselves. If lighting is harsh or glaring, dim or turn off a few lights so audience members will feel more relaxed. Close doors to hallways and other rooms so you're not interrupted. In a large auditorium, don't be afraid to get out from behind the podium. Audience members will view you as more confident and personable and will pay more attention to your speech.

Involve Your Audience

Involving your audience requires careful attention to your listeners' feedback (Chapter 3). Make the audience part of your speech by:

- Referring to what others have said in their speeches ("As Tasha mentioned in her speech last week …").
- Calling on specific audience members ("Hector, what's your reaction to the video clip we just saw?").
- Asking for volunteers ("I need two people to help me demonstrate this process").

nonverbal messages Information that is not communicated with words but rather, through movement, with gesture, facial expression, vocal quality, use of time, use of space, and touch.

As you're speaking, observe the audience, noting if they seem interested, bored, confused, supportive, hostile, uncertain, or the like. **Nonverbal messages**, such as facial expressions and tone of voice, can be ambiguous. So you may want to check your interpretations of audience behaviors. If someone seems confused about a point, you could say, "Anya, you look puzzled. Are you? Other people might be as well, so I can explain that last point in more detail." Some nonverbal behaviors are fairly clear, such as listeners shaking their heads in disagreement or nodding in agreement. Commenting on the behaviors you observe lets audience members know you are interested in their feedback. When you notice those shaking heads, you might say, "Some of you seem to disagree with me. Let me tell you something that might change your mind." If listeners are nodding, you might say, "I can tell by your reactions that some of you have had the same experience." These strategies allow you to integrate audience members into your speech.

Respect the Audience's Time

Remain calm when audience members are disruptive or appear angry.

iStockphoto.com/luoman

Your listeners will expect you to manage your time effectively. Remember, it's *their* time as well. Make the most of your speaking time so you achieve your goals and your listeners feel satisfied with the information you've provided.

When you practice your speech, record your time so you stay within your time limit. Have a general idea of how much time you spend on each part of your speech. This information will help you pace yourself when presenting your speech to your audience.

As you progress through your speech, monitor your time so that each part of your speech receives adequate attention. For instance, if you have three main points and spend half of your speaking time on the first point, you won't be able to develop the other two points fully. In addition, as you adjust to your audience's feedback, you may find it necessary to devote more time to a particular point and leave out other parts of your speech. For example, you might omit an example or shorten a story in your conclusion. That's part of extemporaneous speaking—adapting your speech to your audience and the context during the presentation.

Accommodate Audience Members with Impairments

When presenting a speech to audience members with cognitive, sensory, or physical impairments, accommodate their needs so they can participate fully in the speaking event. Your goal as a speaker is to include everyone and ensure no one is left out. First, check that audience members who require accommodations have them. For example, an audience member with a hearing impairment may need an interpreter. Second, face the audience so everyone can easily see and hear you. Make sure nothing interferes with your voice projection. Third, speak loudly, clearly, and not too rapidly. This is especially important for interpreters, who need a moment or two to translate what you're saying. Fourth, describe the content of any visual materials you use, such as digital slides or overhead transparencies, explaining images as well as text. Finally, if you're not sure what you need to do to accommodate audience members, privately ask them before you start your speech.

Respond Calmly to Rude or Hostile Audience Members

Sometimes audience members express hostility during or after the speech, although this seldom happens in public speaking classes. Some topics can trigger deep emotions. If you're speaking on a controversial topic such as immigration or gun violence, be prepared for negative reactions from audience members who disagree with you. In handling these responses, remain calm. Engaging in a shouting match with audience members will damage your credibility and increase your anxiety level.[40] Let hostile audience members know you understand that they disagree with you. If they don't calm down, suggest that you continue the discussion after you've finished your speech.

Be Prepared for a Question-and-Answer Period

In many cases, once you've finished your speech, audience members will have an opportunity to ask you questions. Researching your audience helps you anticipate those questions; researching your topic helps you answer them. Apply the following guidelines in the question-and-answer session:

- Listen carefully to the question, giving the audience member time to complete it.
- Repeat the question if other audience members couldn't hear it.

- Answer questions as completely as possible.
- If you don't know the answer to a question, admit it and offer to look up the necessary information.

When audience members ask questions, they're most often seeking clarification or more information—they're not evaluating you. Think of the question-and-answer session as a friendly conversation and answer questions as best you can.

Preparing Your Speaking Outline

MindTap®

Go to your MindTap for help with developing your outline.

speaking outline
An outline that distills a complete-sentence outline, listing only the words and phrases that will guide the speaker through the main parts of the speech and the transitions between them.

In the beginning stages of speech development, you use a working outline. The complete-sentence outline, discussed in Chapter 8, elaborates on the working outline by including full sentences detailing all the parts of your speech. The **speaking outline** distills your complete-sentence outline into a list of words and phrases to guide you through the main parts of your speech and the transitions between them. Like the working outline, the speaking outline is brief. Although you may initially create it on your computer or on paper, you'll transfer your speaking outline to note cards, a small tablet, or smartphone to practice and deliver your speech. **Table 12.2** reviews the three types of outlines.

Knowing how to create and use a speaking outline is a fundamental skill for extemporaneous public speaking. The speaking outline allows you to:

- Refer comfortably and precisely to the information you have gathered.
- Present that information in a clear and organized way.
- Engage your audience personally and professionally during the speech.

As you practice your speech, you'll develop the confidence to rely on brief notes while speaking in front of an audience. A speaking outline makes it possible for a well-prepared speaker to deliver an abundance of ideas effectively.

Identify Keywords

keywords
Words that identify a subject or a point of primary interest or concern.

The **keywords** in a speaking outline are very similar to the keywords or search terms you use online: They identify subjects or points of primary interest or concern. Keywords represent the most important points you want to talk about in your speech. Because they're listed in the same order as the sentences in your complete-sentence outline, they indicate the order in which you want to present those points.

Table 12.2 Types of Outlines

Type of Outline	Functions	Key Features	Use When . . .
Working	Assists in initial topic development; guides research.	Includes main points and possible subpoints; revised during research process.	developing your speech topic and conducting your research.
Complete-sentence	Clearly identifies all the pieces of information for the speech; puts ideas in order; forms the basis for developing the speaking outline.	Uses complete sentences; lists all sections of speech and all references; revised during preparation process.	you've completed your research and you're ready to put together your ideas and construct your entire speech.
Speaking	Assists you in practicing and giving your speech.	Uses keywords; revised as you practice your speech; often transferred to note cards for use during practice and the final presentation.	you practice and present your speech.

Although speaking outlines are usually quite short, they can be created only after you've fully researched your topic and developed your complete-sentence outline. The speaking outline captures the essence of your complete-sentence outline in a way that allows you to give your speech extemporaneously. As you use your speaking outline or note cards to practice your speech, you'll find that you need to move back and forth between your complete-sentence outline and your speaking outline, typically making minor revisions in the former and more substantial revisions in the latter. Each time you modify your speaking outline, you'll be challenged to condense your ideas and information into keywords that will trigger your memory as you present your speech. **Figure 12.4** shows an example speaking outline.

Figure 12.4 Sample Speaking Outline

Title: Fireworks: History and Culture

Attention getter: They're loud and bright and sometimes scary. They're used for celebrations around the world, from China's Lantern to Guy Fawkes Day in England to the Fourth of July in the U.S. What are they?

Fireworks! [show first slide with fireworks display]

Thesis: Fireworks have a long and important history in many cultures around the world.

Establish credibility: For example, according to the *Smithsonian Magazine*, Americans first used fireworks to celebrate their independence from Great Britain on July 4, 1777.

Preview: First, I'll give you a brief history of fireworks. Then I'll talk about the importance of fireworks in China, England, and the U.S.

I. History
- A. China: origin—2000 years ago
  1. Needed loud noise—disperse ghosts
  2. Alchemy and chemistry
  3. Firecracker—Northern Song Dynasty
  4. Fireworks—Tang Dynasty
- B. Exported—early 20th century
- C. Most fireworks made in China

II. Culture
- A. China
  1. National holidays
  2. Special occasions (weddings, birthdays)
  3. Business celebrations/events
- B. Great Britain
  1. Bonfire Night or Guy Fawkes Day
     - a. Blow up Houses of Parliament
     - b. Festivals of Light
  2. Hogmanay & New Year
  3. International Festival Concert
- C. U.S.
  1. July 4
  2. Disney & fireworks
  3. Local celebrations

Review: I explained the history of fireworks and how they're a part of Chinese, British, and U.S. culture.

Reinforce purpose: Fireworks have a long history, from their first use to scare away ghosts to their current place in cultural celebrations around the world.

Closure: Fireworks—they're the sounds and lights of people celebrating the important events in their lives. Thank you.

Transfer Your Speaking Outline to Note Cards

Once you've completed your speaking outline, you're ready to transfer the information from your outline to the note cards you'll use during your speech. Write your keywords on the note cards to remind you of the points you want to cover in your speech. Organize and number the cards in the order in which you want to present those points. Make sure the print is large enough for you to read easily as you're giving your speech.

During your presentation, hold your note cards in one hand. The only time you should have both hands on your note cards is when you move from one card to the next. The audience expects you to consult your notes during the speech. Occasionally glancing at your notes shows you planned your speech but didn't memorize it. Maintain eye contact with your audience, glancing at your notes briefly and infrequently.

The speaking outline and note cards are your dependable assistants. When developed and used effectively, the speaking outline helps you give an extemporaneous speech that centers your attention on the audience. Using note cards demonstrates your planning and preparation, keeps you organized, and allows you to create a good rapport with your listeners.

Practicing the Delivery of Your Speech

MindTap®

Watch It: View a video on strategies for practicing your speech.

Too little practice and you won't be ready the day of your speech. Too much practice and your speech loses spontaneity. Moreover, rehearsing your speech over and over will not ensure a successful presentation on speech day.[41] Practicing your speech effectively requires devoting quality time to rehearsing your presentation.

Rather than practicing it just once, you will practice your speech in different ways and at different stages until you are completely ready. But being fully prepared does not mean that the speech you give to your audience will be exactly the same as the speech you practice. You want to present an engaging and dynamic speech, not one that is programmed and predictable.

Give a Version of Your Speech

Think of each speech you give as just one of many possible speeches you could have given with exactly the same information and preparation. You don't have to give a "perfect" speech—you must simply give an excellent version of your speech. If you were to give the same speech tomorrow, and again the next day, you would not deliver those speeches in exactly the same way. The speechmaking method you are learning prepares you to give excellent versions of your speeches adapted to your audience and the speaking context.

With extemporaneous speaking, commit small amounts of your speech to memory, such as the first few and last sentences, transitions, and main points. With thorough preparation and sufficient practice, you'll know what you want to say well enough to say it effectively when you deliver your speech. For example, you will recall certain words and phrases that sounded good when you practiced. You may not say things exactly the same way as you did when you practiced, but you'll feel confident that you know how to make your ideas clear.

Practice Your Speech in Stages

Practicing permeates the entire speech preparation process. As you research your topic (Chapter 6), organize your ideas (Chapter 8), identify the language you'll use in your speech (Chapter 10), and incorporate presentation media (Chapter 11), you'll practice various parts of the presentation, rethinking and revising what you plan to say. Review your complete-sentence outline as you go along, trying out the introduction, main points, transitions, and conclusion to find out how they work or don't work. Make notes for your speaking outline. Practice in stages, section by section. Don't wait until you think you have a finished product.

Practicing Parts of Your Speech During this stage of practice, your goals are to check that your speech makes sense, identify keywords that will best trigger your memory, and try out your presentation materials. When you practice, say the words of your speech out loud to determine if your ideas are clear and if your language and delivery techniques work together to achieve your purpose. By speaking out loud when you practice, you hear your main points and supporting materials and can consider how you might say something more clearly, precisely, humorously, seriously, or persuasively. Practicing out loud allows you to become your own audience, ready to give instant, productive feedback. Try saying small portions of your speech as if you were facing an audience. Listen for how you've organized and supported your ideas, make adjustments, and keep adjusting with the individual segments of your speech.

Practicing your speech during this stage includes practicing with your presentation materials. No matter how briefly you'll be using presentation materials, include them in your practice sessions to find out if they accomplish what you want them to and if you can integrate them into your speech easily.

Practicing Your Whole Speech Now that you've practiced the various parts of your speech, you're ready to practice the entire speech. Practice just like you're giving your speech to the audience: standing up (or sitting, depending on ability), holding your speaking outline on note cards, a tablet, or smartphone, and integrating all your presentation materials. Rehearsing the whole speech with any presentation media you plan to use allows you to observe how your main points flow. You'll also be able to perfect your introduction and conclusion (Chapter 9).

In this stage of practicing, invite friends, family members, coworkers, and others to provide constructive feedback. If you want them to focus on a particular aspect of your presentation, such as transitions or gestures, tell them before you begin your speech. Then be ready to listen to their comments without becoming defensive, knowing they want you to do your best. Research shows that practicing your speech in front of four or more people—either in person or online—improves your presentation on speech day.[42] Recording yourself a few times as you practice can also prove helpful because you'll get an idea of how you look and sound.

Time Your Speech

Your speech should fit within the time allotted and should not go under or over the time limit. When you give your speech, use your time well, presenting the introduction, main points, and conclusion at a comfortable pace that is neither slow nor rushed. During practice sessions, note the time you need for the sections of your speech so you have a rough idea of how long it takes you to get through each part. Then when you deliver your speech, you'll be better able to monitor how you're using your time. Knowing how long your speech will last also gives you confidence and control during the presentation.

MindTap®
Go to MindTap to record, review, and evaluate your speech delivery.

Summary

Delivering your speech brings together all your planning and preparation. Speakers use four delivery methods: impromptu, extemporaneous, manuscript, and memorized. For most speeches, you'll want to speak extemporaneously, balancing careful planning with flexibility.

Several factors influence a public speaker's delivery, including culture and gender. With good preparation, speakers can adapt to the speaking situation and manage negative audience perceptions, regardless of gender and cultural background. Other factors that influence delivery are language fluency, dialect, and physical impairments. Delivering your speech well means effectively managing your voice, your body, and your audience, as well as orally citing your sources.

Careful research, planning, organizing, and preparation provide a solid base for presenting your speech. The speaking outline helps you achieve an organized, engaging, and professional presentation. Practice your speech in stages, distilling your complete-sentence outline into a brief speaking outline. Incorporate any presentation materials into the speech as you practice, making modifications as necessary. Put in quality practice time so that when speech day arrives you're prepared to give an excellent version of your speech. Closely manage your time, adjusting your speech as needed.

> ANALYZE IT

Source: Gardere MLK Jr. Oratory Competition

MindTap®

Watch and analyze this speech on MindTap.

Chase Roberts, First Place Speech at the 2015 Houston 19th Annual Gardere Martin Luther King, Jr., Oratory Competition

Chase Roberts, a fifth grader at Cornelius Elementary School, Houston, TX, won first place for his speech at the 2015 Houston 19th Annual Gardere Martin Luther King, Jr., Oratory Competition. The fourth- and fifth-grade competitors answered the question, "If Dr. King were to win the Nobel Peace Prize today, what would he say in his acceptance speech?" Note how Chase uses several strategies to engage his audience with his delivery.

Am I my brother's keeper? Yes I am. Am I my brother's keeper? Yes I am. Am I my brother's keeper? Yes, I am. If Dr. King were to win the Nobel Peace Prize today, what would he say as his acceptance speech? I believe he would use his acceptance speech as an opportunity to encourage the world. If Dr. King were to win the Nobel Peace Prize today, he would say: first giving honor to God, all the distinguished members and honored guests. Now y'all all know, I'm a Baptist preacher, from the south, and there's no way ya'll could expect to give a Baptist preacher, from the south, three minutes, an audience, and a microphone? And expect him not to preach.

If Dr. King were to win the Nobel Peace Prize today, he would say, as we face this current clash of cultures, we must realize we are our brother's keeper because we are our brother's brother. Whatever affects one directly, affects all indirectly. Now when I use the word brother, it's never cultural, it's always universal. We may not all be brothers and sisters in culture but we are all brothers and sisters in creation. And it is the Creator who seals this unbreakable bond for his creations. His expectations are for us to walk in purpose and live in peace. How do we do that? I'm glad you asked.

If we are to live together as brothers we must activate the power of prayer. Now, I know. Prayer is a delicate subject nowaday, but every time I dig in my pocket and pull out a dollar bill, I read these words: In God We Trust. Every time I stand to recite the Pledge of Allegiance, I say these words, "One nation under God indivisible." If Dr. King were to win the Nobel Peace Prize today, he would say, the Internet has become a major hub for the world's mass media. TV, newspaper, and radio has to take a back seat to the texters, tweeters, and bloggers of today. However, if you're going to text, don't do it while driving. Remember, it can wait. If you're going to tweet, let it be to uplift and not to put down. And if you're going to blog, let it be to encourage and not to endanger. And if you have considerable influence, use it to inspire positive change. If Dr. King were to win the Nobel Peace Prize today, he would say, don't forsake the lessons of the past. Remember how to act. A-C-T. And refrain from reacting. Huh? A-C-T. It is such a small word, but it's packed with powerful, positive, possibilities. A-C-T. Accept the challenge together. A-C-T. Address concerns together. Remember, united we stand, divided we fall.

When faced with an enemy, A-C-T. Approach with compassion and tolerance.

Therefore! I share this award with all my brothers and sisters in Creation, who have stood with me in the past and will stand with me now. To declare the time for change is always now. The time for freedom is always now. And this awesome award serves as our catalyst for a peaceful resolution.

Am I my brother's keeper? Yes I am.
Am I my brother's keeper? Yes I am.
Am I my brother's keeper? Yes, I am.
Thank you.

Questions for Discussion

1. Read through the speech transcript as if you were presenting it. How did you use your voice and body to deliver the speech?
2. Now view the video available and discuss these questions:
    a. What delivery method or methods did Roberts use? How did you identify the method(s)?
    b. How did Roberts use his voice when he delivered his speech? Give examples of how he varied his vocal rate, pitch, and volume.
    c. How did Roberts use his body in delivering her speech?
    d. How did the speaker dress for the occasion? Why do you think he dressed that way?
    e. How did Roberts use eye contact?
    f. What are some examples of facial expressions he used?
    g. How effective was his posture?
    h. How did Roberts use gestures and other movement in his speech? Give a few examples.
    i. Roberts did not use a podium, although one was available. Why do you think that was the case? How effective was his choice?
    j. How did Roberts involve the audience in his speech?
3. View Dr. Martin Luther King, Jr.'s, original Nobel Prize acceptance speech on the Nobel Prize site. In what ways is Roberts' delivery similar to King's? How do they differ? What delivery strategies have endured over time? What are some different expectations that audiences have of a speaker's delivery?
4. What have you learned by analyzing how Chase Roberts delivered his speech that you can use in your own presentations?

> APPLY IT . . .

IN THE WORKPLACE

Speaking Out at Work

Your workplace or other organization provides an excellent venue for you to practice your impromptu public speaking skills. Whether you're in a meeting or having lunch with coworkers, take the opportunity to exercise your voice. For example, if you're in a meeting, consider how you might contribute to the topic under discussion. Respond to these questions with a few brief notes:

1. What are my thoughts about the topic?
2. How do I feel about it?
3. What are my main ideas?
4. In what order do I want to present my ideas?

5. How should I begin in a way that will capture my colleagues' attention?
6. How should I end so I can reinforce my main point?

Your comments need not be lengthy. But practicing your impromptu speaking skills at work will help you learn to quickly articulate your thoughts—and you might just impress your boss! After giving your impromptu speech, evaluate how you did. What went well? How might you improve on your efforts?

IN YOUR COMMUNITY

Helping Others Deliver Their Speeches

One of the best ways to find out if you've really learned something is to teach others about it. In your community's service learning location or other place where you volunteer your time, some people might be interested in learning more about speech delivery. Identify individuals who want advice on speech delivery. Develop a short workshop or module about how to deliver a speech, such as how to use your voice and body to enhance your message. Then follow up in a few weeks by having attendees meet again to present brief speeches. Evaluate the effectiveness of their delivery and your effectiveness as a teacher. What did you learn about speech delivery from teaching others about it? How will you apply what you've learned in your own presentations?

REVIEW IT

MindTap®
Use flashcards to learn key terms and take a quiz to test your knowledge.

Key Terms

articulation 243
delivery 236
dialect 240
extemporaneous speaking 237
impromptu speaking 236
keywords 248
manuscript speaking 237
memorized speaking 237
monotone 243
nonverbal messages 246
pitch 239
posture 244
pronunciation 243
rate 243
speaking outline 248
vocalized pauses 243
vocal variety 243
volume 239

Reflecting on Delivering Your Speech

1. Public speaking classes usually focus on extemporaneous speaking. What are some situations in which you'll likely give extemporaneous speeches in the future? You encounter impromptu speaking situations almost daily, especially in a college classroom. Give an example of a recent experience you had with impromptu speaking. While you're in school, you usually don't do much manuscript or memorized speaking. When might you use these methods in the future?
2. Consider how your own culture, gender, fluency, dialect, and dis/ability may influence how you deliver a speech. How will you address those issues? For instance, if you tend to use a lot of vocalized pauses, how will you reduce them? If you need to adapt your delivery style to accommodate a dis/ability, what will you do?
3. Review your sources for the next speech you'll give. How will you orally cite those sources? Try out a few different ways of citing the same source.
4. Go to the Vocal Warm Ups page of the New York Eye and Ear Infirmary of Mount Sinai website (nyee.edu/patient-care/otolaryngology/voice-swallowing/therapy/vocal-warm-ups). Scroll to the bottom of the page and try out some of the voice warm-up exercises. How do your mouth, tongue, and jaw feel after the exercises? How might you use these exercises to prepare for your next speech?

5. One of the most challenging aspects of delivering a speech is figuring out what to do with your body. Record a brief part of a previous speech you gave or the next one you plan to give. What improvements could you make in your appearance, movement, eye contact, and facial expressions? Try out these changes, recording your practice session. What have you learned about managing your body in public speaking?
6. One aspect of adapting to your audience is accommodating individuals with disabilities. How might you do this in classroom speeches? In speeches outside the classroom?
7. During and after your speech, you may find that audience members challenge your ideas and conclusions. How might you avoid becoming defensive—a natural reaction—and encourage reasoned discussion?
8. How effective were the notes you used in your last speech? How might you improve your speaking outline—your notes—for your next speech?

13 Informative Speaking

READ IT

After successfully completing this chapter, you will be able to:

- Describe the characteristics of informative speaking and explain how informative differs from persuasive speaking.
- Describe the different types of informative speeches.
- Write a specific purpose statement and a thesis statement for your informative speech.
- Select an appropriate organizational pattern for your informative speech.
- Use the guidelines for effective informative speeches to communicate relevance while keeping the speech informative, not persuasive.

MindTap®

Start with a quick warm-up activity and review the chapter's learning outcomes.

To survive and thrive, people need to pass information on to others clearly and convincingly.

James Lull

Their unique ability to exchange thoughts and instructions eventually allowed early humans to become the dominant species in the animal kingdom. Our ancestors' sheer survival depended on communication skill. By using speech and language effectively, they were able to coordinate their efforts to hunt wild animals, teach each other how to make simple tools, and take care of their children.[1] In terms of basic communication, not much has changed over the millennia. To survive and thrive, people still need to pass information on to others clearly and convincingly. Being able to describe or explain something in a way that enables other people to benefit from what you have to say—like what the U.S. National Parks ranger is doing in the photo here—forms a solid foundation for becoming an excellent public speaker.

Today, public speakers have information available to them from a seemingly unlimited range and number of sources. What's more, the information age has morphed into the communication age.[2] From the convenience of gathering information and images to the incredible ease with which you can send information to people almost anywhere on the planet, digital communication technologies give you multiple ways to retrieve and share information.[3] You can find jobs, take classes, research health issues, make and maintain friendships, learn about other cultures, sell products and services, and conduct a host of other information exchanges online.[4] As a public speaker, you can rely on today's extremely rich information environment to research your speech topics, find support for your main points, locate images for presentation media, and refer audiences to additional information and insights about your ideas.

The Image Bank/Getty Images

Characteristics of an Informative Speech

MindTap®

Read, highlight, and take notes online.

informative speaking
Presenting a speech in which the speaker seeks to raise awareness, increase knowledge, or deepen understanding about a topic.

In **informative speaking** situations, the speaker seeks to raise awareness, increase knowledge, or deepen understanding about a topic. When you speak to inform, you want audience members to learn something from your speech. To do this, you share information with them. But you want to do more than just share information; you aim to turn facts into knowledge. Your skill as a speaker is the mechanism that allows you to transfer information accurately in order to create knowledge—your own and that of your audience.[5]

At the root of all human communication is the social connection people make when they share information.[6] When you speak informatively, you make this connection with your listeners. For this to happen, your audience must find the speech meaningful, the information accurate, the message clear, and the scope limited. These four qualities, shown in **Figure 13.1,** form the basis of your competence as an informative speaker.

Personally Meaningful

By effectively relating the topic to the audience, speakers can make their presentations come alive and be personally meaningful. Personalizing your speech begins with the topic you choose, which should be relevant to your audience. You can also personalize your message by using a storytelling approach to organize and present the informative speech topic. Used smartly and sparingly, presentation media can help personalize your information, too.

Even digital media creators try to make the experience of long-distance interaction as personally meaningful as possible for users. Tapping into emotions is key. For example, emoticons (like the original smiley face invented from text) and emojis (tiny cartoonish pictures that display emotion) were invented to warm up online communication. Online marketers microtarget individual consumers by profiling and appealing to their personal feelings, habits, and tastes. Many of the emotional appeals you use to personalize text messages, social media postings, photos, and files can also be used to connect with others in your speeches.

Humor can be a particularly strong emotional technique that binds the speaker to the audience. Being funny, self-effacing, and witty can create emotional closeness with your listeners—just be sure to keep your remarks in good taste and truly humorous. Test out your attempts at humor on your friends before you decide to incorporate humor into a speech. Referring in a positive way to a previous speaker or other class member—the equivalent of a confirming "like" on Facebook—can also create a sense of community, an effective emotional connection. Short, relevant, personal stories and images like those you might reveal on social media can help you win the affection of your audience. Demonstrating concern or empathy for others also affects people positively. You can use any of these personalizing techniques in the spoken words or presentation media that make up your speeches.

Figure 13.1 Characteristics of Competent Informative Speaking

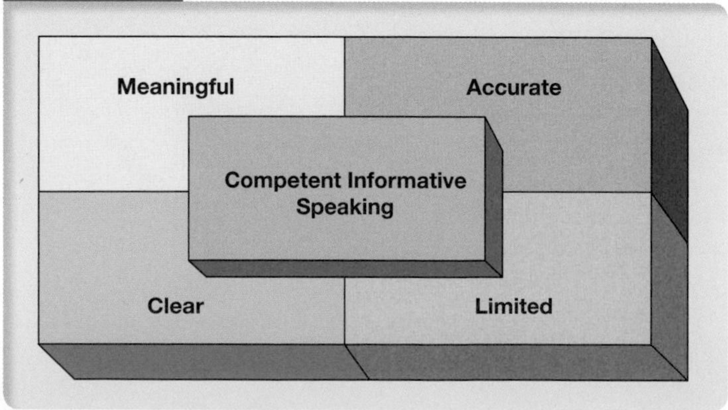

Accurate

Today's robust information environment has heightened the expectations people have about the veracity and legitimacy of the facts they receive. Consequently, today's information sources have to satisfy their audiences' demand for accuracy.[7] Traditional news media have always sought to gain the public's trust by requiring reporters to quote multiple sources on controversial issues and hiring internal fact checkers to verify the truthfulness of their stories. Online independent news outlets, bloggers, and newsgroups keep an eye on the traditional media but are themselves also critically evaluated as information sources.

Gatewatching involves monitoring news sources to analyze and assess the information those sources produce.[8] The principle of gatewatching also applies to informative speaking. Informing your audience effectively requires that you present accurate information. Your individual listeners act as gatewatchers. They expect accuracy in every aspect of your speech: supporting materials, organization, claims, language, delivery, and presentation media.

gatewatching
Monitoring news sources to analyze and assess the information they produce.

Clear

Your audience should not have to work hard to figure out what you're trying to say. If they do, then your message could be lost. Audiences understand and recall information best when it is clearly presented and easy to follow. Clarity unravels confusing and complex ideas, making them unambiguous and coherent. Still, being clear often presents the greatest challenge to informative speakers.[9]

What seems clear to you might not be to your listeners, making it crucial to be strongly audience centered as you prepare your speech. You must be able to explain your topic in terms your audience can easily comprehend. Analyzing your audience, selecting appropriate supporting materials, avoiding technical jargon, and organizing your speech so that it flows logically from one idea to the next will help make your informative speech clear. It also helps to practice out loud in front of friends, family, or roommates and ask whether they understand what you're trying to say.

If you strive to be clear, you'll get another welcome reward: When you give a clear speech and sense that your audience understands you well, your nervousness will decrease.

Limited in Scope

Whenever you speak about any topic, you may be tempted to evaluate the subject matter, give opinions about it, or make a suggestion, particularly if you hold strong feelings about the topic. In an informative speech, however, you should avoid expressing your personal views too strongly.

Don't turn a speech to inform into a speech to persuade. Keep your speech pitched at the level of information sharing. Describe, explain, or demonstrate something, but don't tell the audience specifically what to think or do about it.

Types of Informative Speeches

The five common types of informative speeches are about objects and places, people and other living creatures, processes, events, and ideas and concepts.

These categories represent general topic areas, and you should not consider them to be mutually exclusive. For instance, a speech about a famous person, such as an inventor, would probably include information about the person's best-known ideas. A speech about a place might also be about an event that occurs there, which you would probably want to describe briefly. Still, an informative speech generally has one primary focus you'll highlight in your speech.

MindTap®
Use Outline Builder to help you prepare your informative speech.

Speeches about Objects and Places

An **object** is any nonliving, material thing that the human senses can perceive. **Places** are geographic locations. Here are several speech topics and titles addressing objects and places.

object
Any nonliving, material thing that can be perceived by the human senses.

place
Geographic location.

TOPIC	SAMPLE SPEECH TITLES
3-D TV	"Beyond the Flat Screen: How 3-D TV Works"
	"Will We Ever Have 3-D TV?"
Tijuana	"Tijuana: The Challenges of a Mexican Border Town"
	"The Delights of Tijuana"
Toys for special needs kids	"Choosing Toys for Kids with Special Needs"
	"How Toys Improve Special Needs Kids' Skills"
World Trade Center	"The World Trade Center Complex"
	"Beyond 9/11: America's Memorial and Museum"
Extraterrestrials	"Ancient Beliefs in Extraterrestrials"
	"Humorous Films about Extraterrestrials"
Laser medical technology	"The Latest Advances in Laser Medical Technology"
	"Common Types of Medical Lasers"
The Inca Trail	"Step by Step Along the Inca Trail"
	"Spiritual Journey: Peru's Inca Trail"
Blogs	"What Makes a Successful Blog?"
	"The Daily Read: My Favorite Blogs"
Active volcanoes	"The Active Volcanoes of Latin America"
	"The Causes of Volcanic Eruptions"
Folk art	"Folk Art in Our Community"
	"How Does Folk Art Differ from Commercial Art?"

Your own interests and knowledge can often generate excellent speech topics. Sometimes students worry that the things they know about would not interest an audience. However, with skillful research and delivery, almost anything that is important or interesting to you can be made important or interesting to an audience. Think of the town or area where you grew up. What do visitors consider its main attractions? Could you use presentation media to make those attractions come alive for your listeners? If the place doesn't have a lot of attractions that might interest tourists, what interesting people live there? What important historical events occurred there? Don't immediately discount a topic just because you think it wouldn't interest anyone other than you. Consider how you could *make* it interesting.

Patrick Morisson/Alamy Stock Photo

One World Trade Center is the main building of the new World Trade Center complex in New York City.

Speeches about People and Other Living Creatures

When choosing a topic for an informative speech about people or other living creatures, reflect on the people who fascinate you or the creatures you think your audience would like to learn more about. Who or what would your audience find meaningful? A well-known celebrity or a lesser-known individual? An international figure or someone much closer to home? Would they be interested in an exotic creature, such as the flying squirrel or the banded bamboo shark? Or something more common that they know little about, such as the bald eagle or the bottlenose dolphin? Here are some sample topics and titles for this type of speech.

TOPIC	SAMPLE SPEECH TITLES
Taylor Swift	"Taylor Swift: Her Life Story in Lyrics"
	"How Taylor Swift Became Pop Music's Superstar"
Koko, the "talking gorilla"	"When Gorillas Talk, What Do They Say?"
	"Learning about Human Speech from Koko, the Talking Gorilla"
Bill Maher	"Real Time with Comedian Bill Maher"
	"The Politics of Comedian Bill Maher"
Dinosaurs	"When Dinosaurs Ruled the World"
	"Dinosaurs and the Great Extinction Debate"
Alexander Wang	"Alexander Wang: Fashion's New Icon"
	"The Unique Style of Alexander Wang"
The Dalai Lama	"A Brief Biography of the Dalai Lama"
	"Pathways to Peace According to the Dalai Lama"
Shaun White	"Shaun White: The Heart of a Snowboarding Champion"
	"Shaun White's Snowboarding Techniques"
A local artist	"Insight into the Art of Rolando Diaz"
	"The Struggles and Successes of Local Artist Rolando Diaz"
Tarantulas	"The Truth about Tarantulas"
	"Tarantulas: Evolution of the World's Scariest Spider"
Kathryn D. Sullivan	"Kathryn D. Sullivan: The First American Woman to Walk in Space"
	"The Lesbian Astronaut: Kathryn Sullivan"

For the most part, audiences are highly interested in other people and living creatures—that's why the Biography Channel, History Channel, National Geographic Channel, and Discovery Channel attract lots of viewers. With careful audience analysis, solid research, and presentation media that include images of interesting people and animals, informative speeches about these topics can captivate your audience.

Speeches about Processes

A speech about a **process**—how something is done, how it works, or how it has developed—facilitates an audience's understanding of the process. Depending on the topic you choose, you may want to demonstrate the process yourself. However, for your informative speech you do *not* want to ask the audience to take any specific action. Here are some examples of topics and titles for informative speeches about processes.

process
How something is done, how it works, or how it has developed.

TOPIC	SAMPLE SPEECH TITLES
Matching DNA samples	"How DNA Affects Criminal Prosecutions"
	"DNA and Genetics: Our Genes Tell Our Stories"
Lifeguarding procedures	"What Lifeguarding Techniques Really Work?"
	"Five Steps That Save Lives: A Demonstration"
Testing new cars for safety	"Standards for Testing New Cars for Safety"
	"Test Results on the Safety of New Cars"
Post-traumatic stress disorder	"What Is Post-traumatic Stress Disorder?"
	"The Causes, Symptoms, and Treatment of PTSD"
Removing computer spyware	"Basic Steps for Removing Computer Spyware"
	"Avoiding Common Mistakes in Removing Computer Spyware"
Tattoo removal	"Deciding to Keep or Remove That Tattoo"
	"New Technologies in Tattoo Removal"
Drones	"How Does an Unmanned Aerial Vehicle Fly?"
	"Demonstration: A Close-up Look at a Drone"
Studying abroad	"Real Opportunities for Studying Abroad"
	"Priorities for Considering an International Studies Program"
Tracking global climate change	"The Main Indicators of Global Climate Change"
	"Tracking Global Climate Change over the Centuries"
Popular music	"Symphonic Metal: Innovation in Popular Music"
	"How Nightwish Became Symphonic Metal's Iconic Band"

If your informative speech takes the form of a demonstration, you'll have to prepare your audience first. Especially for topics the audience may not be very familiar with, you have to provide sufficient background information. For instance, before demonstrating the parts of an unmanned aerial vehicle, known commonly as a drone, you'd have to tell your audience briefly about the history of drones, the basic types of drones, and the legal regulations that apply to them. That background information puts your demonstration of how a drone (that you bring into class or show by presentation media) works into context.

Speeches about Events

event
A significant occurrence that an individual personally experiences or otherwise knows about.

An **event** is a significant occurrence you experience personally or otherwise know about. An event can take place in the past, present, or future. It does not necessarily have to occur in public: Important personal or family activities and occurrences like the birth of a child, weddings, or reunions can be events, too. Some events, such as concert tours, holiday rituals, fairs, and athletic contests, take place repeatedly. To call something an event gives it a special

Getty Images Entertainment/Getty Images

Nightwish has led the way in creating a new category of popular music—symphonic metal.

TOPIC	SAMPLE SPEECH TITLES
College graduation day	"Graduation Day: A Great American Ritual"
	"The Changing Nature of Graduation Day"
Mardi Gras	"The Story Behind America's Biggest Party"
	"Mardi Gras in Different World Cultures"
Chinese New Year	"The Ancient Tradition of Chinese New Year"
	"The Best Chinese New Year's Parades in America"
Assassination of President Kennedy	"Why We Remain Fascinated by the Assassination of President John F. Kennedy"
	"How the Assassination of President Kennedy Changed Presidential Security Forever"
World Cup soccer	"World Cup Soccer: Who Gets to Play?"
	"The Cultural Significance of World Cup Soccer"
Career Day on campus	"Successfully Meeting Employers on Career Day"
	"The Basics of Career Day at Our School"
The Grammy Awards	"The Grammy Awards as a Pop Culture Ceremony"
	"The Grammy Awards Yesterday and Today"
The AIDS Walk	"The AIDS Walk: A Response to a Global Crisis"
	"The AIDS Walk in Our Community"

Earth Day	"Why We Celebrate the Earth on April 22"
	"Earth Day: Eco-Activism's Holiday"
Ramadan	"Ramadan: The History of Islam's Holy Ninth Month"
	"The Importance of Fasting during Ramadan"

Jim West/Alamy Stock Photo

Events naturally appeal to audiences because they suggest that something important is taking place, such as the completion of a home for the recipient of a Habitat for Humanity house.

status and makes this category of informative speeches appealing to public speakers and their audiences. Some suggested topics and titles for informative speeches about events appear above and on the previous page.

What would you want to say about an event in your speech? Consider a celebratory event for the recipient of a Habitat for Humanity house. You can talk about what it takes to plan and promote the event, who attends the event and why, or the social significance of the event. In a speech about the Jewish bar mitzvah ritual, you might describe the religious and cultural origins of the event, what the "rites of passage" entail in Jewish culture, and the roles of the various participants in the ritual. When developing an informative speech about an event, consider its many different aspects and choose the ones you think will most interest your audience.

Speeches about Ideas and Concepts

ideas and concepts
Mental activity, including thoughts, understandings, beliefs, notions, and principles.

Mental activity produces **ideas and concepts**, which include thoughts, understandings, beliefs, notions, or principles. Ideas and concepts tend to be abstract rather than concrete. However, over time, an idea or concept may be actualized in the physical world and thus become more concrete. For example, a fundraising event usually starts with someone thinking, "We should raise money so the community center can build a new exercise facility." In another case, a concept car displayed at an auto show begins its life as an automobile designer's idea and may develop into a marketable product later. Initially, however, all ideas and concepts start out as abstractions, and many remain abstract.

When delivering an informative speech about an idea or a concept, the speaker usually explains the origin and main elements of the idea or concept. These aspects of a topic can prove quite extensive and complex, so be sure to select a topic that is manageable within your time frame. Here are some sample topics and titles for informative speeches about ideas and concepts.

TOPIC	SAMPLE SPEECH TITLES
Creativity	"What Does It Mean to Be Creative?"
	"Using Creativity to Solve Problems"
Religious fundamentalism	"The Roots of Religious Fundamentalism"

	"What Is a Religious Fundamentalist?"
The electoral college	"The American Electoral College: How Does It Function?"
	"Tracing the History of the Electoral College"
Marriage	"Views of Marriage across Cultures"
	"How Marriage Has Changed with the Times"
Binge drinking	"Binge Drinking: What Are the Risks?"
	"The Binge Drinking Epidemic on Our Campus"
Individual human rights	"What Are Your Individual Human Rights?"
	"Individual Human Rights: A Guarantee from the United Nations"
Dance therapy	"Dance Therapy as a Psychological Technique"
	"Effective Dance Therapy Techniques"
Cyberbullying	"When Does Online Behavior Become Cyberbullying?"
	"Legal Restrictions against Cyberbullies"
Niche marketing	"How Niche Marketing Developed"
	"Niche Marketing in a Multicultural Society"
Self-driving cars	"How Do Cars Drive Themselves?"
	"The Future of Automotive Transportation"

This list reveals that some subjects for speeches about ideas and concepts can be complex and controversial. That's no reason to avoid such a topic. To the contrary, audiences generally like to learn more about intriguing and provocative topics, especially if you come across as knowledgeable and enthusiastic about the topic. Just make sure you keep your speech informative, not persuasive.

Specific Purposes and Thesis Statements for Informative Speeches

The specific purpose you develop for an informative speech should reflect your general purpose: to raise awareness, increase knowledge, or deepen understanding about a topic. For informative speaking, your general purpose is *to inform,* so your specific purpose should begin with a phrase such as "to help my audience learn" or "to make my audience understand."

As you phrase your specific purpose, ask yourself, "What do I want my audience to learn?" Then, as you phrase your thesis, ask yourself, "What does my audience need to know?" Keep in mind that your specific purpose and thesis should clarify your topic for your audience, make it meaningful, express the main ideas accurately, and pique the audience's interest. **Table 13.1** presents several examples of specific purposes and thesis statements for different types of informative speeches.

Table 13.1 Specific Purposes and Thesis Statements for Informative Speeches

Informative Speech about...	Topic	Specific Purpose	Thesis Statement
Objects and places	Beyond the Flat Screen: How 3-D TV Works	To make my audience understand how the technology of 3-D television differs from that of conventional TV	3-D television differs from conventional digital TV in its technical makeup and viewing requirements.
	The Inca Trail	To educate my audience about the stages of Peru's Inca Trail	The Inca Trail starts at Chilca, Peru, passes through The Sacred Valley, and ends at Machu Picchu, the lost city of the Incas.
People and other living creatures	Taylor Swift: Her Life Story in Lyrics	To help my audience understand how Taylor Swift writes song lyrics to tell her life story	Taylor Swift writes songs that describe her life story including her humble roots, famous boyfriends, and hopes for the future.
	The Truth about Tarantulas	To make my audience understand the truth about tarantulas	True tarantulas are not deadly to humans, usually live a long life, and make great pets.
Processes	How a Dog Show Is Run	To educate my audience about how a professional dog show is run	A professional dog show involves grouping dogs into categories, judging the dogs according to standard criteria, and choosing winners by breed and for the overall show.
	Create Your Own Podcast	To help my audience understand how to create their own podcasts	Creating your own podcast requires creating the content, recording the content, and publishing the podcast.
Events	Career Day	To help my audience understand the features of Career Day on our campus	Career Day on our campus involves meeting with prospective employers, finding out about internships, and enrolling in career-building workshops.
	The Grammy Awards	To make my audience aware of major milestones in the history of the Grammy Awards Ceremony	The major milestones in the history of the Grammy Awards ceremony include the first ceremony in 1959, the first live TV broadcast of the ceremony in 1971, Michael Jackson's sweep of eight Grammy awards in 1984, and the canceled ceremony in 2008.
Ideas and concepts	Binge Drinking	To help my audience understand the risks of binge drinking	Binge drinking is a form of alcohol abuse that poses serious short-term and long-term health risks to the individual.
	Individual Human Rights	To educate my audience about the individual human rights guaranteed by the United Nations	Adopted in 1948, the United Nations' Universal Declaration of Human Rights promotes equal rights, worth, and dignity for all individuals.

Organizational Patterns for Informative Speeches

Nearly all the patterns of organization discussed in Chapter 8 work well for informative speeches, including the chronological, spatial, topical, narrative, and cause-and-effect patterns. When choosing an organizational pattern for your informative speech, pick one that complements your topic and promotes your specific purpose.

The Chronological Pattern

The chronological pattern allows you to explain how someone or something has developed over a period of time. With this pattern, you highlight the importance of each step in that development. This pattern works well with informative speeches about objects and places, people and other living creatures, and processes. Limit your number of main points to no more than four. In the following example, the chronological pattern is used to describe the stages in the life cycle of a living creature.

TOPIC:	The Life Cycle of Jellyfish
GENERAL PURPOSE:	To inform
SPECIFIC PURPOSE:	To help my audience understand the life cycle of jellyfish.
THESIS:	Jellyfish go through four main stages in their life cycle: larva, polyp, strobila, and medua.

MAIN POINTS:

I. The first stage in the life cycle is the jellyfish larva.

II. The second stage is the polyp that attaches itself to the sea floor.

III. The third stage is the strobila, a cluster of tiny jellyfish that emerges from the polyp.

IV. In the last stage, the organism separates from the cluster and swims away to eventually become the medua, a mobile adult jellyfish.

For informative speeches that demonstrate how to do something, the best approach is a chronological pattern that leads the audience through the process step by step. Notice that the speaker in the following example demonstrates how to pack for a trip without trying to convince the audience to travel or take any other direct action. The focus on generally useful information keeps the speech informative, not persuasive.

TOPIC:	Packing for a trip by air
GENERAL PURPOSE:	To inform
SPECIFIC PURPOSE:	To help my audience learn how to pack a carry-on suitcase for a trip by air.
THESIS:	Packing a carry-on for an airplane trip involves making a list of only those things you really need, checking for banned items, using the "roll-up" technique, and putting breakables in plastic containers.

MAIN POINTS:

I. First, make a list of everything you think you'll need for the trip.

II. Second, check the Transportation Security Administration's website for a list of banned items.

III. Third, pack using the "roll-up" technique to conserve space and prevent wrinkling.

IV. Fourth, place breakable items in airtight plastic containers.

The Spatial Pattern

The spatial pattern allows you to describe the physical or directional relationship between or among objects, places, people, or other living creatures. For example, if your specific purpose is to highlight certain locations, areas, or spaces that pertain to a topic, you can use a spatial pattern of organization, as in the following example about people and places.

TOPIC:	Zuni Indian Reservations
GENERAL PURPOSE:	To inform
SPECIFIC PURPOSE:	To familiarize my audience with where Zuni Indians live.
THESIS:	The Zuni Indians live on the Zuni Indian Reservation in western New Mexico and on surrounding lands in New Mexico and Arizona.

MAIN POINTS:

I. The tribal government is based on the Zuni reservation in McKinley County and Cibola County, New Mexico.

II. Some members of the Zuni tribe also live in Catron County, New Mexico, south of the main reservation in the western part of the state.

III. The Zuni tribe has land holdings and residences in Apache County, Arizona, in the eastern part of the state, where it shares territory with Navajo tribes.

The spatial pattern also can be appropriate for organizing informative speeches about processes or events, like the current global shortage of clean drinking water.

TOPIC:	Global water scarcity
GENERAL PURPOSE:	To inform
SPECIFIC PURPOSE:	To educate my audience about where clean drinking water is in short supply
THESIS:	Clean water has become scarce in much of the world.

MAIN POINTS:

I. The global problem of water scarcity.

II. Water scarcity in Africa.

III. Water scarcity in Asia.

IV. Water scarcity in North America.

The Topical Pattern

When using the topical pattern, you divide your topic into subtopics that address the components, elements, or aspects of the topic. Almost any informative speech topic can be organized using this pattern, in which the subtopics become the main points of the speech. For example, when you simply want your audience to understand a process, use the topical pattern to describe the main features of the process.

TOPIC:	Dog shows
GENERAL PURPOSE:	To inform
SPECIFIC PURPOSE:	To make my audience aware of how a professional dog show is run.

THESIS:	A professional dog show involves grouping dogs into categories, judging the dogs according to standard criteria, and choosing winners by breed, group, and best in show.

MAIN POINTS:

I. In professional dog shows, dogs are divided into breeds, and breeds are classified into groups such as sporting or working dogs.

II. Dogs are judged according to conformity with the breed standard, as well as personality, age, and sex within breeds.

III. The winner of each breed then competes within the appropriate group.

IV. The winners of the groups then compete for best in show.

In speeches about concepts and ideas, when you want to explain rather than simply describe important elements of the topic, the topical pattern can help make your explanation clear.

TOPIC:	Globalization
GENERAL PURPOSE:	To inform
SPECIFIC PURPOSE:	To help my audience understand the main differences among the major forms of globalization.
THESIS:	The four forms of globalization are economic, political, cultural, and media globalization.

MAIN POINTS:

I. Trade and commerce between nations represents economic globalization.

II. The flow of international political influence represents political globalization.

III. The movement of cultural goods and ideas from one part of the world to another represents cultural globalization.

IV. Connecting the world with new communication technologies represents media globalization.

Xinhua/Alamy Stock Photo

An informative speech on the scarcity of water can be organized topically by parts of the world. How else might you organize a speech on water scarcity using the topical pattern of organization?

The Narrative Pattern

The narrative pattern allows you to retell events as a story or a series of short stories. This pattern works best with informative speeches about objects, places, people, or other living creatures. The narrative pattern has much in common with the chronological pattern but more strongly emphasizes the dramatic unfolding of events, as in this speech about an object.

TOPIC:	Pluto, a Dwarf Planet
SPECIFIC PURPOSE:	To help my audience understand why Pluto is considered a dwarf planet.
THESIS:	The story of Pluto began with the discovery of Neptune, reached its peak with Pluto's naming as a planet in the early 1900s, and ended recently with Pluto's demotion to dwarf planet.

MAIN POINTS:

I. The story of Pluto began with the discovery of Neptune in the 1840s.

II. In the early 20th century, the planet Pluto was discovered and named.

III. Beginning in 2000, scientists began to doubt that Pluto should have the same status as the other celestial bodies circling the sun.

IV. In 2006, the International Astronomical Union reduced Pluto to a secondary status: dwarf planet.

The narrative pattern works well for turning the chronology of a person's life events into an absorbing story, adding suspense and dramatic flair to the topic.

TOPIC:	Eva Longoria
GENERAL PURPOSE:	To inform
SPECIFIC PURPOSE:	To make my audience aware of major turning points in Mexican American actress Eva Longoria's life.
THESIS:	Eva Longoria was born in Texas, was a motivated student who graduated from college, became a highly successful actress, and used her celebrity to advocate for human rights.

MAIN POINTS:

I. Eva Longoria was born in 1975 in Corpus Christi, Texas, the youngest of four daughters, to poor, working-class parents.

II. A highly motivated student in high school, she received a college degree from Texas A&M University.

III. Beginning with small parts in soap operas and films, Eva won a Golden Globe award for her starring role in *Desperate Housewives* and later became the executive producer and lead actress in *Telenovela*.

IV. Throughout her career, she has been actively involved in philanthropy and human rights politics, advocating for the poor, disabled, immigrants, and women.

The Cause-and-Effect Pattern

The cause-and-effect pattern shows how an action produces a particular outcome. This pattern works well with informative speeches about events—after all, events happen for a reason. This example explains how an alternative holiday now celebrated by the Maoris, the indigenous people of New Zealand, came into being when the country declared independence from Great Britain.

travelstock44/Alamy Stock Photo

What other organizational patterns could you use to give an informative speech about the Matariki celebration? How would changing the pattern change the focus of your speech?

TOPIC:	Matariki: The Maori New Year
GENERAL PURPOSE:	To inform
SPECIFIC PURPOSE:	To raise my audience's awareness of the Maori New Year celebration.
THESIS:	Matariki, the Maori New Year, is now an official celebration in New Zealand, part of an effort to reclaim and celebrate the Maoris' cultural heritage.

MAIN POINTS:

I. The Maoris inhabited New Zealand when it was conquered by the English in the 18th century.

II. Maoris lost much of their cultural heritage in the transition to British rule.

III. In 2001, Matariki, the Maori New Year, became an official day of celebration, resulting in the Maoris reclaiming some of their cultural heritage.

IV. Matariki is now celebrated widely in New Zealand.

Guidelines for Effective Informative Speeches

The success of your speech depends greatly on planning and preparation. The following guidelines will help you prepare an excellent informative speech and add to your repertoire of public speaking skills.

Keep Your Speech Informative

By focusing on your informative purpose, and not straying toward a persuasive purpose, you will be able to give an acceptable informative speech. To do so, choose a topic that interests you. At the same time, determine what you might realistically expect your audience to get out of your speech.

Let's say, for instance, you want to speak on the subject of rain forests. What would be an appropriate specific purpose and thesis for an informative speech about rain forests? What do you want your audience to think or do after listening to you? Given the complexities of the topic and the limited time you have to give your speech, you might reasonably expect only to raise the audience's level of awareness about rain forests generally, focusing on their characteristics.

TOPIC:	Rain forests
GENERAL PURPOSE:	To inform
SPECIFIC PURPOSE:	To educate my audience about the characteristics of a rain forest.
THESIS:	Rain forests are characterized by high levels of rainfall, specific types of trees, and four forest layers.

MAIN POINTS:

I. Rain forests receive extremely high levels of rainfall.
II. Only certain types of trees live in rain forests.
III. Four layers of vegetation exist in a rain forest.

Notice that the main points focus on informing the audience and avoid taking a position on the topic. In this case, the difference between informing and persuading lies in explaining what rain forests are without advocating an environmental policy.

Make Your Speech Topic Come Alive

Informative speeches come alive when speakers demonstrate a positive attitude and connect the topic to the audience in meaningful ways. You can accomplish this by establishing a context for your topic that excites the audience's imagination and by using vivid language to describe the main points. For example, Queen Rania of Jordan opened an exhibit on the ancient Middle Eastern city of Petra at the New York Museum of Natural History with an informative speech on the city's history.[10] Here is part of what she said:

> The magical rose-red city of Petra—whose wonders will enchant you tonight—is like nothing else on earth. It is a remarkable testimony to the human spirit, etched for all time in sandstone and shale....
>
> But Petra is more than just an archaeological treasure. Petra, I believe, offers an enduring message to all mankind. In Petra, human beings—ordinary mortals like you and me—saw potential beauty and grandeur in walls of sheer stone. They imagined the possibility of elegance and splendor where others would see only a barren and desolate wilderness.
>
> Most importantly, they had the vision and courage to attempt the impossible.... Petra teaches us that nothing is impossible and that even the bleakest and most barren situation contains the promise of hope.
>
> It takes a dream, a plan and a supreme effort—but anything is possible. This is the true wonder of Petra, magical and constant through the centuries. In Jordan, we are proud to be the trustees of this heritage of hope ... and bear with pride our responsibility to share it with our region and the entire world.

Notice how, in just a few words, Queen Rania makes the "Lost City of Stone" come alive and provides a context for appreciating the exhibit's art and artifacts. She links the story of Petra to the bleak cultural and political conditions in the region today and then suggests that her nation, Jordan, serves as a bridge between the Islamic Middle East and the more diverse and modern West. The visual exhibit that accompanied her speech further enhanced the appeal of her message.

iStockphoto.com/EdStock

Queen Rania of Jordan

Connect Your Topic to Your Audience

By using techniques that reduce the distance between themselves and their audiences, good speakers encourage audience members to pay attention and focus intently on the topic. For audiences unfamiliar with your topic, you'll have to connect it to audience members' general life experiences.[11] For audiences familiar with your topic, you can attract and maintain attention by reinforcing commonalities between you and your listeners. Help audience members understand how learning about your topic benefits them, and how they can perhaps even incorporate the short lesson into their own lives. Raph Koster, former chief creative officer of Sony Online Entertainment, connected his speech topic, "Theory of Fun for Games," to his audience at a Game Developers Conference with language, examples, and humor.[12]

> Hi, my name is Raph, and I am a gamer. [Audience laughs.] Why do we recognize that reference? Why are we ashamed about "Hi, my name is Raph, and I am a gamer"? Why do we see that connection? Why do we have to defend gaming to people? Why do we have to explain to someone or justify why we do what we do?
>
> *A Theory of Fun* came out of this: a "back to the basics" process of why and how games work....
>
> People are *really good* at pattern matching. I'm going to offer the vast oversimplification that what we think of as "thinking" or consciousness is really just a big memory game. Matching things into sets. Moving things into the right place, and then moving on.... A really good example of this is faces. The amount of data in a face is enormous. Just enormous. We've only just started to figure things about it in the past few decades; when a birdwatcher spots a bird, the face recognition part of the brain goes off. We see faces everywhere....
>
> So when we see a pattern that we get, we do it over and over again. We build neural connections. Now this is what I call *fun.*
>
> Building those patterns is necessary for our survival.... *Fun is the feedback the brain gives while successfully absorbing a pattern.* We need to absorb patterns, otherwise we die. So the brain *has* to give positive feedback to you for learning stuff. We tend to think of fun as being frivolous. The stuff that doesn't matter. And this is the serious games cheer line: I'm here to tell you that fun is not only *not* frivolous but *fundamental to human nature and required for survival.* Therefore what we do as gamers is saving the human race from extinction! [laughs]

Right from the beginning, Koster emphasized the powerful natural relationship he has with his listeners. "Hi, my name is Raph, and I'm a gamer." The audience laughed at this clever introduction because, first, they all knew who he was. Raph Koster is a legendary figure in the world of online gaming, and the audience was there specifically to hear what he had to say. Second, he echoed the way people introduce themselves in 12-step addiction recovery programs. Because gaming is considered an addiction by some, his opening words offered a sly joke. Third, by stating the obvious, "I'm a gamer," he made fun of his own superstar status by suggesting that the audience might not know he plays online games. And, because most audience members were online gamers too, he was able to establish and reinforce a sense of community with them.

Throughout the presentation, the speaker used language that reaffirms the experiences online gamers share. He used the informal language common in gaming culture and constantly referred to online game players as "we." His tone was upbeat and fresh. He hit on a key word—*fun*—as a featured idea. Then he tied gamers' shared appreciation of fun to his thesis: "Fun is the feedback the brain gives while successfully absorbing a pattern."

Inform to Educate

Informative speaking involves more than simply imparting information. A successful speaker informs the audience in a way that educates them. After hearing an informative speech, audience members should understand the nature and importance of the topic.

Educating your audience requires demonstrating the relevance of the speech topic to their lives or values. By nature, people respond better to information that promises to

Yang Lei/PhotoShot

Stephen Hawking appears at the London Paralympic Games opening ceremony.

enhance their lives in some way. As an informative speaker, you must give your audience a reason to listen, as famed theoretical physicist Stephen Hawking did in his opening remarks at the annual "Campus Party" event in Madrid, Spain.[13]

Founded by four young technologists, Campus Party puts on an annual festival that brings people together with one goal: to educate global society about new technologies and the power of the Internet by promoting innovative thinking and responsible participation in digital culture.[14]

Stephen Hawking suffers from a motor neuron disease that forces him to communicate through a speech generating device. He was the subject of the celebrated film, *The Theory of Everything*. Here is part of Hawking's speech:

> The fact that I can greet you today is because of a unique ability that the human race has. Our basic biological building blocks, the DNA and our genetic code, is ninety-eight percent the same as that of the great apes. Yet it is that crucial two percent difference that contains our powers of communicating with each other which has brought to us to where we are today.
>
> [At this point, a video of spectacular natural scenes accompanies his voice.] For millions of years, mankind lived just like the animals. Then something happened which unleashed the power of our imagination. We learned to talk. We learned to listen. Speech has allowed the communication of ideas, enabling human beings to learn together. To build the impossible. Mankind's greatest achievements have come about by talking. His greatest failures, by not talking. It doesn't have to be like this. Our greatest hopes can become reality in the future. With the technology at our disposal, the possibilities are unbounded....
>
> Since [the images I've shown] were made, things have advanced a lot... nearly every young person, and a few old relics as well, has a mobile phone and an Internet connection. We are fast linking up to become part of one global consciousness. This is a new world order. So keep talking!

Stephen Hawking first explained that basic communication skill is what separates human beings from other advanced species. He then described how our basic ability to talk and listen evolved into the invention of mobile communication technology and the Internet. Toward the end of his speech, Hawking made fun of people of his generation ("old relics") while encouraging his young audience to embrace the idea of a new world order based on advanced forms of human communication. That was a message that was surely appreciated by the technology enthusiasts who attended the Campus Party event in person or online.

Use Presentation Media to Inform

Informative speeches frequently include some form of presentation media. However, because you often have only a few minutes to give an informative speech, you have to keep your presentation media very limited and basic. A few well-placed images to introduce your topic or audio or visual references in support of your main points can prove effective. When you limit and carefully select your presentation media, you direct more attention to the images and increase their potential impact.

Developing an engaging delivery rhythm that moves smoothly and confidently between you as the speaker and your presentation media is crucial to becoming an excellent speaker. For example, change your slides at just the right time to illustrate and reinforce the specific points you want to make. When used well, presentation media can help make your informative speech a positive experience for you and your audience.

MindTap®

Watch It: View a video on speaking to inform.

Summary

When you give an informative speech, you seek to raise awareness, increase knowledge, or deepen understanding about a topic. To connect effectively with an audience in order to share information, you must ensure that your speech is meaningful, accurate, clear, and limited in scope. For an informative speech you want to describe, explain, or demonstrate something, but not to tell the audience specifically what to think or do about it. That would be a persuasive speech, which you'll learn about in the next chapter.

Most informative speeches are about objects and places, people and other living creatures, processes, events, or ideas and concepts. The general and specific purposes you develop for an informative speech should reflect your overall goal—to foster understanding about a subject or to explain to your audience how to perform a process. Several patterns of organization work well for informative speeches, including the chronological, spatial, topical, narrative, and cause-and-effect patterns. The pattern you choose for an informative speech should complement your general and specific purposes for that speech.

Five strategies for delivering an effective informative speech are to keep your speech informative rather than persuasive, make your speech come alive with colorful language and a topic that sparks your audience's imagination, connect your topic to your audience in meaningful ways, inform to educate, and use presentation media to enhance the speech content.

ANALYZE IT

Lishan, Chinese Valentine's Day

One of the primary characteristics of a good informative speech is that it is personally meaningful. Responding to his informative speech assignment, Lishan chose a topic that represents his cultural background. As you read the transcript of Lishan's extemporaneous speech, see if he also makes the topic meaningful to his audience—the other students in his introductory public speaking class.

Look at this picture. What do you see? The universe? The stars? Or a romantic story? I see love in this picture. It's the story of Niulang and Zhinü, and that's the origin of Chinese Valentine's Day.

According to the survey I did, 80 percent of you did not know that there is a Chinese Valentine's Day, and 90 percent did not know the origin of it. This does not surprise me. What surprises me is that 90 percent of you know the date of the Western Valentine's Day, but just 10 percent of you know why you have that day.

MindTap®

Watch and analyze this speech on MindTap.

That motivates me to do the research about the Western Valentine's Day and then tell you the story of the Chinese Valentine's Day. I will compare the Western and Chinese Valentine's Day, and I hope that by the end of my speech, you will get to know when the Valentine's Day is and how and why people celebrate the Valentine's Day.

Most of you know that the Western Valentine's Day falls on February 14. But most of you do not know that the Chinese Valentine's Day falls at the seventh day of the seventh lunar month, and it falls on August the 16th this year.

Most of you know why people celebrate Valentine's Day. According to History.com, people in the West celebrate Valentine's Day to remember the death of St. Valentine. St. Valentine was a priest of the third century in Rome. At that time, the Emperor of Rome forbade marriage for young men because he thought young men unmarried made better soldiers. Well, St. Valentine went against that law and performed marriages for young lovers in secret. Another version of this story is that St. Valentine helped Christians escape the harsh Roman prisons where they were often beaten and tortured. In either story, he was bound and sentenced to death.

About the Chinese Valentine's Day. According to chinadaily.com, it's a day when Niulang and Zhinü are allowed to meet with each other. Niulang is a poor, handsome boy, living with his brother and sister-in-law. He owns nothing but an old ox that can talk and is an immortal from the heaven.

Zhinü is the daughter of the emperor of heaven, who is good at handcrafting, especially in weaving clothing. Because the ox is treated nicely by Niulang, the ox wants to fulfill one of Niulang's wishes, so the ox asks Niulang what he wants. "Uh … I want to marry a beautiful girl," that's Niulang's answer. Then the ox takes Niulang to heaven, and there, Niulang meets Zhinü, and they fall in love. After that, they are married and have two kids.

But their story is not like any of the romantic Disney stories. They do not end up living happily together ever since. The marriage between a human and a god is never permitted, so the Emperor of heaven takes Zhinü away from Niulang and her kids. But, he's touched by their love and agrees that they could meet each other once a year. And that day becomes the seventh day of the seventh lunar month.

As we can see, no matter if the Western or the Chinese cultures, people celebrate Valentine's Day all because of love, but they observe that in different ways.

In the West, Valentine's Day is about sharing love with lovers and family members. People send gifts like flowers, chocolates, candy, and love cards to persons they love.

In China, Valentine's Day is more about the longing for love and in the present. Chinese girls offer fruit and incense to Zhinü to pray to have good skills and to find a satisfactory boyfriend. Lovers pray that they could get blessed and also pray for their love and happiness.

Now let's do a review about the Valentine's Day. Western Valentine's Day falls on February 14, and Chinese Valentine's Day falls on the seventh day of the seventh lunar month. And the Western Valentine's Day is about a story about St. Valentine, and the Chinese Valentine's Day is the story of Niulang and Zhinü. And people celebrated Western Valentine's Day by sharing flowers, chocolate, candy, and love cards with the people they love. Chinese people celebrate the holiday to pray for good skills and love.

In conclusion, Western Valentine's Day and Chinese Valentine's Day all contribute to love, although they celebrate that in different ways. The longing for love is a strong thing that Chinese and the Western people share. There are more things we share, even though we come from different cultures. And there will be lots to discover.

Questions for Discussion

1. Lishan began his speech with a digital slide of the night sky. Would the slide and his comments capture your attention and get you interested in the topic from the start? How might he have improved the attention getter?
2. How did Lishan use the results from his audience questionnaire in the speech? What advantage(s) did citing his audience questionnaire give him?
3. What organizational pattern did Lishan use for his informative speech?
4. In what ways do you think Lishan's speech was:
   a. meaningful to the audience?
   b. accurate?
   c. clear?
   d. limited in scope?
5. Was Lishan a credible speaker on the topic? How did he try to build credibility?
6. Lishan referred to historical stories and myths throughout the speech. How did it help you as an audience member to learn about Chinese Valentine's Day and how it compares to Valentine's Day in Western cultures?

> APPLY IT . . .

IN THE WORKPLACE

Written Communication

Learning how to be a clear speaker also helps you become a better writer, and being a good writer is a key to success in the workplace. Like effective speakers, good writers are audience centered. They keep their readers in mind every step of the way. Whether composing a letter, memo, project report, public relations release, letter of recommendation, or any other kind of business communication, you want your writing to be personally meaningful, accurate, clear, and limited in scope for your readers, not just you. What basic principles of effective speechmaking do you think can be applied to written communication? How might writing skills help you advance your particular career goals?

> REVIEW IT

Key Terms

event 262
gatewatching 259
ideas and concepts 264
informative speaking 258
object 259
place 259
process 261

MindTap®
Use flashcards to learn key terms and take a quiz to test your knowledge.

Reflecting on Informative Speaking

1. You want your speech to inform to be meaningful, accurate, clear, and limited in scope. Why might professional public speakers, especially some politicians and business leaders, purposefully avoid being clear about the information contained in their messages? Is that behavior ethical?
2. The difference between an informative speech and a persuasive one can sometimes be difficult for speakers to grasp. Consider the topics you might choose for an informative speech. How would you keep those topics safely inside the boundaries of speaking to inform?
3. Informative speeches are about objects and places, people and other living creatures, processes, events, and ideas and concepts. Some of these categories overlap. So why is it important to keep the focus on one primary category when you develop your speech to inform? How do you plan to keep your informative speech on track?
4. What is the purpose of the thesis statement for a speech to inform? What should the thesis statement contain?
5. The content of your informative speech must be organized into a pattern. Can a single topic be organized into more than one organizational pattern? How will you finally decide which organizational pattern best fits your topic?
6. Good speeches to inform don't just impart information; they engage the audience. What strategies can you use to make your speech to inform really interesting? For your topic, would it help to use presentation media?

14 Persuasive Speaking

READ IT

After successfully completing this chapter, you will be able to:

- Discern between informative and persuasive speaking.
- Explain the difference between practical and issue-based persuasive speaking.
- Distinguish between persuasive speeches of fact, value, and policy.
- Write a specific purpose statement and a thesis statement that reflect one of the three persuasive speech propositions.
- Select an appropriate organizational pattern for your persuasive speech.
- Identify the different types of audiences.
- Construct a persuasive appeal to account for the attitude of the target audience.
- Follow ethical communication guidelines when preparing persuasive speeches.

MindTap®

Start with a quick warm-up activity and review the chapter's learning outcomes.

Persuasive speaking became an evolving art long before today's technology burst onto the scene.

© Kyle Terada-USA TODAY Sports

Effective persuasion depends on the speaker's ability to convince the audience to follow his or her recommendations or instructions. The trusting relationship between the coach of a successful sports team and the players—like Steve Kerr and Steph Curry of the Golden State Warriors—illustrates this basic principle in dramatic form. The success of any kind of team depends on the person in charge having a strong message and the "audience" buying into what the leader says. This fundamental principle of effective persuasive speaking has existed throughout our entire evolutionary history. And in prehistoric times, the stakes were much higher than winning basketball games.

Originating in the northeastern region of Africa, our ancestors learned long ago that working together greatly improved their individual chances for survival.[1] To coordinate their behavior, some form of persuasive communication was needed.[2] For example, an individual might point and make sounds to direct others' attention to an animal hiding in the bush. That individual had to convince the others that the prey was really there before they would decide to pursue it together. Another person may have gestured toward a safe shelter location, signaled the presence of a predator, or revealed a source of water—crucial information for the group to know. Those individuals who could best get others' attention and persuade them to follow their suggestions became the leaders of their primitive tribes.[3] Solid evidence was necessary, too. In order to be considered credible and convincing by their peers, the emerging leaders had to be right more often than not. Human history makes clear that persuasive speaking became an evolving art long before today's communications technology burst onto the scene.

The great Greek philosophers Plato and Aristotle formalized and developed the art of persuasion as the most important public speaking skill for citizens to have during the Classical Era of modern world history (Chapter 1). It remains so today. In a persuasive speech, the speaker attempts to reinforce, modify, or change audience members' beliefs, attitudes, opinions, values, and actions. Two chapters will help you meet this challenge. The chapter you are reading now covers the basics—distinguishing between types of persuasive speeches, developing a thesis, identifying main points, and adopting an organizational pattern that is appropriate for different speech topics and audiences. Chapter 15 then explains how you can apply the primary elements of argument in persuasive situations and avoid common fallacies in reasoning.

Oversnap/Vetta/Getty Images

Defining Persuasion

MindTap®
Read, highlight, and take notes online.

persuasion
Using language, images, and other means of communication to influence people's beliefs, attitudes, opinions, values, or actions.

Persuasion relies on language, images, and other means of communication to influence people's beliefs, attitudes, values, opinions, or actions.[4] We live in a world of persuasive communication. Friends want to make plans with you for the weekend. A coworker texts you for advice on a project. Television constantly tries to sell you products. Family members ask for help. Instructors explain why what they're teaching you is important. Pop-up ads interrupt your online searches. Charitable organizations solicit donations. Indeed, demands for your attention and cooperation never stop.

In addition to being influenced, you also must be able to influence others so you can fulfill your personal needs and be an effective member of society. Modern democratic societies depend on the ability of ordinary citizens to make their voices and opinions heard. Political parties, businesses, nonprofit organizations, media, groups of friends, sporting teams, and even families reward people who can express their views convincingly and motivate others to act. In many ways, *communication is the art of persuasion*.

Persuasion or Coercion?

coercion
Forcing someone to think a certain way or making someone feel compelled to act under pressure or threat.

Persuasion implies choice. **Coercion** does not. Whether attempts to persuade deal with small-scale interpersonal matters or very serious issues that affect large groups, people subjected to social influence must have the freedom to say "no." When people are forced to think a certain way or feel compelled to act under pressure or threat, they are *not* being persuaded. They are being coerced. Brainwashing or intimidating people to get a desired effect is not persuasion. Neither is physically restraining or bullying someone. Free societies are founded on the right of individuals to choose courses of action willfully.

Persuasion or Manipulation?

How does persuasion differ from manipulation? When does a person cross the line from persuader to manipulator?

George Jartos/CartoonStock

To manipulate usually means using dishonest tactics to take advantage of other people. For public speakers, omitting crucial evidence, presenting inaccurate or false information, or intentionally misrepresenting research to your advantage are examples of manipulation. Your audience cannot evaluate your ideas rationally if it is being misled about facts. As an ethical speaker, you want to persuade, not manipulate, your audience.

Persuasive or Informative Speaking?

Informative and persuasive speaking differ in important ways. Informative speakers fulfill the role of *expert* on a topic and seek to facilitate audience understanding about it. In contrast, persuasive speakers take on the role of *promoter* or *proponent*, advocating a particular view on a topic they want the audience to adopt. As a persuasive speaker, you'll become an expert on your topic, but you'll go beyond your expertise to argue for a specific viewpoint you want the audience to accept.

Persuasive speakers voice a clear position on a topic, whereas informative speakers remain neutral. For example, for an informative speech on music-recording technology, the speaker would make the audience more aware of the topic, say, by describing stages in the history of recorded music. In contrast, a persuasive speaker would advocate a particular view of the topic, perhaps arguing that the sound quality of vinyl is superior to that of digital media.

Practical or Issue-Based Persuasion?

When thinking about topics to choose for a **persuasive speech**, you want to consider a wide range of possibilities. Perhaps you believe that regularly giving blood is important and you'd like to motivate your audience to do that. Maybe you've recently joined a campus club and want to encourage your listeners to join, too. Or you went whitewater rafting last summer and you'd love to see others try it out. You might be strongly committed to the idea of equal pay for women and men and want to argue that. Or you believe a wall should be built between the United States and Mexico. Perhaps you support "dying with dignity" laws (sometimes known as "doctor-assisted suicide") and want to make a case for adopting a new policy about this issue in your state.

persuasive speech
A speech in which the speaker attempts to reinforce, modify, or change audience members' beliefs, attitudes, opinions, values, or actions.

See how broad and dissimilar possible topics for a speech to persuade are? Some topics are simply heavier than others. They have a wider impact. Convincing your audience to take up a new sport, join a sorority, or donate time to charity isn't heavy the same way that arguing for or against the death penalty, calling for an end to world poverty, or regulating the flow of immigrants into the United States is. Therefore, we need to distinguish between practical persuasive speech topics that are generally quite personal and those that represent issues that impact society more widely. This chapter helps prepare you to deliver both types of persuasive speeches—practical and issue-based.

Practical Persuasion

Practical persuasion speeches attempt to convince audiences to personally take action on a "do-able" topic. Compared to issue-based topics, practical persuasion topics are more modest in scope. This doesn't mean practical persuasion topics aren't important. For instance, persuading your audience not to text while driving, adopt a more nutritious diet, or reduce the amount of time spent on social media are all worthy subjects for a speech to persuade.

MindTap®
Use Outline Builder to help you prepare your persuasive speech

practical persuasion
A persuasive speech of modest scope that encourages audiences to take action on a "do-able" topic.

Practical persuasion speeches also are *not* simple demonstrations, like how to pack your bags for air travel, compose a great photograph, or administer the new techniques of CPR. Demonstrations like these fall into the category of informative speaking (Chapter 13).

In a practical persuasion speech you try to convince each audience member to do something specific and realizable. To accomplish this, you will likely have to overcome some challenges. Sometimes the audience knows little or nothing about your topic. In that case, you'll have to provide sufficient information about the subject of your speech so audience members can confidently follow your call to action. For example, if you want your audience to try a zumba exercise class you would first have to describe the typical movements and rhythms of zumba and then convince them to try that instead of some other exercise program. Sometimes you have to motivate your audience to do something they know about but haven't tried. The classic case is recommending that audience members improve their eating habits. But you could also present a plan to help your audience use their time more wisely, avoid impulse buying, or keep college costs in check. Depending on the topic you choose, you may also want to explain to the audience how to best accomplish the action you recommend. For instance, if you were to give a speech on how to use social media effectively to find a job, you would describe how to do that.

Specific Purposes, Thesis Statements, and Main Points for Practical Persuasion Speeches

For all persuasive speaking, your general purpose is *to persuade,* so your specific purpose should begin with "To persuade [or convince] my audience to...." For a practical persuasion speech, you want to persuade the audience to do something specific and feasible. So, your specific purpose would be "To persuade my audience to [take some sort of realistic action]." For this kind of persuasive speech your thesis summarizes your feelings about the topic and the call to action for which you advocate.

TOPIC:	Passport
GENERAL PURPOSE:	To persuade
SPECIFIC PURPOSE:	To persuade my audience to obtain a passport
THESIS:	American citizens benefit from having a passport.

The content of practical persuasion speeches should be presented in a straightforward manner. The main points you raise in your speech should directly reflect your specific purpose. For the subject of this speech, some audience members already have a passport, but most probably do not. You could identify main points like these:

MAIN POINTS:

I. A passport allows citizens to travel to other countries legally.
II. Passports differ from visas which are granted by other countries for entry.
III. American citizens should apply for a passport online.

Organizational Patterns for Practical Persuasion Speeches

It's best to organize the main points of a practical persuasion speech in a clear topical manner. After giving your attention getter you identify and describe your topic. Then you provide the audience with reasons to accept your advice. Finally you show the audience how to follow through on the course of action you suggest. Here is an example of a practical persuasion speech including an attention getter, initial working outline, and conclusion:

TOPIC:	Crowdfunding
GENERAL PURPOSE:	To persuade
SPECIFIC PURPOSE:	To persuade my audience to crowdfund a project
THESIS:	Crowdfunding provides opportunities for individuals to have worthy projects supported financially.

MAIN POINTS:

I. Crowdfunding uses Internet sites to provide financial resources for individuals.
II. Various projects are excellent options for crowdfunding solicitations.
III. Individuals can take specific steps to create crowdfunding opportunities.

ATTENTION GETTER:

[*Show close-up photo of Laura on presentation media.*] My friend Laura graduated from our university last spring. She didn't have any great job offers and didn't want to jump into her career right away anyway. Laura wanted to do something meaningful that would also be a challenge and an adventure. She thought it would be cool to go somewhere she could use her education and learn about another culture. As a public health major and Spanish speaker, she thought a poor country in South America would be a great choice. But she didn't have money for a trip like that. *[Dim photo.]* So how did she manage to go? Laura got the money she needed from a crowdfunding site. Today, I'm going to describe the various kinds of crowdfunding sites and the kinds of projects they support. Then I'll explain the steps you need to take to get a project funded this way.

WORKING OUTLINE:

I. Crowdfunding sites
- **A.** Brief history of crowdfunding sites
- **B.** Types of crowdfunding sites
- **C.** How crowdfunding sites work
- **D.** Avoiding scams

II. Crowdfunding projects
- **A.** Personal projects
- **B.** Creative projects
- **C.** Institutional projects
- **D.** Specialty projects
- **E.** Micro-financing projects

III. Steps to get crowdfunded
- **A.** Deciding on a project
- **B.** Choosing the right crowdfunding site
- **C.** The overall funding process
- **D.** Applying online
- **E.** Soliciting pledges

CONCLUSION:

Today, I've given you some practical information about how to fund a project using one of the many crowdfunding websites available to you. I've explained what crowdfunding sites are, what kinds of projects can be funded, and how you can take steps to get your own project funded. [*Show photo of Laura helping native people in Peru while on her project.*] My friend Laura got a lot out of her project personally. And she made a contribution to the country of Peru too. A successful crowdfunding effort can put you in a picture just like this. Good luck with your crowdfunding project, and thank you!

Issue-Based Persuasion

Issue-based persuasive speeches address topics that most people would agree have serious consequences for society. **Issue based persuasion** deals with three types of questions: fact, value, and policy. Although each of these types of speeches has the general purpose of persuading an audience, they differ in the kind of outcome the speaker seeks. The type of issue-based persuasive speech you give influences how you develop your specific purpose and thesis, select main points, and organize your ideas.

MindTap®

Use Outline Builder to help you prepare your issue-based persuasive speech.

issue-based persuasion
A persuasive speech usually with serious consequences for society that addresses questions of fact, value, or policy.

Speeches on Questions of Fact

question of fact
A question that asks whether something is true or false.

A **question of fact** asks whether something is true or false. In speeches addressing questions of fact, the speaker tries to persuade an audience that something did or did not occur, or that one event did in fact cause another. For example, in a criminal court the prosecution attempts to persuade the jury the defendant did engage in illegal activity, while the defense argues the defendant did not.

Chapter 7 defines *facts* as observations you make from your own and others' experiences, and *inferences* as conclusions you draw based on facts. In speeches addressing questions of fact, speakers and listeners must carefully distinguish between facts and inferences. An infamous example of a speech that blurred the line between facts and inferences is former Secretary of State Colin Powell's address to the United Nations—the speech that convinced many Americans the imminent invasion of Iraq would be justified.[5] In his speech, Powell argued that Iraq's leader, Saddam Hussein, possessed weapons of mass destruction and would use them against other countries, including the United States. But much of what Powell presented as fact turned out to be invalid inferences based on information that was not properly verified.[6] Later, after weapons of mass destruction were not found in Iraq, Powell admitted he regretted giving the speech and presenting as facts information he later found out was unreliable.[7] The consequences of Powell's grievous error are still being felt in the Middle East and around the world. Partly because of this grave error, a cottage industry—the "fact-checker"—has become an essential feature of modern journalism and political analysis.

Apart from the heated disputes that define political discourse, individuals tend to agree on what constitutes a fact, especially when the information can be proven to be true or false. But people frequently disagree on exactly what they observe or how the observations were made. For example, one scientific study found that Americans talk regularly about their personal troubles with an average of two people, a finding that was down from three in previous years. However, the questions asked in the survey implied face-to-face communication only, leaving out other ways to interact, including text messages, social media, email, and online chats. The wording of the question skewed the "facts" revealed by the survey. Because facts can be contested, the speaker must persuade the audience that the facts presented are correct and that the means used for ascertaining those facts are valid and reliable.

The persuasiveness of a speech addressing a question of fact thus rests on the speaker's ability to present sound, credible evidence. Facts and statistics typically provide the foundational evidence for speeches on questions of fact. But speakers may also use examples, testimony, definitions, or narratives as supporting evidence. For example, in a persuasive speech arguing that mandatory seat-belt laws save lives, the speaker might include quotes from an interview with a highway patrol officer or tell a story about how wearing a seat belt saved the speaker's life in a car crash.

Heide Benser/Corbis/Getty Images

In a court of law, attorneys for the prosecution and defense each present a version of the "facts" whose veracity is decided by a judge or jury.

Specific Purposes, Thesis Statements, and Main Points for Speeches on Questions of Fact For persuasive speaking, your general purpose is *to persuade,* so your specific purpose should begin with something like "To persuade my audience to [take some sort of action]" or "To convince my audience to [think a certain way]."

When you give a speech on a question of fact, you want the audience to believe or agree with you that something is true or false. You focus mainly on reinforcing or changing how people think, not on how they behave, as the following example shows.

TOPIC:	The Peak in Worldwide Oil Production
GENERAL PURPOSE:	To persuade
SPECIFIC PURPOSE:	To convince my audience that oil production in the world has not yet peaked
THESIS:	Recent evidence shows that worldwide oil production has increased and will continue to increase.

This example demonstrates how the topic, general purpose, specific purpose, and thesis work together to answer a question of fact. In this speech, you're asking, "Has oil production in the world reached its peak?" Your specific purpose and thesis provide the answer you want your audience to accept: "No. Recent evidence shows that worldwide oil production has yet to peak and will continue to increase."

After forming your specific purpose and thesis, you want to develop the main points you intend to cover in the speech. When creating your main points for a speech on a question of fact, ask yourself, "What would make someone think this claim is true (or false)?" For example, in a speech about the causes of autism, the thesis suggests that the speaker will address theories associated with autism's causes.

TOPIC:	Causes of Autism
GENERAL PURPOSE:	To persuade
SPECIFIC PURPOSE:	To convince my audience that the causes of autism are unknown
THESIS:	Current theories about autism have not identified its cause.

MAIN POINTS:

I. Genetic theories of autism suggest the disease is caused by an anomaly in the ways certain genes interact with each other, but the research is inconclusive.

II. Environmental theories suggest that autism is caused by a virus or infection, although research findings are inconsistent.

III. Some biosocial theories, such as the notions that childhood vaccines or poor parenting cause autism, have not been supported.

Organizational Patterns for Speeches on Questions of Fact As with an informative speech, choose a pattern of organization for a persuasive speech that is consistent with your specific purpose and thesis. All the organizational patterns discussed in Chapter 8 can be used for persuasive speeches. For speeches that address questions of fact, speakers usually arrange their main points in a chronological, spatial, topical, or cause-and-effect pattern. The thesis often provides guidance about how best to organize a speech.

Kevin G. Hall/MCT/Newscom

Increased demand for oil is being met by new sources of crude oil, such as the boom underway in North Dakota.

Chronological For example, the thesis for the oil-production speech, shown again here, suggests a chronological pattern, which allows the speaker to trace production trends.

ORGANIZATIONAL PATTERN:	Chronological
TOPIC:	Worldwide Oil Production
GENERAL PURPOSE:	To persuade
SPECIFIC PURPOSE:	To convince my audience that oil production in the world has not yet peaked
THESIS:	Recent evidence shows that worldwide oil production has increased and will continue to increase.

MAIN POINTS:

I. Oil production has been highly variable throughout history.
II. Demand for oil has quadrupled in the past five years.
III. New sources of crude oil have been discovered recently.
IV. Despite competition from alternative energy industries, oil production will continue to increase

Spatial Notice how the thesis statements suggest the appropriate pattern to use for various speech topics.

ORGANIZATIONAL PATTERN:	Spatial
TOPIC:	Health Risks in International Travel
GENERAL PURPOSE:	To persuade
SPECIFIC PURPOSE:	To convince my audience they will encounter health risks when visiting foreign countries
THESIS:	Visiting foreign countries brings various health risks.

MAIN POINTS:

I. When visiting South America, you must consider certain health concerns.
II. When visiting East Asia, you should be aware of regional health risks.
III. U.S. visitors to South Asia encounter specific health risks.
IV. U.S. visitors traveling to Africa face several health risks.

Topical With this organizational pattern, the main points have equal weight and appear in a logical order that supports the thesis.

ORGANIZATIONAL PATTERN:	Topical
TOPIC:	The Effectiveness of Vitamin Pills
GENERAL PURPOSE:	To persuade
SPECIFIC PURPOSE:	To convince my audience that vitamin pills don't improve health

THESIS:	Although vitamin intake through the foods we eat is necessary for good health, vitamin pills are unnecessary and risky to good health.

MAIN POINTS:

I. Vitamin intake is necessary for good health.
II. Sufficient vitamin intake occurs through proper eating habits.
III. Vitamin pills add nothing to natural vitamin intake.
IV. Vitamin pills can create health risks.

Cause and Effect Speakers use the cause-and-effect pattern of organization for speeches on questions of fact when attempting to prove or disprove that one behavior or event causes another. Consider this example about bans on handheld cell-phone use while driving.

TOPIC:	Handheld Cell-Phone Use While Driving
GENERAL PURPOSE:	To persuade
SPECIFIC PURPOSE:	To convince my audience that banning handheld cell-phone use while driving reduces accidents and saves lives
THESIS:	Statistics show that banning the use of handheld cell phones while driving reduces accidents and saves lives.

MAIN POINTS:

I. Many states have banned the use of handheld cell phones for drivers.
II. As indicated by traffic accident statistics, banning handheld phone use while driving reduces accidents and saves lives.

In applying the cause-and-effect pattern of organization to speeches on questions of fact, the speaker must clearly demonstrate causation—that action A led to action B. The handheld cell-phone ban example appears to do that, with statistics showing reduced accidents and fewer lives lost after the ban was enacted. Still, the speaker must not confuse *correlation* with *causation*. Two actions may appear linked, but that does not mean they are causally connected. For example, while it's true that banning handheld phones may save lives, decreases in the number of accidents and deaths on the road may be influenced by other factors, too. For example, at the time the cell-phone ban went into effect, the economy was slowing down. People were driving less and were therefore less likely to get into an accident. In addition, improved safety technology in cars, more sophisticated road engineering, and crackdowns on drunk driving have also contributed to lowering the number of accidents and deaths on U.S. highways.[8]

Speeches on Questions of Value

A **question of value** asks for a subjective evaluation of something's worth, significance, quality, or condition. Questions of value invite the speaker to argue that something is good or bad, right or wrong, beautiful or ugly, boring or engaging, funny or serious—all qualitative judgments about something's significance. Although we share a common humanity, how we respond to questions of value reflects the principles, standards, and behaviors of our particular cultural groups.[9]

question of value
A question that asks for a subjective evaluation of something's worth, significance, quality, or condition.

SPEAKING OF ...

Learn about What Americans Value

What do Americans value? Because the U.S. population is diverse in so many ways, there's no easy answer to that question. The U.S. Department of State provides on its website (iipdigitalusembassy.gov) a wealth of information related to American values. Topics include democracy, civil society, education, economic development, security, environment, science, technology, and health. The site targets an international audience, especially foreign media organizations, government officials, and leaders, as well as the general public. Explore the website. What values is our government attempting to communicate to the international community? How can knowing about these values help you in public speaking?

A question of value therefore addresses individual opinions and cultural beliefs rather than proving something to be objectively true or false. In addition, speeches on question of value may include a call for action, but they don't ask for explicit changes in political or organizational policy. Those kinds of appeals belong to another category of persuasive speaking—questions of policy—that will be taken up next.

Speeches on questions of value can address timeless issues such as the morality of war or more contemporary concerns like the personal or ethical uses of social networking websites. Topics for speeches on questions of value may be serious, as with the best way to address the psychological fear of terrorism, or more lighthearted, as with a critique of a city's worst architecture. Still, any discussion based on applying subjective standards will result in some level of disagreement. Because questions of value can prove contentious, they often make for stimulating persuasive speeches, especially if you and your audience view the topic differently.

The very nature of many values speeches seems to suggest a call for action—if we feel strongly about something, then we should act on our convictions. Concerned that professional athletes who dope themselves set a bad example for young athletes? You could try to persuade your listeners to pressure sports teams and governing organizations to engage in stricter antidoping campaigns and administer more frequent tests. If you worry about the ravages of global climate change, then you might encourage your audience members to change their patterns of consumption. Convinced that young children are not sufficiently protected on the Internet? Encourage listeners to sign an online petition. Worried that the current system for nominating presidential candidates used by political parties is unfair? Tell your audience how to complain to party officials. But not all speeches on questions of value include a well-defined call to action. Thus, two points must be kept in mind:

1. Good speeches on questions of value persuade the audience to believe a certain way. They don't necessarily ask the audience to change their behavior. For instance, a speaker might advocate that society give greater attention to the problem of teenage depression without calling for any particular action to be taken by individual audience members.
2. Speeches about questions of value emphasize the basic principle the issue represents, not formal laws, rules, or codes associated with it. For example, a speaker might argue that parents who deny their children medical care for religious reasons are guilty of murder if the child dies but without calling for changes in laws related to this issue.

Thomas M Perkins/Shutterstock.com

Protecting the well-being of young children while maintaining the constitutional principle of free speech has become a major issue in today's information-driven culture, and an appropriate topic for an issue-based speech to persuade.

Specific Purposes, Thesis Statements, and Main Points for Speeches on Questions of Value In a speech on a question of value, your specific purpose reveals your evaluation of the topic's quality. Do you think something is good or bad, right or wrong, moral or immoral, the best or the worst? Make your position clear so your audience will know exactly what you think after listening to your speech. Then develop a thesis that supports your position.

TOPIC:	Public Art
GENERAL PURPOSE:	To persuade
SPECIFIC PURPOSE:	To convince my audience that public art is good for everyone
THESIS:	Public art is good for everyone because it gives residents a better quality of life, encourages tourism, and energizes local artist communities.

The main points for a speech on a question of value must clearly present and strongly support your position. Some speeches addressing questions of value focus on fairly noncontroversial topics, such as "recycling is good" or "littering is bad." But because questions of value reflect individual judgments, speeches on questions of value more often touch on controversial and sensitive topics such as capital punishment, abortion, the right to die, and animal rights. Your challenge is to make your position on the topic seem reasonable to an audience, especially in cases when you know the group disagrees with you.

As you prepare your main points, ask yourself questions such as "What kinds of supporting materials will best convince my audience to accept my position or change its views? What ideas support my position and how should I organize them? What can I reasonably expect my audience to think or do after listening to my speech about this topic?" The value of school vouchers provides a useful example. One way to address this controversy is to examine how well school vouchers perform here and in other countries.

TOPIC:	School Vouchers
GENERAL PURPOSE:	To persuade
SPECIFIC PURPOSE:	To convince my audience that school vouchers are the best way to solve education problems in K–12 schools
THESIS:	School reform movements in the United States and other countries show that school vouchers are the best way to solve current problems in K–12 schools.

MAIN POINTS:

I. School reform movements in Australia provide support for the superiority of a school voucher program over other choices.

II. Education reform movements in Japan also provide support for school vouchers.

III. Recent changes in Canada's public school system indicate a school voucher program would work in the United States.

IV. Trial programs in U.S. schools show that school vouchers help solve current problems.

Organizational Patterns for Speeches on Questions of Value For speeches that address questions of value, speakers usually arrange their main points in a chronological, spatial, or topical pattern. As with all persuasive speeches, choosing the appropriate organizational pattern for a speech on a question of value influences your ability to convince the audience.

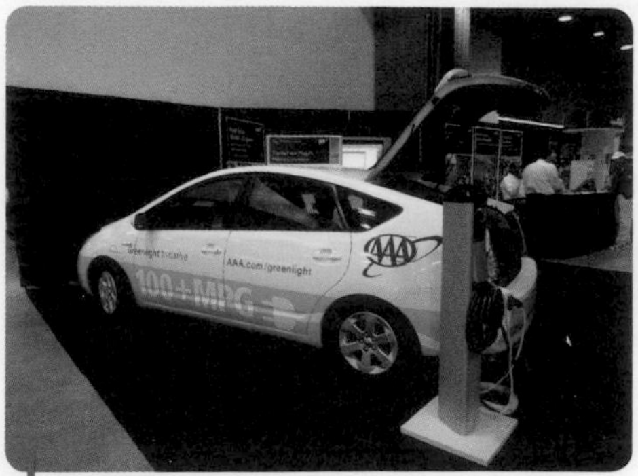

Eric Broder Van Dyke/Shutterstock.com

Automobile technology has evolved to the point where a speaker can argue that electric cars are economically and environmentally superior to traditional vehicles, including hybrids.

Chronological For example, in a speech about electric cars, a chronological pattern allows you to briefly discuss the history of automotive technology, strengthening your argument that electric cars are superior.

ORGANIZATIONAL PATTERN: Chronological

TOPIC: Electric Cars

GENERAL PURPOSE: To persuade

SPECIFIC PURPOSE: To convince my audience that electric cars are superior to gasoline engine or hybrid vehicles

THESIS: Electric cars represent the future of the automobile industry because they perform better overall than gasoline engine or hybrid vehicles.

MAIN POINTS:

I. The original automobile was steam-driven and invented in France in 1769.

II. The prototype of the gasoline-powered automobile was introduced in Austria in 1864.

III. Commercially successful hybrid vehicles entered the U.S. market in the 1960s.

IV. Electric cars are gaining popularity now and will eventually make other vehicle types obsolete.

Topical A topical pattern of organization works well for a question of value speech when the main points are of about equal importance. In the following example, all three points contribute in different but equally important ways to the thesis.

ORGANIZATIONAL PATTERN: Topical

TOPIC: Skin-Lightening Products

GENERAL PURPOSE: To persuade

SPECIFIC PURPOSE: To convince my audience that skin-lightening products are unethical

THESIS: Skin-lightening products are unethical because they can cause physical and psychological harm to users and imply that light skin is better than dark skin.

MAIN POINTS:

I. Cosmetic products used to lighten the skin can cause physical harm to the users.

II. Cosmetic products used to lighten the skin can cause psychological harm to the users.

III. Cosmetic products used to lighten the skin create a racist impression that light skin is preferable to dark skin.

Spatial You can use a spatial pattern of organization for a speech on a question of value when you want to emphasize the breadth of an issue. In this speech about population growth, the speaker wants to focus attention on the widespread nature of the problem.

ORGANIZATIONAL PATTERN:	Spatial
TOPIC:	Global Population Growth
GENERAL PURPOSE:	To persuade
SPECIFIC PURPOSE:	To convince my audience that efforts to control population growth in the future must be concentrated in Africa, South Asia, Europe, and Southeast Asia
THESIS:	Future efforts to control the population in some countries of sub-Saharan Africa, South Asia, Europe, and Southeast Asia will be necessary because they are experiencing extraordinarily high rates of population growth.

MAIN POINTS:

I. Nigeria and Uganda in sub-Saharan Africa have unsustainable population growth.

II. The South Asian countries of India and Pakistan have unsustainable growth in population.

III. In Europe, Great Britain, Holland, and Belgium have exceedingly high population growth.

IV. In Southeast Asia, the Philippines has dangerous levels of population growth.

Speeches on Questions of Policy

Whereas questions of value make judgments about topics and promote the speaker's opinion, a **question of policy** asks what specific course of action should be taken or how a problem should be solved. Note the word *should*—that's your clue that a speech addresses a question of policy rather than a question of fact or value.

question of policy
A question that asks what course of action should be taken or how a problem should be solved.

Questions of policy may reflect current controversies about policy at various levels, such as U.S. immigration reform, the use of body cameras by local police, or teaching creationism in state-funded public schools. These questions also range from the general, such as promoting democracy around the world, to the specific, such as academic integrity policies on your campus.

Speeches on questions of policy ask the audience to personally take (or not take) a particular action or support (or not support) a particular position.[10] Speakers might request immediate involvement, general support for a social or political movement of some kind, disapproval of an idea, or a change in behavior. For example, a speaker might propose that:

- College students should circulate a petition to ban junk food on campuses.
- People should support the animal rights movement.
- Local residents should approve changes in the zoning law.
- People should not buy clothes made in foreign sweatshops.

In a general sense, policies are formal doctrines used by institutions like governments, organizations, schools, teams, and clubs. These policies often take the form of rules, laws, plans, or codes of behavior that institutions create and enforce. Moreover, many questions of policy call for individualized responses, such as recommending that consumers carefully monitor their food and clothing purchases or protect themselves against identity theft.

Many celebrities use their fame to advocate positions on policy. George Clooney has spoken out on Middle East foreign policy, human rights, immigration, and the way Oscar nominees are selected.

The right of individuals to own guns is a classic policy issue in the United States. Speakers who advocate largely unrestricted gun ownership typically argue that any government constraint on the Second Amendment right violates the U.S. Constitution. On the other side of the issue, those who believe that gun violence is out of control in America say at the very least universal background checks on gun buyers should be required and access to military-style guns and large ammunition clips should be banned. Both positions on gun control sharpened after many mass shootings took place in the United States during the past several years.[11]

When choosing a topic for a speech about a question of policy, you need not stick with traditional public policy controversies like gun control, capital punishment, or the right to die. Original, thought-provoking topics or unique positions on well-known subjects are more likely to interest your audience than material they may have heard many times before.

Most important, choose something you truly care about that will resonate with your audience. You might consider, for instance, policy questions involving universal human rights, social justice, or the environment. Do high schools have the right to strip-search students for suspected drugs? Should online sports gambling be legalized and regulated? Should the federal government sue states that fail to provide safe drinking water to their residents?

Or you may want to choose a more specific, local issue affecting your campus, workplace, or community. Are new regulations needed to control the local police department's use of force? Are the visiting rules in your school's dormitories too restrictive? Should smoking be banned everywhere on your campus?

Specific Purposes, Thesis Statements, and Main Points for Speeches on Questions of Policy Unlike speeches on questions of fact and value, speeches on questions of policy often include a call to action, urging the audience to engage in a specific behavior. You may ask your listeners to take immediate action, such as signing a petition, or do something in the future, like carefully reading the fine print when they sign an employment contract. Sometimes you ask your audience simply to lend passive support, as with favoring a campus regulation that establishes open skateboard areas or opposing new cuts in education budgets.

National Rifle Association executive Wayne LaPierre argues against making changes in gun-control policy even in the wake of multiple mass shootings in America. Major news events often stimulate policy debates.

Phrase your specific purpose to indicate clearly what you want your audience to do or agree with. Then develop your thesis so it outlines how you'll support your position. When you create your main points, choose ones that clearly show why a change to an existing policy or situation is necessary, what the benefits of a change are, and what you want the audience to take away from your message. As you're preparing your speech, ask yourself these questions:

- What support can I show for my position?
- How close is my audience to my position—positive, negative, divided, uninformed, or apathetic?
- How does what I suggest solve the problem or move the cause forward in some way?

The following examples—one calling on audience members to take action and the other asking for general support of a position—demonstrate how the main points flow from the thesis.

TOPIC:	Controversial Speakers on Campus
GENERAL PURPOSE:	To persuade
SPECIFIC PURPOSE:	To persuade my audience to oppose a ban on controversial speakers on our campus
THESIS:	Except for hate speech, students should be exposed to a full range of ideas even if it makes them uncomfortable.

MAIN POINTS:

I. The constitutional principle of free speech applies everywhere in America, including college campuses.

II. Free speech does not mean hate speech, which has been defined.

III. Exposure to controversial ideas, even when it makes some people uncomfortable, is an important part of a modern college education.

IV. Our college has banned two controversial speakers from appearing.

V. Students should actively oppose efforts to ban controversial public speakers at our school by signing a petition.

TOPIC:	Year-Round Education in K–12
GENERAL PURPOSE:	To persuade
SPECIFIC PURPOSE:	To persuade my audience to support the institution of year-round education nationwide
THESIS:	Year round K–12 education should be instituted nationwide because of its educational, social, and economic benefits.

MAIN POINTS:

I. The current nine-month school calendar shortchanges students, taxpayers, and society.

II. Having K–12 students attend school year-round provides educational, economic, and societal benefits.

In the first example, the speaker establishes a principle, describes a problem, and then asks listeners to take a specific action. In this way, the main points support the response the speaker seeks from the audience: to allow controversial speakers to appear on campus. In the second example, the speaker simply asks the audience to support the position, first demonstrating why a change is necessary and then describing the benefits of the change.

Organizational Patterns for Speeches on Questions of Policy

Because speeches on questions of policy ask for some sort of change, speakers must clearly articulate why the change must occur and what should be done. Although the organizational patterns previously described can be applied to this type of persuasive speech, three other patterns generally are more effective: problem–solution, problem–cause–solution, and Monroe's motivated sequence.

iStockphoto.com/Kali9

Demonstrating an effective solution to a problem—like a viable alternative to the damaging consequences of corporal punishment, reasoning with a child—can be a powerful persuasive strategy.

Problem–Solution This pattern presents a need or problem and then shows how to solve it, as the following example demonstrates.

TOPIC:	Corporal Punishment by Parents
GENERAL PURPOSE:	To persuade
SPECIFIC PURPOSE:	To persuade my audience that parents never should physically strike their children
THESIS:	Because it's harmful, parents should not strike their children and should use other forms of discipline instead.

MAIN POINTS:

I. Children suffer serious physical and psychological consequences as a result of corporal punishment.

II. Parents should never physically strike their children and should instead use other forms of discipline.

Using this pattern successfully requires clearly establishing the problem's existence. If listeners aren't convinced the problem exists, the solution becomes irrelevant. Once they think there's a problem, the solution must seem reasonable. In the corporal punishment speech, the solution flows naturally from the problem—hitting children harms them, so parents shouldn't do it. However, if you called for long prison sentences to be given to parents who spank their children, most audience members likely would consider your solution too extreme.

Problem–Cause–Solution This pattern of organization extends the problem–solution pattern by adding an additional step: the cause of the problem. Consider this example of a speech about junk food on campuses.

TOPIC:	Junk Food on Our Campus
GENERAL PURPOSE:	To persuade
SPECIFIC PURPOSE:	To encourage my audience to sign a petition banning the sale of junk food on our campus
THESIS:	Junk food should be banned on campus because it contributes to obesity, poor nutrition, and immune-system problems.

MAIN POINTS:

I. Many college students are overweight, eat poorly, and have weak immune systems.

II. Junk food is a major contributing factor to these problems.

III. We must work to ban the sale of junk food on our campus.

The first main point explains the problem: Many college students are overweight, eat poorly, and have weak immune systems. The second point identifies a chief cause of this problem—junk food. The third point provides a solution: Get rid of junk food, at least on campus. Here's another example of a speech about a question of policy that applies the problem–cause–solution pattern.

TOPIC:	Border Security
GENERAL PURPOSE:	To persuade
SPECIFIC PURPOSE:	To convince my audience to support increased border patrols between the United States and Canada
THESIS:	We must have better security to prevent illegal immigrants from crossing the U.S.–Canada border.

MAIN POINTS:

I. Every year, thousands of people cross into the United States illegally from our neighbor to the north, Canada.

II. Security on the U.S.–Canada border is lax, making it easy for people to enter our country illegally.

III. We must increase border patrols between the United States and Canada.

As with the problem–solution pattern of organization, getting the audience to believe a problem exists provides the foundation for the remainder of a speech using the problem–cause–solution pattern. In this example, the idea that so many people cross the border from Canada illegally may surprise many audience members. The speaker must then link the problem with the cause and show that the solution represents a reasonable answer to the problem.

Monroe's Motivated Sequence Your primary challenge in persuasive speaking is to motivate your audience to respond to your speech the way you suggest. You've seen how to do that with the problem–solution and the problem–cause–solution patterns of organization. Monroe's motivated sequence gives you another good option for encouraging your audience to take action.

Developed last century by Alan Monroe, a well-known professor of speech, the motivated sequence draws its core ideas from the philosophy that John Dewey expressed in his classic book, *How We Think*.[12] The motivated sequence mirrors the way we naturally process information and make decisions in our everyday lives.

With Monroe's motivated sequence, you organize your speech in such a way that leads your audience members through a five-step thought process that encourages them to agree with you and take action (Chapter 8). You ask your listeners to grasp the relevance and importance of your topic, understand the problem you describe, become satisfied that the solution you offer is a good one, imagine how the solution could be enacted, and feel motivated to do their part in solving the problem.

The motivated sequence encourages you to take an audience-centered approach to public speaking. When you use this organizational pattern, you focus clearly on what you want the audience to think and do every step of the way throughout

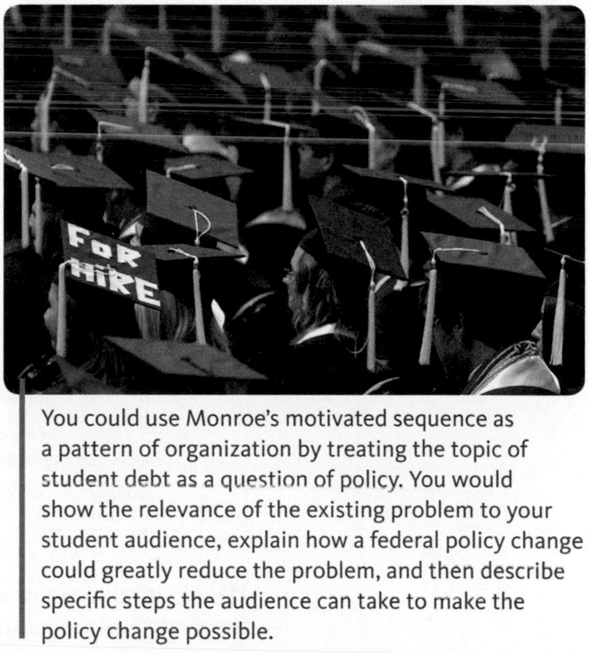

AP Images/Butch Dill

You could use Monroe's motivated sequence as a pattern of organization by treating the topic of student debt as a question of policy. You would show the relevance of the existing problem to your student audience, explain how a federal policy change could greatly reduce the problem, and then describe specific steps the audience can take to make the policy change possible.

Table 14.1 Monroe's Motivated Sequence

Step	Speaker's Action	Audience's Response
Attention	Relate topic to audience to gain attention.	I will listen because this is relevant to me.
Need	Establish the problem or current harm.	There's a problem that needs my attention.
Satisfaction	Describe the solution to the problem.	Here's the solution to the problem.
Visualization	Show benefits of proposed solution or costs of not implementing it or both.	I can visualize the benefits of this solution or the costs of not implementing it.
Action	Explain how audience can implement proposed solution.	I will do this.

your speech.[13] **Table 14.1** indicates what you need to do to get the desired response from your audience at every step of the sequence.

If you're giving a persuasive speech in which you ask your audience to take some sort of action, all five steps of the motivated sequence apply, as in the following example.

TOPIC: Simplify Your Life

GENERAL PURPOSE: To persuade

SPECIFIC PURPOSE: To persuade my audience to take steps to simplify their lives

THESIS: Our consumer culture makes our lives needlessly complex, so we should take concrete steps to simplify our lives.

ATTENTION:

I. We work more hours, spend more time commuting, take fewer vacations, and interact socially more than at any time in the past.

NEED:

II. We buy things we don't need, waste time watching television, check social media too often, and drive to places when we could easily walk.

SATISFACTION:

III. Simplifying your life means figuring out what you value most and focusing on activities that help you fulfill those values.

VISUALIZATION:

IV. Think about all the time you'd have to do what you like if you cut out all the things you do that aren't really necessary.

ACTION:

V. There are specific steps you can take to simplify your life, such as concentrating on a few goals and doing them well, setting aside time for yourself, getting exercise by walking instead of driving, and getting rid of clutter by donating to charity or recycling the things you don't really use.

If you simply want the audience's agreement or support, you can drop the fifth step of the motivated sequence, the action step, as with the following example.

TOPIC:	Cooperation in Video Games
GENERAL PURPOSE:	To persuade
SPECIFIC PURPOSE:	To persuade my audience to support video games that contribute to society by promoting more cooperation and less competition
THESIS:	Video games that encourage players to cooperate with each other rather than compete against each other would benefit our society.

ATTENTION:

I. The stereotypical video game player is a teenage male, but did you know that more than 40 percent of game players are women and the average age of a player is 36?

NEED:

II. Violent video games make the headlines, but another real problem is the lack of games that help players develop the teamwork skills that are so essential in today's world.

SATISFACTION:

III. Video games based on cooperation rather than on competition provide a logical way to facilitate the development of teamwork skills.

VISUALIZATION:

IV. Even if you don't play video games, you recognize that facilitating people's ability to cooperate with others contributes more generally to society, as you've probably experienced yourself when working with a team.

Image Source/Getty Images

Providing evidence that video games encourage social cooperation can lead your audience to imagine how the games contribute something positive to society.

In this example, you're not asking the audience to play or develop cooperation-based video games. Instead, you're asking them to agree with you that such games contribute positively to society. You want your audience to understand your argument and then agree with your point of view. The logical progression of the steps in the sequence helps you meet this goal. Compared with other organizational patterns, the motivated sequence is particularly good at helping audience members understand main points, which helps you persuade them to change their attitudes.

This organizational pattern represented by Monroe's motivated sequence can also be used for practical purposes other than public speaking, including how to compose a convincing business letter[14] or write clear and compelling technical documents.[15]

Persuading Different Types of Audiences

Just as advertisers must know their audiences well and understand how to reach them effectively, you should be aware of where your audience stands on your topic so you can design a message that will encourage them to listen and consider your views. Chapter 5 explains how to analyze an audience for any type of speech. This section provides specific strategies persuasive speakers use to address the beliefs, attitudes, and values of five common audience positions: negative (or hostile), positive (or sympathetic), divided, uninformed, and apathetic.[16] These audience positions and strategies are summarized in **Table 14.2** and explained here.

Table 14.2 Types of Audiences

Type of Audience and View of Topic	Persuasive Strategies
Negative (informed → unfavorable or highly unfavorable)	• Establish credibility • Take common-ground approach • Visualize topic in positive ways • Anticipate and address objections • Keep persuasive objectives within reason
Positive (informed → favorable or highly favorable)	• Rely on engaging evidence to reinforce commitment • Use vivid language and images • Incorporate narratives when possible • Suggest action
Divided (informed → split: half favorable, half unfavorable)	• Acknowledge reasonableness of both sides • Establish credibility • Take common-ground approach • Integrate strategies for negative and positive audiences
Uninformed (uninformed → no opinion)	• Show relevance of topic to audience • Demonstrate expertise and fairness • Use repetition and redundancy • Keep persuasion subtle
Apathetic (informed → not important)	• Gain attention and interest • Show how topic affects audience • Display energy and dynamism • Take a one-sided approach • Use presentation media

The Negative Audience

negative audience
An audience that is informed about a speaker's topic and holds an unfavorable view of the speaker's position; also called a *hostile audience*.

A **negative audience**, also called a hostile audience, is informed about your topic and holds an unfavorable view of it. A negative audience may seem intimidating, but simple exposure to contrasting points of view is where effective persuasion starts for many audience members. Suppose, for instance, you want your audience to support an initiative on your campus to abolish all general education requirements. That goal may seem too radical to most students and faculty, so you might want to argue for a more moderate step, such as reducing the required number of general education units.

When you encounter a high degree of resistance to your position on a topic, several strategies will help you achieve your goal.[17]

- *Establish your credibility with the audience.* Developing a positive relationship with the audience, showing an interest in them, and demonstrating your expertise on the topic all contribute to making a good impression.
- *Take a common-ground approach to the topic.* Identify areas of agreement with the audience, then move to areas of disagreement. If listeners perceive they share similar viewpoints with you, they'll be more open to your message.[18] In a speech favoring single-payer health care, also known as "Medicare for all," you might draw parallels between the right of all citizens to have health care and the abolishment of slavery, passing of laws against child labor, giving women the right to vote, or the right of gays and lesbians to marry, for instance. You could

demonstrate how much resistance there was to each of these changes and then point out that these rights are now considered ordinary by most people.

- *Help your audience visualize your topic in positive ways.* Often just helping the audience get used to a new idea is the first step in effective persuasion. In a speech that advocates renewed funding for space exploration, you might show a few compelling digital slides of the Mars rover or images of distant galaxies to spark the audience's imagination and give them a more favorable impression of the topic.
- *Prepare for a negative reaction to your position.* Consider all the reasons your audience may not agree with you. Then determine how you will confront and overcome those objections in your speech. For example, in a speech on raising the minimum wage in the United States, you could address your listeners' concerns about job loss by pointing to research that shows no such effect. When you acknowledge your listeners' concerns in your speech, you demonstrate an understanding of their perspective, which increases your likelihood of winning them over.
- *Finally, keep your persuasive objectives within reason.* You are not very likely to move your audience to act in a way that conflicts with strong feelings they hold about your topic. In this case, make it your objective to get the audience to start thinking about the topic in a different way. For instance, an audience that is strongly opposed to allowing the U.S. government to issue national identification cards for all citizens is not going to sign a petition in favor of doing that right after listening to your speech advocating the idea. But you might be able to reduce resistance and start your listeners thinking about the advantages you think a national identification card registry provides.

The Positive Audience

A **positive audience**, also called a sympathetic audience, is informed about your topic and has a favorable view of your position. These audience members want to have their views confirmed and reinforced, learn more about the topic, and, in some cases, join a community of like-minded people or find out what they can do personally to advance the cause. Political campaign speeches and religious gatherings commonly attract positive audiences.

positive audience
An audience that is informed about a speaker's topic and has a favorable view of the speaker's position; also called a *sympathetic audience.*

Several proven strategies can help a speaker reinforce the thoughts and behaviors of a positive audience.[19] Consider, for example, how the following strategies could help you promote environmental activism to an already sympathetic audience.

- *Incorporate engaging evidence that reinforces the audience's commitment to the topic.* Use testimony and examples your audience will find captivating; stay away from long lists of facts, endless statistics, and dull definitions. For instance, you might explain how various successful political initiatives—saving forests, rivers, wetlands, and lakes from pollution and urban sprawl—have preserved valuable natural resources and improved the quality of life for all the planet's inhabitants.
- *Use vivid language and images to heighten your audience's enthusiasm for the topic.* Refer to "flourishing, green forests; icy cold, raging rivers; wetlands teeming with wildlife; and cool, inviting lakes" rather than "forests, rivers, wetlands, and lakes." Incorporating a short series of colorful slides displaying the beauty of land and water saved from destruction through political action can also deepen audience members' appreciation for the topic. They're already on your side, so give them something tangible to take away from the speech that confirms their opinion and extends their knowledge on the topic.
- *Rely on narratives to elaborate your points.* Stories work especially well to reinforce the position audience members already hold. For example, if you know that your

Getty Images News/Getty Images

Donald Trump spoke to very enthusiastic, positive audiences during the last presidential primary campaign. His strong message about what to do about Islamic extremism, undocumented immigrants, trade with China, gun ownership, and his opinion of former President Barack Obama resonated with the Tea Party faction of the Republican Party. Trump's call to action was clear: Vote for me.

audience believes in the value of environmental responsibility, a speech promoting environmental activism might begin with a story about the personal experience that got you involved in the topic.

- *When audience members already agree with your view, rally them to take action.* For example, you might encourage your audience to join an environmental group in the community or on campus, participate actively in Earth Day this year, support impending environmental legislation, purchase reusable cloth shopping bags, stop junk mail, or boycott products that degrade the environment.

The Divided Audience

A **divided audience** is informed about your topic but split in its views: About half the members have a favorable view and the rest have an unfavorable one. Speakers are often faced with divided audiences, especially when addressing diverse audiences or speaking about controversial issues. With a divided audience, the main challenge is persuading those audience members who disagree with you. Therefore, you can employ the same basic approach used for a negative audience. This means that you'll want to establish your credibility and connection with the audience clearly, take a common-ground approach, visualize the topic in positive ways for the audience, and confront possible objections.

divided audience
An audience that is informed about a speaker's topic but equally split between those who favor the speaker's position and those who oppose it.

You also want to acknowledge those who agree with you. Relevant narratives, appealing testimony and examples, and engaging images will help you target sympathetic audience members and may appeal to hostile listeners as well.

Suppose you're speaking to a community group in an urban neighborhood that has experienced a high rate of street crime in recent years. The specific purpose of your speech is to convince your audience that video surveillance cameras should be installed throughout the area. Some members of your audience favor the idea as a practical way to reduce crime. Other members oppose the idea, viewing it as an intrusion on their privacy. Here are a few strategies that will help you address the entire audience effectively.

- *Demonstrate that you recognize the legitimacy of the arguments for and against the issue.* Street crime is a problem that must be solved, yet the right to privacy is a fundamental principle of democracy and should be upheld.
- *Establish your credibility* by citing statistics showing that video surveillance does reduce street crime significantly.
- *Establish common ground among all audience members* by saying you are certain everyone in the room agrees with the right to privacy.
- *Integrate strategies for negative and positive audiences.* In this case, you could address the objection that surveillance cameras intrude on the community's right to privacy by saying that the point is not to take away anyone's rights but rather to restore privacy rights that have been taken away by crime itself. You can also reinforce the position of those who agree with you with testimony and examples from places where surveillance cameras are used.

In the end, you encourage the resisters to rethink their position not only by the strength of your argument and supporting evidence but also because you, the speaker, understand what's at stake for individuals' privacy.

The Uninformed Audience

uninformed audience
An audience that is unfamiliar with a speaker's topic and has no opinion about it.

Uninformed audiences are unfamiliar with your topic and therefore have no opinion about it. Audience members potentially could be interested in a topic you care about, but they simply lack exposure to it. For example, people who are not serving in the military often know very little about military benefits. Yet you can argue that members of the armed forces put their lives on the line to protect all of us and deserve to receive decent salaries and benefits. Several strategies will help you provide the information listeners need to facilitate their agreement with you.[20]

- *Show the relevance of your topic to the audience.* By linking audience members with the topic, you can help them realize, "I don't know much about this, but I should." For example, you'd show how not only military families but also audience members would be affected by expanding benefits for veterans. Changing benefits might mean higher costs for all taxpayers, but it's worth it because without military benefits a greater financial burden would fall on local social services. The need to treat veterans for mental health problems resulting from the Iraq and Afghanistan wars has become particularly crucial. Good benefits boost the morale of active duty troops too, and that can affect everyone's security.
- *Demonstrate your expertise on the topic and fairness in addressing all perspectives.* As a persuasive speaker, you will argue one side of the issue or the other—say, supporting increased benefits for military families. Without turning your persuasive speech into an informative one, you must describe the issue. Show you've done your research on the topic and are able to provide listeners with what they need to know to formulate an opinion. Audience members will be much more likely to agree with your position if they believe you have given them a fair and comprehensive sense of the issue.
- *Use repetition and redundancy to reinforce your points.* Your audience is new to this topic, so provide members with basic information about the topic in several forms. In our example about veterans' benefits, you could define the purpose of the benefits, present facts about the services the government currently offers veterans, show statistics comparing those services with the proposed services, offer testimony from a scholar who studies veterans' benefits, and tell a story about a veteran who used those benefits to achieve an important goal, such as completing college. These different types of supporting materials build redundancy into the speech.
- *Keep your persuasion subtle.* Let the audience know your position, but avoid emphatic, inflammatory, or overly passionate statements. Instead, take a matter-of-fact approach. In our example, you might say, "I support the changes to veterans' benefits currently under consideration. Let me tell you why." If you wait too long to let audience members know your position on the topic, they'll feel deceived and might devalue the information you've presented. But if you've motivated your listeners to learn more about the topic and have established yourself as an expert, they'll be more likely to trust you to treat the topic fairly, whatever position you take.

The Apathetic Audience

apathetic audience
An audience that is informed about a speaker's topic but not interested in it.

Apathetic audiences know about your topic but are not interested in it. They are probably apathetic because they think it doesn't affect them. Why bother to pay attention? This type of audience challenges a speaker to forge a positive link between topic and audience.

Let's say that you want to argue that the United States should provide economic support to developing countries. Specifically, you propose that America should

Mike Greenslade/Alamy Stock Photo

The United States Agency for International Development (USAID) provides economic, developmental, and humanitarian assistance around the world in support of U.S. foreign policy goals. A speech that advocates increasing foreign aid would have to provide background information because the audience likely would not be well informed on the topic.

provide startup loans for small businesses in those countries. To get your audience interested, you could apply the basic strategies that help speakers connect with an apathetic audience.

- *Gain their attention and pique their interest.* Even more than with an uninformed audience, you have to show apathetic audience members *why* they should care about the topic. Your audience analysis, or at least your hunch, indicates that your listeners believe the topic has no relevance to their lives. They may have heard something about it, but it hasn't interested them enough to think about it very much. However, you know they give to charity and support strengthening local communities. This convinces you that with the right appeal you'll be able to connect your topic to their sense of social responsibility. Using strong supporting evidence, you might demonstrate the positive impact that economic aid can have on the lives of people who live in the developing world while providing more stability and security for us here at home.
- *Show how the topic affects them specifically.* When listeners identify with a topic and feel it's relevant to them, they're more likely to be persuaded.[21] You might be able to convince your audience to care about this seemingly distant topic by explaining how the health of the U.S. economy depends on the presence of a stable global economic system. You tell them that foreign aid makes up only a tiny fraction of the federal budget. You assert that so long as developing countries struggle economically, the stability of the global economic system is threatened. That precarious condition negatively affects the American economy, the value of the dollar overseas, and our national security. So the question of supporting developing countries directly affects the audience's pocketbook and its safety—primary human motivations.
- *Show your audience how much you care about the topic through your energy and dynamism.* In promoting U.S. economic support for developing countries, you must demonstrate your deep commitment to the topic. So you speak rapidly but clearly, raise your vocal volume a bit, take only short pauses, and gesture and move with energy and purpose. These types of nonverbal behaviors signal your passion for the subject.[22]
- *Take a one-sided approach to the topic.* Although you must make a balanced presentation of information overall, you need not address all perspectives on it, as you would when facing a negative audience. When audience members are generally apathetic, taking a one-sided approach to the topic is both reasonable and ethical. In persuading the audience, you want to advocate a viewpoint that corresponds with the reasons they should care about the topic.
- *Use presentation media.* Incorporating appropriate presentation media helps audience members visualize your topic, stirs their emotions, and is often more persuasive than words alone.[23] In the case of encouraging people to support U.S. economic aid to developing countries, several photographs demonstrating the positive effects of such aid or a 15-second clip from a documentary on life in the developing world could intrigue an apathetic audience.

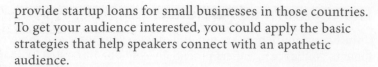

Kayte Deioma/PhotoEdit

Sometimes you have to educate your audience and dramatize your topic with presentation media in order to convince your audience members that it's relevant to them.

The Ethics of Persuasive Speaking

When public speakers attempt to persuade their audiences to think or act in a particular way, they must start and finish their work on firm moral ground. The National Communication Association has established clear standards for ethical communication. Persuasive speakers must adhere to this ethical principle in particular: "We condemn communication that degrades individuals and humanity through distortion, intimidation, coercion, and violence, and through the expression of intolerance and hatred." Ethical speakers do not attempt to deceive or manipulate the audience. Instead, they present their information and arguments truthfully, accurately, and honestly. In addition, they "endorse freedom of expression, diversity of perspective, and tolerance of dissent."[24]

An Example of Ethical Standards

To demonstrate one clear difference between a persuasive speech that meets ethical standards and one that doesn't, consider the subject of DNA testing to determine a person's genetic ancestry. DNA testing has become an indispensable tool for criminologists—in many cases it is the key to helping them accurately identify who did or did not commit a crime. And DNA makes it possible for scientists to determine the age of fossil remains. But the science of DNA has also become available for another purpose: to trace personal genetic history.[25]

Encouraging an audience to subscribe to one of the services that analyzes personal DNA certainly could be developed into an interesting persuasive speech. But what ethical considerations are associated with this topic? An ethical speaker would carefully research how DNA tests are done and properly used to show audience members how they can benefit from the testing process as well as indicate the risks involved. For example, the speaker might discuss how DNA tests can help diagnose a genetic disorder like Huntington's disease, warn of predispositions to addictions, or estimate the risk of passing on a genetic disease to a child. The speaker might try to motivate the audience by explaining how DNA tests can help people find unknown parents, siblings, or other relatives. In addition, the speaker could mention that DNA tests can reveal where every audience member's ancestors come from.

Two categories of potential ethical violation can be identified for this topic: (1) suggesting that DNA tests can deliver something they cannot and (2) failing to mention the drawbacks of DNA testing, which can be serious.

For instance, although the tests can indicate a person's genetic makeup (European, African, Asian, and Native American), they cannot reveal a person's race.[26] Race is an unreliable way of categorizing people by appearance; it is not a scientific category based on genetics. An ethical speaker would not try to convince audience members that DNA testing could help people identify their race.

Perhaps most important, the speaker must warn the audience about the biggest danger associated with DNA testing: the shock many people receive when their DNA results don't match up with their long-held sense of ethnic identity—who they imagined themselves to be. For example, Henry Louis Gates, Jr., professor of African and African American Studies at Harvard University, discovered that his genetic ancestry is as much European as African, completely altering the way he imagined how he descended from his ancestors.[27] Thus, when persuading others, ethical speakers must also consider and address the possible harms their audiences may encounter.

MindTap®
Watch It: View a video on speaking to persuade.

Summary

When you speak to persuade others, you use language and (if desired) presentation media to influence the audience's beliefs, attitudes, values, opinions, or actions. Persuasive speeches are of two basic types—practical and issue-based. Practical persuasion speeches tackle doable topics and suggest a particular action for the audience to take. They generally use a topical pattern of speech organization. Issue-based persuasive speeches focus on topics that have wider social significance. They address questions of fact, value, or policy. Speeches on questions of fact ask whether something is true or not true. Speeches on questions of value take a position on the worth of something. Speeches on questions of policy are concerned with what should or should not be done. Speeches on questions of fact or value are typically organized using topical, chronological, spatial, or cause-and-effect patterns. Because speeches on questions of policy ask for action or passive agreement on the part of the audience, the problem–solution, problem–cause–solution, or Monroe's motivated sequence are the best patterns of organization for such speeches.

In general, persuasive speakers face five types of audiences: negative, positive, divided, uninformed, and apathetic. Each audience type calls for different persuasive strategies. Regardless of their purpose, topic, or audience, ethical public speakers must meet the National Communication Association's standards of ethical communication. Ethical persuasive speakers present their information and arguments truthfully, accurately, and honestly and never try to coerce, deceive, or manipulate the audience.

> ANALYZE IT

PRACTICAL PERSUASION

Carly, Eat Healthier in College

An undergraduate student enrolled in a beginning public speaking class, Carly was asked to prepare a practical persuasion speech on a topic of her choice. Because it was an important issue to her, Carly decided to speak about how to eat healthily while in college—a topic which meets the criteria for practical public speaking and was of interest to her audience.

Have you all heard of the freshman 15? Is it true? Does the average college freshman really gain 15 pounds or is it a myth? Well, according to Doctor Kathleen Zelman, who wrote an article for WebMD, it's a little bit of both. Regardless, though, on whether this 15 pounds of weight gain is fact or fiction, who could argue that eating healthier is not a good idea? Today I'm here to prove to you that eating healthier is easier than you think and that it makes sense. After extensive research on the matter I'm here to encourage you all that this really is your best option. I will show you that there is a need to eat healthier, a simple and straightforward plan to help you accomplish this, and to the benefits you will receive from doing so. Let me start with the need to eat healthier in college.

MindTap®

Watch and analyze this speech on MindTap.

When college students leave home and begin adjusting to independent living, healthy eating behaviors are pushed to the bottom of one's to do list. Still important, however, not enough to be done well. Nanci Hellmich, a journalist for *USA Today*, stated that 76 percent of females eat under stress. This could help explain is most likely to occur due to a change in environment and an increase of stress. According to the U.S. Department of Health and Human Services unhealthy dietary behavior is associated with 5 of the top 10 leading causes of death. And unhealthy dietary behavior is also one of the top six health risk behaviors identified in college students. The problem is that weight gain isn't something that pops up overnight. It's gradual. Sophia Green, a writer for the *Huffington Post*, found out that the average weight gain between freshman year and senior year was an average of 10 pounds. This doesn't sound terrible. However, Sophia Green also argued that the weight gain during college could be the beginning of continuous weight gain throughout one's entire life. And to further this point, Dr. Ardith Brunt, of North Dakota State University, explains that the lifestyles we develop during these transitionary years, which he defines as ages 18 to 24, could impact our future health and the future health of our families.

It's not ideal to eat on campus; however, we still have options available. At the Sub Connection, for instance, you can have an apple or a banana instead of a bag of chips. And you can fill your glass with water instead of soda. It's not ideal at Whitney, either, and it's a little more difficult. However, we have the salad bar or cooked veggies. We also have the option to ask for dismantled food. This means that you can ask for a part of the original meal. I know I do this. Instead of asking for, like, white sauce on my noodles, I'll ask for just my noodles. It's still not very healthy, but it's better than it could have been.

There are also countless benefits to eating healthy that have nothing to do with weight control. Cynthia Sass wrote an article in *The British Journal of Health Psychology* that had five reasons to do with food management that had nothing to do with our weight. One, a better mood. Scientists found that the higher intake of fruits and vegetables resulted in more energy, calm, and greater feelings of overall happiness. Two, sounder sleep. Numerous studies have tied sleep improvements to improvement in overall wellness. Foods tied to better sleep include dark, green, leafy vegetables, nuts, and fish. Three, better workouts. Scientists at the University of Nottingham found several healthy foods that were shown to help build endurance, increase muscle mass, and boost recovery. Glowing skin. A study conducted found that people who ate more fruits and vegetables were rated as more attractive than those with suntans. And, five, improved brain function. I think we'd all be OK with that. In the dieting world the Mediterranean Diet is considered the best of the best. It includes a higher intake of foods, such as fruits and vegetables, and a decrease in foods, such as dairy and refined grains. Researchers found that over six years Mediterranean Diet eaters were 36 percent less likely to have brain damage.

In conclusion, I would like to encourage you all to pay a little bit more attention while you eat. It doesn't have to be all the time and it doesn't even have to be strictly healthy foods, just good changes here and there so it becomes a habit, second nature, and then, when you're ready, maybe you'll take the next step towards a healthier lifestyle. Whatever that may be for you. Today I have shown you the need to eat healthier by showing you how the habits we develop in college could impact our future lives, a straightforward plan to help you accomplish this, and the benefits we receive apart from weight control. I would like to conclude with a quote from Winston Churchill. "Healthy citizens are the greatest asset a country can have." And I would like to believe that our health is our greatest asset." Thank you.

Questions for Discussion

1. Was Carly's attention getter effective for a college audience? Why or why not?
2. What makes Carly's speech a practical persuasive speech instead of an informative speech?
3. Carly refers to the healthy food choices she makes in her own life. Why is it important to choose a persuasive speech topic that is consistent with the way you really do think and act?
4. What were the main points of Carly's speech? Did she preview the main points well? What about her use of transitions between main points?
5. Carly spoke using a key word outline on note cards. How effective was her presentation in terms of delivery? Did she seem well practiced? Enthusiastic about her topic?
6. To be persuasive, a speaker has to be credible. Evaluate Carly's presentation in terms of the four factors of credibility:
   a. competence
   b. trustworthiness
   c. dynamism
   d. sociability

ANALYZE IT

ISSUE-BASED PERSUASION

Alicia, Sexual Assault on University Campuses

Alicia was an undergraduate student enrolled in a beginning public speaking class. Her assignment was to prepare an issue-based persuasive speech on a topic of her choice. She performed so well in class that the speech was entered into a public speaking contest. Alicia spoke forcefully about sexual assault on college campuses. Alicia delivers a passionate speech about a sensitive issue with a clear purpose and thesis. A transcript of Alicia's speech on sexual assault follows.

Emma Sulkowicz is a senior Visual Arts student at Columbia University. According to the *Huffington Post*, on September 3rd, 2014, on the first day of her sophomore year, she was raped by a classmate. The incident took place in her dorm room on her bed. Sulkowicz reported the incident, which then took seven months before an investigative hearing was held by the university, which was marred by officials being confused as to how the sexual assault could have occurred not only in her room but how it could have happened physically. Sulkowicz explains that administrators were unclear as to how anal rape could happen. They requested that she draw a diagram depicting the act. In the end, despite two other female students stepping forward with similar allegations against the same person, her alleged attacker was found not responsible by the university and still remains at school. Since then, Emma has become 1 of 23 students to file a federal complaint against Columbia University for the mishandling of sexual assault cases, but sadly Emma's case is not isolated. The *Washington Post*, on May 1st, 2014, released the names of 55 universities currently under federal review for the mishandling of sexual assault cases. Over the past year, reports of sexual assault on American campuses have skyrocketed. State and federal governments have taken notice and begun to enact legislation that will hopefully help in reducing this problem. But as students like Emma Sulkowicz will now argue this is a problem that cannot wait for a top-down solution. This is a situation that requires us here in this room to become agents of change. So today, we'll first examine the rising problem of sexual assault on university campuses then understand the causes before finally focusing on some solutions and in particular personal solutions that we can take on to help fight back. But first, we will examine the rising problem of sexual assault on university campuses.

According to the Department of Justice last accessed January 25th, 2015, the definition of sexual assault varies from state to state. Generally, sexual assault is defined as any type of sexual contact or behavior that occurs without the explicit consent of the recipient. This can include behaviors such as unwanted touching or kissing, sexual contact with an individual under the influence of drugs or alcohol, and unable to give an informed yes or no, rape, or attempted rape. The previously cited *Washington Post* explains that one in seven women have been or will be sexually assaulted while in college, yet actions to address this issue are slow, which leads us to the second part of this persistent problem, university's violations of Title IX. According to National Public Radio on May 1st, 2014, under Title IX, colleges and universities that receive federal funding, which is nearly all of them, are required to respond to incidences of sexual misconduct, assault, and harassment on campus, and to have policies in place that help prevent such incidences. The 55 universities currently under federal review are being sued by victims of sexual assault stating that the colleges have failed to protect them under Title IX. *The Guardian* of October 28th, 2014, explains that while women have become more confident in reporting sexual assault, universities are failing to protect the victims when it comes to investigating rapes through to successful convictions. Now, let's understand the causes.

First the lack of definition, according to *Time Magazine* on October 29th, 2014, MIT conducted a sexual assault survey on its campus. Results revealed that despite the recent efforts of the Obama administration, many students are still uncertain about what qualifies as sexual assault. Without an agreed upon definition, students cannot become educated about all the forms of sexual assault. Second the lack of qualified policy enforcers on university campuses, according to the *New York Times* of July 12th, 2014; in 2011 the federal government mandated that sexual assaults on college campuses must be processed by the university. So today, colleges are conducting trials often presided over by administrators or professors who know little about the law or a criminal investigation. In the case of Anna, an 18-year-old college freshman at Hobart and William Smith College who was raped by a gang of football players, her trial was presided over by the Assistant Psychology professor, Vice-President of Human Resources, and Director of the Campus Bookstore. According to the Department of Federal Education, a sexual assault investigation typically takes around 60 calendar days. After allegations and overwhelming physical evidence, it took the college 12 days to investigate Anna's rape report and hold a hearing and cleared the football players. This lack of qualified policy enforcers repeatedly demonstrates that colleges cannot or will not deliver justice, thus alleged attackers are released without a record to offend again on the same campus. The final cause of this problem is victims are scared of being punished. The previously cited *New York Times* reports that after Anna's trial, the football team went on to finish undefeated in their conference, while Anna was left to face threats and harassments for accusing members of the most popular sports team on campus. This continued record of failure discourages women from reporting sexual assault and gives the offenders the chance to re-offend. Now that we have a better understanding of the problem and its causes, let's focus on some solutions.

On the governmental level, an agreed upon federal definition of sexual assault should be issued to all university campuses. According to the previously cited National Public Radio, while the government has been successful in raising awareness about sexual assault, administrators have failed to agree upon a federal definition for all universities. By having an agreed upon definition, students will become more educated about all the forms of sexual assault. On a society level, universities need to adopt qualified policy enforcers on campus. According to the *Daily Princeton* of October 13th, 2014, they have hired an external investigator to handle all sexual assault disciplinary proceedings on campus. By adopting this policy, Princeton is in compliance with Title IX, thus insuring that all students have the right to a fair trial with a fair conviction. And finally, as individuals, it is our responsibility to become agents of change. Everyone in this room is a member of the college and university community. This rising problem of sexual assault affects us all. That is why today, I urge each and every one of you to become members of Step Up, which is a bystander intervention program that helps to educate students to be more proactive when helping others. The Department of Defense has adopted the active bystander programs, stating on their website that intervention isn't about stepping in to stop a crime in progress but rather before a crime begins. We need to become active bystanders because we are in the frontlines of this issue. It's great that reform is happening at the top, but it doesn't kick in until after an assault has occurred. That means we're it, the sole force of prevention.

With graduation from Columbia University approaching in the spring, Emma Sulkowicz has begun her senior thesis project titled "Carry That Weight" for what she calls an endurance art piece. She will carry her 50-pound mattress on which she was raped everywhere she goes on campus until her attacker is either expelled or leaves the school. Emma has two rules to her year-long project. She is not allowed to ask for help, but others are allowed to give their assistance and they have. Bystanders have actively stepped in to help Emma carry her burden from one class to another or even for the whole day. Emma Sulkowicz's rapist may never leave on his own accord and likely will never be brought to justice, but in the aftermath she has chosen to step up and fight back and so should we.

Questions for Discussion

1. Alicia begins her speech with a story. Why do you think she chose that particular story? Would it have likely grabbed the attention of her audience? Why or why not?
2. Was this a speech on a question of fact, value, or policy? What makes it so?
3. Issue-based persuasion requires that speakers make their main points clear to the audience. Identify Alicia's first, second, and third main points and describe how she supports them.
4. Were you able to follow the flow of the speech? Can you evaluate Alicia's use of transitions to move from one main point to the next?
5. What organizational pattern did Alicia use for her speech? Was that a good choice? What other organizational patterns could have been used for this speech?
6. Did you find Alicia to be sincerely concerned about the topic of the speech? Why do you feel that way?
7. Specifically, what behavior did Alicia ask her audience to do?
8. How did the way Alicia concluded the speech tie back in to the introduction? Was this an effective technique? What insights did the introduction and conclusion give you about how seriously Alicia prepared her speech?

APPLY IT . . .

IN YOUR COMMUNITY

Be an Advocate!

Why not put your skills as a persuasive speaker to work in your community by advocating for causes you think deserve support? To advocate means to speak in favor of or recommend something. An advocate is a person who argues for, supports, or defends a cause. Many advocates try to influence decisions about government and institutional policies or the use of resources that affect people's lives.[28] Lawyers advocate for their clients. Advocacy groups try to influence policies or sway public opinion on a particular issue. There is plenty of room in a democratic society for individuals to advocate for causes they care about too. Advocates often speak up on behalf of citizens whose interests are not well represented in the legal system—homeless people, for example, or consumers, special needs children, indigenous groups, or an individual who is unfairly accused of a crime. Your public speaking skills help prepare you for getting personally involved in this important form of social activism. What issues or causes that you care about should be advocated publicly by organizations or individuals in your community?

REVIEW IT

MindTap®
Use flashcards to learn key terms and take a quiz to test your knowledge.

Key Terms

apathetic audience 301
coercion 280
divided audience 300
issue-based persuasion 283
negative audience 298
persuasion 280
persuasive speech 281
positive audience 299
practical persuasion 281
question of fact 284
question of policy 291
question of value 287
uninformed audience 301

Reflecting on Persuasive Speaking

1. As a persuasive speaker, what steps must you take to avoid manipulating your audience? As an audience member, how can you make sure speakers don't manipulate you?
2. What key differences distinguish practical persuasion from issue-based persuasion? Specifically, how will these differences influence your choice of topic(s) this term?
3. An issue-based speech to persuade on a question of fact usually focuses on influencing the audience's thinking more than their behavior. Why so? Can you think of exceptions to this general rule? When would a call to action be appropriate for a persuasive speech on a question of fact?
4. How does a call for an active audience response in a speech on questions of value differ from the response a speaker might call for in a speech on questions of policy?
5. The authors recommend three possible organizational patterns for speeches on questions of policy: problem–solution, problem–cause–solution, and Monroe's motivated sequence. Why do these patterns work better than the other organizational patterns for this type of speech?
6. The differences between positive and negative audiences should be clear. But can you explain how divided, uninformed, and apathetic audiences differ? Can you think of topics that would likely fall into all five categories (positive, negative, divided, uninformed, apathetic) for your audience this term?
7. What unique ethical considerations face persuasive speakers when they're addressing questions of fact? What ethical considerations are associated with questions of value? What ethical issues must a persuasive speaker who is addressing a question of policy confront?

15 Understanding Argument

READ IT

After successfully completing this chapter, you will be able to:

- Explain the three major elements of a complete argument.
- Use evidence, reasoning, and qualifiers to develop claims in a persuasive speech.
- Apply logos, ethos, pathos, and mythos effectively in speeches to persuade.
- Distinguish between deductive, inductive, causal, and analogical reasoning.
- Identify and describe common fallacies in argument.

MindTap®

Start with a quick warm-up activity and review the chapter's learning outcomes.

The ability to create a winning argument defines public speaking as an "art." But the power of argument also depends on principles embedded in the scientific method.

thelefty/Fotolia LLC

The foundation of persuasive speaking—argument—evolved gradually over the long span of our social history.[1] As our distant ancestors became better and better communicators, they looked to leaders who could persuade them to take particular courses of action. Even before modern language developed, the emerging leaders of our ancient communities were the ones who were best able to convince others to follow them and their ideas—the ones who could argue well.[2]

The Greek philosopher Aristotle was the first to identify and write comprehensively about the role of argument in public communication. Aristotle said that for a democratic society to advance, its political leaders must be able to argue positions that are supported by compelling evidence and delivered skillfully to an audience. Perhaps no one in modern American history accomplished this more effectively than Dr. Martin Luther King, Jr., the great civil rights advocate of the last century.

Throughout history, the ability to create a winning argument is what best defines public speaking as an "art." But science also comes into play. Aristotle wrote that the power of argument also ultimately depends on principles embodied in the scientific method: the ability to observe the natural world dispassionately and use logic to draw valid inferences (or conclusions) about what is observed. The discipline of Aristotelian thought—especially the crucial role of logic (*logos*) as a path to knowledge—foreshadowed the scientific revolution of Galileo, Newton, Darwin, and many other scientists who have shaped our understanding of the natural world.[3] The link from science to modern public discourse has become clear: Although other factors are involved, an argument stands the best chance of being convincing if it makes good sense—if it is logical.

AP Images/File

What Makes Up an Argument?

MindTap®
Read, highlight, and take notes online.

In common usage, the term *argument* refers to a disagreement or a conflict. But in public speaking, *argument* does not have negative connotations. Individual arguments are developed to support a persuasive speaker's position on questions of fact, value, or policy (Chapter 14). Successful speakers formulate their arguments effectively and present them well.

Figure 15.1 Elements of an Argument

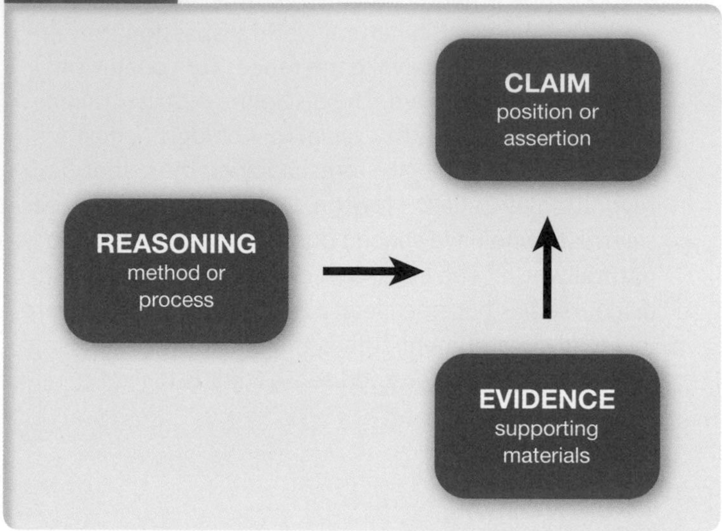

Source: Adapted from Toulmin, S. E. (2003). *The uses of argument* (updated ed.). Cambridge, UK: Cambridge University Press.

An **argument** makes a claim and backs it up it with evidence and reasoning.[4] In public speaking, a **claim** is the position or assertion a speaker wants the audience to accept, and **evidence** refers to the supporting materials—narratives, examples, definitions, testimony, facts, and statistics—that the speaker presents to reinforce the claim. **Reasoning** is the method or process used to represent the claim and arrive at the argument's conclusion.[5] **Figure 15.1** illustrates the elements of an argument.

Effective public speaking, especially persuasive discourse, is artful. The speaker uses language, delivery style, and presentation media—the tools of contemporary rhetoric—to make an argument as convincing as possible to the audience. Good rhetoric does not make an argument more valid; artful language and the clever use of media can be used to persuade us of falsehoods as well as truths. But rhetorical skill can definitely make an argument more persuasive.[6]

This chapter discusses the elements of argument in detail and how they work together to create the foundation of a successful persuasive speech. You'll learn how to craft an argument effectively and avoid fallacies in persuasive speaking.

argument
Presenting claims and supporting them with evidence and reasoning.

claim
A position or assertion that a speaker wants an audience to accept.

Using Claims Effectively

evidence
Supporting materials—narratives, examples, definitions, testimony, facts, and statistics—that a speaker presents to reinforce a claim.

reasoning
The method or process used to link claims to evidence.

Claims go beyond facts and other supporting materials to propose conclusions based on the evidence presented. For example, a speaker might say, "Video games are addictive." That is a claim or a position the speaker is taking. The speaker might then present scientific studies to support that claim. But the claim "Video games are addictive" is still an inference based on the results of those studies. So claims require that listeners make a leap from what is known—the evidence—to some conclusion.[7]

Claims lay the groundwork for the argument that makes up your thesis. They respond to basic questions about your topic and the position you take. Claims answer the question, "What is the speaker asserting?" As you develop your speech, consider the questions your topic raises and how you might respond to them. How you answer those questions will help you identify the claims you'll make in your speech and reveal your position on the topic. **Table 15.1** provides an example of the questions a speaker might ask about a speech on paying collegiate student athletes in the United States and the claims that correspond with those questions.

Table 15.1 Questions and Claims for Speech on Paying College Athletes

Topic Question	Claim
Why should major sport college athletes be paid?	These athletes generate huge profits for their universities.
Aren't these athletes already compensated?	Athletic scholarships do not provide a sufficient level of compensation for the total cost of attending school.
Don't the athletes receive a valuable free education and career opportunities?	Colleges and universities fail to graduate an alarming number of their student athletes. Very few become professionals, and many suffer debilitating injuries.
How do we know paying athletes will improve the situation?	Authoritative, objective studies show that reform would create measurable benefits for the athletes and their schools.

Types of Claims

Arguments include two types of claims: conclusions and premises.

- The **conclusion** is the primary claim or assertion a speaker makes.
- A **premise** gives a reason to support a conclusion.

conclusion
A primary claim or assertion.

premise
A claim that provides reasons to support a conclusion.

Both conclusions and premises are claims, but premises are smaller claims that lead up to a conclusion—the central claim or position the speaker promotes.[8] For example, in a speech supporting new nuclear power plant construction, Eileen Claussen, founder of the Pew Center on Global Climate Change,[9] offered one conclusion and three premises as support.

PREMISE 1:	Climate change is real.
PREMISE 2:	Protecting the global climate is necessary.
PREMISE 3:	All forms of energy have problems.
CONCLUSION:	Nuclear power should continue to be part of the solution to climate change.

For audience members to agree with the conclusion, they must agree with all the premises leading up to it. If they find fault with one premise, they're highly unlikely to support the conclusion.

Specific words, either implied or stated, often identify premises and conclusions. Words indicating a premise include *because, whereas, since, on account of,* and *due to.* Words indicating a conclusion include *therefore, consequently, and so, thus,* and *accordingly.* Think of the relationship between premises and conclusions in this way:

> Because (premise 1), because (premise 2), and because (premise 3), therefore (conclusion).

Claussen asserted that *because* climate change is real, *because* protecting the environment is necessary, and *because* all forms of energy have problems, it is *therefore* right to create a role for nuclear energy in the national energy policy. Although *because* and *therefore* were unstated, Claussen made the relationship between her premises and conclusion clear. **Table 15.2** presents additional examples of premises and conclusions.

Prochasson frederic/Shutterstock.com

If the premise of an argument stipulates that all forms of energy have problems, is that sufficiently convincing? Or would the severity of potential problems need to be taken into account?

Table 15.2 Examples of Premises and Conclusions

Topics	Visual Ergonomics	Globalization and Labor	Online Dating Services
Premises	1. Poor visual ergonomics when using a desktop, laptop, or tablet computer causes eyestrain. 2. Poor visual ergonomics when using a desktop, laptop, or tablet computer leads to neck and shoulder problems.	1. Globalization allows for the free movement of goods between countries. 2. Globalization allows for the free movement of services between countries. 3. Globalization allows organizations to locate freely to other countries.	1. In today's world, single people are too busy to join clubs and organizations to meet other singles. 2. Today, interacting with people online is a normal way to communicate.
Conclusion	Improving visual ergonomics is essential for the health and safety of desktop, laptop, and tablet computer users.	Globalization should also allow for the free movement of individual workers between countries.	Online dating services are a practical way to meet romantic partners in today's world.

enthymemes
An argument in which a premise or conclusion is unstated.

Sometimes an argument's premises or conclusion are implied rather than stated. These kinds of arguments, called **enthymemes,** assume members of the audience will figure out the premise or conclusion on their own. Enthymemes depend on the audience's social information or knowledge to complete the argument.[10] For example, in a speech on a question of policy about downloading music from the Internet, the speaker might argue:

PREMISE:	Downloading music without payment or permission is against the law.
CONCLUSION:	Don't download copyrighted music illegally.

This basic argument leaves out one premise: It is immoral to download copyrighted music without payment or permission because it amounts to stealing someone else's property. But there's no need for the speaker to say that because the audience already knows it.

Speeches on questions of fact or value often leave the conclusion unstated. In a speech on traffic congestion, for example, the speaker might include these premises:

PREMISE 1:	Traffic congestion in our city wastes time.
PREMISE 2:	Traffic congestion in our city wastes resources.
PREMISE 3:	Traffic congestion in our city increases pollution.

The unstated conclusion is that something should be done about traffic congestion. But as this is a speech addressing a question of fact, the speaker is concerned only with whether or not something is true (or false), not with taking some kind of action.

An enthymeme invites audience participation because listeners mentally fill in the missing parts of the argument, facilitating a dialogue between the speaker and the audience.[11] Encouraging these kinds of thought processes can give the audience a better understanding of the topic and a more favorable view of the speaker's argument.[12]

Qualifying Claims

To accept a claim, an audience must view it as reasonable. Because claims are assertions, they can always be challenged. Some claims, such as "smoking causes cancer" and "a college education leads to a better job," are quite easily supported.

Those claims are feasible. But others, such as "U.S. employers don't provide adequate health insurance for their employees" or "Hunting whales does not impact their long-term survival rates," are not so widely accepted. They are "de-feasible"—they could be shown to be wrong.[13] Even topics that seem completely uncontroversial are not always without question. By the 17th century, science had proved Earth revolves around the sun, but 20 percent of Americans today still believe the sun revolves around Earth.[14]

Qualifiers Defined Qualifiers provide a way to make your claims more reasonable to an audience. A **qualifier** indicates the scope of the claim with words such as *probably, likely, often,* and *usually.* These words help you stay away from indefensible assertions or claims that must hold up in every case. Qualifiers answer the question "How strong is the claim?" For example, instead of claiming "Major airline outsourcing of plane maintenance increases the number of plane accidents," you might say, "Major airline outsourcing of plane maintenance *likely* increases the number of plane accidents." Here you acknowledge that outsourcing probably increases accidents, but you're not definitely sure. There may be other factors leading to an increase in accidents, or it may be that accidents haven't increased at all. **Figure 15.2** shows how a qualifier fits in with the elements of argument.

Why Use Qualifiers? As a persuasive speaker, you want to anticipate alternative assertions or claims related to your topic by acknowledging and carefully refuting objections or different points of view in your speech. Considering other claims lets audience members know you are not just single-minded about the topic. Acknowledging positions held by audience members that differ from your view shows you understand their perspective, even if you don't agree with it. This helps you establish a respectful and productive connection with your listeners.[17]

For instance, Eileen Claussen used this strategy in her speech advocating construction of new nuclear power plants. Claussen is well aware that many people, including some environmental groups, oppose further development of nuclear power. After claiming that "nuclear power could make a substantial contribution to our efforts to reduce greenhouse gasses," she said,

> However, there are other things we can't ignore. And these are the potential problems associated with the expanded use of nuclear power in this country and around the world....

She pointed out that the main objections to nuclear power today are the safety of the power plants and the storage of nuclear waste.

To put those problems into perspective, she also briefly discussed the obstacles posed by wind and solar power—public opposition to huge wind farms and solar power's relatively low and intermittent power production.

The strength of her argument, therefore, rests not only on the evidence she presents and the reasoning she uses to weave her ideas together but also in the way she deftly raises objections to her position and then refutes possible counterarguments.

Similarly, a speech designed to convince an audience that globalization helps poor countries raise their standard of living will be stronger if the speaker acknowledges

SPEAKING OF ...

Images and the Naturalistic Enthymeme

Not all claims are expressed with words; some claims involve images. For example, advertisers often use images to advance claims that you should buy their products or services. Soft drink ads, for instance, typically show individuals or groups laughing and enjoying themselves. The claims are

Premise 1:	Everyone likes to have fun.
Premise 2:	Drinking this soft drink is one way to have fun.
Premise 3:	If you drink this soft drink, you'll have fun.
Conclusion:	You should buy this soft drink.

Yet no one has to say anything in the ad—you know how to interpret those visual claims based on your social and cultural experiences. One key reason that visual claims work so well is the *naturalistic enthymeme*—audiences assume that unless there's evidence to the contrary, a camera captures a realistic and natural view of what they would see.[15] Of course, when an image is clearly altered, as with computer-generated imagery in photos, video, or film, the naturalistic enthymeme does not hold true. But even when viewers know images have been staged, as with the soft drink commercials, they still tend to assume that the images represent something real—the first step in visual persuasion.[16]

qualifier
A word or phrase that clarifies, modifies, or limits the meaning of another word or phrase.

Figure 15.2 Elements of an Argument with Qualifier

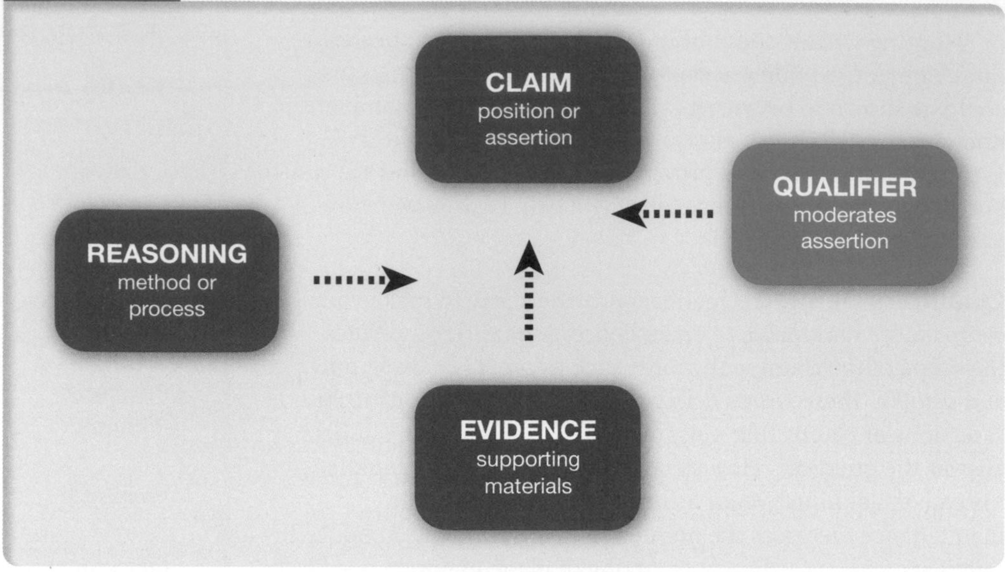

Source: Adapted from Toulmin, S. E. (2003). *The uses of argument* (updated ed.). Cambridge, UK: Cambridge University Press.

that globalization has also widened the gap between rich and poor in many countries. By voicing alternative claims, the speaker gains the trust of the audience for being fair. When speakers ignore or hide information they disagree with or try to mislead the audience about differing viewpoints, they behave unethically and undercut their own position on the topic.

Using Evidence Effectively

A claim answers the question "What is the speaker asserting?" Evidence answers the question "What is the speaker's support for the assertion?" Evidence provides the foundation for your claims. In presenting evidence to support a claim, the persuasive speaker relies on some combination of the four types of appeals that were introduced in Chapter 1. These appeals and the kinds of evidence usually associated with them are summarized in **Table 15.3.**

Logos: Appeals to Logic

Logical appeals, or *logos,* can be a particularly persuasive type of appeal when presented well. The nature of logical appeals is data driven and stems from the world of science and rationality. Audiences expect qualified public speakers to use logical appeals in their speeches for most topics.[18]

Table 15.3 Types of Appeals

Appeal	Brief Definition	Example
Logos	Logical proof	Verifiable facts and statistics
Ethos	Speaker's credibility	References to own expertise on topic
Pathos	Emotional proof	A humorous quote or story
Mythos	Cultural beliefs and values	A well-known fable or morality tale

Factual claims and evidence are always subject to interrogation. Audience members naturally question the legitimacy of what they hear, especially when they are unfamiliar with the topic or disagree with the position taken by the speaker. They ask themselves, "Do the speaker's claims, evidence, and reasoning make sense?"

The power of **logical appeals** therefore relies on the audience believing that the argument made by the speaker is truthful, reasonable, and supported by strong factual evidence.

logical appeals
Use of rational thought based on logic, facts, and analysis to influence an audience; also known as *logos*.

Although logical appeals typically are associated with valid facts and statistics, definitions and testimony may also fit this category of evidence. Generally, logical evidence is verifiable. For example, listeners can research the scientific facts a speaker presents or look up an historical event the speaker describes.

Using Logical Appeals When using logical appeals, effective speakers gather up-to-the-minute statistical data, facts, definitions, or expert opinions. For instance, a just-released poll of Americans' attitudes favoring congressional reform would add considerable weight to an argument calling for changes in campaign financing laws. A damaging new report from the Substance Abuse and Mental Health Service Administration would bolster an argument against consumption of highly caffeinated energy drinks. By demonstrating the currency of research you cite on your topic, you'll earn your audience's respect and keep its members listening to you.

Your audience must be willing to listen carefully and comprehend the logical evidence you present. Long lists of facts and statistics can overwhelm listeners and cause them to lose interest. Good speakers find ways to present logical appeals in ways that are not dry and boring. Speakers should:

- Not apologize for presenting concise statistical or other fact-based information. Make the data interesting by connecting the factual information to the needs and interests of the audience.
- Integrate logical appeals with other kinds of appeals into the argument.
- Avoid jargon and overly-scientific language when describing quantitative information.
- Use presentation media to complement, not just repeat, factual information that is presented orally.

Logical appeals and presentation media were combined effectively by Dr. Nora D. Volkow, director of the National Institute on Drug Abuse, in her speech "Drug Addiction: Free Will, Brain Disease, or Both?"[19]

She presented her speech to city residents at a town hall meeting in Los Angeles. In this part of her speech, she focused on her claim that drug addiction is a brain disease:

> Drug addiction is a developmental disease. What do we mean by that? What we've learned from many years of epidemiological studies is drug addiction develops during these periods of our lives, during adolescence and early adulthood. This is a graph [on a digital slide] that actually describes at what age individuals develop, at first, a dependence on marijuana. Similar graphs occur for cocaine, nicotine, and alcohol. You can see the peak in this case is around age eighteen. By age twenty-five, if you have not become addicted to marijuana the likelihood that you will do so is very minimal. It's not zero but it's very minimal.[20]

Volkow presented data from a large number of studies to support her claim. She used a digital slide to show the statistics, and then explained in clear, nontechnical terms what the statistics mean to the audience.

A. Ramey/PhotoEdit

Presenting verifiable evidence in a thought-provoking and easily understandable way increases the power of your logical appeals.

Ethos: Appeals to Speaker Credibility

appeals to speaker credibility Creating a perception of the speaker as competent, trustworthy, dynamic, and likeable to influence an audience; also known as *ethos*.

The effectiveness of **appeals to speaker credibility**, or *ethos*, rests on the degree to which the audience perceives the speaker as competent, trustworthy, dynamic, and likeable—the speaker's ethos. The elements of speaker credibility were discussed in detail in Chapter 5. As you develop your argument for a persuasive speech, remember that it is the audience's perceptions of your credibility that matters. The speaker's job is to create that favorable impression.

Using Appeals to Speaker Credibility Perceived competence or expertise on the topic has a direct positive impact on a speaker's persuasiveness. If audience members believe you're an expert on your subject matter, you're far more likely to convince them. But speaker credibility also depends on the degree to which listeners trust and feel personally connected to you. If you haven't established a good relationship with your listeners, expertise alone will not convince them.[21]

The degree to which an audience finds a topic personally relevant also influences your persuasiveness as a speaker.[22] Even when audience members consider the source of a message to be competent and trustworthy but find the subject uninteresting, they judge the speaker to be not very persuasive. Similarly, if audience members don't think the topic applies to them, they don't pay much attention to it. Fortunately, a dynamic, engaged delivery of the speech can remedy these potential problems. Your sincere enthusiasm for the topic and your ability to relate *your* topic to *the audience's* interests will keep your listeners on track with your argument.

How you frame your argument is key. Telling people what they will gain from your proposal, not what you personally think about it, works best. Build a new library on campus? Specifically, how will it benefit your audience? Decrease funding for the Department of Defense? What does your audience gain? In favor of a high-speed rail system in your state? How would that help individual members of your audience?

In a persuasive speech titled "The Power of Introverts" author Susan Cain called for greater understanding and appreciation of people like her who naturally direct their thoughts and interests inward more than outward.[23] She proposed specific behaviors people can take to accomplish that goal.

> A third to half of the population are introverts ... so even if you're an extrovert yourself, I'm talking about your coworkers and your spouses and your children and the person sitting next to you right now—all of them are subject to this bias that is pretty deep and real in our society.
>
> Extroverts really crave large amounts of stimulation, whereas introverts feel at their most alive and their most switched-on and their most capable when they're in quieter low-key environments ... but our most important institutions, our schools and our workplaces, are designed mostly for extroverts.

Cain then asked her audience to take three positive steps to develop the power of introversion. First, "Stop the madness of constant group work." She encouraged all her listeners to learn how to work independently with more privacy, freedom, and autonomy. That gives introverts the space they need to create and produce original ideas. It helps extroverts engage in productive deep thought, too.

Second, "Go out to the wilderness." It's not necessary to build a log cabin, but by eliminating constant social distractions, people can "get into their heads a little more often." And third, "Take a good look at what's inside your own suitcase and why you put it there." Extroverts have little trouble showing off the things they love to do—party or skydive, for instance. But introverts should show off the introspective lifestyle they represent, too:

> ... because the world needs you and it needs the things you carry. So I wish you the best of all possible journeys and the courage to speak softly. Thank you.

Susan Cain skillfully appealed to everyone in her audience. She asked the more outgoing people in the group to respect and learn from introverts. She reinforced the less outgoing members of her audience by praising their personality while encouraging them to modestly share the personal rewards and great ideas that can be produced by private, inward thinking.

Pathos: Appeals to Emotion

emotional appeals Use of emotional evidence and stimulation of feelings to influence an audience; also known as *pathos*.

Emotional appeals, or *pathos*, rely on emotional evidence and the stimulation of feelings to influence an audience. Speakers typically use human interest stories, personal examples, and human testimony when appealing to our emotions. Emotional appeals alone seldom work to convince an attentive audience, yet when used in conjunction with other types of appeals they can win over even skeptical listeners.[24]

Appeals to emotion are especially effective when they tap into the audience's beliefs and needs, call up personal associations with the topic, and help listeners identify with and recall the speaker's message.[25] The fundamental, bottom-up principle of human evolution applies here.[26] According to social psychologist Abraham Maslow, humans are motivated by five types of needs, beginning with the most basic requirement—sheer survival.[27]

- *Physiological needs* are those necessary for our body to function, including food, water, and sleep.
- *Safety needs* are associated with the desire to feel free from harm.
- *Love/belonging needs* include wanting to feel part of a group and loved by others.
- *Esteem needs* focus on our status and having others recognize our accomplishments.
- *Self-actualization needs* are concerned with personal growth and self-fulfillment.

You're motivated to fulfill your needs in a hierarchical order, satisfying more basic needs before progressing to higher-order ones (**Figure 15.3**). But no one does this alone. You interact emotionally and connect with others to satisfy your needs. For example, you depend on others to help you feel safe and loved. Even obtaining basic needs such as food and water requires the help of others.[28]

Using Emotional Appeals Telling a story channels emotion and makes it persuasive. The speaker and the listener create the positive effect together. The co-created narrative encourages audience members to relate to ideas and individuals with whom they might not otherwise connect.[30] A touching story about the struggle of a local family to survive the winter might help an audience overcome the idea that real poverty doesn't exist in America. A speaker who recounts the agonizing details of a dying loved one could open minds about doctor-assisted suicide. A heartwarming tale of a young girl who

Figure 15.3 Maslow's Hierarchy of Needs[29]

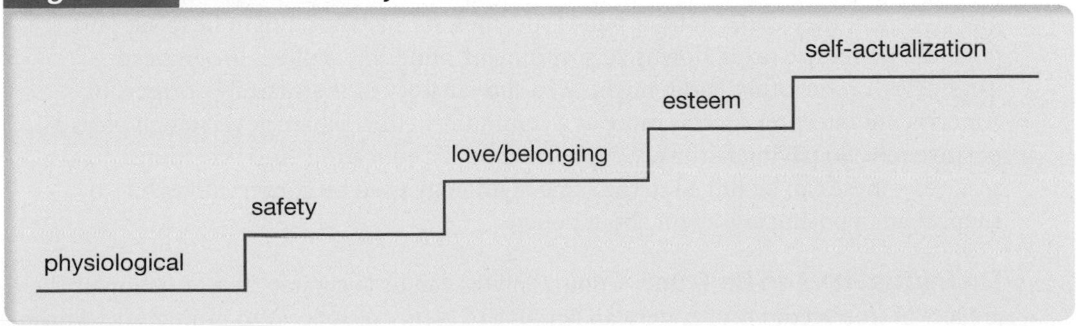

Emotionally gripping stories of the devastating effects of concussions have led to greater public awareness and changes in the rules of football.

volunteered time to help immigrant families adjust to life in her city might encourage others to do the same. Describing how a college football player's disability was caused by repeated concussions might inspire the audience to support stricter safety measures for the sport.

Persuasive speakers often use presentation media to help elicit emotion. For example, to support the claim that your community needs a new theater, you might show slides or a short video clip of an especially powerful performance by the local theater group, presented in its current dilapidated venue. Digital slides of unwanted pets waiting for adoption at the Humane Society can stir feelings of sympathy and buttress the claim that all pets should be spayed or neutered.

Emotional appeals must do more than stimulate an emotional response. Such appeals must serve as evidence—direct support for your claim. When you tell a story, define a term, recite a quote, or show a photograph, you want to be sure you are appealing to your audience's emotions in ways that advance your claim. As with any form of evidence included in your persuasive speech, an emotional appeal must be relevant to your topic and appropriate for your audience.

Mythos: Appeals to Cultural Beliefs

appeals to cultural beliefs Use of values and beliefs embedded in cultural narratives or stories to influence an audience; also called *mythos*.

Telling original stories allows speakers to connect with listeners by arousing their emotions. But retelling existing stories can be very persuasive, too. **Appeals to cultural beliefs**, or *mythos*, rely on values and beliefs embedded in familiar cultural narratives or stories to influence an audience.

All cultures have defining narratives. Creation myths, folk tales, parables, folk songs, legends, *corridos* (Spanish-language ballads), and literature all help cultural groups form coherent identities that are passed from one generation to the next.[31] By referring to these cultural narratives in their presentations, speakers can forge a common bond with their audiences.

But to be persuasive, the cultural stories used by the speaker must also create a positive impression for the argument. For example, the myth of the American hero who does good deeds, works hard, and triumphs over misfortune is deeply engrained in our culture.[32] Stories related to this mythic figure tap into our cultural beliefs about helping others, being industrious, and persevering in the face of adversity. A speaker who can tie the thesis of the speech to this kind of traditional mythology improves the chances the argument will be accepted.

The "immigrant makes good in America" myth has been adopted by many politicians as they tell the story of their ancestors' triumph over hardship. They then link their political platform to that story. For conservative politicians, the cultural appeal might be that learning English, getting an education, starting a small business, and relying mainly on self and family are the key to financial success in America. The argument they make in their public speeches, for instance, might be to support policies that reduce taxes, downsize government, and limit welfare. Progressive candidates, on the other hand, might tell a similar story of their family's origins in America but interpret success more as a community effort where government plays a positive role. So paying fair taxes, supporting public education, and providing social services—these can be linked to the same mythology used by conservatives but to support an opposing argument about policy.

Do Myths Have to Be True? Cultural myths can be verifiably true or fictional. There are lots of true accounts of American heroes and plenty of successful immigrants whose struggles actually happened, for instance. But sometimes myths are fully or partly made up. That doesn't make them less powerful symbolically or necessarily less effective as evidence.

The audience doesn't even have to be personally familiar with the myth. To be effective, however, the myth must resonate with the audience's overall sense of the culture. The myth can then be used to advance the speaker's argument.

For example, consider the West Virginia legend of "John Henry, the Steel Driving Man." The original story was turned into a folk song that has been recorded by dozens of artists from Woody Guthrie to Bruce Springsteen. The story describes the physical prowess of a man born a slave in 1840.[33] Freed after the Civil War, he went to work for the Chesapeake and Ohio Railroad driving steel spikes into the rocky Appalachian countryside to lay tracks.

A thousand men died trying to drill their way through the rough mountainous terrain. But John Henry kept drilling tirelessly with a 14-pound hammer and could sometimes go as far as 10 or 12 feet in a single day.

AP Images/The Register-Herald, Dayton Whittle

The familiar cultural myth of "John Henry, the Steel Driving Man" is commemorated near Talcott, West Virginia. The statue helps legitimize and perpetuate the myth.

> Then one day a salesman came along to the camp. He had a steam-powered drill and claimed it could out-drill any man. Well, they set up a contest then and there between John Henry and that there drill. The foreman ran that newfangled steam-drill. John Henry, he just pulled out two 20-pound hammers, one in each hand. They drilled and drilled, dust rising everywhere.... At the end of 35 minutes, John Henry had drilled two 7-foot holes—a total of 14 feet, while the steam drill had only drilled one 9-foot hole.
>
> John Henry held up his hammers in triumph! The men shouted and cheered. The noise was so loud, it took a moment for the men to realize that John Henry was tottering. Exhausted, the mighty man crashed to the ground, the hammer's rolling from his grasp.... A blood vessel had burst in his brain. The greatest driller in the C&O Railroad was dead.

How might a speaker today use the legend of John Henry as cultural evidence for an argument?

One could make the point, for example, that even though a machine-based, impersonal industrial society (represented by the steam drill) may win out in the end, the spirit and willpower of every single human being can never be diminished. The other side of the issue could also be argued: Try as we may to resist the dehumanizing trend, automation and industrial development make many kinds of manual labor unnecessary. Don't kill yourself: Adapt to new technology when the inevitable confronts you.

The skilled speaker adapts cultural beliefs to fit the specific purpose of the persuasive speech.

Guidelines for Using Evidence in Argument

Follow these guidelines for using evidence effectively in your persuasive speech:

- *Keep your evidence relevant to your topic.* Your audience must be able to grasp quickly and clearly how the evidence you present supports your claim. For example, if you wanted your audience to support a policy of testing elderly drivers more frequently, you would cite statistics concerning the role of advanced age as a factor in causing accidents. You might show how easy it is for the elderly to renew their licenses without having to pass a driving test for many years. But you would not mention other kinds of problems encountered by elderly people. Every piece of evidence you include must directly support your argument.

Juli Hansen/Shutterstock.com

In his bid to become president, Bernie Sanders constantly pointed out the huge differences in pay between bosses and workers in the United States, and how almost all new wealth created in America goes to the top 1 percent.

- *Draw your evidence from highly credible sources.* Credible evidence comes from identifiable, respected sources. If you want to demonstrate the wide gap in pay between chief executive officers (CEOs) and their corporate employees, for example, provide data about average executive and workers' incomes available from the U.S. Labor Department. When conducting interviews about any topic, be sure to choose individuals who are truly experts on your topic—then make your interviewee's impressive credentials clear to your audience during your speech.
- *Select evidence from diverse sources.* Integrating evidence from a variety of sources provides a stronger foundation for your claims, shows you've done your research, and enhances your credibility. For example, in a speech advocating a ban on personal fireworks, you could cite state and local statistics on fireworks-related injuries and property damage, interview the fire chief, and present supportive facts from areas where such a ban is in place.
- *Incorporate evidence addressing multiple types of appeals.* Speeches that include only one type of evidence seldom succeed in persuading the audience. Employing logical appeals, appeals to the speaker's credibility, emotional appeals, and appeals to cultural beliefs provides a broad foundation of evidence to support your claims. Tell the story of someone who was hurt emotionally by a romantic Internet hoax, for example, and then use credible statistics to demonstrate the extent of the problem. You could also add testimony from expert authorities about how fast attraction to an unscrupulous online "friend" can develop.

Using Reasoning Effectively

Reasoning is the method or process speakers use to link their evidence with their claims. Claims answer the question "What is the speaker asserting?" and evidence answers the question "What is the speaker's support for the assertion?" Reasoning then answers the question "How are the support and assertion connected?" Reasoning provides the bridge between the claim and the evidence, indicating to the audience why the evidence presented should be accepted as support for the claim. Although many types of reasoning exist, this section discusses those most relevant to persuasive speaking. **Table 15.4** summarizes the types of reasoning.

Table 15.4 Types of Reasoning

Type	Brief Definition	Strengths	Weaknesses
Deductive	From general principle to specific case	Relies on established formal logic	Invalid premises leading to false conclusions
Inductive	From specific examples to general principle	Visualizes and personalizes argument	Lack of representation, sufficiency, relevance
Causal	One event causes another	Useful for explanation and prediction	Incorrect cause–effect link
Analogical	Draw similarities between two distinct cases	Links the unfamiliar with the familiar	Ignores key differences

Deductive Reasoning

In **deductive reasoning**, the speaker argues from a general principle to a specific instance or case. Persuasive speakers apply deductive reasoning to categories of people, objects, processes, and events, claiming that what applies to the group also applies to the individual: "Compact fluorescent light bulbs save energy and last longer. The light bulb I bought is compact fluorescent, so it will save energy and last longer."

deductive reasoning
Reasoning from a general condition to a specific case.

With deductive reasoning, if the general principle is true, the specific instance must be true as well. You use deductive reasoning in everyday life. For example, you might read research that shows the best way to learn a second language is through immersion learning—where you are permitted to speak only the language you are trying to learn. You reach the conclusion that you should enroll in such a course locally or study abroad. Here you're reasoning from the general—people who successfully learn a second language—to the specific—yourself.

Deductive reasoning relies on formal logic and most commonly follows this pattern: major premise (general condition), minor premise (specific instance), and conclusion. With this form of reasoning, also called a **syllogism**, both premises must hold true for the conclusion to be true. Here are some examples.

syllogism
A form of deductive reasoning consisting of a major premise, minor premise, and conclusion.

MAJOR PREMISE:	All triathletes are in excellent physical condition.
MINOR PREMISE:	Taylor is a triathlete.
CONCLUSION:	Taylor is in excellent physical condition.

MAJOR PREMISE:	All accredited colleges and universities must go through a rigorous assessment process for certification.
MINOR PREMISE:	My college is accredited.
CONCLUSION:	My college went through a rigorous assessment process.

MAJOR PREMISE:	No one in our family missed the reunion.
MINOR PREMISE:	Afarin is part of our family.
CONCLUSION:	Afarin did not miss the reunion.

MAJOR PREMISE:	Citizens may rightfully overthrow a tyrannical government.
MINOR PREMISE:	The king of Great Britain's rule in the American colonies is a tyrannical government.
CONCLUSION:	The citizens of the American colonies may rightfully overthrow the king of Great Britain's government in the colonies.

Validity of Premises To successfully employ an argument based on deductive reasoning, persuasive speakers must demonstrate the validity of their major and minor premises with supporting evidence, then work their way toward the conclusion. If speakers do this well, listeners cannot easily refute the argument. Consider the following example from a student speech advocating a ban on smoking in all public places:

TOPIC:	Smoking Ban in All Public Places
GENERAL PURPOSE:	To persuade
SPECIFIC PURPOSE:	To convince my audience that smoking should be banned in all public areas in our state
THESIS:	Smoking should be banned in all public areas throughout our state because secondhand smoke harms nonsmokers.
MAJOR PREMISE:	One obligation of the state is to keep individuals safe from harm in public places.
MINOR PREMISE:	Smoking in public causes harm to nearby nonsmokers.
CONCLUSION:	Smoking should be banned in all public places in our state.

For the audience to accept the conclusion that smoking should be banned in all public places, the speaker must first show that (1) the state is responsible for protecting people from harm when they're out in public and (2) secondhand smoke harms nonsmokers.

Supporting the major premise may pose a challenge, because the state government cannot protect individuals from all forms of harm. For example, driving, cycling, or walking on a road can be dangerous. Because roads can't be removed, states can only develop laws and regulations that make roads safer, though never completely safe.

For the minor premise, the speaker must demonstrate the magnitude of the harm. Research indicates a strong link between secondhand smoke and several diseases.[34] Still, the speaker's evidence must convince the audience that the minor premise is true. Once the audience accepts both premises, the conclusion becomes logically apparent.

Tribune News Service/Getty Images

In deductive reasoning, conclusions must be based on valid premises, like restrictions on hoverboards (conclusion) based on the proven danger of fiery accidents (valid premises).

Validity of Reasoning For deductive reasoning to be valid, the premises and conclusion must be true, as we saw in the previous examples. Sometimes, however, premises do not guarantee a true conclusion. In those cases, the argument is invalid.[35] Consider the following syllogism:

MAJOR PREMISE:	Reducing stress helps students get good grades.
MINOR PREMISE:	Playing video games reduces stress.
CONCLUSION:	Playing video games helps students get good grades.

The speaker may be able to find evidence supporting the major and minor premises. And for some audience members, the conclusion may also hold true. But for many others, playing video games wastes time that could be spent preparing for tests, writing papers, or doing other things that help ensure good grades. Therefore, the conclusion that playing video games will help students get good grades is not proven. It may be true for some people, but other determining factors limit the conclusion's more general truth. In this case, the conclusion does not necessarily follow from the premises, so the argument is invalid.

In persuasive speaking, there are two keys to applying deductive reasoning when linking claims to evidence:

1. The speaker must have sufficient supporting evidence to convince the audience that the general condition (major premise) and specific instance (minor premise) are true or correct.
2. The speaker must have sufficient supporting evidence to show that the conclusion is the correct one based on the premises.

Inductive Reasoning

Speakers use **inductive reasoning** when they support a claim with specific instances or examples. Also called *reasoning by example*, inductive reasoning asks the audience to accept a general claim based on a few cases or even just one case. People naturally think inductively, using their own experiences to draw conclusions about the world.[36] Suppose you practice a speech for your public speaking class in front of friends and get more out of the experience than when you only practiced by yourself. Based on that single experience, you decide that practicing with an audience is probably always more productive than practicing alone. In this case, you applied inductive reasoning.

inductive reasoning Supporting a claim with specific cases or instances; also called *reasoning by example.*

When speakers use inductive reasoning to make their arguments, they rely on the principle of probability—that the evidence they present in their argument leads to a conclusion that is *probably* correct. Inductive reasoning depends on the quality of the evidence presented and the way speakers make sense of it.

Sampling Quality How do you know when you have enough evidence when reasoning inductively? You can never know for sure. Unlike deductive reasoning or formal logic, where you're certain of your conclusion, inductive reasoning relies on probability—the idea that the conclusion is likely true. So your task as a persuasive speaker is to present enough evidence to show that your position has a high probability of being correct.

But it's more than a numbers game. A small number of examples that represent a population well can make a much stronger case than a large number of examples that only represent a portion of the population. If you were arguing, for instance, that students on your campus should support building a new student center and you interviewed only students who live in campus dormitories you wouldn't have an appropriate sample. But if you interviewed a cross-section of students who live in dorms, sororities, fraternities, apartments off campus, and at home with their spouses or parents you would have much greater confidence in reasoning from those specific cases to the general student population.

Inductive reasoning stimulates human emotion in a way that deductive reasoning rarely does. One strong example—a case study of a severely autistic child, for example—or one compelling story—the devastating effect that gang violence had on one family in South Chicago, for instance—can provoke great interest and sympathy. One example alone, however, seldom convinces an audience of a claim's legitimacy. Inductive reasoning works best when speakers use multiple, diverse, and relevant examples.[37] The examples used must clearly represent the general conclusion they support.

Causal Reasoning

causal reasoning
Linking two events or actions to claim that one resulted in the other.

In **causal reasoning**, the speaker argues that one action or event brought about another action or event.[38] Persuasive speakers use causal reasoning in four ways:

- to *explain why* something happened,
- to identify *who's responsible* for something,
- to determine whether people can *control* an event, and
- to *predict* what might occur in the future.

In each of these cases, the speaker wants to show the cause of something.

People frequently use causal reasoning to make sense of their everyday experiences. You take on an extra project at work, for instance, and after you complete it you get a raise. To explain the salary increase, you point to your efforts on the project as the cause. Causal reasoning also plays an important role in your attempts to predict the future. If you can determine a causal relationship between two events that occurs consistently, you can expect the relationship will continue to occur. You might observe, for instance, that if you take a brief nap during the day you feel more alert in the evening than on the days you skip a nap. You'd predict, then, that in the future taking a nap will help you feel refreshed later in the day.

Strength of the Causal Relation Causal reasoning can prove quite persuasive because humans are naturally inquisitive—they like to know why and how things happen. People also like a sense of stability and predictability in their worlds, which causal reasoning can provide. As a persuasive speaker, however, you must be sure that the two events are indeed related and that one truly causes the other. You must consider, for example, other factors that might lead to a particular result.

For instance, let's say you want to argue that a recent increase in crime on Indian reservations in the Southwest was caused by a dramatic spike in unemployment among Native Americans. You argue that social stress increases when people lose their jobs and that employment opportunities on Indian lands have been hit especially hard. Based on this premise, your thesis is that the government should provide intensive new work programs for these areas.

However, it could also be that increase in crime on the reservations was caused largely by a cutback in funding for local law enforcement, public safety, and tribal courts. This doesn't mean that you couldn't argue a case for more job opportunities for Native Americans. But when you argue a thesis based on causal reasoning, be sure to take all possible factors into account for any phenomenon you try to explain, and do the research necessary to make certain that all the elements of your argument can hold up to alternative explanations.

Analogical Reasoning

An *analogy* is a comparison between two things. Analogies work well when the things being compared share clear points of relevance. For example, most people probably understand the now-classic analogy "The Internet is an information super highway" because both the Internet and highways involve speed, networks, points of access, and

pumkinpi3/Alamy Stock Photo

When you use causal reasoning, think carefully about what the true causes of an event or action are. For example, do violent video games and movies cause people to commit violence? If so, should violent media be censored? Or do other factors—broken homes, substance abuse, high unemployment, or mental illness, for instance—contribute more to violent behavior?

long-distance travel. But the analogy "The Internet is an information country road" likely wouldn't resonate with an audience because the two objects don't have obvious points of comparison.

When persuasive speakers use **analogical reasoning**, they compare similar objects, processes, concepts, or events and suggest that what holds true for one also holds true for the other. The similarities provide the rationale for the conclusion the speaker offers.

analogical reasoning Comparing two similar objects, processes, concepts, or events and suggesting that what holds true for one also holds true for the other.

In a motivational speech given at Occidental College, the founder of Motown Records, Berry Gordy, Jr., used analogical reasoning when he described his struggle to become a successful music producer in Detroit:

> I was a songwriter…I wanted to be the greatest songwriter. I was writing about everything—everything I saw. But I was not making money, and I finally agreed with everyone I ever talked to who knows me, who said, "Boy, you need to get a job—a real one."
>
> So I got a job on the Ford assembly line. And every day I watched how a bare metal frame rolling down the line would come off the other end a spanking, brand-new car. Wow, I thought: what I great idea. Maybe I can do the same thing with my music—create place where a kid off the street can walk in one door an unknown and out the other as a star.
>
> That little thought that came to me while running up and down at Ford Motor Company became a reality you now know as Motown.[39]

As with all arguments, analogical reasoning must reach some conclusion.[40] Barry Gordy, Jr., made an analogy based on his own life experience to insinuate the conclusion he wanted his audience to grasp: You can apply the underlying process that characterizes one thing to something completely unrelated in order to create remarkable possibilities: Producing music isn't that much different than producing cars.

Comparison Suitability When speakers reason by analogy, the two things they compare must have enough similarities to make the comparison believable. For example, a persuasive speaker might argue that alcohol and marijuana are similar, so the latter should be legalized. But the audience must be convinced that the two are truly similar.

In addition, the speaker must recognize differences between the things compared. If the differences are larger or more important than the similarities, the analogy won't work. For example, solutions to environmental problems in one city may not translate to another city because of differences in climate and geography, even if the two locations share similar environmental problems.

Avoiding Fallacies in Argument

fallacy
An error in making an argument.

MindTap®

Watch It: View a video on the elements of argument.

A **fallacy** is an error in making an argument.[41] The error may reside in the claims offered, the evidence presented, or the reasoning process. At first, fallacies may appear valid and reasonable. They may even persuade an uncritical listener.[42] But upon closer inspection, fallacies do not hold up.

Including fallacies in a persuasive speech—even when done unintentionally—reflects poorly on the speaker and can constitute unethical behavior. Effective speakers recognize fallacies in their arguments and eliminate them before they make their presentations.

Fallacies fall into four main categories:

1. Faulty claims
2. Flawed evidence
3. Defective reasoning
4. Erroneous responses

Table 15.5 summarizes common fallacies in public speaking.

Fallacies in Claims

Fallacies stemming from the claims a speaker makes refer to errors in basic assumptions or assertions.

false dilemma fallacy
Argument in which a speaker reduces available choices to only two even though other alternatives exist; also called the *either–or fallacy.*

The False Dilemma Fallacy Also called *either–or thinking,* the **false dilemma fallacy** occurs when a speaker tries to reduce the choices an audience can make to two even though other alternatives exist. For instance, to say that "We must fund this arts program or it is doomed" fails to acknowledge other options, such as supporting parts of the program and eliminating others.

begging the question
Argument in which a speaker uses a premise to imply the truth of the conclusion or asserts that the validity of the conclusion is self-evident; also called *circular reasoning.*

Begging the Question Also referred to as *circular reasoning,* **begging the question** is rooted in a speaker's claims. When speakers beg the question, they imply the truth of the conclusion in the premise or simply assert that the validity of the conclusion is self-evident. For example, in attempting to persuade an audience to support closing some elementary schools to reduce costs, a speaker states, "Closing these schools will save the district money. We will only eliminate schools whose closure will financially benefit the district." But the speaker has provided no support for the premise that closing these schools really will actually reduce costs. Students from the closed schools will have to be educated somewhere. The premise implies the conclusion, which essentially only restates the premise.

slippery-slope fallacy
Argument in which a speaker asserts that one event will necessarily lead to another without showing any logical connection between the two events.

The Slippery-Slope Fallacy When a speaker says that one event will necessarily lead to another without showing any logical connection between the two, the speaker has used the **slippery-slope fallacy**. Although the conclusion might possibly follow from the premise, the speaker skips the steps between them. The speaker argues, for example, "If the government passes a law requiring all citizens to carry a national identification card, it will be a lot easier for the government to invade our private lives in other ways, too." So the claim made is that a national identity card will inevitably lead to the dismantling

Table 15.5 Common Fallacies in Public Speaking

Fallacy	Brief Definition	Example
Fallacies in Claims		
False dilemma	Choices are reduced to just two.	We must either raise student tuition or lay off teachers.
Begging the question	Something is true because it is.	Our program is the best one because we rate it highly.
Slippery slope	One event leads to another without a necessary logical connection.	Passing stricter gun laws is the first step by the government to take away our guns.
Ad ignorantiam	A thing is true because it hasn't been disproved.	Angels and devils must exist because we have no proof that they don't.
Fallacies in Evidence		
Red herring	Distract with irrelevant point or example	Lots of trolls post on social media. We must not use social media to raise awareness of the growing heroin epidemic in our community.
Ad populum	Appeal to popular attitude or emotion	If you're a true progressive thinker, you'll support our petition for gender-neutral restroom facilities.
Appeal to tradition	Support the status quo	In-person college classes are better than online classes because City College has always taught face-to-face classes well.
Comparative evidence	Inappropriate use of statistics	Violent crime in our city *doubled* from last year. [Speaker omits previous year's number, which was very low.]
Fallacies in Reasoning		
Division	Parts of a whole share the same properties.	The Warriors play unselfish team basketball. Deandre is a member of the team so he must be an unselfish player.
Hasty generalization	Insufficient examples or inadequate sample	Two local restaurants have seen an increase in profits since the stadium was built, so all local businesses have benefited.
Post hoc	Misrepresent causal relationship	The year after the department hired a new manager, sales increased.
Weak analogy	Key dissimilarities make the comparison misleading.	Buying stocks is like gambling because both involve money and risk.
Fallacies in Responding		
Ad hominem	Personal attack	That administrator is an idiot so it's no surprise she came to the wrong conclusion.
Guilt by association	Claim linked to objectionable person	Any terrorist would support this crazy idea.
Straw man	Misrepresentation of a claim	My opponent's position would greatly weaken our nation's ability to defend itself. [In reality, the speaker's opponent is calling for limited cuts of outdated Defense Department programs.]
Loaded words	Emotionally laden, misleading language	Hunting is the utterly senseless murder of innocent creatures.

of other privacy rights. This type of argument is fallacious because one event will not necessarily lead to a much larger and more significant event.

***ad ignorantiam* fallacy**
Argument in which a speaker suggests that because a claim hasn't been shown to be false, it must be true; also called an *appeal to ignorance.*

The *Ad Ignorantiam* Fallacy Also called *appeal to ignorance,* the ***ad ignorantiam* fallacy** suggests that because a claim hasn't been shown to be false, it must be true. It is also called the burden-of-proof fallacy. Senator Joseph R. McCarthy famously used this tactic in the 1950s to accuse people, especially Hollywood movie producers, of being communists. He argued that if an individual couldn't disprove his allegations, then the person must be a communist. Claims of UFOs, alien abductions, and paranormal activities also usually rely on the *ad ignorantiam* fallacy: Scientists have no proof that UFOs don't exist; therefore, UFOs probably exist.[43]

Fallacies in Evidence

Even if a speaker presents valid claims, the evidence used to support those claims may be irrelevant, inaccurate, or insufficient.

red herring
Argument that introduces irrelevant evidence to distract an audience from the real issue.

Red Herring When speakers present evidence that has nothing to do with the claim, they create a **red herring**, distracting the audience with irrelevant evidence. To urge the audience to support abolishing all competitive sports on campus, a speaker might argue, "We need to end competitive sports here at our college. The state is in a budget crisis, and tuition is going up." The state's budget crisis and rising tuition are not necessarily related to the cost of competitive sports, but mentioning those points sensationalizes the topic—and takes audience members' minds off the real issue.

comparative evidence fallacy
Argument in which a speaker uses statistics or compares numbers in ways that misrepresent the evidence and mislead the audience.

The Comparative Evidence Fallacy The **comparative evidence fallacy** occurs when speakers compare numbers in ways that mislead the audience and misrepresent the evidence included to support the argument. This may happen unintentionally when a speaker simply misinterprets statistical data. In other cases, the speaker may manipulate the numbers or omit some information and purposefully deceive the audience. For example, some urban universities highlight their low rates of crime by reporting only crimes that occur on the campus itself, leaving out any that are reported even within a block or two of the campus's borders. Although the statistics may be technically accurate, omitting nearby crime incidents may give students, faculty, and staff a false sense of security.

In addition, speakers may favor one kind of evidence too heavily—for example, privileging numbers over other forms of evidence such as testimony, narrative, and examples. Although statistics can provide powerful evidence, they are not always the best choice. Statistics often shed little light on how things work. A speaker may present statistics showing that students who learn math using a new method score higher on tests than do students using an old method. But the reason for the higher scores may be the increased attention that students using the new method received, rather than the method itself. Without additional evidence, the audience can't be sure of what really led to the results.[44]

***ad populum* fallacy**
Argument in which a speaker appeals to popular attitudes and emotions without offering evidence to support claims.

The *Ad Populum* Fallacy Although effective speakers sometimes employ stories and examples from popular culture that touch audience members' emotions, the ***ad populum* fallacy** plays on popular attitudes without offering any supporting material. Speakers may appeal to audience members' cultural prejudices or their desire to be part of a group. Advertisers do this all the time. For instance, to be considered cool you should drive a certain car or use a particular smartphone. Trying to persuade an audience to go on a gluten-free diet because everyone's doing it is another example of the *ad populum* fallacy.

appeal to tradition fallacy
Argument in which a speaker asserts that the status quo is better than any new idea or approach.

The Appeal to Tradition Fallacy When speakers use the **appeal to tradition fallacy**, they argue that maintaining the status quo is inherently better than trying a new idea or approach. Audience members often find this fallacy persuasive because it comfortably reinforces what is familiar and safe. But danger lurks in these situations.

Cultural traditions always represent particular social interests but are not always recognized as such.[45] For instance, the appeal to tradition fallacy has been used to argue against allowing women in all-male colleges and vice-versa. Sometimes traditional ways of doing things are indeed the best course of action. But the speaker must present sufficient evidence to support that contestable point of view.

Fallacies in Reasoning

Fallacies in reasoning involve errors in how the speaker links the evidence and the claims.

The Division Fallacy When they use the **division fallacy**, speakers assume that what's true of the whole is also true of the parts making up the whole. Consider the statement, "Our university has an excellent reputation for scholarship." This image may be widely recognized as true, but it does not necessarily apply to every department on campus. Or, to claim that a food item is "organic" does not always mean that every ingredient is natural.

division fallacy
Argument in which a speaker assumes that what is true of the whole is also true of the parts that make up the whole.

The Hasty Generalization Fallacy When speakers draw a conclusion based on too few examples or from an unrepresentative sample, they've made a hasty generalization, a flaw in inductive reasoning. The **hasty generalization fallacy** occurs when the speaker makes a claim after offering only one or two examples, or when the examples offered don't represent the larger group. For example, a speaker who argues for improving the quality of national disaster relief training by using data drawn only from a couple small cities would not be able to establish convincingly the need for reform at the national level.

hasty generalization fallacy
Argument in which a speaker draws a conclusion based on too few or inadequate examples.

The *Post Hoc* Fallacy Also called the *false cause fallacy,* the ***post hoc* fallacy** involves concluding that a causal relationship exists simply because one event follows another in time. Let's say that the coach of your successful college football team quits to accept a job at another university. Next season, your team fails to win many games. Did the loss of the coach lead to your team's poor performance on the field? Maybe, but many other factors could be involved as well, such as the graduation of key players from your team, the high quality of opponents the following year, and the poor quality of recruits brought in by the former coach. When a speaker argues that one event necessarily caused another, always consider additional possible explanations for why something occurred.

***post hoc* fallacy**
Argument in which a speaker concludes a causal relationship exists simply because one event follows another in time; also called the *false cause fallacy.*

The Weak Analogy Fallacy The **weak analogy fallacy** results when two things have important dissimilarities that make the comparison inaccurate and the analogy faulty. Although it's possible to identify similarities between almost any two things you might want to compare, the similarities must contribute much to the argument and the dissimilarities must not detract from it. A speaker argues, for example, "Graffiti is like any other form of public art and should be supported." But the process for displaying public art is quite different from that for displaying graffiti. With public art, members of the community decide on the type of art and where it should be placed. With graffiti, the person applying the paint is making those choices.

weak analogy fallacy
Argument in which a speaker compares two dissimilar things, ideas, or concepts, making the comparison inaccurate.

Fallacies in Responding

Speakers aren't the only ones who commit logical fallacies. Listeners sometimes make serious errors in judgment when they respond to a speaker's arguments.

The *Ad Hominem* Fallacy Also called the *against the person fallacy*, the ***ad hominem* fallacy** is probably the most common fallacy in responding. This fallacy occurs when a claim is rejected based on perceptions of the speaker's character rather than the evidence. The *ad*

***ad hominem* fallacy**
Argument in which a speaker rejects another speaker's claim based on that speaker's character rather than the evidence the speaker presents; also called the *against the person* fallacy.

AP Images/HALEY/SIPA

Guilt by association is a common fallacy often found in political speech. The most infamous and unfair comparison is with Adolph Hitler.

hominem fallacy typically follows this pattern: "You want me to accept your thesis, but [for whatever reason] I don't like you so I reject your position." Although you should certainly evaluate a speaker's credibility, you must critique the argument based on the evidence presented rather than something about the person that has nothing to do with the topic. Personally attacking the speaker distracts from the merits of a claim and is unethical.

The Guilt-by-Association Fallacy The **guilt-by-association fallacy** suggests something's wrong with people who support the speaker's claim. Also known as the *bad company fallacy,* this fallacy links the thesis with someone the audience finds objectionable, deplorable, or repulsive. For instance, responding to a speaker arguing for national health care, an audience member says, "Fidel Castro set up a government health care system in Cuba. I certainly wouldn't want something in the United States that was designed by a dictator." Of course, all relatively developed democratic countries have some form of tax-supported national health care, but by associating the speaker's claim with someone the audience probably dislikes, the person responding employs the guilt-by-association fallacy.

guilt-by-association fallacy Argument in which a speaker suggests that something is wrong with another speaker's claims by associating those claims with someone the audience finds objectionable; also called the *bad company fallacy.*

straw man fallacy Argument in which a speaker misrepresents another speaker's argument so that only a shell of the opponent's argument remains.

The Straw Man Fallacy The **straw man fallacy** misrepresents a speaker's argument so that just a shell of the original claim, if any of it, remains. Then the argument is easily refuted because it appears implausible or too simplistic.[46] These fallacies often occur in political campaigns when candidates present distorted and exaggerated views of their opponents' positions. For instance, an argument in favor of teaching young people contraceptive methods in public schools to protect them if they choose to have sex might be reduced to "support for birth control just gives our kids license to have sex with no consequences."[47] Or, a candidate for president of student government who advocates revising the grading system might be denounced as calling for an end to grades entirely. In both cases, the original claim is misrepresented so that the argument against it becomes obvious.

loaded word fallacy Argument in which a speaker uses emotionally laden words to evaluate claims based on a misleading emotional response rather than the evidence presented.

The Loaded Word Fallacy The **loaded word fallacy** uses emotionally laden words to distract from the speaker's argument and evaluate claims based on a misleading emotional response rather than the evidence presented.[48] The intent in using such language is to refute a speaker's claims without offering any substantial evidence. Responding to a speaker's claim that our country needs a comprehensive immigration policy by saying, "many immigrants are criminals, rapists, and terrorists" plays on emotions but does nothing to refute the speaker's original argument.

Summary

The well-constructed argument forms the foundation of persuasive speaking. An argument consists of claims, evidence, and reasoning.

Claims lay the groundwork for the thesis of your speech, answering the question "What am I asserting?" Every claim includes at least one premise and a conclusion.

Evidence refers to the supporting materials presented to back up the claim, answering the question "What is the support for my assertion?" Speakers may use logical appeals (logos), appeals to the speaker's credibility (ethos), emotional appeals (pathos), or appeals to cultural beliefs and values (mythos).

Reasoning answers the question "How are my supporting materials and assertions linked together?" and shows the audience how the evidence you've chosen provides justification for your position on the topic. Persuasive speakers rely on four types of reasoning: deductive, inductive, causal, and analogical.

A fallacy occurs when an error is made in constructing an argument. Although fallacies may be persuasive, they are nonetheless a deceptive and unethical approach to convincing an audience. Fallacies may stem from errors in claims, evidence, reasoning, or responding.

> ANALYZE IT

Adam, Together, We Can Stop Cyberbullying

MindTap®

Watch and analyze this speech on MindTap.

Adam was an undergraduate student enrolled in a beginning public speaking class. His assignment was to prepare a persuasive speech on a topic of his choice. His topic is very timely and important to his audience, and his argument is well formed. In particular, notice how Adam handles a requirement his instructor gave him to cite at least four sources in the speech and his call to action.

"I'll miss just being around her." "I didn't want to believe it." "It's such a sad thing." These quotes are from the friends and family of 15-year-old Phoebe Prince, who committed suicide by hanging herself. Why did this senseless act occur? The answer is simple: Phoebe Prince was bullied to death.

Many of us know someone who has been bullied in school. Perhaps they were teased in the parking lot or in the locker room. In the past, bullying occurred primarily in school. However, with the advent of cell phones, text messaging, instant messaging, blogs, and social networking sites, bullies can now follow and terrorize their victims anywhere, even into their own bedrooms. Using electronic communications to tease, harass, threaten, and intimidate another person is called *cyberbullying.*

As a tutor and mentor to young students, I have witnessed cyberbullying first hand, and by examining current research, I believe I understand the problem, its causes, and how we can help end cyberbullying. What I know for sure is that cyberbullying is a devastating form of abuse that must be confronted on national, local, and personal levels.

Today, we will examine the widespread and harmful nature of cyberbullying, uncover how and why it persists, and pinpoint some simple solutions we must begin to enact in order to thwart cyberbullies and comfort their victims.

Let's begin by tackling the problem head on. Many of us have read rude, insensitive, or nasty statements posted about us or someone we care about on social networking sites. Well, whether or not those comments were actually intended to hurt another person's feelings, if they did hurt their feelings, then they are perfect examples of cyberbullying.

Cyberbullying is a pervasive and dangerous behavior. It takes place all over the world and through a wide array of electronic media. According to Susan Keith and Michelle Martin's article in *Reclaiming Children and Youth,* 57 percent of American middle-school students had experienced instances of cyberbullying ranging from hurtful comments to threats of physical violence. Quing Li's article published in the journal *Computers in Human Behavior* noted that cyberbullying is not gender biased. According to Li, females are just as likely as males to engage in cyberbullying, although women are 10 percent more likely to be victimized.

Li noted that Internet and cell-phone technologies have been used by bullies to harass, torment, and threaten young people in North America, Europe, and Asia. However, some of the most horrific attacks happen right here at home.

According to Keith and Martin, a particularly disturbing incident occurred in Dallas, Texas, where an overweight student with multiple sclerosis was targeted on a school's social networking page. One message read, "I guess I'll have to wait until you kill yourself which I hope is not long from now, or I'll have to wait until your disease kills you." What is most disturbing about cyberbullying is its effects upon victims, bystanders, and perhaps even upon bullies themselves.

Cyberbullying can lead to physical and psychological injuries upon its victims. According to an article in the *Journal of Adolescent Health,* Michele Ybarra and colleagues noted that 36 percent of the victims of cyberbullies are also harassed by their attackers in school. For example, the Dallas student with MS had eggs thrown at her car and a bottle of acid thrown at her house.

Ybarra and her colleagues reported that victims of cyberbullying experience such severe emotional distress that they often exhibit behavioral problems such as poor grades, skipping school, and receiving detentions and suspensions. Furthermore, Peter K. Smith and his co-researchers suggested that even a few instances of cyberbullying can have these long-lasting negative effects. What is even more alarming is that, according to Ybarra and colleagues, victims of cyberbullying are significantly more likely to carry weapons to school as a result of feeling threatened. Obviously, this could lead to violent outcomes for bullies, victims, and even bystanders.

Now that we have heard about the nature, scope, and effects of cyberbullying, let's see if we can discover its causes. Let's think back to a time when we may have seen a friend or loved one being harassed online. Did we report the bully to the network administrator or other authorities? Did we console the victim? I know I didn't. If you are like me, we may unknowingly be enabling future instances of cyberbullying.

Cyberbullying occurs because of the anonymity offered to bullies by cell phone and Internet technologies, as well as the failure of victims and bystanders to report incidents of cyberbullying. You see, unlike schoolyard bullies, cyberbullies can attack their victims anonymously.

Ybarra and colleagues discovered that 13 percent of cyberbullying victims did not know who was tormenting them. This devastating statistic is important because, as Keith and Martin noted, traditional bullying takes place face-to-face and often ends when students leave school. However, today, students are subjected to nonstop bullying, even when they are alone in their own homes.

Perhaps the anonymous nature of cyberattacks partially explains why Li found that nearly 76 percent of victims of cyberbullying and 75 percent of bystanders never reported instances of bullying to adults. Victims and bystanders who do not report attacks from cyberbullies can unintentionally enable bullies.

According to De Nies, Donaldson, and Netter of *ABCNews.com,* several of Phoebe Prince's classmates were aware that she was being harassed but did not inform the school's administration. Li suggested that victims and bystanders often do not believe that adults will actually intervene to stop cyberbullying. However, *ABCNews.com* reports that 41 states have laws against bullying in schools and 23 of those states target cyberbullying specifically.

Now that we know that victims of cyberbullies desperately need the help of witnesses and bystanders to report their attacks, we should arm ourselves with the information necessary to provide that assistance. Think about the next time you see a friend or loved one being tormented or harassed online.

What would you be willing to do to help?

Cyberbullying must be confronted on national, local, and personal levels. There should be a comprehensive national law confronting cyberbullying in schools. Certain statutes currently in state laws should be amalgamated to create the strongest protections for victims and the most effective punishments for bullies as possible.

According to Susan Limber and Mark Small's article titled *State Laws and Policies to Address Bullying in Schools,* Georgia law requires faculty and staff to be trained on the nature of bullying and what actions to take if they see students being bullied. Connecticut law *requires* school employees to report bullying as part of their hiring contract. Washington takes this a step further, by protecting employees from any legal action if a reported bully is proven to be innocent. When it comes to protecting victims, West Virginia law demands that schools must ensure that a bullied student does not receive additional abuse at the hands of his or her bully.

Legislating punishment for bullies is difficult. A comprehensive anticyberbullying law should incorporate the best aspects of these state laws and find a way to punish bullies that is both punitive and has the ability to rehabilitate abusers. However, for national laws to be effective, local communities need to be supportive.

Local communities must organize and mobilize to attack the problem of cyberbullying. According to A. S. Green's article published in the *Journal of Social Issues,* communities need to support bullying prevention programs by conducting a school-based bullying survey for individual school districts. We can't know how to best protect victims in our community without knowing how they are affected by the problem. It is critical to know this information as Greene noted, only 3 percent of teachers in the United States perceive bullying to be a problem in their schools.

There are several warning signs that might indicate a friend or loved one is a victim of a cyberbully. If you see a friend or loved one exhibiting these signs, the decision to get involved can be the difference between life and death.

According to Keith and Martin's article *Cyber-Bullying: Creating a Culture of Respect in a Cyber World,* victims of cyberbullies often use electronic communication more frequently than do people who are not being bullied. Victims of cyberbullies have mood swings and difficulty sleeping, they seem depressed or become anxious, victims can also become withdrawn from social activities and fall behind in scholastic responsibilities. If you witness your friends or family members exhibiting these symptoms, there are several ways you can help.

According to Juliana Raskauskas and Ann Stoltz's article in *Developmental Psychology,* witnesses of cyberbullying should inform victims to take the attacks seriously, especially if the bullies threaten violence. You should tell victims to report their attacks to police or other authorities, to block harmful messages by blocking email accounts and cell phone numbers, to save copies of attacks and provide them to authorities.

If you personally know the bully and feel safe confronting him or her, do so! As Raskaukas and Stoltz noted, bullies will often back down when confronted by peers. By being a good friend and by giving good advice, you can help a victim report his or her attacks from cyberbullies and take a major step toward eliminating this horrendous problem. So, you see, we are not helpless to stop the cyberbullying problem as long as we make the choice NOT to ignore it.

To conclude, cyberbullying is a devastating form of abuse that must be reported to authorities. Cyberbullying is a worldwide problem perpetuated by the silence of both victims and bystanders. By paying attention to certain warning signs, we can empower ourselves to console victims and report their abusers. Today, I'm imploring you to do your part to help stop cyberbullying. I know that you agree that stopping cyberbullying must be a priority.

First, although other states have cyberbullying laws in place, ours does not. So I'm asking you to sign this petition that I will forward to our district's State Legislators. We need to make our voices heard that we want specific laws passed to stop these horrific attacks and to punish those caught doing it.

Second, I'm also asking you to be vigilant in noticing signs of cyberbullying and then taking action. Look for signs that your friend, brother, sister, cousin, boyfriend, girlfriend, or loved one might be a victim of cyberbullying and then get involved to help stop it!

Phoebe Prince showed the warning signs, and she did not deserve to die so senselessly. None of us would ever want to say, "I'll miss just being around her," "I didn't want to believe it," "It's such a sad thing," about our own friends or family members. We must work to ensure that victims are supported and bullies are confronted nationally, locally, and personally.

I know that if we stand together and refuse to be silent, we can and will stop cyberbullying.

Questions for Discussion

1. In the introduction of his speech when Adam says, "What I know for sure is that cyberbullying is a devastating form of abuse that must be confronted on national, local, and personal levels" what aspect of argument is he presenting?
2. When Adam says, "According to Susan Keith and Michelle Martin's article in *Reclaiming Children and Youth,* 57 percent of American middle-school students had experienced instances of cyberbullying ranging from hurtful comments to threats of physical violence" what aspect of argument is he presenting?
3. When Adam says, "Perhaps the anonymous nature of cyberattacks partially explains why LI found that nearly 76 percent of victims of cyberbullying and 75 percent of bystanders never reported instances of bullying to adults" what aspect of argument does his evidence include?
4. When Adam says, "What is even more alarming is that, according to Ybarra and colleagues, victims of cyberbullying are significantly more likely to carry weapons to school as a result of feeling threatened. Obviously, this could lead to violent outcomes for bullies, victims, and even bystanders" what aspects of argument is he presenting?
5. When Adam says, "According to Susan Keith and Michelle Martin's article in *Reclaiming Children and Youth,* 57 percent of American middle-school students had experienced instances of cyberbullying ranging from hurtful comments to threats of physical violence" what type of appeal is he making?

6. When Adam says, "As a tutor and mentor to young students, I have witnessed cyberbullying first hand, and by examining current research, I believe I understand the problem, its causes, and how we can help end cyberbullying" what type of appeal is he making?
7. When Adam shares quotes from the friends and family of 15-year-old Phoebe Prince, who committed suicide by hanging herself, and says, "Why did this senseless act occur? The answer is simple: Phoebe Prince was bullied to death" what type of appeal is he making?
8. When Adam says, "Now that we know that victims of cyberbullies desperately need the help of witnesses and bystanders to report their attacks, we should arm ourselves with the information necessary to provide that assistance" what kind of reasoning is he using?

APPLY IT . . .

IN THE WORKPLACE

Effective Communication at Work

Employees try to convince bosses to support an idea they have. Coworkers keep each other happily on track by working effectively in teams. Bosses want to motivate their employees to do their best work for the organization.

No matter what our role at work, we are most likely to succeed when we communicate sensitively with our colleagues—even when we're arguing for something important to us. The principles of effective workplace communication resemble the basics of audience-centered public speaking: Show respect for everyone you interact with. Be aware of cultural differences. Don't just talk, listen attentively. Recognize effort and achievement. Be open and honest. Allow for creativity and freedom of expression. Be positive in your approach to challenges and problems. And don't let the convenience of text messaging and email determine your patterns of interaction with bosses, employees, and colleagues—make it a point to frequently engage others at work in a friendly way face-to-face.

Can you think of any workplace situation in which you feel you could have improved communication? If you have never faced such a situation yourself, can you think of situations that came to your attention where communication could have been improved? For either case, make a note of the circumstances and what should be done differently.

IN YOUR COMMUNITY

Arguing for Alternative Policies

Because they enjoy a very high standard of living, middle class Americans have a special responsibility to contribute something positive to the global community. Nongovernmental organizations (NGOs) offer real opportunities to campaign for social responsibility on a range of issues. Excellent persuasive speaking is central to their success. Spokespersons for NGOs argue for instituting or changing public policy in ways that promote the interests of underserved groups and communities. For example, representatives from the Southern Poverty Law Center (SPLC) speak throughout the United States about the need to "fight hate and bigotry and to seek justice for the most vulnerable members of our society." To accomplish this, the SPLC monitors hate groups and other extremists throughout the United States and exposes their activities to the public, the media, and law enforcement.[49]

> REVIEW IT

Key Terms

ad hominem fallacy 331
ad ignorantiam fallacy 330
ad populum fallacy 330
analogical reasoning 327
appeal to tradition fallacy 330
appeals to cultural beliefs (*mythos*) 320
appeals to speaker credibility (*ethos*) 318
argument 312
begging the question 328
causal reasoning 326
claim 312
comparative evidence fallacy 330
conclusion 313
deductive reasoning 323
division fallacy 331
emotional appeals (*pathos*) 319
enthymemes 314
evidence 312
fallacy 328
false dilemma fallacy 328
guilt-by-association fallacy 332
hasty generalization fallacy 331
inductive reasoning 325
loaded word fallacy 332
logical appeals (*logos*) 317
post hoc fallacy 331
premise 313
qualifier 315
reasoning 312
red herring 330
slippery-slope fallacy 328
straw man fallacy 332
syllogism 323
weak analogy fallacy 331

MindTap®
Use flashcards to learn key terms and take a quiz to test your knowledge.

Reflecting on Understanding Argument

1. Choose a controversial topic you're interested in and identify the claims each side presents. How might speakers on both sides of the issue use evidence and reasoning to make their opposing arguments?
2. Persuasive speakers use qualifying claims to strengthen their arguments. If qualifying claims create doubt about a conclusion, how can that "strengthen" an argument? Can you think of an example where qualifying claims strengthen the conclusion of an argument on a controversial topic? What does the importance of qualifying claims tell us about the complexity of good thinking in general?
3. Excellent persuasive speaking typically involves multiple forms of evidence. How might you use logical and emotional appeals together in a speech that advocates eliminating the death penalty for violent crimes? For increasing the age for selling tobacco products to persons 21 and over?
4. Can you explain the difference between deductive and inductive reasoning? Between causal and analogical reasoning? Where do the weaknesses lie in each of these forms of reasoning and how can you avoid them?
5. Research has found that students who learn the fundamentals of argument are better at detecting fallacies than are students without training in argument. This is true not only of public speaking. How might knowledge of fallacies influence the way you respond to persuasive messages in the future? Where are fallacies in argument most likely to exist?

16 Special Occasion, Distance, and Group Speaking

READ IT

After successfully completing this chapter, you will be able to:

- Describe the main principles for preparing speeches of introduction, nomination, acceptance, award presentations, tributes and eulogies, roasts and toasts, public testimony, after dinner, and elevator speeches.
- Analyze situations where videoconferences, online graphical presentations, and telephone meetings can function as effective distance speaking performances.
- Explain how panel discussions, symposia, oral reports, and forums differ from each other and describe the role of public speaking in each type of group presentation.

MindTap®
Start with a quick warm-up activity and review the chapter's learning outcomes.

Public speakers today must be prepared to participate in special cultural events, present online, and play a role in meetings of all kinds.

CLAYTON DE SOUZA/picture alliance/ESTADAO CONTE/Newscom

Accepting an award at his college alma mater, the Massachusetts Institute of Technology (MIT), Salman Khan delivered an inspiring message when he addressed current students:

> One of my roommates when I was two years out of college, who had formerly been a bit of a track star at MIT, and I had finished watching *Chariots of Fire* one night at 2 A.M. I told him that it made me feel like running. He simply told me, "Don't waste inspiration." I reminded him that it is 2 A.M. He said, "So what; don't waste inspiration." I looked at him for a few seconds and realized that he was dead serious. I jumped off the couch, threw on my running shoes and took to the streets. If you ever feel inspired, take action with it. Don't let anyone tell you why you shouldn't; at least lace up and give it a try.[1]

No American has contributed more to the evolution of higher education in the 21st century than Salman Khan. The Khan Academy, a web-based instructional center founded and directed by the young entrepreneur, provides a high-quality education to anyone, anywhere—and at no cost.

Khan began his online educational venture by tutoring members of his extended family on an interactive electronic blackboard. Positive feedback encouraged him to greatly expand his idea. With a unique and highly effective approach to distance learning, the Khan Academy today hosts more than 4,000 video tutorials online in math, science, economics, humanities, computer science, and test-preparation courses. The academy has delivered millions of self-paced lessons in dozens of languages.[2]

Many of the presentations you'll give in your life will take place on special occasions, such as accepting an award or introducing the main speaker at an event. As a professional person, you'll likely speak during online or telephone meetings and participate in live group presentations. This chapter helps you prepare speeches for various special occasions, provides guidelines for "distance speaking" presentations such as video conferences and telephone meetings, and describes how to speak effectively in various types of small-group events.

iStock/Getty Images

Special Occasion Speeches

MindTap®

Read, highlight, and take notes online.

Special occasion speeches extend the nature of what you do all the time—talk to others about what's going on in your life. When you introduce a friend to someone else, for example, you might say something about your friend as part of the introduction: This is also a common aspect of special occasion speeches. The different types of special occasion speeches are presented here.

Speeches of Introduction

speech of introduction A short speech that introduces someone to an audience.

Whenever you attend a public speech given by a well-known person, you'll probably first hear a short speech that introduces the main speaker to the audience. That's a **speech of introduction**. It should prepare the audience for who and what they came to hear: the main speaker and the main speech. Following some basic guidelines will help make your speech of introduction successful.

- *Prepare the audience.* When introducing the main speaker, keep your remarks brief but also prepare the audience for the speaker and the occasion. The audience has gathered to hear the main speaker, not the introducer. Although it may be tempting to go on and on about the speaker, especially if the person has impressive credentials, there is no need to spend more than a couple of brief minutes on an introduction. Most audience members already know quite a bit about the speaker—that's why they're attending the speech. So when former President Barack Obama was introduced before the commencement address he gave at Barnard College, a women's college in New York, the president of the university linked the American president's political record with the particular interests of the audience. Debora Spar praised the president for signing into law the Lilly Ledbetter Act, which supports equal pay for equal work; for removing "barriers to women" in military service; for "improved access to health services" for women; and for "repeatedly supporting our right to choose." She noted that President Obama appointed Elena Kagan and Sonia Sotomayor to the Supreme Court, and she named the women he had appointed to cabinet positions. To much applause, Spar then congratulated the president on his marriage to Michelle Obama as one of the "greatest slam dunks" of his life.[3]
- *Be accurate and up to date.* Research the speaker as you would any topic. If you're introducing someone you don't know personally, check online for information the person may have posted on a website or social networking site. Search for stories in the popular press and consult sources such as *Who's Who in America.* If possible, interview the speaker by email, phone, or in person to get the most accurate and up-to-date information.
- *Connect with the audience.* Even a speaker the audience knows well needs an introduction in order to properly respect that person and generate maximum enthusiasm among the listeners. When the speaker is less well known, the introducer's role in connecting the speaker with the audience becomes even more important. Making a strong connection between the main speaker and the audience requires that you know enough about the speaker and what the person intends to say so you can skillfully preview the nature of the guest's remarks and gain the audience's interest. At a meeting of the International Women's Media Foundation, famed television journalist Christiane Amanpour introduced

MANDEL NGAN/AFP/Getty Images

A speech of introduction helps an audience get to know the featured speaker and establishes the speaker's credibility.

Amira Hass, an Israeli newspaper columnist and author. Hass was being honored with the organization's Lifetime Achievement Award for her reporting on Israeli–Palestinian relations. Amanpour told the audience:

> She writes what the Palestinian journalists think about their country's leadership but dare not say themselves. She writes what she thinks citizens of Israel should know about their leadership but do not want to hear. Some call her a traitor. It is uncomfortable to hear the truth; it's very uncomfortable to tell the truth. Some say she is the only voice of truth in a polarized conflict. For twenty years she's paid no attention to either of these camps, choosing instead to follow her own path. Amira knows that dictators do not like journalists, but more than that, democracies don't like journalists either.[4]

Speaking to an audience of journalists, Amanpour said that it was Amira Hass's investigative reporting that had exposed the grim realities underlying the conflict between Israel and Palestine. Highlighting the first principle of good journalism—objectivity—she praised Hass for her fearless reporting and commentary.

Acceptance Speeches

Audiences expect individuals who are being recognized, honored, or awarded to give an **acceptance speech** after they step up to the podium or move to the front of the room. If you were to find yourself in the position of being publicly recognized, what do you think you should say? Most individuals who receive honors or awards know in advance that they have won, so you'll have plenty of time to prepare.

acceptance speech
Speech given by an individual who is being recognized, honored, or given an award.

When accepting an award, some general rules apply. Most important, award recipients should thank the presenter, organization, and audience; demonstrate humility; and keep their remarks succinct. In addition, some acceptance speakers may contextualize the award by discussing the work or activity that won them the award or providing a short personal narrative that is relevant to the occasion.

- *Be thankful and humble.* You've seen enough award ceremonies to know what is expected of the winners. First, everyone thanks the people who helped them succeed. Many award winners also minimize their personal accomplishments, demonstrating a sense of perspective, even humility. On the occasion of his induction into the New Jersey Hall of Fame, Bruce Springsteen spoke of the love and gratitude he has for people in his home state. In his unassuming way, "The Boss" made good fun of the state he adores by reciting a "Garden State benediction":

  > Rise up my fellow New Jerseyans, for we are all members of a confused but noble race. We, of the state that never gets any respect. We, who bear the coolness of the forever uncool. The chip on our shoulders of those with forever something to prove. And even with this wonderful Hall of Fame, we know that there's another bad Jersey joke coming just around the corner.[5]

- *Be succinct.* Listeners expect comments made when accepting an award to be brief and to the point. The Webby Awards—the leading international award recognizing excellence on the Internet—likely holds the record for the shortest and funniest acceptance speeches. Recipients are allowed only five words. Recent speeches include "Had we lost, we'd sue," by the American Bar Association (Law category); "Creativity is a renewable resource," Twitter cofounder Biz Stone (Breakout of the Year category); "Thank you for swiping right" by Tinder (Special Achievement Award); and "Me, me, me, me, me," by Stephen Colbert (Person of the Year category).[6] No other award ceremonies call for speakers to say only five

WireImage/Getty Images

Always known for a humble attitude and love for his home state, Bruce Springsteen spoke to fans when inducted into the New Jersey Hall of Fame.

words, but the point still applies: Keep your remarks brief when accepting an award. Accepting a nomination by President Barack Obama to be a U.S. Supreme Court associate justice, Sonia Sotomayor first thanked the "many friends and family who have guided and supported me throughout my life, and who have been instrumental in helping me realize my dreams." She briefly recounted her professional record as a lawyer and lower court judge and stated how her background would guide her service on the Supreme Court if confirmed by the Senate:

> This wealth of experiences, personal and professional, has helped me appreciate the variety of perspectives that present themselves in every case that I hear. It has helped me to understand, respect, and respond to the concerns and arguments of all litigants who appear before me as well as to the view of my colleagues on the bench. I strive to never forget the real-world consequences of my decisions on individuals, business, and government.[7]

Sotomayor finished her short speech by thanking the president for the honor of the nomination. She said she wanted the American public to know she is just "an ordinary person who has been blessed with extraordinary opportunities and experiences" and "looked forward to working with the Senate in the confirmation process."

- *Contextualize the award.* Speakers may provide a context for an award by describing what they did that led to the award or telling a story related to the occasion. These comments, often emotionally touching and inspiring, personalize the award and help the audience feel more connected with the recipient. When Michael Giacchino won an Oscar for the music he wrote for the movie *Up,* he encouraged kids to unleash their creativity:

> Thank you, guys. When I was nine I asked my dad, "Can I have your movie camera? That old, wind-up 8 millimeter that was in your drawer?" And he goes, "Sure, take it." And I took it and I started making movies with it and I started being as creative as I could, and never once in my life did my parents ever say, "What you're doing is a waste of time." Never. And I grew up—I had teachers, I had colleagues, I had people that I worked with all through my life who always told me, what you're doing is not a waste of time. So it was normal to me that it was okay to do that. I know there are kids out there that don't have that support system, so if you're out there and you're listening, listen to me: If you want to be creative, get out there and do it. It's not a waste of time. Do it, okay? Thank you.[8]

After-Dinner Speeches

After-dinner speech
Speech given after a meal designed to add something light-hearted and pleasurable to the occasion.

After-dinner speeches usually serve as a featured part of an organized event. These kinds of events were originally scheduled as dinner gatherings, but today they are just as likely to be scheduled for breakfast or lunch. Whatever the time of day, the goal of the speech is to contribute something pleasurable to the occasion. After-dinner speeches amplify and extend the good feelings the sponsors of the event want to create for everyone in attendance.

The topic for the after-dinner speech can be serious for some occasions, but most of these presentations are upbeat and often humorous. Some after-dinner speeches take place on special personal occasions like weddings, anniversaries, retirements, or graduation parties. As with any other speech, the after-dinner speech must fit the makeup and interests of the group that gathered for the event.

- *Be entertaining and lighthearted.* Humor is a cornerstone of after-dinner speeches, but it isn't the only way to entertain and enlighten an audience. Although after-dinner speeches often include jokes or funny anecdotes, don't force yourself to be funny if you don't feel comfortable in that role. Above all else, after-dinner speakers should try to develop good rapport with their audiences and leave them feeling good about the time they've spent together. Sharing thoughtful reflections, telling a relevant story, making insightful comments about something of interest to the group, and using language creatively can please your listeners just as much as a good joke.

- *Focus on a theme.* Although most after-dinner speeches have an upbeat, enjoyable quality, they should also have a clear point. The audience should feel not only entertained but also enriched in some way. However, this doesn't mean you should drone on and on. Your job is to provide an enjoyable final touch to the event, not to lecture your audience. Imagine, for example, that you've been asked to give an after-dinner speech to your former classmates at a high school reunion. You might good-naturedly tell a few stories about some of your old friends and teachers, but you'd also want to develop a theme. For instance, you might want to speak about how important those high school days were for everyone and how much you've all benefited from knowing each other.
- *Avoid presentation media.* Audiences for after-dinner speeches don't want to be sermonized, challenged too seriously, feel offended, or think they should be taking notes. Except for very special and limited purposes, speakers in these situations should avoid using presentation media. A brief audio or video segment might be appropriate for a speech that focuses on sports, media, music, or fashion, for instance, but even then, speakers must be careful. All the rules that apply to the use of presentation media (Chapter 11) pertain to the after-dinner speech in even greater measure, especially concerning the technical aspects. Unless the room is well equipped for presentation media, speakers should avoid using them.

Tributes and Eulogies

Sometimes people are honored for something they've done, for who they are, for where they've been in life, or for where they're headed. **Speeches of tribute** give credit, respect, admiration, gratitude, or inspiration to a person or group who has accomplished something significant, lives in a way that deserves to be praised, or is about to embark on an adventure. **Eulogies** are a special kind of speech of tribute presented as retrospectives about individuals who have died.

speech of tribute
Speech that gives credit, respect, admiration, gratitude, or inspiration to someone who has accomplished something significant, lives in a way that deserves to be praised, or is about to embark on an adventure.

eulogy
Speech of tribute presented as a retrospective about an individual who has died.

You may very well have occasion to give one or more of these speeches of tribute. Perhaps you've already done so. Weddings, anniversaries, retirements, school reunions, even family birthday parties or welcome home gatherings frequently call for speeches of tribute. The best man or maid of honor, or both, may be asked to give a brief tribute to a newly married couple. A returning veteran from a war zone might be praised by his best friend at a party in his honor. A successful classmate from high school might be recognized at a school reunion. The daughter of a couple celebrating their golden anniversary might speak about her parents' marriage.

You sometimes see and hear impassioned praise of famous people—past presidents, civil rights leaders, sports heroes, or entertainers, for instance—in eulogies that are shown on television and the web. But most eulogies take place much closer to home. Family members and friends often find it appropriate to eulogize deceased loved ones at funeral ceremonies. Eulogies not only praise or shed light on the person who has passed away but also help surviving family members and friends cope with the loss.

The rules for giving an effective speech of tribute are flexible. Some speeches are written in manuscript form and read to the audience, while others are presented extemporaneously. In either case, the speaker must be exceptionally well prepared. Responsibly accepting and executing the challenge of giving a speech of tribute or eulogy

SPEAKING OF ...

Online Tributes

A member of the various communities you belong to may become the subject of a tribute or a eulogy in the future. Even if you are not invited to speak at such an event, you could contribute a tribute or eulogy online. Several companies build and host websites where a speech of tribute or eulogy can be combined with other video, photos, music, and messages from relatives and friends. A Facebook app called Evertalk lets users create digital tributes and share memories of loved ones on the massive social media site. Web-based companies like BCelebrated.com encourage individuals to create legacy sites for themselves, a trend that will grow more and more popular over time.

is greatly appreciated by the audience and particularly rewarding for the speaker. You will enhance your speech of tribute by keeping the following suggestions in mind:

- *Emphasize emotion appropriately.* Tributes and eulogies often are quite emotional. The mood of the tribute depends on the occasion, but speeches of tribute are generally warm, friendly, and positive. After singer Whitney Houston died, her music director for 30 years, Rickey Minor, remembered the superstar in a very personal way:

  > Thirty years ago, I met this young girl with dreams of singing in the music business. And I was a young, 22-year-old hotshot bass player. I was going to show her a few things. And we were going to take the world by storm. . . .
  >
  > It didn't take me long to realize that I love Whitney Houston. Not because she's pretty, I mean she's pretty... That face, that smile, those eyes. But that's not why I love Whitney Houston. I mean, not because the girl can sing. The girl sang, alright? I mean what a voice. Not *a* voice, *the* voice.
  >
  > I love Whitney Houston . . . Could it be the dancing?. . . the hairstyles?. . . the outfits?. . . that smile?. . . that grace? I love Whitney Houston for all those reasons and so much more. Whitney Houston changed my life forever by entrusting me, Rickey from Monroe, Louisiana, with her music career.[9]

  Rickey Minor finished his tribute by recalling how he collaborated with Whitney Houston to produce her famous rendition of the national anthem at the Super Bowl during the Gulf War—which has been viewed more than 7 million times on YouTube.[10]

- *Provide inspiration.* Speeches of tribute often inspire the audience as well as praise the person being honored. Mexican American labor leader Cesar Chavez cofounded the United Farmworkers Union in California in the 1970s. He struggled all his life to improve the lives of immigrant farmworkers who were dying from cancer caused by pesticides sprayed onto crops the immigrants picked. Chavez's tribute to Dr. Martin Luther King, Jr., helped draw attention to the problem faced by immigrant farmworkers and brought about a long-term boycott of grapes:

  > The time for action is upon us. The enemies of justice want you to think of Dr. King as only a civil rights leader, but he had a much broader agency. He was a tireless crusader for... the rights of workers everywhere. My friends, the suffering must end. So many children are dying, so many babies are born without limbs and vital organs, so many workers are dying in the fields. We have no choice; we must stop the plague of pesticides.[11]

Bob Riha Jr/WireImage/Getty Images

Farmworker union leader Cesar Chavez was an inspiring public speaker.

Speeches of Nomination

Speeches of nomination focus on the qualifications or accomplishments of a particular person. **Nomination speeches** demonstrate why that person would be successful at something if given the chance.

For nomination speeches, a few simple guidelines apply. First, deciding on who does the nominating can be just as important as what is said about the nominee. For example, the person who nominates someone for an elected office, position, citation, prize, or award should him- or herself be well respected and liked by the people who will select a winner from a field of nominees.

nomination speech
Speech that demonstrates why a particular individual would be successful at something if given the chance.

The individual who seeks to be nominated for a position or prize usually asks a trusted friend or colleague to make the nomination speech on her or his behalf. At other times, an individual or group approaches a qualified person with the idea of nominating him or her. In either scenario, the speech of nomination can play a determining role in who gets elected or selected. Especially when the stakes are high, nomination speeches should be arranged well in advance. Here are some guidelines for any nomination speech you may give:

- *Be well informed.* The nominator must have accurate, concise, and compelling information about the nominee. Audience members want to know why they should consider a particular candidate favorably. What are the strongest reasons for choosing this person to serve in some capacity or be given recognition for something the nominee has accomplished? The speaker should justify the nomination in a way that creates absolute confidence among listeners that the nominated individual deserves the job or recognition.
- *Get the wording right.* Most nomination speeches are brief. When making a nomination, accurately and clearly identify the nominee, cite the best reasons for selecting the individual, personalize the candidate without being too informal, express confidence in how the nominee will perform, ask for the group's support, and thank the group. For instance, if you were nominating someone for treasurer of a school organization, you might say, "I nominate Rhea Salazar for treasurer of our club. Rhea is an excellent person for the position because she has earned top grades in all her accounting classes and has worked part-time as a bookkeeper for a local retail store. I've known Rhea for several years, and I've observed her dedication to the tasks she sets out to do. She's organized, detail-oriented, and a problem-solver. I know she'll serve our organization well. So please give her your support. Thank you."

Public Testimony

The American system of government and way of life depend on the willingness and ability of individuals to share their knowledge and voice their opinions in public meetings. Through **public testimony** you have many opportunities to participate in discussions that shape the policies that directly affect your world.

public testimony
Factual information and opinions about policy issues presented to government bodies or other public institutions.

Government bodies are usually required by law to consider public opinion during their deliberations. For instance, the mayor of San José, California, notified citizens of their right to express their views about the construction of a new soccer stadium in the city. Two main factions showed up at city council chambers to comment on the proposal: fans of the team, who strongly supported the idea, and families from the neighborhood where the stadium would be constructed, who were generally opposed to construction. Dozens spoke up. Each individual was given one minute to speak.

Don't think one minute is much time? By applying the principles of good speechmaking, you can say a lot in one minute.

- *Narrow your comments down to the basics.* Introduce yourself by name and state any relevant fact or affiliation you may have (for example, "I'm a coach in the Youth Soccer League" or "I live on a street where our quality of life will be directly affected by noise from the stadium.").
- *Contribute something original and useful.* Don't just say "I am in favor. It seems like a really good idea" or "I don't think we need a soccer stadium." If you

Paul Morigi/WireImage/Getty Images

Grammy Award–winning singer Shakira (at left) joins students seeking public support for legislation to establish basic education programs for children in poor nations.

have relevant information, provide it (for example, "New sports venues always stimulate the local economy" or "The freeway in our neighborhood is already loud, and noise is cumulative.").

- *Use key words and phrases you want your audience to remember.* For instance, one supporter of the stadium proposal said, "San José is a big city. Let's make it a *big-league* city. Build the stadium now!" An opponent said, "The stadium will be nothing more than a bright and noisy eyesore in the neighborhood we love!"

Roasts

Comedians are paid to be entertaining and funny, but the rest of us rarely have an opportunity to make a humorous presentation in public. A roast may be your only chance, so why not make the most of it? Although you may not immediately think of a roast as a public speech, it is a spoken-word performance before an audience.

The analogy suggested by the term *roast* fits this kind of public presentation. When you roast a piece of meat, you expose it to slow heat, usually in an oven. That's the idea behind a roast speech, too. The **roast** exposes a guest of honor to ironic and sometimes scathing (but never mean-spirited) remarks in front of others. The idea is to amuse an audience at the guest of honor's expense, but in a good-natured way.

roast
Humorous and good-natured ridicule directed toward the guest of honor at an event.

Speakers for roasts have two audiences—the person being roasted and everyone else in the room. You need to know the "roastee" well enough to come up with good material. Don't take that job lightly, even if you know the person well. Brainstorm. Jot down things you think the audience would also find funny or telling about the roastee. Select particular habits, personality quirks, or behaviors the audience would recognize and appreciate.

At the same time, remember that although you want to poke fun at the roastee, you don't want to humiliate the person or offend the audience. Use good judgment when deciding what to include in your comments—and what to leave out. People attend roasts because they like or appreciate the person being roasted. Because the object of the jokes is a real person, you have to know where to draw the line.

Although you don't have to go through all the steps for outlining a speech when preparing to give a roast, you still want to organize your ideas into a flow that makes sense. Develop a simple keyword outline on an index card, laptop, or tablet computer to prompt you from one comment or brief story to the next.

Concise stories that call attention to unique characteristics of the person being roasted often work well, but only if the audience recognizes the traits you plan to describe. Be sure to practice telling the stories before the event and keep them short. Don't write the stories down. The appeal of storytelling in this situation rests largely on its spontaneous nature, so practice beforehand and trust yourself to tell the story well.

Toasts

Whereas a roast makes good fun of the guest of honor, a **toast** unabashedly celebrates the person or persons being toasted. Although a funny anecdote or comment might be appropriate as part of the toast, consider the seriousness of the occasion. For example, although wedding receptions are often fun and can include lots of humorous moments, weddings are important rituals. These occasions demand an extra level of sensitivity and preparation on the part of the people making the toasts. Whatever you do, don't grab some prewritten, generic toast off the Internet. Use your own thoughts and words. When preparing your remarks for a toast, keep these ideas in mind:

toast
Brief remarks celebrating the accomplishments of a guest of honor at an event.

- *Keep your remarks short and upbeat.* Don't tell stories that only you and the toastee know about, especially not at a wedding; you may think the story is hilarious, but most of the audience won't get it. Stay focused on the person or the couple being toasted and the reason for their being celebrated. If a microphone will be used, coordinate your performance with the technical person in charge and check sound levels ahead of time if possible.[12]
- *Rules for the ritual.* The person giving the toast should stand, and the person being toasted should remain seated. Refer to the person being toasted by name, briefly say something about your relationship to that person, and mention the occasion for which the person is being toasted. Wait until the last second to raise your glass and then finish up with something encouraging or inspiring like, "We are all very proud of you, Charles, and wish you great success in the future. Cheers!"

Roasts and toasts are among the most common public presentations people are asked to make. Welcome the chance to roast or toast your friends or colleagues. Although it's certainly an honor to be the person or persons recognized on these special occasions, it's also a privilege to speak about them—a privilege that comes with responsibility.

The Elevator Speech

No matter what someone's career status or goals are, every serious person should be able to spontaneously give a very brief presentation that impressively explains who you are, what you do, or what you would like to do professionally. On some occasions—like a social gathering or networking event—you should expect to have chances to make a quick presentation; you might even attend a party or function specifically to make your pitch. At other times an opportunity to do so might present itself unexpectedly.

You don't ever want to be caught in a situation fumbling around for the right words when you have a brief moment to tell someone about your current work, an idea you have, or desired employment. So the idea behind the **elevator speech** is that any individual ought to be able to describe her or his work, present an idea, or give a potential employer a positive impression in the amount of time it takes an elevator to descend in a building from the top to the bottom floor—30 to 60 seconds.

elevator speech
Very brief presentation that impressively explains who the person is, what he or she does, or what the individual would like to do professionally.

The basic principles of persuasive speaking apply to these very short, high-impact presentations. You want to get the "audience's" attention, establish your credibility, provide interesting content, and make a call to action. Here are two examples of undergraduate student elevator speeches suggested by the Career Center at the University of Oregon:[13]

> Hi, my name is Samantha Atcheson, and I am a senior Environmental Sciences major. I'm looking for a position that will allow me to use my research and analysis skills. Over the past few years, I've been strengthening these skills through my work with a local watershed council on conservation strategies to support water quality and habitats. Eventually, I'd like develop education programs on water-conservation awareness. I read that your organization is involved in water-quality projects. Can you tell me how someone with my experience may fit into your organization?

> Nice to meet you, I'm Alex Biondo. I'm currently a senior and am studying Computer and Information Science. I hope to become a computer programmer when I graduate. I've had a couple of internships where I worked on several program applications with a project team. I enjoy developing computer applications for simple business solutions. The position you have listed in UO-JobLink seems like it would be a perfect fit for someone with my skills. I'd like to hear more about the type of project teams you have in your organization.

Distance Speaking

Successful public speakers today adapt traditional presentational skills to nontraditional communication settings and situations like online meetings and events. The fundamental principles and techniques of traditional public speaking still apply to online presenting, but in today's communication environment we need to develop fresh ways of thinking and new skills.

distance speaking
The planned and structured presentation of ideas transmitted from one physical location to other locations by means of information and communications technology.

internal communication
The exchange of messages within an organization.

videoconference
Allows people at two or more locations to communicate interactively by means of simultaneous video and audio transmission.

The ability of communications technology to overcome barriers posed by geographical and cultural distance provides speakers with many new opportunities to expand their public speaking skills.[14] **Distance speaking** refers to the planned and structured presentation of ideas transmitted from one physical location to other locations by means of information and communications technology.

Many of the most useful applications of technology for distance speaking take place at the institutional level. Businesses, educational institutions, governments, nongovernmental organizations (NGOs), and civic organizations all use technology in ways that establish new forms and patterns of **internal communication**—the exchange of messages within the organization.[15] The CEO of a multinational corporation, for instance, might introduce a new business plan by means of an encrypted intranet interactive video presentation that thousands of employees in various locations can watch and respond to on their computers—on site or at home, in real time or later. Or anthropology graduate students from universities around the world can gather in a virtual meeting room every week to collectively analyze the findings of their team fieldwork.

Hero Images/Getty Images

Videoconferences allow individuals in remote locations to participate in presentations and meetings.

Videoconferences

A **videoconference** allows people at two or more locations to communicate interactively by means of simultaneous video and audio transmission. The popularity of videoconferencing even at the global level has increased dramatically in recent years.[16]

With cameras standard on personal computers, tablets, and smartphones, video chat and other forms of online video communication have become commonplace for many kinds of meetings and group presentations, even very informal events.[17] In many institutional settings, studio-quality video technology has been installed in meeting rooms to facilitate videoconferences. Like all successful presentations, effective videoconferencing requires careful planning and preparation.

Sometimes videoconferences take asymmetrical form. In these cases, an individual makes a presentation much like a speech or lecture to other participants in the online conference or meeting. The "audience members" listen and ask questions in a manner that approximates the student-teacher relationship in distance learning. Other kinds of videoconferences are more symmetrical. A boss or manager, for instance, might lead a meeting where she or he calls on several individuals to present informational reports or give their opinions about the topic under discussion. Participants can jump in at various junctures during the meeting to contribute to the discussion or ask questions of the other "presenters."

Videoconferences today can be quite dynamic. Television and web technology make it easy to cut back and forth between speaker and graphical material or project multi-screen images that show participants and graphics simultaneously. Today's high-definition, life-size TV images and broadband fiber-optic audio make videoconferencing much more realistic and appealing than ever before.

Graphical Online Presentations

Although videoconferences usually take for granted that participants will be visible, much distance speaking today does not make that assumption. The other major form of distance speaking, a **graphical online presentation**, is a graphics-based talk delivered to an audience by computer and the Internet where the speaker is heard but does not appear on the screen.

graphical online presentation Graphics-based talk delivered by someone using a computer and the Internet where the speaker does not appear on the screen.

Many graphical online presentations take place in virtual meetings held by businesses, governments, and other modern organizations around the world. To facilitate a graphical online presentation, every participant's computer is linked to a shared web address so everyone sees the same visuals. Participants dial in on a special phone number or connect by online audio—Voice over Internet Protocol (VoIP)—in order to establish voice contact with everyone else. After the conference begins, the group leader calls on someone to present. That person launches a sequence of prepared slides on the web and speaks simultaneously over the telephone or VoIP connection. Virtual presentations like this become a series of digital slides that are narrated by an unseen speaker.

Videoconferences and graphical online presentations frequently involve participation by people who already know each other personally or share something important, like working for the same company, government agency, or nongovernmental organization. When conducted effectively, mediated meetings can be even more interactive than face-to-face conferences.[18] Individual videoconferences and online presentations often form part of a regular, ongoing series of virtual meetings, so participants frequently get to know each other quite well in the process, though they may never meet in person.

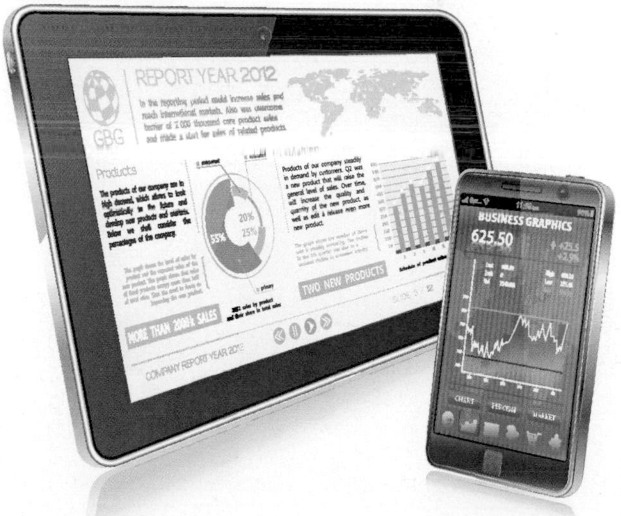

TAlex/Fotolia LLC

Participants in videoconferences and online graphical presentations can view digital slides in full screen, even on mobile devices.

Telephone Meetings

It's actually often better in distance speaking for participants *not* to see each other, and frequently there is no need for the use of graphics either. Lots of important ideas and

telephone meeting Group meetings facilitated by telephone that help members exchange ideas, solve problems, make assignments, set deadlines, and arrange schedules.

information can be presented vocally over the telephone. But can we consider vocal participation in a group meeting over the telephone really a "speech"? It certainly helps to think of it that way. Do we need to prepare and practice for a **telephone meeting**? Yes!

Telephone meetings involving multiple participants can be extremely good ways to get feedback on ideas, clarify issues for team members, suggest ways to solve problems, make assignments, set deadlines, and arrange schedules. Telephone meetings keep everyone in touch with each other, helping to make sure everyone has the same information as they begin or continue work on a project. Talking with each other keeps people engaged not only about the work being done, but with each other as people. Good human relationships invariably improve the quality of any shared task. Communication is the key to making that positive development happen.

For all these reasons, many organizations schedule regular, frequent telephone meetings. If you are asked to participate, you should be ready to perform effectively during these calls. Know what will be expected of you beforehand. Develop an informal presentation or keyword outline to keep close at hand during the call. Practice out loud ways of concisely expressing your views with impact before the call begins. During the phone meeting, listen attentively to everything that is being said so you can offer relevant input or respond to questions directed to you or to the group.

You will very likely become a participant in distance speaking in whatever profession you enter, if you're not doing so already. By applying the principles of effective public speaking to these less formal but equally important occasions, you'll make your participation in videoconferences, graphical online presentations, and telephone meetings more valuable to others and more rewarding to yourself (**Table 16.1**).

Table 16.1 **Distance Speaking Types and Advantages**

Type	Advantages
Videoconferences	Flexible: allows for speech or interactive meeting Popular, familiar form Speaker and slides visible Very engaging for participants Vocal and nonverbal cues revealed Creates professional aura Realistic, high definition Slides can be shared Event can be archived
Graphical online presentations	Emphasizes visual detail Less formal than videoconference Less technologically demanding Realistic, high definition Slides can be shared Event can be archived
Telephone meetings	Inexpensive: minimal technology needed Less formal: speaker not visible Spontaneous; less setup needed Good for planning, scheduling, assigning tasks Unlimited number of possible participants Participants can drop in and out easily as needed Helps maintain professional working relationships

Guidelines for Distance Speaking

What might a typical videoconference or graphical online presentation situation look like? Imagine that you work as a graphic designer for an advertising agency. You've been brainstorming with your colleagues in marketing to develop an approach for a television advertising campaign to launch a new product for your client. You've created what you and your bosses think is an effective concept.

Now it's time for you to present your design ideas to the client for approval. The agency manager, marketing director, sales manager, media production supervisor, and the client, all in different locations, maybe even in different countries, meet with you by videoconference. Acting as host of the meeting, the agency manager calls on you to present your series of graphical images—a storyboard that shows what the television commercials would look like if they were to be produced. After being introduced by your boss, you explain the overall concept of the campaign vocally and then show and describe each slide. That kind of performance is what anyone who takes part in a videoconference would be expected to do.

Preparation and Practice Just because you don't normally stand in front of a live audience when taking part in a videoconference or graphical online presentation doesn't mean you don't have to prepare just as thoroughly. In some respects, you'll have to prepare more rigorously than you would for a classroom speech or public presentation.

Just like good classroom speakers, successful online presenters prepare their slides well in advance. The basic principles of visual design for classroom presentations remain the same when transmitting visuals online (Chapter 11). But some additional rules apply.

Online audiences tend to tune out speakers unless something interesting is happening on the screen. Do everything you can to avoid boring your audience by making the slides visually captivating. Minimal text, easy-to-read fonts, clean and clear graphical material, compelling images, and complementary colors, etc., will help.

When designing slides, leave ample space on the margins so that none of your information gets lost because of browser differences. Be sensitive to how you format the images, especially if your audience will be using mobile devices. Then, configure, upload, and practice with your slides well in advance of your presentation. Test annotation tools, make speaker notes, and prepare any URLs or other applications you intend to share with the group beforehand.

Visuals suffer when the audio goes bad. Make sure you are using a quality microphone and, if using VoIP, that your Internet speed and connection are sufficient. Good presenters in any situation prepare note cards based on a keyword outline and rehearse their entire speech—including remarks to be made when visuals are displayed. Expect some nervousness, of course, just as you would before a classroom speech. Manage your anxiety by using the re-labeling, visualization, and breathing techniques described in Chapter 2.

Successful Presenting Unless you are simply going to give a speech by standing or sitting in front of a video camera, the success of your distance presentation will depend largely on how well you establish rapport with your audience, the quality of your visual material, how well you display it, and how effectively you come across vocally during the presentation. Not surprisingly, research shows that individuals who are better prepared for their videoconference session have a much more positive and productive experience.[19]

Create a comfortable environment for the audience from the start by describing your goals for the presentation, reviewing the basics of the tool being used to present, and, depending on the purpose of the event, encouraging active audience engagement. To ensure speed and machine compatibility, ask all participants to close other applications they may have running on their computers or smart devices before you begin.

Make sure to use a quality microphone and, if using VoIP, that your Internet speed is sufficient and your connection is good. Especially when your audience is large (20 or more participants), insist that participants' VoIP or phone connection be muted to avoid background noise, except, of course, when you solicit vocal feedback from your audience. Check to be sure everyone can see the opening visual and can hear you easily.

During the presentation speak clearly and with sufficient volume into the microphone or telephone. Online presentations are often made to speakers of diverse languages. Stay away from colloquialisms, humor, or local examples they won't understand. Speak somewhat more slowly, but not to the point where you appear to be simplifying so as to be understood. Use language that travels understandably from one language or cultural group to another.[20]

Just as in classroom presentations, never just say what's on the screen. Provide important detail to fill out and strengthen the ideas that are summarized in the visuals. To liven up the visuals, annotate the slides as you speak by using circling and highlighting techniques. Incorporating video or launching a live website during a presentation also helps break the monotony of slide-based presentations.

To stimulate active involvement from your audience, encourage the participants to use the various interactive tools at their disposal. The "question manager" and "hands up" features for participants in web-based meetings, for instance, facilitate smooth interactions between the speaker and others in the group. Speakers can ask audience members to share files, go into break-out sessions, or take part in task-oriented, timed events conducted within the framework of the presentation. If possible, keep track of how the audience is reacting to your presentation as you go along by setting up sidestream survey questions that allow participants to discretely give you feedback while you speak. Adjust your presentation accordingly.

Social media can help keep audience members engaged in online presentations too. For instance, speakers can team up with experts to provide the audience with a twitter handle so they can tweet about your presentation. In this way participants can ask questions or comment on your presentation and the topic in real time. This backchannel capacity encourages participation by audience members who may be reluctant to speak up vocally.[21] If a social media integration like this is not possible, speakers can use the chat feature available on most online presentation software to encourage immediate feedback and interaction among participants.

As You Conclude Many online presentations take place in professional or vocational contexts, so participants are usually motivated to take away something that is truly useful from the experience. Encourage participants to ask questions after you present, especially the ones who are less likely to speak up. Be ready to provide additional information and resources participants might need or want for their work. The question-and-answer session that follows your formal remarks in online presentations should serve to make sure everyone's expectations are met.

Just as audience members have ethical responsibilities to the speaker and to each other in classrooms and other offline settings, so too must they participate responsibly in videoconferences and other kinds of online presentations. If you are an audience member, ask questions. Provide clarifying comments. Support good ideas. Demonstrate appreciation for good work and impressive presentations.

Presenting in Small Groups

With the popularity of partnerships and teams in organizations on the rise, you'll encounter many situations that require you to work with others and then present information as a group to an in-person audience.[22] Group presentations usually involve both interacting within the group and speaking to those outside the group. A **small group** is a collection of individuals who interact and depend on one another to solve a problem, make a decision, or achieve another common goal.

Effective group presentations emphasize group rather than individual effort. So when preparing your group's presentation, focus on the way you fit together as a cohesive whole. In addition to the qualities expected in any excellent oral presentation—that it be well researched, audience centered, and effectively delivered—the performance should truly reflect a group endeavor.[23] The coherence of your group's performance will rest on how well prepared you are as a group, how well you coordinate the presentation, how effectively you listen to each other and to the audience, how many clear references you make to the group, and how well you achieve your group's goal together.

Working in groups in a classroom setting and giving group presentations will prepare you for participating in team-based organizations and other professional contexts.[24] For example, your instructor might assign some kind of group presentation in your public speaking class. This section explains how to give five types of traditional group presentations.

MindTap®

Watch It: View a video on giving group presentations.

small group
A collection of individuals who interact and depend on one another to solve a problem, make a decision, or achieve a common goal or objective.

Panel Discussion

You've likely viewed **panel discussions** on campus or television. A moderator or facilitator asks questions to direct the group's interaction, which occurs in front of an audience. Group members are experts on the subject and know beforehand what will be covered. The moderator provides an introduction, giving an overview of the topic and stating the purpose of the discussion. The moderator may then briefly recite each person's credentials or ask panelists to introduce themselves. The moderator or facilitator then also assumes primary responsibility for the smooth flow of discussion.

Although panel discussions are not rehearsed, they are not entirely impromptu either. Participants often refer to notes during the discussion. Some questions may be unexpected and the responses spontaneous. Still, participants prepare carefully and don't simply "wing it" during the discussion. Listeners expect group members to avoid interrupting or talking over each other, and each speaker should provide a smooth transition to the next presenter. Some standardization among the speakers gives the audience an impression of continuity and prior planning.[25] An effective opening overview and closing summary give the presentation a sense of cohesion.[26]

panel discussion
A discussion in which a moderator asks questions of experts on a topic in front of an audience.

Round-Table Discussion

Unlike panel discussions, **round-table discussions** do not have audiences—only the group members are present. All group members participate in the discussion, which may or may not have a leader or facilitator. Because speakers are experts on the topic, responses are impromptu. Nevertheless, speakers arrive prepared, knowing the

round-table discussion
A discussion in which expert participants discuss a topic in an impromptu format without an audience present.

topic and often the other participants, too. Round-table discussions often address a challenge that faces a community. The discussions rely on a free flow of information among speakers that produces possible solutions to the challenge that has been identified.

The setting for a round-table discussion is generally informal, with speakers sitting in a circle to facilitate dialogue and engaged participation. The facilitator or host first describes the purpose of the discussion, outlines procedures for conducting the round table, and sets a time limit. At the conclusion of the event, the facilitator or host summarizes the main themes that emerged from the discussion and indicates what will be done with the information. In addition, the discussion is recorded or someone is assigned to take notes so the information participants generate can be used at a later date.

Round-table discussions provide a means for individuals to exchange information and ideas about a topic of common interest. All discussants are encouraged to participate, maximizing the opportunity to consider different points of view on the subject. Sometimes round-table discussions are convened to generate new ideas or create innovative approaches to a problem. For example, in an effort to develop strategies for stimulating the local economy, the *Akron Beacon Journal* brought together local experts to discuss promoting entrepreneurship, small-business growth, and start-up businesses in northeastern Ohio. The product of that round-table discussion was a list of recommendations distributed to community leaders.[27]

Symposium

symposium
A presentation format in which each member of a group presents a speech about a part of a larger topic.

If you're giving a group presentation in your public speaking class, you're probably using a symposium format. In a **symposium**, the group chooses a topic and divides it into different areas. Each group member then presents a speech on the subtopic assigned to him or her. For example, your group might choose popular music and identify hip-hop, country, metal, and alternative rock as the subtopics. Speakers usually follow the same organizational pattern in order to provide continuity among the speeches. In the music example, each speaker might discuss the music genre's history, identify two or three key artists or groups, and provide a few musical examples.

Symposiums require the most preparation as a group. Planning the format thoroughly in advance is essential. For example, group members must discuss whether or not to use a podium, the formality of their attire, the presentation media they may use, how they will structure their speeches, how they will open and close the symposium, and how they will transition from one speaker to the next.

Although group members talk about their own particular subtopics, those subtopics must form a coherent whole in the overall presentation. For example, suppose a group chooses the topic of unusual team sports such as canoe polo, curling, and korfball as the subtopics. Before beginning in-depth research, group members must agree on the main points they'll cover in their speeches. Each one might, for instance, talk about his or her sport's general description, history, and what makes it especially unique or interesting. Once the groundwork for the symposium is complete, group members work independently to prepare their individual speeches. In the later stages of speech preparation, group members practice together and make any necessary adjustments.

The group should avoid having one person discussing only history, another covering only how the game is played, and a third focusing solely on why the audience might want to learn how to play the game. Clear references to the group provide mechanisms for linking together the parts of any group presentation. In a symposium, a speaker might say, "As Sheila remarked in her presentation. . . " or "Similar to what Marco found. . ." These comments help demonstrate how the different pieces of the presentation fit together.

Marcin Balcerzak/Shutterstock.com

Although only one group member delivers an oral report, it's a good idea for members to work together to prepare the report. This ensures that the entire group contributes to the speech and can help answer questions after the formal presentation.

Oral Report

When a group presents an **oral report**, one representative from the group gives the entire report. Various members of an organization's work team develop the report, and then one group member presents the findings to the audience.

Effective oral reports clearly recognize the contributions of all group members. The speaker might refer to specific aspects of the project individual group members worked on. These brief acknowledgments personalize the report and indicate how different members of the group contributed to the project. The speaker should use pronouns such as *we* and *us* to indicate that the group, rather than the individual, produced the report. In addition, the speaker makes specific references to group members or units in the organization that wrote the report in order to acknowledge everyone's contributions. The speaker must be fully versed in all aspects of the report ahead of time, asking group members for clarification where needed.

oral report
A report in which one member of a group presents the group's findings.

forum
The question-and-answer session following a group's formal presentation.

The oral report format provides consistency and smooth transitions between the sections of a presentation. Oral reports avoid the inherent disruptions associated with each team member taking a turn at speaking. Audience members need only orient themselves to one person's speaking style.

Forum

After listening to a panel discussion round table, symposium, or oral report, audience members often want to ask questions. The question-and-answer session that follows a formal group presentation is a **forum**. In these situations, the main speaker or group members must listen attentively and be ready to answer audience members' questions thoroughly and honestly, just as they would after individual speeches.

Coordinating group members' responses can prove challenging in forums because you don't want to appear disorganized or unsure of your answers. When appropriate, decide before the presentation which group members will handle which question areas. Choose someone to facilitate the forum. After a panel discussion or round table, the facilitator would probably also serve as the moderator. In symposiums, anyone who participated may lead the question-and-answer session. For oral reports, the group may choose the presenter or ask another group member to coordinate the responses. Group members should decide in advance who is responsible for questions in specific topic areas. This avoids two problems: (1) several group members responding to a question at the same time and (2) all group members having blank looks with no one responding. Here

SPEAKING OF ...

Effective Listening

Effective listening plays a key role in the success of any group presentation. No matter what the setting, group members should display active listening skills, such as giving the speaker their complete attention, nodding, looking at the speaker, taking brief notes, and showing interest in what each speaker has to say. During the group performance, individual members should not work on their own presentations, talk or whisper with each other, or check their mobile devices.

Careful listening is especially important in round-table and panel discussions because participants likely do not know exactly what others will say. Appropriately responding to other speakers requires close attention to the discussion. In addition, round-table and panel discussions typically include speakers with different—often opposing—viewpoints, making critical listening essential. In these types of group presentations, audience members expect participants to carefully examine other speakers' ideas and supporting evidence.

ZUMA Press Inc/Alamy Stock Photo

A forum is the question-and-answer session that follows a formal group presentation.

are some tips that will help you and others in your group establish rapport with the audience in a forum:

- Maintain good eye contact with the questioner. A head nod or smile makes the questioner feel appreciated and listened to.
- When listening to a question, quickly make a note that reflects the questioner's concern or is something you or another person in the group wants to say in response.
- Thank the questioner and don't become defensive, even when responding to hostile questions. (And as an audience member asking a question, be sure not to disrespect the speaker or the position taken.)

Summary

Many special occasions call for some type of speech. Speeches of introduction prepare the audience to listen to the main speaker. Speakers accepting awards make brief comments to show thanks and demonstrate humility. After-dinner speeches are meant to entertain. Tributes and eulogies respect the person being honored and often provide inspiration. Speeches of nomination focus on the qualities that make the nominee the best person for the position or award. Public testimony allows speakers to participate in discussions that shape policies that affect their world. Roasts amuse an audience at the guest of honor's expense in a good-natured way. Toasts celebrate another person. Elevator speeches concisely promote an individual's professional interests.

Today's communications technology makes it possible for speakers to connect with audiences that don't share the same physical space. Distance speaking allows people at two or more locations to communicate interactively by means of simultaneous video and audio transmission. Businesses, educational institutions, governments, nongovernmental organizations, and civic organizations use videoconferences and graphical online presentations to exchange messages internally and externally. Telephone meetings involving multiple participants can also help organizations solve problems and keep projects on track. All distance learning applications require a level of preparation and performance that is very similar to preparing and giving speeches to a live, in-person audience.

Groups may give several types of in-person presentations, including a panel discussion, round-table discussion, symposium, oral report, or forum. Panel discussions involve a moderator asking questions of experts on a topic in front of an audience. Round-table discussions also include expert speakers but focus on an exchange of ideas among participants, so an audience is not present. Symposiums are the most common form of classroom group presentations where participants each present a subtopic of the group's overall subject to an audience. For an oral report, one member of the group presents the entire report. Forums are question-and-answer sessions that may stand alone or occur after an oral report, panel discussion, or symposium.

ANALYZE IT

Tara, My Grandfather, John Flanagan Sr.

Tara gave this speech of tribute in an introductory public speaking class at Colorado State University. Her assignment was to give a three- to five-minute commemorative speech about a person she admired. As you read Tara's speech, consider how effective her use of language is and how well she commemorates her grandfather.

As I wiped the streams that flooded down my face, I saw out of the corner of my eye a group of homeless men enter the room. My sadness turned to anger as I watched these uninvited guests interrupt *my grandfather's* funeral. They were like unwanted ants invading a family picnic. After our pastor concluded his eulogy, I went to the back of the room to ask them to leave. "Excuse me," I said, "but this is my grandfather's funeral, and only invited guests are allowed inside." And one of the men looked at me, and he said, "You must be Tara. Your grandfather carried a picture of you in his wallet." Much to my surprise, these homeless men were friends of my grandfather. My grandfather was never a good judge of people. He was just better at not judging them at all.

As I walked around the room, I saw many people that neither my family nor I recognized, but each one of them had a story on how my grandfather had touched them with his love and kindness. My grandfather was a loving, brave man with an amazing sense of humor, and these virtues never shone brighter for me than they did on the day of his funeral.

From the funeral home, our entourage headed to the cemetery to place my grandfather in his final resting place. It was a hot July day, and the sun was just pounding down on our car. We were following the white hearse when all of the sudden it stopped, and this terrible, white smoke began billowing out of the hood. It laid there like a huge, immovable beached whale.

My father began laughing as the cars piled up behind us, and he said, "I bet your grandfather had something to do with this." My grandfather had an amazing sense of humor. This incident reminded us of the many jokes he told and pulled on our family. Making his own hearse break down on the day of his funeral to give us all a good laugh wasn't beyond him.

MindTap®

Watch and analyze this speech on MindTap.

I remembered a time when my grandfather cheered me up when I was younger. I was visiting my father for the summer, and I was incredibly homesick. I missed my mom and my sister very badly. He spent the entire afternoon telling me silly knock-knock jokes and doing random things just to make me laugh. And I remember feeling so much better. My homesickness melted away. My grandfather always had a way of making our family laugh and feel better, and the day of his funeral was no exception.

When we finally got the white whale back on the road, we drove into the lush cemetery. There were flowers blossoming and a gentle stream that ran through the middle. It was like a scene out of the Garden of Eden. There to greet us were several gentlemen dressed in their Marine best. They carried with them large guns and gave my grandfather his twenty-one–gun salute. After the service I spoke with them, and they told me of my grandfather's bravery while he served in World War II. One of the men had actually served with my grandfather. He told me a story about how my grandfather had saved his life, and they ended up being the only two men out of the entire platoon to survive. At the end of the war they even saw the famous raising of the flag at Iwo Jima.

Living, laughing, loving life: My grandfather was an amazing man who taught me so much about humor, courage, and compassion. Even though his funeral was the saddest day of my life, I was uplifted by all the lives that he had touched. I hope that someday I can learn to love people more than I judge them, just like he did.

Questions for Discussion

1. Tributes should shed light on the individual being praised. After reading Tara Flanagan's speech about her grandfather, do you feel you learned important things about him? What things stand out in your mind?
2. How did Tara use emotion to enhance the quality of her speech? Were the emotional elements she used appropriate for this speech? How did they help you appreciate her grandfather?
3. Tributes can inspire the audience to think about something in a different way. Her introductory story about the presence of uninvited guests at her grandfather's funeral was an attempt to do this. What was she trying to accomplish by telling that story?
4. Tara said she wanted to impart a sense of her grandfather's compassion, humor, and courage in her tribute to him. Did she provide enough material in the speech to accomplish this three-part objective?

APPLY IT . . .

IN THE WORKPLACE

The Multipurpose Elevator Speech

A well-crafted elevator speech doesn't just help college graduates looking for a good job, it also helps people make a favorable impression after they've settled into a vocational and professional situation. In a very concise way, the elevator speech embodies much of what you're learning about effective communication in your public speaking class. Knowing how to create a good elevator speech can also help you contribute something important in meetings, consultations, panel discussions, videoconferences, and any occasion in the workplace when you have a limited amount of time to positively affect others with your information and ideas. Keep these guidelines in mind: economy of language, enthusiastic delivery, focused ideas, and an action plan.

If you've already crafted an elevator speech in preparation for a job interview, review it in light of these guidelines. If you don't have such a speech ready, prepare one, and ask yourself: How can I adapt my elevator speech to different situations? Can I make it more concise? Give it more impact? Tighten its focus? And make crystal clear what my goal is?

> REVIEW IT

Key Terms

acceptance speech 341
after dinner speech 342
distance speaking 348
elevator speech 347
eulogy 343
forum 355
graphical online presentation 349
internal communication 348
nomination speech 345
oral report 355
panel discussion 353
public testimony 345
roast 346
round-table discussion 353
small group 353
speech of introduction 340
speech of tribute 343
symposium 354
telephone meeting 350
toast 347
videoconference 348

MindTap®
Use flashcards to learn key terms and take a quiz to test your knowledge.

Reflecting on Special Occasion, Distance, and Group Speaking

1. Which types of speeches for special occasions can you imagine yourself giving? Why?
2. How might you use distance speaking methods—videoconferences, graphical online presentations, and telephone meetings—in the line of work you plan to be in or in which you are currently employed?
3. In what ways does distance speaking resemble traditional public speaking in front of a live audience? Explain the steps you'd take to make a successful presentation during a videoconference.
4. The moderator or facilitator of a small group presentation plays a vital role in the coordination and performance of the group. What specific responsibilities does the moderator–facilitator have for panel discussions, symposiums, oral reports, and forums?

Glossary

acceptance speech Speech given by an individual who is being recognized, honored, or given an award.

ad hominem fallacy Argument in which a speaker rejects another speaker's claim based on that speaker's character rather than the evidence the speaker presents; also called the *against the person* fallacy.

ad ignorantiam fallacy Argument in which a speaker suggests that because a claim hasn't been shown to be false, it must be true; also called an *appeal to ignorance.*

ad populum fallacy Argument in which a speaker appeals to popular attitudes and emotions without offering evidence to support claims.

After-dinner speech Speech given after a meal designed to add something light-hearted and pleasurable to the occasion.

alliteration Repetition of a sound in a series of words, usually the first consonant.

analogical reasoning Comparing two similar objects, processes, concepts, or events and suggesting that what holds true for one also holds true for the other.

analogy A type of comparison that describes something by comparing it to something else that it resembles.

anecdote A brief narrative.

antithesis Juxtaposition of two apparently contradictory phrases that are organized in a parallel structure.

apathetic audience An audience that is informed about a speaker's topic but not interested in it.

appeals to cultural beliefs Use of values and beliefs embedded in cultural narratives or stories to influence an audience; also called *mythos.*

appeals to speaker credibility Creating a perception of the speaker as competent, trustworthy, dynamic, and likeable to influence an audience; also known as *ethos.*

appeal to tradition fallacy Argument in which a speaker asserts that the status quo is better than any new idea or approach.

argument Presenting claims and supporting them with evidence and reasoning.

arrangement The way ideas presented in a speech are organized.

articulation The physical process of producing specific speech sounds to make language intelligible.

attention getter The first element of an introduction, designed mainly to create interest in a speech.

attitude How an individual feels about something.

audience-centered Describes a speaker who acknowledges the audience by considering and listening to the diverse and common perspectives of its members before, during, and after the speech.

audience-research questionnaire A questionnaire used by speakers to assess the knowledge and opinions of audience members; can take the form of email, web-based, or in-class surveys.

audience analysis Obtaining and evaluating information about your audience in order to anticipate its members' needs and interests and designing a strategy to respond to them.

audience centered Acknowledging an audience's expectations and situations before, during, and after a speech.

audience The intended recipients of a speaker's message.

begging the question Argument in which a speaker uses a premise to imply the truth of the conclusion or asserts that the validity of the conclusion is self-evident; also called *circular reasoning.*

belief Something an individual accepts as true or existing.

bibliographic information A source's complete citation, including author, date of publication, title, place of publication, and publisher.

body The middle and main part of a speech; includes main and subordinate points.

brainstorming The free-form generation of ideas for speech topics and content in which individuals think of and record ideas without immediately evaluating them.

call number The number assigned to each book or bound publication in a library to identify that book in the library's classification system.

captive audience Individuals who feel they must attend an event.

causal reasoning Linking two events or actions to claim that one resulted in the other.

cause-and-effect pattern A pattern that organizes a speech by showing how an action produces a particular outcome.

channel A mode or medium of communication.

chronological pattern A pattern that organizes a speech by how something develops or occurs in a time sequence.

claim A position or assertion that a speaker wants an audience to accept.

cliché An expression so overused it fails to have any important meaning.

closed-ended question A question that limits the possible responses, asking for very specific information.

coercion Forcing someone to think a certain way or making someone feel compelled to act under pressure or threat.

coherence An obvious and plausible connection among ideas.

communication climate The psychological and emotional tone that develops as communicators interact with one another.

comparative evidence fallacy Argument in which a speaker uses statistics or compares numbers in ways that misrepresent the evidence and mislead the audience.

competence The qualifications a speaker has to talk about a particular topic.

complete-sentence outline A formal outline using full sentences for all points developed after researching the speech and identifying supporting materials; includes a speech's topic, general purpose, specific purpose, thesis, introduction, main points, subpoints, conclusion, transitions, and references.

conclusion A primary claim or assertion.

conclusion The end of a speech, in which the speaker reviews the main points, reinforces the purpose, and provides closure.

connotative meaning A unique meaning for a word based on an individual's own experiences.

context The situation within which a speech is given.

convergence When people interact in multiple communications spheres simultaneously.

copyright A type of intellectual property law that protects an author's original work (such as a play, book, song, or movie) from being used by others.

copyright information A statement about the legal rights of others to use an original work, such as a song (lyrics and melody), story, poem, photograph, or image.

credibility An audience's perception of a speaker's competence, trustworthiness, dynamism, and sociability.

cultural norms Prescriptions for how people should interact and what messages should mean in a particular setting.

deductive reasoning Reasoning from a general condition to a specific case.

definition A statement that describes the essence, precise meaning, or scope of a word or a phrase.

delivery The public presentation of a speech.

demographics The ways in which populations can be divided into smaller groups according to key characteristics such as, gender, ethnicity, age, and social class.

denotative meaning An agreed-upon definition of a word found in a dictionary.

dialect The vocabulary, grammar, and pronunciation used by a specific group of people, such as an ethnic or regional group.

dialogue Occurs when communicators are sensitive to each other's needs and communicative goals, actively listen, and respond appropriately and effectively.

digital divide The gap between groups that have a high level of access to and use of digital communications technology and groups that have a low level of access and use.

direct quote Comments written in response to open-ended questions in an audience-research questionnaire.

distance speaking The planned and structured presentation of ideas transmitted from one physical location to other locations by means of information and communications technology.

divided audience An audience that is informed about a speaker's topic but equally split between those who favor the speaker's position and those who oppose it.

division fallacy Argument in which a speaker assumes that what is true of the whole is also true of the parts that make up the whole.

document cameras A projection device that uses a video camera to capture and display images.

dynamism An audience's perception of a speaker's activity level during a presentation.

elevator speech Very brief presentation that impressively explains who the person is, what he or she does, or what the individual would like to do professionally.

emotional appeals Use of emotional evidence and stimulation of feelings to influence an audience; also known as *pathos*.

enthymemes An argument in which a premise or conclusion is unstated.

environment The external surroundings that influence a public speaking event.

ethnocentrism The belief that your worldview, based on your cultural background, is superior to others' worldviews.

ethos Appeals to the speaker's credibility.

eulogy Speech of tribute presented as a retrospective about an individual who has died.

euphemism A word used in place of another word that is viewed as more disagreeable or offensive.

event A significant occurrence that an individual personally experiences or otherwise knows about.

evidence Supporting materials—narratives, examples, definitions, testimony, facts, and statistics—that a speaker presents to reinforce a claim.

example An illustration or case that represents a larger group or class of things.

extemporaneous speaking A type of public speaking in which the speaker researches, organizes, rehearses, and delivers a speech in a way that combines structure and spontaneity.

external noise Conditions in the environment that interfere with listening.

fact An observation based on actual experience.

fair use Using someone else's original work in a way that does not infringe on the owner's rights, generally for educational purposes, literary criticism, and news reporting.

fallacy An error in making an argument.

false dilemma fallacy Argument in which a speaker reduces available choices to only two even though other alternatives exist; also called the *either–or fallacy*.

feedback Audience members' responses to a speech.

flip chart A large pad of paper that rests on an easel, allowing a speaker to record text or drawings with markers during a speech.

forum The question-and-answer session following a group's formal presentation.

gatewatching Monitoring news sources to analyze and assess the information they produce.

gender-fair language Words that are not associated with or do not privilege either sex.

general purpose The speaker's overall objective: to inform, to persuade, or to entertain.

goodwill An audience's perception that a speaker shows he or she has the audience's true needs, wants, and interests at heart.

graphical online presentation Graphics-based talk delivered by someone using a computer and the Internet where the speaker does not appear on the screen.

guilt-by-association fallacy Argument in which a speaker suggests that something is wrong with another speaker's claims by associating those claims with someone the audience finds objectionable; also called the *bad company fallacy.*

handout Sheets of paper containing relevant information that are distributed before, during, or after a speech.

hasty generalization fallacy Argument in which a speaker draws a conclusion based on too few or inadequate examples.

hate speech Words that attack individuals or groups based on their race, gender, ethnic background, religious affiliation, dis/ability, or sexual orientation.

hedges Qualifiers, such as *probably* and *maybe*, that make statements ambiguous.

human assistant A person who plays a supportive part in a speech.

ideas and concepts Mental activity, including thoughts, understandings, beliefs, notions, and principles.

idiom An expression that means something other than the literal meaning of the words.

illusion of transparency The tendency of individuals to believe that how they feel is much more apparent to others than is really the case.

impromptu speaking A type of public speaking in which the speaker has little or no time to prepare a speech.

inclusive language Words that don't privilege one group over another.

inductive reasoning Supporting a claim with specific cases or instances; also called *reasoning by example.*

inference An interpretation of facts.

information literacy The ability to access, select, evaluate, and use information effectively and responsibly.

information overload Occurs when individuals receive too much information and are unable to interpret it in a meaningful way.

informative speaking Presenting a speech in which the speaker seeks to raise awareness, increase knowledge, or deepen understanding about a topic.

Interactive whiteboard Also called *smart board*, a device that can maximize active student involvement in learning; can be very useful in certain situations.

internal communication The exchange of messages within an organization.

internal consistency A logical relationship among the ideas that make up any main heading or subheading in a speech.

internal noise Thoughts, emotions, and physical sensations that interfere with listening.

internal summary A review of main points or subpoints given before going on to the next point in a speech.

interview guide A list of all the questions and possible probes an interviewer asks in an interview, as well as notes about how the interviewer will begin and end the interview.

introduction The beginning of a speech, including an attention getter, a statement of the thesis and purpose, a reference to the speaker's credibility, and a preview of the main points.

invention Discovering what you want to say in a speech, such as by choosing a topic and developing good arguments.

invitation to imagine Asking listeners to create a scene or situation in their minds.

issue-based persuasion A persuasive speech usually with serious consequences for society that addresses questions of fact, value, or policy.

jargon Technical language used by members of a profession or associated with a specific topic.

keyword A term associated with a topic and used to search for information related to that topic.

keywords Words that identify a subject or a point of primary interest or concern.

language The system of words people use to communicate with others.

listening anxiety Anxiety produced by the fear of misunderstanding, not fully comprehending, or not being mentally prepared for information you may hear.

loaded word fallacy Argument in which a speaker uses emotionally laden words to evaluate claims based on a misleading emotional response rather than the evidence presented.

logical appeals Use of rational thought based on logic, facts, and analysis to influence an audience; also known as *logos.*

logos Appeals to logic.

manuscript speaking A type of public speaking in which the speaker reads a written script word for word.

memorable message A sentence or group of sentences included in the conclusion of a speech, designed to make the speaker's thesis unforgettable.

memorized speaking A type of public speaking in which the speaker commits a speech to memory.

memory Using the ability to recall information about all aspects of public speaking to give an effective speech.

message The words and nonverbal cues a speaker uses to convey ideas, feelings, and thoughts.

metaphor A language device that demonstrates the commonalities between two dissimilar things.

metaphor A figure of speech that makes an implicit comparison between two things.

metasearch engine A search tool that compiles the results from other search engines.

mindfulness Occurs when individuals actively focus their attention on themselves and others in the present moment.

mindlessness Occurs when individuals view something as unimportant, trivial, routine, or habitual and fail to focus their attention on it.

monologue Occurs when communicators are concerned only with expressing their own ideas and their own individual goals.

monotone A way of speaking in which the speaker does not alter his or her pitch.

Monroe's motivated sequence A five-step pattern of organization that requires speakers to identify and respond to what will motivate an audience to pay attention.

mythos Appeals to cultural beliefs and values.

narrative A story used in a speech or other form of communication.

narrative pattern A pattern that organizes a speech by a dramatic retelling of events as a story or a series of short stories.

negative audience An audience that is informed about a speaker's topic and holds an unfavorable view of the speaker's position; also called a *hostile audience.*

noise Anything that interferes with the understanding of a message.

nomination speech Speech that demonstrates why a particular individual would be successful at something if given the chance.

nonverbal messages Information that is not communicated with words but rather, through movement, with gesture, facial expression, vocal quality, use of time, use of space, and touch.

object Any nonliving, material thing that can be perceived by the human senses.

open-ended question A broad, general question, often specifying only the topic.

opinion A way of thinking or judgment about something.

optimized speaker A public speaker who consciously selects relevant topics, adapts to the audience, speaks personally and conversationally, and uses technology when appropriate.

oral citation A source of information that a speaker mentions, or cites, during a speech.

oral report A report in which one member of a group presents the group's findings.

panel discussion A discussion in which a moderator asks questions of experts on a topic in front of an audience.

parallelism Using the same phrase, wording, or clause multiple times to add emphasis.

pathos Appeals to emotion.

pattern of organization A structure for ordering the main points of a speech.

persuasion Using language, images, and other means of communication to influence people's beliefs, attitudes, opinions, values, or actions.

persuasive speech A speech in which the speaker attempts to reinforce, modify, or change audience members' beliefs, attitudes, opinions, values, or actions.

pervasive communication environment The ability to access and share information in multiple forms from multiple locations in ways that transcend conventional ways of thinking about time and space.

physical model A copy of an object, usually built to scale, that represents the object in detail.

pitch The highness or lowness of a speaker's voice.

place Geographic location.

plagiarism Presenting someone else's ideas and work, such as speeches, papers, and images, as your own.

positive audience An audience that is informed about a speaker's topic and has a favorable view of the speaker's position; also called a *sympathetic audience.*

post hoc fallacy Argument in which a speaker concludes a causal relationship exists simply because one event follows another in time; also called the *false cause fallacy.*

posture The way speakers position and carry their bodies.

practical persuasion A persuasive speech of modest scope that encourages audiences to take action on a "do-able" topic.

premise A claim that provides reasons to support a conclusion.

presentation media Technical and material resources ranging from presentation software and real-time web access (RWA) to flip charts and handouts that speakers use to highlight, clarify, and complement the information they present orally.

presentation software Computer software that allows users to display information in multimedia slide shows.

preview of main points The final element of the introduction, in which the main points to be presented in the body of the speech are mentioned.

primacy effect An audience is more likely to pay attention to and recall what speakers present at the beginning of a speech than what they present in the speech body.

primary source Information that expresses an author's original ideas or findings from original research.

problem–solution pattern A pattern that organizes a speech by describing a problem and providing possible solutions.

process How something is done, how it works, or how it has developed.

pronunciation The act of saying words correctly according to the accepted standards of the speaker's language.

psychographics Psychological data about an audience, such as standpoints that draw from a person's values, attitudes, and beliefs.

public speaking When an individual speaks to a group of people, assuming responsibility for speaking for a defined length of time.

public testimony Factual information and opinions about policy issues presented to government bodies or other public institutions.

qualifier A word or phrase that clarifies, modifies, or limits the meaning of another word or phrase.

question of fact A question that asks whether something is true or false.

question of policy A question that asks what course of action should be taken or how a problem should be solved.

question of value A question that asks for a subjective evaluation of something's worth, significance, quality, or condition.

rate The speed at which a speaker speaks.

real-time web access (RWA) Employing a live Internet feed as a visual media or information resource during a public speech.

reasoning The method or process used to link claims to evidence.

recency effect An audience is more likely to remember what speakers present at the end of a speech than what they present in the speech body.

red herring Argument that introduces irrelevant evidence to distract an audience from the real issue.

relabeling Assigning more positive words or phrases to the physical reactions and feelings associated with speech anxiety.

relevance How closely a webpage's content is related to the keywords used in an Internet search.

review of main points The portion of the conclusion of a speech in which the main points presented in the body of the speech are briefly mentioned again.

rhetoric Aristotle's term for public speaking.

rhyme Using words with similar sounds, usually at the end of the word, to emphasize a point.

roast Humorous and good-natured ridicule directed toward the guest of honor at an event.

round-table discussion A discussion in which expert participants discuss a topic in an impromptu format without an audience present.

search engine A sophisticated software program that hunts through documents to find those associated with particular keywords.

secondary source Others' interpretations or adaptations of a primary source.

signpost A transition that indicates a key move in the speech, making its organization clear to the audience.

simile A language device that compares two things that are generally dissimilar but share some common properties, expressed using *like* or *as*.

slang Informal, nonstandard language, often used within a particular group.

slippery-slope fallacy Argument in which a speaker asserts that one event will necessarily lead to another without showing any logical connection between the two events.

small group A collection of individuals who interact and depend on one another to solve a problem, make a decision, or achieve a common goal or objective.

sociability The degree to which an audience feels a connection to a speaker.

spatial pattern A pattern that organizes a speech by the physical or directional relationship between objects or places.

speaker The person who assumes the primary responsibility for conveying a message in a public communication context.

speaking outline An outline that distills a complete-sentence outline, listing only the words and phrases that will guide the speaker through the main parts of the speech and the transitions between them.

specific purpose A concise statement articulating what the speaker will achieve in giving a speech.

speech anxiety Fear of speaking in front of an audience.

speech of introduction A short speech that introduces someone to an audience.

speech of tribute Speech that gives credit, respect, admiration, gratitude, or inspiration to someone who has accomplished something significant, lives in a way that deserves to be praised, or is about to embark on an adventure.

spotlight effect An overestimation of how much others are paying attention to you, your appearance, your actions, and what you say.

standpoint The psychological location or place from which an individual views, interprets, and evaluates the world.

statistics Numerical data or information.

straw man fallacy Argument in which a speaker misrepresents another speaker's argument so that only a shell of the opponent's argument remains.

style The language or words used in a speech.

summary statistics Information in the responses to an audience-research questionnaire that reflects trends and comparisons.

supporting material Evidence used to demonstrate the worth of an idea.

syllogism A form of deductive reasoning consisting of a major premise, minor premise, and conclusion.

symbol Something, such as a word, that stands for something else, such as a person, place, thing, or idea.

symposium A presentation format in which each member of a group presents a speech about a part of a larger topic.

tag questions Questions added onto the ends of declarative statements that lessens the impact of those statements.

target audience The particular group or subgroup a speaker most wants to inform, persuade, or entertain.

telephone meeting Group meetings facilitated by telephone that help members exchange ideas, solve problems, make assignments, set deadlines, and arrange schedules.

testimony An individual's opinions or experiences about a particular topic.

thesis A single declarative sentence that captures the central idea of a speech.

toast Brief remarks celebrating the accomplishments of a guest of honor at an event.

tone Use of language to set the mood or atmosphere associated with a speaking situation.

topical pattern A pattern that organizes a speech by arranging subtopics of equal importance.

topic The main subject, idea, or theme of a speech.

traditional whiteboard A smooth whiteboard that can be written or drawn on with markers.

transition A word, phrase, sentence, or paragraph used throughout a speech to mark locations in the organization and clearly link the parts of a speech together.

transparency An acetate page displayed by means of an overhead projector.

trustworthiness An audience's perception of a speaker as honest, ethical, sincere, reliable, sensitive, and empathic.

uncertainty reduction theory A theory that posits when individuals face an uncertain or unfamiliar situation, their level of anxiety increases.

uninformed audience An audience that is unfamiliar with a speaker's topic and has no opinion about it.

values Enduring concepts of what is good, right, worthy, and important.

videoconference Allows people at two or more locations to communicate interactively by means of simultaneous video and audio transmission.

visualization Imagining a successful communication event by thinking through a sequence of actions in a positive, concrete, step-by-step way.

vocalized pauses "Ah," "um," "you know," and other verbal fillers that speakers use when they're trying to think of what they want to say.

vocal variety Changes in the volume, rate, and pitch of a speaker's voice that affect the meaning of the words delivered.

volume The loudness of a speaker's voice.

voluntary audience Individuals who can choose to attend or not attend a speaking event.

weak analogy fallacy Argument in which a speaker compares two dissimilar things, ideas, or concepts, making the comparison inaccurate.

web directory An online list that organizes webpages and websites hierarchically by category; also called a search index.

webidence Web sources displayed as evidence during a speech, found by using real-time web access or webpage capture software.

working outline An outline that guides you during the initial stages of topic development, helping to keep you focused on your general purpose and clarify your specific purpose.

References

CHAPTER 1

1 Naomi (2008). Eight classes I should have taken in college [weblog message]. Retrieved from http://www.eduinreview.com/blog
2 Common Sense Media (2012). Teens on social media: Many benefits to digital life, but downsides too. Retrieved from http://www.commonsensemedia.org
3 Mehl, M., Vazire, S., Holleran, S. E., & Clark, C. S. (2010). Eavesdropping on happiness: Well-being is related to having less small talk and more substantive conversations. *Psychological Science, 21,* 539–541.
4 Frobish, T. (2000). Jamieson meets Lucas: Eloquence and pedagogical model(s) in *The Art of Public Speaking. Communication Education, 49,* 239–252.
5 Lull, J., & Neiva, E. (2012). *The language of life: How communication drives human evolution.* Amherst, NY: Prometheus.
6 Johanson, D., & Edgar, B. (2006). *From Lucy to language.* New York: Simon & Schuster.
7 Stringer, C., & Andrews, P. (2005). *The complete world of human evolution.* New York: Thames & Hudson.
8 Fritz, C. A. (1922). A brief review of the chief periods in the history of oratory. *Quarterly Journal of Speech Education, 8*(1), 26–48.
9 Kaiser Family Foundation (2010). *Generation M2: Media in the lives of 8- to 18-year-olds.* Retrieved from http://www.kkf.org
10 Pew Research Center (2015). Internet user demographics. Retrieved from http://www.pewinternet.org/data-trend/internet-use/latest-stats/
11 Smith, A. (2012). *Reaching your audience in the digital age: Key research trends to watch.* Pew Internet Project Florida Governor's Conference on Tourism. Transcript retrieved from http://www.slideshare.net
12 Baron, L. (2001). Why information literacy? *Advocate, 18*(8), 5–7.
13 Smith, C. R. (2003). *Rhetoric and human consciousness: A history.* Prospect Heights, IL: Waveland.
14 Smith, C. R. (2003); Herrick, J. A. (2012). *History and theory of rhetoric.* New York: Routledge.
15 Habinek, T. (2005). *Ancient rhetoric and oratory. Oxford, UK:* Blackwell.
16 Borchers, T. (2013). *Persuasion in the media age* (3rd ed.). Long Grove, IL: Waveland.
17 Gross, A. G., & Dascal, M. (2001). The conceptual unity of Aristotle's rhetoric. *Philosophy and Rhetoric, 34,* 275–291.
18 Hoogestraat, W. E. (1960). Memory: The lost canon? *Quarterly Journal of Speech, 46,* 141–147.
19 Ishii, S. (1992). Buddhist preaching: The persistent main undercurrent of Japanese traditional rhetorical communication. *Communication Quarterly, 40,* 391–397.
20 Dessalles, J.-L. (2007). *Why we talk: The evolutionary origins of language* (p. 27). Oxford, UK: Oxford University Press.
21 Fisher, W. R. (1987). *Human communication as narration: Toward a philosophy of reason, value, and action.* Columbia: University of South Carolina Press; Sprague, A. (2004). *The wisdom of storytelling in an information age.* Lanham, MD: Scarecrow Press.
22 Dutton, D. (2009). *The art instinct* (p. 103). New York: Bloomsbury.
23 Ford, W. S. Z., & Wolvin, A. D. (1993). The differential impact of a basic communication course on perceived communication competencies in class, work, and social contexts. *Communication Education, 42,* 215–223.
24 Ford & Wolvin (1993).
25 Fox, S. (2006). *Online health search 2006.* Retrieved 2007 from http://www.pewinternet.org
26 Seibold, D. R., Kudsi, S., & Rude, M. (1993). Does communication training make a difference? Evidence for the effectiveness of a presentation skills program. *Journal of Applied Communication Research, 21,* 111–131.
27 Langer, E. (1998). *The power of mindful learning.* New York: Perseus.
28 Perelman, L. (2009). Communicating across the curriculum. *Massachusetts Institute of Technology Faculty Newsletter.* Retrieved from http://web.mit.edu/fnl/volume/221/perelman.html
29 Addley, E. (2005, June 5). Office hours: Stand up and be counted: Although we may hate public speaking, it's a vital skill, says Esther Addley. *The Guardian,* p. 2; Krapels, R. H., & Davis, B. D. (2003). Designation of "communication skills" in position listings. *Business Communication Quarterly, 66*(2), 90–96; Maes, J. D., Weldy, T. G., & Icenogle, M. J. (1997). A managerial perspective: Oral communication competency is most important for business students in the workplace. *Journal of Business Communication, 34,* 67–80.
30 Robinson, K. (2011). *Out of our minds: Learning to be creative.* New York: Capstone.
31 Ford & Wolvin (1993).
32 Wirtz, C. (2003, April–May). Public speaking: An accounting marketing tool. *The National Public Accountant,* 14–15.
33 Gittlen, S. (2004, July 26). The public side of you: Be it for budget negotiations, project updates or industry conference panels, great public skills speaking will get you noticed—and promoted. *Network World,* p. 1; Green, M. C., & Brock, T. C. (2005). Organizational membership versus informal interaction: Contributions to skills and perceptions that build social capital. *Political Psychology, 26,* 1–25; Lublin, J. S. (2004, October 5). To win advancement, you need to clean up any bad speech habits. *Wall Street Journal,* p. B1.
34 Hassam, J. (2002). Learning the lesson—Speaking up for communication as an academic discipline too important to be sidelined. *Journal of Communication Management, 7*(1), 14–20; Murphy, T. A. (2005). Deliberative civic education and civil society: A consideration of ideals and actualities in democracy and communication education. *Communication Education, 53,* 74–91.
35 McMillian, J. J., & Harriger, K. J. (2002). College students and deliberation: A benchmark study. *Communication Education, 51,* 237–253; West, M., & Gastil, J. (2004). Deliberation at the margins: Participant accounts of face-to-face public deliberation at the 1999–2000 World Trade protests in Seattle and Prague. *Qualitative Research Reports in Communication, 5,* 1–7.
36 Laswell, H. (1948). The structure and function of communication in society. In L. Bryson (Ed.), *The communication of ideas.* New York: Harper & Row.
37 Schramm. W. (1954). *The processes and effects of communication.* Urbana: University of Illinois Press; Berlo, D. (1960). *The process of communication.* New York: Holt, Rinehart, & Winston; Barnlund, D. (1970). A transactional model of communication. In K. Sereno & C. D. Mortensen (Eds.), *Foundations of communication theory* (pp. 83–102). New York: Harper & Row.
38 Beck, U., & Beck-Gernsheim, E. (2002). *Individualization.* Newbury Park, CA: Sage; Lull, J. (2002). Superculture for the communication age. In J. Lull (Ed.), *Culture in the communication age.* London: Routledge.
39 Coopman, T. M. (2009). Toward a pervasive communication environment perspective. *First Monday 14.* Retrieved from http://www.firstmonday.org

CHAPTER 2

1 Addison, P., Ayala, J., Hunter, M., Behnke, R., & Sawyer, C. (2004). Body sensations of higher and lower anxiety sensitive speakers anticipating a public presentation. *Communication Research Reports, 21,* 284–290; Dwyer, K., & Davidson, M. M. (2012). Is public speaking really more feared than death? *Communication Research Reports, 29*(2), 99–107; Huey, A. (2012). The painful art of public speaking. *O'Dwyer's, 26*(1), 24; Phillips, G. C., Jones, G. E., Rieger, E. J., & Snell, J. B. (1997). Normative data for the personal report of confidence as a speaker. *Journal of Anxiety Disorders, 11,* 215–220.
2 Hancock, A. B., Stone, M. D., Brundage, S. B., & Zeigler, M. T. (2010). Public speaking attitudes: Does curriculum make a difference? *Journal of Voice, 24*(3), 302–307; Hunter, K. M., Westwick, J. N., & Haleta, L. L. (2014). Assessing success: The impacts of a fundamentals of speech course on decreasing public speaking anxiety. *Communication Education, 63*(2), 124–135; Liao, H. L. (2014). Examining the role of collaborative learning in a public speaking course. *College Teaching, 62*(2), 47–54.
3 Bodie, G. D. (2010). A racing heart, rattling knees, and ruminative thoughts: Defining, explaining, and treating public speaking anxiety. *Communication Education, 59*(1), 70–105.

4 Behnke, R. R., & Sawyer, C. R. (2001). Patterns of psychological state anxiety in public speaking as a function of anxiety sensitivity. *Communication Quarterly, 49,* 84–94; Harris, K. B., Sawyer, C. R., & Behnke, R. R. (2006). Predicting speech state anxiety from trait anxiety, reactivity, and situational influences. *Communication Quarterly, 54,* 213–226; MacIntyre, V. A., MacIntyre, P. D., & Carre, G. (2010). Heart rate variability as a predictor of speaking anxiety. *Communication Research Reports, 27*(4), 286–297; Rowa, K., Paulitzki, J. R., Ierullo, M. D., Chiang, B., Antony, M. M., McCabe, R. E., & Moscovitch, D. (2015). A false sense of security: Safety behaviors erode objective speech performance in individuals with social anxiety disorder. *Behavior Therapy, 46*(3), 304–314.

5 Witt, P. L., & Behnke, R. R. (2006). Anticipatory speech anxiety as a function of public speaking assignment type. *Communication Education, 55,* 167–177.

6 Beatty, M. C., & McCroskey, J. C. (1998). Interpersonal communication as temperamental expression: A communibiological paradigm. In J. C. McCroskey, J. A. Daly, M. M. Martin, & M. J. Beatty (Eds.), *Communication and personality: Trait perspectives* (pp. 41–67). Cresskill, NJ: Hampton Press; Hickson, M., & Stacks, D. W. (2010). Biological views of communication. *Review of Communication, 10*(4), 263–275; Hye Yoon, J., & McCroskey, J. C. (2004). Communication apprehension in a first language and self-perceived competence as predictors of communication apprehension in a second language: A study of speakers of English as a second language. *Communication Quarterly, 52*(2), 170–181.

7 Hazel, M., Keaten, J., & Kelly, L. (2014). The relationship between personality temperament, communication reticence, and fear of negative evaluation. *Communication Research Reports, 31*(4), 339–347; Kelly, L., & Keaten, J. A. (2000). Treating communication anxiety. Implications of the communibiological paradigm. *Communication Education, 49,* 45–57; Vevea, N. N., Pearson, J. C., Child, J. T., & Semlak, J. L. (2009). The only thing to fear is ... public speaking? Exploring predictors of communication in the public speaking classroom. *Journal of the Communication, Speech & Theatre Association of North Dakota, 22,* 1–8.

8 McCroskey, J. C. (1970). Measures of communication-bound anxiety. *Speech Monographs, 37,* 269–277.

9 Shikatani, B., Antony, M. M., Cassin, S. E., & Kuo, J. R. (2015). Examining the role of perfectionism and intolerance of uncertainty in postevent processing in social anxiety disorder. *Journal of Psychopathology and Behavioral Assessment.* doi:10.1007/s10862-015-9516-8; Witt & Behnke (2006).

10 MacIntyre et al. (2010).

11 Barjesteh, H., Vaseghi, R., & Neissi, S. (2012). Iranian EFL learners' willingness to communicate across different context and receiver types. *International Journal of English Linguistics, 2*(1), 47–54; Honour, D. (2007). Speech performance anxiety for non native speakers. *Florida Communication Journal, 36*(2), 57–66; Khan, S. M. (2015). Influence of speech anxiety on oral communication skills among ESL/EFL learners. *Advances in Language and Literary Studies, 6*(6), 49–53.

12 Bodie (2010); Martinez-Pecino, R., & Durán, M. (2013). Social communication fears: Factor analysis and gender invariance of the short-form of the personal report of confidence as a speaker in Spain. *Personality and Individual Differences, 55*(6), 680–684.

13 Finn, A. N., Sawyer, C. R., & Behnke, R. R. (2009). A model of anxious arousal for public speaking. *Communication Education, 58*(3), 417–432; Fodor, E. M., & Wick, D. P. (2009). Need for power and affective response to negative audience reaction to an extemporaneous speech. *Journal of Research in Personality, 43*(5), 721–726.

14 Nelson, E. A., Deacon, B. J., Lickel, J. J., & Sy, J. T. (2010). Targeting the probability versus cost of feared outcomes in public speaking anxiety. *Behaviour Research and Therapy, 48*(4), 282–289.

15 Field, A. P., Hamilton, S. J., Knowles, K. A., & Plews, E. L. (2003). Fear information and social phobic beliefs in children: A prospective paradigm and preliminary results. *Behaviour Research and Therapy, 41,* 113–123.

16 Byrne, M., Flood, B., & Shanahan, D. (2012). A qualitative exploration of oral communication apprehension. *Accounting Education, 21*(6), 565–581.

17 Hook, J. N., Valentiner, D. P., & Connelly, J. (2013). Performance and interaction anxiety: Specific relationships with other and self-evaluation concerns. *Anxiety, Stress, & Coping, 26*(2), 203–216; Horvath, N. R., Moss, M. N., Xie, S., Sawyer, C. R., & Behnke, R. R. (2004). Evaluation sensitivity and physical sensations of stress as components of public speaking state anxiety. *Southern Communication Journal, 69,* 173–181; Nicolas, F., Andrew C., P., Crystal, S., Vivien, T., & Christopher, W. (2008). Speaker overestimation of communication effectiveness and fear of negative evaluation: Being realistic is unrealistic. *Psychonomic Bulletin & Review, 15*(6), 1160–1165.

18 Fortune, J. L., & Newby-Clark, I. R. (2008). My friend is embarrassing me: Exploring the guilty by association effect. *Journal of Personality and Social Psychology, 95*(6), 1440–1449; Goberman, A. M., Hughes, S., & Haydock, T. (2011). Acoustic characteristics of public speaking: Anxiety and practice effects. *Speech Communication, 53*(6), 867–876.

19 Edwards, C. C., Myers, S. A., Hensley-Edwards, A., & Wahl, S. (2003). The relationship between student pre-performance concerns and evaluation apprehension. *Communication Research Reports, 20,* 54–61.

20 Cruess, D. G., Finitsis, D. J., Smith, A., Goshe, B. M., Burnham, K., Burbridge, C., & O'Leary, K. (2015). Brief stress management reduces acute distress and buffers physiological response to a social stress test. *International Journal of Stress Management, 22*(3), 270–286; U.S. Department of Health and Human Services. (2013, February). *Relaxation techniques for health: An introduction.* Retrieved from nccih.nih.gov/health/stress/relaxation.htm

21 Jerath, R., Crawford, M. W., Barnes, V. A., & Harden, K. (2015). Self-regulation of breathing as a primary treatment for anxiety. *Applied Psychophysiology and Biofeedback, 40*(2), 107–115.

22 Cosnett, G. (2003). Just breathe: Taking in a bit of fresh air isn't as easy as you think. *Training and Development Journal, 56*(9), 17–18; Donnet, N. (1989) Letting nervousness work for you. *Training and Development Journal, 43*(4), 21–23; Patient handout: Relaxation techniques. (2003). *Alternative Medicine Alert, 6*(7), 81–82.

23 Hubbard, K. K. (2015). *The impact of stress and anxiety and effects of progressive muscle relaxation on working memory and academic performance in health science graduate students* (Doctoral dissertation, Northcentral University); Kaur, R. (2015). Quasi experimental study to evaluate the effectiveness of progressive muscle relaxation therapy to reduce anxiety among nursing students. *International Journal of Psychiatric Nursing, 1*(1), 26–28.

24 Rains, J. (2013). *Meditation illuminated: Simple ways to manage your busy mind.* Bethesda, MD: Whole Earth Press.

25 Goldman, R. (2014, December 2). What is Jacobson's relaxation technique? *Healthline.* Retrieved from healthline.com

26 20 interesting human tongue facts. Facts Legend. Retrieved from factslegend.org/20-interesting-human-tongue-facts

27 Galante, J. G., Galante, I., Bekkers, M., & Gallacher, J. (2014). Effect of kindness-based meditation on health and well-being: A systematic review and meta-analysis. *Journal of Consulting and Clinical Psychology, 82*(6), 1101–1114.

28 Hanley White, K., Howard, M. C., Zhong, B., Soto, J. A., Perez, C. R., Lee, E. A., & ... Minnick, M. R. (2015). The Communication Anxiety Regulation Scale: Development and initial validation. *Communication Quarterly, 63*(1), 23–43.

29 Brooks, A. W. (2014). Get excited: Reappraising pre-performance anxiety as excitement. *Journal of Experimental Psychology: General, 143*(3), 1144–1158; Docan-Morgan, T., & Schmidt, T. (2012). Reducing public speaking anxiety for native and non-native English speakers: The value of systematic desensitization, cognitive restructuring, and skills training. *Cross-Cultural Communication, 8*(5), 16–19.

30 Moore-Russo, D., Viglietti, J. M., Chiu, M., & Bateman, S. M. (2013). Teachers' spatial literacy as visualization, reasoning, and communication. *Teaching and Teacher Education, 29,* 97–109; Slof, B., Erkens, G., Kirschner, P. A., & Helms Lorenz, M. (2013). The effects of inspecting and constructing part-task-specific visualizations on team and individual learning. *Computers & Education, 60*(1), 221–233; Westermann, G. A., Verheij, F., Winkens, B., Verhulst, F. C., & Van Oort, F. A. (2013). Structured shared decision-making using dialogue and visualization: A randomized controlled trial. *Patient Education & Counseling, 90*(1), 74–81.

31 Ayres, J., & Sonandré, D. M. A. (2003). Performance visualization: Does the nature of the speech model matter? *Communication Research Reports, 20,* 260–268; Choi, C. W., Honeycutt, J. M., & Bodie, G. D. (2015). Effects of imagined interactions and rehearsal on speaking performance. *Communication Education, 64*(1), 25–44; Honeycutt, J. M., Choi, C. W., & DeBerry, J. R. (2009). Communication apprehension and imagined interactions. *Communication Research Reports, 26*(3), 228–236.

32 Honeycutt et al. (2009).

33 Duff, D. C., Levine, T. R., Beatty, M. J., Woolbright, J., & Sun Park, H. (2007). Testing

public anxiety treatments against a credible placebo control. *Communication Education, 56,* 72–88; Choi et al. (2015).
34 Price, M., & Anderson, P. L. (2012). Outcome expectancy as a predictor of treatment response in cognitive behavioral therapy for public speaking fears within social anxiety disorder. *Psychotherapy, 49*(2), 173–179.
35 Behnke, R. R., & Sawyer, C. R. (1999). Public speaking procrastination as a correlate of public speaking communication apprehension and self-perceived public speaking competence. *Communication Research Reports, 16,* 40–47.
36 Bodie (2010).
37 Ayres, J. (1996). Speech preparation processes and speech apprehension. *Communication Education, 45,* 228–235.
38 MacIntyre, P. D., & Thivierge, K. A. (1995). The effects of audience pleasantness, audience familiarity, and speaking contexts on public speaking anxiety and willingness to speak. *Communication Quarterly, 43,* 456–466.
39 Chen, J., Mak, R., & Fujita, S. (2015). The effect of combination of video feedback and audience feedback on social anxiety. *Behavior Modification, 39*(5), 721–739.
40 Goberman et al. (2011); Smith, T. E., & Frymier, A. B. (2006). Get "real": Does practicing speeches before an audience improve performance? *Communication Quarterly, 54,* 111–125.
41 Choi et al. (2015); Smith, T. E., & Frymier, A. B. (2006). Get "real": Does practicing speeches before an audience improve performance? *Communication Quarterly, 54,* 111–125.
42 Addison, P. (2003). Worry as a function of public speaking state anxiety tips. *Communication Reports, 16,* 125–131.
43 Priem, J. S., & Solomon, D. (2009). Comforting apprehensive communicators: The effects of reappraisal and distraction on cortisol levels among students in a public speaking class. *Communication Quarterly, 57*(3), 259–281.
44 Brooks, A. W. (2014); Shi, X., Brinthaupt, T. M., & McCree, M. (2015). The relationship of self-talk frequency to communication apprehension and public speaking anxiety. *Personality and Individual Differences, 75,* 125–129.
45 Deiters, D. D., Stevens, S., Hermann, C., & Gerlach, A. L. (2013). Internal and external attention in speech anxiety. *Journal of Behavior Therapy and Experimental Psychiatry, 44*(2), 143–149.
46 Witt, P. L., Brown, K. C., Roberts, J. B., Weisel, J., Sawyer, C. R., & Behnke, R. R. (2006). Somatic anxiety patterns before, during, and after giving a public speech. *Southern Communication Journal, 71*(1), 87–100.
47 Goberman et al. (2011).
48 MacIntyre, P. D., & MacDonald, J. R. (1998). Public speaking anxiety: Perceived competence and audience congeniality. *Communication Education, 47,* 359–365.
49 Chen, N. M., Thomas, L. M., Clarke, P. F., Hickie, I. B., & Guastella, A. J. (2015). Hyperscanning and avoidance in social anxiety disorder: The visual scanpath during public speaking. *Psychiatry Research, 225*(3), 667–672.
50 Heigl, K. (2012, June 7). Tribute to Shirley MacLaine at the American Film Institute. Retrieved from youtube.com /watch?v=TUClh5qacQc
51 Finn, A. N., Sawyer, C. R., & Schrodt, P. (2009). Examining the effect of exposure therapy on public speaking state anxiety. *Communication Education, 58,* 92–109.

CHAPTER 3

1 2015 San Luis Valley Rural Philanthropy Days Listening Tour Report. Retrieved from crcamerica.org/wp-content/uploads/2015 -San-Luis-Valley-Listening-Tour-Report.pdf
2 Brownell, J. (2012). *Listening: Attitudes, principles, and skills* (5th ed.). New York: Pearson; Purdy, M. (1991). What is listening? In D. Borisoff & M. Purdy (Eds.), *Listening in everyday life: A personal and professional approach* (pp. 3–19). Lanham, MD: University Press of America; Wolvin, A. D., & Coakley, C. G. (2000). Listening education in the 21st century. *International Journal of Listening, 14,* 143–152.
3 Zelko, H. P. (1954). An outline of the role of listening in communication. *Journal of Communication*, 471–475.
4 McRae, C. (2012). Listening to a brick: Hearing location performatively. *Text and Performance Quarterly, 32*(4), 332–348.
5 Brownell, J. (2012).
6 Bawden, D., & Robinson, L. (2009). The dark side of information: Overload, anxiety and other paradoxes and pathologies. *Journal of Information Science, 35*(2), 180–191; Haase, R. F., Jome, L. M., Ferreira, J. A., Santos, E. R., Connacher, C. C., & Sendrowitz, K. (2014). Individual differences in capacity for tolerating information overload are related to differences in culture and temperament. *Journal of Cross-Cultural Psychology, 45*(5), 728–751.
7 Coopman, S. (1997). Personal constructs and communication in interpersonal and organizational contexts. In G. Neimeyer & R. Neimeyer (Eds.), *Advances in personal construct psychology* (Vol. 4, pp. 101–147). Greenwich, CT: JAI Press; Zohoori, A. (2013). A cross-cultural comparison of the HURIER listening profile among Iranian and U.S. students. *International Journal of Listening, 27*(1), 50–60.
8 Clark, A. J. (1989). Communication confidence and listening competence: An investigation of the relationships of willingness to communicate, communication apprehension and receiver apprehension to comprehension of content and emotional meaning in spoken messages. *Communication Education, 38,* 237–248.
9 Bodie, G. D., Vickery, A. J., & Gearhart, C. C. (2013). The nature of supportive listening, I: Exploring the relation between supportive listeners and supportive people. *International Journal of Listening, 27*(1), 39–49.
10 Hammond, S. C., Anderson, R., & Cissna, K. N. (2003). The problematics of dialogue and power. In P. J. Kalbfleisch (Ed.), *Communication yearbook 27* (pp. 125–157). Mahwah, NJ: Erlbaum; Montague, R. R. (2012). Genuine dialogue: Relational accounts of moments of meeting. *Western Journal of Communication, 76*(4), 397–416; Phillips, L. (2011). *The promise of dialogue: The dialogic turn in the production and communication of knowledge.* Amsterdam/Philadelphia: John Benjamin.
11 Arnett, R. C., Arneson, P., & Bell, L. M. (2007). Communication ethics: The dialogic turn. In P. Arneson (Ed.), *Exploring communication ethics: Interviews with influential scholars in the field* (pp. 143–184). New York: Peter Lang.
12 Forward, G. L., Czech, K., & Lee, C. M. (2011). Assessing Gibb's supportive and defensive communication climate: An examination of measurement and construct validity. *Communication Research Reports, 28*(1), 1–15.
13 Dannels, D. P., Housley Gaffney, A. L., & Martin, K. (2011). Students' talk about the climate of feedback interventions in the critique. *Communication Education, 60*(1), 95–114.
14 Arneson, P. (2008). A dialogic ethic in the public rhetoric of Angelina Grimké. In K. G. Roberts & R. C. Arnett (Eds.), *Communication ethics: Between cosmopolitanism and provinciality* (pp. 139–154). New York: Lang.
15 Purdy, M. W., & Manning, L. M. (2015). Listening in the multicultural workplace: A dialogue of theory and practice. *International Journal of Listening, 29*(1), 1–11.
16 Ala-Kortesmaa, S., & Isotalus, P. (2014). Relational tensions and optimal listening in the communication relationships of American and Finnish legal professionals. *Journal of Intercultural Communication Research, 43*(3), 173–193.
17 Arasaratnam, L. A., & Banerjee, S. C. (2011). Sensation seeking and intercultural communication competence: A model test. *International Journal of Intercultural Relations, 35*(2), 226–233; Neuliep, J. W. (2012). The relationship among intercultural communication apprehension, ethnocentrism, uncertainty reduction, and communication satisfaction during initial intercultural interaction: An extension of Anxiety and Uncertainty Management (AUM) Theory. *Journal of Intercultural Communication Research, 41*(1), 1–16.
18 Kang, O., & Rubin, D. (2009). Reverse linguistic stereotyping: Measuring the effect of listener expectations on speech evaluation. *Journal of Language and Social Psychology, 28,* 441–456.
19 Lund, D. (2006). Rocking the racism boat: School-based activists speak out on denial and avoidance. *Race, Ethnicity and Education, 9,* 203–221; Talmy, S. (2010). Becoming "local" in ESL: Racism as resource in a Hawai'i public high school. *Journal of Language, Identity and Education, 9*(1), 36–57.
20 Huston, D. C., Garland, E. L., & Farb, N. S. (2011). Mechanisms of mindfulness in communication training. *Journal of Applied Communication Research, 39*(4), 406–421; Liang, Y. L., Lee, S. A., & Jang, J. (2013). Mindlessness and gaining compliance in Computer-Human Interaction. *Computers in Human Behavior, 29*(4), 1572–1579.
21 Sarampalis, A., Kalluri, S., Edwards, B., & Hafter, E. (2009). Objective measures of listening effort: Effects of background noise and noise reduction. *Journal of Speech, Language and Hearing Research, 52*(5), 1230–1240.
22 Froemming, K. J., & Penington, B. A. (2011). Emotional triggers: Listening barriers to effective interactions in senior populations. *International Journal of Listening, 25*(3), 113–131; Rane, D. B. (2011). Good listening skills make efficient business sense. *IUP Journal of Soft Skills, 5*(4), 43–51.
23 Nichols, R., & Stevens, L. M. (1957). Listening to people. *Harvard Business Review, 35,* 85–92.
24 Treasure, J. (2011, July). 5 ways to listen better. Talk presented at TEDGlobal 2011. Retrieved from ted.com
25 Goh, E. S. (2012). Integrating mindfulness and reflection in the teaching and learning of

listening skills for undergraduate social work students in Singapore. *Social Work Education, 31*(5), 587–604.

26 Brownell, J. (2012).

27 King, P. E., & Behnke, R. R. (2004). Patterns of state anxiety in listening performance. *Southern Communication Journal, 70,* 72–80.

28 Makany, T., Kemp, J., & Dror, I. E. (2009). Optimising the use of note-taking as an external cognitive aid for increasing learning. *British Journal of Educational Technology, 40*(4), 619–635.

29 Purdy, M. W., & Manning, L. M. (2015). Listening in the multicultural workplace: A dialogue of theory and practice. *International Journal of Listening, 29*(1), 1–11.

CHAPTER 4

1 Cronkhite, G. (1986). On the focus, scope, and coherence of the study of human symbolic activity. *Quarterly Journal of Speech, 72,* 231–246; Kellermann, K. (1992). Communication: Inherently strategic and primarily automatic. *Communication Monographs, 59,* 288–300; Motley, M. T. (1990). On whether one can(not) not communicate: An examination via traditional communication postulates. *Western Journal of Speech Communication, 54,* 1–20.

2 Keith, W. (2004). Planning a no-sweat presentation. *Government Finance Review, 20*(4), 55–56.

3 Williams, G. (2002). Looks like rain: If you've thought and thought and still haven't come up with any great ideas, don't sweat. *Entrepreneur, 30*(9), 104–110.

4 Osborn, A. F. (1957). *Applied imagination.* New York: Scribner; Prendergast, K. (2003, September 29). The ideal setting for ideas. Brainstorming sessions can be productive if done the correct way. *The Press Enterprise,* p. A7; Wellner, A. S. (2003). A perfect brainstorm. *Inc., 25*(10), 31–35.

5 Kupperman, M. A (2003). Perfect brainstorm *Inc., 25*(10), 31–32, 35.

6 Snyder, A., Mitchell, J., Ellwood, S., Yates, A., & Pallier, G. (2004). Nonconscious idea generation. *Psychological Reports, 94,* 1325–1330.

7 Sutton, R. I., & Hargadon, A. (1996). Brainstorming groups in context. *Administrative Science Quarterly, 41*(4), 685–718.

8 Guerrero, L. K., & Afifi, W. A. (1995). Some things are better left unsaid. Topic avoidance in family relationships. *Communication Quarterly, 43*(3), 276–296; Caughlin, J., & Golish, T. (2002). An analysis of the association between topic avoidance and dissatisfaction: Comparing perceptual and interpersonal explanations. *Communication Monographs, 69*(4), 275–295.

9 Kollins, T. K. (1996). Tips for speakers. *Association Management, 48*(8), 175–179.

10 Ogden, H. V. S. (1948). On teaching the sentence outline. *College English, 10*(3), 152–158.

11 Higbee, R. W. (1964). A speaking approach to composition. *The English Journal, 53*(1), 50–51.

12 House, J. (1993). The first shall be last: Writing the essay backwards. *The English Journal, 82*(6), 26–28.

13 Watkins, K. J. (2005). Will they throw eggs? *Journal of Accountancy, 199*(4), 57–61.

14 Johnson, S. (2010). *Where Good Ideas Come From.* New York: Riverhead Books.

15 Sutton, R. I., & Hargadon, A. (1996). Brainstorming groups in context. *Administrative Science Quarterly, 41,* 685–718; Paulus, Paul B. (2006). Putting the brain back in brainstorming. Associations Now. Center for Association Leadership. Retrieved from https://www.asaecenter.org/Resources/ANowDetail.cfm?ItemNumber=20824

CHAPTER 5

1 Barkow, J. H., Cosmides, L., & Tooby, J. (1992). *The adapted mind: Evolutionary psychology and the generation of culture.* New York: Oxford University Press.

2 Gates, B. (2005, October). Remarks by Bill Gates, Founder and Chief Software Architect, Microsoft Corporation, University of Michigan, Ann Arbor, MI. Retrieved from http://www.microsoft.com/billgates/speeches.asp; Gates, B. (2014). Remarks by Bill Gates, Founder and Chief Software Architect, Microsoft Corporation, Stanford University. Retrieved from http://news.stanford.edu/news/2014/june/gates-commencement-remarks-061514.html; Gates, B. (2005, October 13). Remarks by Bill Gates, Founder and Chief Software Architect, Microsoft Corporation, University of Waterloo, Waterloo, Ontario, Canada. Retrieved from http://www.microsoft.com/billgates/speeches.asp

3 Morgan, N. (2003). *Working the room.* Cambridge, MA: Harvard Business School Press.

4 Nightingale, V. (2011). *The handbook of media audiences.* Boston: Wiley Blackwell.

5 Haynes, W. L. (1990). Public speaking pedagogy in the media age. *Communication Education, 38,* 89–102.

6 Park-Fuller, L. M. (2003). Audiencing the audience: Playback Theatre, performative writing, and social activism. *Text and Performance Quarterly, 23,* 288–310.

7 Weissman, J. (2003). *Presenting to win: The art of telling your story.* Harlow, Essex, UK: Financial Times Prentice Hall.

8 Villaraigosa, A. R. (2006, April). *Accelerating our ambitions.* State of the City address, Los Angeles, CA. Retrieved from http://www.lacity.org/mayor/

9 Bennett, S. (1998). *Theatre audiences.* London: Routledge; Jamieson, K. H., & Campbell, K. K. (2000). *The interplay of influence.* Belmont, CA: Wadsworth; McQuail, D. (1997). *Audience analysis.* London: Sage; Traudt, P. (2004). *Media, audience, effects: An introduction to the study of media content and audience analysis.* Boston: Allyn & Bacon; Yopp, J. J., & McAdams, K. C. (2002). *Researching audiences.* Boston: Allyn & Bacon.

10 McCarty, H. (1998). *Motivating your audience.* Boston: Allyn & Bacon.

11 Myers, F. (1999). Argumentation and the composite audience: A case study. *Quarterly Journal of Speech, 85,* 55–71.

12 National Center for Education Statistics. (2012). *Digest of education statistics: Postsecondary education,* table 237. Retrieved from http://www.nces.ed.gov

13 Carnevale, E. P., & Fry, R. A. (2000). *Crossing the great divide: Can we achieve equity when Generation Y goes to college?* Princeton, NJ: Educational Testing Service.

14 Pew Research Center. (2015). Women's college enrollment gains leave men behind. Retrieved from http://www.pewresearch.org/fact-tank/2014/03/06/womens-college-enrollment-gains-leave-men-behind/

15 Ibid.

16 College Campus Explorer. (2015). LGBT college statistics. Retrieved from http://www.campusexplorer.com/college-advice-tips/DC54CA9B/LGBT-College-Statistics/

17 Pew Research Center. (2015). Millennials increasingly are driving growth of 'nones.' Retrieved from http://www.pewresearch.org/fact-tank/2015/05/12/millennials-increasingly-are-driving-growth-of-nones/

18 National Center for Education Statistics. (2015). Students with disabilities. Retrieved from https://nces.ed.gov/fastfacts/display.asp?id=60%

19 Wall Street Journal. (2015). International students stream into U.S. colleges. Retrieved from http://www.wsj.com/articles/international-students-stream-into-u-s-colleges-1427248801

20 Brown, L. I. (2004). Diversity: The challenge for higher education. *Race Ethnicity and Education, 7,* 21–34; Bylander, J., & Rose, S. (2007). Border crossings: Engaging students in diversity work and intergroup relations. *Innovative Higher Education, 31,* 251–264; Engberg, M. E. (2007). Educating the workforce for the 21st century: A cross-disciplinary analysis of the impact of the undergraduate experience on students' development of a pluralistic orientation. *Research in Higher Education, 48*(3), 283–317; Mor Barak, M. (2005). *Managing diversity: Towards a globally inclusive workplace.* Thousand Oaks, CA: Sage; van Knippenberg, D., & Schippers, M. D. (2007). Work group diversity. *Annual Review of Psychology, 58,* 515–541.

21 Myers, F. (1999). Political argumentation and the composite audience: A case study. *Quarterly Journal of Speech, 85,* 55–71.

22 DeFrancisco, V. P. (2007). *Communicating gender diversity.* Thousand Oaks. CA: Sage; Harding, S. (2003). *The feminist standpoint reader.* New York: Routledge; Orbe, M. P. (1998). From the standpoint(s) of traditionally muted groups: Explicating a co-cultural communication theoretical model. *Communication Theory,* 8, 1–26; Wood, J. T. (2008). *Gendered lives: Communication, gender and culture.* Boston: Wadsworth.

23 Atkinson, J. (2005). Conceptualizing global justice audiences of alternative media: The need for power and ideology in performance paradigms of audience research. *The Communication Review, 8,* 137–157; Harding, S. (1991). *Whose science? Whose knowledge? Thinking from women's lives.* Ithaca, NY: Cornell University Press.

24 Orbe, M. P., & Warren, K. T. (2000). Different standpoints, different realities: Race, gender, and perceptions of intercultural conflict. *Qualitative Research Reports in Communication, 1*(3), 51–57.

25 Dietz, T., Kalof, L., & Stern P. C. (2002). Gender, values, and environmentalism. *Social Science Quarterly, 83,* 353–364.

26 Fowler, G. A., Steinberg, B., & Patrick, A. O. (2007, March 1). Mac and PC's overseas adventures: Globalizing Apple's ads meant tweaking characters, clothing, and body language. *The Wall Street Journal,* p. B1.

27 Yook, E. L. (2004). Any questions? Knowing the audience through question types. *Communication Teacher, 18,* 91–93.

28 *Michael Beschloss speaks at 172nd commencement.* Retrieved from http://www.lafayette.edu/news.php/viewnc/10374
29 Myers, S. A. (2004). The relationship between perceived instructor credibility and college student in-class and out-of-class communication. *Communication Reports, 17,* 129–137; Myers, S. A., & Bryant, L. E. (2004). College students' perceptions of how instructors convey credibility. *Qualitative Research Reports in Communication, 5,* 22–27.
30 Miller, A. (2002). An exploration of Kenyan public speaking patterns with implications for the American introductory public speaking course. *Communication Education, 51,* 168–182.
31 Smith, C. R. (2003). *Rhetoric and human consciousness: A history.* Prospect Heights, IL: Waveland.
32 Haskins, W. (2000). Ethos and pedagogical communication. *Current Issues in Education, 3,* 1–9.
33 Rosenberg, A., & Hirschberg, J. (2005). Acoustic prosodic and lexical correlates of charismatic speech. *Proceedings of Interspeech* 2005, 513–516.
34 Aune, R. K., & Kikuchi, T. (1993). Effects of language intensity similarity on perceptions of credibility, relational attributions, and persuasion. *Journal of Language and Social Psychology, 12,* 224–237; Myers & Bryant (2004); Pfau, M., & Kang, J. G. (1991). The impact of relational messages on candidate influence in televised political debates. *Communication Studies, 42,* 114–128.
35 Nunberg, S. (2012). Convocation address. Given at the University of Chicago. Retrieved from https://college.uchicago.edu/story/class-2012 graduation speeches
36 Miller, N. (2007). Snack attack: Minifesto for a new age. *Wired, 15.03,* 124–135.
37 Johnson, S. (2007). Snacklash. *Wired, 15.03,* 178.

CHAPTER 6

1 Biddix, J., Chung, C., & Park, H. (2011). Convenience or credibility? A study of college student online research behaviors. *Internet and Higher Education, 14*(3), 175–182; Head, A. J., & Eisenberg, M. B. (2011). How college students use the Web to conduct everyday life research. *First Monday, 16*(4). Retrieved from firstmonday.org; Lawrence, K. (2015). Today's college students: Skimmers, scanners and efficiency-seekers. *Information Services & Use, 35*(1/2), 89–93; Timpson, H., & Sansom, G. (2011). A student perspective on e-resource discovery: Has the Google factor changed publisher platform searching forever? *Serials Librarian, 61*(2), 253–266.
2 Rennis, L., Mcnamara, G., Seidel, E., & Shneyderman, Y. (2015). Google it!: Urban community college students' use of the internet to obtain self-care and personal health information. *College Student Journal, 49*(3), 414–426.
3 Bloom, B., & Deyrup, M. M. (2015). The SHU research logs: Student online search behaviors trans-scripted. *Journal of Academic Librarianship, 41*(5), 593–601; Booker, L. D., Detlor, B., & Serenko, A. (2012). Factors affecting the adoption of online library resources by business students. *Journal of the American Society for Information Science and Technology, 63*(12), 2503–2520; D'Couto, M., & Rosenhan, S. H. (2015). How students research: Implications for the library and faculty. *Journal of Library Administration, 55*(7), 562–576.
4 Tsai, M. (2009). Online information searching strategy inventory (OISSI): A quick version and a complete version. *Computers & Education, 53,* 473–483.
5 He, D., Wu, D., Yue, Z., Fu, A., & Vo, K. (2012). Undergraduate students' interaction with online information resources in their academic tasks: A comparative study. *Aslib Proceedings, 64*(6), 615–640.
6 Mussell, J., & Croft, R. (2013). Discovery layers and the distance student: Online search habits of students. *Journal of Library & Information Services in Distance Learning, 7*(1/2), 18–39; D'Couto & Rosenhan (2015).
7 Head, A. J., & Eisenberg, M. B. (2010). How today's college students use Wikipedia for course-related research. *First Monday, 15*(3). Retrieved March 15, 2010, from firstmonday.org
8 Garrison, J. C. (2015). Getting a "quick fix": First-year college students' use of Wikipedia. *First Monday, 20*(10). Retrieved from firstmonday.org
9 Anagnostopoulos, I. (2010). A capture–recapture sampling standardization for improving Internet meta-search. *Computer Standards & Interfaces, 32,* 61–70.
10 Maxwell, C. (2015). Going beyond Google again: Strategies for using and teaching the invisible web. *Internet Reference Services Quarterly, 20*(1/2), 61–62; Zheng, Q., Wu, Z., Cheng, X., Jiang, L., & Liu, J. (2013). Learning to crawl deep web. *Information Systems, 38*(6), 801–819.
11 Free, D. (2015). ProQuest scholarly content now discoverable in Google Scholar. *College & Research Libraries News, 76*(9), 481; Orduna-Malea, E., Ayllón, J., Martín-Martín, A., & Delgado López-Cózar, E. (2015). Methods for estimating the size of Google Scholar. *Scientometrics, 104*(3), 931–949.
12 Internet live stats. (2015, October 29). Total number of websites. Retrieved from internetlivestats.com; The size of the World Wide Web. (2015, October 29). WorldWideWebSize.com. Retrieved from worldwidewebsize.com
13 Georgas, H. (2015). Google vs. the library (part III): Assessing the quality of sources found by undergraduates. *Portal: Libraries & the Academy, 15*(1), 133–161.
14 Chen, Y. (2015). Testing the impact of an information literacy course: Undergraduates' perceptions and use of the university libraries' web portal. *Library & Information Science Research (07408188), 37*(3), 263–274; Ludovico, C., & Wittig, C. (2015). A universe of information, one citation at a time: How students engage with scholarly sources. *Journal of Library & Information Services in Distance Learning, 9*(1/2), 30–39.
15 Vallano, J. P., & Compo, N. (2011). A comfortable witness is a good witness: Rapport-building and susceptibility to misinformation in an investigative mock-crime interview. *Applied Cognitive Psychology, 25*(6), 960–970.
16 Stax, H. P. (2004). Paths to precision: Probing turn format and turn-taking problems in standardized interviews. *Discourse Studies, 6*(1), 77–94.
17 El-Gawley, N., & O'Donnell, P. (2009). Listening, journalism and community voices— Nadyat El-Gawley in conversation with Penny O'Donnell. *Continuum: Journal of Media & Cultural Studies, 23*(4), 519–523.
18 Lanning, S. (2012). *Concise guide to information literacy.* Santa Barbara, CA: Libraries Unlimited.
19 Johannsen, R. L., Valde, K. S., & Whedbee, K. E. (2008). *Ethics in human communication* (6th ed.). Prospects Heights, IL: Waveland.
20 Olson, S. (2005). Schools face prevalence of online plagiarism: Educators try to thwart growing cheating problem as Web sites make it easy for students to purchase papers. *Indianapolis Business Journal, 26*(13), 17; Parker, K., Lenhart, A., & Moore, K. (2011, August 28). *The digital revolution and higher education.* Retrieved from pewinternet.org; Tillman, L. (2009, August 9). Students nationwide say they cheat. *The Brownsville Herald.* Retrieved from http://www.brownsvilleherald.com
21 Belter, R., & du Pré, A. (2009). A strategy to reduce plagiarism in an undergraduate course. *Teaching of Psychology, 36,* 257–261; Craig, P. A., Federici, E., & Buehler, M. A. (2010). Instructing students in academic integrity. *Journal of College Science Teaching, 40*(2), 50–55; Gullifer, J., & Tyson, G. (2014). Who has read the policy on plagiarism? Unpacking students' understanding of plagiarism. *Studies in Higher Education, 39*(7), 1202–1218; Williams, S., Tanner, M., & Beard, J. (2012). How to cure the cheating pandemic. *Bized, 11*(4), 58–59.
22 Turnitin. (2015). *White paper: The plagiarism spectrum: Instructor insights into the 10 types of plagiarism.* Retrieved from turnitin.com
23 Lipson, C. (2008). *Doing honest work in college: How to prepare citations, avoid plagiarism, and achieve real academic success* (2nd ed.). Chicago: University of Chicago Press.
24 Ludwig, M. (2008, March 31). UTSA honor code not original: Copied parts are an oversight, student says. *Houston Chronicle.* Retrieved from http://www.houstonchronicle.com
25 Lipson (2008).
26 Lerner, M. (2015, March 5). The thin line between plagiarizing and paraphrasing. *Star Tribune* (Minneapolis, MN). Retrieved from startribune.com
27 American Psychological Association. (2009). *Publication manual of the American Psychological Association* (6th ed.). Washington, DC: Author; Gibaldi, J. (2009). *MLA handbook for writers of research papers* (7th ed.). New York: Modern Language Association of America.

CHAPTER 7

1 Smith, C. R. (2009). *Rhetoric and human consciousness: A history* (3rd ed.). Prospect Heights, IL: Waveland.
2 Anthony, S. B. (1873). On women's right to vote. The History Place: Great Speeches Collection. Retrieved from historyplace.com/speeches/anthony.htm
3 Irwin, M. (2013). "Their experience is the immigrant experience": Ellis Island, documentary film, and rhetorically reversible whiteness. *Quarterly Journal of Speech, 99*(1), 74–97; Ivie, R., & Giner, O. (2009). American exceptionalism in a democratic idiom:

Transacting the mythos of change in the 2008 presidential campaign. *Communication Studies, 60*(4), 359–375; Valenzano, J. J., & Engstrom, E. (2014). Cowboys, angels, and demons: American exceptionalism and the frontier myth in the CW's Supernatural. *Communication Quarterly, 62*(5), 552–568; Van Gorp, B., & van der Goot, M. J. (2012). Sustainable food and agriculture: Stakeholder's frames. *Communication, Culture & Critique, 5*(2), 127–148.

4 Ling, L. (2015, May 24). Carthage College commencement speech. Transcribed by S. J. Coopman. Retrieved from youtube.com/watch?v=U0xb6k_KHbE

5 Fisher, W. R. (1987). *Human communication as narration: Toward a philosophy of reason, value, and action.* Columbia: University of South Carolina; Hamby, A., Daniloski, K., & Brinberg, D. (2015). How consumer reviews persuade through narratives. *Journal of Business Research, 68*(6), 1242–1250; Limon, M. S., & Kazoleas, D. C. (2004). A comparison of exemplar and statistical evidence in reducing counterarguments and responses to a message. *Communication Research Reports, 21,* 291–298; Moyer-Gusé, E., & Nabi, R. (2010). Explaining the effects of narrative in an entertainment television program: Overcoming resistance to persuasion. *Human Communication Research, 36,* 26–52.

6 Aruffo, C. (2015). Turning scientific presentations into stories. *Journal of College Science Teaching, 45*(1), 32–35; Randall, D., & Harms, A. (2012). Using stories for advantage: The art and process of narrative. *Strategy & Leadership, 40*(1), 21–26.

7 Cohen, S. D. (2011). The art of public narrative: Teaching students how to construct memorable anecdotes. *Communication Teacher, 25*(4), 197–204; Lucas, K., & Rawlins, J. D. (2015). PechaKucha presentations: Teaching storytelling, visual design, and conciseness. *Communication Teacher, 29*(2), 102–107.

8 Springsteen, B. (2012, March 28). SXSW keynote address. Retrieved from rollingstone.com

9 Chang, C. (2015, April 21). Lead On Conference 2015 keynote. Transcribed by S. J. Coopman. Retrieved from watermarkconferenceforwomen.org/candy-chang-at-the-2015-lead-on-conference-for-women

10 Burns, K. (2015, May 15). 2015 commencement address, Washington University, Saint Louis. Retrieved from commencement.wustl.edu/speakers-honorees

11 McCormick, S. (2014). Argument by comparison: An ancient typology. *Rhetorica, 35*(2), 148–164; Yopp, D., & Ely, R. (2016). When does an argument use a generic example? *Educational Studies in Mathematics, 91*(1), 37–53.

12 Hoeken, H., Šorm, E., & Schellens, P. J. (2014). Arguing about the likelihood of consequences: Laypeople's criteria to distinguish strong arguments from weak ones. *Thinking & Reasoning, 20*(1), 77–98; Hornikx, J. (2007). Is anecdotal evidence more persuasive than statistical evidence? A comment on classic cognitive psychological studies. *Studies in Communication Sciences, 7*(2), 151–164.

13 Aoki, K. (2006). A study of Franklin Delano Roosevelt's persuasive communication within the fireside chat: An analysis of language and style. *Human Communication, 9*(1), 71–81.

14 Roosevelt, F. D. (1936, September 6). On drought conditions. Retrieved from www.mhric.org/fdr/fdr.html

15 Robinson, M. (2012, August 5). Freedom, truth, democracy: Citizenship and common purpose. Retrieved from nelsonmandela.org/news/entry/transcript-of-mary-robinsons-nelson-mandela-annual-lecture

16 Laurens, S. (2012, July 26). Weathering the transition … Keeping the faith. Keynote address presented at the Romance Writers of America National Convention, Anaheim, CA. Retrieved from stephanielaurens.com/rwa12keynote.html

17 Sandberg, S. (2012). Commencement address to the Harvard Business School Class of 2012. Retrieved from www.hbs.edu/videos/sheryl-sandberg-addresses-class-of-2012.html

18 Hill, M. (2012, September 23). The science of cooking. *San Jose Mercury News,* pp. E1, E6.

19 Braverman, J. (2008). Testimonials versus informational persuasive messages: The moderating effect of delivery mode and personal involvement. *Communication Research, 35*(5), 666–694; Tobin, S., & Raymundo, M. M. (2009). Persuasion by causal arguments: The motivating role of perceived causal expertise. *Social Cognition, 27*(1), 105–127.

20 Evans, A. T., & Clark, J. K. (2012). Source characteristics and persuasion: The role of self-monitoring in self-validation. *Journal of Experimental Social Psychology, 48*(1), 383–386.

21 Blodget, H. (2012, May 25). And here's the secret reason Apple is crushing Google . . . *Business Insider.* Retrieved from businessinsider.com/and-heres-the-secret-reason-apple-is-crushing-google-2012-3

22 Federal Trade Commission. (2015). *Consumer Sentinel Network Data Book: January–December 2014.* Retrieved from ftc.gov

23 Nwakanma, N. (2014). Keynote address. Presented at NETmundail. Retrieved from webfoundation.org/2014/04/nnenna-nwakanma-delivers-keynote-speech-at-opening-ceremony-of-netmundial/

24 Hoeken, H., & Hustinx, L. (2009). When is statistical evidence superior to anecdotal evidence in supporting probability claims? The role of argument type. *Human Communication Research, 35*(4), 491–510; Hornikx, J. (2008). Comparing the actual and expected persuasiveness of evidence types: How good are lay people at selecting persuasive evidence? *Argumentation, 22*(4), 555–569; Petty, R. E., & Briñol, P. (2015). Emotion and persuasion: Cognitive and meta-cognitive processes impact attitudes. *Cognition & Emotion, 29*(1), 1–26.

CHAPTER 8

1 Borchers, T. (2013). *Persuasion in the media age* (3rd ed.). Long Grove, IL: Waveland.

2 Slagell, A. (2013). Why should you use a clear pattern of organization? Because it works. *Communication Teacher, 27*(4), 198–201.

3 A brief history of the Internet of things. (n.d.). Retrieved from postscapes.com/internet-of-things-history; Leiner, B. M., Cerf, V. G., Clark, D. D., Kahn, R. E., Kleinfock, L., Lynch, D. C., Postel, J., Roberts, L. G., & Wolff, S. (2012). Brief history of the Internet. Retrieved from http://internetsociety.org/internet/what-internet/history-internet/brief-history-internet

4 Blinne, K. C. (2012). Making the familiar strange: Creative cultural storytelling within the communication classroom. *Communication Teacher, 26*(4), 216–219; Cohen, S. D. (2011). The art of public narrative: Teaching students how to construct memorable anecdotes. *Communication Teacher, 25*(4), 197–204.

5 Campbell, K. K., Huxman, S. S., & Burkholder, T. R. (2015). *The rhetorical act: Thinking, speaking, and writing critically* (5th ed.). New York: Cengage.

6 The Atlantic City Convention & Visitors Authority. (2013). Atlantic City Boardwalk: A stroll on the wooden way is steeped in history. Retrieved from atlanticcitynj.com; The history of Atlantic City. (2006, January 8). Atlantic City Free Public Library. Retrieved from acfpl.org; The real "Boardwalk Empire": Atlantic City during Prohibition in the 1920s. (2013). *New York Daily News.* Retrieved from nydailynews.com

7 German, K. M., Gronbeck, B. E., Ehninger, D., & Monroe, A. H. (2013). *Principles of public speaking* (18th ed.). New York: Pearson.

8 Collins, P. (2012). *The art of speeches and presentations: The secrets of making people remember what you say.* Chichester, UK: Wiley.

9 Baaijen, V. M., Galbraith, D., & de Glopper, K. (2014). Effects of writing beliefs and planning on writing performance. *Learning & Instruction, 33,* 81–91.

10 de Smet, M. R., Brand-Gruwel, S., Leijten, M., & Kirschner, P. A. (2014). Electronic outlining as a writing strategy: Effects on students' writing products, mental effort and writing process. *Computers & Education, 78,* 352–366; Staneart, D. (2013). *Mastering presentations: Be the undisputed expert when you deliver presentations (even if you feel like you're going to throw up).* Hoboken, NJ: Wiley.

11 American Psychological Association. (2009). *Publication manual of the American Psychological Association* (6th ed.). Washington, DC: Author; Gibaldi, J. (2009). *MLA handbook for writers of research papers* (7th ed.). New York: Modern Language Association of America.

CHAPTER 9

1 Truth, S. (1853). Suppose I am about the only colored woman that goes about to speak for the rights of colored women. Speech presented at the Fourth National Woman's Rights Convention, New York City. Retrieved from gos.sbc.edu/t/truth2.html

2 Chisholm, S. (1969, May 21). Equal rights for women. Speech presented to the U.S. House of Representatives, Washington, DC. Retrieved from gos.sbc.edu/c/chisholm.html

3 Obama, M. (2015, March 19). Address at Let Girls Learn joint partnership announcement, Tokyo, Japan. Retrieved from americanrhetoric.com/speeches/michelleobamaletgirlslearnjapan.htm

4 Anselmi, P., Vianello, M., & Robusto, E. (2011). Positive associations primacy in the IAT: A Many-Facet Rasch Measurement analysis. *Experimental Psychology, 58*(5), 376–384; Jeong, Y., Tran, H., & Zhao, X.

(2012). How much is too much? The collective impact of repetition and position in multi-segment sports broadcast. *Journal of Advertising Research, 52*(1), 87–101; Yongick, J., & Hai, T. (2014). Detecting pod position effects in the context of multi-segment sport programs: Implications from four Super Bowl broadcasts. *Sport Marketing Quarterly, 23*(1), 5–16.

5 Miller, J. K., Westerman, D. L., & Lloyd, M. E. (2004). Are first impressions lasting impressions? An exploration of the generality of the primacy effect in memory for repetitions. *Memory & Cognition, 32,* 1305–1315.

6 Little, A. C., Jones, B. C., & DeBruine, L. M. (2014). Primacy in the effects of face exposure: Perception is influenced more by faces that are seen first. *Archives of Scientific Psychology, 2*(1), 43–47.

7 Kraljic, T., Samuel, A., & Brennan, S. (2008). First impressions and last resorts: How listeners adjust to speaker variability. *Psychological Science, 19,* 332–338.

8 Dahl, L. C., Brimacombe, C., & Lindsay, D. (2009). Investigating investigators: How presentation order influences participant–investigators' interpretations of eyewitness identification and alibi evidence. *Law and Human Behavior, 33*(5), 368–380; Lee, H., Mozer, M. C., Kramer, A. F., & Vecera, S. P. (2012). Object-based control of attention is sensitive to recent experience. *Journal of Experimental Psychology: Human Perception and Performance, 38*(2), 314–325; Polyn, S. M., Erlikhman, G., & Kahana, M. J. (2011). Semantic cuing and the scale insensitivity of recency and contiguity. *Journal of Experimental Psychology: Learning, Memory, and Cognition, 37*(3), 766–775.

9 Price, H. L., & Dahl, L. C. (2014). Order and strength matter for evaluation of alibi and eyewitness evidence. *Applied Cognitive Psychology, 28*(2), 143–150.

10 Logan, S. W., & Fischman, M. G. (2015). The death of recency: Relationship between end-state comfort and serial position effects in serial recall: Logan and Fischman (2011) revisited. *Human Movement Science, 44,* 11–21.

11 Van De Mieroop, D., de Jong, J., & Andeweg, B. (2008). I want to talk about … A rhetorical analysis of the introductions of 40 speeches about engineering. *Journal of Business and Technical Communication, 22*(2), 186–210.

12 Kamga, C. T. (2012, July). 2012 scholar award acceptance speech. Retrieved from congress.cpsociety.org/cynthias-2012-scholar-award-acceptance-speech

McGonigal, J. (2010, February). *Gaming can make a better world.* Speech presented at the 2010 TED Conference, Long Beach, CA. Retrieved from ted.com/talks/jane_mcgonigal_gaming_can_make_a_better_world.html

13 Davis, V. (2015, September 20). Emmy acceptance speech. Retrieved from vulture.com/2015/09/viola-davis-emmys-acceptance-speech.html

14 Adichie, C. N. (2012, March 15). Connecting cultures. Commonwealth Lecture presented in The Guildhall, London, UK. Retrieved from commonwealthfoundation.com/Howwedeliver/Events/CommonwealthLecture

15 Chigumadzi, P. (2015, August 17). Of coconuts, consciousness and Cecil John Rhodes: Disillusionment and disavowals of the Rainbow Nation. Presented at the Ruth First Memorial Lecture, University of the Witwatersrand, South Africa. Retrieved from journalism.co.za/projects-a-fellowships/ruth-first/

16 DeCamp, E. (2015). Humoring the audience: Performance strategies and persuasion in Midwestern American stand-up comedy. *Humor: International Journal of Humor Research, 28*(3), 449–467.

17 Barnett, M. D., & Deutsch, J. T. (2016). Humanism, authenticity, and humor: Being, being real, and being funny. *Personality and Individual Differences, 91,* 107–112; Greatbatch, D., & Clark, T. (2003). Displaying group cohesiveness: Humour and laughter in the public lectures of management gurus. *Human Relations, 56,* 1515–1544; McRoberts, D. A., & Larson-Casselton, C. (2006). Humor in public address, health care, and the workplace: Summarizing humor's use using meta-analysis. *North Dakota Speech and Theatre Journal, 19,* 26–33.

18 Frymier, A., Wanzer, M., & Wojtaszczyk, A. (2008). Assessing students' perceptions of inappropriate and appropriate teacher humor. *Communication Education, 57,* 266–288; Lee, S. (2011). Understanding truth in health communication. *Journal of Mass Media Ethics, 26*(4), 263–282; Moyer-Gusé, E., Mahood, C., & Brookes, S. (2011). Entertainment-education in the context of humor: Effects on safer sex intentions and risk perceptions. *Health Communication, 26*(8), 765–774.

19 Abrams, J. R., & Bippus, A. (2011). An inter-group investigation of disparaging humor. *Journal of Language and Social Psychology, 30*(2), 193–201; Abrams, J. R., Bippus, A. M., & McGaughey, K. J. (2015). Gender disparaging jokes: An investigation of sexist-nonstereotypical jokes on funniness, typicality, and the moderating role of ingroup identification. *Humor: International Journal of Humor Research, 28*(2), 311–326; Hackman, M. Z. (1988). Audience reactions to the use of direct and personal disparaging humor in informative public address. *Communication Research Reports, 5*(2), 126–130; Hackman, M. Z. (1988). Reactions to the use of self-disparaging humor by informative public speakers. *Southern Speech Communication Journal, 53,* 175–183.

20 Hodges, S. (2012, October 16). Founder's Day speech transcript. Retrieved from artslehigh.wordpress.com/2012/10/19/founders-day-sam-hodges-13-speech-transcript/

21 Chen, Z., Mo, L., Honomichl, R., & Sohn, M. (2010). Analogical symbols: The role of visual cues in long-term transfer. *Metaphor and Symbol, 25*(2), 93–113; Kool, W., Conway, A., & Turk-Browne, N. (2014). Sequential dynamics in visual short-term memory. *Attention, Perception & Psychophysics, 76*(7), 1885–1901; Page, M. P. A., Cumming, N., Norris, D., Hitch, G. J., & McNeil, A. M. (2006). Repetition learning in the immediate serial recall of visual and auditory materials. *Journal of Experimental Psychology: Learning, Memory, and Cognition, 32,* 716–733.

22 Brown, R. M. (n.d.). Retrieved from quotationspage.com

23 McGonigal (2010).

CHAPTER 10

1 Henry, P. (1775, March 23). Liberty or death. Speech presented at the Second Virginia Convention, St. John's Church, Richmond, VA. Retrieved from patrickhenrycenter.com/Speeches.aspx

2 Suu Kyi, A. S. (2013, October). Full transcript: Daw Aung San Suu Kyi accepts Sakharov Prize. Retrieved from allmyneighbors.org/2013/10/22/full-transcript-daw-aung-san-suu-kyi-accepts-sakharov-prize/

3 BBC. (2014). Languages of world. Retrieved from bbc.co.uk/languages/guide/languages.shtml

4 Ogden, C. K., & Richards, I. A. (1923). *The meaning of meaning: A study of the influence of language upon thought and of the science of symbolism.* New York: Harcourt, Brace.

5 *DOD Dictionary of Military Terms.* (2015). CAR. Retrieved from dtic.mil/doctrine/dod_dictionary; InvestorWords (2016). Car. Retrieved from investorwords.com/739/car.html; *Merriam-Webster* (2015). Car. Retrieved from merriam-webster.com/dictionary/car; *The Free Dictionary.* (2016). Car. Retrieved from thefreedictionary.com/car

6 Global Language Monitor. (2014). Homepage. Retrieved from languagemonitor.com

7 American Dialect Society. (2016). Words of the year. Retrieved from americandialect.org/woty

8 Manovich, L. (2001). *The language of new media.* Cambridge: MIT Press.

9 FreeThesaurus.net. (2016). *Speak; Listen.* Retrieved from freethesaurus.net

10 Eckert, P., & McConnell-Ginet, S. (2013). *Language and gender* (2nd ed.). Cambridge: Cambridge University Press.

11 Bailly, S., Nassau, G., & Divoux, A. (2015). Analysing advising dialogue from a feminist perspective: Gendered talk, powerless speech or emotional labour? *Studies in Self-Access Learning Journal, 6*(1), 32–49; Blankenship, K., & Craig, T. (2007). Powerless language markers and the correspondence bias: Attitude confidence mediates the effects of tag questions on attitude attributions. *Journal of Language and Social Psychology, 26,* 28–47; Fandrich, A. M., & Beck, S. J. (2012). Powerless language in health media: The influence of biological sex and magazine type on health language. *Communication Studies, 63*(1), 36–53; Jules, S. J., & McQuiston, D. E. (2013). Speech style and occupational status affect assessments of eyewitness testimony. *Journal of Applied Social Psychology, 43*(4), 741–748.

12 Hosman, L. A., & Siltanen, S. A. (2011). Hedges, tag questions, message processing, and persuasion. *Journal of Language and Social Psychology, 30*(3), 341–349; McGlone, M. S., & Pfiester, R. A. (2015). Stereotype threat and the evaluative context of communication. *Journal of Language and Social Psychology, 34*(2), 111–137; Palomares, N. (2009). Women are sort of more tentative than men, aren't they? How men and women use tentative language differently, similarly, and counterstereotypically as a function of gender salience. *Communication Research, 36,* 538–560; Ye, Z., & Palomares, N. A. (2013). Effects of conversation partners' gender-language consistency on references to emotion, tentative language, and gender salience. *Journal of Language and Social Psychology, 32*(4), 433–451.

13 Benson, E. J., Kemp, T. D., Pirlott, A., Coughlin, C., Forss, Q., & Becherer, L. (2013). Developing a nonsexist/nongendered language policy at the University of Wisconsin–Eau Claire. *Feminist Teacher, 23*(3), 230–247; Koeser, S., Kuhn, E. A., & Sczesny, S. (2015). Just reading? How gender-fair language triggers readers' use of gender-fair forms. *Journal of Language and Social Psychology, 34*(3), 343–357.
14 Association of American Medical Colleges. (2014). *The state of women in academic medicine 2013–2014.* Retrieved from aamc.org/members/gwims/statistics; The Henry J. Kaiser Family Foundation. (2016, January). Distribution of physicians by gender. Retrieved from kff.org/other/state-indicator/physicians-by-gender/
15 Koeser, S., & Sczesny, S. (2014). Promoting gender-fair language: The impact of arguments on language use, attitudes, and cognitions. *Journal of Language and Social Psychology, 33*(5), 548–560.
16 Angelini, J. R., MacArthur, P. J., & Billings, A. C. (2014). Spiraling into or out of stereotypes? NBC's primetime coverage of male figure skaters at the 2010 Olympic Games. *Journal of Language and Social Psychology, 33*(2), 226–235; Aull, L. L., & Brown, D. W. (2013). Fighting words: A corpus analysis of gender representations in sports reportage. *Corpora, 8*(1), 27–52; Billings, A. (2007). From diving boards to pole vaults: Gendered athlete portrayals in the "Big Four" sports at the 2004 Athens Summer Olympics. *Southern Communication Journal, 72,* 329–344; Bystrom, D., & Dimitrova, D. V. (2014). Migraines, marriage, and mascara: Media coverage of Michele Bachmann in the 2012 Republican presidential campaign. *American Behavioral Scientist, 58*(9), 1169–1182; Hayes, D., Lawless, J. L., & Baitinger, G. (2014). Who cares what they wear? Media, gender, and the influence of candidate appearance. *Social Science Quarterly (Wiley-Blackwell), 95*(5), 1194–1212.
17 Campo, J. L. (2015, July 8). Opening ceremony speech. Presented at the 5th Parapan American Games, Toronto. Retrieved from paralympic.org/news/toronto-2015-opening-ceremony-speech-jose-luis-campo-apc-president
18 Pinckard, C. (2015, December 22). Steve Harvey's gaffe at Miss Universe 2015 Pageant: Social media erupts. Retrieved from cleveland.com
19 Fanning, L. (2015, December 16). CorpsAfrica: Peace Corps for Africans. Talk presented at the Commonwealth Club, San Francisco. Retrieved from commonwealthclub.org/events/archive/podcast/corpsafrica-peace-corps-africans
20 McCormick, S. (2003). Earning one's inheritance: Rhetorical criticism, everyday talk, and the analysis of public discourse. *Quarterly Journal of Speech, 89,* 109–131.
21 Sczesny, S., Moser, F., & Wood, W. (2015). Beyond sexist beliefs: How do people decide to use gender-inclusive language? *Personality and Social Psychology Bulletin, 41*(7), 943–954.
22 Spotorno, N., & Bianchi, C. (2015). A plea for an experimental approach on slurs. *Language Sciences, 52,* 241–250.
23 Chong, D. (2006). Free speech and multiculturalism in and out of the academy. *Political Psychology, 27(1),* 29–54; Dickter, C. (2012). Confronting hate: Heterosexuals' responses to anti-gay comments. *Journal of Homosexuality, 59*(8), 1113–1130; Dickter, C. L., & Newton, V. A. (2013). To confront or not to confront: non-targets' evaluations of and responses to racist comments. *Journal of Applied Social Psychology, 43,* E262–E275; Harell, A. (2010). Political tolerance, racist speech, and the influence of social networks. *Social Science Quarterly (Blackwell Publishing Limited), 91*(3), 724–740.
24 Garcia, J. V. (2015, May 17). Commencement address 2015. Retrieved from smith.edu/events/commencement_speech2015.php
25 Alameda County Water District. (2014). 2014 slogan winners. Retrieved from acwd.org/index.aspx?NID=537
26 Parran, A. (2012, May). Keynote speech, Stephens College Commencement. Retrieved from stephens.edu/news/commencement/2012/May/
27 Jenkins, S. P. (2005, March). Raising the bar on integrity. Retrieved from boeing.com. Emphasis added.
28 Yousafzai, M. (2014, December 10). Nobel lecture. Retrieved from nobelprize.org/nobel_prizes/peace/laureates/2014/yousafzai-lecture_en.html
29 Nussbaum, M. C. (2003, May 16). *Compassion and global responsibility.* Commencement address at Georgetown University, Washington, DC. Retrieved from humanity.org/voices/commencements/martha-nussbaum-georgetown-university-speech-2003
30 DeCamp, E. (2015). Humoring the audience: Performance strategies and persuasion in Midwestern American stand-up comedy. *Humor: International Journal of Humor Research, 28*(3), 449–467; McRoberts, D., & Larson-Casselton, C. (2006). Humor in public address, health care and the workplace: Summarizing humor's use using meta-analysis. *North Dakota Journal of Speech & Theatre, 19,* 26–33.
31 DeNeal, D. (2004, October 12). Katabasis and Anabasis: A four-year journey. *Wabash Magazine* (Summer/Fall). Retrieved from wabash.edu/magazine
32 Abrams, J. R., & Bippus, A. (2011). An intergroup investigation of disparaging humor. *Journal of Language and Social Psychology, 30*(2), 193–201; Hackman, M. Z. (1988). Reactions to the use of self-disparaging humor by informative public speakers. *Southern Speech Communication Journal, 53,* 175–183; Montemurro, B., & Benfield, J. A. (2015). Hung out to dry: Use and consequences of disparagement humor on American Idol. *Humor: International Journal of Humor Research, 28*(2), 229–251.
33 Hirst, R. (2003). Scientific jargon, good and bad. *Journal of Technical Writing and Communication, 33,* 201–229.
34 Edwards, C., & Myers, S. (2007). Perceived instructor credibility as a function of instructor aggressive communication. *Communication Research Reports, 24,* 47–53; Linvill, D. L., & Mazer, J. P. (2013). The role of student aggressive communication traits in the perception of instructor ideological bias in the classroom. *Communication Education, 62*(1), 48–60; Matthews, N. C. (2016). The influence of biological sex on perceived aggressive communication in debater–judge conflicts in parliamentary debate. *Western Journal of Communication, 80*(1), 38–59.

CHAPTER 11

1 California Academy of Sciences. (2013, January). "Asteroids: Science with Impact" Hohfield Hall, Golden Gate Park, San Francisco.
2 Aristotle. (1991). *On rhetoric.* (G. A. Kennedy, Trans.). Oxford, UK: Oxford University Press.
3 Kelly, K. (2010). *What technology wants.* New York: Viking.
4 Kress, G. (2006). *Reading images: The grammar of visual design.* New York: Routledge.
5 James, K. E., Burke, L., & Hutchins, H. M. (2006). Powerful or pointless? Faculty v. student perception of PowerPoint effectiveness in business education. *Business Communication Quarterly, 69,* 374–396.
6 Szabo, A., & Hastings, N. (2000). Using IT in the undergraduate classroom. *Computers and Education, 35,* 175–187.
7 Cyphert, D. (2004). The problem of PowerPoint: Visual aid or visual rhetoric? *Business Communication Quarterly, 27,* 80–84.
8 Mahin, L. (2004). PowerPoint pedagogy. *Business Communication Quarterly, 27,* 219–222.
9 DuFrene, D. D., & Lehman, C. M. (2004) Concept, content, construction, and contingencies: Getting the horse before the PowerPoint cart. *Business Communication Quarterly, 27,* 64–88.
10 Mahin (2004).
11 DuFrene & Lehman (2004).
12 Jones, J. H. (2004). Message first: Using films to power the point. *Business Communication Quarterly, 27,* 88–91.
13 Stark, D. & Paravel, V. (2008). PowerPoint in public. *Theory, Culture and Society, 25,* 30–55.
14 Blokzijl, W., & Naeff, R. (2004). The instructor as stagehand. Dutch student responses to PowerPoint. *Business Communication Quarterly, 27,* 70–77.
15 White, C., Easton, P., & Anderson, C. (2000). Students' perceived value of video in a multimedia language course. *Educational Media International, 37,* 167–175.
16 Pew Internet & American Life Project. (2009). *The audience for online video-sharing sites shoots up.* Retrieved from http://www.pewinternet.org/Reports/2009/13
17 Pew Research Center: Internet, Science and Tech. (2013). *Photo and video sharing grow online.* Retrieved from www.pewinternet.org/2015/3/13
18 Wormald, K. E. (2004). Pump up your presentations. *OfficeSolutions, 21*(2), 48–49.
19 Lull, J. (1985). On the communicative properties of music. *Communication Research, 12,* 363–372; Lull, J. (Ed.) (1992). *Popular music and communication.* Newbury Park, CA: Sage.
20 Bell, S. (2004). End PowerPoint dependency now! *American Libraries, 35*(6), 56–59.
21 Marx, M. (2016). Getting Off Oil. Presented to Creative Video Services seminar, Newark, California.

CHAPTER 12

1 Houghton, H. G. (1916). *The elements of public speaking.* Boston: The Atheneum Press.

2 Houghton. (1916). p. vi.
3 Schmalzle, R., Hacker, F. K., Honey, C. J., & Hasson, U. (2015). Engaged listeners: Shared neural processing of powerful political speeches. *Social Cognitive and Affective Neuroscience, 10*(8), 1137–1143.
4 Ivic, R. K., & Green, R. J. (2012). Developing charismatic delivery through transformational presentations: Modeling the persona of Steve Jobs. *Communication Teacher, 26*(2), 65–68; Jacks, J. Z., & Lancaster, L. C. (2015). Fit for persuasion: The effects of nonverbal delivery style, message framing, and gender on message effectiveness. *Journal of Applied Social Psychology, 45*(4), 203–213; Johnstone, C. L. (2001). Communicating in classical contexts: The centrality of delivery. *Quarterly Journal of Speech, 87,* 121–143; McCorkle, B. (2012). *Rhetorical delivery as technological discourse: A cross-historical study.* Carbondale: Southern Illinois University Press.
5 Yale, R. N. (2014). The impromptu gauntlet: An experiential strategy for developing lasting communication skills. *Business and Professional Communication Quarterly, 77*(3), 281–296.
6 Rumbough, T. B. (1999). The effects of impromptu speech exercises in reducing trait and situational communication apprehension. *New Jersey Journal of Communication, 7*(2), 206–215.
7 Cope, E. M. (2015). "Inspiration of Delivery": John A. Broadus and the Evangelical underpinnings of extemporaneous oratory. *RSQ: Rhetoric Society Quarterly, 45*(4), 279–299.
8 Householder, B. D., & Louden, A. D. (2013). Extemporaneous speaking competitions: Investigating the impact of conventional extemporaneous speech organization and judge experience on speaker ratings. *Forensic, 98*(1), 17–34.
9 Miller, A. (2002). An exploration of Kenyan public speaking patterns with implications for the American introductory public speaking course. *Communication Education, 51,* 168–182.
10 Dilbeck, K., McCroskey, J., Richmond, V., & McCroskey, L. (2009). Self-perceived communication competence in the Thai culture. *Journal of Intercultural Communication Research, 38*(1), 1–7.
11 Croucher, S. M., Sommier, M., Rahmani, D., & Appenrodt, J. (2015). A cross-cultural analysis of communication apprehension. *Journal of Intercultural Communication, 38.* Retrieved from immi.se/intercultural/nr38/croucher.html; Mansson, D. H., & Myers, S. A. (2009). A reexamination of Swedish and American college students' communicative attributes. *Journal of Intercultural Communication Research, 38*(1), 9–22.
12 Zarrinabadi, N. (2012). Self-perceived communication competence in Iranian culture. *Communication Research Reports, 29*(4), 292–298.
13 Hsu, C. (2010). Acculturation and communication traits: A study of cross-cultural adaptation among Chinese in America. *Communication Monographs, 77*(3), 414–425.
14 Hsu. (2010); Merkin, R. S. (2009). Cross-cultural communication patterns—Korean and American communication. *Journal of Intercultural Communication, 20,* 5.
15 Natalle, E. J., & Bodenheimer, F. R. (2004). *The woman's public speaking handbook.* Belmont, CA: Wadsworth.
16 Brann, M., & Himes, K. L. (2010). Perceived credibility of male versus female television newscasters. *Communication Research Reports, 27*(3), 243–252.
17 Martín-Santana, J. D., Muela-Molina, C., Reinares-Lara, E., & Rodriguez-Guerra, M. (2015). Effectiveness of radio spokesperson's gender, vocal pitch and accent and the use of music in radio advertising. *Business Research Quarterly, 18*(3), 143–160.
18 Sellnow, D. D., & Treinen, K. P. (2004). The role of gender in perceived speaker competence: An analysis of student peer critiques. *Communication Education, 53,* 286–296.
19 Wagner, T. R. (2013). The effects of speaker eye contact and gender on receiver's assessments of the speaker and speech. *Ohio Communication Journal, 51,* 217–235.
20 Pearson, J. C., Child, J. T., DeGreeff, B. L., Semlak, J. L., & Burnett, A. (2011). The influence of biological sex, self-esteem, and communication apprehension on unwillingness to communicate. *Atlantic Journal of Communication, 19*(4), 216–227.
21 Weeks, J. W., Lee, C., Reilly, A. R., Howell, A. N., France, C., Kowalsky, J. M., & Bush, A. (2012). "The sound of fear": Assessing vocal fundamental frequency as a physiological indicator of social anxiety disorder. *Journal of Anxiety Disorders, 26*(8), 811–822.
22 Natalle & Bodenheimer (2004).
23 The Stuttering Institute. (2016). Stuttering facts and information. Retrieved from stutteringhelp.org/faq
24 Panico, J., Healey, E. C., & Knopik, J. (2015). Elementary school students' perceptions of stuttering: A mixed model approach. *Journal of Fluency Disorders, 45,* 1–11; St. Louis, K. O., Williams, M. J., Ware, M. B., Guendouzi, J., & Reichel, I. K. (2014). The Public Opinion Survey of Human Attributes-Stuttering (POSHA-S) and Bipolar Adjective Scale (BAS): Aspects of validity. *Journal of Communication Disorders, 50,* 36–50.
25 Healey, E. (2010). What the literature tells us about listeners' reactions to stuttering: Implications for the clinical management of stuttering. *Seminars in Speech and Language, 31*(4), 227–235; Jackson, E. S., Yaruss, J. S., Quesal, R. W., Terranova, V., & Whalen, D. (2015). Responses of adults who stutter to the anticipation of stuttering. *Journal of Fluency Disorders, 45,* 38–51; Plexico, L., Manning, W., & Levitt, H. (2009). Coping responses by adults who stutter: Part II. Approaching the problem and achieving agency. *Journal of Fluency Disorders, 34*(2), 108–126.
26 Bloomquist, J. (2015). The minstrel legacy: African American English and the historical construction of 'black' identities in entertainment. *Journal of African American Studies, 19*(4), 410–425; Hamilton, K. (2012). Mother tongues and captive identities: Celebrating and "disappearing" the Gullah/Geechee Coast. *Mississippi Quarterly, 65*(1), 51–68; Moody, S. (2015). New perspectives on African American English: The role of black-to-black contact. *English Today, 31*(4), 53–60; Nero, S. (2015). Language, identity, and insider/outsider positionality in Caribbean Creole English research. *Applied Linguistics Review, 6*(3), 341–368.
27 Purnell, T., Raimy, E., & Salmons, J. (2009). Defining dialect, perceiving dialect, and new dialect formation: Sarah Palin's speech. *Journal of English Linguistics, 37,* 331–355.
28 Fuertes, J. N., Gottdiener, W. H., Martin, H., Gilbert, T. C., & Giles, H. (2012). A meta-analysis of the effects of speakers' accents on interpersonal evaluations. *European Journal of Social Psychology, 42*(1), 120–133.
29 Centers for Disease Control and Prevention. (2015). Vision health initiative: National data. Retrieved from cdc.gov/visionhealth/data/national.htm
30 National Institute on Deafness and Other Communication Disorders. (2015, April 20). Quick statistics. Retrieved from nidcd.nih.gov/health/statistics/pages/quick.aspx
31 Omansky, B. (2006, August 2). Personal communication.
32 Czajkowski, A. L., & Greasley, A. E. (2015). Mindfulness for singers: The effects of a targeted mindfulness course on learning vocal technique. *British Journal of Music Education, 32*(2), 211–233.
33 Shapira, A. (2015, June 30). Breathing is the key to persuasive public speaking. *Harvard Business Review.* Retrieved from hbr.org
34 Cameron, P. (2000). Enchancing your classroom delivery using oral interpretation techniques. *Community Review, 18,* 28–36.
35 Martín-Santana, J. D., et al. (2015).
36 Laukka, P., Linnman, C., Åhs, F., Pissiota, A., Frans, Ö., Faria, V., et al. (2008). In a nervous voice: Acoustic analysis and perception of anxiety in social phobics' speech. *Journal of Nonverbal Behavior, 32*(4), 195–214.
37 Christenfeld, N. (1995). Does it hurt to say um? *Journal of Nonverbal Behavior, 19*(3), 171–186; Engstrom, E. (1994). Effects of nonfluencies on speakers' credibility in newscast settings. *Perceptual and Motor Skills, 78,* 739–749; Galili, L., Amir, O., & Gilboa-Schechtman, E. (2013). Acoustic properties of dominance and request utterances in social anxiety. *Journal of Social & Clinical Psychology, 32*(6), 651–673.
38 Geonetta, S. C. (1981). Increasing the oral communication competencies of the technological student: The professional speaking method. *Journal of Technical Writing and Communication, 11*(3), 233–244.
39 Goldin-Meadow, S., & Alibali, M. W. (2013). Gesture's role in speaking, learning, and creating language. *Annual Review of Psychology, 64*(1), 257–283.
40 Fodor, E. M., & Wick. D. P. (2009). Need for power and affective response to negative audience reaction to an extemporaneous speech. *Journal of Research in Personality, 43,* 721–726.
41 Smith, T. E., & Frymier, A. B. (2006). Get "real": Does practicing speeches before an audience improve performance? *Communication Quarterly, 54,* 111–125.
42 Smith & Frymier. (2006); Lee, S. (2013). Can speaking activities of residents in a virtual world make difference to their self-expression? *Journal of Educational Technology & Society, 16*(1), 254–262.

CHAPTER 13

1 Johanson, D., & Edgar, B. (2006). *From Lucy to language.* New York: Simon & Schuster; Hrdy, S. (2010). *Mothers and others.* Cambridge, MA: Harvard University Press.
2 Lull, J. (ed.) (2001). *Culture in the communication age.* London: Routledge.
3 Castells, M. (2009). *Communication power.* Oxford, England: Oxford University Press.

4 U.S. Department of Commerce. (2004). *Entering the broadband age: A nation online.* Retrieved from http://www.ntia.doc.gov
5 Reddy, W., & McCarthy, S. (2006). Sharing best practices. *International Journal of Health Care Quality Assurance, 19,* 594–598.
6 Lull, J., & Neiva, E. (2012). *The language of life: How communication drives human evolution.* Amherst, NY: Prometheus.
7 Gillmor, D. (2004). *We the media: Grassroots journalism by the people, for the people.* Sebastopol, CA: O'Reilly.
8 Bruns, A. (2005). *Gatewatching: Collaborative online news production.* New York: Lang.
9 Rowan, K. E. (1995). A new pedagogy for explanatory public speaking: Why arrangement should not substitute for invention. *Communication Education, 44,* 236–250.
10 Al-Abdullah, Rania, Queen of Jordan (2003, October). *Petra: Lost city of stone—excerpts.* Speech presented at the New York Museum of Natural History, New York, NY. Retrieved from http://www.queenrania.jo
11 Kalfadellis, P. (2005). Integrating experiential learning in the teaching of cross-cultural communication. *Journal of New Business Ideas and Trends, 3,* 37–5.
12 Koster, R. (2005, March). *Keynote: A theory of fun for games.* Retrieved from http://www.crystaltips.typepad.com/wonderland/2005/03/raphs_keynote.html
13 Hawking, S. (2006). Stephen Hawking Inaugural Address. Retrieved from http://lockerz.com/u/20853946/decalz/9067531/stephen_hawking_campus_party_speech_2
14 Campus Party. (2013). Retrieved from http://www.campus-party.eu/2012/index.html

CHAPTER 14

1 Coyne, J. (2010). *Why evolution is true.* New York: Penguin Books; Dawkins, R. (2011). *The Magic of Reality.* New York: Free Press; Dawkins, R. (2009). *The greatest show on earth: The evidence for evolution.* New York: Free Press; Stringer, C. & Andrews, P. (2005). *The complete world of human evolution.* New York: Thames & Hudson.
2 Tomasello, M. (2014). *A natural history of human thinking.* Cambridge, MA: Harvard University Press.
3 Dessalles, J.-L. (2007). *Why we talk: The evolutionary origins of language.* New York: Oxford.
4 Borchers, T. A. (2005). *Persuasion in the media age* (2nd ed.). New York: McGraw-Hill.
5 Powell, C. (2003, February). *Iraq: Denial and deception.* Speech presented to the United Nations Security Council, New York. Retrieved from http://www.whitehouse.gov/news/releases/2003/02/20030205-1.html
6 Hanley, C. J. (2003, August 10). U.S. justification for war: How it stacks up now. *Seattle Times,* p. A4.
7 Weisman, S. R. (2005, September 9). Powell calls his U.S. speech a lasting blot on his record. *The New York Times,* p. A10.
8 National Safety Council, http://www.nsc.org; Utility Consumers' Action Network, http://www.ucan.org
9 Lull, J. (2000). *Media, communication, culture.* Cambridge, UK: Polity Press.
10 Simons, H. W. (2001). *Persuasion in society.* Thousand Oaks, CA: Sage; Tracy, L. (2005). Taming hostile audiences. *Vital Speeches of the Day, 71*(10), 306–312.
11 LaPierre, W. (2012, December 21). National Rifle Association Press Conference. Retrieved from http://www.nytimes.com/interactive/2012/12/21/us/nra-news-conference-transcript.html; Obama, B. (2012, December 19). Press conference on gun violence. Retrieved from http://www.dailypress.com/news/breaking/hc-obama-press-conference-on-gun-violence-20121219,0,6519049.story
12 Dewey, J. (1997/1910). *How we think.* Belmont, CA: Wadsworth.
13 Micciche, T., Pryor, B., & Butler, J. (2000). A test of Monroe's motivated sequence for its effects on ratings of message comprehension and attitude change. *Psychological Reports, 86,* 1135–1138.
14 Plung, D. L. (1980). Writing the persuasive business letter. *Journal of Business Communication, 17*(3), 45–49.
15 Broadhead, G. J., & Wright, R. R. (1987). Problem/solution cases in technical writing. *Journal of Advanced Composition, 6,* 79–88.
16 The expanded approach to audience analysis for persuasive speaking presented here is based on Lull, J., & Cappella, J. (1981). Slicing the attitude pie: A new approach to attitude measurement. *Communication Quarterly, 7,* 67–80.
17 Simons (2001)
18 Neuman, Y., Bekerman, Z., & Kaplan, A. (2002). Rhetoric as the contextual manipulation of self and nonself. *Research on Language and Social Interaction, 35,* 93–112.
19 Simons (2001).
20 Simons (2001).
21 Claypool, H. M., Mackie, D. M., Garcia-Marques, T., McIntosh, A., & Udall, A. (2004). The effects of personal relevance and repetition on persuasive processing. *Social Cognition, 22,* 310–335.
22 Lewis, T. V. (1988). Charisma and media evangelists: An explication and model of communication influence. *Southern Communication Journal, 54,* 93–111.
23 Goossens, C. (2003). Visual persuasion: Mental imagery processing and emotional experience. In Scott, L. M., & Batra, R. (Eds.), *Persuasive imagery: A consumer response perspective* (pp. 129–138). Mahwah, NJ: Lawrence Erlbaum.
24 National Communication Association. (1999). NCA credo for ethical communication. Retrieved from http://www.natcom.org
25 Brown, K. (2002, March 1). Tangled roots? Genetics meets genealogy. *Science, 295,* 1634–1635; Jasanoff, S. (2006). Just evidence: The limits of science in the legal process (DNA fingerprinting and civil liberties). *Journal of Law, Medicine & Ethics, 34,* 328–241; Mulligan, C. J. (2006). Anthropological applications of ancient DNA: Problems and prospects. *American Antiquity, 71*(22), 365–380.
26 Ossorio, P. N. (2006). About face: Forensic genetic testing for race and visible traits. *Journal of Law, Medicine & Ethics, 34,* 277–292.
27 Kalb, C. (2006, February 6). In our blood; DNA testing: It is connecting lost cousins and giving families surprising glimpses into their pasts. Now scientists are using it to answer the oldest question of all: Where did we come from? *Newsweek,* p. 46.
28 McKerrow, R. E., Gronbeck, B. E., Ehninger, D., & Monroe, A. H. (2003). *Principles and types of public speaking* (15th ed). Boston: Allyn & Bacon.

CHAPTER 15

1 Dunbar, R. (2014). *Introduction to human evolution.* London: Penguin.
2 Tomasello, M. (2008). *Origins of human communicaiton.* Boston: MIT Press; Scott-Phillips, T. (2014). *Speaking our minds.* London: Palgrave.
3 Dawkins, R. (2009). *The greatest show on Earth.* New York: Free Press.
4 Munson, R., & Conway, D. A. (2001). *Basics of reasoning.* Belmont, CA: Wadsworth.
5 Toulmin, S. E. (2003). *The uses of argument* (updated ed.). Cambridge, UK: Cambridge University Press.
6 Baggini, J. (2003). *Atheism.* New York: Sterling.
7 Campbell, K. K., & Huxman, S. S. (2003). *The rhetorical act* (2nd ed.). Belmont, CA: Wadsworth.
8 Munson & Conway (2001).
9 Claussen, E. (2007, November). Reality before the renaissance. Making nuclear power part of the solution. Address given at the American Nuclear Society/European Nuclear Society international meeting, Washington, DC.
10 Brugidou, M. (2003). Argumentation and values: An analysis of ordinary political competence via an open-ended question. *International Journal of Public Opinion Research, 15,* 413–430; Dickinson, G., & Anderson, K. V. (2004). Fallen: O. J. Simpson, Hillary Rodham Clinton, and the re-centering of White patriarchy. *Communication and Critical/Cultural Studies, 1,* 271–296; Smith, C A. (2005). President Bush's enthymeme of evil: The amalgamation of 9/11, Iraq, and moral values. *American Behavioral Scientist, 49,* 32–47.
11 Bitzer, L. F. (1959). Aristotle's enthymeme revisited. *Quarterly Journal of Speech, 45,* 399–408.
12 Walker (2006). The place of theory in ancient rhetoric. In L. Montefusco (ed.), *Papers on rhetoric VII.* Rome: Herder; Williams, M. A. E. (2003). Arguing with style: How persuasion and the enthymeme work together in *On Invention,* Book 3. *Southern Communication Journal, 68,* 136–151.
13 Baggini (2003), p. 36.
14 Moore, J. W. (2006). Science literacy and science standards. *Journal of Chemistry Education, 83*(3), 343.
15 Finnegan, C. A. (2001). The naturalistic enthymeme and visual argument: Photographic representation in the "Skull Controversy." *Argumentation and Advocacy, 37,* 133–149.
16 Messaris, P. (1996). *Visual persuasion: The role of images in advertising.* Thousand Oaks, CA: Sage Publications.
17 Simons, H. W. (2001). *Persuasion in society.* Thousand Oaks, CA: Sage; Tracy, L. (2005). Taming hostile audiences. *Vital Speeches of the Day, 71*(10), 306–312.
18 Artz, N., & Tybout, A. M. (1999). The moderating impact of quantitative information on the relationship between source credibility and persuasion: A persuasion knowledge model interpretation. *Marketing Letters, 10*(1), 51–62; Lindsey, L. L. M., & Ah Yun, K. (2003). Examining the persuasive effect of statistical messages: A test of mediating

relationships. *Communication Studies, 54,* 306–321.
19 Volkow, N. D. (2006). Drug addiction: Free will, brain disease, or both? *Vital Speeches of the Day, 72*(16/17), 505–508.
20 Volkow (2006), p. 506.
21 Pornpitakpan, C. (2004). The persuasiveness of source credibility: A critical review of five decades' evidence. *Journal of Applied Social Psychology, 34,* 243–281.
22 Bordia, P., DiFonzo, N., Haines, R., & Chaseling, E. (2005). Rumors denials as persuasive messages: Effects of personal relevance, source, and message characteristics. *Journal of Applied Social Psychology, 35,* 1301–1331; Eckstein, J. J. (2005). Conversion conundrums: Listener perceptions of affective influence attempts as mediated by personality and individual differences. *Communication Quarterly, 53,* 401–419.
23 Cain, S. (2012). The power of introverts. TED Conference, Long Beach, CA. Retrieved from http://www.ted.com/talks/susan_cain_the_power_of_introverts.html
24 Perse, E. M., Nathanson, A. I., & McLeod, D. M. (1996). Effects of spokesperson sex, public service announcement appeal and involvement on evaluations of safe-sex PSAs. *Health Communication, 8,* 171–189.
25 Braun-Latour, K. A., & Zaltman, G. (2006). Memory change: An intimate measure of persuasion. *Journal of Advertising Research, 46*(1), 57–72; Page, T. J., Thorson, E., & Heide, M. P. (1990). The memory impact of commercials varying in emotional appeal and product involvement. In S. J. Agres, J. H. Edell, & T. M. Dubitsky (Eds.), *Emotion in advertising: Theoretical and practical explorations* (pp. 255–268). Westport, CT: Quorum Books.
26 Dawkins, R. (2009).
27 Maslow, A. H. (1954). *Motivation and personality.* New York: Harper; Maslow, A. H. (2000). *The Maslow business reader.* New York: Wiley; Maslow, A. H., with Stephens, D. C., & Heil, G. (1971). *Maslow on management.* New York: Wiley; Maslow, A. H. (1999). *Toward a psychology of being* (3rd ed.). New York: Wiley; Rowan, J. (1998). Maslow amended. *Journal of Humanistic Psychology, 38*(1), 81–92.
28 Hanley, S. J., & Abell, S. C. (2002). Maslow and relatedness: Creating an interpersonal model of self-actualization. *Journal of Humanistic Psychology, 42*(4), 37–57.
29 Adapted from Maslow (1999).
30 Wilson, T. (2011). Redirect. *The surprising new science of psychological change.* New York: Little, Brown.
31 Tomasello, M. (2008). *Origins of human communication.* Cambridge: MIT Press.
32 Dorsey, L. G. (1997). Sailing into the "wondrous now": The myth of the American navy's world cruise. *Quarterly Journal of Speech, 83,* 447–465; Winfield, B. H., & Hume, J. (1998). The American hero and the evolution of the human interest story. *American Journalism, 15*(2), 79–99.
33 Schlosser, S. E. (2013). John Henry: The steel-drivin' man. Retrieved from http://americanfolklore.net/folklore/2010/07/john_henry.html
34 Centers for Disease Control and Prevention. (2004). *Surgeon General's 2004 report: The health consequences of smoking on the human body.* Retrieved from http://www.cdc.gov/Tobacco/sgr/sgr_2004/sgranimation/flash/
35 Munson, R., & Conway, D. A. (2001). *Basics of reasoning.* Belmont, CA: Wadsworth.
36 Lin, T., & McNab, P. (2006). Cognitive trait modeling: The case of inductive reasoning ability. *Innovations in Education & Teaching International, 43*(2), 151–161.
37 Heit, E., & Feeney, A. (2005). Relations between premise similarity and inductive strength. *Psychonomic Bulletin & Review, 12,* 340–344.
38 Epstein, R. L. (2006). *Critical thinking* (3rd ed.). Belmont, CA: Wadsworth; Munson & Conway (2001).
39 Gordy, B. (2007). Occidental College commencement address. Retrieved from http://tootalltodd.blogspot.com/2007/07/i-was-songwriter-i-was-struggling-and-i.html (excerpt appears in http://www.nytimes.com/2007/06/10/us/10commencement.html?pagewanted=all&_r=0)
40 Epstein (2006).
41 Ikuenobe, P. (2004). On the theoretical unification and nature of fallacies. *Argumentation, 18,* 189–211.
42 Hansen, H. V. (2002). The straw thing of fallacy theory: The standard definition of "fallacy." *Argumentation, 16,* 133–155; Neuman, Y., Glassner, A., & Weinstock, M. (2004). The effect of a reason's truth-value on the judgment of a fallacious argument. *Acta Psychologica, 116*(2), 173–184.
43 Walton, D. (1999). The appeal to ignorance, or *argumentum ad ignorantiam. Argumentation, 13,* 367–377.
44 Broadfoot, P. (2004). "Lies, damned lies, and statistics!": Three fallacies of comparative methodology. *Comparative Education, 40,* 3–6.
45 Giddens, A. (2003). *Runaway world.* New York: Routledge.
46 Munson & Conway (2001), p. 82.
47 "Straw man fallacy." Retrieved from http://grammarist.com/rhetoric/straw-man-fallacy/
48 Munson & Conway (2001), p. 83.
49 Southern Poverty Law Center (SPLC). Retrieved from www.splcenter.org

CHAPTER 16

1 Khan, S. (2012, June 8). Sal Khan's commencement address. Retrieved from http://web.mit.edu/newsoffice/2012/commencement-khan-address-0608.html
2 Khan Academy. (2016). Retrieved from https://www.khanacademy.org/
3 Spiering, C. (2012, May 14). Gushing Barnard college president an Obama donor. Retrieved from http://washingtonexaminer.com/gushing-barnard-college-president-an-obama-donor/article/1291741
4 Amanpour, C. (2009, October 21). Introduction of Amira Hass, Lifetime Achievement Award, International Women's Media Foundation. Retrieved from http://www.democracynow.org/2009/10/21/israeli_journalist_amira_hass
5 Springsteen, B. (2009). Acceptance speech for induction into New Jersey Hall of Fame. Retrieved from http://www.youtube.com/watch?v=Wt7TKLqX_SE
6 Webby Awards. (2016). Archived winner speeches. Retrieved from http://www.webbyawards.com/press/archived-speeches.php
7 Sotomayor, S. (2009). Full text: Judge Sonia Sotomayor's speech. *Time.* Retrieved from http://www.time.com/time/printout/0,8816,1900940,00.html
8 Giacchino, M. (2010). Acceptance speech. Retrieved from http://www.Oscars.org
9 Minor, R. (2012). CNN Live Event/Special. Whitney Houston: Her life, her music. Retrieved from http://transcripts.cnn.com/TRANSCRIPTS/1202/18/se.04.html
10 Whitney Houston sings the national anthem—Star Spangled Banner. Retrieved from http://www.youtube.com/watch?v=Z1QmeEdFOSc
11 Chavez, C. (1990). Lessons of Dr. Martin Luther King, Jr. Retrieved from http://www.ufw.org/_board.php?mode=view&b_code=cc_his_research&b_no=3654
12 Feiler, B. (2012). The art of the wedding toast. *The New York Times,* Sunday Style section, p. 2.
13 University of Oregon Career Center. (2016). Elevator speech—30 seconds to interview. Retrieved from http://career.uoregon.edu/blog/students/2010/04/elevator-speech-30-seconds-interview
14 Robart, M. (2008). Wainhouse research: Videoconferencing market to set record growth. Retrieved from www.tmcnet.com; Videoconferencing sees record growth. (2007). *Business Communications Review, 37*(8), 6.
15 Holz, S. (2003). *Corporate conversations: A guide to crafting effective and appropriate internal communications.* New York: AMACOM; Dawkins, J. (2005). Corporate responsibility: The communication challenge. *Journal of Communication Management, 9*(2), 108–119; Kosonen, M., Henttonen, K., & Ellonen, H-K. (2007). Weblogs and internal communication in a corporate environment. *International Journal of Knowledge and Learning, 3*(4–5), 437–449.
16 Towey, R. (2016). Global video conferencing and telepresence market shows clear growth. Retrieved from eyenetwork.com
17 Videoconferencing sees record growth. (2007). *Business Communications Review, 37*(8), 6.
18 Anderson, A. H. (2006). Achieving understanding in face-to-face and video-mediated multiparty interactions. *Discourse Processes, 41,* 251–287.
19 Anderson (2006).
20 Adams, T., & Scollard, S. (2006). *Internet effectively: A beginner's guide to the World Wide Web.* Boston: Pearson; St. Amant, K. (2002). When cultures and computers collide. *Journal of Business and Technical Communication,16* (2), 196–214; Bentley, J. P. H., Tinney, M.V., & Chia, B. H. (2005). *Educational Technology and Research Development, 53*(2), 117–127.
21 Gabriel, T. (2011). Speaking up in class, silently, using social media. Retrieved from www.nytimes.com

22 LaFasto, F., & Larson, C. E. (2001). *When teams work best: 6,000 team members and leaders tell what it takes to succeed.* Thousand Oaks, CA: Sage; Pettigrew, A. M., & Fenton, E. M. (2000). *The innovating organization.* London: Sage

23 Light, W. H. (2007). Reframing presentation skills development for knowledge teams. *Organization Development Journal, 25,* 99–110.

24 Chen, G., Donahue, L. M., & Klimoski, R. J. (2004). Training undergraduates to work in organizational teams. *Academy of Management Learning & Education, 3*(1), 27–40; Greenberg, L. W. (1994). The group case presentation: Learning communication and writing skills in a collaborative effort. *Medical Teacher, 16,* 363–367.

25 Hanke, J. (1998). Presenting as a team. *Presentations, 12*(1), 74–78.

26 Bayless, M. L. (2004). Change the placement, the pace, and the preparation for the oral presentation. *Business Communication Quarterly, 67,* 222–225.

27 Business Roundtable. (2006, February 5). Discussion transcript. *Akron Beacon Journal.* Retrieved from http://www.ohio.com

Index

Page numbers followed by f indicate figures; followed by t indicate tables

C

D

E

F

M

P

Q